IT on Valentines Day
Salisbury MD.

Feb. 24, 2018

Habeas Corpus in Wartime

Habeas Corpus in Wartime

*From the Tower of London
to Guantanamo Bay*

AMANDA L. TYLER

OXFORD
UNIVERSITY PRESS

OXFORD
UNIVERSITY PRESS

Oxford University Press is a department of the University of Oxford. It furthers the University's
objective of excellence in research, scholarship, and education by publishing worldwide. Oxford is a
registered trademark of Oxford University Press in the UK and certain other countries.

Published in the United States of America by Oxford University Press
198 Madison Avenue, New York, NY 10016, United States of America.

© Oxford University Press 2017

Library of Congress Cataloging-in-Publication Data
Names: Tyler, Amanda L., author.
Title: Habeas corpus in wartime: from the Tower of London to Guantanamo Bay / Amanda L. Tyler.
Description: New York : Oxford University Press, 2017 | Includes index.
Identifiers: LCCN 2017018855 | ISBN 9780199856664 ((hardback) : alk. paper)
Subjects: LCSH: Habeas corpus—United States—History. | Habeas corpus—England—History.
Classification: LCC KF9011 .T958 2017 | DDC 345.73/056—dc23
LC record available at https://lccn.loc.gov/2017018855

1 3 5 7 9 8 6 4 2
Printed by Edwards Brothers Malloy, United States of America

Note to Readers

This publication is designed to provide accurate and authoritative information in regard to the subject
matter covered. It is based upon sources believed to be accurate and reliable and is intended to be current
as of the time it was written. It is sold with the understanding that the publisher is not engaged in rendering
legal, accounting, or other professional services. If legal advice or other expert assistance is required, the
services of a competent professional person should be sought. Also, to confirm that the information has
not been affected or changed by recent developments, traditional legal research techniques should be
used, including checking primary sources where appropriate.

*(Based on the Declaration of Principles jointly adopted by a Committee of the
American Bar Association and a Committee of Publishers and Associations.)*

You may order this or any other Oxford University Press publication
by visiting the Oxford University Press website at www.oup.com.

For my children, my greatest joy

We cannot yield to this, that [the King] should have power to commit any, and within "convenient time" he shall declare the cause; . . . if it be per mandatum domini regis, or "for matter of state"; . . . then we are gone, and we are in a worse case than ever. If we agree to this imprisonment "for matters of state" and "a convenient time," we shall leave Magna Carta and the other statutes and make them fruitless, and do what our ancestors would never do.

SIR EDWARD COKE PROMOTING THE PETITION
OF RIGHT IN PARLIAMENT (1628)

Contents

PART TWO: *Incorporating the Suspension Framework
into American Law*

Acknowledgments

I OWE MY appreciation to a very long list of people who helped make this project come to life. In order to unearth and compile the historical materials necessary to tell the story of the habeas privilege in Anglo-American legal history, I received invaluable assistance from a number of librarians along the way. These include Ellen Gilmore, Marci Hoffman, Michael Levy, Edna Lewis, and I-Wei Wang at the University of California, Berkeley School of Law Library. I owe a great debt as well to the librarians and archivists who assisted me in my research on site at Lincoln's Inn, the British Library, the British National Archives, the British Parliamentary Archives, and the Library of Congress. I also wish to recognize the librarians who aided my research efforts with respect to earlier articles leading up to this book: Kasia Solon, Jason Hawkins, and Germaine Leahy, all previously or currently of George Washington University Law School's Jacob Burns Law Library, and Terri Gallego-O'Rourke of the Harvard Law School Library.

This book has benefited from the superb work of many research assistants over the years, including former Berkeley Law students Easha Anand, Jordan Bock, Lauren Freeman, Neda Khoshkhoo, John Maher, Kassandra Maldonado, Taylor Reeves, James Matthew Rice, and Anuradha Sivaram. I also wish to thank former George Washington University Law School students Devin Anderson, Jonathan Bond, Russell Gold, Benjamin Kapnik, Derek Lawlor, and Sean Sherman for their work on several articles that provided the foundation upon which the book is built.

I am also grateful to the many friends and colleagues who encouraged me to pursue this project, engaged in spirited discussions of the subject (either in academic presentation or one-on-one), and who toiled through drafts of some or all of this manuscript and the articles that launched me on this line of inquiry. This list includes Michael Abramowicz, Janet Alexander, Brad Clark, Tom Colby, Richard Fallon, Daniel Farber, Mark Gergen, Jack Goldsmith, Tom Green, Paul Halliday, Philip Hamburger, John Harrison, Chris Kutz, Carlton

Larson, David Lieberman, Michael Lobban, Chip Lupu, Gerard Magliocca, John Manning, Maeva Marcus, Jenny Martinez, Justin McCrary, Daniel Meltzer, Henry Monaghan, Trevor Morrison, Caleb Nelson, William Nelson, Gerald Neuman, Anne Joseph O'Connell, James Pfander, Saikrishna Prakash, Jack Rakove, Russell Robinson, Stephen Schulhofer, David Shapiro, Jonathan Siegel, Peter Smith, Larry Solum, Karen Tani, Mark Walters, G. Edward White, William Wiecek, and John Yoo. (I am sure that I have mistakenly omitted some names; my gratitude to those who I have neglected to mention is no less.) I owe special appreciation to Brad Clark, Gerard Magliocca, and David Shapiro, who devoted extensive time to reading and commenting on multiple versions of this manuscript; the late Daniel Meltzer, who first introduced me to habeas corpus jurisprudence when I was his student at Harvard and with whom I had many enlightening conversations about matters explored in this book; and Paul Halliday, who gave enormously helpful feedback on the manuscript and whose masterful work on habeas corpus in the English legal tradition has taught me a great deal, as have our many rich discussions on the subject. Finally, I am grateful to Lord Nicholas Wilson of the Supreme Court of the United Kingdom, who generously arranged for me to view the four original copies of Magna Carta joined together on their 800th anniversary alongside the original copies of the English Bill of Rights and English Habeas Corpus Act of 1679, an experience I will not soon forget.

I also wish to thank my assistant for several years at George Washington University Law School, Frances Arias, and my assistant at the University of California, Berkeley School of Law, Amatullah Alaji-Sabrie, both of whom helped me in countless ways as this project unfolded. This work has been supported by several Deans at two institutions, George Washington University Law School, where I developed the idea for the book, and the University of California, Berkeley School of Law, where I wrote the book. Special appreciation goes to former GW Law dean Frederick Lawrence, who kept telling me "I think there is a book here," and former Berkeley Law dean Christopher Edley, who provided generous research support for my efforts when I joined the Berkeley Law faculty. I also wish to acknowledge the Law Department of the London School of Economics and Political Science, where I had the privilege of being a Visiting Senior Fellow in early 2017 as I completed this manuscript.

I am grateful as well to the wonderful editorial team at Oxford University Press, all of whom kindly took me under their wings and shepherded this book to print.

Finally, I owe my greatest appreciation to my family. Throughout the process of writing this book, my husband has been an unwavering and generous source of support and encouragement and my children have been patient enough to share me with my work while also cheering on my efforts.

I BECAME INTERESTED in this subject some years ago after mooting counsel for the petitioner in *Hamdi v. Rumsfeld* and later sitting in the gallery of the Supreme Court of the United States watching oral arguments in the case. My ambition in writing this book, if nothing else, has been to unearth the extensive historical backdrop to *Hamdi* and more generally the Suspension Clause, with the hope that what I have recovered and presented here will better inform such debates going forward.

Portions of material included have been published previously in the *California Law Review, Harvard Law Review, Indiana Law Review, Notre Dame Law Review, Stanford Law Review*, and *Yale Law Journal*. Of course, any errors herein are mine.

Introduction

ON APRIL 15, 2013, two pressure-cooker bombs went off in close succession near the finish line of the Boston Marathon. The blasts killed three victims and severely injured hundreds of others, many of whom lost limbs. What had been a scene of triumph and celebration quickly turned into, as one victim described it, a "war zone."

After a four-day manhunt that saw nearby towns put into unprecedented lockdown, law enforcement finally captured alive one of the two suspects in nearby Watertown. Almost immediately, public debate began as to how to treat the suspect, Dzhokhar Tsarnaev. (The second suspect, his older brother, died in the police shootout leading to Tsarnaev's capture.) United States senators John McCain and Lindsey Graham, among others, believed that Tsarnaev should be labeled and treated as an "enemy combatant." As they viewed matters:

> It is clear the events we have seen over the past few days in Boston were an attempt to kill American citizens and terrorize a major American city. The accused perpetrators of these acts were not common criminals attempting to profit from a criminal enterprise, but terrorists trying to injure, maim, and kill innocent Americans. . . . Under the Law of War we can hold this suspect as a potential enemy combatant.[1]

Others, however, argued that the criminal justice system could, and *should*, be the forum for detaining and ultimately trying Tsarnaev. In the end, the latter voices largely prevailed,[2] and in time Tsarnaev stood trial on a host of federal criminal charges. Almost two years to the day after the bombings, a jury convicted Tsarnaev of all charges and weeks later recommended a death sentence.

But what if those voices that argued in favor of treating Tsarnaev as an "enemy combatant" had prevailed and the government had detained him in military custody without affording him a criminal trial? Was such a course a legally viable option for the government? Or was the government legally required to prosecute Tsarnaev, a naturalized U.S. citizen, in civilian courts in order to justify his detention?

Habeas Corpus in Wartime. Amanda L. Tyler.
© Oxford University Press 2017. Published 2017 by Oxford University Press.

Only a few years earlier, the Bush administration had faced similar questions and concluded that no such requirement existed with respect to hundreds of detainees—including two U.S. citizens—who had been captured after the devastating terrorist attacks of September 11, 2001. In one such case, President George W. Bush declared that José Padilla, a U.S. citizen arrested at Chicago's O'Hare International Airport, was an "enemy combatant" who should be detained in military custody, rather than charged criminally and prosecuted.

In making this declaration, the president wrote that he had "DETERMINE[D]" that Padilla "[was] closely associated with al Qaeda, an international terrorist organization with which the United States is at war"; had carried out "warlike acts, including conduct in preparation for acts of international terrorism" against the United States; "possesse[d] intelligence" that might assist the government in its counterterrorism efforts; and "represent[ed] a continuing, present and grave danger to the national security of the United States," such that his immediate detention "[was] necessary to prevent him from aiding al Qaeda in its efforts to attack the United States."[3]

Extensive litigation followed over the lawfulness of Padilla's detention. In a petition for a writ of habeas corpus, Padilla's lawyers argued that his detention violated the Suspension Clause of the U.S. Constitution. That provision declares that "[t]he Privilege of the Writ of Habeas Corpus shall not be suspended, unless when in Cases of Rebellion or Invasion the public Safety may require it."[4] Specifically, Padilla argued that because the government had not suspended the privilege of the writ of habeas corpus in the wake of the attacks of September 11—as, for example, President Abraham Lincoln had done during the Civil War—the government had no authority to hold him unless it charged him with a crime and prosecuted him in due course.

Padilla's case reached the Supreme Court only to be dismissed on jurisdictional grounds. Two years later, when Padilla again sought review in that court, the government rendered the case moot by indicting Padilla on various criminal charges and transferring him to the control of civilian authorities for prosecution. Accordingly, the Court declined to take up the case anew.[5] In the meantime, the government had detained Padilla in military custody without pending criminal charges for over three years.

Meanwhile, in 2004, the Supreme Court reached the merits in another case raising many of the same issues. *Hamdi v. Rumsfeld* involved a habeas petition filed on behalf of a U.S. citizen who had been captured by U.S. allies in Afghanistan where he was reportedly fighting with the Taliban against U.S. forces. Like Padilla, Hamdi argued that his detention as an enemy combatant on American soil violated the Constitution. A fractured Supreme Court disagreed, ultimately concluding that "[t]here is no bar to this Nation's holding one of its own citizens as an enemy combatant."[6]

Hamdi was a case of first impression, but the foundations of its holding date back to World War II. In the months following the Japanese bombing of Pearl Harbor, the U.S. government ordered over 120,000 Japanese Americans living in the western United States—including over 70,000 citizens—to evacuate their homes and report to Relocation Centers for long-term detention. Under the auspices of Franklin Delano Roosevelt's infamous Presidential Order 9066, the military regulations that set these events in motion were predicated upon generalized suspicion that Japanese Americans—including those who were U.S. citizens—might spy on behalf of the enemy Japanese Empire. As one of its many legacies, this episode in American history established a precedent that the government may detain U.S. citizens for national security purposes outside the criminal process in the absence of a suspension.

These precedents suggest that the Constitution poses no bar to the detention of U.S. citizens outside the criminal process for national security purposes. It would seem to follow that detaining Dzhokhar Tsarnaev as an enemy combatant was a legal option for the government in the wake of the Boston Marathon bombings. But what if the Constitution dictates otherwise?

QUESTIONS LIKE THESE—regarding the scope of executive power to arrest and detain in times of war and the meaning of the Suspension Clause and the constitutional habeas privilege—implicate enormously important issues involving the role of the U.S. Constitution in wartime. Unfortunately, however, modern debates over these matters have taken place largely in a historical vacuum. But as these pages reveal, many of the questions implicated in modern debates have arisen before and, accordingly, there exists a wealth of Anglo-American legal and historical experience that can inform and enrich our understanding today.

This book sets out to recover that neglected history and recount it here. Specifically, the book identifies and explains the origins of the privilege of the writ of habeas corpus in English legal tradition, documents how those origins heavily influenced the development of early American law and the drafting of the U.S. Constitution, and then traces how both the privilege and the concept of suspension have been understood over the course of American history. Later chapters explore how the challenges posed by modern warfare have placed considerable strain on long-standing conceptions of the privilege and the role of suspension, resulting in what the book calls "the forgotten Suspension Clause."

This undertaking is the first of its kind to lay out as comprehensively as possible the full story of the legal and political history of the constitutional privilege of the writ of habeas corpus in wartime. The story begins in England before American independence—where the origins of American law may be found—before crossing the Atlantic to take the story forward on American shores, first in the American colonies and then in the independent United States. To piece together its many parts, the book draws upon a wealth of original and, in many cases, heretofore untapped historical and archival resources to shed light on the purpose and role of the Suspension Clause in the U.S. Constitution.

As is revealed in these pages, this forgotten history has much to contribute to modern debates. The history detailed here provides insight on many important questions, including: What are the origins of the privilege of the writ of habeas corpus in the Anglo-American legal tradition? What protections does the privilege embody? Who may lay claim to the privilege? Is affirmative provision of that privilege guaranteed by the Constitution? How far does the privilege reach? Does it go beyond U.S. borders? What is the role of suspension and which branch of government may declare a suspension? Can the suspension power be delegated? Can the courts review exercises of the suspension authority, or are such decisions so political in nature as to be immune from judicial review? How does the suspension power relate to martial law? And finally, what do the protections long associated with the privilege tell us about the propriety of employing military tribunals to try individuals without affording them the safeguards of the criminal process and independent courts? Each of these questions is explored in the pages that follow in the course of recounting the story of the privilege and suspension throughout Anglo-American history.

Part I begins by tracing the origins of the privilege in England. The story of habeas corpus begins hundreds of years ago, with the most important events in its evolution taking place in the seventeenth century. During the early decades of that century, John Selden and Sir Edward Coke argued against the king's power to detain persons *per mandatum domini regis*, or "for matter of state." In so doing, they set in motion a series of significant events, which culminated in the passage of the English Habeas Corpus Act of 1679.[7] This enormously important Act followed from Parliament's desire both to limit the authority of the king and his ministers to detain individuals outside the criminal process and to constrain the royal courts from countenancing such practices, and therefore accompanied the rise of parliamentary supremacy. To accomplish this end, the Act's seventh section provided that it was only through timely prosecution and conviction that a person who could claim the protection of domestic law could be detained for criminal or national security purposes. If a person detained on such a basis was not timely prosecuted, moreover, the Act promised the remedy of discharge and provided that judges violated its mandates under threat of penalty. It is no wonder that decades later, in lectures that were read by virtually every early American studying law, Blackstone glorified the Habeas Corpus Act as a "bulwark" of "per[s]onal liberty" and declared it a "second *magna carta*."[8]

As Part I also shows, the English Habeas Corpus Act included no exception for times of war. Thus, it took little time for Parliament to invent the concept of suspension in the face of war and recurrent threats to the throne, enacting the first suspension in the wake of the Glorious Revolution just ten years after passage of the Habeas Corpus Act. As Part I concludes, this uneasy conceptual pairing of the Act's protections and their suspension in times of crisis created the model that came to govern on both sides of the Atlantic during the American Revolutionary War.

Following the story from England to American shores, Part II details how the Crown's position that the Act did not apply in the American colonies constituted a major complaint about British rule and contributed to the movement for independence. In 1774, for example, the Continental Congress decried the fact that colonists were "the subjects of an arbitrary government, deprived of trial by jury, and when imprisoned cannot claim the benefit of the habeas corpus Act, that great bulwark and palladium of English liberty."[9] The Americans wanted to enjoy the benefits and protections of this "second *magna carta*" too. Accordingly, the importation of the English Habeas Corpus Act into early American jurisprudence followed quickly in the wake of independence. Examples on this score abound. To take but one, Georgia included in its Constitution of 1777 express provision that "[t]he principles of the *habeas-corpus* act shall be a part of this constitution."[10] (To make all the more clear that the English Act proved the basis of its Constitution's habeas provision, Georgia's legislature annexed verbatim copies of the Act to the original distribution of the 1777 Constitution.[11]) And just three months before the Constitutional Convention convened in Philadelphia in 1787, New York passed a statute practically identical to the 1679 English Habeas Corpus Act.[12] By 1833, the English Act's influence was so pervasive that Justice Joseph Story wrote in his famous *Commentaries on the Constitution of the United States* that it "has been, in substance, incorporated into the jurisprudence of every state in the Union."[13]

This was the backdrop against which the Founding generation wrote the Constitution and adopted the Suspension Clause. As Part II reveals, references to the English Habeas Corpus Act pervaded the ratification debates and highlight how the Act and the English suspension model proved the foundation for the Clause's terms. Alexander Hamilton, for example, celebrated and promoted the draft Constitution in the *Federalist Papers* specifically because it "provided . . . in the most ample manner" for "trial by jury in criminal cases, aided by the *habeas corpus* act."[14] Indeed, the protections of the Act were so important to the Founding generation that they called the habeas "privilege" nothing less than "essential to freedom."[15] At the same time, the Founding generation understood all too well the extraordinary nature of suspension, as Parliament had enacted a series of suspensions to legalize the detention of American "Rebels" in England during the war "like other prisoners of war."[16] Thus, the Constitution included strict limitations on when the power to suspend could be invoked—namely, only "when in Cases of Rebellion or Invasion the public Safety may require it." Part II describes how these same concerns regarding the potential abuse of the suspension power informed early debates and led Congress to reject the first proposed suspension under the new Constitution, which President Thomas Jefferson had requested to address the Burr Conspiracy.

With the Civil War, however, suspension finally became part of the American constitutional experience. As described in Part III, President Abraham Lincoln wasted little time in the face of what he viewed as a "clear, flagrant, and gigantic case of Rebellion"[17] to claim the suspension power for himself, soon provoking a confrontation with Chief Justice Roger B. Taney. Relying heavily on the English Habeas Corpus Act, Taney ruled in Ex parte *Merryman* that the president could not suspend in the absence of congressional action and that Lincoln's claim to the contrary asserted that "the constitution of the United States has conferred upon him more regal and absolute power over the liberty of the citizen, than the people of England have thought it safe to entrust to the crown. . . ."[18] After two years of debating suspension, Congress finally passed legislation, delegating much of its administration to Lincoln. Although many members of Congress disagreed with the president's view that he could proclaim a suspension on his own, Congress's 1863 Act was fully consistent with Lincoln's belief that a suspension was necessary to hold both the disaffected and Confederate soldiers as prisoners outside the criminal process.[19] This position followed from the fact that the Union viewed the secession of the Confederate States as illegal, and considered those who supported the Confederacy to be traitors who needed to return to their proper allegiance.[20] As is also detailed in Part III, the Confederacy witnessed its own series of suspensions—three in total—and they provide a fascinating point of comparison to events unfolding in the North. For his part, Confederate president Jefferson Davis never once claimed the power to suspend on his own (and indeed criticized Lincoln for doing so). Further, late in the war, the Confederate Congress took the position that the suspension authority could never be delegated in any form to its president. Nonetheless, the North and

South alike viewed suspension as a necessary predicate to detain persons who could claim the protection of domestic law outside the criminal process.

Following the war, suspension returned to the national stage when Congress authorized President Ulysses S. Grant to suspend the privilege to combat the rise of Ku Klux Klan violence in the South.[21] President Grant referred to the legislation as conferring upon him "extraordinary powers" that he would invoke only "reluctant[ly]" as needed "for the purpose of securing to all citizens . . . enjoyment of the rights guaranteed to them by the Constitution and laws."[22] Under the suspension, military officers employed their expanded powers to infiltrate the Klan by arresting its members in droves. As things unfolded, consistent with the long-standing operation of the suspension model, everyone at the time understood that with the lapsing of the suspension, those in custody had to be charged criminally or released.

As Part IV reveals, however, in the twentieth and twenty-first centuries, this long-established understanding of the Suspension Clause fell by the wayside. During World War II, under the auspices of President Roosevelt's Order 9066,[23] the military forced over 120,000 Japanese Americans—including over 70,000 citizens—to leave their homes on the West Coast and report to barren camps called "Relocation Centers" that were surrounded by barbed wire and armed guards for detentions averaging three years in length. As noted above, these policies were predicated solely upon a generalized suspicion that such persons might spy on behalf of the enemy Japanese Empire. The policies also lacked any factual basis, a point recognized by many government officials at the time, including Federal Bureau of Investigation Director J. Edgar Hoover. Further, many government lawyers—including Attorney General Francis Biddle—argued during this period that such a policy, at least as applied to U.S. citizens, would violate the Suspension Clause. As Biddle put it, "unless the writ of habeas corpus is suspended, I do not know any way in which Japanese born in this country, and therefore American citizens, could be interned."[24] When Ex parte *Endo*, a habeas case directly challenging the constitutionality of the camps, finally made its way to the Supreme Court, the Court delayed handing down its decision for political reasons and ultimately avoided wading into the constitutional issues in play, instead deciding the case in favor of the petitioner by narrowly interpreting the military's governing regulations.[25] In the meantime, the internment of Japanese Americans created a precedent that gave constitutional sanction to "a policy of mass incarceration under military auspices."[26]

As explained in Part IV, this precedent laid the groundwork for events that followed in the wake of the attacks of September 11, 2001. During this period, as noted above, the government detained two U.S. citizens as enemy combatants on American soil, and in its 2004 decision in *Hamdi v. Rumsfeld*, the Supreme Court sanctioned the idea that the Constitution poses no bar to such detentions. But as the extensive history set forth in these pages demonstrates, *Hamdi*'s recognition of the concept of a citizen enemy combatant overlooks the enormously important influence of the English Habeas Corpus Act and suspension model on the development of Anglo-American habeas law and stands at odds with the Founding generation's expectations as to how the Constitution would operate in times of war. Indeed, as the history set forth in these pages reveals, well through the Reconstruction period, the dominant legal and political view of the habeas privilege constitutionalized in the Suspension Clause understood it to preclude the government, in the absence of a valid suspension, from detaining persons who could claim the protection of domestic law outside the criminal process.

Part IV concludes by discussing the most recent Supreme Court decision on the Suspension Clause, *Boumediene v. Bush*.[27] In a 5-4 ruling, the *Boumediene* Court concluded that alien detainees held at the U.S. military installation at Guantanamo Bay, Cuba, enjoyed "the constitutional privilege of habeas corpus, a privilege not to be withdrawn except in conformance with the Suspension Clause." At the same time, however, the Court did not afford such detainees the traditional remedy of release from custody. Rather, the Court concluded that the detainees were entitled to greater opportunities to challenge their designation as enemy combatants in federal court than Congress had provided them in governing statutes. As Part IV explores, *Boumediene* presented the Court with a series of difficult questions that lacked any close historical analogies. Thus, the Court relied upon larger structural considerations and cited "the particular dangers of terrorism in the modern age" to support its holding. In so doing, the Court interpreted the Suspension Clause to promise access to a tribunal to contest the underlying lawfulness of detention, with the legality of the detention to be defined by law external to the Suspension Clause. (In other words, the Court never questioned the premise that some detainees could be held as enemy combatants; the holding instead promised detainees greater process to challenge that classification.) This aspect of *Boumediene* may have unnecessarily conflated the Court's Suspension Clause jurisprudence with its modern due process case law—a result that could in turn limit the relief available and pose conceptual problems in future Suspension Clause cases.

FINALLY, A WORD on the role of history in constitutional interpretation is in order. Although legal jurists and scholars argue over whether history should be the decisive factor in ascertaining the meaning and application of the Constitution, no one seriously questions that history is deeply relevant to the debate. With respect to the Suspension Clause, moreover, the Supreme Court has repeatedly declared in recent years that " 'at the absolute minimum,' the Clause protects the writ as it existed when the Constitution was drafted and ratified."[28] This proposition necessarily invites reference to history when interpreting and applying the Suspension Clause, an idea that is hardly new. Chief Justice John Marshall wrote long ago that understanding the role of habeas corpus in the U.S. Constitution requires looking to the privilege's origins in English law. As he put it, the phrase "privilege of the writ of habeas corpus" was "used in the constitution, as one which was well understood." Thus, to interpret the Suspension Clause, Marshall counseled, one must look to "that law which is in a considerable degree incorporated into our own"—namely, "the celebrated *habeas corpus* act" of 1679.[29]

More generally, it is hard to imagine how one could even begin to understand the meaning of the Suspension Clause without turning to history. After all, the Clause itself adopts terms of art taken directly from English legal tradition and therefore surely invites inquiry into the English backdrop that informed its drafting, not unlike the text of the Seventh Amendment, which expressly does so.[30] At a minimum, therefore, any discussion of how to interpret the Suspension Clause should begin with that backdrop. To be sure, as many have recognized, the Founding generation may not have fully worked out every aspect of the Constitution's application at the time of its ratification. James Madison, for one, called the Constitution "nothing more than the draught of a plan . . . until life and validity were breathed into it,"[31] and he suggested that its meaning might be "considered as more or less obscure and equivocal, until . . . liquidated and ascertained by a series of particular discussions and adjudications."[32] On this view, then, the early history of the Suspension Clause and the periods when it first came to be tested during the Jefferson, Lincoln, and Grant administrations also have much to contribute to debates over the Clause's role in the constitutional framework.

In the end, this book largely—although not entirely—leaves it to others to decide how to employ the full historical account of the Suspension Clause set forth in its pages. Because the modern understanding of the role of habeas corpus in wartime has departed so dramatically from the model that had long governed in Anglo-American law and that which the Founding generation sought to achieve in adopting the Suspension Clause, the current state of habeas jurisprudence should trouble anyone who cares about the Constitution. It follows, the book argues, that the time has come to reconsider the proper role of the Suspension Clause in our constitutional framework going forward.

PART ONE

Origins

The Privilege of the Writ of Habeas Corpus and Suspension in English Law

Many of those who framed the United States Constitution, participated in its ratification, and expounded its early meaning were lawyers trained in the English tradition. To understand the role of the privilege of the writ of habeas corpus in the American legal tradition, it is therefore necessary to understand its role in English law. As will be shown, the English historical backdrop provides a wealth of clues concerning what the Founding generation hoped to achieve in adopting their Constitution and particularly its habeas provision, the Suspension Clause.

Those who wrote the Constitution were keenly aware of the long and celebrated role of the writ of *habeas corpus ad subjiciendum et recipiendum* in English law. Translated as "to undergo and receive" the "corpus," or body, of the prisoner, the writ was by its origins a judicial creation and served as the basis for courts to demand cause for a prisoner's detention from his jailer. As historian Paul Halliday's work shows, the common law writ came into regular use in the seventeenth century as a "prerogative writ"—that is, as the embodiment of royal power invoked by the Court of King's Bench in aid of the monarch's obligation to look after his subjects. For the writ to evolve into something that would override the royal command as sufficient cause for detention would take additional developments. Specifically, it would take the English Habeas Corpus Act of 1679, a parliamentary creation intended to harness the common law writ and constrain the Crown from detaining outside the criminal process. Parliament's adoption of the Habeas Corpus Act was but one aspect of the rise of parliamentary supremacy and played a major role in a broader parliamentary effort to wrestle control over matters of detention from the king and his courts.

With the Act, Parliament now controlled and defined what constituted legal cause to detain. In the process, the royal command ceased to suffice as good cause. But in the face of war and Jacobite threats to the throne, Parliament soon created a tool for setting aside the Act's protections—namely, *suspension*. In a series of suspensions spanning from the late seventeenth century through the eighteenth century, Parliament set aside the Habeas Corpus Act and all related legal protections in order to legalize arrests made outside the criminal process—arrests that otherwise would have resulted in discharge of the prisoner under the terms of the Habeas Corpus Act.

The Founding generation knew a great deal concerning the benefits provided by the Act—indeed, denial of the Act's protections to the colonists constituted a major complaint about British rule and contributed to the movement for independence. The colonists read Blackstone to glorify the Act as a "bulwark" of "personal liberty" and a "second *magna carta*," and they wanted to enjoy the benefits of this second *Magna Carta* too.

But before turning to the Founding generation, it is necessary to trace the roots of the "privilege" that they would eventually come to adopt as their own.

I

The Making of the Privilege

*[I]f any person be restrained of his liberty . . . he shall, upon
demand of his coun[sel], have a writ of habeas corpus. . . . And
by . . . the habeas corpus act, the methods of obtaining this
writ are so plainly pointed out and enforced, that, so long as
this statute remains unimpeached, no subject of England can
be long detained in prison, except in those cases in which the
law requires and justifies such detainer.*

BLACKSTONE'S COMMENTARIES[1]

THE STORY OF the writ of habeas corpus in Anglo-American jurisprudence is
a complicated one. Part of the problem lies in the fact that historically, English
law recognized both a common law and a statutory writ of habeas corpus. The
former, the product of judicial creation, was at its origins a prerogative writ
that enabled the royal courts to act as an arm of the king in "demand[ing an]
account for his subject who is restrained of his liberty."[2] The statutory writ, by
contrast, was the product of parliamentary efforts to constrain the executive's
authority. Much of modern American habeas scholarship has downplayed the
role of the statutory writ in the development of American habeas jurisprudence, but as the chapters that follow reveal, the English Habeas Corpus Act
played a central role in that very development, wielding extensive influence
over early American law. Indeed, no less than Blackstone, in the 1765 publication of his law lectures that were read by virtually every early American studying law, glorified the Habeas Corpus Act as a "bulwark" of "personal liberty"
and a "second *magna carta*."[3]

Yet here lies yet another complication in the story of habeas corpus.
Although without question over time habeas corpus would come to be associated with the protection of individual liberty, at its origins, habeas corpus
was about *power*. Specifically, as this and the next chapter explore, the Habeas
Corpus Act was caught up in ongoing struggles between Parliament and the
Crown that dominated the better part of the seventeenth and eighteenth centuries. Thus, although much of what follows tells a story cloaked in the language

Habeas Corpus in Wartime. Amanda L. Tyler.

of individual rights, the English Habeas Corpus Act must be viewed as part of a larger movement away from the royal absolutism that defined earlier periods in English history. Further, Blackstone's glorification notwithstanding, at its origins, the Habeas Corpus Act was an imperfect safeguard of personal liberty. Indeed, after the Act's adoption, Parliament continued to wield its attainder power to circumvent the Act and detain persons without formal process. Only ten years after passing the Act, moreover, Parliament invented the concept of suspension to set aside the Act's protections in times of war and in the face of threats to the throne. In short, Parliament itself did not always adhere to the constraints it had imposed on the executive's authority to detain with the Habeas Corpus Act.

Nonetheless, it was during the important decades chronicled in this chapter that the seeds of the association of habeas corpus with individual liberty were sown by the likes of Coke and Selden and with Parliament's adoption of the English Habeas Corpus Act. In time, with the birth of a new country across the Atlantic and its constitutional framework that enshrined the privilege and provided for independent courts, the protections associated with the Habeas Corpus Act would finally warrant Blackstone's praise.

Tracing the Origins of the Privilege

Modern accounts often tie the origins of the writ of habeas corpus to those of Magna Carta—the "Great Charter of the Liberties of England"—sealed by King John at Runnymede in 1215. Chapter 39 of the Great Charter declared:

> No free man shall be taken or imprisoned or dispossessed, or outlawed, or banished, or in any way destroyed, nor will we go upon him, nor send upon him, except by the legal judgment of his peers or by the law of the land.[4]

Like almost every major development in the story of the privilege, the Great Charter emerged from a period of unrest and civil war in England. It represented a bargain of sorts between rebelling English nobility and King John, who was to remain in power in exchange for recognizing the liberties set forth in the compact.[5] The concept of due process, so important to modern Anglo-American civil liberties jurisprudence, is grounded in the declarations set forth in Chapter 39 of Magna Carta.[6]

Picking up the story in the seventeenth century, Sir Edward Coke's highly influential *Institutes on the Law of England* connected Chapter 39 with the writ of habeas corpus, positing: "Now it may be demanded, if a man be taken, or committed to prison *contra legem terrae*, against the law of the land, what remedy hath the party grieved?" To this, he answered: "He may have an *habeas corpus.* . . ."[7] Presiding over a habeas case on King's Bench, Chief Justice Coke added: "By the law of God, none ought to be imprisoned, but with the cause expressed. . . ."[8] The narrative that has emerged to describe this early view of habeas corpus goes something like this: the writ of habeas corpus was designed to ensure that a prisoner receives the due process promised by the Great Charter, which in turn demanded that a jailor present legal cause for a prisoner's detention. This was the function of the common law writ, known more specifically as the writ of habeas corpus *ad subjiciendum et recipiendum*, which translates as "to undergo and receive" the "corpus," or body, of the prisoner. Courts used other common law writs of habeas corpus to compel the appearance of witnesses, move prisoners, and demand responses in civil proceedings. Common law writs were judicial creations and, as already noted, were born as prerogative writs in aid of the king's obligation to look after his subjects.

But as will be seen in the chapters that follow, the story of the privilege as it came to America is far more complex than this account reveals, in large measure because of the important influence that the English Habeas Corpus Act of 1679 wielded upon the development of early American law and the limits that the common law writ encountered in the decades immediately preceding the Act's passage. Indeed, as is explored below, in the century leading up to the Act, royal command commonly sufficed as sufficient cause for detention or, at the least, precluded judicial inquiry into the same. But the privilege that came to be enshrined in the U.S. Constitution—based as it was primarily upon the privilege associated with the English Act—was not simply the embodiment of a promise of some process before a tribunal only to meet defeat in the face of executive command. Instead, the habeas privilege born out of the English Act constituted a far more significant check on the power of the executive to arrest and detain. As will be seen, the privilege associated with the Act and imported into the American legal tradition functioned to limit dramatically the causes for which the executive could legally detain persons who could claim the protection of domestic law. Specifically, the Act required that one be charged criminally and proceeded against in due course, even in times of war, and it rejected outright the proposition that the royal command, standing alone, would suffice as lawful cause to detain.

It was, of course, not always so. For example, the return in "*Darnel's Case*" in 1627—sometimes called the "Case of the Five Knights"—stated nothing more than that the prisoners were held "*per speciale mandatum Domini Regis*"—in other words, by the special command of the king.[9] When Parliament refused to fund King Charles I's plans for continued English participation in the

Thirty Years' War, he demanded that the rich nobles of England "loan" him money to support his military objectives. When several knights refused the forced loans, Charles had them thrown in London's Fleet Prison. Represented by some of the English bar's finest, the nobles petitioned the Court of King's Bench, the judges of which served at the pleasure of the king, for writs of habeas corpus to win their release.[10] The central question posed by their case concerned whether the king's vacuous return would suffice as lawful cause for their imprisonment.

The knights' counsel attacked the position that the royal command on its own represented the law of the land, or "*legem terrae*," contemplated by Magna Carta. Celebrated parliamentarian, lawyer, and legal scholar John Selden developed this argument most fully on behalf of the knights. Referencing Chapter 39 of the Great Charter, Selden asserted that "if it were fully executed as it ought to be, every man would enjoy his liberty better than he doth."[11] He continued: "The law saith expressly, 'No freeman shall be imprisoned without due process of the law.'" Although recognizing that the words "legem terrae" could be interpreted to permit the king's return to stand, Selden contended that there were limits on what should be granted the force of law in justifying detention. Specifically, Selden argued that the best interpretation of Magna Carta posited that "[n]o freeman shall be imprisoned without due process of the law"—which he defined as comprising "due course of law, to be either by presentment or by indictment."[12] In so arguing, Selden equated due process with the specific process governing the initiation of formal criminal charges.

Selden's argument was not entirely without support. Indeed, almost three hundred years earlier, during the reign of Edward III and in conjunction with adoption of the treason statute that governed for many centuries, Parliament had essentially embraced the very same proposition when it declared:

> Whereas it is contained in the Great Charter . . . that none shall be imprisoned nor put out of his Freehold, nor of his Franchises nor free Custom, unless it be by the Law of the Land; It is accorded assented, and stablished, That from henceforth none shall be taken by Petition or Suggestion made to our Lord the King, or to his Council, unless it be by Indictment or Presentment of good and lawful People of the same neighbourhood where such Deeds be done, in due Manner, or by Process made by Writ original at the Common Law . . . and forejudged of the same by the Course of the Law. . . .[13]

Selden invoked this statute and others to challenge head-on the idea that the king's word alone constituted the "law of the land."

But Attorney General Robert Heath countered the argument forcefully in defending the king's authority to imprison the knights. Heath conceded that Magna Carta "is the foundation of [English] Liberties."[14] But any definition of "legem terrae," he argued, must recognize that:

> [Th]e king is the head of the same fountain of justice, which your lordship administers to all his subjects; all justice is derived from him, and what he doth, he doth not as a private person, but as the head of the common wealth, as *justiciarius regni*, yea, the very essence of justice under God upon earth is in him. . . .

Heath continued by all but labeling Selden's arguments fanciful, at one point asserting that "no learned man" would agree with the assertion that "no man should be committed, but first he shall be indicted or presented." Then, after offering a lengthy recitation of why the statutes and precedents relied upon by the knights did not support their position, Heath defended the king's power to detain prisoners for "state reasons." Finally, he concluded by drawing upon a wealth of precedents and current practices supporting the position that the king's command constituted the law of the land.[15]

All involved appreciated the momentousness of the case. During arguments, Lord Doderidge, one of the justices on King's Bench, declared: "This is the greatest cause that ever I knew in this court."[16] Similarly, Chief Justice Hyde labeled the case "of very great weight and expectation."[17] In the end, however, the *Cobbett's State Trials* version of the proceedings reports that King's Bench viewed the precedents as supporting the king, holding that his word constituted the "law of the land" and therefore justified the prisoners' remand to the Fleet. For their release, they would have to look elsewhere—specifically, to the very person who had imprisoned them in the first instance. In the words of Chief Justice Hyde, "we make no doubt but the king, if you seek to him, he knowing the cause why you are imprisoned, he will have mercy."[18]

King's Bench may well have reached a different result had Charles not removed its chief justice, Randolph Crewe, the previous year, reportedly because Crewe had shown "no zeal for the advancement of the Loan[s]."[19] Reports suggest that Crewe had informed the king through intermediaries that he believed that "no tax . . . can be laid upon the people without the authority of parliament, and that the King cannot imprison any of his subjects without a warrant specifying the offense with which they are charged."[20] Of course, if Crewe held this view and remained on King's Bench, Selden's arguments would have fallen upon sympathetic ears. It seems that Crewe's dismissal may well have sealed the knights' respective fates. This being said, many historians suggest that the decision makes perfect sense in terms of accepted "contemporary legal justification[s]" for detention and a wealth of precedents.[21]

And so, Selden's argument did not prevail on this occasion. He therefore took his cause to another forum—Parliament—enlisting the support of fellow House of Commons member and great English jurist Sir Edward Coke, among others, in the process. Parliament adopted the Petition of Right the following year, but only after extensive debates that pitted Selden and Coke up against Heath once more. Coke's remarks during the debates shed considerable light on his view of the law. He began by invoking Saint Paul, quoting the Acts of the Apostles for the proposition that " '[i]t is against reason to send a man to prison without shewing a cause.' "[22] Turning to the specific problem posed by the Case of the Five Knights, Coke argued that if a detention be upheld *"per mandatum domini regis,* or 'for matter of state' . . . then we are gone, and we are in a worse case than ever. If we agree to this imprisonment 'for matters of state' and 'a convenient time,' we shall leave Magna Carta and the other statutes and make them fruitless, and do what our ancestors would never do." Notably, here Coke argued that existing law *already* denied the king the power to detain for "state reasons" absent specific cause, yet he also promoted the Petition as going further to clarify the point.[23]

Given its impetus, it is hardly surprising that the Petition essentially embraced Selden's arguments from the Case of the Five Knights and repudiated King's Bench's resolution of the matter. Specifically, after quoting Chapter 39 of the original Magna Carta, the Petition set forth the following grievance and demand:

> [Y]our subjects have of late been imprisoned without any cause shewed: And when for their deliverance they were brought before your justices by your Majesties writts of habeas corpus . . . , no cause was certified, but that they were deteined by your Majesties speciall comaund signified by the lords of your privie councell, and yet were returned backe to severall prisons without being charged with any thing to which they might make aunswere according to the lawe. . . . They . . . pray . . . that no freeman in any such manner as is before mencioned be imprisoned or deteined.[24]

The Petition also responded more broadly to the events that had preceded *Darnel's Case* by, among other things, purporting to restrict declarations of martial law, ban forced quartering of soldiers, and prohibit unilateral taxation by the king.[25] It was, in this respect, very much a repudiation of Charles's attempts to govern without Parliament, and embedded within the power struggle between Parliament and the monarchy that came to define much of seventeenth-century England.[26]

A king increasingly at odds with his Parliament, Charles I had resisted initial efforts to enact portions of what became the Petition of Right in the form of legislation. Under Coke's leadership, however, the House of Commons pushed ahead with the Petition in order to register its grievances. The king reluctantly accepted the Petition, presumably with the intention of securing greater parliamentary support for his military objectives going forward.[27] Within a year, however, the king was once again at war with the Houses over his demand for taxes of tonnage and poundage, which Parliament had denied him but had not denied his predecessors. As part of this long-standing dispute, Charles dissolved Parliament yet again.[28] It would be decades before the Petition would evolve from mere aspiration and eventually provide a foundation for limiting the monarch's authority to detain, in part due to the debatable legal status of the Petition itself.[29] Indeed, as if to drive home the point that the Petition had changed little, Charles I threw John Selden and eight other members of Parliament in the Tower of London in 1629 for their open opposition to his actions. Some in the group had prevented the House speaker, John Finch, from leaving his chair to adjourn the Commons in keeping with the king's command but over the protest of its members.[30] Among this group was Sir John Eliot, a regular foe of Charles, who had promoted the Petition of Right and led a campaign against the right of the king to levy tonnage and poundage.[31] It was not Eliot's first visit to the Tower, but it would be his last.

When Selden and the other prisoners went before King's Bench to seek their freedom via writs of habeas corpus, Attorney General Heath responded with a flurry of arguments against bailing the prisoners. First, he cited backdated royal warrants as cause for imprisonment. Second, he argued that "[a] petition in parliament is not law" and thereby denied that the Petition of Right had any legal force. Under this view, it followed that the royal command sufficed as legal cause.[32] Finally, he levied general accusations of treasonous conduct.[33] In response, Edward Littleton countered on behalf of Selden (with his client's able assistance) that the Petition of Right was both enforceable and had changed the state of the law, making the case very simple. As he put it, "[t]o detain the prisoner, by the command of the king singly, is against the Petition of Right." Littleton spoke with some authority on the topic, having played a significant role in the Commons' drafting of the grievances set forth in the Petition. In Littleton's view, the Petition required that "out of the Return, the substance of the offence ought always to appear . . . [and provide] cause upon which any indictment might be drawn up." Following the levying of formal criminal charges, moreover, Littleton understood the Petition to guarantee that the prisoner "shall have his trial." It followed, Littleton concluded, that if the king had true cause to believe treason was afoot, the proper procedure was to indict the prisoners on charges, not detain them on the sole basis of royal command.[34]

Once again, Selden's attack on the king's authority to detain outside the criminal process would fail, but not without garnering some legal traction. There was drama as well. One chronicler of the period reports:

> When the Court was ready to have delivered their Opinions in this great business, the Prisoners were not brought to the bar, according to the rule of the court. Therefore proclamation was made for the Keepers of the several prisons to bring in their Prisoners; but none of them appeared, except the Marshal of the King's-Bench, who informed the Court, that [a prisoner] . . . in his custody, was removed yesterday, and put in the Tower of London by the king's own warrant: and so it was done with the other prisoners; for each of them was removed out of his prison [and put in the Tower by royal warrant]. . . .[35]

Why had the king removed all the prisoners to the Tower? As another writer of the period, Bulstrode Whitelocke (whose father served on King's Bench during the case) recorded:

> The Judges were somewhat perplexed about the Habeas Corpus for the Parliament-men, and wrote an humble and stout Letter to the king, "That by their oaths they were to bail the Prisoners; but thought fit, before they did it, or published their Opinions therein, to inform his majesty thereof, and humbly to advise him (as had been done by his noble progenitors in like case) to send a direction to his Justices of his bench, to bail the prisoners."[36]

Unsurprisingly, "the king . . . was not pleased with their determination, [and] commanded them not to deliver any opinion in this case without consulting with the rest of the judges; who delayed the business." It was at this point that the king removed all the prisoners not already there to the Tower, communicating to King's Bench that he had done so "because of their insolent carriage at the bar."[37] With no prisoners before them, there was little King's Bench could do:

> [N]otwithstanding [the absence of the prisoners], it was prayed by the counsel for the prisoners, that the Court would deliver their Opinion

as to the matter in law: but the Court refused to do that, because it was to no purpose; for the Prisoners being absent, they could not be bailed, delivered, or remanded.[38]

In the end, although potentially prepared to change the course of habeas law and restrict executive power, King's Bench never announced its opinion in the case.[39] The prisoners remained in the Tower for the summer until Charles—perhaps eager to avoid his court finally wading into the political thicket—offered the prisoners bail upon the giving of sureties for good behavior. Led by Selden, who now argued his cause personally, the prisoners refused, for they viewed the requirement of a surety as imputing their guilt. Instead, Selden declared: "We demand to be bailed in point of Right."[40] The king was unmoved. From this point, the prisoners' stories diverged: some were charged and convicted of sedition; two remained imprisoned until 1640; Selden languished for two more years in prison, and Eliot famously suffered three severe years in the Tower, where he died and is buried.[41]

Selden's plight instructs that one should not view the Petition as having dramatically altered the course of English law in any immediate fashion.[42] All the same, the Petition clearly influenced the thinking of leading contemporary jurists, introduced rights-based language to the English legal tradition, and set in motion important developments in English statutory law that would come to pass over the next few decades.

The Habeas Corpus Act of 1679

But change takes time. Indeed, it would take five decades before Parliament finally adopted a statute that made real the aspirations of the Petition of Right and constrained the executive's ability to detain outside the criminal process—the Habeas Corpus Act of 1679. Legislative efforts leading up to the 1679 Act go as far back as Parliament's unsuccessful attempts to pass habeas legislation in 1621 and 1624. By contrast, 1641 finally witnessed some progress. That year, by statute, Parliament "absolutely dissolved" the "Court commonly called the Star Chamber" and all the conciliar courts for having acted beyond their authority and levying punishments not warranted by law. Parliament invoked as authority for its legislation the principles set forth in the Petition of Right and various statutes from the reign of Edward III, including the famous provision tethered to the long-standing treason statute. Significantly, the 1641 law, known as the Star Chamber Act, declared that any person imprisoned by the king, his Council Board, or any member of the Privy Council had the right to challenge that detention through a writ of habeas corpus before the Courts of

King's Bench or Common Pleas. The Act called upon those judges to "examine and determine whether the cause of . . . commitment appearing upon
the . . . return be just and legall." Finally, to enforce its mandate that the jailor
be bound to make a return, the law provided that anyone acting "contrary to
the direction and true meaning" of the Act did so at the risk of suffering liability to the prisoner for treble damages.[43]

The Star Chamber Act marked an important development by clearly subjecting executive detention to judicial review and setting forth statutorily-based
procedures for certain habeas cases. It is no surprise that the law came during
a time when Parliament generally sought to claim for itself powers previously
claimed by the king.[44] Indeed, during this period and beyond, Parliament continued to assert—and exercise—the power to imprison individuals at its pleasure, completely free of judicial scrutiny through attainder and impeachment
proceedings.[45]

In the immediate wake of the Star Chamber Act, Charles attempted to
arrest six members of Parliament on charges of treason, thereby bringing the
power struggles between the monarch and the Houses to a head.[46] The English
Civil War followed (and, with it, the execution of Charles I), ushering in the
rule of Oliver Cromwell along with a dramatic rise in the frequency of both
executive and parliamentary imprisonment of political enemies without process of any kind. During this period, those in power also increasingly employed
the practice of sending prisoners to "legal islands" (whether true islands or
the Tower of London) to escape the reach of writs of habeas corpus.[47] While
Parliament considered adopting habeas legislation to regulate the practice,[48]
Cromwell died and more war followed, leading to the Restoration of the monarchy under Charles II, son of Charles I. His reign would witness the greatest
advancements in statutory habeas law, while also laying the foundation for a
period of extended unrest that would highlight its limitations.

Several events in the 1660s reveal increased parliamentary attention to the
unsettled nature of both the reach and scope of protections inherent in the
law of habeas corpus. In 1667, for example, the House of Commons began
impeachment proceedings against the Earl of Clarendon for his role in sending prisoners to "remote islands, garrisons, and other places, thereby to prevent them from the benefit of the law."[49] In the midst of a disagreement with
the House of Lords over whether Clarendon should be imprisoned pending
the proceedings, one member of the Commons (who was no less a disciple
of John Selden) claimed that parliamentary-ordered detention in cases of
suspected treason did not violate Magna Carta because "Parliaments are confined to no rules or precedents, where there is a concern of their own safety."[50]
To be sure, this statement is deeply troubling from a modern civil liberties

perspective. But during this period, Parliament's claim to act independent of the supervision of the royal courts must be viewed against the backdrop of decades of a parliamentary struggle for privilege and protection from what it viewed as the "oppress[ive] . . . power of the crown."[51]

Indeed, to emphasize the tension between the royal courts and Parliament, in 1667, the Commons charged the chief justice of the Court of King's Bench, Sir John Kelyng, with employing "an arbitrary and illegal Power . . . of dangerous Consequences to the Lives and Liberties of the People of England" and "vilif[ying] . . . *Magna Charta*, the great Preserver of our Lives, Freedoms, and Property."[52] One of the more specific complaints levied against the chief justice focused on his actions in a recent case in which he prevented "a *Habeas Corpus* and a *Plures* to be issued out, so that the party was constrained to petition the King."[53] John Milward, a member of Parliament who kept a diary during this period, described the chief justice's defense of his denial of bail to the habeas petitioner as follows: "[H]e answered that he did it in a time of danger, and the person whom it was denied was a dangerous person and had formerly been in rebellion, and although the Act of Oblivion had pardoned his former offences, yet he did not think it safe to suffer a person of such ill principles to go at large in a time so full of danger."[54]

Milward was likely describing "Feimer's Case," reported in Sir Edward Northey's Notebooks as having presented King's Bench with a petition for habeas corpus filed by a state prisoner who had already spent five years in the Tower based solely on a conciliar order. As Northey reports, King's Bench was no more welcoming to the petition than it had been to the petitions in the case of the Five Knights some forty years earlier. In ordering the prisoner remanded, Northey's Notebooks state that Kelyng declared:

> Likely he is a dangerous person. We know not what times we live in. We must use a justifiable prudence and not strain the strict rules of law to enlarge those persons which will use their liberties to get the kingdom in a flame.[55]

In the immediate wake of these events, Parliament returned its attention in 1668 to habeas corpus legislation directed at constraining the courts in such cases. That year, Lord St. John introduced a bill "to prevent the denying *habeas corpus*." Although the bill died with the proroguing (or adjournment) of Parliament, it seems to have laid the groundwork for the 1679 Act insofar as "[i]t directed that no man should be kept in prison above six months, but should be brought to his trial, and if then he was not legally proceeded against within six months he should have his *habeas corpus* upon the first moving for it."[56] Parliament next considered habeas legislation in 1674 directed at "prevent[ing] imprisonment beyond [the] sea" and establishing regular procedures for habeas proceedings. This bill also failed, but only after passing the Commons and introducing additional concepts that would eventually make their way into the successful 1679 legislation.[57]

Debates preceding the 1674 bill shed light on the problems that concerned Parliament during this period, including the common practice of sending prisoners to places where writs could not run.[58] More fundamentally, however, the bill picked up where Selden and Coke left off with the Petition of Right. Promoting the legislation, Sir Thomas Clarges complained that there were "[m]ore warrants to the Tower under the king's hand now, than in 200 years before."[59] Clarges posited that he "[w]ould have men committed to legal prisons" and allow "a man [to] know his accuser" rather than continue the current state of affairs, in which "the subject can have no remedy" for imprisonment by royal command.[60] Joining rank with Clarges, Colonel John Birch also complained of the common practice "to commit by the King's or some great Minister's warrant," while positing that "it is not reasonable" in such cases that the king *should be both Party and Judge.*"[61]

Arguing against the legislation, Attorney General Francis North saw "no need of such a Law."[62] Secretary of State Henry Coventry in turn invoked the security of the state as reason to proceed with caution. "Suppose," he suggested, there is "war here, and a correspondency; and suppose the King receives a letter, 'that he is betrayed by his Secretary,' and he imprisons him; if he must have a deliverance, you can never have any intelligence."[63] When the debates resumed a few days later, Coventry asked if "the King's warrant" will no longer suffice as "cause," what might his secretaries do "in case a man would kill the King"?[64] In other words, Coventry suggested that limiting the king's power to imprison by expanding habeas corpus protections would undermine crucial intelligence-gathering efforts and the ability to thwart assassination attempts. As will be seen, Coventry's arguments foreshadowed the debates that followed in 1696 in the wake of an assassination plot and the broader debates that continue to this day surrounding the role of the habeas privilege in wartime.

The year 1677 witnessed a renewed effort by the Commons to enact a habeas bill, but once again the Lords failed to pass it before the end of the parliamentary session. Then, finally, in 1679, circumstances favored the passage of habeas legislation. Some commentators have cautioned against overemphasizing the role of the Habeas Corpus Act of 1679 in the story of the privilege. English historian Henry Hallam, for one, wrote that the Act "introduced no new principle, nor conferred any right upon the subject."[65] Without question, the Act complemented the common law writ of habeas corpus, using the preexisting writ as a vehicle for enforcing its terms. The common law writ, as Blackstone noted, also continued to serve as the vehicle for redress available in "all . . . cases of unjust imprisonment" that were not covered by the Act.[66] Likewise, it is fair to suggest that the courts had already adopted some of the procedural aspects of the Act. (Not unrelated is the fact that the king had replaced Chief Justice Kelyng by this point with Sir Mathew Hale, a judge who demonstrated a tendency to be far more progressive on this score.[67])

But it would be wrong to view the Act as having changed nothing. Indeed, the Act accomplished two very important things. First, it imposed substantial limitations on the scope of lawful detention by the executive. Second, because these constraints could only be disregarded by English judges under the threat of penalties prescribed in the Act, the Act also dramatically curtailed judicial discretion. In so doing, the privilege associated with the Act came to hold a fixed status that its common law ancestor, which permitted judges far greater discretion in deciding when to grant relief to petitioners, had never known. These significant constraints—unyielding as they were—quickly became apparent to Parliament, leading it to invent the concept of suspension in order to displace the Act's protections in times of war.

Further, it was the Habeas Corpus Act of 1679 that gave the writ its celebrated status in Blackstone's *Commentaries on the Laws of England*, published between 1765 and 1769 and widely read, particularly in the American colonies. Blackstone—building on Coke's *Institutes*—linked the privilege with the Great Charter's guarantee that one may be detained only in accordance with due process.[68] In Blackstone's words, "*Magna carta* . . . declared, that no man shall be imprisoned contrary to law: the *habeas corpus* act points him out effectual means . . . to release himself."[69]

Accordingly, it is no accident that the Act came to play a central role in the development of early American habeas corpus jurisprudence, given the profound influence of Blackstone and Coke on American legal development more generally and the timing of Blackstone's publication, coming as it did only a few years before the Declaration of Independence. Also influential was Henry Care's popular treatise on *English Liberties*, first published in London in the late seventeenth century and reprinted and widely circulated in the American colonies in the eighteenth century, which called the Act a "*most wholesome Law*" and championed it as a cure for the failings of the common law writ. As Care wrote:

> The Writ of *Habeas Corpus* is a Remedy given by the Common Law for such as were unjustly detained in Custody, to procure their Liberty: But before this Statute was rendered far less useful than it ought to be,

partly by the Judges, pretending a Power to grant or deny the said
Writ at their Pleasure, in many Cases; and . . . [who] would oft-times
alledge, That they could not take Bail, because the Party was a Prisoner
of State. . . .[70]

In the period leading up to and encompassing the Revolutionary War, moreover, Americans came to appreciate all too well the importance of the Act as
central to the story of habeas corpus. As is explored in Chapter 3, the American
colonists decried the Crown's refusal to grant them the protections of the
Habeas Corpus Act in the American colonies. Those Americans unlucky
enough to be captured and brought to English soil during the war, moreover,
were subject to a suspension of the Act's protections and therefore detained
outside the reach of the Act.

As a threshold matter, there is the long-standing question whether
Parliament actually passed the law in the first place. Contemporary lore had
it that at the time of a crucial vote in the House of Lords, one of the tellers,
Lord Grey, was set to count the Lords favoring the bill as they passed through
a doorway to re-enter the House. The story goes that Grey decided to test the
other teller's attentiveness by counting one generously-sized Lord as ten and,
when the joke went unnoticed, he recorded the number, thereby securing the
requisite votes in favor of the bill. In support of the story, one writer points to
inconsistencies between the vote numbers and the reported attendance in the
Lords' Chamber that day.[71]

It is a great story, but as Professor Helen Nutting once observed, it is
also "highly improbable." After all, James II was soon to take the throne and
designate the Habeas Corpus Act as one of two laws that he wished to see
repealed—surely he would "have taken advantage of a real miscount to overturn the act." In addition, the attendance lists of the period were "notoriously
inaccurate," the Lords had passed earlier versions of the bill without incident,
and the Lords had the final say on the terms of the bill as it emerged from the
Conference with the House.[72]

This being said, the statute came during a period of great unrest in English
history. Many in Parliament were highly critical of Charles II's repeated proroguing of the Houses to render impossible the passage of legislation with
which he did not agree. After speaking against the practice, Francis Jenkes
found himself sent to the Gatehouse by the Privy Council. When, in turn, the
Earl of Shaftsbury defended Jenkes and argued that adjourning Parliament for
longer than a year was unlawful, the Lords sent him to the Tower of London.
He languished in the Tower for a year before finally agreeing to apologize to the
king and Lords.[73] Shaftsbury's failure to secure relief in the courts for his own

detention highlights the reality of the period—namely, control over the law of detention was much more about power than individual liberty. Specifically, when Shaftsbury sought relief in the form of a writ of habeas corpus from King's Bench, the justices declared that the House of Lords was superior to them and therefore its orders were not subject to review before their court.[74]

Meanwhile, the question whether James—Duke of York, brother of Charles II, and a Catholic convert—would succeed to the throne on Charles's death controlled most political affairs. Concerns over his ascendency had already fueled legislation barring Catholics from membership in the Houses of Parliament and generated witch-hunts for supporters of the so-called "Popish Plot," which allegedly sought to usher in Catholic rule by speeding Charles II's demise. One finds interspersed with the Commons' debates over the habeas bill the introduction of bills to discover and convict "Popish Recusants" along with votes in favor of declaring the Duke of York a "Papist" who "has given the greatest Countenance and Encouragement to the present Conspiracies and Designs of the Papists against the King. . . ." Likewise one finds records of the ongoing impeachment trials of the "Five Popish Lords" who had been ordered to the Tower of London by the very same Earl of Shaftesbury after being deemed guilty by the House of treason against the state.[75] Professor Nutting's work aptly highlights the irony that the Habeas Corpus Act came at a time "when men seemingly were more interested in getting their fellow Englishmen into jail than out of it."[76]

Who drafted the bill remains the subject of dispute. According to some historians, it may have been Attorney General William Jones.[77] Many helped move the bill along in the Commons, including Sir Thomas Clarges who had previously promoted the 1674 bill. Shaftsbury, an exclusionist who openly sought to block the Duke of York from inheriting the throne, is often credited with having shepherded the bill through the Lords. In so doing, he had help from various colleagues, including Baron Holles, who years earlier had secured passage of the Star Chamber Act in 1641.[78] Once introduced, the bill quickly moved through the Commons but stalled in the face of numerous amendments at the hands of the Lords, which created the need for more than one conference between the chambers to settle terms. The bill passed when the Commons accepted most of the Lords' amendments, probably spurred on by the fact that the king was on his way to the House of Lords to give his assent to all outstanding bills, including the Habeas Corpus Act, before calling the parliamentary session to an end.[79]

Given that the legislation was written to curtail royal powers and promoted by those who would curtail his line, it is curious that Charles II gave his assent to the Act. English Whig historian Thomas Macaulay wrote that although the king did not favor the legislation, "he was about to appeal from his Parliament to his people on the question of the succession, and he could not venture, at so critical a moment, to reject a bill which was in the highest degree popular."[80] Others have suggested that the king's assent came in part because many of the Act's terms were no longer controversial in light of evolving judicial practices and by assenting to the law, the king hoped to secure leniency from Parliament in its treatment of his close adviser Lord Danby, whom Parliament had recently sent to the Tower.[81]

The Houses entitled the legislation "An Act for the better securing the Liberty of the Subject, and for preventing of Imprisonments beyond the Seas" and declared that it was intended to address "great delays" by jailers "in making Returns to Writts of Habeas Corpus to them directed" as well as other abuses undertaken "to avoid . . . yielding Obedience to such Writts." By its terms, the Act sought to remedy the fact that "many of the Kings [sic] Subjects have beene and hereafter may be long detained in Prison, in such Cases where by Law they are baylable." Toward that end, the Act declared that it was "[f]or the prevention whereof and the more speedy Releife of all persons imprisoned for any such criminall or supposed criminall Matters." In defining its scope as such, the Act did not speak to cases of civil detention, but limited its reach to those cases involving "*all persons imprisoned for any such criminall or supposed criminall Matters*"—a category that very soon would come to be understood as embracing not just ordinary criminals, but domestic enemies of the state as well.[82]

In an attempt to codify regular procedures for such cases, the second section of the Act set forth how courts and jailers should respond upon the filing of a petition for a writ of habeas corpus. The law provided that the jailer "shall within Three dayes after the Service" of a writ "make Returne of such Writt" and bring "the Body of the Partie soe committed or restrained" before the relevant court while "certify[ing] the true causes of his Detainer or Imprisonment." The third section of the Act set forth procedures for obtaining writs during the vacation periods of the courts. This was in response to recent events, including the Francis Jenkes case in 1676, in which vacation writs had been denied even where bail likely should have been granted.[83] The fifth section of the Act, building on the model established in the Star Chamber Act, set forth escalating penalties to be paid to the prisoner in cases where jailers violated the obligation to make a return and produce the prisoner. The sixth and ninth sections curtailed the common abuses of recommitting discharged prisoners for the same offense and moving prisoners to escape a court's jurisdiction. The Act's tenth section made clear that judges violated the Act under threat of financial penalty. Its eleventh section in turn clarified that the writ would run to various islands and "privileged places" within the kingdom notwithstanding the judicial precedents that had previously deemed these places the equivalent of legal islands. To reach yet further abusive practices by the king and his ministers, the twelfth section declared that the imprisonment of any "Subject of this Realme" in Scotland, Ireland, Jersey, Guernsey, Tangier (a common destination for prisoners condemned by the Earl of Clarendon), or "Parts Garrisons Islands or Places beyond the Seas . . . within or without the Dominions of His Majestie," is "hereby enacted and adjudged to be illegal."[84]

Many of these provisions are most significant for providing a measure of certainty as to habeas procedures and the availability of the writ—whether in vacation term or from privileged places, for example.[85] But the seventh section of the Act did much more than this. That section both connected the writ of habeas corpus with the criminal process and placed specific limits on how and when the executive lawfully could detain the most serious of criminals—even alleged traitors. By its terms, the section covered "any person or persons . . . committed for High Treason or Fellony." Where a prisoner committed on this basis was not indicted within two court terms (a period typically spanning only three-to-six months), the Act provided that the justices of King's Bench and other criminal courts "are hereby *required* . . . to sett at Liberty the Prisoner upon Baile." Going further, section 7 also declared that "if any person or persons committed as aforesaid . . . shall not be indicted and tryed the second Terme . . . or upon his Tryall shall be acquitted, he *shall be discharged* from his Imprisonment."[86] In other words, the Act promised the most dangerous of suspects the remedy of discharge where they were not timely tried and convicted. Referring to this section fifteen years after its passage, Chief Justice John Holt wrote that "the design of the Act was to prevent a man's lying under accusation of treason, &c. above two terms."[87]

Going back to the reign of Edward III, high treason had long included, among other things, plotting the demise of the monarch or his or her line, levying war against the Crown, and adhering or providing aid to the Crown's enemies.[88] As Blackstone elaborated in his *Commentaries*, treason encompassed a whole range of acts that today would be viewed as taking up arms against the government or the equivalent of terrorism. It followed that high treason not only encompassed aiding "foreign powers with whom we are at open war," but also providing assistance to "foreign pirates or robbers, who may happen to invade our coasts, without any open hostilities between their nation and our own"[89]—that is, aiding nonstate actors hostile to the throne. Blackstone also instructed that high treason "most indisputably" included adhering to or aiding "fellow-subjects in actual rebellion at home."[90] The common aspects of treason included "giving the [enemy] intelligence, . . . sending them pro-visions, . . . selling them arms, . . . treacherously surrendering a fortress, or the like."[91] Each of these acts was most likely to occur in time of war, yet the Habeas Corpus Act did not include any exception for wartime. For this very reason, Charles II's successor and brother James II viewed the Act as "a great misfortune," lamenting that "it oblige[d] the Crown to keep a greater force on foot th[an] it needed otherwise to preserve the government" and deal with the "disaffected, turbulent, and unquiet spirits" and "their wicked designs."[92]

It was because the crime of high treason was so serious—it was gener-ally a capital offense with no opportunity for bail—that Blackstone counseled that its sanctions must be safeguarded from abuse by the government. Thus, Blackstone wrote that high treason must be "the most precisely ascertained" of crimes, for if it "be indeterminate, this alone . . . is sufficient to make any government degenerate into arbitrary power." He likewise cautioned that the "opportunity to create abundance of constructive treasons" was equally dan-gerous to liberty.[93] Chief Justice Mathew Hale also cautioned against deviating from the settled legal framework for punishing treason:

> How dangerous it is by construction and analogy to make treasons, where the letter of the law has not done it: for such a method admits of no limits or bounds, but runs as far as the wit and invention of accusers, and the odiousness and detestation of persons accused will carry men.[94]

In recognition of the importance of safeguards in treason cases, Parliament passed the Trial of Treasons Act in 1696. Following on the heels of the Habeas Corpus Act, the legislation instituted additional protections for those charged with the crime of high treason.[95] These included the requirement of two wit-nesses to an overt act, a requirement later imported into the Treason Clause in the U.S. Constitution,[96] and other protections that had not been previously granted to those accused of common law crimes, including the right to coun-sel and to compel witnesses for one's defense.[97]

Viewing all of these developments together, it was no stretch for Henry Care's popular treatise on English law to point to Magna Carta, the Habeas Corpus Act, and the 1696 treason statute as the guardians of English liber-ties.[98] It is also true, however, that much of this legal framework was not so much the result of a deep concern for civil liberties *per se*, but represented instead the product of a concerted effort by Parliament to protect its privileges and wrestle control of such matters from the monarch.[99]

THUS, AT LONG last Selden and Coke's aspiration to constrain the executive's power to detain outside the criminal process came to be. No longer did the king and his ministers enjoy free reign to detain without proceeding toward criminal trial, nor did the royal courts enjoy any longer the discretion to disregard these limitations on executive detention when ruling on habeas corpus petitions. Instead, by the terms of the Habeas Corpus Act, Parliament claimed for itself control over the relevant legal framework for the detention of prisoners. In this regard, the Act was part of the rise of parliamentary supremacy, including Parliament's assertion of much greater control over matters of war and foreign affairs during this period.[100] On the ground, the Act proved a powerful check on the king and the royal courts. No longer would the royal command suffice as justification for operating outside the constraints of parliamentary law. In time, Scotland and Ireland adopted the same habeas protections in their own acts—Scotland in 1701 and Ireland in 1782.[101]

For American colonists studying English law during this period, the inability to claim the benefits of the Habeas Corpus Act and related legal protections such as trial by jury and the various protections of the Trial of Treasons Act—all of which the Crown denied them—would foster a deep resentment of English rule. Indeed, in the period leading up to the Revolutionary War, Americans were steeped in Henry Care's treatise on *English Liberties* and Blackstone's recently published *Commentaries*, which glorified the Habeas Corpus Act as a "second *magna carta*"[102] and celebrated its promise that "no man is to be arrested, unless charged with such a crime, as will at least justify holding him to bail, when taken."[103] Blackstone also rejected general warrants "to apprehend all persons suspected, without naming or particularly describing any person in special" as "illegal and void."[104] Whether so-called Whig History or not, Care and Blackstone's work dominated the popular and political discourse surrounding habeas corpus during this period with the effect of making the Habeas Corpus Act the central component of the story.

But the American experience did not know many of the rights and protections that were glorified by Care and Blackstone. In the period leading up to the Revolutionary War, American colonists suffered the increasing issuance of general search warrants (called writs of assistance) and, James Otis's eloquent protests notwithstanding, were repeatedly told by the Crown that they did not enjoy the same rights as their English counterparts across the Atlantic. There, Blackstone instructed, the Habeas Corpus Act had made "the remedy . . . now complete for *removing* the injury of unjust and illegal confinement," and being "apprehended upon suspicion" alone was no longer legal anywhere the Act remained in force.[105] It would take a revolution for these principles to take hold in America.

An Imperfect Safeguard

Even where the Act did apply, its limitations quickly came to light. For example, following its passage, the practice of moving prisoners to so-called "legal islands" (even those specifically mentioned in the Act) continued. In 1683, when the government learned of the so-called Rye House Plot to murder Charles II and James, the Duke of York, it arrested a number of alleged conspirators, including twelve Scotsmen. Although these prisoners had been arrested in England on suspicion of treason committed there, the Scots Privy Council, presided over by the king, ordered the prisoners dispatched to Scotland. Upon arrival, some were tried, but others were never tried and instead tortured repeatedly for intelligence. The decision to deport the prisoners appears to have been driven entirely by the absence of the governance of the Habeas Corpus Act in Scotland at that time and therefore highlights the geographic limitations of the Act that would become increasingly important in the next century.[106]

It is also the case that during this period the exceptions to the Act's coverage—even where it applied—proved substantial. Consider the story of Charles II's illegitimate son, the Duke of Monmouth, who had been exiled from England in 1683 following the failed Rye House Plot, in which he had played a role. In the immediate aftermath of the death of the king and the crowning of his brother as James II two years later, Monmouth returned to England determined to foster rebellion and wrestle the throne from his uncle.

The execution of the Duke of Monmouth on Tower Hill, 1685
Credit: London in the Time of the Stuarts by Sir Walter Besant (artist unknown), Adam & Charles Black, London 1903.

After Monmouth was defeated in battle and captured, James ordered him sent to the Tower of London. Monmouth never enjoyed a criminal trial, but instead, within days of his capture, Parliament passed a bill of attainder declaring him summarily guilty of treason and ordering his execution.[107] His gruesome public beheading on Tower Hill followed in due course, and scores of his followers were executed or sold into slavery without trial. Parliament would continue to wield its potent and essentially unchecked attainder power for some time to come.[108]

With the flight of James II from the throne only a handful of years later and in response to attempts by those loyal to him to retake the throne for his line, Parliament would create yet another means of sidestepping the mandates of the Habeas Corpus Act. Ironically, in so doing, Parliament would both confirm and underscore the potency of the Act's protections where they could not be so evaded.

2

Suspension

LEGISLATING AN EMERGENCY POWER

If an Angel came from Heaven that was a Privy-Counsellor,
I would not trust my Liberty with him one moment.

SIR WILLIAM WHITLOCK TO THE HOUSE
OF COMMONS (1690)[1]

THE UNREST IN the period leading up to James II's reign would also be his undoing. Religious tensions hardly evaporated with his crowning and were fueled all the more by James's efforts to reverse many of Parliament's anti-Catholic policies adopted during his brother's reign. When James's second wife gave birth to a Catholic son and likely heir to the throne, opposition nobility formalized an invitation to William of Orange to invade. William wasted little time, landing on English shores in 1688. Rather than fight, James fled to France where he sought refuge in the protection of his cousin, Louis XIV.

The crowning of William and his wife Mary, James II's daughter from his earlier Protestant marriage, marked the Glorious Revolution. Their reign witnessed the restoration of a Protestant monarchy, the continued rise of parliamentary supremacy, and the adoption of the Declaration of Rights. It did not, however, bring a settled peace. Despite their king having fled, James II's supporters remained eager to engineer his return. It was to defeat the plotting of these so-called Jacobites that Parliament would invent a tool for setting aside the very protections that it had secured with the Habeas Corpus Act of 1679. They would call it *suspension*.

The first suspension of the Habeas Corpus Act, which came only months into the reign of William and Mary, established a precedent to which future Parliaments would look when contemplating similarly dramatic legislation. Together, the historical context and debates preceding adoption of the English suspensions of the seventeenth and eighteenth centuries, their terms, and how the executive and courts interpreted their operation, all shed considerable light not only on the prevailing understanding of suspension during this

Habeas Corpus in Wartime. Amanda L. Tyler.
© Oxford University Press 2017. Published 2017 by Oxford University Press.

important period, but also on the Habeas Corpus Act itself. The entire point of these suspensions was to set aside the protections promised by the Act. Thus, by studying the suspensions of the Habeas Corpus Act, one can discern precisely which of the Act's protections warranted displacement in times of war.

As shown below, the suspensions during this period confirm that the protections inherent in the Habeas Corpus Act placed significant constraints on the executive's authority to detain persons, even in times of war. This explains why the purpose consistently animating the Act's suspension was born out of a parliamentary desire to empower the executive to arrest suspected traitors outside the criminal process. Correspondingly, studying this period highlights that in the absence of suspension, the Act's seventh section was understood to demand that suspects—even those believed to pose a threat to the state— be timely tried on criminal charges or else released. Notably, however, this model applied only to those who fell within the protection of domestic law and not to formal prisoners of war, an important caveat that is explored at the end of this chapter. Examining the debates and judicial decisions surrounding the suspensions of this period underscores the importance of the statutory privilege of the writ of habeas corpus as a check on executive authority.

It remained the case during this period that much of habeas corpus jurisprudence was not so much about the protection of individual liberty as it was about Parliament expanding its power. Indeed, during this period, Parliament not only devised suspension, but as the dramatic story of John Bernardi told here highlights, it also repeatedly employed its attainder power as a separate means of circumventing the Habeas Corpus Act. As matters unfolded, the understanding that emerged from this period of the respective roles of the Habeas Corpus Act and suspension in the English legal framework proved enormously important to the story of habeas corpus in America. In time, much of this framework would come to be incorporated directly into the U.S. Constitution.

What Parliament Gives, It May Take Away

Almost immediately upon taking the throne, William and Mary had to confront the threat posed by James. James had been received by his cousin at the French Court and, with the help of the French and a powerful group of his English supporters, had begun plotting his return to England. In the meantime, Ireland—preferring a Catholic to a Protestant king—was in full-fledged revolt; Scotland, meanwhile, appeared to be on the brink of unraveling. A dramatic series of events followed. On March 1, 1689, William delivered a message to the House of Commons through an emissary, Richard Hampden, a member of the Privy Council. As Paul Halliday has written, it "was a sign of how much political circumstances had changed" that Hampden delivered the king's message, for he had been "an active supporter" of the Habeas Corpus Act just ten years earlier.[2]

The king intended his message to inform the Commons of the severity of the threat that James and his supporters posed and convey the Crown's need for expanded powers to address the situation.[3] Hampden reported that William had reason to believe that supporters of James were meeting in and around London. Hampden also relayed that by the Crown's orders, persons had already been arrested on suspicion of treasonous activities, and that William expected that there might be reason to arrest more. Speaking of those already imprisoned, he observed:

> If these should be set at liberty, 'tis apprehended we shall be wanting to our own safety, the Government, and People. The King is not willing to do any thing but what he may be warranted by Law; therefore, if these persons deliver themselves by *Habeas Corpus*, there may arise a difficulty. Excessive Bail you have complained of. If men hope to carry their great design on, they will not be unwilling to forfeit their Bail. The King asks your Advice, and hopes you will give it, as likewise the Lords. I forgot to tell you, some are committed on suspicion of Treason only.[4]

Thus, Hampden conveyed that the king did not want to violate the law and feared that persons detained without formal charges would be "deliver[ed] by *Habeas Corpus*." As a new monarch eager to buttress his legitimacy, William may have believed it especially necessary to work within the law.

Debate in the House of Commons followed. It opened with Charles Boscawen noting that disaffection had invaded military ranks and expressing concern that English soldiers might join the enemy in Scotland. He then remarked:

> [T]he King has sent for your Advice, and he knows well enough how the Law stands, which ought to be inviolable, and I am always for keeping it. Therefore I would make immediate application to the King, to take up such persons as he shall suspect to be obnoxious; likewise I would have a short Bill, for two or three months, to enable the King to commit such persons as he shall have cause to suspect, without the benefit of *Habeas Corpus*.[5]

The suggestion naturally encountered significant opposition. Some reacted with alarm to the idea of repealing the protections of the Habeas Corpus Act, as Sir Thomas Clarges called it, "a thing so sacred!" Clarges's reaction was emblematic of the resistance many felt to setting aside a "sacred" Act passed only ten years earlier after such a long struggle. Clarges, who had played a key role in securing the Act's passage after promoting earlier habeas legislation unsuccessfully, questioned whether setting excessive bail was instead the appropriate means to keep suspicious persons under lock and key. Clarges's resistance followed in part from his equating the concept of suspension with a state of "Martial Law."[6] In response to the suggestion that setting excessive bail would suffice to address the current situation, more than one member of the House pointed out that only two weeks earlier the Declaration of Rights repudiated the practice.[7] Heneage Finch then suggested another reason for pause, noting that regardless of any protections enjoyed by reason of the Habeas Corpus Act, no judges had yet been installed by the new government, and therefore it was not obvious that any practical avenue for securing the privilege existed.[8] But Hampden pressed on. He noted that the king—in contrast to his predecessors—held the belief that the writ ran to the Tower, where some of the prisoners were being held. For them to remain committed, he continued, the House needed "to have a Vote for a Bill for the King to commit, without benefit of *Habeas Corpus*, [for] [th]ree months."[9] In other words, Hampden asked Parliament to declare the detentions lawful.

The House of Commons quickly read a draft bill twice and committed it.[10] Meanwhile the same day, through another emissary, William informed the House of Lords that:

> He had secured some Persons, as dangerous to the Government; and thought it might be convenient to secure more: But, being extreme tender of doing any Thing that the Law doth not fully warrant, had given Order that this House might be acquainted with what He had thought Himself obliged to do, for the Public Peace and Security of the Government.

In response, the Lords communicated to the Commons that they wished to authorize the king to "secure[] all such suspected Persons, as may effectually prevent any Disturbance of the Public Peace; and that such Persons as are, or shall be, so committed may be detained until the First Day of the next [court] Term."[11]

Within days—and after inserting a provision excepting their own members from the bill's coverage[12]—both Houses passed the first suspension of the

Suspension

39

Habeas Corpus Act. They entitled it: "An Act for Impowering His Majestie to Apprehend and Detaine such Persons as He shall finde just Cause to Suspect are Conspireing against the Government." The legislation provided:

> For the secureing the Peace of the Kingdome in this Time of Imminent Danger against the Attempts and Trayterous Conspiracies of evill disposed Persons
>
> Bee it Enacted . . . That every Person or Persons that shall be committed by Warrant of Their said Majestyes most Honourable Privy Councill Signed by Six of the said Privy Councill at least for Suspition of High Treason may be detayned in safe Custodie till [April 17, 1689], without Baile or Mainprize[13] and that noe Judge or other Person shall Baile or Try any such Person or Persons soe Committed without Order from Their said Majestyes Privy Councill Signed by Six of the said Privy Councill . . . any Law or Statute to the contrary notwithstanding.
>
> Provided alwayes That from and after the said [April 17] the said Persons soe Committed shall have the Benefitt and Advantage of [the Habeas Corpus Act of 1679[14]] and alsoe of all other Laws and Statutes any way relateing to or provideing for the Liberty of the Subjects of this Realme.[15]

This first suspension accomplished many things. First, it explicitly set aside "the Benefitt and Advantage" of the Habeas Corpus Act for those "persons"[16] suspected of High Treason who were committed by a warrant signed by six members of the Privy Council. Thus, from the beginning, suspension was linked inextricably to the Habeas Corpus Act. Second, it set aside "all other Laws and Statutes any way" relating to the liberty of the subject, establishing the principle that suspension also set aside laws and practices that were complementary to the Act—including the common law writ of habeas corpus. Third, by its plain terms it prohibited any "Judge or other Person" from bailing or trying such prisoners. Finally, by its title, it purported to "impower" the Crown to order the arrests of those it believed were "conspiring against the government." Undoubtedly aware that they were handing the Crown a potent emergency authority—namely, the ability to arrest and detain suspected traitors without trial—Parliament provided that the suspension would last for only one month.

Additional arrests on suspicion followed immediately after passage of the suspension. The King's Privy Council wasted little time on that score—ordering on the very same day that the suspension received the king's assent that "all magistrates of the Severall Ports of the West of England to Stop all

Irish Papists endeavoring to make their escape that way and to keep them in Safe Custody."[17] The Council also labeled those who had gone to James as "Rebells and Traytors" and ordered all those in a position to do so to "use their best and utmost Endeavors . . . to resist, Repell, and Suppress" the rebellion and "seize and Prosecute" such persons "according to the utmost rigors of the law."[18] In so doing, the Council both issued a sweeping order to suppress the rebellion and seize perpetrators and suggested that it harbored the goal of eventually prosecuting such persons. As the suspension continued, however, this goal would become less important to those ordering arrests.

During the brief period that this initial suspension ran, James, enjoying the support of France, had landed in Ireland where the Irish Parliament declared that he remained king. James in turn made preparations to invade Scotland. Scores of Protestants fled Ireland for England and its Protestant ruler, and hidden among them came many Irish Catholics who supported the Jacobite cause. At home, "disaffection was rife in the army," and there was a mutiny at Ipswich. Meanwhile, the suspension lapsed at the start of the new court term and several prisoners quickly sought relief in the courts, requesting that they be bailed or tried as promised by the Habeas Corpus Act.[19]

Before the courts could act, Parliament immediately took up a bill to extend the suspension one additional month while also expanding its scope. Both Houses passed the extension and the king signed it the same day.[20] The extension differed in two important respects from the original bill. First, the extension empowered the executive to arrest and commit not only on suspicion of high treason but also more generally on suspicion of so-called "Treasonable Practices." Second, the new legislation expanded the scope of those who were given the power to commit prisoners to include either of the two secretaries of state.[21]

The day following its passage, the king in Council ordered the principal secretary of state to "Recommitt the Prisoners now in the Tower of London" as well as "the Roman priests now Prisoners in Newgate," while explicitly tying the Crown's authority to issue such orders to the suspension act passed by Parliament one day earlier.[22] (To ensure coverage of those prisoners already in custody, moreover, the extension specifically covered "every Person or Persons that Shall be in Prison at or upon the [25th of April, 1689] or after.") This new round of warrants prevented the relevant prisoners from invoking the benefits of the Habeas Corpus Act before the courts. In the wake of the extension, the Crown also issued warrants for new arrests, along with several general warrants that provided broadly for the arrest of so-called "suspicious persons."[23] Meanwhile, William formally declared war against France and James II moved closer to undertaking a military strike to retake the English throne.[24] These developments triggered a debate in Parliament over a proposal to extend the suspension yet a third time.

Hampden once again led off discussion in the Commons. His remarks are illuminating as to the animating purpose of the suspension:

> Dangers usually come not in a day; growing dangers, and the conse-quences, are in the dark, when it is too late to prevent. What is the mean-ing of all the intelligence that comes out of the Country, of ill-affections to the Government? And have we not a body here that are mutinying against the Government? In *Lancashire*, since the *Irish* were disbanded, they meet in parties, and you have no way to obviate this danger but by this Bill. You are willing to go home; what will the King do? Dangerous persons will be delivered out of prison of course, if this Bill prevent it not; and they may act to the Subversion of the Government. . . . And if people conspire, the King cannot keep them in prison; since they must come out by *Habeas Corpus*, if you prevent it not by this Bill. We are in War, and if we make only use of that remedy as if we were in full Peace, you may be destroyed without remedy. This Bill is for present occasion, and for a short time only I move it.[25]

Unlike the prior two bills, this proposal provoked extensive debate in the Commons. Whether for or against the measure, speakers uniformly equated suspension with empowering the Crown to arrest outside the criminal proc-ess those persons thought to be working with the enemy. Likewise, all appear to have assumed that those imprisoned would have enjoyed a criminal trial in the absence of a suspension.[26]

As the debate unfolded, Sir John Hawles defended the bill as necessary to confine the disaffected and thereby prevent them "from doing mischief." In his remarks, Hawles also emphasized the fact "that the King and Government will not do it [that is, detain the disaffected] without an Act."[27] Colonel John Birch in turn cautioned that "[w]e are in a state of War . . . [with] disaffected persons in every corner" and urged that the bill was necessary to address the fact that many prisoners "that disturb the Government have been picked up, but not tried, in two or three months."[28] Of course, the only reason the lack of trial was significant was that the Habeas Corpus Act, which Birch labeled as not "practicable" in such times, promised a timely trial to those who could claim its protections. Birch therefore pleaded for continuing the suspension to render detention without trial lawful.

Sir Christopher Musgrave opposed the extension. As he noted, with its sweeping terms, the bill "suspends not only the *Habeas Corpus*, but the Law that was before it." Musgrave counseled: "We hear of several clapped up, and no prosecution against them. . . . We are told of some going to King *James*; if that be so, you have a Law to punish them; and if any break in upon your Army, 'tis Rebellion, and you may punish them."[29] Thus, in Musgrave's view, rebellion and treason called for criminal prosecution in the ordinary course; there was no need for suspension. Clarges, still championing the Habeas Corpus Act, agreed, arguing "'[t]is so much against the privilege of the subject that any man may be imprisoned upon a bare suggestion, and not have benefit of *Habeas Corpus*." For his part, he "would not have any man committed, by this Bill, but by Oath, and that the accuser do give security to prosecute."[30]

Also opposing the measure, Sir Robert Cotton detailed the connection between the privilege and the protections inherent in criminal procedure:

> Laws are made that a man may be safe, that a man may know his crime before he be committed to prison, and may recover his Liberty in a legal manner, as the Law appoints. If this was for . . . any ground of reasonable suspicion; but when the suspicion has no ground, but upon private resentments, and that not so open, and not know why suspected, this alters the very reason of the Law of *Habeas Corpus*.[31]

Here, Cotton equated the function of "the Law of *Habeas Corpus*" with ensuring that "a man may know his crime before he be committed to prison" and be permitted to test the sufficiency of the grounds of the charges against him during that process.

Whether for or against the bill, everyone in Parliament seemed to appreciate that they were creating a precedent for the future, and many remained strongly opposed to setting aside protections hard won in the Act just ten years earlier. In one particularly colorful statement, Sir Robert Napier observed: "This Mistress of ours, the *Habeas Corpus* Act, if we part with it twice, it will become quite a common Whore."[32] Ultimately, despite substantial opposition, the bill passed in both Houses, received the royal assent, and extended the suspension for five additional months.[33] Like the first extension, it permitted commitment on suspicion of high treason as well as suspicion of "Treasonable Practices."

When this extension finally lapsed, the legal framework of the Habeas Corpus Act returned immediately to effect. As one historian reviewing records from the period reports, "[i]mmediately after the expiration of the Suspension Act, we find numerous mentions of writs of Habeas Corpus being granted. . . ."[34] Indeed, as Paul Halliday shows in his work surveying King's Bench following the lapse of this suspension, that court bailed or discharged some 80 percent of those who sought writs of habeas corpus before it during the period.[35]

Notwithstanding the flurry of activity before King's Bench, certain prisoners remained in custody following the lapsing of the suspension. They did so based upon one of two justifications—either they were proceeding toward trial on criminal charges[36] or they had been imprisoned by direct order of Parliament, which continued to act beyond the reach of the Habeas Corpus Act. Indeed, just two days after the suspension ended, upon learning that some of James's key supporters were in the process of being bailed from the Tower of London by King's Bench "by virtue of a *Habeas Corpus*," the House of Commons directed the Serjeant at Arms to take the prisoners into custody so that it could determine their fates.[37] The next day, the Commons learned of additional Tower prisoners who were before King's Bench invoking the Habeas Corpus Act "in order to their Bailing." Once again, the House ordered the prisoners brought before it and then re-committed two of them to the Tower on warrants charging High Treason.[38] Suspension, it seems, was only one of the weapons in Parliament's arsenal of detention powers.

An attempt to revive this first experiment with suspension failed in the spring of 1690. What little information is available about the proposal suggests that the members of Parliament recognized the drastic nature of what they had created in suspension, for it is here that one finds Sir William Whitlock's dramatic observation: "If an Angel came from Heaven that was a Privy-Counsellor, I would not trust my Liberty with him one moment."[39] Within weeks of this debate, William sailed for Ireland where he personally commanded the English army in its defeat of James II at the Battle of the Boyne, spurring James II's return to France. Meanwhile, however, the English were reeling from the French fleet's important victory over English and Dutch ships at the Battle of Beachy Head, from which the French emerged in temporary control of the English Channel.[40]

The Assassination Plot and the Plight of John Bernardi

The years that followed witnessed ongoing war with France and Jacobite threats to retake the throne, although whether such attempts could have succeeded remains the subject of considerable debate among historians who study the period. Regardless, citing the repeated threats to the throne posed by the Jacobites, Parliament passed numerous additional suspensions in the decades that followed. By 1696, James II had returned to France from Ireland, where he remained just long enough to assemble troops to prepare for an attempted invasion of England.[41] In February of that year, William learned of a plot to assassinate him the night before it was to be carried out. He reacted first by arresting several conspirators, and second by summoning the Commons to the House of Lords to inform them that:

> I have received several concurring Informations of a Design to assas-
> sinate me; and that our Enemies, at the same time, are very forward in
> their Preparations for a sudden Invasion of this Kingdom. . . . Some of
> the Conspirators against my Person are already in Custody; and Care
> is taken to apprehend so many of the rest as are discovered; and such
> other Orders are given, as the present Exigency of Affairs does abso-
> lutely require at this Time, for the publick Safety.[42]

William then called upon the Houses "to do every thing which you shall judge proper for our common Safety."[43] In other words, instead of claiming the power to act outside the legal constraints of the Habeas Corpus Act, William went to Parliament to ask, once again, that it set aside the Act's protections and thereby expand his power to arrest and detain outside the criminal process to address the emergency at hand.

In immediate response, the Houses declared in a joint resolution that they "humbly desire[d] his Majesty to give speedy Order for securing such Persons, with their Horses and Arms, as he shall have just Reason to suspect are Enemies to his Person and Government" and they assured the king that they would "give all possible Dispatch to all the publick Business now depend-ing before them." Unsurprisingly, the very first order of business to follow this resolution and a conference of the Houses was an order granting leave to introduce a suspension of the Habeas Corpus Act.[44] Within days, both Houses passed and the king signed new suspension legislation modeled on the sec-ond and third suspension acts of 1689.

The 1696 suspension provided that it would run for six months. The Act's preamble cited the "time of imminent Danger" and stated that it was intended to reach "Traiterous Conspiracies of Evil disposed Persons," including per-sons already in custody.[45] As with earlier suspensions, this one by its terms empowered the Crown, through the secretaries of state or Privy Council, to arrest and detain suspects outside the criminal process "for Suspicion of High Treason or treasonable Practices." Thus, the Act served to expand executive power for a temporary period. Likewise, the Act provided that "noe Judge or Justice . . . shall bail or try any such Person or Persons soe committed without Order [signed by six members of] His said Majesties Privy Council." The sus-pension made clear that upon its expiration, all persons then in custody would

once again "have the Benefitt and Advantage" of "An Act for the better securing the Liberty of the Subject and for Prevention of Imprisonment beyond
the Seas" (namely, the Habeas Corpus Act), along with "all other Laws and
Statutes any way relating to or providing for the Liberty of the Subject of this
Realme." Accordingly, although the Habeas Corpus Act and any other means
for securing bail or trial were displaced for the duration of the suspension,
Parliament provided that they would spring back to life immediately upon its
expiration.

The legislation does not appear to have met with any opposition in
Parliament,[46] and unsurprisingly, a wave of arrests followed its passage.
Indeed, in the days immediately preceding and following enactment of the
suspension, the Privy Council entry book is replete with warrants for the seizure of persons on suspicion of High Treason and Treasonable Practices, typically ordering their detention in safe custody either in the Tower of London or
the Gatehouse.[47] When certain suspects eluded capture, the Council ordered
all English subjects to arrest on sight the most notable of them, including Lord
Montgomery and Sir John Fenwick. The Council also ordered that possible
hiding places, including most notably Lincoln's Inn, be searched for "concealed" suspects.[48]

Although the 1696 suspension granted the Crown the power to detain
without trial those suspected of involvement in the assassination plot, the
government nonetheless prosecuted several of the suspects while the suspension remained in effect, securing convictions in many cases.[49] As for Sir
John Fenwick, who was finally caught, he managed to escape conviction by a
jury for high treason because key witnesses against him had successfully fled
England.[50] No matter, Parliament responded by invoking its power of attainder
once again—and, upon lapsing of the suspension, it attainted Fenwick guilty
of high treason and ordered him beheaded on Tower Hill.[51] In a remarkable
twist of fate, Fenwick's horse, "Sorrel," confiscated on his attainder and given
to the king, would later stumble on a mole hill and cause the fall that ultimately led to William's death.[52]

When the assassination plot suspension lapsed, King's Bench ordered the
release of a first wave of prisoners who had been detained on the basis of
Crown warrants and against whom the government did not initiate prosecutions.[53] When counsel took on the case of another group implicated in the
assassination plot and it appeared that they too would win release, Parliament
again turned to its attainder powers to circumvent the Habeas Corpus Act.
Among this group of prisoners was John Bernardi, whose story demonstrates
dramatically the significance of suspension and attainder as the two primary
means of avoiding the Habeas Corpus Act's mandates. Thirty-three years into

his detention at Newgate and yet to enjoy a criminal trial, he recorded what
happened in the immediate wake of the assassination attempt:

> [N]ine . . . being executed,[54] there still remained many close prison-
> ers in Newgate . . . ; but evidence being wanted to convict any more
> of them, the Habeas Corpus Act was suspended for nine months, to
> prevent them from gaining their liberty by law; and this was done
> with a view of finding out evidence against them within that time. The
> suspension of the act expiring, several of them entered their prayer
> at the then next sessions and term, to be tried and admitted to bail.
> The first who entered such their prayer . . . were all bailed out and
> discharged. . . . The remaining number in confinement [including
> Bernardi] . . . could neither communicate or do any thing for them-
> selves in order to their liberty . . . : But the good success of those before
> mentioned caused their friends abroad officiously to enter prayers for
> them at the second sessions after the Habeas Corpus act came in force;
> whereupon they were all of them taken out of their close holes, and
> were carried to the Old-Baily, in order to be tried or bailed. . . .
>
> As soon as they were produced in court in order to be tried or bailed,
> the solicitor of the treasury stood up and whispered the judges upon
> the bench: and though that sessions, being a sessions of gaol-delivery,
> could not lawfully be determined without either trying or bailing these
> state-prisoners . . . , yet upon the whispering motion of the solicitor of
> the treasury, the judges adjourned the court for a fortnight, and imme-
> diately after a bill was brought into parliament, and an act passed within
> that time to confine them for a twelvemonth, on a supposed probability
> still of finding out some evidence against them in that time. . . .[55]

When Parliament's special act continuing Bernardi's detention lapsed, it
passed another, and still another.[56] Some forty years later, Bernardi died in
Newgate, never having enjoyed a trial, his habeas corpus petitions repeatedly
thwarted by bills of attainder passed against him interspersed with additional
acts of suspension.[57] Perhaps more than any other, Bernardi's case drove home
the reality that Parliament now wielded total control over matters of detention
and, with no formal constraints on its power, prisoners were at its mercy.[58]

Meanwhile, another prisoner implicated in the 1696 assassination plot,
Lord Aylesbury, filed his motion for relief under the Habeas Corpus Act
almost five years too late. This produced an opinion from King's Bench in
which it concluded that one committed for treason during a suspension must
pursue relief under the Habeas Corpus Act during "the first week of the term

or day of the sessions after the expiration of [the suspension]." Despite denying Aylesbury the "benefit of the Habeas Corpus Act," the court nonetheless
exercised its discretion to bail him because of ill health.[59]

More Suspensions and the Tower Prisoners

In the years that followed, war with France and continuing Jacobite efforts to
reinstate the Stuart line resulted in suspension becoming a not uncommon—
though always short-lived—state of affairs. Thus, Parliament adopted suspensions in 1708, 1715, 1722, 1744, and 1745. Although certain Jacobite efforts
posed genuinely serious threats during this period, it is also true that the
Whigs had a strong partisan interest to inflate those threats so as to maintain
the royal patronage and political power that they enjoyed under the reign of
the Hanovarian line.

The 1708,[60] 1715,[61] and 1722[62] suspensions each followed a series of events
similar to those that had preceded earlier ones. In each case, Queen Anne,
Mary's sister and successor, and later King George I (who inherited the throne
as Anne's closest Protestant relative upon her death in 1714), learned that the
Jacobites were plotting to reinstate the Stuart line to the throne by installing
James II's Catholic son, James Edward Stuart, popularly known as "the Old
Pretender." In all three cases, the suspension acts targeted plots transpiring in
Scotland and provided that for those imprisoned on suspicion of high treason
or treasonable practices, "no Judge or Justice shall bail or try any such Person
or Persons so committed" without an order from the Privy Council. Further,
all three acts expressly "suspended" the Scottish Habeas Corpus Act of 1701.[63]
The 1708 suspension, more detailed than the two suspensions that followed
it, also provided that upon its expiration, all "Persons so committed shall have
the Benefit and Advantage of all Laws and Statutes any way relating to or providing for the Liberty of the Subjects of this Realm."

Although the threat in 1708 never truly materialized,[64] the 1715 threat
proved more substantial. That year witnessed portions of Scotland proclaim
James Edward Stuart as their king along with the first major battles between
royal troops and the Jacobites.[65] Among those detained during the 1715 suspension was Sir William Wyndham, a leading Jacobite who had been committed to the Tower for high treason by the secretary of state. Wyndham's initial
attempt to win bail from King's Bench failed, coming as it did during the
suspension. When the suspension lapsed, Wyndham tried again. This time
he succeeded, with King's Bench holding that in light of the passage of four
terms since his commitment and "there being no prosecution against him, he
must be admitted to bail."[66] Wyndham's case confirmed what earlier episodes

had already instructed—namely, when suspension ends, the mandates of the Habeas Corpus Act immediately return to force and constrain the executive's power to detain.[67] Wyndham's case also established an important judicial precedent respecting the role of the courts in enforcing the terms of the Habeas Corpus Act, and its timing in this respect may have been connected to recently adopted protections put in place to enhance the independence of the courts by distancing them from the Crown's control.[68]

After a brief respite, the Jacobites regrouped. Sir Robert Walpole, leader of the House of Commons during this period, informed the House that a renewed conspiracy had begun in late 1721, when Jacobite leaders approached "some Potentates abroad, for an assistance of 5000 men," and carried over to the spring of 1722, when they repeated their request, this time for the aid of 3,000 men. "[B]eing again disappointed in their expectations from foreign assistance," Walpole continued, "they resolved desperately to go on, confiding in their own strength, and fondly depending on the disaffection in England" to advance their cause. By May of 1722, Walpole told the House, "the government had undoubted informations of this Plot . . . ; but nevertheless thought fit not to take up any body, because there being then two terms coming on together, the conspirators would have had the benefit of the Habeas Corpus act and so the apprehending them was put off until the long vacation."[69]

Thus, wait the Administration did. Once the law courts were in vacation, the king's council ordered a number of leading suspects, including the Bishop of Rochester, the Earl of Orrery (Lord Boyle), and Lord North and Grey, to be arrested and committed to the Tower on suspicion of High Treason. When the new Parliament convened in October, the king opened the session by making the chambers aware of the details surrounding the alleged conspiracy and informing the Houses that some of the conspirators were in custody and that others remained at large. The House of Lords immediately took up a bill to suspend the Habeas Corpus Act for one year, and within a matter of days the bill passed both houses and received the king's assent.[70] Accordingly, the suspension came into effect well before the "Prisoners in the Tower," as the conspirators came to be known, were ever in a position to claim the benefit of the Habeas Corpus Act.[71]

The passage of the 1722 bill was not without dissent, however. Several members of Parliament protested that the length of the suspension—one year—extended longer than all prior suspensions and set a dangerous precedent of empowering the Crown for too lengthy a period to "imprison[] the subjects at will."[72] Opponents also compared the power granted in the bill to that once wielded by Roman dictators.[73] Nonetheless, the administration successfully defended the bill as necessary to "strengthen[] the hands of his

Majesty's ministers, in order to a full detection and entire suppression of those traitorous designs and practices."[74] Contemporary descriptions of the debates highlight the claims of its defenders that the bill was necessary "to grant the executive power, for a time, a right to apprehend and detain the persons . . . suspected to have a part in [the conspiracy]." Toward that end, supporters championed the suspension as "absolutely necessary to the preservations of the [Habeas Corpus] act itself, and all the privileges of it. . . . For what indeed avails it to have a good constitution, if there be not in that constitution somewhere lodged a power of preserving itself by extraordinary methods, upon extraordinary occasions?"[75]

Following enactment of the 1722 suspension, several of the Tower prisoners nonetheless petitioned King's Bench for their release under the Habeas Corpus Act. Their efforts were doomed from the start. The report of the court's decision in the case opens by noting that the seventh section of the Habeas Corpus Act "was at this time suspended for a time." It then recounted the arguments in the case, beginning with the prisoners' contention that the suspension legislation, which provided that "no Judge or justices shall bail or try" persons detained for high treason, should not be read to encompass King's Bench acting as a court. The prisoners further argued that the court's "jurisdiction is invested with an ordinary and extraordinary power, which cannot be taken away by implication in any statute." On the other side, the king's counsel pointed out that "if this Court is not restrained, the Act of Suspension will be eluded." Agreeing with the government that the suspension had set aside not only the protections of the Habeas Corpus Act but any and all discretion the courts might otherwise possess to grant relief to the prisoners (including any common law remedies), King's Bench denied the prisoners relief and observed that it "would not try [the prisoners] until they had an order from the King, as the Act directs."[76] This important decision confirmed that even the jurisdiction of the great King's Bench and its majestic writ of habeas corpus existed at the mercy of Parliament.[77]

The Fall of the Jacobites

In 1744, Parliament once again proclaimed the existence of a "threatened . . . Invasion by a *French* power, in concert with disaffected Persons at Home."[78] In fact, Louis XV had approved a plan of invasion and summoned from Rome James II's grandson Charles Edward Stuart—popularly known as "Bonnie Prince Charlie" and the "Young Pretender"—to play a role. Within days of sightings of the French fleet in the English Channel, Parliament moved to defend against the impending attack and address renewed support for rebellion in Scotland by enacting a suspension providing that "[p]ersons in Prison may be detained for Treason, or Suspicion" without trial for a period of two months. In addition, just as it had done in every prior suspension with respect to either the English or Scottish Habeas Corpus Acts, Parliament expressly "suspended" the Scottish Habeas Corpus Act, which had been adopted in 1701.[79] Formal declarations of war by France and Britain followed shortly thereafter.[80]

Although the French sailing failed miserably (largely due to weather-inflicted destruction of large portions of its fleet), in the months that followed, France won several battles on the Continent. This fueled concern in England that France would revisit plans to invade, which in turn distracted the Crown from the fact that Charles Edward Stuart had by this point landed in Scotland and raised the Jacobite standard. Before long, Stuart was leading, as Parliament would later describe it, a full-fledged "wicked and unnatural Rebellion" in the north to reinstate his line. Although there is evidence to suggest that he landed in Scotland without the tacit approval of the French court, he viewed Scotland as fertile ground for mounting a substantial uprising and believed that once it was underway, the French would "have every incentive to supply men and arms to restore the Stuart dynasty."[81] Before long, Jacobite forces had taken Edinburgh and were marching south under Stuart's direction for London, where he hoped to be joined by supporters and met by French invasion forces.

Now plainly focused on the threat posed by Stuart, Parliament again declared a suspension "for the preservation of his Majesty's Sacred Person, and the securing the Peace of this Kingdom in a Time of so much Danger, against all traiterous Attempts and Conspiracies whatsoever." The terms of the new law provided that "[p]ersons imprison'd for Suspicion of High Treason may be detained without Bail" until the following year. Parliament also once again expressly "suspended" the Scottish Habeas Corpus Act.[82] As the suspension approached its initial expiration date, the British Army routed the Jacobites on Culloden Moor in April 1746. In time, the Battle would mark the end of the Jacobite cause.[83] Nonetheless, in the immediate wake of Culloden, Parliament passed the first of two extensions of its 1745 suspension legislation.

Meanwhile, the Crown had to sort through the numerous prisoners taken in battle and captured in its aftermath. Bonnie Prince Charlie, like his father and grandfather before him, managed to escape to France, never to return to Great Britain. Others who were captured suffered a range of fates: many of the wounded were killed, the French fighting with the Jacobites were mostly exchanged, some of the "Rebels" were impressed in the British Army, and many prisoners were sent to England for trial. As had occurred during earlier periods of suspension, treason trials went ahead over the summer, even as the suspension continued in effect. Many of the prisoners pleaded guilty and hoped for mercy; others went to trial only to be convicted in droves. To take but one example, "in one day the judges at York passed sentence of death on 70 Rebels who had been found guilty."

For the rebels, it was of no moment to their legal defense that they had purported to renounce their allegiance to the king and sworn fidelity to Charles.[84] Indeed, when the chief justice of King's Bench, Sir William Lee, pronounced the judgments following the London trials of one group of rebels, he chastised the defendants for "falsely pretending that they were entitled to the same Treatment as the Subjects of a Foreign Prince taken Prisoners of war." Instead, he declared, they were guilty of "one of the most heinous [crimes] that could be committed by mankind in endeavouring to destroy their lawful Sovereign," and he ordered a punishment that was heinous in its own right.[85] (As is discussed at the end of the chapter, this episode is indicative of the way English law treated the bond of allegiance.) For its part, Parliament attainted as traitors many of the leading Jacobites. Among the most prominent of those to fall before Parliament was Lord Lovat, who was impeached for High Treason after extensive proceedings and subsequently beheaded on Tower Hill.[86] In time, almost one thousand prisoners were banished to the American colonies while many of those who remained eventually won their freedom under an act of indemnity passed in June 1747.[87]

In the wake of the Scottish uprisings, suspension departed the English political-legal framework for a time, but it would return thirty years later in response to events transpiring across the Atlantic Ocean.

"Extreme Emergencies," Parliamentary Supremacy, and Governing within the Law

The suspensions of this period were consistent on several scores. To begin, every suspension by its express terms "impowered" the executive to arrest and detain certain classes of persons—specifically, those believed to be engaged in treasonous acts in concert with the king's enemies at home or abroad. In so doing, the suspensions altered the underlying law of detention by bestowing expanded powers upon the executive during periods of instability and war.[88] The executive's expanded powers came by reason of suspension's express and temporary displacement of the operation of the Habeas Corpus Act (whether in England or Scotland)—and more specifically, the suspension of the Act's promise of a speedy trial or discharge. As the early suspensions and King's Bench decisions from this period also made clear, suspension likewise set aside any related protections and judicial practices that might otherwise be invoked to check the executive.

During this period, the relationship between the privilege of the writ of habeas corpus associated with the Habeas Corpus Act and its suspension was well established and widely chronicled. For example, pamphleteers stressed the limited nature of a suspension along with the legal constraints governing the Crown's power to detain that operated in the absence of suspension. As one contemporary pamphlet supporting the 1722 suspension argued:

> [T]he time limited by the *Habeas Corpus Act* for the Tryal of Persons committed to Prison for Capital Crimes, is so short and insufficient, in Cases of High Treason, that notwithstanding the Administration may have information in general of a Man's being engaged in Traiterous Practices against the Government, yet if it has not such a particular Knowledge of the Affair, as to be able to convict him according to the ordinary method of Law, the Act ordains, That the Second Term after his Commitment, he shall be discharged. It is almost impossible therefore, while this Act is in force, to discover thoroughly any Conspiracy, or to punish the Conspirators. It seldom happens that Plots are detected, at least they can never be wholly unraveled, but by Persons concern'd In them; and when a suspected Persons is taken up, if the Administration has not Authority to keep him confined as long as is necessary to provide sufficient Evidence against him, which in such Cases is generally extremely difficult to get, as he knows they cannot detain him beyond the time limited by the Laws, and that thro' the insufficiency of them his own Life is safe, it will not be easy to induce him to discover his Accomplices; and so a Plot may take effect, and the Nation be ruined, because, out of an extraordinary Regard for our Liberties, we would not lodge a reasonable Power in the Hands of the Administration to put it in a Capacity of preventing it.
>
> . . . [Through] the Suspension of this Act . . . , tho' his Majesty has a power to imprison whom he shall have Reason to suspect to be dangerous Persons, and Enemies to the Government, the time of keeping them under Confinement is limited by Parliament, and his Majesty is divested of that Authority as soon as it can reasonably be supposed the Occasion for which it was granted him will be over. . . .[89]

Blackstone's highly influential *Commentaries* described the English legal framework in the same way. Specifically, in a passage later relied upon by

Alexander Hamilton in the *Federalist Papers*, Blackstone emphasized the importance of individual liberty along with the role of "*the habeas corpus act*" in the English legal tradition, pursuant to which "the methods of obtaining this writ are so plainly pointed out and enforced." He recognized, however, that in certain circumstances the law may nonetheless permit vesting in the executive discretionary control over that liberty:

> Of great importance to the public is the preservation of this personal liberty: for if once it were left in the power of any, the highest, magistrate to imprison arbitrarily whomever he or his officers thought proper . . . , there would soon be an end of all other rights and immunities. . . . To bereave a man of life, or by violence to confiscate his estate, without accusation or trial, would be so gross and notorious an act of despotism, as must at once convey the alarm of tyranny throughout the whole kingdom; but confinement of the person, by secretly hurrying him to gaol, where his sufferings are unknown or forgotten, is a less public, a less striking, and therefore a more dangerous engine of arbitrary government. And yet sometimes, when the state is in real danger, even this may be a necessary measure. But the happiness of our constitution is, that it is not left to the executive power to determine when the danger of the state is so great, as to render this measure expedient; for it is the parliament only, or legislative power, that, whenever it sees proper, can authorize the crown, by suspending the *habeas corpus act* for a short and limited time, to imprison suspected persons without giving any reason for so doing; as the senate of Rome was wont to have recourse to a dictator, a magistrate of absolute authority, when they judged the republic in any imminent danger. . . . In like manner this experiment ought only to be tried in cases of extreme emergency; and in these the nation parts with its liberty for a while, in order to preserve it forever.[90]

Blackstone's writings, studied in earnest by the American founding generation, confirm what the historical episodes of suspension in the seventeenth and eighteenth centuries teach us—namely, that suspension's effect was to "suspend[] the *habeas corpus act* for a short and limited time." He likewise made clear that suspension was a parliamentary power, not an executive one.[91] More specifically, Blackstone reinforced that the power of the executive to arrest persons suspected of treasonous activities outside the criminal process followed exclusively from invocation of the suspension authority and the displacement of the protections inherent in the Habeas Corpus Act.

Correspondingly, the evidence of this period demonstrates that the Habeas Corpus Act played a far more important role in checking executive authority than has been recognized by both jurists and scholars, for it was only by setting aside the Act's protections that suspensions could empower the executive to detain outside the criminal process. By illuminating the Act's core protections through its relationship with suspension, this period shows that the writ of habeas corpus promised by the Act encompassed far more than merely access to judicial process. Indeed, not only did the evolving understanding of the Act place specific limitations on what would be deemed legitimate "cause" for detention and therefore dramatically constrain the executive's authority, it embodied and made real a host of specific procedural rights later enshrined in the American Bill of Rights, including the right to bail and speedy trial. By the end of the eighteenth century, taking all of these developments together, English law had come to embrace a settled legal framework under which the Crown and Privy Council were denied "the power to lock up, without laying a criminal charge, those who were considered to be dangerous to the security of the State" when no "emergency legislation conferr[ed] such power."[92] Notably, however, as discussed above, one also finds many examples of persons who could be held without trial during suspensions being tried nonetheless, even while a suspension remained in effect. Consider in this regard the 1696, 1722, and 1746 episodes.

Worth questioning in all of this is why Parliament invented suspension at all. During this period, as British jurist and constitutional theorist A.V. Dicey later wrote, Parliament enjoyed "the right to make or unmake any law whatever."[93] Put another way, as one pair of scholars writing more generally about the period observed, the rise of parliamentary supremacy "raises the issue of why [that body] would not then proceed to act just like the king."[94] As their work shows, the answer likely stems from the political and economic context of the late seventeenth and eighteenth centuries, which witnessed the rise of judicial independence coincide with a greater commitment to the protection of private rights. Respect for the latter transcended many contexts and was perhaps most pronounced during this period as part of the growth of a stable market for public debt. Indeed, in the wake of the Glorious Revolution, Parliament appreciated that if it made credible commitments to honor its financial obligations and operate within a stable legal framework that honored such commitments, economic growth would follow.[95] Suspension stands as another example of Parliament attempting to honor its prior commitments and work within the law—rather than outside of it—during this period.

The Relevance of Allegiance

During this same period, English law placed great emphasis on allegiance. A review of seventeenth- and eighteenth-century practices shows that allegiance to the Crown was inextricably linked to the availability of the protections of the Habeas Corpus Act, especially during wartime. British subjects owed such allegiance and could not easily divest themselves of it. This, in turn, rendered subjects susceptible to prosecution for treason and yet entitled to claim the protections of the Habeas Corpus Act. The status of aliens—that is, non-British subjects—was far more complicated. Relevant considerations with respect to aliens and the application of the Habeas Corpus Act included whether or not they were citizens or subjects of an enemy nation, the asserted basis of their detention, and whether or not they resided within the realm at the time of their detention.

Blackstone wrote in the eighteenth century that "alien-enemies have no rights, no privileges, unless by the king's special favour, during the time of war."[96] Those deemed to owe allegiance, by contrast, enjoyed extensive rights under domestic law, along with important *obligations*, the violation of which exposed them to domestic penal sanctions. Sir Matthew Hale, chief justice of King's Bench during the early years of the Habeas Corpus Act, observed that "those that raise war against the king may be of two kinds, subjects or foreigners, the former are not properly enemies but rebels or traitors. . . ."[97] Hale echoed Lord Coke, who had earlier written that those owing allegiance who take up arms against the king "shall be punished as Traytors"—not treated and detained as wartime enemies.[98] During this period, treason was understood as "an Offense committed against the Duty of Allegiance"[99] committed by a "member of the community."[100] It followed that protection and allegiance to the Crown were understood to be "reciprocal Obligations."

These reciprocal obligations allowed persons who could claim the protection of domestic law to enjoy the full benefits of the Habeas Corpus Act when it was not suspended, but such persons in turn had to answer for violating the obligation of allegiance. It was also the case that where a violation of allegiance amounted to treason, the guilty often suffered a terrible death as punishment.[101] Those who could not claim allegiance and who were easily classified as enemy aliens, by contrast, fell outside of this framework. There was no need to suspend the Habeas Corpus Act to hold such persons in a preventive posture because any rights owed to them derived from the law of nations, not domestic law. It followed that when properly held as prisoners of war as contemplated under the law of nations, such persons could not invoke the benefits of the Habeas Corpus Act before the English courts.

The actions of the Privy Council and the courts during the seventeenth and eighteenth centuries highlight the importance that was assigned to distinguishing lines of allegiance for these legal purposes. In 1694, for example, the Privy Council issued "Proposalls for the more easy Conviction of Traytors & Pirates" to be implemented during the battles with the Jacobites and France. The Proposals set forth instructions for "all Commanders of his Majesty's Men of Warr & Privateers" to identify more easily those English subjects in the act of treason. The policy called upon Commanders to "carefully . . . examine all Prisoners which they May suspect to be English, Scotch or Irish as soon as they are taken"; take declarations regarding the "Place of the Nativity" of prisoners when necessary; take "particular Notice of such Prisoners as shall either owne themselves to be borne within his Majesty's Dominions, or are suspected so to be . . . to the end, that they may upon a Tryall be able to [testify]"; and "secure all Papers" when taking a ship, including the "List of Seamens Names."[102]

Why was subjecthood so important? Because often that threshold classification proved determinative as to how an individual case would proceed. Thus, the remaining instructions provide that "such Prisoners as are found or suspected to be his Majesty's Subjects be set on Shoar as near to the Port of London as conveniently may be, and . . . immediately carried before a Magistrate to be Examined" together with witnesses. The instructions directed the magistrate, in turn, to examine the circumstances of the prisoner's capture, along with his "Nativity, Habitation, Reputation or Parentage or any Circumstances whereby it may be presumed that they are his Majesty's Subjects. . . ." Finally, with respect to those who could be tried as "Traytors" or Pirates under the treason statute of Henry VIII, the Privy Council called for their "Tryalls [to] be had at [the] usuall time of azzizes" when the judges ride circuit, recognizing that where this is not possible, prisoners could be tried in London.[103]

Accordingly, during this period, the Privy Council viewed the distinction between those who could be deemed subjects of the Crown and those who could not as enormously significant for purposes of deciding how to proceed with prisoners captured in battle at sea. The former were to proceed to trial as traitors or pirates; the latter were, as a general proposition, to be detained and exchanged as prisoners of war. This followed long-standing practices dating back to the early seventeenth century,[104] and is exemplified in the numerous Privy Council entries from this period that routinely classified French subjects captured in battle as prisoners of war and ordered their exchange for English prisoners held by France.[105]

Paul Halliday's review of King's Bench practices during this period also reveals the importance of the concept of allegiance in English law. As he describes it, habeas corpus served as a "sorting function" during this time, dividing along the lines of allegiance those who could invoke the protections of the Habeas Corpus Act and those who could not. Once "sorted" as an alien and prisoner of war, a prisoner's attempts to invoke the Act were essentially doomed. Take, for example, the 1759 case of a Swede named Barnard Schiever, who was the "subject of a neutral power, taken on board of an enemy's ship." In petitioning for a writ of habeas corpus before King's Bench, Schiever's counsel argued that Schiever had left his home country to serve on an English merchant ship only to see that ship captured by a French privateer, on which Schiever was then forced to serve as part of its crew. When an English ship captured the French privateer in turn, Schiever was "sent to the town-gaol of Liverpool, as a prisoner of war" where he remained "detained . . . for no other cause than the cause aforesaid." Schiever's counsel argued that "it would be very hard upon this man, to be kept in prison" and petitioned for his client's discharge so that he could return to the service of an English merchant ship. All of this was of little moment to the court, which "thought this man, upon his own showing, clearly a prisoner of war, and lawfully detained as such. Therefore they Denied the motion."[106]

During the American Revolutionary War, a period explored more fully in the next chapter, King's Bench would face a similar case and reach the same conclusion. In 1779, three Spanish sailors had been taken prisoner off of a Spanish privateer at sea. When offered a spot on another ship heading for England upon the promise of "immediate exchange by cartel upon their arrival," they agreed to enter on board the merchant vessel, only to be paid nothing for their labor and turned over as prisoners of war upon landing in England. King's Bench concluded that "these men, upon their own shewing, are alien enemies and prisoners of war, and therefore not entitled to any of the privileges of Englishmen; much less to be set at liberty on a habeas corpus."[107] As Halliday's survey of hundreds of cases during the seventeenth and eighteenth centuries concludes, King's Bench "never released a person it concluded had been properly designated as a POW."[108]

By contrast, those who could claim allegiance could successfully challenge their classification as prisoners of war and invoke the protection of the Habeas Corpus Act—but they did so at the risk of answering for violations of their duty of obedience. Garrett Comberford appears to have been one of the lucky ones in this regard. Detained as a prisoner of war in the 1690s for several years, Comberford sought a petition for a writ of habeas corpus to win his discharge. An intervening Privy Council order suggests that he owed allegiance, so the fact that the return to his writ mentioned no criminal charges against him is likely what drove King's Bench to bail him from custody.[109]

John Golding was not so fortunate. As Halliday reports, in 1692, the English captured the Irishman at sea serving as second-in-command of a Jacobite vessel "flying French colors." The return to his writ relayed these details and stated that he was being held as a "prisoner of war." In response, King's Bench bailed Golding on his "giving surety to appear at the next Admiralty sessions," where he was then tried for treason.[110] Among his many defenses advanced at trial, Golding claimed that he was a Frenchman, presumably to escape the reach of the treason statute. His confession when first arrested, combined with his pledge of loyalty to King James II, appears to have done him in on this score.

Golding's case, posing the question of how to treat subjects captured in battle fighting under commissions of the French king or James II, is illustrative of a common practice during this period—namely, to refer such persons to the criminal process rather than permit them to escape from the obligations of their native allegiance or, for that matter, permit the Crown to hold them as prisoners of war outside the framework of the Habeas Corpus Act.[111] Cases such as Golding's also demonstrate that allegiance was not easily cast off. The case of six other Irish prisoners also captured at sea and tried shortly after Golding in the Admiralty courts underscores the latter point. Their defense to charges of piracy was reported as follows: "The prisoners insisted that they were no Pirats but had King James's Commission, which they said was a lawfull Commission, and those that fought under it in Ireland were allw'd to be treated and exchanged as Prisoners of Warr & no reason that they should be try'd as Pirats." In response, one of the Admiralty judges instructed the jury that it "cannot be deceived in this point, for there is no Commission of King James's that can take force against the Government." The jury wasted little time in finding the prisoners guilty of piracy and robbery.[112]

The trials of the Scottish rebels in 1746, discussed earlier, tell a similar story. In particular, the trial of one of Bonnie Prince Charlie's key supporters during this period highlights the difficulty of casting off allegiance. Notably, the case also appears to have wielded considerable influence on early American legal thinking about allegiance. Indeed, the Reporters' Note to an early American case relates the story. Riding circuit in 1799, Chief Justice Oliver Ellsworth presided over *Williams' Case*, involving a native-born American who claimed that he had renounced his allegiance to the United States and ceased to be a citizen when he moved to France and took an oath of allegiance to that country. These facts, Williams argued, rendered his subsequent acceptance of a French commission to fight against the king of Great Britain beyond the reach of American law, which criminalized acts of hostility taken against Britain by Americans because such acts violated existing treaties between the United States and Britain. Ellsworth declined to give any legal effect to Williams's naturalization as a French citizen and rejected the notion that "a citizen may . . . renounce [on] his own, and join himself to a foreign country." Instead, Ellsworth posited, Congress must consent under the "compact" that binds "all the members of civil community."[113]

The Reporter's Note to *Williams' Case* deemed Ellsworth's conclusion consistent with the case of Æneas MacDonald, one of the so-called "Seven Men of Moidart" who had accompanied Charles on his voyage from France to Scotland and who had been captured in the wake of Culloden.[114] MacDonald's case comprised "an illustration of the severity of the rule" against casting off one's native allegiance so easily:

> Aeneas Macdonald was a native of Scotland. At a very early period he had been taken to France; had passed there all the earlier portion of his life; and had entered the service of the king of France. He took part in the rebellion of 1745, and served under the Pretended at Culloden. Being taken after that battle, he was indicted for high treason. He claimed the treatment due by the laws of war to an alien enemy. But the judges all held, that notwithstanding his removal to France, he still remained a subject, and the jury found him guilty of high treason.[115]

In this respect, MacDonald's case contributes to a substantial body of evidence from the seventeenth and eighteenth centuries revealing that domestic law, as opposed to the law of war, governed the relationship between the Crown and its subjects, who bore an obligation of allegiance.

This being said, the rules governing the treatment of aliens during this period were not always so clear. To begin, as a general matter, protection and obligation were not limited exclusively to subjects of the Crown, and aliens sometimes came within the protection of domestic law under the idea of temporary or "local" allegiance. As Sir Edward Coke once wrote from the bench: "when an alien . . . cometh into England, because as long as he is within England, he is within the King's protection; therefore so long as he is here, he oweth unto the King a local obedience or ligeance, for that the one (as has been said) draweth the other."[116] (In his famous *Institutes*, Coke was all the more clear that the obligation of allegiance permitted even those owing only a local allegiance to "be punished as Traytors."[117]) There is also evidence from this period suggesting that even the potential classification of someone as an alien enemy did not always exempt that person from the reach of domestic penal laws. During the war with France in 1696, for example, the

Privy Council ordered the detention of a "Frenchman" named John Vienne for "Treasonable Words and Practices."[118] The following year, King's Bench took up "The Case of Du Castro a Foreigner" in which it rejected the argument that the defendant's foreign citizenship placed him beyond the protection of the Habeas Corpus Act. As the report of the case summarizes the court's decision: "This Du Castro was committed by order of the Secretary of State for a spy, and had been imprisoned a year and a half, and then admitted to bail, and now no prosecution against him, so he was discharged."[119] The outcome suggests that where a prisoner was captured on domestic soil and committed in a criminal posture but not tried, he too might enjoy the benefit of all of the protections of domestic law under the concept of "local" allegiance.

Another case from many years later offers a more extensive explanation of how the lines of protection and allegiance operated during this period. In 1781, upon discovering that François Henri de la Motte was sending sensitive military information to the French during the American Revolutionary War, the Crown ordered de la Motte arrested, committed to the Tower, and tried for high treason before King's Bench. In introducing the charges, the attorney general, James Wallace, explained:

> The prisoner is supposed to be a Frenchman by birth; he certainly is not a natural-born subject of this country: but I must inform you, that whilst he is under the protection of the laws of this kingdom, he owes allegiance to it equal to that of any natural-born subject. It has been the custom of modern times, during war and hostilities, not to drive out of this country the subjects of the enemy who are resident in it [as de la Motte was], or even to prevent others from coming . . . : but it has ever been understood, that, whilst they are here under the protection of the laws and government, they do nothing detrimental to the state, and that they owe the same allegiance to the king, during the time they stay, as any natural-born subject whatever.[120]

At the end of de la Motte's trial, Justice Buller declared that the prisoner had enjoyed "the protection of the laws of the land" during his residency in England, and chastised him that "[a]s such, you owed a duty to those laws, and an allegiance to the king whose laws they are." Because de la Motte had "thought fit to abuse that protection which [he] received" by supporting the French king in war against Britain, he was found guilty and executed.[121]

De la Motte's trial confirms that the lines of protection could sweep well beyond subjecthood to include those who had come within the "local allegiance" of the king. But de la Motte's trial goes further in suggesting that the obedience of aliens was sometimes demanded (and its violation severely punished) even when the alien's sovereign was at war with the Crown.[122] The critical point for present purposes is that the ability to invoke the Habeas Corpus Act—and the need to suspend the same to hold persons outside the criminal process—was linked inextricably to the bond of allegiance as that term was then understood. But as will be seen, where the Habeas Corpus Act did not reach, all bets were off.

3
Rebellion and Treason

*[I]t had been customary upon similar occasions of rebellion,
or danger of invasion, to enable the king to seize suspected persons. . . . But as the law stood . . . it was not possible at present officially to apprehend the most suspected person. . . . It
was necessary for the crown to have a power of confining them
like other prisoners of war.*

LORD FREDERICK NORTH, speaking to the British
House of Commons in 1777[1]

IN THE WAKE of the final defeat of the Jacobite cause, Great Britain enjoyed
some measure of peace, or at the least respite from the constant suspensions
that plagued the first half of the eighteenth century. It would not last, for revolution was brewing in America. In 1775, British troops met local colonial militia at Lexington and Concord, and then Bunker Hill. Before long, the colonists
formed the Continental Army and royal officials were fleeing America. With
battles came prisoners. The treatment of the American "rebels" would pose
a series of very intricate and difficult questions about the reach and framework of English law. How the British addressed these questions would come
to wield considerable influence over the subsequent development of early
American law.

As this and the next chapter explore, the centerpiece of the legal calculus
governing the detention of prisoners during the war—both in Great Britain
and in the United States—was the English Habeas Corpus Act of 1679. The
war also confirmed the Act's limitations on two scores. First, well before
Americans claimed independence, Parliament had denied the Act's application in the colonies, thereby taking the position that its geographic sweep did
not follow British rule wherever it went. Second, during the war, Parliament
suspended the Act's application to Americans held on English soil, thereby
denying them its benefits even where it otherwise would have applied to anyone claiming subjecthood. But as will be seen, with independence, the United

Habeas Corpus in Wartime. Amanda L. Tyler.
© Oxford University Press 2017. Published 2017 by Oxford University Press.

States would finally lay claim to the protections inherent in the Act as their own and, in time, constitutionalize them.

The Habeas Corpus Act in Colonial America

From the beginning of English settlement in North America, the colonists claimed to possess "all the rights, liberties and immunities of free and natural-born subjects, within the realm of England."[2] But this claim rarely equated with the reality on the ground. Despite attempts by several colonies to adopt or invoke the protections of the Habeas Corpus Act as their own, the Crown consistently denied colonists outside England the "privilege" of the benefits of the Act. The story of New York's efforts is instructive. In 1684, that colony submitted its Charter of Liberties and Privileges to the royal Committee of Trade and Plantations (part of the Privy Council) for approval, having secured the approval of the then-Duke of York. In the Charter, the New York colonists claimed the general right to "be governed by and according to the Laws of England." Within a month of inheriting the throne from his brother, the Duke of York—now crowned James II—vetoed the Charter on the stated basis that "[t]his Priviledge is not granted to any of His Ma[ts] Plantations where the Act of Habeas Corpus and all such other Bills do not take Place."[3]

In 1692, the Massachusetts colony attempted to pass a Habeas Corpus Act that essentially copied the 1679 English Act. The Privy Council disallowed this attempt as well, decreeing in 1695:

> [W]hereas . . . the writt of Habeas Corpus is required to be granted in like manner as is appointed by the Statute 31 Car. II. in England, which priviledge has not as yet been granted in any of His Maj[tys] Plantations, It was not thought fitt in His Maj[tys] absence that the said Act should be continued in force and therefore the same hath been repealed.[4]

To the extent that any doubt remained on this score, Massachusetts's colonial governor declared in 1699 that the "Habeas corpus act [is] not to be in force in the colonies."[5]

Against this backdrop, it was not uncommon for colonial governors to claim detention powers more expansive than those enjoyed by the Crown. In one case from 1699, New York governor Lord Bellomont advised his lieutenant governor with respect to two prisoners who had been taken into custody, "commit 'em to gaol without baile or mainprize, which I am positive you can legally justifie, and there's no removing them by Habeas corpus, for there is no such law in force in any of the Plantations."[6] In an earlier case from 1687,

prisoners jailed for their town's vote objecting to taxation by the royal council reported that they were "denied the privilege of Habeas Corpus," along
with the benefit of "the Magna Charta . . . and the statute laws that secure the
subjects' properties and estate" by a court that included Chief Justice Joseph
Dudley of the Dominion of New England. By the prisoners' account, Dudley
told them: "[W]e must not think the Laws of *England* follow us to the ends
of the earth . . . [Y]ou have no more privileges left you than not to be sold as
slaves."[7] One sees why the prominent New England Puritan minister Cotton
Mather could have complained during this time: "Wee are Slaves, without the
Habeas Corpus-Act."[8]

Over time, the denial of the protections of the Habeas Corpus Act to the
colonists became a major source of complaint regarding British rule. In 1774,
for example, the Continental Congress documented a number of complaints
about British rule in a letter to the people of Great Britain. The Congress
decried the fact that colonists were "the subjects of an arbitrary government,
deprived of trial by jury, and when imprisoned cannot claim the benefit of the
habeas corpus Act, that great bulwark and palladium of English liberty."[9] That
same year, while soliciting Canadian support for the cause of independence,
the Continental Congress declared the right to be governed by representatives
of the people's choosing, the right to trial by jury, and the privilege of habeas
corpus among the most fundamental rights.[10] In its words, "[t]hese are the
rights, without which a people cannot be free and happy."[11] These complaints
underscore the importance of the denial of habeas corpus and related rights
in fueling the movement for independence, as well as explain their centrality
to the subsequent development of the American legal framework governing
individual liberties. During this period and the subsequent Founding period,
moreover, it was the Habeas Corpus Act that was central to colonial thinking
about such liberties. As one pair of scholars noted in studying this period:

> Latter-day students of the use of the writ in Colonial times have argued
> that it derived from the common—not the statute—law [and] even that
> repeals of the various charters of liberty and declarative acts of rights
> and privileges lessened the basic liberties of the Colonists not at all. The
> Colonists themselves were not so indifferent.[12]

As the Revolutionary War unfolded, the colonists came to appreciate all the
more the importance of the Act as a limitation on executive detention authority. It is no wonder that upon breaking away from the "cord" that bound them
to the Crown (namely, their allegiance to the same), they would soon claim the
Act's benefits for themselves.

Rebel Detention Policy and
the Habeas Corpus Act

In the wake of Bunker Hill, the Second Continental Congress convened in 1775 to make one final attempt at reconciliation with Great Britain through the Olive Branch Petition. Realistic about its chances of success, the Congress established the Continental Army at the same time. King George III responded in August by issuing a proclamation declaring that "many of Our Subjects in divers Parts of Our Colonies and Plantations in *North America* . . . , forgetting the Allegiance which they owe to the Power that has protected and sustained them . . . , have at length proceeded to an open and avowed Rebellion, by . . . traitorously preparing, ordering and levying War against us." He ordered all officers and "obedient and loyal Subjects" to suppress the rebellion with the objective of "bring[ing] the Traitors to Justice" and "Punishment."[13] There was no question, it seems, that the Americans were traitors who needed to be reminded of their obligations as royal subjects and punished for their intransigence. Indeed, just one year earlier, Attorney General Edward Thurlow and Solicitor General Alexander Wedderburn had advised secretary of state for American affairs, the Earl of Dartmouth, that the colonists' acts surrounding the Boston Tea Party events "amount to the crime of high treason"—specifically, "the levying of war against His Majesty."[14]

But of course, suppressing the rebellion and "bring[ing] the Traitors to Justice" would not to be that simple. With war now waging on multiple fronts, it was only a matter of time until the British were forced to address the status of Americans taken prisoner in battle—a question that itself did not admit of easy answers.

The matter came to a head with the capture of none other than Ethan Allen and his famed "Green Mountain Boys." In September 1775, after having seized the important strategic post of Fort Ticonderoga in New York, Captain Allen and his Boys headed north into Canada in an ill-fated attempt to take Montreal. After his capture, Allen was turned over to British general Richard Prescott, who, Allen recorded in his journal, treated him poorly and threatened him with a traitor's execution.[15] By November, British lieutenant governor Cramahé had ordered Allen and several of his fellow "Rebel Prisoners" aboard Royal Navy ships bound for England, "having no proper Place to confine them in, or Troops to guard Them" in Canada.[16] On board, according to Allen's *Narrative*, the Rebels were "shackled together by pairs, viz. two men fastened together by one hand-cuff, being closely fixed to one wrist of each of them, and treated with the greatest severity, nay as criminals."[17] The prisoners landed in Falmouth, England, days before Christmas in December 1775. They would not stay long.

Meanwhile, General Prescott had been captured and taken into the custody of the Continental Army. With news of Allen's harsh treatment at the hands of the British having reached the Americans, General George Washington wrote to British general William Howe on December 18, declaring that Prescott would suffer the same treatment as his former prisoner. Washington complained specifically about the fact that Allen had been reportedly "thrown into irons and suffers all the hardships inflicted upon common felons." This was not the first time that the Americans had threatened retaliation, nor would it be the last. Indeed, Washington had previously threatened retaliatory treatment of British prisoners in the wake of reports of British mistreatment of American prisoners in August, and Thomas Jefferson soon penned a "Declaration on the British Treatment of Ethan Allen" threatening retaliation, particularly upon Prescott.[18] Washington suggested in his letter to Howe that the time had come for the parties to enter a cartel for the exchange of prisoners[19]; American practice, after all, viewed British soldiers taken in arms "as prisoners of war" who could be held in a preventive posture and who were amenable to exchange under the Law of Nations.[20]

Upon arrival in England, Allen and his fellow prisoners were imprisoned at Pendennis Castle in Cornwall. Allen was already something of a legend by this point and his notoriety only grew during his brief stint at the castle. Allen's *Narrative* describes, for example, how on a daily basis persons "came in great numbers out of curiosity, to see me."[21] During his time in England, Allen wrote that he "was treated as a criminal . . . , and continued in irons . . . in consequence of the orders which the commander of the castle received from General Carlton."[22]

Allen's case posed significant legal questions for his British captors. Was he truly a criminal, as the irons and other aspects of his detention (including the failure of the British to make any distinctions among their prisoners based on military rank) suggested? Or was he a prisoner of war? And if he was the former, could he be held without criminal charges or did the Habeas Corpus Act apply? The handling of Allen's case suggests that the British were still working through these questions and that political considerations factored heavily into the calculus. In short order, however, the British stood firm to the claim that the Americans were rebels and traitors—most assuredly *not* wartime prisoners of a foreign sovereign—and as such, they were criminals. This explains Allen's detention in irons. Whether the Americans could be detained without criminal trial posed a more complicated question. As matters unfolded, the answer turned entirely on the reach of the Habeas Corpus Act.

Immediately upon Allen's landing, the British legal elite began debating what to do in his case.[23] On the morning of December 27, Solicitor General Wedderburn, who later served as attorney general for much of the Revolutionary War, wrote a letter to his cousin William Eden, under-secretary of state, sharing his views on Allen's case. Wedderburn wrote the letter only hours before attending a cabinet meeting that had been called by the Earl of Suffolk, Secretary of State for the Northern Department, to determine the fate of Allen and his fellow prisoners. Wedderburn informed Eden that his view of "the Business does not differ much" from that of the attorney general, Lord Thurlow. He then continued:

> I am persuaded that some unlucky incident must arise if Allen & his People are kept here. It must be understood that Government does not name to execute them, the Prosecution will be remiss & the Disposition of some People to thwart It very active. I would therefore send them back, but I think something more might be done than merely to return them as Prisoners to America.

Wedderburn went on to question Allen's loyalty to the American cause. He suggested that if Allen's lands (of which he had been dispossessed due to a Council order settling the boundary between Hampshire and New York) were restored, Allen might be convinced "not only [to] have his pardon from Gen[eral] Howe [but also] a Company of Rangers" to lead in the British cause. Wedderburn concluded by suggesting that even if Allen was not immediately amenable to the proposal, "there is still an Advantage in finding a decent reason for not immediately proceeding ag[ainst] him as a Rebel"—namely, that "[s]ome of the People who came over in the Ship with Him ... might easily settle this bargain" with him. Nonetheless, Wedderburn also recognized that if Allen "does not accept" the terms of the offer, "he & they [his men] must be disposed of as the Law directs."[24]

What transpired at the cabinet meeting was not recorded. It is clear that Allen's presence was viewed with displeasure by the administration, and it appears that those participating in the meeting decided to send Allen and his fellow prisoners back to America immediately.[25] Indeed, the very same day, Lord Suffolk signed a warrant for the delivery of the prisoners along with an order that they be sent to Boston. Also that same day, Lord George Germain, Secretary of State for the Americas, wrote to the Lords of the Admiralty that it was "The King's Pleasure" that Allen and the other prisoners be removed to his Majesty's ship *Solebay*, which should "put to Sea with the first fair wind" setting course for Boston, where the prisoners were to be turned over to General

Howe.[26] Within days, the men were put on the *Solebay* and the ship sailed for America by way of Ireland in the early days of January 1776.[27]

Why was Allen sent back to America so quickly? A review of contemporary evidence suggests many possible reasons. To draw upon one source, in March 1776, two months after the *Solebay* sailed for America, members of Parliament discussed Allen's case while debating the use of foreign mercenaries in the Revolutionary War. Lord Richmond, a regular antagonist of the North administration, called for clear terms on the exchange of prisoners in the war while asserting that the government had avoided bringing Allen to trial "either because they knew that he could not be legally tried, or feared an English jury could not be prevailed on to find him guilty."[28] In response, the Earl of Suffolk, who had convened the meeting of December 27 to determine Allen's fate, deemed Richmond's observations in error. "I do assure his grace," Suffolk declared, "that . . . we neither had a doubt but we should be able legally to convict [Allen], nor were we afraid that an English jury would have acquitted him; nor further, was it out of any tenderness to the man, who I maintain had justly forfeited his life to the offended laws of his country." Instead, Suffolk explained, the fact that the "rebels had lately made a considerable number of prisoners" comprised the "true motives" for sending Allen back. Suffolk continued by explaining that "we accordingly avoided bringing him to his trial from considerations of prudence; from a dread of the consequences of retaliation; not from a doubt of his legal guilt, or a fear of his acquittal by an English jury."[29]

Suffolk's statements suggested that Allen and his fellow prisoners offered more value as barter for prisoner exchanges in America than as convicted criminals in England. Subsequent internal administration correspondence is in tension with Suffolk's claim about the lack of concern over the ability to prosecute Allen successfully, but either way, it is clear that political considerations animated the decision at least in part.[30] The administration's earlier decision to decline to prosecute the principals in the Boston Tea Party, despite deeming their actions treasonous, lends further support to the idea that the administration was generally concerned over its ability to prosecute rebels successfully. (That decision followed reportedly based on Thurlow and Wedderburn's "doubt whether the evidence was sufficient to convict them."[31]) Still more support may be found in the Earl of Dartmouth's directive to General Thomas Gage, who commanded the British forces in North America and had been appointed to serve as Governor of the Massachusetts Colony in 1774, to investigate treasonous acts by the colonists. In deciding whether to bring prosecutions for treason, Dartmouth instructed Gage to take into account the "prejudices of the people": "[H]owever clear and full the evidence might be," if such prejudices "would in all probability prevent a conviction," then it "would be better to desist from prosecution, seeing that an ineffectual attempt would only be triumph to the faction and disgraceful to government."[32]

Various contemporary sources—including Allen's own *Narrative* and a letter sent from England to the Continental Congress[33]—suggest that in addition to political calculations, the mere threat of a writ of habeas corpus sought on Allen's behalf may have influenced the decision to send him back. Specifically, Allen wrote that once on board the *Solebay*, his irons were removed and "[t]his remove was in consequence, as I have been since informed, of a writ of habeas corpus, which had been procured by some gentlemen in England, in order to obtain me my liberty."[34] Numerous other contemporary sources suggest that at a minimum, a habeas action was in the works. *The Annual Register* for 1775, for example, reported of the prisoners: "whilst their friends in London were preparing to bring them up by *habeas corpus*, to have the legality of their confinement discussed, they were sent back to North America to be exchanged." Immediately following this report, moreover, the *Register* noted that another "American rifleman, who was taken prisoner [in Quebec]" had been "discharged, as no crime was alleged against him."[35] The *London Evening Post* ran similar stories, including one on January 2, 1776, in which it reported that Allen and his fellow prisoners "have sent up to their friends in town to sue out the writ of Habeas Corpus, to know on what law or authority they are detained in their present state, at a distance from the capital."[36] And days later, the *Post* ran a passage drafted by a so-called "friend to the CONSTITUTIONAL LAW of this country" that "call[ed] upon the yet *remaining Sons of Liberty* immediately to set on foot a public subscription for trying the right of transporting British subjects above three thousand miles from their own country (as has been done in the *bringing over* and *confining* Mr. Ethan Allen, and others of the Provincials)."[37] Meanwhile, two other British newspapers reported that matters had evolved to where counsel had been retained on behalf of the Americans, reporting: "Mr. Dunning and Mr. Alleyne are retained as Council in behalf of Ethan Allen, and the rest of the prisoners lately brought from America."[38]

The newspaper reference is to John Dunning, opposition member of Parliament and former solicitor general, and John Alleyne. Both had made appearances on either side of the proceedings in the famous *Somersett's Case*, which involved a habeas petition challenging the legality of slavery.[39] Alleyne, moreover, had only a few months earlier represented American Stephen Sayre in his habeas proceedings; later, he would represent American Ebenezer Smith Platt in a similar attempt to win his discharge from British detention during the Revolutionary War.[40] (Both cases are discussed below.) In short,

Dunning and Alleyne, both experts in habeas practice and connected to the American cause, were the logical candidates for the job of representing Allen and his cohort in any habeas proceedings.

How far any legal efforts on behalf of the American prisoners went is unclear. There is no record of a writ being sought on Allen's behalf in the Old Bailey, nor is there any archival record of a writ, return, or entry in the Court of King's Bench records of the period. King's Bench would have been on vacation from the end of November well into January, so the only means of obtaining a writ on his behalf during his time in England would have been to obtain a vacation writ issued by an individual justice.[41] If such a writ was filed with King's Bench, however, no record exists of it in the bound writs preserved from that period.[42]

The lack of record in these courts suggests—though by no means proves, given the imperfect record-keeping of vacation writs during the period—that no one ever filed a petition for a writ of habeas corpus on Allen's behalf during the less than two weeks he spent in England. It says nothing, however, about whether a petition was in the works—as a wealth of contemporary reports suggest—or whether even the mere possibility of such a filing may have influenced the decision to send Allen back to America. All this being said, the reports linking counsel with habeas experience and a record of representing Americans to Allen's case strongly suggests that opposition circles had taken up the legal plight of the prisoners, and it is fair to presume that the administration was well aware of the same.

There is, moreover, significant evidence to suggest that the administration felt considerable pressure to make the problems posed by Allen's detention in England go away—and fast. As one Admiralty Lord wrote the Earl of Sandwich, head of the Lords of the Admiralty, on December 29: "The principal object being to *get the prisoners out of reach as soon as possible*, one of the Secretary of State's messengers set out yesterday morning at 2 o'clock with our orders to the Solebay at Plymouth to call at Falmouth. He was to proceed with a warrant to Pendennis Castle to deliver them to the Solebay or any other ship that may call there for them. . . ."[43] Time, it seems, was of the essence, but it is hard to imagine that politics alone warranted such urgency. To the contrary, the letter to the Earl of Sandwich implies that the administration was deeply concerned that a petition would be filed on Allen's behalf to invoke the protections of the Habeas Corpus Act and thereby force his trial or discharge. Contemporary commentary in at least one London newspaper, moreover, pointed to the administration's desire "to elude the Habeas Corpus Act" as the very reason for sending Allen back to America.[44] In short, extensive evidence suggests that the possibility that counsel representing Allen would invoke the protections of the English Habeas Corpus Act played a major role in the decision to send him quickly back to America.

It is also the case that the filing of a habeas petition in Allen's case—true or not—quickly became the stuff of American lore and influenced the direction of early habeas law. As noted, Allen connected his being sent home to the filing of a habeas petition in his *Narrative*, a book that was widely read in the colonies upon its first publication in 1779.[45] Even before this time, in 1777, Chief Justice Thomas McKean of the Pennsylvania Supreme Court, who would later serve as President of Congress, granted habeas relief to twenty Quakers held without charges in Philadelphia who were suspected of passing information to the British. The decision was widely unpopular, especially in Congress, so much so that McKean felt compelled to defend his actions in a letter to John Adams. He did so in part by claiming that "No gentleman thought it amiss in the judge, who allowed the habeas corpus for Ethan Allen and his fellow-prisoners upon the application of Mr. Wilks &c."[46]

The suggestion that John Wilkes would have been behind any legal efforts made on Allen's behalf is highly plausible. Wilkes was Lord Mayor of London, a controversial member of Parliament, and a prominent American sympathizer who that same year had compared the American Revolution to the Glorious Revolution.[47] Wilkes himself had spent time in the Tower of London for criticizing George III.[48] And Wilkes had been a driving force behind the successful invocation of the Habeas Corpus Act in American Stephen Sayre's case just two months prior to the arrival of Allen and his fellow prisoners in England. Finally, Wilkes had strong ties to both Alleyne and Dunning.[49]

Sayre's case was a precursor to Allen's and likely influenced the administration's handling of Allen and his fellow American prisoners. Sayre was an American banker living in London who had been heavily involved in London-based pro-American causes with his friend Wilkes. In October 1775, he was arrested and charged with directing a plot to kidnap and detain King George III in the Tower of London before forcing the monarch to leave the country. When a lieutenant of American birth reported the story to the principal secretary of state, the Earl of Rochford, claiming that Sayre had attempted to enlist him in the scheme, Rochford wasted little time in issuing a warrant ordering Sayre's arrest on charges of high treason. Rochford, however, could not secure the second witness necessary to sustain the charges. This led him to reduce Sayre's charge to "treasonable practices" in a new warrant that directed the Earl of Cornwallis, Constable of the Tower of London, to take Sayre and keep him in "close custody."[50] Per these terms, Sayre was denied the benefit of visits from anyone other than his wife. But this did not stop Sayre's friends, including the same John Alleyne who later reportedly took on the case of Ethan Allen, from petitioning for a writ of habeas corpus to secure Sayre's release from the Tower. On October 28, 1775, five days after Sayre's arrest, Lord Mansfield, chief justice of King's Bench, released Sayre on bail following a makeshift hearing at Mansfield's house on Bloomsbury Square. Reportedly, Mansfield "called for the warrant of commitment, and immediately on perusing it, pronounced that he had not the least doubt of Mr. Sayre's being entitled to bail; as he observed, [the] gentleman was only charged with treasonable practices."[51]

Why was Sayre released? As the account of Lord Mansfield's words suggests, his case presented a straightforward application of the right to bail as promised by the Habeas Corpus Act. It was apparently of no relevance that Sayre was charged with participation in a scheme that directly threatened the king. Within weeks, another of Sayre's attorneys, Arthur Lee—a prominent member of Wilkes's opposition circles in London and later American Commissioner representing the United States in France—successfully moved at the Old Bailey to discharge Sayre's recognizance when it became obvious that the government would not prosecute him.[52]

By the following summer, Sayre had borrowed a tactic from his friend Wilkes and sued Rochford for false imprisonment, winning one thousand pounds before the judgment was thrown out on the basis of pleading errors.[53] Presiding in Sayre's civil case in the Court of Common-Pleas, Lord Chief Justice de Grey observed that the "present was a cause of the utmost importance, as it involved in it these two very material points, the safety of the government, and the safety and security of the subject."[54] Parliament would soon have to confront this very same tension in addressing increasing numbers of American prisoners brought to English shores.

The Need for a Clear Legal Framework

The same month that Allen and his fellow prisoners arrived in England, Vice Admiral Graves, then in command of the North American Station, sent another group of "Rebels" to England on board the *Tartar*. The group of prisoners consisted of seventy Americans who had been captured from an American privateer sailing under a Commission issued by the Continental Congress. Along with details of the prisoners' capture, Graves wrote the Lords of Admiralty with a plea for direction as to how to handle American prisoners going forward, highlighting the problems with keeping prisoners in America. First, Graves noted that "there is no Commission in Boston to try prisoners Guilty of Acts of Rebellion or High Treason committed on the High Seas." Second, he informed the Lords that "many inconveniences will arise from keeping Prisoners on board and in the present state of things a few only can be kept Prisoners in Boston."[55]

Nonetheless, the North administration quickly ordered the officers returned to America (the privates having entered the king's service rather than remain prisoners). It did so, in Lord Germain's words, "for the same obvious reasons that induced the sending back the Rebel Prisoners taken in Arms upon the attack of Montreal"—a reference to Allen's case. In a letter to General William Howe (who had relieved Gage on the land, while his brother Admiral Richard Howe had relieved Graves on the sea), Lord Germain wrote that he hoped the prisoners could be exchanged for British prisoners in American custody. But Germain also reminded Howe that "it cannot be that you should enter into any Treaty or Agreement with the Rebels for a regular Cartel for the Exchange of Prisoners." Instead, Germain entreated Howe to rely on his "Discretion" to determine the "means of effecting such an Exchange without the King's Dignity & Honor being committed, or His Majesty's Name used in any Negotiation for that purpose."[56]

Why was Howe precluded from entering into a formal cartel? Because doing so would be tantamount to recognizing that the American prisoners were in the service of a foreign sovereign, rather than traitors who needed to return to their proper allegiance. Because British policy was quite clear on this point—namely, that the Americans were traitors and criminals—Howe would have to avoid entering into a formal cartel and instead effect exchanges in his own name through direct agreements with George Washington. Washington, for his part, insisted that the American prisoners be recognized as prisoners of war.[57] As the war progressed, notwithstanding the informal sanctioning by the British government of prisoner exchanges in America, Howe steadfastly refused to enter any formal cartel lest it "imply an acknowledgement inconsistent with the claims of the English Government."[58] His successor, Sir Henry Clinton, likewise refused to enter any formal cartel lest it "acknowledg[e] independency," and instead declared that personal agreements between Washington and him would govern prisoner exchanges in America.[59] Throughout the war, moreover, the British engaged in sustained efforts to bring the wayward Americans back into allegiance by offering the king's pardon to those who would pledge to quit their support for the American cause.[60]

Meanwhile, on the seas, the British continued to capture American ships and with them, American prisoners. Despite the North government's initial practice of sending such prisoners back to America almost immediately following their arrival in England, British ships continued to bring American prisoners to English ports. It became necessary for the administration to settle the legal framework that governed the American prisoners held on English soil.

To do so, the North administration would consult a regular advisor, the chief justice of King's Bench and great English jurist Lord Mansfield, the same judge who had earlier bailed American Stephen Sayre from the Tower of London.[61] On August 6, 1776, Lord Germain wrote to Mansfield for guidance concerning how to treat four American officers of the Boston sloop called the *Yankee*, which was now at the port of London.[62] Commanded by Henry Johnson, the *Yankee* had been "fitted out and armed for the purpose of intercepting British ships," a task at which it had achieved some success, having captured two British prizes and taken on some of their respective crews as prisoners. On July 3, 1776, however, several of the British prisoners "turned the captors into prisoners," confining the Americans in irons below deck and setting sail for England. Upon arrival, they sailed the *Yankee* right up the Thames River to London, where the Americans were put on display for all to see.[63]

The Americans consisted of four officers and their crew, the latter of whom Germain had no problem putting into service on one of the king's ships heading to East India. In Germain's view, however, there were "several obvious objections to giving the same treatment to the other four, and it is perhaps a decisive one that it would certainly expose His Majesty's commissioned officers to a cruel and disgraceful retaliation." "[S]end[ing] them back" was certainly an option, Germain noted, "as was very wisely suggested and practiced with regard to the Canada prisoners who were brought to Pendennis Castle," again a reference to Ethan Allen and his fellow prisoners. Germain took pains to note, however, that the two situations did not present the same considerations. First, "the motives which then made it the duty of government to temporize no longer exist in the same degree and will, it may be expected, totally cease in the course of the present campaign." Second, Germain observed, "the crime of these men is very different from that of Ethan Allen and his associates, and a tendency of leaving it unpunished is infinitely more interesting and extensive."

He continued by distinguishing the present situation from Allen's treatment:

> The rebels, engaged in a land service in which there is no plunder to be gained nor any better return than sixpence a day for all the hardships and hazards which they undergo, will whenever the interval comes for cool reflection find sufficient discouragement in the mere circumstances of their situation. But the reasoning of rebels who turn to piracy is very different; they expose themselves to little or no personal danger in the attacking of unarmed vessels, and if they make one valuable capture they acquire according to their ideas immense fortunes. If, added to this, they find that when accidentally or otherwise taken prisoners,

they are to be dismissed without punishment, they will then have the complete and irresistible temptation of great probable gain without any possible risk. These considerations are too obvious to escape our merchants, who are at this moment particularly interested in the subject. And the illegal acts, which in the case of Allen had the tacit approbation of the kingdom, would I apprehend be very differently considered if extended to the four men abovementioned.

Germain, it seems, viewed both cases as involving "illegal acts" and "crime[s]." But the political circumstances surrounding the two situations differed on at least two scores and counseled against sending the Yankee officers back to America for exchange or putting them into the king's service. First, Germain believed that declining to punish rebels such as the *Yankee* officers would have the effect of only encouraging more attacks on unarmed British merchant vessels by American privateers. Second, he suggested that unlike the case of Allen and his associates, here the plight of the American prisoners had engendered little sympathy—or, in his word, "approbation"—within the kingdom. On this point, Germain hinted that the administration felt the pressure of British merchants to punish these prisoners for their acts.[64]

Nonetheless, Germain suggested that perhaps the best course was to "keep[] the men aboard a guardship for the present" while noting that "if any factious man should force us to commit them, that the trial can be forced on in the Admiralty courts. . . ." Germain closed by posing three specific questions to his friend:

1. Whether to give up all Idea of commencing a legal Prosecution against these Men for their Crime. 2. Whether to keep them in a guardship 'till the Turn of the Campaign is more decided. 3. Whether to commit them at once for the Piracy.[65]

Lord Mansfield replied two days later. He wrote to Germain: "The subject of your letter is important and in every light attended with difficulty." Mansfield thought it "might be the best expedient" if the officers would ask for leave to enter the service of the king in the East Indies, but he also recognized that the officers were unlikely to do so. He continued:

Their crime abstractedly and upon the face of it is piracy, and it is better so to treat it, though under all the collateral circumstances I take them to be guilty of high treason in levying war. It seems most clear that they ought not to be set at liberty. I am not able to answer the many

objections to sending them back. There is no analogy between the reason and circumstances which wisely prevailed in the case of Allen etc.
and the present.[66]

Mansfield said nothing more on the comparison with Ethan Allen's case.

As for the prospect of trying the four officers, Mansfield informed Germain
that "[t]here cannot be an Admiralty session in the ordinary course till about
January next." If the administration committed them to Newgate for piracy,
though, "it is possible to throw upon this step the colour of a trial and execution." "But," Mansfield continued, "if it be clear that they should not be dismissed or sent back, though perhaps these men may never . . . be thought the
object of execution or even trial, the only deliberation is how to keep them." In
other words, Mansfield now set out to tackle the question how the administration might keep the four officers in custody *without* trying them. His remarks
on this point are noteworthy:

> If they were prisoners of war the King might keep them where he
> pleased; consequently aboard a guardship no *habeas corpus* could
> deliver them. It is tenderness to avoid treating them as rebels or pirates,
> and in sound policy prudent to suspend any extensive acts either way. If
> these 4 are so wickedly advised as to claim to be considered as subjects
> and apply for a *habeas corpus*, it is their own doing; they force a regular
> commitment for their crime. Upon the return to the writ, if they are not
> committed before, opposition should be made to their discharge on the
> part of the Attorney-General upon information of their crime properly
> sworn, as a ground for their commitment.

Here, Lord Mansfield confirmed the legal distinction between prisoners of
war and subjects who could invoke the Habeas Corpus Act. In so doing, he
warned Germain that to the extent that the captured Americans claimed royal
subjecthood, their commitment on English soil could be defended against a
petition for discharge under the Habeas Corpus Act only by sworn criminal
charges presented against them. Notably, Lord Mansfield here also noted that
"[d]uring the last rebellion and after . . . , many French officers were in gaol as
rebels, being either born in the King's dominions or if born abroad the sons of
British subjects; they were tried and condemned."[67] Putting on the French uniform, it seems, had not relieved the British subjects of their duty of allegiance,
for which they were in turn held criminally accountable.

In the end, Mansfield advised his friend "to direct the 4 to be kept aboard
[a guardship] till further order, always being prepared in case of a *habeas*

corpus...."[68] The administration followed the advice, with Lord Suffolk reporting to the Lords of the Admiralty only days later that he had been "directed to signify ... the King's Commands" that the four officers "aboard the Rebel Privateer call'd the Yankee of Boston, be properly secured for the present aboard such Vessel belonging to His Majesty as your Lordships may find most convenient."[69] Within two weeks, Captain Johnson had escaped, as did another *Yankee* officer some months later. (The latter was recaptured only to escape a second time from British imprisonment.[70]) The other officers also attempted to win their freedom via escape, but it seems that only one succeeded.[71]

The Prisoners Keep Coming

Mansfield's advice was nothing more than a stopgap measure. The time by which the British would have to confront the role of the Habeas Corpus Act as it applied to American prisoners being brought to English shores was fast approaching. By late 1776, ships delivering American prisoners to England were now arriving in a constant stream. Lord Suffolk, inundated with requests from the Lords of Admiralty as to how to proceed in such cases, repeatedly advised that all prisoners be detained "in safe Custody 'till further Orders."[72]

One such American was Ebenezer Smith Platt, whose story suggests that the Habeas Corpus Act was indeed very important—and well known—to Americans. Platt had been involved in the first capture of a British ship in the colonies, although it was only some time later that the British took him into custody in Jamaica. His transport from Jamaica to England followed aboard the *Pallas*. The administration initially detained Platt, like the officers of the *Yankee*, on a ship at port rather than on land, having moved him to the *Centaur* from the *Pallas*.[73] During this time—before he had even set foot on English soil—Platt requested permission to "send for an attorney ... so that I may lay before him a State of my Case, in order to have the benefit of the Habeas Corpus Act ... and want nothing but to be tried by the Laws of my King & Country."[74] Mansfield's concern over an American claiming the benefits of the Act had finally come to pass. The way that Platt's case unfolded demonstrates that Platt's confidence in the Act was not unfounded, just naive.

When Platt landed in England in December 1776, his requests for an attorney caused sufficient concern that Lord Suffolk sought the advice of the attorney and solicitor generals as to how best to proceed in the matter.[75] Thurlow and Wedderburn responded by stressing the importance of being able to prove that Platt's actions bore "a connection with the treasonable force ... in arms within [Georgia]." "Supposing that to be the case," they continued, "[i]t will be proper to commit him for trial in the ordinary course." But, they noted, "[t]he temper of our Laws certainly requires that every Prisoner should be allowed the means of suing out a Habeas Corpus." Concluding, they advised: "[I]t seems better to proceed to His examination; and to discharge Him, if nothing appears in proof against Him; or to commit Him regularly if a sufficient foundation be laid for that."[76] In other words, Thurlow and Wedderburn counseled the administration to levy charges, if they could be substantiated, or else be prepared to see a court discharge Platt upon his invocation of the protections of the Habeas Corpus Act.

Notably, Platt's captors also delivered three witnesses to testify to his treason—specifically, officers of the British ship *Philippa*, which Platt and others purportedly had captured outside Savannah and stripped of its stock of gunpowder for the use of the American rebels.[77] On this basis, the administration committed Platt to Newgate Prison in London on January 23, 1777, pursuant to a warrant issued by Justice of the Peace William Addington charging Platt with "High Treason at Savannah in the Colony of Georgia in North America."[78] But Platt remained determined to win his discharge by invoking the Habeas Corpus Act in the British courts. What he may not have known at the time was that his early chances of success were substantial, given that the original three witnesses against him had escaped from custody and fled in late December.[79]

Platt's litigation strategy, however, turned out to be disastrous. In February, his counsel—the very same John Alleyne who had reportedly earlier taken on Ethan Allen's case—presented Platt's petition for habeas corpus to the Court of Oyer and Terminer, and General Gaol Delivery at the Old Bailey. This made sense insofar as the Old Bailey immediately bordered Newgate. But it was a catastrophic jurisdictional mistake in light of the governing law of treason and what soon transpired in Parliament. On the first point, the treason statute of Henry VIII provided that all treasons committed outside the realm of England would be heard before the Court of King's Bench or else before a special commission set up for the purpose.[80] Because this meant that only King's Bench could grant Platt bail or discharge, the Justices of Gaol Delivery declared that his petition "to a Court of Gaol Delivery, who have no power at all to try the prisoner, is nugatory and void." Nonetheless, the justices studying Platt's case were quite clear that he was entitled to the full benefits of the Act. As they put it, "the prisoner may apply, under the *Habeas Corpus* Act, to the Court of King's Bench, to be tried or bailed; and if not tried in two terms after his prayer is received, he will be intitled to his discharge." "[B]ut," the justices wrote, "this Court cannot interpose."[81] In short, Platt just had to file his writ in the proper court. But before Platt could do so, Parliament intervened.

Revisiting Suspension

While Platt's counsel was arguing on his behalf at the Old Bailey, Parliament began discussing a bill that would render the proceedings all but moot. In early February, debate began on a bill to suspend the Habeas Corpus Act with respect to American prisoners detained in England. Prime Minister North explained why such a bill was necessary when he introduced the measure in the House of Commons:

> [T]here had been, during the present war in America, many prisoners made, who were in actual commission of the crime of high treason; and, there were persons, at present, guilty of that crime, who might be taken, but perhaps for want of evidence could not be kept in gaol. That it had been customary upon similar occasions of rebellion, or danger of invasion, to enable the king to seize suspected persons. . . . But as the law stood . . . it was not possible at present officially to apprehend the most suspected person. . . . *It was necessary for the crown to have a power of confining them like other prisoners of war.*[82]

Another account of Lord North's speech reports that he set forth among the "purposes of the bill" the necessity of being able to confine the prisoners "in the same manner that was practiced with respect to other prisoners of war, until circumstances might make it advisable to proceed criminally against them."[83]

The next day in the Commons, Lord Germain read the proposed bill, which by design responded to the commission of "acts of treason and piracy" by "certain of his Majesty's colonies" and the fact that "many persons have been seized and taken, who are expressly charged or strongly suspected of . . . treasons and felonies, and many more such persons may be hereafter so seized and taken." Germain noted that because it was simply not possible "to proceed forthwith to the trial of such criminals," the bill permitted detention of such persons without bail or mainprize for as long as it remained in force.[84]

The bill, like the war that produced it, was controversial from the start. Governor Johnstone agreed that it was necessary to "bring[] back the Americans to their allegiance," but thought this possible "without the dangerous measure of attacking the grand palladium of the British constitution, the freedom of men's persons."[85] Others ridiculed the asserted basis for the legislation, drawing sharp contrasts with prior episodes of suspension. To take one example, the very same John Dunning who had reportedly taken on Ethan Allen's cause pointed to the earlier eighteenth-century episodes of rebellion in Scotland as creating a "necessity" for suspension. Here, however, he argued that there was no "rebellion within the kingdom." "Are we," he asked, "afraid that the people American will pass the Atlantic on a bridge, and come over and conquer us?" Still others feared that the law would be used to detain not just those taken in arms, but any person from the rebellious colonies.[86]

Dunning echoed comments made by many others when he raised the concern that the law would "empower[]" the Crown to "apprehen[d], solely on suspicion."[87] To this, Attorney General Thurlow expounded that "nothing more was meant by the Bill, than to apprehend, commit, and confine persons actually charged, or suspected of committing, the crime of high treason in American, or on the high seas, or of piracy." This being said, Thurlow also noted that "the present Bill . . . was meant to prevent mischief, not with a view to rigorous punishments. . . ."[88] There was some tension between Thurlow's two remarks—he claimed that the bill targeted persons actually charged with or suspected of committing treason, and yet acknowledged that its objective was not necessarily punishment. As will be seen, however, the way in which the administration executed the law ultimately largely supported Thurlow's vision.[89]

Opponents trotted out the case of Stephen Sayre as an example of the abuse of power that the bill would permit. In response, Lord North defended the handling of Sayre's case while also highlighting that the bill would constrain magistrates from releasing on bail any person charged on suspicion of treason. North next made his case for the necessity of "entrust[ing] such extraordinary powers" in the "King's servants" that "would not be proper on ordinary occasions."[90] Those in the opposition were not convinced, and raised the specter of gross abuses on the part of the very same "servants" that North wanted them to trust.[91] Thurlow once again rose in response, noting that if "powers should be abused, that would be a very proper subject for parliament hereafter to enquire into."[92]

Unsurprisingly, the bill's opponents in the Commons included John Wilkes, who cited the case of Ebenezer Platt in arguing against the bill, referring to it as "another violation of the law, an evasion of the Habeas Corpus Act." Platt, Wilkes observed, had yet to face his accusers and had been moved from ship-to-ship upon his arrival in England, allegedly to defeat the service of earlier writs of habeas corpus upon his custodians. Wilkes accordingly moved that the bill be amended to require "an oath of two witnesses to the charge [of treason], and of their being confronted with the prisoner" before any person could be committed.[93] The proposal went nowhere and instead triggered reactionary proposals to expand the bill's reach. Richard Rigby, for example, thought it better to pass "a general suspension of the Habeas Corpus Act" to reach "covert" support for the Americans wherever it may be discovered. Temple Luttrell, in turn, cited a recent case in Dublin in which merchants sending arms to Americans had won bail "for want of a law of this kind" as reason to expand the bill's reach to "this kingdom and Ireland."[94]

Throughout the debate in the Commons, members routinely referred to the proposed legislation as a "suspension of the Habeas Corpus Act" and conceived of the bill as a natural outgrowth of the earlier suspension acts.[95] (Attorney General Thurlow, for example, invoked the case of William Wyndham and Parliament's 1715 suspension, claiming that the present bill was modeled on that earlier episode.[96]) But from what appears to have been a concern that any domestic application of the Act would trigger protest, the administration was careful not to promote or write the bill as an outright suspension of the Habeas Corpus Act.[97] Members nonetheless articulated great reservations about the bill on this score,[98] leading to approval of an amendment to clarify that the bill should not be read to apply to persons suspected of aiding the American cause from England, but instead only to persons "who shall have been out of the Realm at the Time or Times of the Offence or Offences wherewith he or they shall be charged."[99] With the amendment, the bill passed the Commons by a vote of 112-33.[100] What little information is available about the debates in the House of Lords suggests that they largely tracked those of the Commons before the chamber also passed the bill.[101]

As passed, the legislation provided:

WHEREAS a Rebellion and War have been openly and traiterously levied and carried on in certain of his Majesty's Colonies and Plantations
in *America*, and Acts of Treason and Piracy have been committed on the
High Seas, and upon the Ships and Goods of his Majesty's Subjects, and
many Persons have been seised and taken, who are expressly charged
or strongly suspected of such Treasons and Felonies, and many more
such Persons may be hereafter so seised and taken: And whereas such
Persons have been, or may be brought into this Kingdom, and into
other Parts of his Majesty's Dominions, and it may be inconvenient in
many such Cases to proceed forthwith to the Trial of such Criminals,
and at the same Time of evil Example to suffer them to go at large; be
it therefore enacted . . . That all and every Person or Persons who have
been, or shall hereafter be seised or taken in the Act of High Treason
committed in any of his Majesty's Colonies or Plantations in *America*,
or on the High Seas, or in the Act of Piracy, or who are or shall be

charged with or suspected of the Crime of High Treason [committed in the same domains], or of Piracy, and who have been, or shall be committed, in any Part of his Majesty's Dominions, for such Crimes . . . or for Suspicion of such Crimes, or any of them, by any Magistrate having competent Authority in that Behalf . . . shall and may be thereupon secured and detained in safe Custody, without Bail or Mainprize, until the first Day of *January*, [1778]; and that no Judge or Justice of Peace shall bail or try any such Person or Persons without Order from his Majesty's most honourable Privy Council [during this period]; any Law, Statute, or Usage, to the contrary in anywise notwithstanding.[102]

Thus, the Act applied only to acts "committed in any of his Majesty's Colonies or Plantations in *America*, or on the High Seas." It also plainly governed those engaged in piracy—a clause included to reach the acts of American privateers, for Parliament would never acknowledge such persons as sailing under proper letters of marque issued by an independent foreign government.

Like the suspensions that preceded it, this legislation granted temporary allowance for detention without trial and conviction of "[p]ersons" who were either charged with high treason or more generally "suspected" of the same. As its terms made clear, the entire purpose of the suspension was to permit the detention of prisoners during the war outside the normal criminal process. Parliament declared that it was adopting the Act because "it may be inconvenient in many such Cases to proceed forthwith to the Trial of such Criminals"—that is, the rebellious American colonists—"and at the same Time of evil Example to suffer them to go at large." Toward that end, the legislation, which came to be known as "North's Act," called for the designation of "one or more Places of confinement within the Realm, for the Custody of such Prisoners," such that they would not be kept in "the Common Gaol[s]."[103]

Here again, one finds reinforcement of key lessons of earlier periods of unrest in English history. First, the episode highlights the important relationship between the Habeas Corpus Act's promise of a timely trial and the suspension of that right by Parliament. Second, the limited nature of North's Act—applying as it did only to Americans imprisoned in England based on actions taken in America or on the high seas—reveals that the geographic reach of the Habeas Corpus Act mattered enormously in constructing the legal framework governing the treatment of American prisoners. Finally, as with earlier episodes of English suspensions, it is Parliament and not the executive who controlled the terms of British detention policy, at least where the Habeas Corpus Act governed.

The New Legal Landscape—Suspension
for American Rebels Detained in England

Lord Suffolk wasted little time in notifying the Lords of the Admiralty of the new legislation. On the day that the law received the king's assent, Suffolk immediately sent notice to the Lords of its passage and asked them to designate "one or more Place or Places of Confinement within the Realm for the Custody of such Prisoners . . . to be appointed in the Manner & for the Purposes [set forth in the Act]—instead of the Common Gaols."[104] In response, the Lords recommended Mill Prison in Plymouth and Forton Prison in Portsmouth, both of which had been "used for the Custody of Prisoners during the last War."[105] Within weeks, the attorney and solicitor generals had drafted general warrants for detaining prisoners who fell within the terms of North's Act at the two prisons. Lord Suffolk then ordered that "all persons subject to the provisions of the said Act" who had already been brought to England along with "all others subject to the said provisions, who may hereafter be brought . . . be committed to one of the [two] Places of Confinement."[106] Within months, Mill and Forton held hundreds of American prisoners.

On the other side of the Atlantic, reaction to North's Act was swift and angry. To take but one prominent example, just a few months after the Act's passage, George Washington's widely published 1777 "Manifesto" complained that "arbitrary imprisonment has received the sanction of British laws by the suspension of the Habeas Corpus Act."[107] And, as almost three thousand Americans subsequently detained in England during the war would learn, suspension meant indefinite detention without trial.

This brings us back to Ebenezer Platt, who remained at Newgate throughout the debates over North's Act. By the time that Platt refiled his petition for a writ of habeas corpus with the Court of King's Bench at the start of Easter Term on April 16, 1777, suspension had become the law.[108] It followed that Platt's petition was doomed from the start. His request to be tried, bailed, or discharged came before King's Bench on May 12, the last day of Easter Term. Attorney General Thurlow, aided by James Wallace and James Mansfield, argued for the Crown. Their case was straightforward. Relying up North's Act, they asserted that "[p]ersons suspected to be guilty, of High Treason in *America, or Piracy on the High Seas . . . shall be imprisoned and secured without Bail or Mainprize till the 1st of* January, 1778, *and that no Judge or Justice of the Peace shall bail or try* such Persons, unless under License from the Privy Council, signed by six Privy Counsellors."[109] Platt's counsel nonetheless repeated an argument made years earlier by the prisoners held in the Tower during the 1722 suspension (a group that included the Bishop of Rochester)—namely, that the words of the statute, speaking as they did to judges in the singular, did not bind the judges of the Court of King's Bench acting together. Once again, the argument failed, though not before levying some good points. "If any Law is to be construed strictly," Platt's counsel argued, "surely that is which acts in direct Contradiction of that great Bulwark of our Liberties the Habeas Corpus Act . . . which affects an unfortunate Man denied the Privilege of evincing his Innocence to the World, and that boasted Birth-Right of every *Englishman*, a Trial by his Peers."[110]

In an opinion by Lord Mansfield, King's Bench told Platt that it was powerless to grant him any relief. Mansfield began by observing that in relevant part, the Habeas Corpus Act was "made to accelerate the Trial of Persons committed for Treason or Felony." Nonetheless, Mansfield noted, on several occasions, Parliament had set aside that promise, and those acts, "from the Effect that they had . . . have always been called Suspensions of the Habeas Corpus Act." This followed, Mansfield observed because "the Act of Habeas Corpus says *they shall be tried or bailed* under this Proviso; these temporary Acts say *during a limited Time they shall not be tried*, nor consequently for Non-Trial *shall not be bailed*; that has been the Effect of them, and therefore they have obtained that Name." As to whether North's Act could be construed as not applying to the Court of King's Bench, Mansfield again relied on historical practice, noting that "there is not a single Instance alleged of one Man . . . who has had the Benefit of this Clause of the Habeas Corpus Act, by Virtue of its not extending to the Court of King's Bench."[111] Indeed, as Mansfield observed, notes from the Bishop of Rochester's case in 1722 show that King's Bench had earlier rejected the very same argument.[112]

Mansfield next remarked that "[t]he purpose of the Act is to prevent the Necessity of the Trial," which itself derived from the positive law that constituted the Habeas Corpus Act. As the 1777 Act set aside the commands of that law, he declared, "of course it extends to the Judges of the Court of *King's Bench*." Any other construction "would destroy the whole Meaning" of the suspension legislation.[113] Finally, Mansfield declared that he was "clear, without a Particle of Doubt," that Platt's petition for relief was the kind of case "that the Act . . . was particularly made to prevent."[114] The court ordered Platt remanded to Newgate and "kept in safe Custody until he shall be from thence discharged by due course of law."[115]

Platt's frustration with his plight is revealed in a letter he wrote to Benjamin Franklin just days after his appearance before King's Bench. Franklin was then heading up diplomatic efforts from Paris on behalf of American prisoners held in England. Platt reported: "Since my Confinement here I have taken every Legal step to Indeavour to be brought to tryall but could not, and fear

I shall not be, as I am now detained under that Accursd, and Arbitrary Law, for the suspention of the Habeous Corpus Act until January 1778."[116] In fact, Platt languished at Newgate even longer in light of Parliament's decision to extend North's Act through 1778. (Parliament would renew the extension five times, leaving the Act in place through the year 1782.[117]) It was not until April 1778 that the diplomatic efforts of Benjamin Franklin and the Committee for American Prisoners in Paris finally succeeded in negotiating Platt's release.[118]

In the wake of the passage of North's Act, hundreds of other American prisoners were committed to Mill and Forton Prisons. Meanwhile, early efforts directed by Benjamin Franklin out of Paris for the exchange of American prisoners in Europe met great resistance. Lord Stormont would not entertain such proposals, reportedly saying: "I never treat with rebels, unless to receive submission."[119] By the autumn of 1777, debates in Parliament over whether to extend North's Act witnessed the opposition drawing attention to the inconsistent treatment of American prisoners depending upon what side of the Atlantic they were held. In the Commons, for example, Edmund Burke complained of the failure to reach a cartel for the exchange of American prisoners in Europe, and charged that North's Act was "only to save appearances."[120] In the House of Lords, the Duke of Richmond once again raised the plight of Ebenezer Platt, noting that "[a]ll he asks is to be brought to trial."[121] But the administration remained firm in its conviction that North's Act remained both a necessary and prudent course for dealing with American prisoners detained within the realm. Thus, in defending the first extension of North's Act, Lord Chancellor Henry Bathurst observed:

> It was certainly necessary that some punishment should be inflicted on persons taken in the act of enmity against us; but what ought it to be? since it was plainly not expedient that they should be discharged, and not political, from the apprehension of retaliation, to put them to immediate death. What was the alternative? [T]he only just medium had been adopted: that of preserving them until the conclusion of the war, so that they might retain the power of punishment without doing it at a time when the consequences might fall upon such of our subjects as were now in a similar situation in America.[122]

Similar defenses were advanced in support of subsequent renewals of North's Act throughout the war.[123]

Evidence suggests that in compliance with the terms of North's Act, at least initially, the government took measures to screen prisoners before their committal. Thus, in one of the prisoner narratives preserved from this period,

William Russell notes that upon arrival in England, he was told "to go on shore to be examined" and that he was then "[e]xamined by 2 justices and committed to Mill Prison in Plymouth for Piracy, Treason, and Rebellion against his Majesty on the High Sea."[124] Another prisoner, Charles Herbert, described a similar commitment procedure. After being called together with a group of American prisoners before "the judges and examined," Herbert recorded, the prisoners were asked about the location of their birth, whether they had a commission from Congress, and the details of their service and capture. Later, he reported, "we were called up a second time, one at a time, and asked the same questions, to which we answered." After being examined still a third time, Herbert wrote, "we were called up together, as at the first, and our commitments were read to us and delivered to the constable."[125] As late as 1780, moreover, Russell wrote in his journal that a number of Americans who had not been properly committed were turned away from Mill Prison at the gate.[126] For those ordered committed, the examiners issued warrants charging them with treason.[127]

Although William Russell would refer to Mill Prison as a "Castle of Despair," the reality is that conditions were dramatically better at Mill and Forton Prisons than on the floating prison ships on which the British kept countless American prisoners in the New York Harbor. There, disease and death rates were staggering.[128] (There is little wonder that many referred to the worst of these "prison ships," the HMS *Jersey*, as "Hell Afloat.") All the same, the British government regularly made a point of reminding the Americans detained in England that they were not prisoners of war, as that term was understood under the Law of Nations, but instead criminals and "rebels" still bound by "the cord." This reminder took many forms, including giving the American prisoners lesser food rations than their French counterparts,[129] who, by contrast, were deemed prisoners of war once the two countries were in a declared state of war.[130] The differential treatment also encompassed subjecting American prisoners to irons as a disciplinary measure and requiring the lucky few who benefited from the sporadic prisoner exchanges negotiated successfully by Benjamin Franklin to request the king's pardon before they would be released.[131] Of the approximately three thousand Americans ultimately detained in Britain during the war, only about three hundred enjoyed their release as a result of such exchanges before the end of hostilities.[132] The much higher rates of exchange in America resulted largely from the fact that there was simply nowhere for the British to detain many of the captured rebels there. For those Americans who remained imprisoned in England, the government had no obligation to bring them to trial given the numerous extensions of North's Act, and it followed that the British government never did try any American for treason.[133]

Lord Germain's papers from this period underscore the administration's determination to treat the Americans as criminals and not as prisoners of war. Interestingly, they also reveal adherence (at least on his part) to the idea that even within the context of a suspension, prisoners should not be committed without sufficient evidence to support formal charges of treason or piracy, thereby bringing them within the strict terms of North's Act. Thus, in one notable exchange, Lord Germain wrote to Quebec governor Frederick Haldimand in March 1780 complaining that a rebel had been sent over without any evidence "to justify his detention," thereby compelling the prisoner's discharge. Germain advised:

> [U]pon this occasion I think it proper to observe to you, that the sending of Persons to England of whose disaffection you have not full proof & that proof being authentically transmitted along with them is only exposing the weakness of Government . . . , for no person can be kept in Confinement in this Country unless committed upon a Criminal Charge verified by the Oath of one or more credible Witness, nor can they without such Charge be restrained from quitting the Kingdom. . . .[134]

Here, one finds evidence of a determination to address wayward subjects within the constraints imposed by domestic criminal law. To make the point all the more clear, Germain continued:

> The Revolted Provinces not being on the foot of a Foreign Enemy their Prisoners are not deemed Prisoners of War in England but are committed for High Treason upon proof of their having borne Arms against The King such proof therefore it will be necessary for you to transmit with any that you think proper to send to England, but as exchanges are more readily made from New York, I should recommend to you to avail yourself of such Conveyances as offer to send those You have thither.[135]

Once again, the basis for British policy was clear—the Americans were traitors. Viewing them as prisoners of war in the service "of a Foreign Enemy" would have implicitly recognized American independence, something the British were unwilling to do at this stage of the war.

Germain's advice that Governor Haldimand curtail sending more prisoners to England and instead exchange them in North America had little influence. By October of that same year, Haldimand was still sending ships of rebel prisoners to England. As he explained to Lord Germain, "every Post Capable of Lodging Prisoners was full, they consumed a Quantity of Provisions and employed many Troops to guard them, whom I wished to imploy on more useful Service." One reason that the prisoner ranks had grown so much, Haldimand wrote, was because General Carlton "had refused to enter upon any cartel" with the enemy—a decision of which Haldimand approved.[136] The governor was concerned that in the event of an exchange, rebel sailors would immediately return to service and disrupt the province's trade. Haldimand, however, did comply with Germain's request that he send prisoners with better proof, for he assured Germain that this group was "accompanied with sworn Certificates of their being taken in Arms."

One prisoner dispatched from the Canadian coast to England during this period would warrant special attention upon his arrival in London.

From President of Congress to the Tower of London: The Plight of Henry Laurens

Per Lord Suffolk's direction, the Admiralty Lords detained most American prisoners brought to England at either Mill or Forton Prisons. The administration detained a handful of more prominent American prisoners, however, in London. The administration lodged the most prominent of them all, Henry Laurens, in England's most famous prison, the Tower of London. The British captured Laurens, who had served as President of the Continental Congress and been appointed ambassador to Holland, in September 1780 off the coast of Newfoundland en route to the Netherlands to negotiate a loan to support the war effort. While under chase from the twenty-eight-gun British ship *Vestal*, Laurens burned or dumped overboard most of his papers in a desperate effort to destroy evidence of the purpose of his voyage. Nonetheless, his captors were able to recover sufficient papers, including a draft treaty, to discern his charge and condemn him as a traitor. Based in part on this discovery, the British declared war on the Netherlands within months.[137]

The British took Laurens prisoner and transported him aboard the *Vestal* to England.[138] Upon his arrival there, Laurens protested to no avail that because he was an ambassador, imprisoning him violated the Law of Nations.[139] Of course, the British did not view him as an ambassador but as a traitor. In short order, Lords Stormont and Hillsborough, principal secretaries of state, issued a warrant on October 6, 1780, for Laurens's commitment to the Tower of London as a "close" prisoner. (This meant that Laurens was to be kept under constant watch and denied both pen and ink as well as visitors in the absence of prior approval.) The warrant charged Laurens with high treason, "committed at Philadelphia in the Colony of Pensylvania in America and on the High Seas." As one archived copy of the document shows, Solicitor General James Mansfield personally signed the warrant.[140]

Laurens resided in a two-room apartment at the Tower of London for fifteen long months during which his health deteriorated considerably. (His secretary, meanwhile, had been sent to Forton Prison, from which he managed to escape in early 1782.[141]) By December 1781, encouraged by Benjamin Franklin, Edmund Burke initiated efforts to win Laurens's exchange. Although Lord North was reportedly willing to consider an exchange for General Burgoyne, Lord Hillsborough contended that Laurens "could not be discharged & his condition changed from that of State prisoner to a prisoner of War without the intervention of a pardon." Laurens steadfastly refused to seek a pardon and communicated through Burke his expectation that he be "treated as a prisoner of War."[142]

Henry Laurens, President of the American Congress, Prisoner at the Tower of London, 1781

Credit: Lemuel Francis Abbott (artist), United States Senate, Cat. no. 31.00010.000.

Burke next took Laurens's cause to Parliament as part of a broader effort to end what he called the "disgraceful and inconvenient" suspension legislation and substitute in its place a formal policy for the "exchange of prisoners of war" between the British and Americans.[143] Burke recognized that Laurens's commitment followed from North's Act, but he protested the harsh conditions under which Laurens had been detained (all at Laurens's expense, no less) and the patchwork legal framework governing the detention of American prisoners.[144] North's Act, in his view, "made no distinctions, such as wisdom and justice required . . . but was confined solely to distinctions purely geographical." Burke continued: "Thus it depended not on the enormity of each captive's suspected guilt, but on the place where he was taken, and the place to which he was conveyed, whether he should be considered as a traitor, a pirate, or a mere prisoner of war."

"In America," Burke observed, "the prisoners were exchanged upon an equal and a liberal principle." But by reason of the suspension legislation, "when American prisoners were brought here, they were not suffered to be free as prisoners of war on parole, but were either sent to confinement under commitments as pirates, or on a charge of high-treason." It was "to put justice on a more equal footing" Burke said, that he intended to push a bill for equal treatment of all American prisoners and their designation as prisoners of war.[145] When parliamentary discussions of Laurens's case continued days later, Solicitor General James Mansfield did not dispute Burke's description of the legal patchwork that governed the British treatment of American prisoners. To the contrary, he defended the commitment of Laurens as a "state prisoner" rather than as a "prisoner of war," declaring that "[i]t was . . . not only lawful, but *necessary*, to confine him as a criminal" in England.[146]

The Laurens family knew all too well how these legal distinctions worked. Laurens's son John, a lieutenant colonel in the Continental Army, had been captured in May 1780 after the fall of Charleston. Instead of facing prison like his father, because he remained on American soil, the younger Laurens was quickly paroled and by November 1780 had been exchanged as part of the succession of informal exchanges between Generals Clinton and Washington.[147] But while the son enjoyed his freedom, the father languished in the Tower of London. Because attempts to negotiate the senior Laurens's exchange with General Burgoyne had stalled, Burke suggested that Laurens petition directly to Lord North and the House of Commons for his release, which Laurens did.[148] The petition triggered renewed discussions of an exchange, but by then the administration had someone else in mind—namely, the constable of the Tower where Laurens was being held prisoner, Lord Cornwallis. This was the very same Cornwallis whose defeat at Yorktown just a few weeks earlier had turned the tide of the war decisively in favor of the Americans and triggered the commencement of peace negotiations.

The actual process by which Laurens obtained his release from the Tower underscored the administration's determination to treat Laurens as a criminal and not as a prisoner of war, even as the tide of the war had turned dramatically against Britain by this point. Specifically, instead of being paroled as Cornwallis had been by the Americans, Laurens was made to go before Lord Mansfield for a bail hearing on December 31, 1781. This followed after Lord Hillsborough, now concerned with Laurens's deteriorating health, had sought advice from Attorney General Wallace as to whether Laurens might be amenable to bailing. Wallace responded that Laurens "may be legally admitted to Bail, by one of the Judges of His Majesty's Court of King's Bench during vacation time under an Order from His Majesty's most Honourable Privy Council."[149] Thus, by the terms of North's Act, Laurens had to seek the consent of the Privy Council to be bailed from the Tower.

By his own account of the proceedings before Lord Mansfield that followed, once bail was settled, "when the words of the Recognizance 'Our sovereign Lord the King' were repeated," Laurens declared, "not my sovereign lord."[150] As part of the proceedings or "farce"—Laurens's term—he was ordered to put up a sizeable bond and agree to appear at Easter Term of the Court of King's Bench for his trial on the charge of high treason.[151] By the spring of 1782, with the North administration having fallen and peace negotiations well underway, the British finally dropped any pretense of trying Laurens, discharged his obligation to appear before King's Bench, and ultimately agreed to his exchange for General Cornwallis.[152] In what can only be described as an incredibly ironic conclusion to Laurens's story, he reported that Lord Shelburne (with whom he had begun discussions in the spring of 1782 over a possible peace) told him:

> Well Mr Laurens if we must acknowledge your Independence I shall be grieved as I have already said for your own sakes, you will lose the benefit of the Habeas Corpus Act.[153]

Never mind that Laurens had never enjoyed the Act's benefits, having first been denied its application in the colonies and subsequently confined without trial in the Tower of London under a suspension of the Act.

Coinciding with Laurens's October 1780 commitment to the Tower, the administration, under Lord Stormont's signature, issued a warrant similar to those issued in March 1777 with respect to Mill and Forton Prisons. The new warrant "order[ed] & appoint[ed] the Tower of London to be a Place of Confinement for the Custody of all & every Person or Persons who have been or shall hereafter be seized or taken in the Act of High Treason committed in any of His Majesty's Colonies or Plantations in America or on the High Seas, or of Pyracy, & who shall be liable to be committed to any Prison for any of the said Crimes." The warrant was issued "[i]n Pursuance of" North's Act.[154] It does not appear that any other American prisoners were sent to the Tower, but the order suggests that Laurens's capture had given the administration some optimism that other high-profile prisoners might soon join him.

One of those who might have joined Laurens—but ultimately chose not to do so on grounds of fiscal prudence—was John Trumbull, son of Connecticut governor Jonathan Trumbull. The younger Trumbull had left his post as personal aide to General Washington at the start of the war and taken up the study of art. Determined to study under Benjamin West in London, he traveled there by way of France in 1780. His timing was regrettable to say the least. American Loyalists met his arrival in July with protests and reported his presence, already known, to the authorities. Initially, the authorities left Trumbull alone, but that changed when news of the hanging of British major John André by the Americans reached London in November. Soon the administration issued warrants for the arrest of both Trumbull and another American officer of similar rank, Major John Steel Tyler. Tyler escaped, so "Trumbull was taken up for high Treason" in his place and committed to prison.[155]

The administration chose not to charge Trumbull with spying in England, but instead committed him on the charge of bearing arms against the king "within His Majesty's Colonies and Plantations in America."[156] These grounds brought his detention within the terms of North's Act. Trumbull wrote of this period that he was set on "forc[ing] myself to a legal trial," believing that by this point in England, "no jury could be found, who would enforce the penalty of the law." Accordingly, Trumbull consulted "an eminent lawyer," John Lee, who was king's counsel and would eventually serve as both solicitor and attorney general. As Trumbull recounts the meeting, Lee told him "that the suspension of the act of the habeas corpus, rendered such a measure impossible, and that my only hope was, by impressing the minds of ministers . . . and thus inducing them to release me."[157] It followed that Trumbull could not force a trial; instead, he remained imprisoned for almost eight months before the intervention of Edmund Burke resulted in an order by the king in Council to bail Trumbull on the condition that he leave England.[158]

The Significance of Geography to the Legal Calculus

One final story of American prisoners taken during the war and brought to England for detention drives home the central role that the Habeas Corpus Act and its suspension played in the British legal framework during this period. In February 1781, the British captured the Dutch island of St. Eustatius in the Caribbean, a crucial source of arms and ammunition for the Americans, with American ships filling its harbor.[159] (Notably, in November 1776, St. Eustatius had also been the first foreign entity to recognize American independence.) In the wake of the quick surrender of the island to the British, the search of a ship bound for Holland turned up correspondence from two men on the island addressed to the American ambassador in Holland, John Adams. Admiral George Rodney ordered the two men, Samuel Curson and Isaac Gouverneur, arrested and transported to England as "prisoners of state."[160]

By July, the prisoners had arrived in Portsmouth, causing Lord Germain to write Attorney General James Wallace and Solicitor General James Mansfield for advice on the matter. In his letter, Germain noted that Rodney had discovered prior correspondence between the two prisoners and, as Germain called him, "John Adams, the Rebel Agent in Holland." Likewise, he noted that it appeared that the two prisoners had sent considerable supplies from the island to the American "Rebels." Germain inquired of his legal officials their "[o]pinion of the nature of the Crime [the prisoners] are liable to be charged with and in what manner they ought to be proceeded against in order to their Conviction & Punishment."[161]

In response, Wallace and Mansfield informed Germain that they had learned that the two prisoners were "natural born Subjects of His Majesty." Specifically, Curson and Gouverneur were Americans who had been stationed in the Caribbean as agents of the Continental Congress to arrange shipments of supplies to America. Continuing, Wallace and Mansfield wrote that they believed that "the extracts from the Copy Book of Letters referred to, by Sir George Rodney, if that Book can be properly authenticated contains direct proof of treasonable Acts committed by them in supplying His Majesty's Rebellious Subjects in America with Arms and Military Stores." "[B]ut," they added, it was not entirely clear that the papers *could* be authenticated in England, a fact that obviously posed a significant problem if the goal was to prosecute the two for treason. Indeed, Wallace and Mansfield noted that because "the Acts charged upon them were done in the Island of St. Eustatius a Dutch Settlement," exposing them "to a prosecution for High Treason committed out of the Realm," the prisoners "will be intitled to force on their Tryal,

probably before sufficient evidence to support the prosecution may be collected, or their being bailed or discharged."

They further explained: "It appears however to us, that altho' there may not
be at present legal Evidence to convict them of the Crime of High Treason, yet
that the circumstances of the Case furnish sufficient ground to committ them
to Prison." What circumstances might those be? In a passage underscoring
the vital role that the suspension legislation had played in setting aside the
obligation derived from the Habeas Corpus Act to furnish a timely trial in
cases of suspected treason, they advised:

> But as some of the Supplies sent by them to America, no doubt arrived
> safe at the place of Destination, we think Curson and Governeur may
> be deemed to have committed Treason in His Majesty's Rebellious
> Colonies in America, and that it will be expedient to committ them
> as being suspected of High Treason committed by them in one of the
> Colonies to which they sent supplies for the use of the Rebels.[162]

In other words, Wallace and Mansfield offered Germain a means to buy
time to build a case against the prisoners. Given that existing evidence
against them could not be presently authenticated and that their allegedly
treasonous acts had been committed in St. Eustatius (falling beyond the
reach of North's Act), the prisoners were well situated to win their freedom
by invoking the Habeas Corpus Act's protections. But, as his legal advisers
instructed Germain, if instead he saw to it that the charges against Curson
and Gouverneur were formally predicated upon treasonous acts committed
in the American colonies, then the two could be held without trial under the
auspices of North's Act, and the lack of proper evidence to convict would no
longer pose a problem.

The administration followed this advice and detained Curson and
Gouverneur under the authority of North's Act, never affording them a
trial. To win their freedom, like Platt, Laurens, and Trumbull before them,
the two would turn to the diplomatic efforts of Edmund Burke and William
Hodgson, the latter a London merchant who worked closely with Benjamin
Franklin throughout the war to lend aid to the American prisoners held
in England.[163] Hodgson reported to Franklin in December 1781 that he had
effected the "removal" of Gouverneur specifically by following the advice of
Lord Mansfield. As he wrote, "alltho ministers were willing [Gouverneur]
shoud be removed they knew not how to do it & it was by suggestions of Lord
Mansfield I obtained the Sign Manual for a Habeas where the Law actually
forbids one to Issue."[164]

Only seven years later, Isaac Gouverneur's cousin—a delegate to the Constitutional Convention by the name of Gouverneur Morris—drafted the U.S. Constitution's language strictly limiting the circumstances under which the new federal government could suspend "the privilege of the writ of habeas corpus."[165] One is left to ponder whether and to what extent the experience of his cousin may have influenced Morris's actions at the Convention.

Finally, Americans as Prisoners of War

As already noted, in the wake of the British defeat at Yorktown in October 1781, the tide of the war had turned decisively in favor of the Americans. Indeed, it is reported that Lord North met the news of Cornwallis's surrender by crying: "Oh God! It is all over!" By the following March, Lord North's government had fallen and Lord Rockingham's administration had taken its place. The latter was not disposed to continue in pursuit of a losing cause[166] and as part of its march toward a negotiated end to the war and recognition of American independence, the administration threw its support behind legislation that Edmund Burke had proposed the prior December to alter the status of American prisoners held in England.

This significant shift in British policy came in March 1782. Instead of extending North's Act, the most recent extension of which was set to expire on January 1, 1783, Parliament addressed the legality of the continuing detention of the "*American* Prisoners brought into *Great Britain*" during the "present Hostilities" by adopting an approach that better coincided with the direction of peace negotiations. Specifically, Parliament passed "An Act for the better detaining, and more easy Exchange, of *American* Prisoners brought into *Great Britain*." The Act noted that "Exchanges of Prisoners taken in *America*, or conveyed to *America*, have been there regularly made." In keeping with that practice, Burke's Exchange Act posited that "it may be likewise convenient . . . that *American* prisoners brought into *Great Britain* should be detained, and exchanged, in the same manner." Toward that end, the statute declared that "it may and shall be lawful for his Majesty, during the Continuance of the present Hostilities, to hold and detain . . . as *Prisoners of War*, all Natives or other Inhabitants of the Thirteen revolted Colonies not at His Majesty's Peace." The Act likewise authorized the discharge or exchange of such prisoners "according to the Custom and Usage of War, and the Law of Nations . . . any Warrant of Commitment, or Cause therein expressed, or any Law, Custom, or Usage, to the contrary notwithstanding." Finally, the Act permitted discharging prisoners "detained as Prisoners or Prisoners of War, either absolutely, or upon such

Conditions, and with such Limitations, or for such a Time, as His Majesty shall deem proper."[167]

Thus, as part of the shift toward recognition of American independence, Parliament allowed its suspension legislation to lapse and altered the status of American prisoners held on English soil from prisoners of state to "prisoners of war"—a concept that under the Law of Nations recognized the American prisoners to be in the service of a foreign enemy. For this very reason, in writing John Adams one month later, Benjamin Franklin pointed to this legislation as "a renunciation of the British Pretensions to try our People as Subjects guilty of High Treason and to be a kind of tacit acknowledgement of our Independency." "Having taken this step," Franklin surmised, "it will be less difficult for them to acknowledge it expressly."[168]

Immediately on the heels of passage of this Act, peace negotiations began in April in Paris. Also that month, the Crown indicated that it was open to a general prisoner exchange, with Lord Shelburne conveying to Franklin through Hodgson that "the first official Act he did in his Department was to give directions that the Prisoners shou'd be exchanged."[169] Toward that end, as Franklin reported to Adams that month, the British were "now preparing transports to send the Prisoners home." By summer, Lord Shelburne (who had taken over the ministry in the wake of Rockingham's death), acknowledged that Britain should recognize American independence.[170] In November, the British and Americans agreed to preliminary articles of peace that formally recognized that independence and called for the freeing of "all prisoners on both sides."[171] (The group that negotiated on behalf of the Americans included Henry Laurens and Benjamin Franklin, among others.) Exchanges increased considerably in the wake of passage of the 1782 legislation, and by March 1783, the British had delivered all American prisoners remaining in England to France.[172]

Coinciding with their conversion to the status of prisoners of war, the Americans detained in England reportedly finally enjoyed full rations while awaiting their exchange. Thus, William Russell, detained at Mill Prison, recorded in his journal just one month after passage of the March 1782 Act that "Mr. Cowdry informed us that we are to have a full diet tomorrow. So we are no longer *Rebels* but *Prisoners of War*."[173] Likewise, the reward offered for the capture of escaped American prisoners was no longer commensurate with their previous criminal status, but was instead reduced to the much lesser amount typically offered for the return of escaped prisoners of war.[174] Nonetheless, British practice was not entirely consistent with respect to the new status of American prisoners, for despite the legislation declaring that they were now prisoners of war, King George III still requested a list of American prisoners to pardon before they would be set at liberty.[175]

This latter point underscores the lingering tensions between formal British policy and practice. Nonetheless, the legal framework governing American prisoners held by the British shifted dramatically as the tide of the war changed in early 1782 and American victory appeared a foregone conclusion. Indeed, once the British recognized the inevitability that the lines of allegiance would be severed with the Americans, British law understood the wartime acts of the former colonists as those of enemy soldiers in the service of a foreign sovereign, rather than treason. It followed that the relationship between the American "prisoners of war" and Great Britain was no longer governed by domestic law, including the English Habeas Corpus Act, but instead by the Law of Nations.

Meanwhile, the Americans had already begun constructing their own independent legal frameworks, importing the protections they associated with the Habeas Corpus Act and, sometimes (though not always), the idea of suspension. In so doing, they would finally claim the Act as their own.

PART TWO

Incorporating the Suspension Framework into American Law

On the other side of the Atlantic, the newly-declared independent states embraced the English Habeas Corpus Act as their own, while some states during the Revolutionary War also declared suspensions to confront the problem of disaffection. In studying the legal frameworks of the original states, one finds extensive evidence that the idea of a core habeas privilege was linked inextricably to the English Act, and a number of those states quickly moved to adopt formally the Act's terms as part of their new constitutions and codes. Highlighting the pervasive influence of the English Habeas Corpus Act on the development of early American law, the great New York jurist and legal commentator Chancellor James Kent observed in 1827 that "the statute of 31 Charles II. c. 2 is the basis of all the American statutes on the subject."

Of the many state codes embracing the terms of the English Act, surely the most significant statutory adoption of the English Act's terms occurred just three months before the Constitutional Convention convened in Philadelphia in 1787, when New York passed a statute almost identical to the 1679 Act. Such was the backdrop against which the delegates at the Constitutional Convention began their deliberations over a habeas clause.

When their work was done, the result was the Suspension Clause, which provided: "The Privilege of the Writ of Habeas Corpus shall not be suspended, unless when in Cases of Rebellion or Invasion the public Safety may require it." As Alexander Hamilton reported in the *Federalist Papers*, in this and related provisions, the delegates had amply provided for "trial by jury in criminal cases, aided by the *habeas corpus act*." Only a few decades later, the great chief justice John Marshall referenced the English statute as the basis of the constitutional privilege, counseling that in interpreting the Suspension Clause, it is necessary to look to "that law which is in a considerable degree incorporated into our own"—specifically, "the celebrated *habeas corpus* act" of 1679.

4

Forging a New Allegiance

With regard to the writ of Habeas Corpus, they wished that its privileges should be more accurately defined and more liberally granted, so that citizens should not be subject to confinement on mere suspicion.

BOSTON'S RETURN TO THE DRAFT HABEAS CLAUSE
IN THE MASSACHUSETTS CONSTITUTION (1780)[1]

DURING THE REVOLUTIONARY War, the British were not the only side that had to work through difficult questions surrounding the status of prisoners. The states comprising the upstart United Colonies faced the very same questions during the war when detaining British soldiers and the disaffected "Loyalists" among their ranks. In constructing new legal frameworks to govern these matters, the states drew heavily on the English model that had governed before the war and under which so many of their legal elite had trained— sometimes importing its concepts wholesale and sometimes reacting to its perceived failings by charting a different course. Reviewing the developing legal frameworks of the United Colonies during the revolutionary period reveals two important lessons. First, the concept of allegiance—dividing those falling "within protection" and those outside of it—played a crucial role in triggering the application of domestic law. Second, the newly independent states wasted little time in formally claiming the rights and privileges that had come to be associated with the English Habeas Corpus Act of 1679 as their own, setting the stage for the drafting of a federal Constitution in 1787 that would enshrine the privilege and carefully limit the opportunities for its suspension. This chapter chronicles the story of the long-standing struggle of the states to claim the Act's protections for themselves, highlighting the pervasive influence of the Act—including especially its seventh section—on early American habeas jurisprudence.

The fact that the English Habeas Corpus Act played such a central role in early American habeas jurisprudence is hardly surprising. British general Thomas Gage, reporting from his post in Boston in 1768, counseled

Habeas Corpus in Wartime. Amanda L. Tyler.
© Oxford University Press 2017. Published 2017 by Oxford University Press.

his British superiors against oppressing the people of a "Country[] where every Man Studys Law."[2] And in the immediate lead-up to the war, Edmund Burke observed to his fellow members of the Commons: "In no country perhaps in the world is the law so general a study."[3] Many leaders of the colonial bars had taken their training at the English Inns of Court.[4] The colonists had also studied the leading commentators on English law—Coke, Hale, and Blackstone—along with all the pillars of English law—including, of course, Magna Carta, and also the Habeas Corpus Act. They were heavily steeped in law and had studied Blackstone's glorification of the Act as one of the great pillars of liberty in his *Commentaries*, which were published and widely circulated in the United States in the 1770s. They also read Henry Care's treatise, which lauded the Act and reprinted it in full.[5] Against this backdrop, it is easy to see how the Founding generation saw great injustice in their denial of many of the liberties enjoyed by their English counterparts, and why in the wake of the Declaration of Independence those very same protections quickly became imported into early American law.[6]

Claiming the English Habeas Corpus Act as Their Own

The colonists had long declared themselves to be "entitled to all the inherent rights and liberties of [the crown's] natural-born subjects, within the kingdom of Great Britain," a claim reiterated in 1765 by the Congress of the Nine Colonies, and again in 1774 by the Continental Congress.[7] But as explored in the last chapter, the reality was different. Under the prevailing understanding of English law during this period, those living outside the formal British realm commonly enjoyed many fewer rights than those living within the realm.[8] Thus, the English Habeas Corpus Act may have been, as Blackstone wrote, a "second *magna carta*,"[9] but the Americans did not know its benefits. As noted, several attempts by the colonists to claim the benefit of the English Act failed by way of royal veto. In 1684, for example, King James II denied efforts by the people of New York to claim the full protections of English law in their Charter of Liberties and Privileges, responding in turn that "[t]his Priviledge is not granted to any of His Ma[ts] Plantations where the Act of Habeas Corpus and all such other Bills do not take Place." The Crown next disallowed efforts in Massachusetts to adopt the Act in 1696, declaring that the "privilege has not as yet been granted in any of his majesty's plantations."[10] As one chronicler of the period wrote, during the seventeenth century, the colonists "did not happily know" the "effectual remedy, the writ of habeas corpus"[11]—or at least the writ associated with the English Habeas Corpus Act. (In this respect, the American experience of numerous failed attempts to adopt the English Habeas Corpus Act bore resemblance to the Irish experience. Ireland witnessed seventeen failed attempts by the Irish House of Commons, spanning some ninety years, to adopt the English Act, before the Privy Council finally approved an Irish Act in 1782.[12]) As explored in the last chapter, moreover, the Crown's denial of application of the English Act on American soil played an important role in the Revolutionary War legal framework governing the detention of prisoners during the war.

Notwithstanding failed efforts early on in New York and Massachusetts to secure formal recognition of the English Habeas Corpus Act in the colonies, the eighteenth century witnessed attempts by multiple colonies to import the Act's principles into their legal frameworks. Such efforts proceeded along a number of different paths. Notably, some actually had their impetus in royal instructions, thereby standing in tension with the Crown's formal resistance to the Act's extension to the colonies, while other efforts to embrace the Act's principles occurred in quiet defiance of the Crown's position. In sifting through the historical evidence from this period, one thing becomes clear— by the time that the Founding generation convened to draft the Constitution in 1787, the American colonists were determined to claim the benefits and protections of the English Habeas Corpus Act—and particularly its seventh section—for themselves. They wanted to enjoy this "second *magna carta*" too.

Colonial examples of the Act's influence sweep well beyond New England. In the curious case of Virginia, for example, Lieutenant Governor Alexander Spotswood in 1710 declared that it was Queen Anne's pleasure that the inhabitants of Virginia should "have free liberty to petition . . . for a writt of Habeas Corpus." The details of the governor's proclamation, however, show that he had bestowed far fewer benefits on the Virginians than those embodied in the English Act, instead conveying protections that were easily circumvented. (For example, bail was left to the complete discretion of judges and penalties for non-issuance of writs were far less than those found in the Habeas Corpus Act.)[13] The governor's proclamation also stood in tension with the Crown's often-conveyed position to royal governors that they should not endorse any assembly bills that might prejudice the royal prerogative. But the seeds of adoption of the Act's principles had been planted in Virginia all the same, and in time they would bear fruit.

The Carolinas appear to have adopted the English Habeas Corpus Act not once, but twice, during the colonial period—first in 1692, and later in 1712. The 1712 legislation provided that the executive and judicial officers of the colony were "authorized, impowered and required, to do, act and put in execution the said Act, commonly called the Habeas Corpus Act, and every matter, clause and thing therein contained. . . ." So as to drive the point home, the legislation concluded by declaring that "all and every person which now is or hereafter shall be within any part of this Province, shall have to all intents, constructions and purposes whatsoever, and in all things whatsoever, as large ample and effectual right to and benefit of the said act, commonly called the Habeas Corpus Act, as if he were personally in the said Kingdom of England."[14] But it is unclear if the Crown even knew of the law's existence and there is good reason to suspect that it did not. In all events, the lack of royal record, combined with the failed attempts to adopt the Act before this point in New York and Massachusetts and later in North Carolina, strongly suggest that the 1712 statute never enjoyed the formal sanction of the Crown.[15] (Perhaps, in this regard, North Carolina's colonial practice mirrored Rhode Island's—the latter colony having often taken great pains to insulate the specific terms of its legal codes from Crown review.[16])

This being said, the Crown did allow for habeas protections in the Carolinas a few years later, and subsequent events suggest that the Act's terms began to take hold in the two colonies' jurisprudence. In 1730, one year after the division of the Carolinas, the Council of Trade and Foreign Plantations, with the approval of the Privy Council, instructed the colonial governors of both Carolinas to extend the right to petition for habeas corpus to the colonists in those jurisdictions.[17] These instructions were the same as those given earlier to Virginia's royal government and later to Georgia's government in 1754. Notably, the instructions introduced many of the core concepts of the English Habeas Corpus Act, including the promise of bail to those "committed for any criminal matters," where the offense in question was "bailable by the law of England," along with the promise of trial within two court terms for those committed for treason or felony. Likewise, the instructions directed that "no prisoner being set at large by an habeas corpus be recommitted for the same offense." All the same, as noted above with respect to the Virginia instructions, the directives did not address the problem of excessive bail and provided far lesser penalties for noncompliance than the original Act.[18] Nonetheless, the foundation had been established for incorporation of the Act's principles into the legal frameworks of the two colonies.

Indeed, notwithstanding the limitations of the royal instructions, evidence from the years following their issuance demonstrate that both Carolinas held fast to their embrace of the English Act, and that in time its protections firmly took hold. In 1733, for example, the South Carolina colonial assembly passed a controversial indemnity bill to shield public officials from suit "on Account of the Habeas Corpus Act."[19] The Council of Trade and Foreign Plantations reacted by recommending its disallowance to the king.[20] The king, through his Privy Council, repealed and voided the law without explanation.[21] This disallowance could be read as defending the Habeas Corpus Act's protections from encroachment (and thereby confirming the Act's applicability), although the Crown's subsequent disallowance of the Act to North Carolina in 1754, discussed below, calls such a conclusion into question.[22] Either way, by March 1776, when South Carolinians inaugurated a new independent government (and elected Henry Laurens vice president of their colony), the Act was so firmly rooted in its legal framework that the General Assembly took up as one of its very first matters the adoption of an "Ordinance to vest the several Powers . . . formerly granted to the Council of Safety in the President and Privy Council to suspend the Habeas Corpus Act. . . ."[23] Accordingly, the Assembly's early work took for granted that the English Habeas Corpus Act governed in the colony and, to the extent any doubt remained on that score, a catalog compiled in 1814 of English statutes remaining in force in the state confirmed this, reprinting as it did the English Act verbatim.[24]

The experience in North Carolina tells a similar story. In 1715, the colonial assembly declared that "all statute laws of England providing for the privileges of the people . . . are and shall be in force here, although this province or the plantations in general are not named."[25] In 1730, as explored above, the Council of Trade and Foreign Plantations instructed the colonial governor to ensure that the colonists enjoy "free liberty to petition . . . for a Writ of Habeas Corpus."[26] But as was also noted, these instructions fell short of granting the full scope of the English Act's many protections. Likely for this reason, in 1749, the North Carolina General Assembly adopted the English Habeas Corpus Act expressly as part of broader legislation laying claim to many English acts.[27] Just as with New York and Massachusetts, however, the king declared North Carolina's Act of 1749 "void and of no[] effect."[28] Even still, by the time North Carolina adopted its constitution in 1776, commentators report that "England's Habeas Corpus Act . . . was accepted as part of the state's common law."[29]

During this period, often "[u]sage, precedent and practice were mightier forces than legislation, in extending English law" to the colonies.[30] Thus, colonies often embraced the English Habeas Corpus Act's principles in the period before the Declaration of Independence through incorporation "in practice"—namely, through judicial action rather than express legislation.[31] Maryland provides one such example. Although records from as early as 1725 demonstrate the established understanding in that state that "the received opinions of the best lawyers of England . . . and several adjudged cases" were against the applicability of the Habeas Corpus Act in the colonies, "[t]hese opinions . . . were not acquiesced in by the people, and there were several proceedings which would shew, if it was necessary, the adoption of this statute; in one of which, it was defended even in the Upper House, as the birth right of the inhabitants."[32] Although "[n]o act of assembly was passed on this subject, in the provincial government," in time the Act nonetheless became a recognized pillar of Maryland law through judicial practice. Indeed, leaving little doubt on the point, when Maryland enacted suspension legislation in 1777 during the Revolutionary War, the law expressly suspended "the *habeas corpus* act." The need formally to suspend the Act likely derived from the state's recognition of its force through its 1776 Constitution, which declared that the people are entitled to "the benefit of such of the English statutes" both by reason of their enactment and their "use[] and practi[ce] by the courts," and/or numerous earlier statutory resolutions laying claim to the common law and such English statutes "as are securitative of the Rights and Liberties of the Subject. . . ."[33] In all events, by 1809, Maryland formally codified the terms of Section 7 of the English Habeas Corpus Act as part of a broader habeas statute.[34]

The Pennsylvania experience is more complicated, but the result similar. The process by which the Act's concepts came to be rooted in pre-Revolutionary Pennsylvania is difficult to determine with certainty. There is, however, no question that by the time of the Revolutionary War, the English Habeas Corpus Act was a pillar of Pennsylvania law. Indeed, in framing the plan of its new government, the Pennsylvania Constitutional Convention of 1776 "recommended to the first general assembly of this state, to make a law similar to the *habeas corpus* act of England, for the security of the personal liberty of the inhabitants."[35] And although adoption of a detailed Pennsylvania statute closely tracking the English Act did not occur until 1785,[36] state law nonetheless clearly recognized the Act as in force during the war, as is demonstrated by the important role that the Act played in a famous case involving the detention of some twenty Quakers in the early days of the Revolutionary War.[37] In describing the case of the Quakers in a letter to his friend John Adams, the chief justice of the Pennsylvania Supreme Court, Thomas McKean, reported that the English Act had controlled his disposition of the matter. McKean, who had been the final signatory on the Declaration of Independence and would later serve as President of Congress, noted first that "[t]he writs were applied for in form, agreeable to the directions of the statute of the 31 Car. 2 ch. 2. [the English Habeas Corpus Act]; and the only authority for the confinement, that I saw, was the copy of a letter from the Vice-President to Colo: Lewis Nicola." McKean continued:

The habeas corpus Act forms a part of the Code of the Pennsylvania laws, and has been always justly esteemed the palladium of liberty. . . . By the statute all discretionary power is taken away, and a penalty of £500 sterling imposed for a refusal of any judge in the vacation to allow the writ: so that if I had forgot the oath I had taken but a few days before, common prudence would have prevailed upon me not to have incurred the forfeiture of ten thousand pounds sterling, and also as a judge to have subjected myself to the just censure of the judicious and dispassionate. . . .

I acquainted the Vice-President with every particular of what had happened by an Express sent for the purpose; enquired of him, if the habeas corpus act had been suspended, or was about being suspended, for a limited time; and requested, if an act had passed for that purpose, to favor me with an exemplified copy. I told him, that, in almost every war since the making the statute, the like had been done in England, and that it was now in fact done there.[38]

Thus, McKean believed that in the absence of criminal charges and without a suspension, his court was bound under the Habeas Corpus Act to give the Quakers their freedom. And, just as had been true in English history, it was of no moment that the state was in the midst of fighting a war for its very existence. As he observed, suspension was a necessary predicate to detain persons in such a posture. Responding swiftly, the Pennsylvania Assembly adopted a suspension to address the case of the Quakers, declaring its intent "to restrain for some limited Time the Operation of the *Habeas Corpus* Act."[39]

Georgia, like Virginia and the Carolinas, witnessed introduction of certain aspects of the English Habeas Corpus Act by its royal governor. This followed from royal instructions given to Georgia's governor in 1754 similar to those given to Virginia and the Carolinas.[40] Then, following the break with England, Georgia wasted little time in claiming the full benefit of the Act. Indeed, as though to drive home the continuing and profound influence that the English Act wielded on early American law, the Georgia Constitution of 1777 expressly provided that "[t]he principles of the Habeas Corpus Act, shall be part of this Constitution" and annexed verbatim copies of the English Habeas Corpus Act to its original distribution.[41] Well until the Civil War, moreover, the terms of the English Act remained part of the codified laws of Georgia.[42]

Taken together, these stories illustrate the early determination of many of the colonies and then the states to import the English Habeas Corpus Act's terms and protections. Even in the states such as New York, which did not succeed in formally adopting the Act as part of their legal frameworks prior to

independence, there is evidence suggesting that the Act influenced both parties and courts during that period.[43] Further, as discussed below, in the immediate wake of the war, the states moved quickly to adopt the relevant terms of
the English Act as their own.

Declaring Independence and Forging a New Allegiance

The Crown's refusal to afford the protections of the Habeas Corpus Act to the
colonists constituted but one of many denials to them of basic liberties that
were enjoyed by their fellow subjects across the ocean. The fact that in 1774
the British Parliament had voted down extending the benefit of the Habeas
Corpus Act to the province of Quebec only served to fuel the belief held by
the colonists that they were the subjects of a tyrannical government. Indeed,
anger over developments in Quebec ran so deep as to bear mention in the
Declaration of Independence.[44] As they marched toward war, the colonists
decried their status as "subjects of an arbitrary government" who had been
denied both "trial by jury [and] the benefit of the habeas corpus Act, that great
bulwark and palladium of English liberty."[45] These were rights, they declared,
"without which a people cannot be free and happy." Thus, the Americans
resolved: "These are the rights . . . which we are, with one mind, resolved
never to resign but with our lives."[46]

It was in the early days of that fateful year of 1776 that the movement
to form a new allegiance formally took root. In January of that year, the
Continental Congress declared that "those who refuse to defend their country should be excluded from its protection."[47] "Their country" to which the
proclamation referred was "the United Colonies"—*not* Great Britain. By May
1776, the Congress had declared that "all the powers of government" should be
"exerted under the authority of the people of the colonies."[48] By June, with war
now unfolding, the Congress declared that "all persons abiding within any of
the United Colonies, and deriving protection from the laws of the same, owe
allegiance to the said laws." This new allegiance came with not only "the protection from the laws," but also the same obligation of loyalty as it had under
English law. Thus, the Congress declared:

> That all persons . . . owing allegiance to any of the United Colonies . . .
> who shall levy war against any of the said colonies within the same, or
> be adherent to the king of Great Britain, or others the enemies of the
> said colonies, or any of them . . . giving to him or them aid and comfort,
> are guilty of treason against such colony. . . .[49]

This resolution effectively embodied a renunciation of English subject-hood and the creation of a new union just as much as did the Declaration of Independence, which followed only days later and declared: "The good People of these Colonies . . . are Absolved from all Allegiance to the British Crown."[50]

In its June 24 resolution, the Continental Congress also "recommended to the legislatures of the several United Colonies" that they "pass laws for punishing . . . any of the treasons before described."[51] Most colonies responded quickly in turn, borrowing heavily from the English conception of treason. There was, of course, a compelling need to address the problems of treason and disaffection during this period. Persons with Crown sympathies—so-called "Loyalists"—were ubiquitous in the colonies and hard to differentiate from those loyal to the movement for independence. Further, thousands of Loyalists joined the British military effort. Colonists also often traded with the enemy, "shared intelligence, harbored clandestine intruders, and joined in acts of sabotage, looting, and violence of the sort that today might be called 'terrorism.' "[52]

Against this backdrop, it is notable that where a habeas privilege derived from and associated with the protections of the English Habeas Corpus Act had taken root—as it had in many of the colonies by this time—the dominant understanding of the formal law contemplated that persons owing allegiance could be detained only on criminal charges in the absence of a suspension or state of martial law. Indeed, even when the Continental Congress empowered General George Washington "to arrest and confine persons who . . . are otherwise disaffected to the American cause," it ordered him to "return to the states of which they are citizens, their names, and the nature of their offences, together with the witnesses to prove them"—presumably so that such persons could be tried on criminal charges in the ordinary course.[53] Supporting this interpretation is a subsequent resolution by the Congress declaring that those persons deemed to owe allegiance to the American cause who were captured fighting with the British should be sent to their home states "to be dealt with [under] the laws thereof."[54]

Further, just as English legal tradition had, the Continental Congress made regular practice of distinguishing between those persons owing allegiance and those who fell outside the protection of domestic law. In one early example, the Congress resolved:

> That all persons, not members of, nor owing allegiance to, any of the
> United States of America, as described in a resolution of Congress of
> the 24th of June last, who shall be found lurking as spies in or about
> the fortifications or encampments of the armies of the United States,

or of any of them, shall suffer death, according to the law and usage of
nations, by sentence of a court martial, or such other punishment as
such court martial shall direct.[55]

By this resolution, those "not members of, nor owing allegiance to" the
United States were left to rely upon the "law and usage of nations" for their
protection. This explains the practice of treating the British Redcoats, labeled
"Enemies in War" in the Declaration of Independence, as falling outside the
realm of domestic law. Practices on the ground conformed to this understanding. Accordingly, captured Redcoats were held as prisoners of war and, where
their actions warranted it (as in certain cases of spying), they were punished
within the framework of the Law of Nations. During this period, Thomas
Paine echoed Hale in highlighting the importance of the lines of allegiance in
his widely-circulated pamphlet *Common Sense*. There, he argued that "[a] line
of distinction should be drawn between English soldiers taken in battle, and
inhabitants of America taken in arms. The first are prisoners, but the latter
traitors. The one forfeits his liberty, the other his head."[56]

The laws of the newly formed states generally drew this same distinction.
Responding to the Continental Congress's June 24 resolution, many states
enacted laws defining and criminalizing treasonous activity.[57] These statutes
generally differentiated between persons from whom allegiance was expected
and those who fell outside protection. Pennsylvania's 1777 treason statute
is typical on this score. The legislation by its terms applied to persons falling "under the protection of [the state's] laws" but expressly did *not* apply to
"prisoners of war."[58] North Carolina's 1777 treason statute drew the same distinction, declaring that "all and every Person and Persons (Prisoners of War
excepted) now inhabiting or residing within the limits of the State of North-
Carolina, or who shall voluntarily come into the same hereafter to inhabit or
reside, do owe, and shall pay Allegiance to the State of North Carolina."[59]

With War Comes Suspension

As the war unfolded, the Continental Congress further urged state executives
"to apprehend and secure all persons . . . who have, in their general conduct
and conversation, evidenced a disposition inimical to the cause of America."[60]
In the midst of war, however, there was simply no way that all of the disaffected could be brought to trial. It is no wonder, then, that at least six of those
states that had imported the protections of the Habeas Corpus Act into their
legal frameworks responded just as English tradition had taught them to do—
they enacted suspensions.

These suspensions are noteworthy for several reasons. First, they confirm the centrality of the English Habeas Corpus Act to early American legal thinking about habeas and executive detention and underscore the fact that many of the states recognized by this point a robust habeas privilege derived from the Act's seventh section. Second, these suspensions offer a window into Founding-era thinking about the sweep and purpose of suspension, revealing that suspension served the same function during this period as it had within the English legal framework in the prior century. Specifically, suspension served to legalize wartime detentions outside the ordinary criminal process of persons who could claim the protections of domestic law. Finally, by design, each of the Revolutionary War American suspensions ran for a finite period (often through the next legislative session), suggesting an appreciation of the profound ramifications of suspension on individual liberty.

By their common terms, the Revolutionary War suspensions adopted in the states bestowed authority on state executives to arrest and detain persons preventively based on suspicion of supporting the Crown. Often the suspensions coincided with the imminent threat of invading British troops and the perceived need to grant the executive expanded powers in such circumstances. One example from early in the war may be found in Pennsylvania, when, in 1777, its General Assembly enacted a suspension for the "preservation of th[e] state" at a time of threat of "hostile invasion." The suspension was unquestionably triggered by the Quaker episode detailed above along with the landing of the British Navy at the head of the Chesapeake Bay and its anticipated attack on Philadelphia, which soon followed and led to the city's temporary occupation.[61]

As already noted, the Pennsylvania Assembly passed the suspension in order "to restrain for some limited Time the Operation of the Habeas Corpus Act."[62] By its terms, the law declared that it was a response to the fact that "there are . . . persons among us, who cannot at this juncture be safely trusted with their freedom," specifically referencing the Quakers then in custody. To legalize their detention and possibly others, the act provided that "it shall and may be lawful" for the state's executive and council:

> [T]o arrest any person or persons within this commonwealth who shall
> be suspected from any of his or her acts, writings, speeches, conversa-
> tions, travels or other behavior, to be disaffected to the community of
> this or all or any of the United States of America, or to be a harbinger of
> the common enemy who is at our gates, or to give mediate or immedi-
> ate intelligence and warning to their commanders . . . or by discourag-
> ing people from taking up arms for the defense of their country.

The law expressly empowered the executive "to confine" such persons, to banish them, or to demand that they subscribe an "oath or affirmation of allegiance and fidelity to [the] state." Here, consistent with English legal tradition, the law tied suspension to the lines of allegiance. Finally, in conjunction with bestowing such broad powers on the executive, the act by its plain terms prohibited judges from "issu[ing] or allow[ing] any writ of habeas corpus . . . to obstruct the proceedings of the said executive council."[63]

The Continental Congress had already raised concerns about the Quakers, resolving that it was "certain . . . that those persons are, with much rancor and bitterness, disaffected to the American cause." At the same time, the Congress "earnestly recommended to the supreme executive council of the State . . . forthwith to apprehend and secure" various Quaker leaders.[64] The council responded in turn by taking the leaders into custody. The council also took the position that the Quakers had renounced "all the privileges of citizenship" because they had failed to take oaths of allegiance. This renunciation, the council believed, rendered the Quakers outside the legal protection of domestic law such that they could be held without charges like other prisoners of war.[65] But when the matter came before the Pennsylvania Supreme Court, Chief Justice McKean concluded that the Quakers fully enjoyed their rights of citizenship. As he described in his correspondence with John Adams, quoted extensively above, McKean believed that the principles of the Habeas Corpus Act, incorporated into the law of Pennsylvania, rendered the Quakers' confinement without charges unlawful in the absence of a suspension. The Assembly responded immediately by adopting one. At this point, McKean concluded there was nothing left for him to do in the case: "I could no more. On Tuesday last a law was enacted for the purpose . . . and delivered to my express the same day, which has relieved me from any farther difficulties."[66]

Developments in several other battlefield states also triggered suspensions. In Maryland, for example, the legislature responded to the same sightings of the British Navy in the Chesapeake by enacting a suspension in 1777 providing that in the event of an invasion by the British, the governor shall assume "full power and authority to arrest . . . all persons whose going at large the governor . . . shall have good grounds to believe may be dangerous to the safety of this state, and the same persons to confine." The statute further declared "that during any invasion of this state by the enemy, the *habeas corpus* act shall be suspended, as to all such persons. . . ."[67] Notably, the law both established invasion as a necessary predicate to suspension (something that the U.S. Constitution would soon also do) and confirmed the connection forged between suspension and those protections derived from "the *habeas corpus* act," which the suspension expressly displaced. The Maryland legislation followed just one day after the Continental Congress urged the state's legislature and executive (as well as those of Delaware) "to apprehend and remove all persons of influence, or of desperate characters," within certain counties "who have betrayed or manifested a disaffection to the American cause."[68]

As the war continued, so suspension spread. In 1778, with Lord Germain having instructed General Clinton to invade South Carolina, the state's legislature responded to "this time of public danger, when this State is threatened with an invasion by the enemy," by enacting a suspension for the express purpose that "the hands of the executive should be strengthened." Toward that end, South Carolina's legislation declared it "lawful" for the executive "by warrant under his hand and seal, to arrest, secure and commit to safe custody all such persons as now are in, or hereafter shall come into this State, and whose going at large may, in the opinion of the [executive] endanger the safety of this State." The law further provided that neither the courts nor any judge "shall bail or try any person so as aforesaid to be committed" until the suspension expired.[69] Just as under the English model, in South Carolina, suspension equated with the temporary displacement of the demand that persons within protection be tried on criminal charges in a timely manner. (This suspension came on the heels of the state legislature having confirmed its power "to suspend the Habeas Corpus Act," as discussed above.[70])

Also in 1778, New York created a Board of Commissioners, empowering it with the authority:

> to send for persons and papers and administer oaths and to apprehend and confine or cause to be apprehended and confined in such manner and under such restrictions and limitations as to them shall appear necessary for the public safety all persons whose going at large shall in the judgment of the said commissioners or any three of them appear dangerous to the safety of this State.

Although it did not mention the protections of the Habeas Corpus Act that New Yorkers had tried to adopt so many years earlier, the legislation specifically prohibited the granting of bail by judges or magistrates to those individuals confined by the commissioners.[71] In this respect, it operated similarly to a suspension.

Across the Hudson River, the New Jersey legislature enacted a suspension in 1780. It targeted those persons apprehended for trading with the enemy, crossing enemy lines, or aiding the enemy more generally. The law came at a curious time, as New Jersey by this point had seen the last of any significant Revolutionary War battles on its soil. All the same, it suggests that recognition of a robust habeas privilege was well established in the state by this time, as the law directed that for those apprehended aiding the enemy, "the Privilege of the Writ of *Habeas Corpus*" was "suspended and made void, during the Continuance of [the] Act."[72]

Suspension next came to Virginia in May 1781. It followed closely on the heels of the British, who had turned their sights just months earlier toward the Commonwealth, in part—or so the story goes—because General Cornwallis believed that his army would be a welcome sight to many Virginians.[73] The legislature responded swiftly in this "time of public danger" to the invading British troops with a suspension that declared a need to "invest the executive with the most ample powers, both for the purpose of strenuous opposition to the enemy, and also to provide for the punctual execution of laws." The statute provided:

> The governor, with advice of the council, is . . . hereby empowered to apprehend . . . and commit[] to close confinement, any person or persons whatsoever, whom they may have just cause to suspect of disaffection to the independence of the United States or of attachment to their enemies, and such person or persons shall not be set at liberty by bail, mainprize or *habeas corpus*.[74]

Like Pennsylvania's legislation, Virginia's law also "empowered" the governor and his council "to send within the enemy's lines" persons "who hath or have heretofore refused to take the oaths of allegiance" and "whom they shall have good cause to suspect . . . [are] inimical to the independence of the United States." Weeks later, the British attempted to capture Virginia's then-governor Thomas Jefferson in a raid on Charlottesville. (He escaped, but some members of the legislature were not so fortunate.[75]) Within months, however, the tide had turned with the defeat of Cornwallis's troops at Yorktown.

Massachusetts: The Precursor to 1787

Three Massachusetts suspensions during this period, along with the state's adoption of its constitution in 1780, deserve special attention. Early in the war, with the British having "invaded some of our neighbouring states, and threaten[ing] an invasion of this state," the Massachusetts legislature, known as the General Court, passed suspension legislation in 1777. The law broadly empowered the executive and his council to issue warrants for the apprehension and commitment of "any person whom the council shall deem the safety of the Commonwealth requires should be restrained of his personal liberty, or whose enlargement within this state is dangerous thereto." Those persons captured were subject to being "continued in imprisonment, without bail or mainprize," until discharged by order of the council or General Court.[76]

Three years later, the people of Massachusetts debated and adopted a constitution that included express recognition of the privilege of habeas corpus along with the power to suspend. (The 1780 Constitution followed a failed effort to adopt a constitution in 1777.) The convention's numbers were so great that a subcommittee was given the task of penning a draft constitution, which in turn appointed John Adams, Samuel Adams, and James Bowdoin to do the real work. Once the draft constitution was ready for circulation, the convention circulated it to the towns for approval. Rather than a tally of up or down votes, the towns returned to the committee a mass of highly detailed comments on the draft's various sections. As historian Jack Rakove writes of the events, at this point, the convention delegates "had no handy formula to reduce these unwieldy materials to one simple result." Accordingly, "the convention threw up its hands and declared the constitution ratified."[77] Although failing to influence changes to the constitution, the returns are nonetheless enormously significant to the modern reader. This is because they provide a unique window into how a broad segment of the population at the time of the Founding viewed, among other things, the role of habeas corpus and suspension within their emerging legal framework.

The proposed habeas clause, which survived unaltered in final form, recognized both an express right to habeas corpus along with a power to suspend it in emergencies. It read:

> The privilege and benefit of the writ of Habeas Corpus shall be enjoyed in this Commonwealth in the most free, easy, cheap, expeditious and ample manner; and shall not be suspended by the Legislature, except upon the most urgent and pressing occasions, and for a limited time not exceeding twelve months.[78]

Once circulated with the draft constitution, the clause triggered extensive commentary in the town returns. For their part, Boston's delegates generally supported the proposed constitution, but they expressed specific concerns about the habeas clause. As their Return stated:

> [T]he Suspension of this security of personal Liberty or freedom from Imprisonments [should be limited] to times of War, invation and rebellion. . . . It was not conceived that any cause could possibly exist in time of peace, that could justify imprisonments *without allegation or charge;*

and the granting a Power in a season of tranquility liable to such gross abuse, and which might be attend with consequences destructive of the dearest priviledges and best interest of the Subject was deemed incompatable with every Principle of Liberty.[79]

As English legal tradition had taught them, suspension equated with imprisonment "without allegation or charge"; for this reason, the delegates believed it crucial to limit strictly when suspension could be declared.

Lest there be any doubt concerning the contemporary linking of the privilege with the right of citizens not to be detained outside the criminal process—and more specifically with the protections derived from the English Habeas Corpus Act—the returns of several other towns drove home the point. For example, Milton's Return posited that a suspension should occur only "in times of war, or threatned Invasion, and then for a time not exceeding six months. . . . [S]ix months is fully sufficient for any Legislature to ascertain the precise crime, and to procure the evidence against any Individual, in order to bring him for Trial."[80] The town of Waltham proposed that the draft habeas clause be amended to clarify that "the Habeas Corpus Act be not suspended for a Longer Time than six months as in that Time they think any Person may be brought to his Tryal or admitted to Bail."[81] Lexington's Return also connected the privilege specifically with the Habeas Corpus Act.[82] Finally, Groton's Return proposed a time limit on any potential suspension that derived from the very protections embodied in the 1679 Act. Specifically, Groton argued that whether a prisoner is charged with a crime or not, no suspension may "opperate against any one Subject after the Superior Court hath Set Two Terms" in the relevant county, positing that "in Either Case he shall be delivered before the Second Term is over."[83]

Taken together, these returns constitute compelling evidence of a contemporary understanding that equated the availability of the privilege with the right of persons not to be detained in the absence of timely criminal trial. They also underscore the continuing influence and centrality of the English Habeas Corpus Act to early American habeas jurisprudence. Ultimately, despite the fact that numerous returns had sought to limit invocation of the suspension power specifically to times of war, invasion, or rebellion, rather than the less precise wording of "urgent and pressing occasions," the Massachusetts clause maintained its original wording.

Although Massachusetts was not the first state to constitutionalize habeas corpus (Georgia having done so in 1777), it was the first to recognize (and at the same time limit) the power of suspension within such a framework. In this respect, the Massachusetts experience, which witnessed two suspensions in the years immediately following adoption of its constitution, provided an important reference point for those who wrote the U.S. Constitution seven years later in Philadelphia. The second of these suspensions was especially significant in this regard, as it came in response to Shays's Rebellion, an episode that proved to be a major "catalyst in the movement for the Constitution and for its ratification."[84]

But before Daniel Shays, there was Samuel Ely. In the early 1780s, Ely led a small band of armed malcontents in western Massachusetts who had sworn opposition to the government. Their complaints were similar to those later advanced by Shays: taxes were too high, the government was spending too much, currency was next to worthless, and debtors were being run over in court. Ely and his followers rioted, seized government property taken in execution of debts, and attempted to keep the courts from sitting.[85] Notwithstanding its relatively small size, Ely's movement was the subject of great concern in Boston. Alarm followed in part from the widespread—though likely inaccurate—perception that Ely was allied with the British, who were still in the Maine territory on Massachusetts's northern border and viewed as a continuing threat by state leaders in Boston.[86]

To address the situation, the Massachusetts General Court enacted its first suspension in 1782. By its terms, the legislation expressly "suspend[ed] the privilege of the writ of habeas corpus" and "authorised and empowered" the governor and his council "to apprehend and secure . . . without Bail or Mainprize, any Person or Persons whose being at large may be judged" by the executive "to be Dangerous to the Peace and Well-being of this or any of the United States."[87] When, six months into the suspension, the "Disturbances" and "Opposition to the legal Authority" of the state continued unabated, the General Court extended the suspension for an additional four months. The renewal legislation clarified the effect of the suspension—positing that "the *Benefit* derived to the Citizens from the issuing of Writs of Habeas Corpus should be suspended for a limited Time in certain Cases." The governor, meanwhile, was "authorised and empowered by Warrant . . . , by him subscribed, to apprehend and secure" anyone believed to pose a danger to the state.[88]

With order temporarily restored, the General Court turned its attention to codifying much of the English Habeas Corpus Act in early 1785. The statute that resulted adopted key aspects of Section 7 of the English Act, requiring that those persons held on suspicion of the most serious crimes be tried or discharged within two terms.[89] Soon, however, the General Court employed its suspension power to displace these protections in response to a larger and far more alarming movement developing in the western part of the state. Under the leadership of Daniel Shays, Luke Day, and others, insurgents prevented several Commonwealth courts from sitting and attempted to seize a federal arsenal.[90] Unlike Ely's band, "the Shaysites were short on political theory and long on military organization."[91] With each passing day, the movement took on "more and more tokens of real insubordination and anarchy."[92] Once again, those in power feared—again without substantiation—that the British were behind the uprising.[93]

This concern triggered a special session of the General Court in September 1786. There, Governor James Bowdoin, who had presided over the drafting of the Massachusetts Constitution, urged the chambers to give him expanded powers to put down the uprising. Only after an offer of pardon to the insurgents met no response did the Senate respond by passing a suspension. The House, however, was not yet ready to act.[94] This reluctance reportedly "occasioned very great alarm[]" among those who supported more stringent measures "to prevent [more insurrections] in [the] future."[95] Indeed, reports suggest there was a prevailing fear that the situation could unravel into civil war.[96] Once it became clear that existing measures were failing to stem the tide of the growing insurgency, the House finally passed the suspension bill.[97]

By its terms, the law responded to the ongoing "violent and outrageous opposition, which hath lately been made by armed bodies of men . . . to the Constitutional Authority" of the state. As it had done for the Ely Riots, the General Court declared that the "*benefit* derived to the Citizens from the issuing of Writs of Habeas Corpus, should be suspended for a limited time." Likewise, the legislature "authorised and empowered" the governor and his council, by issuance of their own state warrants, to arrest and detain "any person or persons whatsoever, whom [they], shall deem the safety of the Commonwealth requires should be restrained of their personal liberty, or whose enlargement is dangerous thereto." Further, the Act declared that "any Person who shall be apprehended and imprisoned" under its terms "shall be continued in imprisonment, without Bail or Mainprize, until he shall be discharged therefrom by order of the Governor, or of the General Court." Finally, it made clear that the grant of executive authority controlled "any Law, Usage or Custom to the contrary notwithstanding." In other words, as many English suspensions had done before, the law set aside any and all legal protections that a prisoner might invoke to procure his or her freedom.[98]

Governor Bowdoin finally had his expanded powers, and he wasted little time using them. In the immediate wake of the suspension, the governor and his council issued state warrants for a number of suspected insurgents to be held pending restoration of order.[99] Efforts to enforce state warrants upon the insurgency's rank and file met with frustration, as many had gone into hiding. But contemporary reports suggest that one expedition to enforce state warrants against principals was "a very important event," the effect of which was to make "precarious" their "personal safety."[100] Meanwhile, state leaders issued a general warning to Shays's followers that unless they laid down their arms, they "would be dealt with in a summary manner."[101] As events unfolded, the state militia secured key victories, ultimately leading the rebels to disband and flee. A chronicler of the period reports that at this point, "the General Court found it a suitable time for providing for the trials of such as were in custody," and trials of key figures in the insurgency followed in due course.[102] With the restoration of order and lapsing of the suspension, it appears that it was simply taken for granted that those in custody had to be referred to the criminal process. This explains why one contemporary writer observed that without the suspension, the "ringleaders" of the rebellion held solely on state warrants would have been able to secure their freedom through habeas corpus.[103] But suspension had altered the legal landscape by eliminating that possibility. As another contemporary account observed, the General Court viewed the Rebellion as warranting a suspension that placed "every man's liberty" in "the discretion of the Supreme Executive, without legal remedy."[104]

In the end, most of those arrested during Shays's Rebellion were pardoned.[105] But the experience weighed heavily on those promoting the need for a new Constitution to replace the failing Articles of Confederation, and they would cite the Rebellion as an example of the need for a stronger central government. Indeed, Shays's Rebellion is mentioned in no fewer than six of *The Federalist Papers*.[106] And in the lead-up to the Constitutional Convention, George Washington wrote to James Madison referencing Shays's Rebellion, asking "[w]hat stronger evidence can be given of the want of energy in our governments than these disorders?"[107]

The Continuing Influence of the English Habeas Corpus Act

As the history detailed here reveals, the English Habeas Corpus Act wielded great influence over the development of early American law in the newly independent states. Under British rule, a number of states had tried—mostly unsuccessfully—to claim the English Habeas Corpus Act as their own. Then, in the wake of the Declaration of Independence, many states moved quickly to adopt the express terms of the Act as part of their new law, whether by expressly incorporating the Act into their constitutions, as Georgia did, or by expressly guaranteeing "the privilege and benefit" of habeas corpus in their constitutions, as Massachusetts did. Other state constitutions generally laid claim to the benefit of many important English statutes.[108] During and shortly after the war, several states also constitutionalized limitations on the suspension authority, whereas other states, aware of the dramatic power that suspensions granted an executive, banned suspensions outright.[109] Additional evidence of the strong influence of the English Habeas Corpus Act and the English suspension framework may be found in the suspensions adopted by at least six states during the Revolutionary War.

Further, underscoring the Act's profound influence over the development of early American habeas law, in the wake of the Revolutionary War, a large number of states formally adopted habeas statutes predicated upon and incorporating key sections of the English Habeas Corpus Act. For example, in 1784, Virginia adopted a statute loosely modeled on the English Act.[110] Confirming the already entrenched application of the Act on its jurisprudence, Pennsylvania adopted a statute in 1785 that encompassed the protections of Section 7 and many other key aspects of the English Act.[111] As noted, Massachusetts adopted a habeas statute in 1785 closely tracking the English Act and codifying Section 7's requirement that one held on suspicion for treason or felony must be tried within two terms or discharged.[112] Delaware (1793),[113] New Jersey (1795),[114] and North Carolina (1837)[115] adopted key aspects of the Act's protections in turn, including the core requirements of its seventh section. Indeed, North Carolina's statute, which expressly codified the state's practice of adhering to the English Act, cited the English Act repeatedly, and well into the nineteenth century, North Carolina courts cited the English Act as the basis of the state's habeas statute.[116] Georgia, having constitutionalized the English Act by its title and appended its terms to the original circulation of its constitution, thereafter codified the Act verbatim as part of a digest of early Georgia Laws published in 1819.[117] In 1798, Rhode Island's General Assembly adopted a declaration of rights that linked the rights to bail, habeas corpus, and speedy trial on criminal charges.[118] And, as already noted, Maryland and South Carolina adopted statutes tracking the English Act and embracing the terms of its seventh section in 1809 and 1814 respectively, with South Carolina adopting the English Act verbatim.[119]

Arguably the most significant incorporation of the English Habeas Corpus Act by a state took place just three months before the 1787 Constitutional Convention when New York passed a statute almost identical to the 1679 Act. The legislation, tracking the seventh section of its English predecessor, made express the requirement that any person "committed for any treason or felony" who is not "indicted and tried [by] the second term [of the] sessions of oyer and terminer, or gaol delivery, after his commitment . . . shall be discharged from his imprisonment."[120] It had taken a little over one hundred years, but New Yorkers finally enjoyed the rights and protections associated with the English Habeas Corpus Act.

Highlighting the pervasive influence of the English Act on the development of early American law, the great New York jurist and legal scholar Chancellor James Kent observed in 1827 that "the statute of 31 Charles II. c. 2 . . . is the basis of all the American statutes on the subject."[121] Along the same lines, Justice Joseph Story wrote in his famous *Commentaries on the Constitution of the United States* that by 1833 the English statute "has been, in substance, incorporated into the jurisprudence of every state in the Union."[122] Throughout this early American period, moreover, a notable shift had taken root regarding the nature of habeas corpus. What had originated in England as part of the struggle for power between Parliament and the Crown was now routinely referred to as a "writ of right" and associated with Blackstone's description as a "great bulwark of personal liberty."[123] In so doing, American law drew upon its English origins to incorporate and bolster the privilege as one of the most important protections of individual liberty.

Just months after the Shays's Rebellion suspension and New York's adoption of a Habeas Corpus Act modeled on its English predecessor, delegates convened in Philadelphia to write a new national constitution. They would draw heavily on this backdrop when providing for a privilege derived from the English Act and recognizing the need for its suspension on truly extraordinary occasions—and *only* on such occasions.

5

Enshrining a Constitutional Privilege

This privilege ... is essential to freedom, and therefore the
power to suspend it is restricted.

JUDGE INCREASE SUMNER TO THE MASSACHUSETTS
CONVENTION ON THE ADOPTION OF THE FEDERAL
CONSTITUTION (1788)[1]

ONE YEAR AFTER the Declaration of Independence, the Continental Congress drafted the Articles of Confederation, declaring the new country the United States of America. It took four years for every one of the original states to ratify the compact and, by then, its shortcomings were apparent. Among other things, the Articles gave the national government very limited powers, failed to provide for an executive or judicial branch at the federal level, and required the unanimous consent of the states to amend. Because the Articles failed to grant general legislative authority to the Continental Congress, moreover, the legislative body had to work through the states to implement any policy objectives. The Articles also failed to include anything resembling a bill of rights or a habeas clause, presumably because the national government enjoyed little power to flex at the expense of individual rights. That said, the Articles did promise the "free inhabitants" of the member states entitlement to "all privileges and immunities of free citizens in the several States."[2] By May 1787, when delegates convened in Philadelphia ostensibly to propose amendments to the Articles, the failings of the current structure had convinced most of them that the time was ripe for a new constitutional framework. And so they set to work.

The new Constitution that emerged created a much stronger central government, and for the first time established national courts. It also included the Suspension Clause, which provided: "The Privilege of the Writ of Habeas Corpus shall not be suspended, unless when in Cases of Rebellion or Invasion the public Safety may require it."[3] As explored below, a wealth of evidence from this period demonstrates that in the Suspension Clause, the Founding generation sought to constitutionalize the protections associated with the seventh section of the English Habeas Corpus Act and import the English

Habeas Corpus in Wartime. Amanda L. Tyler.
© Oxford University Press 2017. Published 2017 by Oxford University Press.

suspension model, while also severely limiting the circumstances when the suspension power could be invoked.

Drafting a New Compact

The framework of the federal government that emerged from Philadelphia was decidedly different from the one that existed under the Articles. First and arguably of greatest importance, the delegates resolved that the new federal government would be empowered to act directly upon the people, rather than exclusively through member states.[4] Next, based largely on a plan drafted principally by James Madison and introduced by Virginia governor Edmund Randolph, the basic contours of three separate branches of government took form, albeit after extensive debates over such key questions as whether to have single or multiple executives, whether the states would maintain equal representation in the new Congress, and how federal law would be enforced against conflicting state laws. Few questioned the need at this point for a stronger national government. Those who saw such a need included George Washington, who had reached this conclusion after reading about Shays's Rebellion, and who served as head of the Convention.[5]

Among the many innovations embodied within the constitutional framework was the formal separation of powers—a marked departure from the British model—as well as the creation of a Supreme Court and authorization for inferior national courts that would operate independently of the political branches.[6] (The Articles had failed to create national courts, although the plan had authorized their temporary creation by the Continental Congress for interstate disputes.) Alexander Hamilton later famously promoted the idea of independent courts in *The Federalist Papers* by arguing that " 'there is no liberty, if the power of judging be not separated from the legislative and executive powers.' "[7] More specifically, as he described the judicial role: "the courts were designed to be an intermediate body between the people and the legislature, in order, among other things, to keep the latter within the limits assigned to their authority."[8] Among their most important tools for achieving this end was the storied writ of *habeas corpus*.

Constitutionalizing the Privilege and Carefully Limiting the Potential for Its Suspension

Within the larger conversation about the judicial branch, the delegates turned to two cherished liberties that British rule had denied the colonists: the protections associated with the English Habeas Corpus Act and the right to a jury trial. Possibly weighing on the minds of some of them was the fourth letter in a series published in Philadelphia in the spring of 1776, in which the author proclaimed:

> A CONSTITUTION should . . . perfect liberty of conscience, security of person against unjust imprisonments, similar to what is called the Habeas Corpus act; the mode of trial in all law and criminal cases; in short, all the great rights which man never mean, nor ever ought, to lose, should be *guaranteed*, not *granted*, by the Constitution.[9]

The delegates may have also been influenced by a draft set of amendments to the Articles that had been prepared by a committee for consideration by the Continental Congress. Although never formally considered, these amendments promoted as "sacred . . . the benefits of the writ of *Habeas Corpus*."[10]

More generally, as explored in the last chapter, the delegates met following the Revolutionary War in which they had known suspension, as well as in the wake of Shays's Rebellion and the Massachusetts suspension enacted to put it down. Further, a wave of states had constitutionalized and/or enacted statutes guaranteeing protections derived from the English Habeas Corpus Act in the years since the formal declaration of independence. This list included New York, which just months before the Convention passed a statute modeled extensively on the English Act that embraced almost verbatim the protections of its seventh section. And up north, after prolonged efforts, Quebec had finally adopted much of the English Habeas Corpus Act almost word-for-word, including the terms of its seventh section.[11]

As matters unfolded, there was only limited discussion at the Convention of what ultimately became the Suspension Clause. On May 29, 1787, four days after the Convention came to order, Charles Pinckney introduced a draft plan to the Convention that received no reported discussion. Pinckney, a veteran of the war who had been captured by the British after the fall of Charleston, included in his draft plan a habeas clause that reportedly provided: "The legislature of the United States shall pass no law on the subject of religion, nor touching or abridging the liberty of the press; nor shall the privilege of the writ of *habeas corpus* ever be suspended, except in case of rebellion or invasion."[12] Although the speech and religion aspects of Pinckney's original proposal would not find their way into the original Constitution (but instead came later as part of the First Amendment to the Constitution), his proposed limitation of suspension to cases of rebellion or invasion survived in the final draft. One possible source for the restriction on the suspension power was the Irish adoption of the English Habeas Corpus Act in 1781, subsequently approved by the Irish Committee of the English Privy Council in 1782. The Irish Act imported much of the language of the 1679 Act verbatim, with the notable addition of a provision expressly empowering while also constraining the Irish Council to suspend the Act "during such time only as there shall be an actual invasion or rebellion in this kingdom or Great Britain."[13] In all events, Pinckney's "Observations" on his proposed plan pressed for protection of the privilege, the jury trial right, and freedom of the press as "essential in Free Governments."[14]

Surviving notes from the Convention record no further discussion of habeas and suspension until months later.[15] On August 20, Pinckney moved again for recognition of the habeas privilege. James Madison's notes of the debates reported only that Pinckney had submitted a proposal "securing the benefit of the habeas corpus." *Max Farrand's Records of the Federal Convention of 1787*, borrowing from the Journal of the Convention, reports that Pinckney proposed the following language:

> The privileges and benefit of the Writ of Habeas corpus shall be enjoyed in this Government in the most expeditious and ample manner; and shall not be suspended by the Legislature except upon the most urgent and pressing occasions, and for a time period not exceeding [——] months.[16]

The wording of this proposal closely tracked the habeas provision in the Massachusetts Constitution of 1780. It also bore striking similarities to the habeas provision that New Hampshire had adopted in its Constitution of 1784.[17]

Pinckney introduced his new habeas provision on the same day that the delegates debated the basic framework of the Treason Clause, which was largely the product of James Wilson's hand and derived its core terms directly from English law.[18] The conceptual pairing of the privilege with treason makes sense, given the historical connection between alleged treason and the suspension of the Habeas Corpus Act. But it was not until eight days later that the delegates debated Pinckney's revised habeas proposal on the Convention floor. Madison's notes describe Pinckney as then "urging the propriety of securing the benefit of the Habeas corpus in the most ample manner" and "mov[ing] 'that it should not be suspended but on the most urgent occasions, & then only for a limited time not exceeding twelve months.'" Pinckney, it seems, had finally settled on a specific time limit for any suspension. But more than one delegate remained unconvinced of the need to recognize a suspension authority at the federal level under any circumstances. For example, Madison's notes report that another South Carolinian, John Rutledge, "was for declaring the Habeas Corpus inviolable—He did (not) conceive that a suspension could ever be necessary at the same time through all the States."[19]

Madison's notes next report that Gouverneur Morris introduced his own proposed language for a habeas clause that read:

> The privilege of the writ of Habeas Corpus shall not be suspended, unless where in cases of Rebellion or invasion the public safety may require it.[20]

Morris surely had some familiarity with the concept of suspension. Recall that Morris's cousin, Isaac Gouverneur, had been transported from St. Eustatius during the Revolutionary War to England. There, after internal discussions over whether evidence of Gouverneur's alleged treason could be properly authenticated, the British held him without trial within the terms of North's Act, the British suspension applicable to American rebels that governed during much of the war. Perhaps his cousin's experience influenced Morris's proposal to limit the circumstances within which a suspension could be invoked. Either way, the language of "rebellion or invasion" probably came from Pinckney's original May proposal, the Irish Habeas Corpus Act, or both. In all events, Morris certainly appreciated the danger of leaving this potent legislative power unchecked, remarking at the Convention that "[t]he public liberty [is] in greater danger from legislative usurpations than from any other source."[21]

Following Morris's proposal, Madison reports that James Wilson "doubted whether in any case (a suspension) could be necessary, as the discretion now exists with Judges, in most important cases to keep in Gaol or admit to Bail."[22] Thus, like certain members of Parliament during the debates over the first English suspension in 1689, Wilson appears to have believed that the criminal justice system was equipped to address any crisis, given that judges enjoyed the discretion to grant or refuse bail with respect to persons under criminal indictment. Even as he doubted the need for a suspension authority, however, Wilson looked to the criminal process to deal with those who posed a threat to the state. There is good reason to think that Wilson had the crime of treason in mind when he made this statement. Wilson, who would eventually sit on the Supreme Court as one of President Washington's first nominees, was a native of Scotland who had grown up in the wake of the last of the Jacobite suspensions that governed there under Parliament's 1745 Act. Wilson was also a renowned expert on treason law who had contributed to the drafting of the Continental Congress's June 24, 1776, resolution demanding allegiance to the new Republic and declaring that adherence to the Crown constituted treason. Further, as noted above, he had been a principal drafter of the Constitution's Treason Clause.[23]

At this point, Madison's notes recount that the delegates took a vote on Morris's proposal. All agreed on the first part that, standing alone, prohibited suspension under any circumstances: "The privilege of the writ of Habeas Corpus shall not be suspended. . . ." It was the second part of the proposed clause, recognizing the power to suspend "in cases of Rebellion or invasion [where] the public safety may require it," that elicited dissent. Specifically, North Carolina, South Carolina, and Georgia voted against including such recognition in the clause.[24] In reporting on this debate to his home legislature in Maryland, Luther Martin described those opposed to the Suspension Clause (in whose camp he fell) as resting on two principal objections. First, they were skeptical of the need to recognize the power at the federal level, given that states possessed the ability to address any invasions by wielding the same authority. Second, the power to suspend was subject to abuse. Specifically, Martin reported:

> Nothing could add to the mischevious tendency of this system more than the power that is given to suspend the Act of Ha: Corpus—Those who could not approve of it urged that the power over the Ha: Corpus ought not to be under the influence of the General Government. It would give them a power over Citizens of particular States who should oppose their encroachments, and the inferior Jurisdictions of the respective States were fully competent to Judge on this important priviledge; but the Allmighty power of deciding by a call for the question, silenced all opposition to the measure as it too frequently did to many others.[25]

Martin's comments suggest that although Madison's notes may not have captured the full breadth of the debates over the Suspension Clause, those debates were all the same quite brief. It bears highlighting, moreover, that Martin specifically referred to the Clause as permitting the suspension of "the Act of Ha: Corpus," and it seems most likely the case that Pinckney and Rutledge had also meant to refer to the Act in the Convention debates when they referenced "the Habeas Corpus," given that Martin used the phrases interchangeably.

During their debates, the Convention delegates also left a trail of evidence suggesting that they recognized an important connection among habeas corpus, suspension, and criminal prosecution. For example, the jury trial right had been the subject of discussion immediately before the drafters took up discussion of the Suspension Clause on August 28.[26] Further, the delegates initially placed the Suspension Clause in the judiciary article (then-Article XI) alongside the guarantee that "[t]he trial of all crimes (except in cases of impeachment) shall be by jury."[27] It was only when the Committee of Style, led by Gouverneur Morris, reorganized the articles of the Constitution that it separated the two clauses. At this point, it moved the Suspension Clause to the legislative article, Article I, and left the guarantee of a jury trial in criminal cases in the judiciary article, in what became Article III.[28] Meanwhile, the Committee of Style also changed the word "where" to "when" in the Suspension Clause without explanation.[29] One is left to wonder if the alteration signified a shift from a focus on geography to a focus of time, but the Committee of Style was not, at least by its formal charge, supposed to alter substantive meaning in carrying out its work.

The linking of the jury trial right with the privilege of the writ of habeas corpus makes sense when one considers how the Founding generation viewed the jury right in criminal cases. Just like the privilege of the writ of habeas corpus, the "great object" of trial by jury, Justice Story wrote in his famous *Commentaries on the Constitution of the United States*, first published in 1833, was "to guard against a spirit of oppression and tyranny on the part of rulers, and against a spirit of violence and vindictiveness on the part of the people."[30] As with the privilege, the right to trial by jury had long served to keep the government in check, and both were understood during this period as "bulwark[s] of . . . civil and political liberties" to be guarded "with an unceasing jealousy."[31] As the Continental Congress had phrased it in 1774, the privilege of the writ of habeas corpus and the right to trial by jury were among the most important rights in a free society "without which a people cannot be free and happy."

Further, in the final draft of the Constitution, the Committee of Style placed the Suspension Clause alongside the Bill of Attainder Clause, which prohibited outright any legislative acts of attainder.[32] Of course, such acts had served as the main legislative vehicle other than suspension for circumventing the Habeas Corpus Act. (Recall the discussion in Chapter 2 of the plight of John Bernardi, who languished in prison some forty years without trial as a result of the combination of suspensions and bills of attainder passed against him.) As Justice Story noted in his *Commentaries*, "the right to pass bills of attainder in the British parliament still enables that body to exercise the summary and awful power of taking a man's life, and confiscating his estate, without accusation or trial."[33] Thus, a prohibition on bills of attainder, as well as on ex post facto laws, proved a necessary complement to the Suspension Clause if the latter was to achieve the objective of precluding legislative circumventions of the criminal process.

Debating Ratification

Upon concluding their work in September 1787, the Convention delegates delivered their draft to the Continental Congress. After declining to censure the delegates for exceeding their mandate to amend the Articles, the Congress then circulated the draft Constitution to the state legislatures, which the plan charged with convening ratification assemblies. By the Constitution's terms, it would take effect upon its ratification by nine states, a process that ultimately took some ten months. (With Rhode Island having declined even to attend the Philadelphia Convention, a requirement of unanimous approval had been long ago rejected.) Reviewing the debates that took place during this period further underscores the close relationship between the criminal process and the privilege, as it was understood by the Founding generation.[34]

During the debates, discussion of the Suspension Clause proceeded within the larger debate between Federalists and Anti-Federalists over the allocation of power between the proposed federal government and the states, as well as within the debate over the specific enumeration of individual rights in the new Constitution. Anti-Federalists were critical of the draft's failure to include a Bill of Rights. They also pointed to the Suspension Clause and bans on bills of attainder and ex post facto laws as proving the need for additional enumerated protections. The popular antifederalist essays written by Brutus and published in New York conveyed the argument this way:

> If every thing which is not given is reserved, what propriety is there in these exceptions? Does this constitution any where grant the power of suspending the habeas corpus, to make expost facto laws, pass bills of attainder, or grant titles of nobility? It certainly does not in express terms. The only answer that can be given is, that these are implied in the general powers granted. With equal truth it may be said, that all the powers, which the bills of right, guard against the abuse of, are contained or implied in the general ones granted by this constitution.[35]

In other words, given that the Constitution nowhere specifically empowered the federal government to suspend the privilege, why was there a need for specific language limiting the exercise of that power? Or, as Patrick Henry phrased the argument in the Virginia debates, "if it had not said so, they could suspend it in all cases whatsoever. . . . If the power remains with the people, how can Congress supply the want of an affirmative grant? They can do it but by implication, which destroys their doctrine."[36] The argument proved a common refrain for those pushing for a Bill of Rights during the ratification debates.[37]

One response offered to this argument came from Governor Edmund Randolph in the Virginia debates, who had introduced the plan at the Convention around which the basic structure of the government had taken form. He argued that "by virtue of the power given to Congress to regulate courts, they could suspend the writ of *habeas corpus*," and constitutional protection of the privilege was "therefore an exception to that power" as opposed to more general legislative powers.[38] In the New York debates, meanwhile, one speaker suggested that the Clause was thought "not necessary" but nonetheless "inserted for greater caution."[39]

As the debates unfolded, proponents and opponents went on the offensive in the public newspapers. Among the most prominent efforts was a series of essays now read together as the *Federalist Papers*, penned anonymously by Alexander Hamilton and James Madison, with a handful of additional contributions from John Jay. Although the influence of the essays is debated to this day, they were circulated in New York in an attempt to influence that state's ratification vote and were also sent to influence debates in at least one other key state, Virginia. Regardless of their contemporary influence on the debates, the essays bear close study as a window into the views of prominent members of the Founding generation, including two delegates to the Constitutional Convention, Hamilton and Madison.

For his part, Hamilton responded to the Anti-Federalist concerns relating to the Suspension Clause in several ways. First, he reiterated the Federalist position defending the absence of an enumerated bill of rights that "the people surrender nothing; and as they retain everything they have no need of particular reservations."[40] Second, Hamilton lauded the Suspension Clause as providing for "the establishment of the writ of *habeas corpus*" and celebrated the writ as one of the "greate[st] securities to liberty and republicanism" in the Constitution.[41] Significantly, Hamilton also specifically referenced the protections embodied in the English Habeas Corpus Act as having been provided for in the plan of the Convention, and connected the Suspension Clause and the Act with the jury trial right. As he explained in *Federalist 83*:

> Arbitrary impeachments, arbitrary methods of prosecuting pretended offenses, and arbitrary punishments upon arbitrary convictions have ever appeared to me to be the great engines of judicial despotism; and these have all relation to criminal proceedings. The trial by jury in criminal cases, aided by the *habeas corpus* act, seems therefore to be alone concerned in the question. And both of these are provided for in the most ample manner in the plan of the convention.[42]

Hamilton also promoted the Suspension Clause in *Federalist 84*. There, he observed that "the practice of arbitrary imprisonments, have been, in all ages, the favorite and most formidable instruments of tyranny." But, referencing "the judicious Blackstone," Hamilton noted that "as a remedy for this fatal evil [Blackstone] is everywhere peculiarly emphatical in his encomiums on the *habeas corpus* act, which in one place he calls 'the BULWARK of the British Constitution.' "[43] Hamilton's words provide yet more evidence of Blackstone's enormous influence on early American law as well as the centrality of the Habeas Corpus Act to the story of the Suspension Clause.

Indeed, the provision for the many protections associated with the Habeas Corpus Act in the original body of the Constitution proved an important aspect of Hamilton's argument that there was no need for express recognition in the Constitution of the protections later encompassed within the Bill of Rights.[44] With the benefit of knowing what the Founding generation understood the habeas privilege to embody, it is easy to understand how Hamilton could have taken this position. At the time he was writing, the privilege associated with the Habeas Corpus Act embodied, among other things, the right to presentment or indictment and the right to a speedy trial. Indeed, even the antifederalist publication the *Federal Farmer*, which was deeply critical of the draft Constitution over its omission of a Bill of Rights, pointed to the Suspension Clause and its neighboring provisions as "a partial bill of rights" and celebrated the fact that the Constitution "recognize[d] or re-establish[ed] the benefits [of] that writ, and the jury trial in criminal cases."[45] (A few decades later, Chief Justice John Marshall would also point to Article I, Section 9, which encompasses the Suspension Clause, as "enumerat[ing], in the nature of a bill of rights, the limitations intended to be imposed on the powers of the general government."[46])

Providing yet more contemporary evidence that the Suspension Clause constitutionalized the protections long associated with the English Habeas Corpus Act, the antifederalist *Federal Farmer* also explained that: "The people by adopting the federal constitution, give congress general powers to institute a distinct and new judiciary, new courts, and to regulate all proceedings in them, under [various limitations, including] that the benefits of the *habeas corpus act* shall be enjoyed by individuals."[47] Widespread evidence from the ratification debates also underscores the link. Thus, opponents such as Jasper Yeates noted that supporters in the Pennsylvania debates held out the Clause as "part of the bill of rights" for "directing that the privilege of the *habeas corpus* act shall not be suspended except in times of immediate danger," a position that Yeates believed highlighted the need for a longer bill of rights.[48] In the same debates, John Smilie similarly called for explication of more rights, while also highlighting that in the draft Constitution, "[t]rial by jury in criminal cases" was "reserved," as was "the privilege of the *habeas corpus* act."[49] For his part, Luther Martin, the Marylander who was among the few delegates at the Convention who refused to sign the draft Constitution, criticized the Suspension Clause in his widely circulated *Genuine Information* for bestowing the power on the federal government to "suspend[] the habeas corpus act."[50] At the Massachusetts convention, Theophilus Parsons, a federalist supporter of the Constitution, "made a Loud Speech on the Habeas Corpus act" and the proposed terms for its suspension.[51] And in Virginia, the writings of "A Native of Virginia" in support of the Constitution referred to the Suspension Clause as "[t]he article respecting the habeas corpus act" and defended its terms as born out of a recognition that "circumstances might arise to render necessary the suspension of the habeas corpus act."[52]

More generally, the ratification debates reveal that other participants associated the constitutional privilege with a privilege of parliamentary creation[53] and the criminal process, suggesting further that the English Act provided the foundation of the constitutional privilege.[54] Still others appear to have invoked the Act as the basis for the Suspension Clause by repeatedly referencing "the Habeas Corpus." This list includes John Adams, who wrote in defense of the draft Constitution that in it, "[t]he habeas corpus is in full force,"[55] as well as James Iredell, who observed in the North Carolina debates: "As to criminal cases, I must observe that the great instrument of arbitrary power is criminal prosecutions. By the privileges of the *habeas corpus*, no man can be confined without inquiry; and if it should appear that he has been committed contrary to law, he must be discharged."[56] As set forth below, James Madison and Thomas Jefferson also invoked this shorthand in their correspondence with one another. Further, in the Virginia debates, Governor Randolph specifically linked the phrase to the English Act, explaining:

> [T]he habeas corpus is at least on as secure, and good a footing as it is in England. In that country, it depends on the will of the legislature. That privilege is secured here by the Constitution, and is only to be suspended in cases of extreme emergency.[57]

Randolph was joined by George Nicholas, who used the phrase specifically in reference to the English Act when he called it "the Habeas Corpus under Charles II."[58]

As the debates unfolded, there were many calls for wording the Clause in a manner that expressly guaranteed a habeas right, as had been done in some state constitutions, such as the Massachusetts document.[59] Further, four ratifying conventions proposed the addition of a declarations of rights to the draft Constitution that included a variation on language proposed by Virginia, which read: "That every freeman restrained of his liberty is entitled to a remedy to inquire into the lawfulness thereof, and to remove the same, if unlawful, and that such remedy ought not to be denied or delayed."[60] A common response suggested that such language was unnecessary, for, as James Wilson phrased it in the Pennsylvania debates, "the right of habeas corpus was secured [in the draft] by a particular declaration in its favor."[61]

Other participants in the debates found fault with the lack of express time limitation on exercises of the suspension authority.[62] New York's Convention went so far as to propose an amendment prohibiting the suspension of "the privilege of the Habeas Corpus . . . for a longer term than six months, or until twenty days after the [next] meeting of the Congress."[63] A common response to such objections was that offered by Judge Francis Dana in the Massachusetts debates. Dana suggested that a time limit would be pointless because Congress would always have the option of "continu[ing] the suspension of the writ from time to time."[64]

Finally, more than one participant in the debates raised concerns that without greater constraints on the invocation of the suspension authority, it could prove a potent vehicle for oppression. For example, Luther Martin saw "no reason for giving such a power to the general government," given its potential as "an engine of oppression in its hands" that could be wielded against those who "should oppose its views" or "excite the opposition." Martin feared that Congress would wield the suspension power in order to "imprison [those in opposition] during its pleasure."[65] Here, too, Judge Dana's response to these concerns is representative of the position that ultimately prevailed:

> The safest and best restriction," he said, "arises from the nature of the cases in which Congress are authorized to exercise that power at all, namely, in those of rebellion or invasion. These are clear and certain terms, facts of public notoriety, and whenever these shall cease to exist, the suspension of the writ must necessarily cease also.[66]

Along similar lines, James McHenry argued in the Maryland debates that although "[p]ublic Safety may require a suspension of the Ha: Corpus in cases of necessity: when those cases do not exist, the virtuous Citizen will ever be protected in his opposition to power."[67] Going further, Chief Justice William Cushing of the Massachusetts Supreme Judicial Court opined that "the clause appears to me so plain, that if a Judge should refuse a citizen his hab. Corps., after a rebellion was over, or the invasion at an end; I think *he* ought to be impeached & degraded from his office. . . ." In other words, Cushing believed that judges were obliged to recognize the privilege at all times in the absence of a valid suspension,[68] a position echoed in St. George Tucker's important early treatise on American law.[69]

Jefferson and Madison on Suspension

During this same period, Thomas Jefferson and James Madison corresponded extensively about habeas corpus and suspension. Although Jefferson was not in attendance at the Convention, he followed its work closely and wrote Madison repeatedly about the draft Constitution, joining camp with those who urged the inclusion of a Bill of Rights. In commenting on the draft Suspension Clause and this larger debate, for example, Jefferson opined, "I do not like . . . the omission of a bill of rights providing clearly & without the aid of sophism for . . . the eternal & unremitting force of the habeas corpus law. . . ." Additional letters written by Jefferson during this period reiterate his desire for a Bill of Rights as well as his view that the Constitution should decline to recognize any suspension authority.[70] (As discussed in the next chapter, Jefferson later strayed from this position as president when he sought a suspension to address the Burr Conspiracy.)

Jefferson's doubt over the need for recognition of a suspension power followed from his view that the criminal process was well equipped to address any future crisis and concerns over its potential abuse. Writing to Madison, Jefferson pondered:

> Why suspend the Hab. corp. in insurrections and rebellions? The parties who may be arrested may be charged instantly with a well defined crime. Of course the judge will remand them. If the publick safety requires that the government should have a man imprisoned on less probable testimony in those than in other emergencies; let him be taken and tried, retaken and retried, while the necessity continues, only giving him redress against the government for damages.[71]

Jefferson's comments echo those made at the convention by James Wilson, with whom Jefferson had worked in drafting the Continental Congress's resolution on allegiance and treason. The idea was simply this: if the public safety required it, the government could work within the criminal process to detain persons under suspicion and, to the extent that the government abused that process, those harmed possessed a remedy at law for damages.[72]

In the next section of his letter to Madison, Jefferson also highlighted the important link between suspension and treason and the dangers of recognizing a suspension authority at all. Lawyers and historians have overlooked this part of his letter, but it speaks volumes about how these concepts, now imported into the constitutional framework, related to one another:

> Examine the history of England: see how few of the cases of the suspension of the Habeas corpus law have been worthy of that suspension. They have been either real treasons wherein the parties might as well have been charged at once, or sham-plots where it was shameful they should ever have been suspected. Yet for the few cases wherein the suspension of the hab. corp. has done real good, that operation is now become habitual, and the minds of the nation almost prepared to live under it's [*sic*] constant suspension.[73]

Jefferson's remarks highlight the Founding generation's familiarity with the English Habeas Corpus Act ("the Habeas corpus law") and Parliament's many suspensions. They also reveal a contemporary understanding that grounded the privilege in the English Habeas Corpus Act and viewed suspension as derived from English tradition. They also reveal that at the time of Ratification, Jefferson believed that even if English history included some episodes in which "the suspension of the hab. corp. has done real good," the better course was simply to leave the matter to the criminal process.

For his part, Madison was generally skeptical of the need and efficacy of a Bill of Rights, observing to his friend that any enumeration of individual rights was unlikely to be effective "when opposed to the decided sense of the public." Turning specifically to the habeas privilege, Madison remarked: "Should a Rebellion or insurrection alarm the people as well as the Govt, and a suspension of the Hab Corp be dictated by the alarm, no written prohibitions on earth would prevent the measure."[74] Notwithstanding his skepticism over the need for a Bill of Rights, Madison soon authored a list of draft amendments to appease the concerns of Anti-Federalists over the original draft, although he omitted any additional language tied to the habeas privilege.[75]

As for Madison's skepticism over how effective "written prohibitions" on the power to suspend would be in times of "alarm," in time future wars would validate his doubts.

Reading the Suspension Clause in Context

The ultimate placement of the Suspension Clause in Article I, the Constitution's legislative article, was surely no accident. The protections associated with the English Habeas Corpus Act and their suspension had always been controlled by Parliament. In time, President Lincoln would act on his own ahead of Congress in suspending the privilege during the Civil War, but his position that the executive possessed unilateral authority to suspend stands at odds with both the entire history of the suspension framework and the placement of the Clause in Article I.

More questions abound as to how the suspension authority fits into the larger constitutional structure. Recall Governor Randolph suggesting that suspension follows from Congress's authority to regulate the courts. If one understands suspension as at least in part a jurisdictional matter—after all, it strips courts of the power to issue the writ—that may well be correct. Others have suggested that the suspension power is best understood as "an ancillary power to implement one of Congress's substantive powers that is relevant to the particular emergency." This view posits that it is the marrying of the Suspension Clause to other enumerated emergency powers—such as the war power and the authority to put down insurrections and repel invasions—that together comprise a "power to detain."[76] Still others have observed that it is "the addition of the Necessary and Proper Clause [that gives] further textual grounding to legislative measures designed to prevail in domestic wars."[77]

Then there is the question whether the Clause affirmatively promises the availability of the protections associated with the privilege or merely regulates the power to suspend. The Clause is framed in the negative and so the argument could be made that it merely prevents Congress from suspending any habeas remedies available in the state courts.[78] In support of this view is the fact that the Constitution "presupposed a going legal system, with ample remedial mechanisms."[79] Further, as was explored in the previous chapter, by the time of the Constitutional Convention, most states had well developed habeas law that embraced the core protections of the seventh section of the English Habeas Corpus Act. Surely the Clause comprises at least a constraint upon Congress with respect to state habeas remedies. But there is also considerable language in the ratification debates to suggest that many understood the Suspension Clause to promise outright these protections as a federal constitutional matter. Thus, for example, as noted above, James Wilson declared in the Pennsylvania debates that "the right of habeas corpus was secured [in the draft] by a particular declaration in its favor."[80] And Alexander Hamilton wrote in the Federalist Papers that with respect to "[t]he trial by jury in criminal cases, aided by the *habeas corpus* act . . . both of these are provided for in the most ample manner in the plan of the convention."[81] Yet more support for this reading may be found in the many references made equating the Suspension Clause with a partial bill of rights.

In all events, whether it was constitutionally obliged to do so or not, the First Congress vested original habeas jurisdiction in the federal courts in Section 14 of the Judiciary Act of 1789. With the exception of the handful of suspensions in American history and more recent legislation passed as part of the war on terrorism, this jurisdiction has existed ever since. Chief Justice John Marshall once suggested the need for congressional intervention to provide for habeas jurisdiction, writing in Ex parte *Bollman* that "the power to award the writ by any of the courts of the United States . . . must be given by written law."[82] But then Marshall continued by observing that the First Congress, "[a]cting under the immediate influence of th[e] [Suspension Clause], must have felt, with peculiar force, the *obligation* of providing efficient means by which this great constitutional privilege should receive life and activity; for if the means not be in existence, the privilege itself would be lost, although no law for its suspension should be enacted."[83] This obligation follows from the historical linkage of the privilege associated with the Habeas Corpus Act to the many rights and protections that it advanced as well as more generally the Founding-era understanding that the independent federal courts would serve an important checking role with respect to the political branches. (The latter reasoning informed the 2008 Supreme Court decision in *Boumediene v. Bush*, discussed in Chapter 11, which held outright that the Suspension Clause promises an affirmative right to the privilege.[84])

The Continuing Influence of English Law

In studying the ratification debates, it becomes quickly apparent that throughout the states, participants evinced considerable knowledge of the English backdrop that informed the Suspension Clause. In the Virginia debates, for example, George Nicholas highlighted the "renew[al], enlarge[ment], and confirm[ation]" of the "Great Charter" in legislation such as "the Habeas Corpus under Charles II., and Declaration of Rights under William and Mary,—the latter limiting the prerogative of the crown, the former establishing the personal liberty of the subject."[85] Alexander Hamilton quoted extensively from Blackstone in describing the history and effect of suspension, while also glorifying the Habeas Corpus Act just as Blackstone had. And in his famous Law Lectures given a few years after the Constitutional Convention, James Wilson lamented that the benefit of the Habeas Corpus Act had been denied to the colonies, detailing the story of the failed attempt in the Massachusetts Colony to adopt the Act.[86]

It should come as no surprise, therefore, that the English Habeas Corpus Act remained a central and profoundly influential part of the development of American habeas law during the Founding period, and proved to be the reference point for the protections enshrined in the Suspension Clause. This conclusion seems almost obvious—after all, it was the *Act* with which the concept of suspension has been associated from its inception. Nonetheless, given that modern case law and scholarship have downplayed or ignored the Act's influence, it bears emphasizing the Act's profound influence on the Suspension Clause all the same.

In constitutionalizing the protections associated with the Habeas Corpus Act and the suspension framework, the Founding generation accomplished two things. First, they constitutionalized a prohibition on government detention outside the criminal process of persons who could claim the protection of domestic law. In this respect, the Constitution's habeas privilege encompasses more than simply a promise of access to judicial review of one's detention, and instead imposes significant constraints on the power of the executive to detain persons within protection. As English history had shown and future chapters will highlight, moreover, these constraints have important ramifications with respect to the detention of prisoners in times of war. Second, in the Suspension Clause, the Founding generation constitutionalized a well-entrenched framework for addressing the inevitable emergencies that would come to pass—adopting a suspension model derived from the English practice that leaves it to the political branches to balance the needs of national security against individual liberty in times of crisis, but only permitting such balancing in truly extraordinary circumstances—namely, in "Cases of Rebellion or Invasion [when] the public Safety may require it."

In writing his *Commentaries* some forty years after ratification, Justice Story highlighted the importance of the English Act in the story of the Suspension Clause. Specifically, after noting that the English Act "has been frequently considered, as another magna charta" and noting that the "statute has been, in substance, incorporated into the jurisprudence of every state in the Union," Story also stressed that "the right to it has been secured in most, if not all, of the state constitutions by a provision, similar to that existing in the constitution of the United States."[87] Continuing, Story pointed to the Suspension Clause as an example that reveals the importance of reading technical terms in the Constitution with "common sense." As Story explained: "No one would doubt, when the constitution has declared, that 'the privilege of the writ of *habeas corpus* shall not be suspended, unless' under peculiar circumstances, that it referred, not to every sort of writ, which has acquired that name; but to that, which has been emphatically so called, on account of its remedial power to free a party from arbitrary imprisonment."[88] In other words, a common sense reading of the Suspension Clause requires two things. First, one must bring to bear an understanding of the English backdrop against which it was written and from which American habeas jurisprudence has developed. Second, one must recognize the centrality of the protections associated with the English Habeas Corpus Act in giving content to the habeas privilege recognized in the Constitution. Indeed, the privilege was so important to the Founding generation that they provided for its protection in a document that, as John Marshall once wrote, was "designed to be permanent."[89]

6

The Suspension Clause in the Early Republic

> *The English judges, being originally under the influence of the crown, neglected to issue this writ where the government entertained suspicions which could not be sustained by evidence; and the writ when issued was sometimes disregarded or evaded, and great individual oppression was suffered in consequence of delays in bringing prisoners to trial. To remedy this evil the celebrated* habeas corpus *act of the 31st of Charles II. was enacted, for the purpose of securing the benefits for which the writ was given.*
>
> CHIEF JUSTICE JOHN MARSHALL IN *EX PARTE* WATKINS (1830)[1]

THE PERIOD FOLLOWING ratification of the Constitution is possibly most significant for the fact that it did not witness any suspensions at the federal level, notwithstanding the occurrence of two insurrections that challenged the authority of the federal government and at least one major war of international character on American soil. Nonetheless, there is much to be learned from this period as to how the Founding generation understood the Suspension Clause to function within the new constitutional framework. Studying the government's handling of the Whiskey and Fries Rebellions, the Burr Conspiracy, and the War of 1812, as well as early Supreme Court opinions, reveals many important insights into how the meaning of the Suspension Clause came to be "liquidated"—to borrow James Madison's phrase—during the early Republic.[2]

As explored here, the government's treatment of suspected traitors during the events of this period underscores that all three branches understood the Suspension Clause to adopt the English suspension model and embrace a constitutional privilege born out of the English Habeas Corpus Act that required charging the disaffected criminally in the absence of a suspension. As is also detailed in this chapter, important early decisions

Habeas Corpus in Wartime. Amanda L. Tyler.
© Oxford University Press 2017. Published 2017 by Oxford University Press.

from the Marshall Court highlight the continuing and profound influence of the English Habeas Corpus Act and its "incorporat[ion]" into American constitutional law.

Treason in the Early Republic

In the immediate wake of Ratification, the first Congress enacted a statute providing for the "Punishment of certain Crimes against the United States." This statute declared both treason and misprision of treason to be federal crimes. (Notably, early Congresses expressly criminalized little else.) In so doing, the treason statute relied heavily on the same important concept that had informed the law of treason in England and the early Republic—the obligation of allegiance. Specifically, the law defined a traitor as "any person . . . owing allegiance to the United States of America [who] shall levy war against them, or shall adhere to their enemies."[3] In his famous law lectures given during this period, James Wilson pointed to English law as the source of the related concepts of allegiance—the obligation which he termed "obedience"—and the reciprocal protection that established the foundations of the law of treason. Reducing the concepts to their essence, "[o]f obedience," Wilson said, "the antipode is treason." And, because citizens unquestionably owed obedience to the United States, treason stood as a fundamental violation of that obligation. In his lectures, Wilson also explicated his understanding of "levying war" against the United States and giving aid to the enemy. Among other things, treason included "join[ing] with rebels in a rebellion, or with enemies in acts of hostility," and aiding the enemy encompassed "giv[ing] intelligence to enemies," sending them "provisions," and "sell[ing] arms to them."[4]

Defining treason from the early days of the Republic was important because during this period, charging individuals with the crime of treason proved to be the conventional approach to dealing with rebels and other persons who took up arms against the state or aided its enemies. There is no evidence, for example, that President Washington even considered calling for a suspension to aid his efforts to put down the Whiskey Rebellion, even though the uprising required the assembling of a substantial militia to quash.[5] President John Adams followed the same course a few years later in putting down Fries's Rebellion. Further, in both cases, when the military sought to commit captured insurgents, it handed suspects over to civilian authorities for criminal prosecution. Thus, although both episodes witnessed citizens in armed conflict with government troops, there is no indication that the government ever sought to hold captured insurgents as "enemies of the state" or "prisoners of war" during this period.

During the Whiskey Rebellion, for example, President Washington called forth the militia on the basis that the insurgents had proven "too powerful to be suppressed by the ordinary course of judicial proceedings or by the power vested in the [United States] marshals. . . ."[6] In so doing, Washington gave specific orders to his general, Henry Lee, that the leaders of the rebellion were "to be delivered to the civil magistrates" to be evaluated for criminal prosecution.[7] Further, Washington specifically rejected the suggestion that the insurgents be brought before military tribunals,[8] instead setting forth that General Lee should carry out his orders to quash the uprising "in two ways—1. By military force[, and] 2. By judiciary process, and other civil proceedings."[9] Correspondingly, in speaking to his military leaders, "Washington . . . sought constantly to get [them] to impress on their troops the necessity for proper conduct and strict observance of their roles as assistants to the civil authority."[10] "He assured us," said one chronicler of the episode, "that the army should not consider themselves as judges or executioners of the laws, but as employed to support the proper authorities in the execution of them."[11]

Accordingly, during the first two presidential administrations, suspension remained a lever of extraordinary authority that government leaders eschewed. Even the return of the British to American soil and the War of 1812 did not witness a suspension of habeas corpus (not counting then-Major General Andrew Jackson's effective declaration of a suspension in New Orleans, discussed below). Instead, in keeping with the model established during Washington's presidency, the Madison administration and the courts took the position that citizens suspected of aiding the British during the war could not be detained in the absence of criminal charges and could not be tried by military tribunals.

In one case arising during the war, for example, the U.S. military detained an American citizen on suspicion of passing information to the British regarding troop movements on the Great Lakes front of the war. Notwithstanding the dramatic nature of the charges and the fact that the alleged acts helped the British during a "critical" time in the war,[12] the celebrated jurist and constitutional scholar Chief Justice James Kent of New York's Supreme Court of Judicature found it deeply troubling that the military was "assuming criminal jurisdiction over a private citizen." It did not help the military's case that the commander to whom the writ had issued filed an evasive response and claimed that he could not produce the prisoner. As Kent wrote:

The pretended charge of treason, (for upon the facts before us we must consider it as a pretext,) without being founded upon oath, and without any specification of the matters of which it might consist, and without any colour of authority in any military tribunal to try a citizen for that crime, is only aggravation of the oppression of the confinement.

Kent continued by deeming it "the indispensable duty" of the court "to act as a faithful guardian of the personal liberty of the citizen, and to give ready and effectual aid to the means provided by law for its security." "One of the most valuable of those means," he wrote, "is this writ of *habeas corpus,* which has justly been deemed the glory of the *English* law." Finally, observing that "[i]f ever a case called for the most prompt interposition of the court to enforce obedience to its process, this is one," Kent presented the government with a choice—either discharge the prisoner outright or bring him before a commissioner in compliance with the writ that had issued, presumably to be discharged by that process.[13] Two years later, the same New York court upheld an action for false imprisonment against the military officials who had detained a naturalized American citizen on similar terms.[14]

In another prominent case arising out of the War of 1812, the military tried and convicted an American citizen before a court martial on charges of spying predicated on allegations that he had passed information to the British. In response, President Madison "direct[ed]" that the prisoner, "being considered a citizen of the U.S. & not liable to be tried by a court martial as a spy, . . . unless he should be arraigned by the civil court for treason or a minor crime under the laws of the state of New York, . . . must be discharged."[15] During this period, the use of military tribunals was reserved for those in military service and persons not deemed to owe allegiance. Specifically, just as the resolution of the Continental Congress had in 1776, the American Articles of War, enacted in 1806, provided:

> That in time of war, all persons not citizens of, or owing allegiance to the United States of America, who shall be found lurking as spies, in or about the fortifications or encampments of the armies of the United States, or any of them, shall suffer death, according to the law and usage of nations, by sentence of a general court martial.[16]

Against this backdrop, President Madison's directive is hardly surprising, given the fact that there existed no statutory basis for a court martial to preside over the trial of a citizen under these circumstances. (By contrast, such jurisdiction did exist with respect to those not "owing allegiance," whose rights the law declared were governed by "the law and usage of nations.") But the president's comments and actions can be interpreted to reflect a more general understanding that ordinary citizens—even alleged traitors in time of war—could only be detained and prosecuted through the standard criminal process of the civilian courts in the absence of a valid suspension. His response to one of the most famous episodes to occur during the War of 1812 supports this interpretation.

As the story goes, Andrew Jackson—then-major general of the Tennessee militia—unilaterally declared martial law in New Orleans in the final months of the War of 1812. He also effectively suspended the privilege, given that he not only ignored a writ of habeas corpus ordering the release of a prisoner in his custody, but he also ordered the jailing of the judge who had issued the writ. In defending his actions to the president, Jackson chose words eerily similar to those that Abraham Lincoln would use to justify his own actions a few decades later. Jackson was compelled, he argued, to take "'measures of necessity . . . without which the country must have been conquered, and the Constitution lost.'" Madison's response, delivered by his acting secretary of war Alexander James Dallas, emphatically rejected the notion that necessity trumped legal principles, even in times of war. As Madison viewed things:

> In the United States there exists no authority to declare and impose Martial law, beyond the positive sanction of the Acts of Congress. To enforce the discipline and to ensure the safety, of his garrison, or his camp, an American Commander possesses indeed, high and necessary powers; but all his powers are compatible with the rights of the citizens, and the independence of the judicial authority. If, therefore, he undertakes to suspend the writ of Habeas Corpus, to restrain the liberty of the Press, to inflict military punishments, upon citizens who are not military men, and generally to supercede the functions of the civil Magistrate, he may be justified by the law of necessity, while he has the merit of saving his country, but he cannot resort to the established law of the land, for the means of vindication.[17]

The Burr Conspiracy and the First Federal Debate over Suspension

Despite the reluctance even to consider suspension as a wartime tool during early episodes of insurrection or the War of 1812, the early days of the Republic did witness one occasion on which Congress came close to suspending the privilege. The events leading up to this point are well known, but the story of the role that a proposed suspension played in them is not nearly so familiar. Aaron Burr had served as vice president during President Thomas Jefferson's first term, but as someone for whom President Jefferson never held much regard, he and Jefferson had parted ways by the time Jefferson's second term began in 1805. Not long after, Burr set out to explore the western territories. What he sought to accomplish in his travels remains the subject of debate to this day. What is known is that President Jefferson informed Congress that he believed that Burr was spearheading "an illegal combination of private individuals against the peace and safety of the Union, and a military expedition planned by them against the territories of a Power in amity with the United States."[18] More specifically, in correspondence, Jefferson described Burr as heading up "an armed body," the object of which was "to seize New Orleans, [and] from thence attack Mexico," with the goal of "add[ing] Louisiana to his empire, and the Western States from Alleghany if he can."[19] To reach these conclusions, Jefferson had relied heavily on information received from General James Wilkinson in Louisiana, a person whose own loyalties the gloss of history has now shown to be highly questionable.[20]

As things quickly unfolded, General Wilkinson instituted martial law in New Orleans and ordered the arrests of several of Burr's alleged co-conspirators, including Erick Bollman, Samuel Swartwout, and Peter Ogden, directing that they be kept in military custody.[21] Wilkinson next ordered Bollman and Swartwout transported by warship to the East Coast. Upon their arrival in Washington, they remained in military custody, all this time in the absence of a warrant.[22] Meanwhile, back in New Orleans, a judge ordered Ogden discharged in response to his petition for a writ of habeas corpus. Never one to be second-guessed, General Wilkinson ordered Ogden arrested again, along with the lawyer, James Alexander, who had sought the writ on Ogden's behalf. Wilkinson then sent Ogden to Baltimore, where he won his freedom by petitioning for habeas relief, as did former Kentucky governor and senator John Adair, also caught up in the affair, "there being no evidence [of criminal activity] against either of them."[23]

For his part, Jefferson made no claim that the military arrests were lawful—indeed, he plainly recognized that they were not. Nonetheless, he wrote at the time to his friend, the Louisiana governor: "On great occasions, every good officer must be ready to risk himself in going beyond the strict line of law, when the public preservation requires it."[24] In other words, Jefferson viewed these extralegal acts as warranted in the name of "public preservation." (Here, Jefferson advanced an argument later revived by President Abraham Lincoln during the Civil War.) But Jefferson was also sensitive to the politics of the times. Concerned that arrests "going beyond the strict line of law" would be indulged by the public only in a handful of prominent cases, Jefferson instructed Wilkinson to keep in New Orleans those prisoners who were not central figures in the conspiracy and "against whom there is only suspicion, or shades of offence not strongly marked. In that case," Jefferson wrote, "I fear the public sentiment would desert you; because, seeing no danger here, violations of law are felt with strength."[25] Speaking to the cases of Alexander and Ogden specifically, Jefferson acknowledged that "the evidence yet received will not be sufficient to commit them."[26]

Only days before writing these letters, on January 22, 1807, Jefferson had sent a message to Congress lamenting the fact that one of the "principal emissaries of Mr. Burr, whom the General [Wilkinson] had caused to be apprehended . . . had been liberated by *habeas corpus*," and that a "premature attempt to bring Burr to justice" in Kentucky had failed "without sufficient evidence for his conviction." Jefferson's statement to Congress also expressed concerns over whether there existed sufficient evidence to sustain arrest warrants for the main conspirators upon their delivery to civil authorities for prosecution. As Jefferson stated: "little has been given under the sanction of an oath, so as to constitute formal and legal evidence. It is chiefly in the form of letters, often containing such a mixture of rumors, conjectures, and suspicions."[27] The very next day, Senator William Branch Giles of Virginia introduced a bill to suspend the writ of habeas corpus.[28] Several scholars have suggested that Giles acted at Jefferson's request.[29] There is scarce direct evidence supporting this claim, but the timing and import of Jefferson's January 22 message to Congress (complaining about the "liberat[ion]" of one of Burr's "principal emissaries" by "*habeas corpus*"), the fact that Giles was known as the administration's leader in the Senate,[30] and the Senate's passage of a suspension on the very next day (January 23) together suggest coordination. In all events, Jefferson very likely supported the measure. Assuming this to be true, Jefferson thereby embraced a position in considerable tension with his Ratification-era opposition to any recognition of a suspension power in the draft Constitution, along with his promise at the time of his First Inaugural to honor as among the "essential principles of our Government . . . freedom of the person under the protection of the habeas corpus, and trial by juries impartially selected."[31]

Such was the backdrop against which the first extensive debate followed in Congress over whether to suspend the privilege of the writ of habeas corpus.[32] The Senate took up the matter first and, after suspending its normal rules to hold a closed-door session, quickly and overwhelmingly enacted a suspension bill.[33] The debate was not recorded and provides only hints about what some senators thought about the privilege, suspension, and the propriety of the military arrests that the executive had undertaken. We know from Senator William Plumer's account that Senator James Bayard of Delaware opposed the measure, observing that its "principal object seems to be to hold Bollman & Swartout in custody . . . that they may bear witness against Mr. Burr," while doubting that "the *public safety* at this time require[d] [the] measure." Bayard apparently expressed the concern, repeated numerous times in the subsequent House debates, that a suspension on this occasion would form a "precedent[] danger-ous to free men."[34] Plumer's notes also report that Senator Giles rose to speak in favor of his bill and that Samuel Smith of Maryland defended the bill as a necessary "preventive measure." As for John Quincy Adams, Plumer's account states that he was *"passionately zealous* for its passage," while also acutely aware that something extraordinary was at stake—namely, the temporary suspen-sion of "the great palladium of our rights." Nonetheless, Adams reportedly said: "[Y]et on extraordinary occasions I beleive its temporary suspension is equally as essential to the preservation of our government [and] the priveledges of the people."[35] As for Plumer himself, he supported the bill for similar rea-sons, observing that although the writ "is designed to secure our rights . . . its temporary suspension in such a state of things will most effectually secure its object—*public security*." His notes from the period likewise underscore his belief that without the imprimatur of a suspension, the military arrests would ultimately be deemed unlawful in actions for false imprisonment, exposing those who had carried out the arrests to personal liability.[36]

As passed, the Senate bill provided:

> That in all cases, where any person or persons, charged on oath with trea-son, misprision of treason, or other high crime or misdemeanor, endan-gering the peace, safety, or neutrality of the United States, have been or shall be arrested or imprisoned, by virtue of any warrant or author-ity of the President of the United States, or from the Chief Executive Magistrate of any State or Territorial Government, or from any person acting under the direction or authority of the President of the United States, the privilege of the writ of *habeas corpus* shall be, and the same hereby is suspended, for and during the term of three months. . . .[37]

Several aspects of the bill bear highlighting. By its terms, the bill covered existing and future arrests by order of the executive, although it also required that such persons be "charged on oath" with one of the designated crimes endangering the national security. By applying in part retroactively, the bill reached those persons, such as Bollman and Swartwout, already in military custody, purporting to legalize their ongoing military detentions. Nonetheless, the bill suspended habeas corpus for only a very brief period of three months, suggesting that even in its haste to pass the measure, the Senate understood the dramatic nature of the bill. Finally, unlike the later suspensions enacted by Congress during the Civil War and Reconstruction, this bill purported to suspend habeas corpus outright, rather than delegating the ultimate decision whether to do so to the president.

The Senate having passed the bill on a Friday, the House took up the bill the following Monday, January 26, 1807. Unlike those in the Senate, the House debates were reported in the *Annals*, and they offer a rich glimpse into the Founding-era understanding of the content of the privilege and the objectives behind its suspension.[38] More specifically, the debates reveal that all engaged in the debate viewed suspension as necessary to hold the alleged conspirators outside the formal criminal process, and that many in the House possessed great skepticism that existing circumstances warranted such a dramatic response.

The House debates opened with Representative John W. Eppes—Jefferson's son-in-law—moving to reject the bill without even referring it to committee. Next, his fellow Virginian William Burwell observed that Jefferson had promised to turn over the prisoners to "the civil authority" for prosecution, a fact that he argued obviated any need for a suspension. Noting that during the Whiskey and Fries's Rebellions no one had ever proposed to suspend the writ of habeas corpus, Burwell cautioned against creating a dangerous precedent by doing so here. (Later, John Randolph would make the same argument.[39]) Instead, Burwell believed that the criminal process should be left to run its course. As he argued:

> With regard to those persons who may be implicated in the conspiracy, if the writ of habeas corpus be not suspended, what will be the consequence? When apprehended, they will be brought before a court of justice, who will decide whether there is any evidence that will justify their commitment *for farther prosecution*.[40]

Here, Burwell drew upon the English suspension model to equate suspension with the power to detain outside the criminal process, while recognizing that without a suspension, continued detention of the Burr conspirators turned on whether sufficient evidence existed to sustain criminal charges against them.

Further, in Burwell's view, the dramatic nature of suspension rendered it an entirely inappropriate response to current circumstances:

> Nothing but the most imperious necessity would excuse us in confining to the Executive, or any person under him, the power of seizing and confining a citizen, upon bare suspicion, for three months, without responsibility, for the abuse of such unlimited discretion. . . . [M]en, who are perfectly innocent, would be doomed to feel the severity of

confinement. . . . What reparation can be made to those who shall thus suffer? The people of the United States would have just reason to reproach their representatives with wantonly sacrificing their dearest interests, when . . . it seems the country was perfectly safe, and the conspiracy nearly annihilated. Under these circumstances, there can be no apology for suspending the privilege of the writ of habeas corpus. . . .

Thus, faith in the criminal process, along with a belief that the conspiracy had run its course by this point led Burwell to join Eppes in opposing the bill.[41]

James Elliot of Vermont likewise doubted that circumstances warranted "suspend[ing], for a limited time, the privileges attached to the writ of habeas corpus," a proposition that he deemed "the most extraordinary . . . that has ever been presented for our consideration and adoption." Along these lines, Elliot equated suspension of the privilege with "a temporary prostration of the Constitution itself" that "gives the power of dispensing with the ordinary operation of the laws. . . ." After invoking the English Habeas Corpus Act to deem habeas corpus a "writ of right," Elliot next turned to Blackstone, borrowing the assertion that suspension of the "writ of liberty . . . ought never to be resorted to but in cases of extreme emergency."[42] It followed, in his view, that suspension was appropriate only when "the existing invasion or rebellion, in our sober judgment, threatens the first principles of the national compact, and the Constitution itself. In other words, we can only act, in this case, with a view toward national self-preservation." Those who wrote the Constitution, in Elliot's view, "never contemplated the exercise of such a power, under circumstances like the present."[43]

Many House members rose to echo these sentiments. For his part, Eppes strongly opposed the "extraordinary measure":

I cannot, however bring myself to believe that this country is placed in such a dreadful situation as to authorize me to suspend the personal rights of the citizen, and to give him, in lieu of a free Constitution, the Executive will for his charter. I consider the provision in the Constitution for suspending the habeas corpus as designed only for occasions of great national danger. . . . [I]t ought never to be resorted to, but in cases of absolute necessity. . . .[44]

Mindful that suspension constituted "one of the most important powers vested in Congress by the Constitution" and deeply skeptical that such a measure was necessary to "suppress[] a few desperadoes," Eppes moved that the bill be immediately voted down.[45]

In the face of these arguments, the measure nonetheless drew some support in the House. Joseph Varnum of Massachusetts, one of those supporting the bill, had served under General Benjamin Lincoln in putting down Shays's Rebellion and clearly had the earlier episode in mind when he spoke:

> I know a particular State of the Union who did consider the measure necessary, in the case of an insurrection which occurred within her limits; and I think it very doubtful whether that insurrection would have so happily closed, if it had not been for her suspension of the writ of habeas corpus.

Drawing on this experience, Varnum questioned whether without a suspension the government would here be able "to trace the conspiracy to its source" and accomplish "a full discovery of those concerned" in the Burr affair. Along these lines, Varnum deemed it too great a risk that without the suspension, "the head of [the] conspiracy"—presumably Burr—could "be set at liberty by the tribunals of justice" if there existed "no evidence . . . of the crime charged to him."[46] (Later in the debates, Representative Barnabas Bidwell, also of Massachusetts, would echo these points.[47]) Thus, like everyone else who spoke in the debates, Varnum understood that without the suspension, the administration was bound to proceed criminally against Burr and his counterparts.

Varnum also argued that the suspension would not "have the injurious effects that some gentlemen seem to apprehend"; instead, he maintained that the bill would "only more effectually consign the guilty into the hands of justice." And if, in its application, an "innocent man will have a finger laid upon him," Varnum believed that so long as "the public good requires the suspension of the privilege, every man . . . will be surely willing to submit to this inconvenience for a time, in order to secure the public happiness."[48] (One wonders whether someone so affected would agree.)

But Varnum had few like-minded colleagues. Overwhelmingly those who spoke during the House debates questioned the need for such a dramatic measure and worried of its abuse. For example, Roger Nelson of Maryland equated suspension with permitting "confining a man in prison without a cause" or "on vague suspicion." It was better to preserve the "writ of right" and leave matters to the criminal process, he argued, where so long as "from the evidence, there [are] sufficient grounds to suspect that [the prisoner] is guilty of offence, he will not be discharged."[49] For his part, John Smilie of Pennsylvania equated suspension with "repealing . . . the 'palladium of personal liberty.'"[50] Well versed in English legal tradition (perhaps because he had been born in Ireland), Smilie compared the suspensions of 1715 and 1745 as following from far more serious threats to government, while holding out post-Revolutionary War British suspensions that followed arguably from political motives as good reason to proceed with caution. Indeed, Smilie openly feared that under the auspices of such a bill, the "personal liberty" of those not in Jefferson's party "would be endangered."[51] Notably, in arguing for preserving habeas corpus and against suspension, Smilie specifically noted that the Suspension Clause was predicated upon the English Habeas Corpus Act, observing: "We have taken from the statute book of [England], this most valuable part of our Constitution."[52]

Interspersed within the debates one also finds a heavy dose of criticism of the administration's actions leading up to the proposed suspension. John Randolph of Virginia, for example, believed that "the military ha[d] . . . usurped the civil authority" and decried the bill under debate as "calculated to give a softening and smoothing over to this usurpation." "[O]n this ground," Randolph stated, "I cannot assent to it."[53] Representative Samuel Dana of Connecticut, the last to speak before the House vote, spoke more generally against the measure, deeming "the privilege of the writ of habeas corpus as the most glorious invention of man" and asserting that "[i]f treason was marching to force us from our seats, I would not agree to do this."[54]

In the end, the House debates reveal that all were operating under the assumption that it required a suspension by Congress for the executive to enjoy the power to arrest and detain outside the criminal process. In this regard, everyone assumed that the effect of a suspension would be to set aside, for a time, the normal legal constraints imposed by the criminal process on the executive's power to arrest and detain. But because most in the House were deeply skeptical of the need for such dramatic legislation, and perhaps because they disapproved of the secret expedited process by which the Senate had approved it, the bill failed overwhelmingly by a vote of 113-19 without ever being sent to committee.[55]

Meanwhile, during the weekend that fell between the Senate's passage of the suspension bill and the House taking it up, an attorney for Bollman and Swartwout filed a petition for a writ of habeas corpus in the federal Circuit Court for the District of Columbia.[56] During this time, the two prisoners remained in military custody in Washington, DC, where Bollman had been personally interrogated by Jefferson shortly after his arrival. As reported by Chief Judge Cranch, the petition argued that the attorney

> had called on Colonel Wharton, the commandant of the marine corps, and requested a copy of the warrant or cause of commitment, who replied that he had no warrant of commitment, but that the prisoners

were delivered in the usual military mode, and that they were merely under his care for safe keeping.

In other words, the military held the prisoners in its custody in the absence of any warrant for their arrest.

At the administration's behest, the federal prosecutor responded to the petition with a request that the court issue a warrant to commit Bollman and Swartwout on formal charges of treason.[57] Over Chief Judge Cranch's passionate dissent, a divided court granted the government's motion just one day after the House voted down the suspension.[58] In his dissent, Cranch lamented the court's abdication of its duty "to be peculiarly watchful lest the public feeling should reach the seat of justice, and thereby precedents be established which may become the ready tools of faction in times more disastrous."[59] Cranch also made clear his view that the commitment violated the Suspension Clause, positing:

> I can never agree that executive communications not on oath or affirmation, can, under the words of our constitution, be received as sufficient evidence in a court of justice, to charge a man with treason, much less commit him for trial. If such doctrines can be supported, there is no necessity of a suspension of the privilege of the writ of habeas corpus. . . .[60]

The matter next went to the Supreme Court, coming on the heels of the habeas case of one John Atkins Burford, who had been detained as "an evil doer and disturber of the peace" but in the absence of formal criminal charges. In Burford's case, the Court asked the basic question at the heart of any habeas inquiry: "[W]hat authority has the jailor to detain him?" The Court then explained, "To ascertain this, we must look to the warrant of commitment only. It is that only which can justify his detention." But, the Court emphasized, Burford's warrant "states no offence." It followed, the Court held, that "the warrant of commitment was illegal" and Burford was entitled to his discharge from custody.[61] In this respect, *Burford* reaffirmed the continuing influence of the seventh section of the English Habeas Corpus Act on American law and specifically its guarantee that one could not be detained outside the criminal process in the absence of a valid suspension.

In contrast to Burford, Bollman and Swartwout were now committed on formal charges. Thus, the question presented in their case asked whether there existed a legally sufficient basis supporting the charges. In Chief Justice John Marshall's view, this inquiry called on the Court to decide whether the prisoners had a constitutional claim to habeas relief. As he wrote in Ex parte *Bollman*, "when we say *the writ of habeas corpus*, without addition, we most generally mean that great writ which is now applied for; and in that sense it is used in the constitution." Further, because Congress had failed to enact a suspension, Marshall noted, "this court can only see its duty, and must obey the laws"—in other words, the Court had no choice but to ensure that the commitments of Bollman and Swartwout were lawful.[62] The Court then proceeded to hold additional argument and conduct an extensive review of the evidence that had been presented before the lower court in support of Bollman and Swartwout's commitments on charges of treason. Deeming the evidence insufficient to support the required elements of treason, the Court ordered the prisoners discharged from custody. (The Court declined to rule out the possibility that "fresh proceedings" could be initiated upon stronger evidence.[63]) The Court's decision highlighted both that the Constitution requires initiation of criminal charges to detain suspects such as Bollman and Swartwout and that the Suspension Clause contemplates a checking role for the courts to ensure that charges are not levied as a pretext to circumvent its mandate.

As for Burr, the government eventually captured him and charged him with treason in a case that was populated with notable figures. Jefferson himself handled much of the prosecution, while Burr's defense counsel included Luther Martin and Edmund Randolph, both having served as delegates to the Constitutional Convention and, in Randolph's case, formerly as attorney general of the United States.[64] Representative John Randolph served as grand jury foreman in Burr's case, whereas Senator Giles—who, recall, had introduced the Burr suspension bill—withdrew as a grand juror following a challenge to him sitting being raised by Burr's defense team.[65] Chief Justice Marshall presided over preliminary matters and Burr's trial. In that role, Marshall initially rejected the government's motion to commit Burr on charges of treason, citing insufficient evidence, although he did order Burr's commitment on a lesser charge. Marshall also excluded some evidence that the government sought to introduce at trial. Jefferson in turn criticized Marshall's decisions and reportedly called for the chief justice's impeachment. In the end, the jury returned verdicts of not guilty in Burr's case.[66]

Aside from the questionable conduct of President Jefferson during the entire Burr episode,[67] the affair reveals much about late Founding-era conceptions of the privilege and its suspension. To begin, everyone in Congress simply took for granted that it was for them to decide—and not the president— whether circumstances warranted a suspension.[68] For his part, Jefferson appears to have agreed, given that his administration responded to the failed suspension immediately by charging the alleged conspirators and proceeding against them criminally. Jefferson is noteworthy in this regard for taking a decidedly different view of which branch possesses the power to suspend than President Lincoln did during the Civil War. Second, President Jefferson and Congress viewed suspension as a necessary predicate for detaining persons deemed to owe allegiance outside the criminal process. Along the same lines, the public discourse surrounding the Burr episode underscores that American constitutional law had incorporated key aspects of the English suspension model, for once the suspension failed to pass, everyone took for granted that the detention of the citizen-conspirators suspected of treasonous plotting with Burr turned entirely on whether sufficient evidence existed to sustain criminal charges against them.[69] Finally, General Wilkinson's conduct prior to that point—specifically the military arrests and detentions outside the civilian criminal law framework—was widely criticized. As Chief Judge Cranch wrote at the time:

> Never before has this country, since the Revolution, witnessed so gross a violation of personal liberty, as to seize a man without any warrant or lawful authority whatever, and send him two thousand miles by water for his trial out of the district or State in which the crime was committed—and then for the first time to apply for a warrant to arrest him. . . .[70]

The Continuing Influence of English Law

As with earlier periods in American legal development, in the initial decades following Ratification, one finds overwhelming evidence of the continuing and pervasive influence on American law of both the English model of suspension that had developed during the seventeenth and eighteenth centuries and the English Habeas Corpus Act. During this period, prominent jurists and influential American legal scholars uniformly subscribed to the view that the Suspension Clause could not be interpreted any other way but in reference to the English legal developments that preceded it.

In discussing the reference to the privilege of the writ of habeas corpus in the Suspension Clause, for example, Chief Justice Marshall wrote in Ex parte *Watkins*: "The term is used in the constitution, as one which was well understood."[71] Marshall confirmed what common sense suggests—namely, that it would be impossible to interpret the Suspension Clause without some understanding of the development of habeas law that preceded its adoption. Notably, moreover, recognition of the important role that the English Habeas Corpus Act played in this development figured prominently in Marshall's early interpretation of the Suspension Clause. As the chief justice observed in Ex parte *Watkins*:

> This general reference to a power which we are required to exercise, without any precise definition of that power, imposes on us the necessity of making some inquiries into its use, *according to that law which is in a considerable degree incorporated into our own.* The writ of *habeas corpus* is a high prerogative writ, known to the common law, the great object of which is the liberation of those who may be imprisoned without suffi-cient cause. It is the nature of a writ of error, to examine the legality of the commitment. The English judges, being originally under the influence of the crown, neglected to issue this writ where the government enter-tained suspicions which could not be sustained by evidence; and the writ when issued was sometimes disregarded or evaded, and great individual oppression was suffered in consequence of delays in bringing prisoners to trial. To remedy this evil the celebrated *habeas corpus* act of the 31st of Charles II. was enacted, for the purpose of securing the benefits for which the writ was given. This statute . . . enforces the common law.[72]

Here, Marshall recognized that the Suspension Clause and original grant of habeas jurisdiction to the federal courts in Section 14 of the 1789 Judiciary Act came "without any precise definition" of the habeas "power" vested in the courts. To give content to those provisions, Marshall instructed that we must look to "that law which is in a considerable degree incorporated into our own"—specifically, the "the celebrated *habeas corpus* act" of 1679, which had "secur[ed] the benefits" that the writ was originally designed to achieve.[73] Years later, in an important habeas decision handed down during Reconstruction, the Supreme Court would again highlight the English Habeas Corpus Act's centrality to the story of the Suspension Clause, pointing to the Act as "firmly guarantee[ing]" the "great writ" and highlighting that the Act "was brought to America by the colonists, and claimed as among the immemorial rights descended to them from their ancestors," after which they gave it "prominent sanction in the Constitution."[74]

IN THE WAKE of the Burr Conspiracy, suspension departed the political-legal landscape for over fifty years. But in the face of a "clear, flagrant, and gigan-tic case of Rebellion"[75]—to borrow President Lincoln's words—suspension would finally become part of the American constitutional experience.

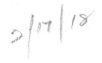

PART THREE

Suspension

With the Confederate attack on Fort Sumter on April 12, 1861, and the onset of the Civil War, the United States finally witnessed its first exercise of the dramatic suspension authority contemplated by the U.S. Constitution. President Abraham Lincoln famously invoked the authority on his own and continued to do so for the next two years until Congress finally enacted suspension legislation in 1863. In so doing, Lincoln triggered a major public debate over the constitutionality of his actions.

President Lincoln viewed suspension as a necessary predicate to arresting outside the criminal process. As he phrased the matter: "Of how little value the constitutional provision . . . will be rendered, if arrests shall never be made until defined crimes shall have been committed. . . ." Notably, because Lincoln held fast to the view that secession was illegal and the Confederates owed a continuing duty of allegiance to the Union, his suspension proclamations specifically encompassed persons held in military custody as "prisoners of war"—that is, Confederate soldiers captured on the battlefield. Congress subscribed to the same view in its 1863 suspension legislation.

During the war, suspension was not the exclusive province of the Union. Although the secessionist states claimed a greater devotion to the cause of liberty than the Union and criticized Lincoln's proclivity to suspend the privilege, it did not take long for the Confederacy to follow the example of its neighbor to the north and enact its own suspensions. But in stark contrast to Lincoln, Jefferson Davis viewed suspension as a legislative power and never suspended ahead of his Congress.

As the country rebuilt and the Union was made whole again, Congress once again authorized suspension, this time toward a very different end. At President Grant's request, Congress conferred upon him "extraordinary powers" to be wielded "for the purpose of securing to all citizens . . . the peaceful enjoyment of the rights guaranteed to them by the Constitution and laws." In so doing, Grant took an old emergency power and retooled it for a new purpose—namely the advancement of the cause of civil rights.

- Ex Parte = on one side only;
    for one party — on behalf of.

- Ex Parte hearing = hearings in which
  the court or tribunal hears only
  one side of the Controversy.

- Ex Parte proceeding = ref a temporary
  restraining order.

7

Civil War and the "Great Suspender"

> *If the president of the United States may suspend the writ,*
> *then the constitution of the United States has conferred upon*
> *him more regal and absolute power over the liberty of the*
> *citizen, than the people of England have thought it safe to*
> *entrust to the crown.*
>
> CHIEF JUSTICE ROGER B. TANEY IN
> *EX PARTE MERRYMAN* (1861)[1]

IT WAS NOT until the Confederate attack on Fort Sumter on April 12, 1861, and the beginning of the Civil War that the United States witnessed its first suspension at the federal level. President Lincoln viewed the secession of the Confederate States as illegal, and considered those who supported the Confederacy to be traitors who needed to return to their proper allegiance.[2] In this regard, the Union view of the secessionists mirrored that held by the British of the American rebels years earlier. For this reason and largely (though not entirely) consistent with prior practice, the president quickly—and controversially—turned to suspension as the basis for detaining Confederate soldiers and sympathizers in the absence of criminal charges.

Within days of the attack on Fort Sumter, Lincoln authorized Union military leaders to suspend habeas wherever they believed it necessary to protect key geographic areas. Lincoln did so famously on his own and without congressional approval. To be sure, initially Congress was unable to meet to grant him this authority, but well after the body reconvened and for the next two years while it debated passing suspension legislation, Lincoln kept right on authorizing suspensions. Initially, the suspensions targeted only concentrated areas of particular military importance. By the fall of 1862, however, Lincoln had proclaimed a suspension applicable to every prisoner in military custody. Lincoln's unilateral assumption of what had always been a legislative power—suspension, after all, owed its very creation to Parliament—soon provoked a showdown between the president and the chief justice of the Supreme Court and, in its wake, widespread public debate over the allocation of emergency powers in wartime.

Habeas Corpus in Wartime. Amanda L. Tyler.
© Oxford University Press 2017. Published 2017 by Oxford University Press.

As explored in this chapter, although Lincoln was wrong to lay claim to the suspension power, his understanding of the necessity of suspension to legalize arrests made outside the criminal process was fully consistent with the long-standing historical view of the suspension model. The same understanding informed the suspension finally enacted by Congress in 1863, in which Congress purported to reach all those disaffected to the Union cause along with Confederate soldiers captured in battle. More generally, studying the debates over suspension that pervaded the Civil War period reveals the continuing and profound influence of the English Habeas Corpus Act and suspension framework on American law. Surveying this period also shows that the role of allegiance in the English legal tradition heavily influenced the Supreme Court's assessment of the use of military tribunals to try civilians during the war and provided the foundation for the Court's decision in Ex parte *Milligan* holding that "[t]he Constitution of the United States is a law for rulers and people, equally in war and in peace. . . ."

The Case of John Merryman

Just days after the Confederate assault on Fort Sumter, mobs attacked the Sixth Massachusetts Infantry while it traveled through Baltimore heading south, resulting in the deaths of four soldiers and many civilians. Meanwhile, although the Maryland legislature had formally voted against secession, state officials took numerous steps to frustrate Union efforts, including refusing to reopen rail lines to the north and pushing for the withdrawal of federal troops from the state. Matters escalated to the point that the governor deployed the state militia and purportedly approved the mayor of Baltimore's orders that several key bridges be destroyed for the purpose of thwarting Union troop movements through the state.

Without the ability to move troops through Maryland, the capital in Washington, DC, would be completely cut off from the north. Recognizing the crucial importance of keeping transportation lines open through Maryland to allow Union troops to pass through the state, President Lincoln authorized his commanding general in the area, Winfield Scott, to do whatever necessary to counteract open resistance. Specifically, Lincoln informed Scott that "[i]f at any point on or in the vicinity of the military line . . . between the City of Philadelphia and the City of Washington . . . , you find resistance which renders it necessary to suspend the writ of Habeas Corpus for the public safety, you, personally or through the officer in command at the point where the resistance occurs, are authorized to suspend the writ."[3] It did not take long for the military to invoke its authority.

One person believed to play a role in destroying several bridges was a Maryland farmer by the name of John Merryman, a first lieutenant in a secessionist group called the Baltimore County Horse Guards. A few weeks after the bridge attacks and on orders from an army general in Pennsylvania, Union troops arrested Merryman at his home in Baltimore in the early morning hours of Saturday, May 25, 1861. From there, they transported Merryman to Fort McHenry for imprisonment. It does not appear that the government ever drew up a warrant for Merryman's arrest, nor did the government level any formal charges against Merryman at this point. This is surely because George Cadwalader, the Union military commander in Maryland, did not believe that he needed a warrant to hold Merryman in light of the declared suspension.

But others were not so sure. That same Saturday, a relative of Merryman's who was a lawyer began preparing a habeas petition on Merryman's behalf, swearing to it before the United States Commissioner in Baltimore and then arranging for its presentation in Washington to the chief justice of the Supreme Court of the United States, Roger B. Taney. (Taney was also the circuit justice for the area encompassing the Baltimore region; the petition was addressed to him in both capacities.) On Sunday, the chief justice ordered General Cadwalader to appear and produce the body of John Merryman at a hearing to be held the next day to ascertain whether Cadwalader had legal justification to detain Merryman. Taney traveled to Baltimore to hold the hearing, doing so, in his words, so as not to "withdraw General Cadwalader . . . from the limits of his military command."[4] Cadwalader nonetheless declined to appear, instead sending a representative to present his position. According to Cadwalader, the military was detaining Merryman as a suspected traitor engaged in hostilities against the government under the authority of the suspension in effect in the relevant area, which was necessary "for the public safety." Through his representative, Cadwalader also requested more time as he awaited further instructions from the president. Taney, however, was unwilling to delay matters and quickly found Cadwalader in contempt. Taney then decided the case the next day.[5]

And so it was that on Tuesday, May 28, 1861, Taney announced his decision before a packed courtroom, rejecting the position that the president on his own could suspend the habeas privilege, and more generally that military authorities could detain a civilian without criminal charges.[6] Days later, the chief justice followed up with a lengthy written opinion. He began by making clear that his position remained the same as before:

As the case comes before me . . . , I understand that the president not only claims the right to suspend the writ of habeas corpus himself, at

his discretion, but to delegate that discretionary power to a military officer, and to leave it to him to determine whether he will or will not obey
judicial process that may be served upon him. . . . I certainly listened to
it with some surprise, for I had supposed it to be one of those points of
constitutional law upon which there was no difference of opinion, and
that it was admitted on all hands, that the privilege of the writ could not
be suspended, except by act of congress.[7]

Taney knew his history, referring first to the debates surrounding the proposal
to suspend habeas in response to the Burr Conspiracy. In those debates, Taney
noted, "no one suggested that Mr. Jefferson might exercise the power himself,
if, in his opinion, the public safety demanded it." Next, Taney explored the
developments leading up to adoption of what he called "the great habeas corpus act" during the reign of Charles II. Taney related the story of the Petition of
Right and the plight of John Selden, whose detention without criminal charges
in the Tower of London, as discussed in Chapter 1, had both laid the groundwork and highlighted the need for habeas legislation in the seventeenth century. "It is worthy of remark," Taney wrote, "that the offences . . . relied on as
a justification for [Merryman's] arrest and imprisonment, in their nature and
character, and in the loose and vague manner in which they are stated, bear
a striking resemblance to those assigned in the warrant for the arrest of Mr.
Selden." Even in Selden's time, Taney emphasized, the delay of the judges in
granting his discharge had "excited the universal indignation of the bar." But,
Taney continued, the Habeas Corpus Act addressed such failings: "The great
and inestimable value of the habeas corpus act of the 31 Car. II. is, that it contains provisions which compel courts and judges, and all parties concerned,
to perform their duties promptly, in the manner specified in the statute."[8]
As Taney explained, that "manner" (or tradition) served as the foundation of
American habeas law and specifically established two important benchmarks
of constitutional law.

The first such principle, Taney wrote, was that only the legislative body
possessed the power to suspend habeas. To support this conclusion, Taney
cited the Suspension Clause's placement in the legislative article of the
Constitution, Article I. In addition, Taney quoted extensively from Blackstone,
whose Commentaries taught that in English tradition "'it is not left to the executive power to determine when the danger of the state is so great as to render
[suspension] expedient.'" Instead, "'[i]t is the parliament only or legislative
power that, whenever it sees proper, can authorize the crown by suspending
the habeas corpus for a short and limited time, to imprison suspected persons

without giving any reason for so doing.'" Continuing, Taney labeled the president's position as all but impossible to square with this English history:

> [N]o one can believe that, in framing a government intended to guard still more efficiently [than English law] the rights and liberties of the citizen, against executive encroachment and oppression, they would have conferred on the president a power which the history of England had proved to be dangerous and oppressive in the hands of the crown, and which the people of England had compelled it to surrender after a long and obstinate struggle on the part of the English executive to usurp it and retain it.[9]

The second principle, which Taney grounded in the incorporation of the English Habeas Corpus Act into American law, was that in the absence of a valid suspension the government must charge someone such as Merryman with a crime and try him in due course. Where the government fails to do so, Taney wrote, a court is duty-bound to order the prisoner's release. In English legal tradition, he explained, "if a person were imprisoned, no matter by what authority, he had a right to the writ of habeas corpus, to bring his case before the king's bench; if no specific offence were charged against him in the warrant of commitment, he was entitled to be forthwith discharged." Here, Taney also highlighted that "the statute of 31 Car. II., commonly known as the great habeas corpus act . . . , secured [this] right."[10] Accordingly, Taney concluded, because Merryman had not been charged with any crime, his detention violated the Constitution.

Almost as though smarting for confrontation, Taney concluded his opinion by noting that he had arranged for his opinion to be delivered to President Lincoln directly. The president, Taney wrote, would then be left "to determine what measures he will take to cause the civil process of the United States to be respected and enforced." The administration responded by indicting Merryman on a number of charges, including treason, although for various reasons he was never tried.[11]

Notwithstanding the change of course in Merryman's particular case, Lincoln had hardly backed down from his position. Indeed, he openly rejected Taney's opinion as wrong and proclaimed numerous additional suspensions over the course of the next two years prior to Congress's passage of legislation governing the matter. Lincoln's suspensions culminated in a suspension applicable to every military prisoner in custody.[12] Lincoln also defended before Congress the president's unilateral power to suspend, asserting that "[i]t was not believed that any law was violated."[13] His attorney general Edward Bates likewise submitted a defense of the president's actions to Congress.[14]

Taney's opinion in *Merryman* was widely published and circulated in legal publications and newspapers. Almost immediately, the opinion triggered an extensive public debate over the separation-of-powers questions raised in the case. Press coverage of *Merryman*, which was substantial, tended to critique or celebrate Taney's opinion in keeping with geographic and political sympathies. Thus, many Northern papers, such as the *New York Times*, pointed to the decision as proving that Taney "serves the cause of rebellion," and Horace Greeley's *New York Tribune* "advise[d]" the remaining members of the Supreme Court to "leave the task of overthrowing this formidable conspiracy against Liberty and Law to the military and naval forces of the United States."[15] Other papers more sympathetic to the Confederate cause lauded Taney's opinion. The *Baltimore American and Commercial Advertiser*, for example, found it "eminently proper that a Government which is fighting to maintain the integrity of the Constitution should interpose no arbitrary action to suspend or interfere with rights plainly guaranteed under it."[16] *Merryman* also led to the publication of a host of pamphlets taking sides on the question whether suspension is an executive or legislative power, including most famously Horace Binney's two-part publication defending Lincoln's actions.[17]

Chief Justice Taney's tenure on the Supreme Court is hardly the subject of celebration—he authored the *Dred Scott* decision, after all—but he was most assuredly right in *Merryman* about which branch possesses the authority to suspend habeas. To begin, his conclusion was the same as that reached by Chief Justice Marshall (albeit in dictum) years earlier as well as Justice Story in his famous *Commentaries on the Constitution*.[18] It was also consistent with President Madison's view of suspension, which, as discussed in the last chapter, led him to rebuke Andrew Jackson for suspending by military order during the War of 1812. Presumably, President Jefferson subscribed to the same view as well, given that Jefferson accepted Congress's decision not to pass suspension legislation during the Burr Conspiracy. Further, as Taney noted, the Committee of Style placed the Suspension Clause in Article I—the legislative article[19]—and suspension was, from its origins, a legislative creation born out of a movement to wrestle control over matters of detention from the Crown. (Indeed, one of the most influential sources consulted by the Founding generation on English law, Blackstone, emphasized this point.)[20] Additionally, the very first suspension in English history arose out of King William of Orange's request that Parliament take the dramatic step of expanding the Crown's powers to arrest and detain. (This

THE KNIGHT OF THE RUEFUL COUNTENANCE.

President Abraham Lincoln, the Constitution, Law, and Habeas Corpus

Credit: The Knight of the Rueful Countenance wood engraving cartoon of Abraham Lincoln by Adalbert J. Volck, 1862, Chicago History Museum, ICHi-022097.

request, moreover, came hand-in-hand with the King's acceptance of the English Declaration of Rights, the first provision of which declared "[t]hat the pretended power of suspending the laws or the execution of laws by regal authority without consent of Parliament is illegal."[21]) The idea that the executive could suspend without legislative involvement is at odds both with the entire history of the suspension framework and the Founding genera- tion's deep suspicion of concentrated executive authority.[22] (On this point, for example, note that the original Articles of Confederation did not even provide for an executive branch.) Further support for this conclusion may be found in the fact that many of the original state constitutions restricted all power to suspend laws to the state legislative body[23] and/or expressly recognized suspension of the privilege as a legislative power.[24] Finally, viewing the power as residing in the legislature is consistent with the Founding generation's desire that suspension only be invoked in the most extraordinary of circumstances.[25]

All the same, some have argued in favor of recognizing a limited and temporary executive authority to suspend where Congress is unable to assemble and circumstances are truly dire. Indeed, this is how President Lincoln defended his initial suspensions at the outset of the Civil War.[26] Of course, this justification quickly passed once Congress returned to session. Taney's failure to account for the fact that Lincoln's actions leading up to *Merryman* came during a period in which Congress was not in session may justify some of the criticism that his opinion has received.[27] Notably, in the extensive public debates that followed *Merryman*, several prominent voices defended a limited role for the president to act when Congress cannot do so itself. In the House debates, for example, Thaddeus Stevens, although firm in his position that suspension is a legislative power, nonetheless suggested that a protective exercise of the power by the executive might sometimes be appropriate.[28] A critic of such a position might argue that such an exception could quickly swallow the proverbial rule. The fact that the Constitution expressly grants the president the power, "on extraordinary Occasions, [to] convene both Houses," moreover, further suggests that the president can call upon Congress to engage with the matter in a timely fashion.[29]

Whether to recognize a temporary protective suspension power presents a terrifically difficult question. At most, any such recognition should sweep no further than to cover a period when Congress is unable to convene. Where Congress *is* able to take up the question whether suspension is constitutionally justified and appropriate, the executive cannot be said to be functioning in a protective posture. In such circumstances, the Constitution plainly contemplates that the decision whether to suspend, or to continue a suspension declared during an emergency period, resides solely within the legislative branch. Given that we live in an age of instant electronic communication, moreover, it is likely that members of Congress could convene remotely if necessary, a prospect that counsels that any decision of this magnitude can and should be made by the legislature in the first instance.

In all events, Lincoln appears to have lost little sleep over his decision to act ahead of Congress and likely anyone else in Lincoln's position would have done the same to protect critical areas at the outset of the war. But it should not go overlooked that Lincoln's actions and particularly his decision to keep authorizing suspensions once Congress returned to session clearly strained the Constitution. Necessity, moreover, does not equate with legality. As Justice Story once wrote:

> It may be fit and proper for the government, in the exercise of the high discretion confided to the executive, for great public purposes, to act on a sudden emergency, or to prevent an irreparable mischief, by summary measures, which are not found in the text of the laws. Such measures are properly matters of state, and if the responsibility is taken, under justifiable circumstances, the Legislature will doubtless apply a proper indemnity. But this Court can only look to the questions, whether the laws have been violated; and if they were, justice demands, that the injured party should receive a suitable redress.[30]

Nevertheless, in analyzing Lincoln's actions during the Civil War, his famous defense of his actions should give pause to any critic,[31] as should the argument that although Lincoln's actions may not have been strictly legal, they could be easily defended on moral grounds.[32] Finally, it should not go overlooked that Congress bears some of the blame for delaying two years before enacting a suspension in the face of a war that was tearing apart the Union.[33]

The Sweep of Suspension

Lincoln was mistaken about which branch possessed the authority to suspend, but he certainly appreciated the dramatic nature of suspension and understood its necessity as a means of legalizing arrests that otherwise would be unconstitutional in the ordinary course. In a widely-published letter, Lincoln wrote that the Suspension Clause "plainly attests to the understanding of those who made the constitution that . . . the purpose" of suspension was so that "men may be held in custody whom the courts acting on ordinary rules, would discharge."[34] The "ordinary rules" to which Lincoln was referring comprised the protections inherent in the criminal process. Thus, as Lincoln explained, "Habeas Corpus, does not discharge men who are proved to be guilty of defined crime; and its suspension is allowed by the constitution on purpose that, men may be arrested and held, who can not be proved to be guilty of defined crime, 'when in cases of Rebellion or Invasion the public Safety may require it.'"[35]

Continuing, Lincoln posited that in these dire circumstances, "arrests are made, not so much for what has been done, as for what probably would be done. [They are made] for the preventive. . . ." Any other conclusion, Lincoln observed, would negate the entire purpose of suspension. As he phrased it: "Of how little value the constitutional provision I have quoted will be rendered, if arrests shall never be made until defined crimes shall have been committed. . . ." Finally, to drive home his understanding of the role of suspension, Lincoln offered a concrete example. What if, Lincoln asked, the Union had arrested those Confederate military leaders within Union grasp and known to be "traitors" at the outset of the war?

> Unquestionably if we had seized and held them, the insurgent cause would be much weaker. But no one of them had then committed any crime defined in the law. Every one of them if arrested would have been discharged on Habeas Corpus, were the writ allowed to operate.

In light of these examples, the President concluded by suggesting that "the time [is] not unlikely to come when I shall be blamed for having made too few arrests rather than too many."[36]

Over the course of the war, military officials, acting under Lincoln's orders, arrested thousands of civilians.[37] Many were Confederate residents who were trapped in the North or who came from border states.[38] (Suspension was also wielded as a potent tool to enforce conscription.) As historian James G. Randall has written: "The arrests were made on suspicion. Prisoners were not told why they were seized. . . . [T]he purpose of the whole process was temporary military detention."[39] As the war progressed, formal prosecutions for treason were undertaken on a highly selective basis for fear of encountering sympathetic juries and creating martyrs for the Confederate cause. Further, Attorney General Bates subscribed to the view that for deterrence purposes, "[t]he penitentiaries will be far more effectual than the gallows."[40] With suspension, of course, came the power to detain. No trial was necessary, at least so long as the war continued.

Because President Lincoln firmly believed that the Confederate states could not legally secede from the Union, it followed in his view that southerners retained their duty of allegiance to the Union. This explains why the Lincoln administration was reluctant to enter formal cartels for the exchange of prisoners, just as Great Britain had been during the Revolutionary War—cartels implied recognition that the opposing soldiers were in the service of a foreign sovereign.[41] This also explains why the president held the view that the detention of Confederate soldiers and civilian supporters outside the criminal process required a suspension. Thus, on September 24, 1862, Lincoln proclaimed a sweeping suspension, the terms of which reached virtually every prisoner who might be captured in the war. Specifically, he ordered:

> That the writ of habeas corpus is suspended in respect to all persons arrested, or who are now, or hereafter during the rebellion shall be, imprisoned in any fort, camp, arsenal, military prison, or other place of confinement by any military authority or by the sentence of any court-martial or military commission.[42]

Although Lincoln's proclamation (like earlier ones) met many critics, the *New York Times* heralded his announcement as "restrain[ing] and defin[ing] and mitigate[ing] the operation of a system which is already in active use."[43] Indeed, this proclamation followed on the heels of an August proclamation that was similarly sweeping in nature, applying as it did to draft evaders and "all persons arrested for disloyal practices."[44] In the immediate wake of that earlier proclamation, there were "sweeping and uncoordinated arrests" that had a "momentous effect on civil liberties."[45]

By the next spring, after actively debating suspension for two years, Congress finally passed legislation in March 1863 that it hoped would put to rest the controversy over whether the president could suspend without its authorization. Part of what finally spurred Congress to act was the existence of a large number of lawsuits brought against federal officials for false imprisonment. These suits, like one brought by John Merryman against General Cadwalader, often cited Chief Justice Taney's *Merryman* opinion to argue that military arrests under presidential order were unconstitutional.[46] The growing number of suits proved to be of grave concern not only to the individual defendants (typically Union military officials), but also to the president, and led the attorney general to draft and deliver proposed legislation to Congress a year before that body finally acted.[47]

In the resulting legislation, entitled "An Act relating to Habeas Corpus, and regulating Judicial Proceedings in Certain Cases," Congress provided:

> That, during the present rebellion, the President of the United States, whenever, in his judgment, the public safety may require it, is authorized to suspend the privilege of the writ of habeas corpus in any case throughout the United States, or any part thereof. And whenever and wherever the said privilege shall be suspended, as aforesaid, no military or other officer shall be compelled, in answer to any writ of habeas corpus, to return the body of any person or persons detained by him by authority of the President ... so long as said suspension by the President shall remain in force, and said rebellion continue.[48]

Congress intended its chosen wording (stating that the president "is autho-rized" rather than "is hereby authorized") to be ambiguous on the question whether the bill was an investiture of the power in the president or a valida-tion of the president's prior acts.[49] This being said, members almost uniformly subscribed to the same position as the president's with respect to the necessity of a suspension to legalize detention—even of those suspected of treason—outside the criminal process.[50]

Congress's suspension authorization, however, came with substantial strings attached. Specifically, in Section 2 of the Act, Congress required, among other things, that lists of all prisoners be provided by the executive to the local federal court in states "in which the administration of the laws has continued unimpaired in the said Federal courts." In such states, if the next sitting grand jury failed to indict any "state or political prisoners" in custody, they were to be released upon taking an oath of allegiance to the Union. If pris-oners falling into this description were not so released, the Act commanded the courts to order their discharge. Violation of this provision subjected an officer of the United States to indictment for a misdemeanor along with a fine and imprisonment.[51] Further, in response to the flood of civil lawsuits that had been filed against Union military officials, Congress included a provision in the Act declaring that following a presidential order was a valid defense to any "civil or criminal" proceeding that attacked "any search, seizure, arrest, or imprisonment" made pursuant to such an order "or under color of any law of Congress."[52]

Now unquestionably armed with the authority to suspend in the face of the rebellion, Lincoln issued his most sweeping suspension in September 1863. Notably, Lincoln cited the 1863 Act as the basis of his authority, practically con-ceding the questionable constitutionality of his earlier proclamations. In this proclamation, he declared:

> [I]n the judgment of the President, the public safety does require that
> the privilege of the said writ shall now be suspended throughout the
> United States in the cases where, by the authority of the President of
> the United States, military, naval, and civil officers of the United States,
> or any of them, hold persons under their command or in their custody,
> either as prisoners of war, spies, or aiders or abettors of the enemy. . . .[53]

The proclamation specifically encompassed persons held in military cus-tody and deemed "prisoners of war"—clearly a reference to Confederate sol-diers captured on the battlefield. This is noteworthy because it shows that both Congress and Lincoln did not believe that the executive had inherent authority to detain such persons in the absence of a suspension. This position was of course consistent with Lincoln's view that the Confederate states could not legally secede and that its members still owed a duty of allegiance to the Union. Likewise, it mirrored precisely the stance that the British had taken toward the American rebels during the Revolutionary War. This was also how Congress viewed the matter. Specifically, the 1863 Act distinguished "state or political prisoners" from "prisoners of war"—the latter surely a reference to Confederate soldiers—and although the Act authorized the detention of prisoners of war under Section 1, it provided that they were not covered by the requirements of Section 2.[54]

In the wake of Lincoln's newest proclaimed suspension, Union military officials continued to arrest and detain individuals across the country, including both civilians and Confederate soldiers captured in battle.[55] Only a portion of those detained during the war were ever tried for criminal conduct and, in a great number of cases, those trials occurred before military tribunals[56]—a practice, as discussed below, that implicates a host of additional constitutional issues. Meanwhile, with one possible exception, Randall's research of contemporary court records and War Department files failed to reveal any lists of prisoners being turned over to the courts in compliance with Section 2 of the 1863 Act. He therefore concluded that Section 2 of "the act seems to have had but little practical effect."[57] Executive officials were either unfamiliar with the terms of the Act,[58] construed it narrowly,[59] or simply chose not to honor it.[60] As matters unfolded, Lincoln's suspension remained in place in some states as late as a full year after General Robert E. Lee surrendered to General Ulysses S. Grant at Appomattox Court House. Only then did President Andrew Johnson finally lift the last of the suspension's reach.[61]

Ex parte Milligan *and Military Trials*

The use of military tribunals during the war proved another controversial aspect of Lincoln's agenda, earning the postwar rebuke of the Supreme Court in its 1866 decision in Ex parte *Milligan*. From the outset, the case's importance was obvious to all involved, leading the Court to preside over six days of oral arguments.

The case was an outgrowth of the trial of Lamdin Milligan, a lawyer and former candidate for governor of Indiana, and others before a military commission in Indiana for a range of charges relating to their Copperhead activities and support of the Confederacy. The charges included "violat[ing] the laws of war," conspiracy, inciting insurrection, and disloyal practices. Many of the charges could not be grounded in existing federal criminal statutes enacted by

Congress but were announced in the first instance by the commission.[62] (The trial of the Lincoln conspirators, explored below, likewise reveals that the creation of new crimes by Civil War military tribunals was a common practice.) Further, the commission procedures only required a two-thirds majority to issue a death sentence and the punishments awarded often far exceeded what federal law authorized civilian courts to issue.[63]

Milligan had been tried, convicted, and sentenced to death by military officers as opposed to a jury. Thereafter, Milligan (joined by two others) pursued habeas corpus relief in federal court challenging the legitimacy of his conviction. When the case eventually came before the Supreme Court, Milligan's attack on the military commission prevailed. Justice David Davis's majority opinion for five justices began by noting that "in Indiana[,] the Federal authority was always unopposed, and its courts always open to hear criminal accusations and redress grievances." (Interestingly, the Court contrasted Virginia, "where the national authority was overturned and the courts driven out," an observation that suggests the five justices in the majority were imminently comfortable rendering an opinion as to whether wartime conditions in certain areas warranted emergency measures.[64]) It did not matter to the majority that Milligan had been charged with violations of the laws of war. Such laws, they concluded, "can never be applied to citizens in states which have upheld the authority of the government, and where the courts are open and their process unobstructed."[65]

More specifically, the majority rejected the argument that martial law justified Milligan's military trial and sentencing:

> Martial law, established on such a basis, destroys every guarantee of the Constitution, and effectually renders the "military independent of and superior to the civil power"—the attempt to do which by the King of Great Britain was deemed by our fathers such an offence, that they assigned it to the world as one of the causes which impelled them to declare their independence.[66]

Accordingly, five members of the Court held that in areas in which civilian courts were "open and their process unobstructed," civilians must be tried by those courts and given the full panoply of constitutional rights relating to criminal procedure, including a jury trial—even in the face of ongoing civil war. In so holding, the Court rejected the government's argument that the Bill of Rights were "peace provisions" that "like all other conventional and legislative laws and enactments, are silent amidst arms, and when the safety of the people becomes the supreme law." More generally, in an oft-quoted passage, the majority wrote, "[t]he Constitution of the United States is a law for rulers and people, equally in war and in peace, and covers with the shield of its protection all classes of men, at all times, and under all circumstances."[67]

The majority's understanding of the limits of martial law and application of military law to civilians is consistent with the example set by President Washington during the Whiskey Rebellion, when, as discussed in the last chapter, he ordered military officials to refer those arrested to the civilian authorities for prosecution. Likewise, it accords with the positions of both President Madison and Chief Justice Kent during the War of 1812. More generally, *Milligan* stands as an important precedent taking a limited view of the role and legitimacy of martial law. Mindful as the Court was of the dramatic effects of such a regime on civil liberties, it staked out an exceedingly narrow view of when martial law might be appropriate, positing that where civilian courts are up and running, there can be no such state of affairs. As will be seen in Chapter 10, this precedent wielded considerable influence over the Supreme Court's later rejection of the declaration of martial law in the Hawaiian Territory during World War II. (Although, as is discussed in Chapter 11, *Milligan* came under fire in the middle of that same war.)

The *Milligan* Court also rejected the argument that the existence of a nationwide suspension validated Milligan's trial before a military commission. Suspension, the Court held, only permits *detention* during its duration; it says nothing about the propriety of military versus civilian courts, nor does it legitimate the denial of standard procedural protections. As Justice Davis phrased it, "[t]he Constitution goes no further. It does not say after a writ of *habeas corpus* is denied a citizen, that he shall be tried otherwise than by the course of the common law. . . . [The Founding generation] limited the suspension to one great right, and left the rest to remain forever inviolable."[68] As a separate matter, the Court rejected the argument that Milligan's detention (separate and apart from his trial and resulting sentence) had been authorized by the terms of the 1863 Act, holding that the requirements of Section 2 had not been satisfied in his case.[69] Finally, the Court dismissed out of hand the assertion that Section 2's procedural requirements did not apply to Milligan because he could be treated as a prisoner of war:

> It is not easy to see how he can be treated as a prisoner of war when he lived in Indiana for the past twenty years, was arrested there, and had not been, during the late troubles, a resident of any of the states in rebellion. If in Indiana he conspired with bad men to assist the enemy, he is punishable for it in the courts of Indiana; but, when tried for the offence, he cannot plead the rights of war, for he was not engaged in

legal acts of hostility against the government, and only such persons, when captured, are prisoners of war. If he cannot enjoy the immunities attaching to the character of a prisoner of war, how can he be subject to their pains and penalties?[70]

The *Milligan* decision proved immensely controversial, in part because many appreciated the grave threat it posed to the legitimacy of the temporary military governments established during Reconstruction in most of the former Confederate States.[71] Indeed, Radical Republican Thaddeus Stevens assailed the decision as "far more dangerous in its operation upon the lives and liberties of the loyal men of this country" than the "infamous . . . Dred Scott decision."[72] Within months, Congress reacted to *Milligan* by passing legislation to protect those officers involved with the commissions by declaring that their actions should be treated as though they followed under prior congressional authorization. As the debates preceding the 1867 indemnity legislation made clear, it came in direct response to *Milligan* and revealed that Congress agreed with Lincoln and the separate opinion of the four concurring justices in *Milligan* that it possessed the authority to authorize the military trials of civilians.[73] As things unfolded, military trials continued in the wake of *Milligan*, although predominantly, if not entirely, such trials involved Union soldiers or were held in former Confederate States and territories under military rule.[74]

Notably, a full year before *Milligan*, many in the administration were already nervous about the potential for Supreme Court rebuke of military trials, and this nervousness translated to a series of extraordinary decisions in the days following President Lincoln's assassination. (It may also have been responsible for the order issued on behalf of the president by Secretary of War Edwin M. Stanton in May 1865 throwing out all existing sentences by military tribunals.[75])

Lincoln's Assassination: Military Courts and Legal Islands

On April 14, 1865, only five days after General Lee's surrender, John Wilkes Booth shot President Lincoln at Ford's Theatre. Taken to a house across the street from the theater, Lincoln died the next day. In the days that followed, the military apprehended most of the conspirators believed to have helped Booth in plotting and carrying out the assassination, although Booth himself died during the attempt to capture him. Almost immediately, executive officials began debating how to prosecute the so-called Lincoln conspirators—specifically, whether to try them before a military tribunal or civilian court.

Despite resistance from some quarters, once those arrested were winnowed down to a list of eight,[76] President Johnson signed an order directing their trial before a military commission composed of nine military officers.[77] Critics included members of the president's own cabinet and the same attorney general who had earlier defended Lincoln's unilateral suspensions to Congress. Specifically, former attorney general Edward Bates was highly critical of the decision to try the conspirators before a military tribunal, believing that "[s]uch a trial is not only unlawful, but it is a gross blunder in policy: It denies the great, fundamental principle, that ours is a government of *Law*, and that the law is strong enough, to rule the people wisely and well." He added, "if the offenders be done to death by that tribunal, however truly guilty, they will pass for martyrs with half the world."[78] Within the current cabinet, Navy Secretary Gideon Welles similarly held the view that the conspirators should be tried by a civilian court, and recorded in his diary that Treasury Secretary Hugh McCulloch subscribed to the same position. By contrast, Secretary of War Edwin M. Stanton reportedly held the view that "the proof [of guilt] is clear and positive" and he "was emphatic" in his support for a military commission.[79] New attorney general James Speed similarly pushed for a commission, and later defended this position on the basis that "the commander of an army in time of war has the same power to organize military tribunals and execute their judgments that he has to set his squadrons in the field and fight battles."[80] (Cabinet members engaged in a similar debate just two months later over whether to try Jefferson Davis before a commission or civilian court. As things turned out, Davis never stood trial in either forum.[81])

Ten days after President Johnson signed the order directing the conspirators' trial by military commission, proceedings began at the Old Arsenal Penitentiary in Washington, DC.[82] The President's Order authorized the commission and empowered it to "establish such order or rules of proceeding as may avoid unnecessary delay and conduce to the ends of public justice." Exercising that authority, the commission adopted rules that, among other things, provided that a majority vote of the officers would sustain a guilty verdict and that a two-thirds majority vote could sustain a death sentence. Further, the rules provided that the only possible appeal on the part of the defendants came in the form of seeking clemency or a pardon from President Johnson.[83]

Before the tribunal, the prosecution team included Representative John Bingham, who just one year later would serve as the primary drafter of the Fourteenth Amendment to the Constitution. Bingham argued from the outset of the proceedings that the due process guarantee in the Fifth Amendment was "only the law of peace, not of war." "[I]n war," Bingham contended, "it must be, and is, to a great extent, inoperative and disregarded."[84]

In response, one of the defense lawyers, Maryland senator Reverdy Johnson, argued that military trial of the conspirators violated the Constitution. As legal scholar Gerard Magliocca has written, "Johnson's logic was simple. The defendants were citizens, and the courts were open. Thus, the accused were entitled to a jury trial and the other criminal procedure guarantees in the Bill of Rights."[85] Specifically, Johnson asserted that fundamental liberties " 'are more peculiarly necessary to the security of personal liberty in war than in peace. All history tells us that war, at times, maddens the people, frenzies government, and makes both regardless of constitutional limitations of power. Individual safety, at such periods, is more in peril than at any other.' "[86] Only members of the military, Johnson argued, could be constitutionally tried by military commission.

But Bingham had yet another argument to press. He believed that suspension meant that in times of war, " 'the rights of each citizen, as secured in time of peace, must yield to the wants, interests, and necessities of the nation.' "[87] Congress's 1863 suspension legislation, he contended, implicitly authorized use of military commissions for civilian trials until the president and Congress declared that the rebellion had ended. Further, President Lincoln had declared martial law and authorized such commissions back in 1862—well before Congress intervened with legislation—and, in all events, Bingham observed, courts were only open in the District " 'by force of the bayonet.' " Many of Bingham's arguments would be rejected one year later by the Supreme Court in *Milligan*, but for the time, they carried the day.

After a seven-week trial, the military officers found all eight defendants guilty of various conspiracy-related charges, including the charge of traitorously conspiring to commit murder, a crime not codified in federal law but one that instead had been announced by the officers for the case at hand. (In this respect and others, many parallels to the *Milligan* case may be drawn.) Four of the defendants were sentenced to death, three received life sentences, and one (Spangler) received a six-year sentence.[88] Days later and just over two months after President Johnson had ordered the creation of the military tribunal, the government hanged Mary Surratt, Lewis Payne, David Herold, and George Atzerodt on July 7, 1865.[89]

It was the four conspirators who lived that caused the most concern to the Johnson cabinet. The decision to assign the fate of the conspirators to a military tribunal rather than a civilian court had been immensely controversial and its legality widely questioned.[90] Many in government recognized, moreover, the possibility that a habeas court might intercede on behalf of the living conspirators and overturn their convictions as unconstitutional under logic similar to that subsequently adopted by the Supreme Court in *Milligan*. Indeed, Mary Surratt's lawyers had already tried to obtain habeas relief in an effort to halt her execution by challenging the constitutionality of the military tribunal that had overseen her trial. In seeking relief, Surratt's lawyers emphasized that "she was a private citizen of the United States" and that her offense was "in no manner connected with the military authority of the same."[91] Her habeas petition, filed the night before Surratt's scheduled hanging, resulted in an overnight issuance of the writ by Justice Andrew Wylie of the Supreme Court of the District of Columbia calling upon the government to produce Surratt in court the next morning and defend her commitment and sentence. But instead of producing Surratt, the official upon whom the writ had been served, Major-General W. S. Hancock, appeared in court alongside Attorney General Speed and produced an "Indorsement" prepared by President Johnson for Hancock "declar[ing] that the writ of *habeas corpus* has been heretofore suspended in such cases as this."[92] It further proclaimed: "I do hereby especially suspend this writ, and direct that you proceed to execute the order heretofore given upon the judgment of the Military Commission, and you will give this order in return to the writ." In response, the court quickly ruled that the suspension curtailed its jurisdiction to review the case and "yielded" to the president.[93] The hangings followed less than two hours later.

But habeas remained a very serious threat to the legitimacy and enforceability of the sentences of the four conspirators who lived. Accordingly, during an excursion to visit the Navy sloop USS *Pawnee* on July 11, 1865, Secretary Stanton pulled Secretary Welles aside to ask "if the Navy could not spare a gunboat to convey some prisoners to Tortugas." According to Welles, when he asked the secretary why he "did not send them by one of his own transports," Stanton:

> told me he wanted to send the persons connected with the assassination of President Lincoln to Tortugas, instead of a Northern prison, that he had mentioned the subject to the President, and it was best to get them into a part of the country where old Nelson or any other judge[*] would not try to make difficulty by *habeas corpus*.[94]

---

[*] The reference is presumably to Supreme Court Justice Samuel Nelson. Justice Nelson had been a critic of expansive notions of executive authority during the Civil War. For example, Nelson had dissented in the *Prize Cases* in part on the basis that Lincoln's blockade of Southern ports was illegal because it occurred before Congress declared war. See 67 U.S. (2 Black) 635, 687–689 (1862) (Nelson, J., dissenting).

Adjusting the Ropes for Hanging the Lincoln Assassination Conspirators
Credit: Photograph by Alexander Gardner, "Washington, D.C. Adjusting the ropes for hanging the conspirators," July 7, 1865. Library of Congress.

And so, perhaps drawing on the example of the British sending Ethan Allen and his Green Mountain Boys back to the Americas to avoid habeas proceedings in their case during the lead-up to the Revolutionary War, Welles arranged transport of the remaining conspirators—Samuel Arnold, Dr. Samuel Mudd (known for having set John Wilkes Booth's broken leg after the assassination), Michael O'Laughlin, and Edward Spangler—to the military prison at Fort Jefferson, located on an island in the remote Dry Tortugas off the coast of Florida. The Earl of Clarendon, famous for his proclivity for sending English prisoners in the seventeenth century to "remote islands' garrisons and other places, thereby to prevent them from the benefit of the law,"[95] would have been proud.

The Johnson administration was right to worry about the potential for habeas proceedings. As early as June 1866, Samuel Mudd's wife had met with lawyers about petitioning for habeas relief on her husband's behalf.[96] And, notwithstanding the remote location of their prison, Mudd, Arnold, and

Fort Jefferson in the Dry Tortugas Today
Credit: National Park Service.

Spangler succeeded in filing habeas petitions in federal district court in Florida, arguing that their trial and convictions were unconstitutional and, accordingly, that they were entitled to their freedom. (O'Laughlin, who had received a life sentence, had died in the meantime.) Nonetheless, the court rejected their claims without even awaiting a return from the government. In so doing, the court distinguished *Milligan*, reasoning:

> There is nothing in th[at] opinion . . . , nor in the third article of the Constitution, nor in the [1863 Act] to lead to the conclusion that if any army had been encamped in the State of Indiana (whether in the immediate presence of the enemy or not,) and any person, a resident of Indiana or any other State (enlisted soldier or not) had, not from any private animosity, but from public reasons, made his way within the army lines and assassinated the commanding general, such a person could not have been legally tried for his military offence by a military tribunal, and legally convicted and sentenced.

Accordingly, because "[i]t was not Mr. Lincoln who was assassinated, but the Commander in Chief of the army for military reasons," the court concluded that *Milligan* was inapposite.[97]

Early on in the war, Chief Justice Taney observed in dictum in *Merryman* that suspension did not justify the use of military tribunals, rejecting one of the key arguments advanced by Bingham to defend the commission that tried the Lincoln conspirators. By the war's conclusion, Taney's dicta became the holding of the Court in *Milligan*. But in the interim, Mary Surratt's habeas petition, which unquestionably raised serious and unresolved constitutional questions, evaded judicial review because Justice Wylie held that suspension precluded his jurisdiction entirely. With Surratt being halfway to the gallows by the time her lawyers filed her habeas petition, perhaps it is unsurprising that the judge declined to review her case. Nonetheless, the court's decision equating suspension with the power to sentence and execute a person by military tribunal free of all judicial review was wrong, plain and simple. From its origins, suspension was conceived of as a legal means by which to justify temporary detention without trial, and nothing more. Indeed, looking back on earlier episodes of suspension in English history, one finds a flurry of trials in the wake of their lapsing. To be sure, at least three episodes of suspension in English history encompassed trials of suspected traitors during the pendency of the suspension,[98] but there is nothing in that history to suggest that the suspects enjoyed lesser protections in their trials than they would have received in the absence of a suspension. Nor is there any support to be found in the Revolutionary War suspensions or the Founding period for the proposition that a suspension's effects sweep beyond legalizing detention without trial during the extreme circumstances that justify the suspension. In short, there exists no historical support for the proposition that suspension legalizes streamlining trial and punishment outside the standard criminal process.

As for the underlying merits of Surratt's petition, the questions posed are more difficult. Unlike Justice Wylie in Surratt's case, the district judge presiding over the habeas petitions of Mudd, Arnold, and Spangler did decide their constitutional objections, finding *Milligan* distinguishable. This narrow reading of *Milligan* suggested that the assassination of the president in any state, including Indiana where the courts were open and the Union unopposed, likely would have justified military trial of the conspirators. Of course, if the judge's debatable reasoning is correct, then the fact that the assassination occurred in Washington, DC, is of no moment. But it seems wrong to read *Milligan* in such a cramped fashion. *Milligan* was much more concerned with the geographic realities of the area in question than the particular crime or victim at issue. Thus, whether Washington, DC, was in or near the theater of war was relevant, as of course was the question whether the District stayed loyal to the Union and maintained operating civilian courts. On the one hand, the proximity of the capital to Virginia battlefields where the war waged on into the spring of 1865 supported the trial of the conspirators by military tribunal. On the other, however, General Lee had surrendered before the assassination, the District remained tied to the Union throughout the war, and courts had been operating in the District well before the conspirators' trial. (To be sure, Bingham argued during the conspirators' trial that this was only "by force of the bayonet.")

These difficult questions are worthy of their own extensive analysis. Given that Lee had surrendered and civilian courts were open (seriously weakening any argument that martial law prevailed in the District), the conspirators' trial by military tribunal ran afoul of the Constitution at least under the precedent of *Milligan*. The broader question whether *Milligan* is itself correct raises its own, much more difficult, set of questions. As is discussed in Chapter 11, *Milligan* has been limited in Supreme Court decisions rendered during World War II and more recently.[99] Nonetheless, Justice Davis's opinion in *Milligan* is consistent with historical understandings animating habeas jurisprudence in the Anglo-American tradition. As explored in earlier chapters, that tradition had long distinguished between application of domestic law to those who clearly could claim its protections and those with whom the state's relationship has traditionally been governed by the law of nations and therefore the law of war. If that same distinction carries over to the question of procedural rights during criminal trial—and there is little reason to believe that it should not—then there are serious constitutional problems with prosecuting citizen civilians before military commissions for violations of the laws of war. To borrow from Justice Davis, if the Constitution can be so easily evaded in times of national emergency, then maybe "it is not worth the cost of preservation."[100]

Complications of the Civil War Example: The Laws of War, Lines of Allegiance, and Martial Law

This complex narrative of Union actions during and immediately after the Civil War suggests a shifting and pragmatic (if not opportunist) understanding of where the lines of allegiance fell. Many in the North at the time argued that those tied to the Confederacy had forsaken their allegiance and could be treated akin to foreigners who fell outside the protection of domestic law.[101] Further, members of Congress and the president moved increasingly toward the position that those fighting with the Confederacy or living within its borders could be denied the privileges of citizenship and treated as enemies under the international laws of war.[102] It was this reasoning that led to the decision to try the Lincoln conspirators (deemed "enemy belligerents" subject to the laws of war by Attorney General James Speed) before a military tribunal.

In keeping with this idea, early in the war, a divided Supreme Court upheld the president's blockade of Southern states in the *Prize Cases* by deferring to the president's decision to treat those aligned with the Confederacy as belligerent enemies under the law of nations and, as such, the laws of war.[103] In so doing, the Court posited that "it is not necessary to constitute war, that both parties should be acknowledged as independent nations or sovereign States. A war may exist where one of the belligerents, claims sovereign rights as against the other." The Court continued to cite Vattel for the proposition that

> [a] civil war breaks the bands of society and government, or at least suspends their force and effect: it produces in the nation two independent parties, who consider each other as enemies. . . . Those two parties, therefore, must necessarily be considered as thenceforward constituting, at least for a time, two separate bodies, two distinct societies. Having no common superior to judge between them, they stand in precisely the same predicament as two nations who engage in a contest and have recourse to arms.[104]

Notably, the Court's reasoning rested in part on the assumption that such persons had "cast off their allegiance" to the Union,[105] and it followed that legislation often required persons who had sided with the Confederacy to renew their allegiance to the Union during the war in order to regain full enjoyment of its protections.[106]

Because the president could treat the insurrection as war, the Court concluded, the president could lawfully treat those who supported the Confederacy as belligerent enemies. It followed that over the course of the Civil War, the Union invoked its authority under the laws of war to kill or capture Confederate soldiers on the battlefield, take and destroy certain Confederate property, and control captured Confederate territory by military rule. Yet many examples from the war, including even the blockade at issue in the *Prize Cases*, highlight the uneasy tension among domestic law, the laws of war, and the role of allegiance during this period. Thus, even when implementing the blockade of southern ports, Lincoln declared that captured private vessels operating under Confederate commissions would be treated criminally as pirates, rather than as privateers who could claim the protection of the laws of war.[107] Further, by the war's end, the Johnson administration once again treated those who sided with the Confederacy as traitors who owed allegiance; that, at least, would seem to be the premise on which President Johnson pardoned "all and every person who participated, directly or indirectly, in the late insurrection or rebellion" for "the offence of treason against the United States or of adhering to their enemies during the late civil war."[108] (Johnson also required Confederate soldiers to take an oath of allegiance before being discharged.[109]) The role of suspension also implicated this uneasy tension. On the authority of the *Prize Cases*, one could certainly argue suspension was unnecessary to hold enemy soldiers as prisoners of war. But, as explored above, the Civil War suspensions, whether proclaimed by the president or Congress, encompassed Confederate "prisoners of war" within their terms. In so doing, they followed the model established during the Revolutionary War, when the British enacted a series of suspensions to hold American rebels in such a posture.

The Civil War also raised questions about the relationship between martial law and suspension. In many of the areas that saw the worst of the war and accordingly witnessed the greatest number of arrests of Confederate soldiers, martial law prevailed because civilian courts had been shuttered as a result of the war.[110] As a pre-Civil War opinion by Attorney General Caleb Cushing had described it, a proclamation of martial law "must be regarded as the statement of an existing fact, rather than the legal creation of that fact" and follows where "civil authority has become suspended . . . by the force of circumstances."[111] (Martial law is discussed further in Chapter 10.) Indeed, without functioning courts, a suspension could be viewed as superfluous. Further, in practice, the Lincoln administration often referred to suspension and martial law interchangeably.[112] But where courts were open and functioning, no one—not even the "Great Suspender"—questioned the need for a suspension to detain persons deemed to owe allegiance outside the criminal process.

BECAUSE THE UNION was not entirely consistent in its treatment of those who aligned with and supported the Confederacy, reasonable people can disagree about the extent to which the Civil War period provides insights into broader questions of the meaning and application of the Suspension Clause. Further, the scale and devastation of the Civil War was unprecedented in many respects. Regardless, there is much to learn from studying the Civil War period. Perhaps the most significant lesson is that even in the face of the direst of circumstances, the formal understanding held by the president and Congress of the relationship between the privilege and the suspension power remained overwhelmingly consistent with that which the Founding generation imported from English tradition. Specifically, where it was believed that allegiance remained unbroken in the eyes of the law and where courts remained open, President Lincoln and Congress held fast to the position that it was only by a suspension that the president lawfully could claim the power to detain persons owing allegiance as so-called "prisoners of war" or "for State reasons"—namely, outside the criminal process. To be sure, that position did not always hold in related contexts, including the application of military law to civilians. But here it was understood, as one contemporary commentator explained, that "[w]hen the term of suspension has passed, the right to apply for the Writ, or the privilege or benefit of the Writ revives; and any one in confinement, who has not been tried, may demand it, in order to bail or trial."[113] In the end, despite the myriad legal complications posed by the horrors of the Civil War, it should not be surprising that Lincoln and Congress worked within the Suspension Clause framework. After all, the Clause's express terms list "Rebellion" as one of only two justifications for a suspension.

8

Liberty in the Shadow Constitution

SUSPENSION AND THE CONFEDERACY

Must the independence for which we are contending, the
safety of the defenseless families of the men who have fallen
in battle and of those who still confront the invader, be put in
peril for the sake of conformity to the technicalities of the law
of treason?

JEFFERSON DAVIS TO THE CONGRESS OF THE
CONFEDERATE STATES OF AMERICA (1864)[1]

WITH THEIR DEPARTURE from the Union, the secessionist states formed
the Confederate States of America and adopted their own Constitution,
importing much of the U.S. Constitution verbatim. There were, however,
notable and important differences between the two constitutions. To begin,
the Confederate Constitution was replete with references to slavery and provisions protecting the rights of slaveholders. To take another example, the
Confederate Constitution limited its president to one six-year term. But the
Confederate Constitution's Suspension Clause mirrored its counterpart in
the U.S. Constitution word for word. The same was true with respect to the
Confederate Constitution's Treason Clause, with the obvious change in reference to the Confederate States as opposed to the United States.[2] Notably, the
Confederate Constitution copied and moved the first eight amendments of
the U.S. Constitution's Bill of Rights alongside the Suspension Clause and
other provisions in Article I, Section 9, lending support to Founding-era and
Marshall Court declarations that the clauses in Article I, Section 9 comprised
a partial bill of rights.

Some might question the relevance of the Confederacy's experience with
the privilege. It is told here in an effort to shed additional light on the working understandings that informed how both sides conceived of the privilege
during the Civil War period. As legal scholar David Currie once observed,
the Confederate Constitution "provides a tailor-made subject of comparative

Habeas Corpus in Wartime. Amanda L. Tyler.

study; a source of alternative interpretation of often identical terms."[3] In this regard, studying the Confederate experience with the privilege and suspension in wartime proves a highly fruitful exercise. As explored here, the Confederate experience provides further evidence that English legal tradition heavily influenced the understanding of the constitutional privilege and suspension that controlled during the Civil War period. Just as in the North, the South viewed suspension as a necessary predicate to detaining persons outside the criminal process. Further, in keeping with the ratification debates and the decisions of the Marshall and Taney Courts, the Confederacy recognized the English Habeas Corpus Act as the foundation of the American constitutional privilege. Likewise, consistent with the majority view in Ex parte *Milligan*, the dominant view in the Confederacy did not view suspension as a justification for military trials. There was, however, one notable exception to the consistency in the stories between the North and South with respect to suspension—namely, a difference in views over which branch of government possesses the power to suspend. Throughout the war, Confederate president Jefferson Davis never once questioned that the power resided in the Confederate Congress.

Davis took office as provisional president of the Confederate States in 1861. After being elected to that office later that year, his inauguration followed on February 22, 1862 (the anniversary of George Washington's birthday). In his inaugural address, Davis decried the Union for "a long course of class legislation, directed not to the general welfare, but to the aggrandizement of the Northern section of the Union" and the North's actions that "threatened to destroy the sovereign rights of the States." The Confederate States, Davis claimed, would "better secure the liberties for the preservation of which that Union was established." Davis criticized the "malignity and barbarity of the Northern States in the prosecution of the existing war," and he particularly condemned the Union's "disregard . . . for all the time-honored bulwarks of civil and religious liberty." To support his aspersions, he cited so-called "[b]astiles filled with prisoners, arrested without civil process or indictment duly found" and the fact that "the writ of *habeas corpus* [was] suspended by Executive mandate."[4] Rebuking the North's supposed lesser devotion to civil liberties—and particularly President Lincoln's proclivity to suspend the privilege—was common practice in the South. Along these lines, Confederate newspapers regularly labeled the U.S. government despotic. What made it so? The papers asserted: "One thing, and one thing alone—the *suspension of the writ of habeas corpus.*"[5]

In his inaugural address, Davis also contrasted the Confederacy with the Union, claiming that his government had done nothing "to impair personal liberty or the freedom of speech, of thought, or of the press." Further, he emphasized, in the South, "[t]he courts have been open, the judicial functions fully executed, and every right of the peaceful citizen maintained as securely as if a war of invasion had not disturbed the land."[6] This statement glossed over the fact that military arrests were already part of the Confederate experience.[7] In all events, such grandstanding would not last in the face of the realities of the unfolding war.

Suspension Comes to the Confederacy

Only five days after Davis made these remarks, the Confederate Congress passed its first suspension legislation. The Act of February 27, 1862, empowered Davis to suspend habeas corpus and declare martial law in those areas witnessing the worst of the war. Drafted in response to "th[e] present invasion of the Confederate States," the legislation declared that "the President shall have power to suspend the privilege of the writ of *habeas corpus* in such towns, cities, and military districts as shall, in his judgment, be in such danger of attack by the enemy as to require the declaration of martial law for their effective defence."[8]

Starting that same day and spanning the next few weeks, Davis declared martial law in several areas of Virginia, including the capital city of Richmond, as well as East Tennessee and portions of South Carolina. In every case, he also proclaimed a suspension of the privilege.[9] To counter the threat of invasion, Davis's Virginia proclamations targeted several counties bordering the Chesapeake Bay. In Richmond, military officials received orders from the War Department to "imprison all persons against whom there is well-grounded suspicion of disloyalty."[10] The more general effect of Davis's orders was to displace civil government in large measure with military rule, drastically limiting the domain of civilian courts.[11] Additional suspensions and presidentially-authorized proclamations of martial law followed in other states over the next few months.[12] Meanwhile, several controversial declarations of martial law by military generals in other locations led the War Department to instruct generals in August 1862 that they had no authority to declare martial law or suspend the privilege absent presidential orders.[13]

Considering how Confederate public debates had disparaged Lincoln for his "despotic" suspension proclamations, unsurprisingly Davis's imposition of martial law and suspension proved deeply controversial on the home front.[14] By March 1862, a member of the Confederate Congress had moved "to secure the rights of the public and of individuals without a general suspension of the habeas corpus."[15] Additional detractors emerged, and this chorus likely contributed to Davis's reluctance to expand his early proclamations of martial law and suspension into new areas.

By April—only two months after enacting the original suspension legislation—the Confederate Congress scaled back the powers that it had vested in Davis. Specifically, it passed "An Act to limit the Act authorizing the suspension of the Writ of Habeas Corpus." By its terms, the new legislation provided that the prior authorization was "hereby limited to arrests made by the authorities of the Confederate Government, or for offences against the same." The Congress also added a sunset provision, providing that the prior authorization "shall continue in force for thirty days after the next meeting of Congress, and no longer."[16] In the wake of this limiting legislation, the executive declared additional proclamations of suspension, including one in North Carolina in June and one in Atlanta in September.[17]

In the waning days of this first suspension period, concerns over the sweep and effect of martial law led the House Judiciary Committee to prepare an extensive report on the subject. Although the Report recognized that Davis had "used this power with exemplary moderation," it nonetheless concluded that because "the phrase 'martial law' is, at best, ambiguous . . . , it is wiser in our legislation to substitute for it such positive regulations as may be deemed necessary." In discussing the difference between martial law and suspension, the Report highlighted the prevailing view that

> to suspend th[e] writ is not to establish martial law with its summary proceedings and absolute power. Although, when the writ is suspended the citizen may be restrained of his liberty, he can be tried and punished only according to the laws of the land.[18]

Thus, the House Report, like the Supreme Court's decision in Ex parte *Milligan*, posited that suspension could not justify summary criminal proceedings. It also suggested that martial law poses a greater threat to civil liberties than suspension.[19] Surely aware that widespread sentiment against martial law was brewing on the ground and in the Congress, Davis issued General Order No. 66 in September on the eve of issuance of the House Report. The Order "annulled all proclamations of martial law by military commanders."[20] Ultimately, the Report recommended that the suspension legislation be permitted to lapse in September, and the Confederate Congress followed that course.

Within a matter of weeks, however, the Confederate Congress enacted new suspension legislation. Adopted in October 1862, this legislation combined the terms of the original suspension authorization and its clarifying legislation. The concerns set forth in the House Report of a month earlier likely explain why the new statute did not expressly confer the authority to "declar[e] . . . martial law," as the original suspension legislation had. Still, this second suspension broadly empowered the Confederate president "to suspend the privilege of the writ of habeas corpus in any city, town, or military district, whenever in his judgment the public safety may require it." As with the earlier clarifying legislation tethered to the first suspension authorization, this Act provided that suspension only applied "to arrests made by the authorities of the Confederate Government, or for offences against the same."[21]

Because the second suspension, like its predecessor, granted Davis broad authority to determine when circumstances justified suspension, some, including David Currie, have questioned its legality. As he viewed the matter, "Congress appeared to have handed the President its entire power to decide—raising a serious question, one might have thought, of the delegation of the legislative authority."[22] There are striking similarities between this Act and the Union Congress's 1863 suspension act, which granted Lincoln the power to suspend the privilege "whenever, in his judgment, the public safety may require it." Also similar is the Reconstruction-era suspension passed by Congress, discussed in the next chapter, which included an almost identical authorization. Currie's concerns would seem to apply equally to those suspensions.

As events unfolded, reports suggest that President Davis invoked his powers under the October 1862 suspension legislation "very sparingly,"[23] although it did not take long for one sweep of arrests of persons suspected of disloyalty in North Carolina to trigger protests from that state's governor.[24] Davis was also clearly mindful of the distinction between martial law and suspension, as well as his military commanders' inability to appreciate the same. Accordingly, during this period, the War Department issued a directive emphasizing, just as the earlier House Report had done, that suspension "is not to be considered as authorizing the trial by military courts of civilians for the offenses committed, but only as holding them in duress for those offenses."[25] As noted, this position was consistent both with historical emphasis on differentiating the two concepts and the majority holding that emerged in *Milligan*. (It was, however, entirely at odds with the position advanced by the Johnson administration in *Milligan*, which argued that suspension *does* legitimate military trial.)[26]

Davis also complied with requirements in the October 1862 legislation that he institute procedures for reviewing detentions ordered under the suspension to ensure that they fell within the terms of the statute. Specifically, the second section of the Act required that the president "cause proper officers to investigate the cases of all persons so arrested; in order that they may be discharged, if improperly detained, unless they can be speedily tried in due course of law."[27] This language is notable for providing that trial "in due course of law" should remain the goal behind arrests. In all events, this requirement led to the formalization of internal review procedures that had already been established by the Confederate War Department.[28]

As is suggested by the statute's required review of arrests, throughout this period, suspension and martial law remained deeply controversial in the Confederacy. For this reason, the Confederate Congress permitted the second suspension to lapse five months after its passage, on February 11, 1863, and declined to adopt new authorizing legislation in its place. (A bill to extend the suspension, sent to committee, received no action.[29]) The timing of the change in course in the South is noteworthy, coming as it did shortly before the U.S. Congress finally passed suspension legislation in the North. For the next year, while President Lincoln enjoyed congressional authorization to suspend the privilege and proclaimed a nationwide suspension, Davis enjoyed no suspension authority and endured repeated and hostile legislative inquiries into the impact of military operations on civil liberties.[30]

The Final Confederate Suspension

The following year, Davis again requested suspension legislation from his Congress. Davis's remarks at the time shed considerable light on the contemporary understanding of how suspension and the law of treason functioned in the Confederate Constitution. As Davis argued, the power to suspend was necessary to address "citizens of well-known disloyalty" seeking to "accomplish treason under form of the law." The problem, as he described matters, was that "through too strict regard to the technicalities of the law," such persons must "be permitted to go at large till they have perfected their treason by the commission of an overt act." Even then, he continued, "the evidence is often unattainable because within the enemy's lines." He lamented: "Again and again such persons have been arrested, and as often they have been discharged by the civil authorities, because the Government could not procure testimony from within the lines of the enemy." Davis went on to cite specific cases in which, because of such failings, persons aiding the enemy had nonetheless been "discharged on habeas corpus," rendering it pointless for the government to arrest known spies against which appropriate evidence could not be collected.[31] (Here, Davis was referring to activities in North Carolina, among other places.[32]) Finally, Davis decried that certain well-known judges had issued writs directed at military officials to produce soldiers seeking to avoid conscription and, in one case, summoned a commandant away from his command to appear.[33] Davis argued that suspension was the appropriate remedy for such "threatening evils," and he believed that it was the Congress's "duty" to respond accordingly. Observing that "history contains no parallel case," Davis concluded by invoking English history to contend that the present conditions were far worse than those "repeatedly" cited as justification for suspension in that country.[34]

Having received Davis's message while meeting in secret session, the Confederate Congress responded by enacting a third and final suspension statute in February 1864. Significantly, this legislation read very differently from its predecessors. To begin, in its preamble, the Act declared that "the power of suspending the privilege of said writ, as recognized in said article first, is vested solely in the Congress, which is the exclusive judge of the necessity of such suspension."[35] In other words, by the Act, the Confederate Congress did what the U.S. Congress would not do—it expressly rejected President Lincoln's position that the executive possesses the unilateral power to suspend. The statute also sounded a retreat from the delegation model that had informed earlier Confederate suspensions as well as the 1863 Act in the North. Specifically, instead of delegating to the executive the ultimate decision when and where to impose a state of suspension, the statute suspended the privilege outright throughout the Confederacy. In rejecting a delegation model, the final Confederate suspension mirrored that passed by the Senate (though not the House) during the Burr Conspiracy.

Despite its geographic breadth, the third Confederate suspension limited the kinds of arrests outside the criminal process that it authorized. Covered cases included arrests of persons suspected of treason, aiding the enemy, fostering insurrection, spying, and trading with the enemy. The list also included those aiding prisoners of war in the custody of the Confederate military, "advising or inciting others to abandon the Confederate cause," deserting from military service "or encouraging desertions, of harboring deserters, and . . . attempt[ing] to avoid military service."[36] This list underscores that draft resistance was a major impetus for this suspension.[37] Indeed, Davis heralded the legislation for "preventing the abuse of the writ for the purpose of avoiding military service by men whose plain duty it is to defend their country."[38]

Likely also to curtail the scope of military arrests, the Act limited its coverage to "cases of persons arrested or detained by order of the President, Secretary of War, or the general officer commanding the Trans-Mississippi Military Department." Further, like the second suspension, the third required that the president set up internal procedures to investigate cases and release persons "improperly detained."[39] Finally, the legislation again included a sunset provision, providing that its authorization would lapse after six months.[40]

Notably, the original version of the bill made clear that "the purpose of Congress in the passage of this act is to provide more effectually for the public safety, by the restraint of persons, even when the proof is not complete, and when the ordinary process of law is insufficient for the public safety. . . ."[41] Here, one finds yet more evidence that it remained the settled understanding of suspension that its purpose was to empower the executive to detain persons outside the criminal process and relieve the government from the obligations imposed by that process, including the provision of a timely trial on specific charges with sufficient evidence to sustain both an arrest and ultimately a conviction. Even so, in implementing internal procedures for reviewing arrests under this suspension, the War Department instructed its appointed commissioners to turn prisoners over for prosecution to federal or state courts if prosecution appeared "as efficient and convenient a mode of redress" as detention without charges.[42] This policy likely followed in part from the controversial status of suspension in the Confederacy. In all events, it reveals a very different approach than that followed in the North during the war.

Ending Suspension in the Confederacy

With the 1864 suspension set to lapse on August 1, 1864, Davis urged the Confederate Congress to extend it. Davis argued that "it would be perilous, if not calamitous, to discontinue the suspension," which he maintained had been "so effectual" in achieving its objectives, including "restraining those who were engaged in treasonable practices and in dangerous complicity with our enemies." (Davis also claimed that he had ordered "very few" arrests under the 1864 suspension.[43]) A Majority Report from the Confederate House Judiciary Committee also supported extending the Act and offers additional insights into contemporary thinking regarding the privilege. In particular, the Report traced the origins of the Confederate Constitution's privilege to the English Habeas Corpus Act of 1679.[44] The Report further recognized that the "obvious purpose" behind guaranteeing that privilege in the Constitution "is to tie the hands of the Executive and make the judiciary paramount in questions affecting the restraint of persons." Only when "a rebellion or invasion occurs, and . . . the legislature, if the public safety requires it," suspends the privilege, will that "release executive power from judicial control, so far as the writ of *habeas corpus* is an instrument of control." Further, the Report observed that although the 1864 suspension Act did not, "in direct terms, empower [the President] or any other officer to order arrests," it "may fairly be construed . . . as legalizing the orders."[45] Notably, the Report took pains to emphasize that a role remained for the courts even during periods of suspension—specifically, it observed, "the question of the constitutionality of the act" could not "be withdrawn by any action of the Executive or of Congress" from judicial evaluation.[46] As will be seen in Chapter 10, some federal courts agreed and reviewed the propriety of the suspension that governed in the Hawaiian Territory during World War II.

Despite Davis's appeal, the Confederate Congress permitted the third suspension to lapse. Nor did the Congress pass legislation when Davis sought a suspension in November 1864 and again in March 1865, despite the House sending the bills forward. (Both bills failed in the Senate.[47]) In calling for the latter bill, Davis deemed suspension as "not simply advisable and expedient, but almost indispensable to the successful conduct of the war."[48]

Davis's inability to bring along the Confederate Congress likely stemmed from the fact that by 1864, suspension and martial law had become rallying points both for critics who charged Davis's administration with military despotism and those who more generally opposed the administration, the war, or both. As one historian wrote of the period, it was "one of the bitterest, and in some respects most disastrous, conflicts of the whole war between Confederate and state authorities."[49] War weariness and collapsing morale in the Confederacy also loomed large in the background.[50] State officials and several state legislatures opposed suspension, often calling it unconstitutional. One of the most fertile grounds for such criticism was Georgia, where its General Assembly passed a resolution in March 1864 "declaring the late act of Congress for the suspension of the writ of habeas corpus unconstitutional."[51] This resolution followed on the heels of a three-hour speech given before the Assembly by Confederate Vice President Alexander Stephens in which he condemned the February 1864 suspension as "unwise, impolitic and unconstitutional" and "exceedingly dangerous to public liberty." Stephens, a leading antagonist of the president, equated the suspension with "tending toward a dictatorship in this country."[52] North Carolina, Mississippi, Alabama, and Louisiana leveled similar criticism of the administration, with additional legislatures passing resolutions condemning suspension.[53]

This period marked the final decline of the Confederacy. Although the reasons for its ultimate defeat were many and have provoked volumes of writing, the extensive and prominent dissention over various war measures, including martial law and suspension, clearly reflected larger problems of internal discord among the Confederate States. These problems in turn played at least some role in the Confederacy's ultimate downfall.[54]

In total, the Confederate Congress delegated President Davis suspension authority on two occasions and suspended outright on a third, for a combined seventeen months, with the final suspension lapsing in August 1864.[55] The total length of time stands in dramatic contrast to suspension in the North, where President Lincoln proclaimed suspensions (first without, and later with, congressional approval) throughout the war. Following from this fact, Confederate records suggest that the number of political prisoners arrested during periods of suspension were far fewer than in the North.[56] Historian Mark Neely has argued, however, that the statistics are misleading and that in the Confederacy, "liberty was more severely restricted for longer periods and over larger areas than mere legislative history suggests."[57]

Comparing Two Constitutions and Two Approaches to War

As a contemporaneous point of comparison to President Lincoln, it is noteworthy that Davis never acted ahead of his Congress in suspending the privilege—apparently believing that he could not do so.[58] Likewise, the Confederate Congress went on record to reject the assertion that the executive could suspend the privilege unilaterally. Also unlike Lincoln, Davis went to his Congress every time he sought a suspension and, like Thomas Jefferson decades earlier, acquiesced when his Congress denied him the authority to suspend. Thus, the Confederate experience further undermines Lincoln's arguments defending a unilateral presidential power to suspend.

More generally, the contrasting approaches of the two presidents reflect different approaches to waging war. As discussed in the last chapter, Lincoln believed that he had to act swiftly to defend the capital and prevent important border states from joining the Confederacy. Davis, by contrast, had heralded the Confederate government as more respectful of civil liberties than the Union government. Doing so followed from Davis's need to play "salesman" to advance the cause of the Confederacy and attract border states and international recognition of the Confederate government.[59] The result, for better or worse, was that the Confederacy witnessed far less sweeping proclamations of suspension and martial law, both geographically and temporally, than the North.

Also noteworthy is the Confederate Congress's decision to cease delegating decisions regarding the imposition and scope of suspension to the president when it revisited suspension in 1864. This change of course may have resulted in part from the influence of several prominent officials who argued that the Congress could not legally delegate any aspect of the suspension decision to the executive. This group included former Mississippi supreme court justice William Sharkey and Vice President Alexander Stephens.[60] Stephens had argued before the Georgia Legislature that "Congress alone, under the constitution, has the power to suspend the privileges of the writ. They cannot confer this power upon the President or anybody else."[61] This was also the position set forth in the House Judiciary Committee's Minority Report opposing the extension of the 1864 suspension.[62]

Studying this distinction, David Currie argues that direct legislative suspension in the Confederacy "proved a far blunter tool and far more destructive of liberty than if Congress had empowered the President, as before, to suspend the writ selectively on a finding of need." Continuing, Currie observes that the fact that the third Confederate suspension "contained no geographic limitation" meant that it could be read to suspend across the Confederacy, which "arguably was more than the public safety could reasonably be thought to require."[63] Either way, it is not at all clear that one approach is necessarily more protective of liberty than the other. After all, Congress's delegation of the suspension authority to President Lincoln during the Civil War also resulted in a sweeping nationwide suspension. As explored in the next chapter, it was not until Reconstruction that a delegation of the suspension power resulted in the kind of on-the-ground responsiveness that marked the early days of Lincoln's unilateral proclamations and Davis's initial proclamations under the first Confederate suspension.

Another interesting point of comparison during the Civil War period relates to the courts' role in times of war, and specifically to the important question whether state courts could direct habeas writs to federal officials. In the North, decisions spanning the period immediately preceding the Civil War through Reconstruction developed the principle that state courts lacked the authority to command federal officials to submit returns to habeas writs. Starting with the fugitive slave case of *Ableman v. Booth* and culminating in a conscription challenge brought in *Tarble's Case*, the Supreme Court held that state courts may not inquire into the custody of persons held "under the authority, or claim and color of the authority, of the United States, by an officer of that government."[64] These decisions are in tension with the fact that many state courts had exercised such jurisdiction since the Founding period.[65] (Indeed, as discussed in Chapter 6, the New York courts issued writs of habeas corpus to federal officials during the War of 1812 and Maryland's chief justice discharged two suspected Burr conspirators from federal custody at Fort McHenry during the Jefferson administration.[66]) Today, the holding in *Tarble's Case* remains the subject of debate. Specifically, it is unclear whether its preclusion of state court jurisdiction to issue writs to federal officers was predicated upon constitutional limitations sounding in federalism or instead constituted an interpretation of the grant of habeas jurisdiction to federal courts as impliedly exclusive of the state courts.[67]

A similar debate waged in the South over the power of state courts to issue writs running to Confederate officials. In the Confederacy, where most of the adult male population was drafted for military service, countless petitioners sought relief in habeas proceedings by claiming to fall within various exemptions to the conscription laws, laws that the Confederate Congress continually updated and expanded. Although Confederate district courts had supplanted the formerly operating U.S. district courts in Confederate States,[68] many petitioners went to the state courts, targeting judges well known for granting relief. Because, moreover, a Confederate Supreme Court never came into being, any victory achieved in the state courts was final.

In keeping with the holding in *Tarble's Case*, some in the South believed that the state courts could not issue writs to federal officers. Further, as one historian who surveyed the habeas cases of this period concluded, in "most" matters, state courts respected that a suspension extinguished judicial authority to review any case plainly falling within its terms.[69] But a number of state courts and judges subscribed to the position that it was well within their power to issue writs to Confederate officials, particularly in cases of contested conscription. In one such case, the Georgia Supreme Court concluded:

> Where the power of imprisonment is exercised by one claiming authority, other than judicial, under an Act of Congress, within the limits of a State, any magistrate of that State having authority to issue the writ of *habeas corpus* may inquire into its legality, and even military officers are not exempt from this jurisdiction, but owe obedience to the final judgment.[70]

In the same decision, the Georgia Supreme Court emphasized that the preamble to the Confederate Constitution preserved the role of "each State acting in its sovereign and independent character" along with the obligation of states to their citizens for "protection against illegal restraint of their personal liberty."[71] The Court also pointed to a decision binding federal officers issued by celebrated scholar and New York jurist James Kent during the War of 1812.[72]

Accordingly, it was not uncommon for state judges to grant discharge requests from petitioners challenging their conscription, even in the face of a suspension.[73] Further, some state court decisions granted relief to persons detained by Confederate officers as suspected traitors.[74] The most notable state court decisions came out of North Carolina, and they came from the pen of that state's chief justice, Richmond Pearson. Pearson was not only legendary for routinely issuing writs against Confederate officials (with one commentator remarking that he "discharged man after man from the army" and another saying that Pearson's action rendered the Confederate conscription laws "almost a nullity in North Carolina"[75]), he regularly did so during periods of suspension. This followed from Pearson's view that suspension legislation could not reach cases of contested conscription under any circumstances. Thus, in one such case, Pearson concluded that a suspension could not apply to a petitioner who had filed "an application for a civil remedy" (namely, relief from conscription) and had not been "charged with the commission of, or an intention to commit, any crime." In Pearson's view, it was "perfectly clear that the clause of the Constitution giving power to Congress to suspend the writ of *habeas corpus* refers only to the writ of *habeas corpus ad subjiciendum* when a person stands committed or detained as a prisoner for a crime within [the terms of the English Habeas Corpus Act], and does not include other writs." Continuing, Pearson cited Parliament's Revolutionary War suspension and observed that "[n]o precedent can be found among the rolls of Parliament, where the suspension has ever been made to extend to civil cases or the writs used in such cases."[76] In another case, Pearson also labeled suspension as "an act in derogation of common right" that should be "construed strictly" in favor of the habeas petitioner.[77] Many of these decisions were decided in chambers, as was common for that court during the period.[78] In time, Pearson's two colleagues went on record to reject his position, concluding instead that courts were bound to respect the Congress's criminalization of the avoidance of military duty and enactment of a suspension encompassing such cases.[79]

In the North, state courts increasingly hesitated to interfere in federal conscription matters.[80] It surely helped that Congress provided in the 1863 suspension legislation for removal to federal court of suits brought against federal officers in state courts.[81] But even in the face of the 1863 Act's terms, some border state courts resisted removal of habeas proceedings more generally, and at least one state's legislature passed laws forbidding its judges from honoring removals.[82] As for the question whether any Northern court outside the border states openly disregarded the nationwide suspension in a conscription case on the basis of Chief Justice Pearson's reasoning, research has failed to uncover any examples.[83] Indeed, although Pearson was not off base in observing that pre-Ratification English suspensions were not designed to facilitate conscription but instead more generally to target the disloyal, his colleague Justice Matthias Evans Manly was probably correct to focus instead on the long-standing link between suspension and alleged criminal conduct more generally, a link that was at the heart of the seventh section of the English Habeas Corpus Act. The real question presented in such cases, Justice Manly argued, is whether the legislature had the power to criminalize avoidance of conscription in the first place, which, he concluded, it did.[84] (Notably, some took the opposite position during the war, including the Pennsylvania Supreme Court.[85])

One final point of comparison between the North and South merits highlighting. Throughout the war, the Confederate Congress pushed back consistently against declarations, and broad definitions, of martial law. In so doing, the Confederate Congress, unlike its counterpart in the North,[86] never formally approved of the military trial of civilians.[87] Beyond the lack of congressional action on this score, one prominent opinion issued by Acting Attorney General Wade Keys in November 1863 concluded that under the Articles of War, civilians charged with treason must be tried in civilian courts.[88] But as is common in times of war, exceptions may be found. In particular, Secretary of War Judah Benjamin blurred the distinction between those subject to the law of treason and prisoners of war, and ordered military trials of civilians for violations of the laws of war.[89] It was not uncommon, moreover, for native civilians arrested for acts of disloyalty to be treated as having sided with the Union at the time of secession, permitting their classification by Confederate officials as enemy aliens.[90] In this respect, the blurring of the lines of allegiance by Confederate authorities reflected practices in the North and underscores the extraordinary pressures that war places on deeply enshrined constitutional principles.

In short order, piecing the Union back together would place similar pressures on the Constitution in its soon-to-be expanded form.

9

Reconstructing the Union and Suspending in the Name of Civil Rights

The effects of the late civil strife have been to free the slave and make him a citizen. Yet he is not possessed of the civil rights which citizenship should carry with it. This is wrong, and should be corrected. To this correction I stand committed, so far as Executive influence can avail.

ULYSSES S. GRANT, SECOND INAUGURAL ADDRESS (1783)[1]

AS THE BATTLEFIELDS of the Civil War smoldered, the job of reconstructing the Union began. As part of that effort, lessons hard learned during the preceding period called upon the Constitution to play a new role. As originally drafted, the founding document had focused almost exclusively on the potential of the new federal government to infringe upon individual liberties. The Civil War and the spotlight that it put on sectional politics and slavery, however, had taught that states as well as individuals posed their own threat to those very liberties. Thus came the Thirteenth, Fourteenth, and Fifteenth Amendments, ratified in 1865, 1868, and 1870, respectively. The Thirteenth prohibited slavery and involuntary servitude and gave Congress the power to enforce its mandate.[2] The Fourteenth promised citizenship to "[a]ll persons born or naturalized in the United States" and commanded that "[n]o State . . . shall abridge the privileges or immunities of citizens . . . ; nor . . . deprive any person of life, liberty, or property, without due process of law; nor deny to any person within its jurisdiction the equal protection of the laws." As with the other Reconstruction Amendments, here too the Constitution expressly vested Congress with an enforcement power.[3] Finally, the Fifteenth guaranteed that the "right of the citizens . . . to vote shall not be denied or abridged by the United States or by any State on account of race, color, or previous condition of servitude."[4] In the years following the Civil War, these profound alterations to

Habeas Corpus in Wartime. Amanda L. Tyler.
© Oxford University Press 2017. Published 2017 by Oxford University Press.

the original compact met dramatic resistance in many portions of the country that had once comprised the Confederacy.

As is explored below, this resistance led the victorious Union general-turned-president Ulysses S. Grant to request a suspension from his Congress in order to infiltrate the Ku Klux Klan and combat Klan violence. Studying the Reconstruction period reveals that the understanding of the constitutional privilege and suspension remained consistent with Anglo-American legal tradition. In carrying out the suspension on the ground, military officers employed their expanded powers to engage in preventive detention of Klan members and to protect the new civil rights enshrined in the Reconstruction Amendments. By the same token, everyone understood that with the lapsing of the suspension, no one could be held outside the criminal process. The Reconstruction period also underscores the continuing influence of the English Habeas Corpus Act on American constitutional habeas jurisprudence. Notably, however, the Reconstruction period tells a very different narrative about the ends to which the suspension power may be wielded—namely, the advancement of civil rights.

The Rise of Klan Violence

In the wake of the Civil War, in many parts of the South—particularly northern counties in South Carolina—the Ku Klux Klan had become a domestic terrorist organization of tremendous consequence. Klan violence in certain areas was shocking in its scope and brutality. Night riders engaged in scores of murders, whippings, attacks, and rapes of African Americans and more generally anyone who opposed the organization. These routine occurrences met little if any resistance or prosecution from local authorities.[5] To advance its reign of terror, the Klan targeted anyone who dared to testify against its members and also controlled many arms of local government, rendering some Southern states "unable to provide even the semblance of criminal law enforcement."[6] The Klan also wielded considerable influence on at least some federal courts in the South and they controlled many of the wires by which federal officials communicated in the region.[7] As Attorney General Amos T. Akerman reported to Congress, "[i]n some parts of the country . . . [Klan] operations have been marked by an atrocity that is without precedent in the previous history of the United States."[8]

This state of affairs led President Grant in March 1871 to "urgently recommend" emergency legislation for two reasons. First, he argued that "the power to correct these evils is beyond the control of the State authorities." Second, Grant maintained that it was "not clear" whether "the power of the

Executive of the United States, acting within the limits of existing laws, is sufficient for present emergencies. . . ."[9] Congress responded with what came to be known as the Ku Klux Klan Act of 1871, the third in a series of important legislative initiatives aimed at supporting the new Reconstruction Amendments.

The Act's first section created a civil cause of action for "any person" deprived by a state actor of "any rights, privileges, or immunities secured by the Constitution."[10] Today, this important civil rights provision is codified at 42 U.S.C. § 1983. The second and fifth sections of the Act criminalized a range of conduct threatening civil rights.[11] The third and fourth sections responded to Grant's request by giving him potent new enforcement powers. Specifically, the Act's third section empowered the executive to employ "the militia or the land and naval forces of the United States" to suppress "insurrection[s], domestic violence, or combinations." The Act's fourth section authorized the executive, "when in his judgment the public safety shall require it, to suspend the privileges of the writ of habeas corpus" in order to put down any "rebellion" orchestrated by "unlawful combinations" and designed to "overthrow or set at defiance the constituted authorities. . . ." The Act defined "unlawful combinations" to encompass, among other things, those designed to oppose the government or to interfere with the enjoyment of the rights secured by the Reconstruction Amendments. Underscoring the long-standing view that suspension was necessary to detain outside the criminal process, the Act's terms provided that suspension could be invoked only with respect to a district in which "the conviction of . . . offenders and the preservation of the public safety shall become . . . impracticable."[12]

At the same time, Congress strictly cabined the emergency powers that it had just conferred upon the executive. Specifically, the 1871 Act required that prior to suspending habeas in any jurisdiction, the president must order insurgents to disperse, a requirement that Grant honored as events unfolded. Congress also provided that the suspension authorization would lapse at the end of its next regular session, thereby ensuring that any extension of the authority would require reauthorization. (This sunset provision may have been influenced by Congress's omission of a sunset provision in the Civil War suspension, discussed in Chapter 7, which left that suspension in place until President Johnson finally revoked the last of its geographic sweep in 1866—a full year after the Confederacy's surrender.) Finally, the Act incorporated the same conditions included in the 1863 Civil War suspension legislation, requiring that the executive furnish local courts with a list of prisoners and that all prisoners, unless labeled "prisoners of war," be discharged by the courts if not indicted by the next sitting grand jury.[13]

The debates over the legislation that became the 1871 Act took place in a highly partisan environment, yet participants uniformly appreciated the dramatic authority that the bill would grant the executive. Throughout the debates, both supporters and opponents of the bill equated suspension with placing "unbounded trust" in the executive's judgment and vesting him with broad discretion along with "tremendous power" over individual liberty.[14] The debates turned instead on two other issues. First, members of Congress argued over whether conditions in the South warranted such a dramatic course of action, with some contending that the language of Section 4 went beyond the requirement in the Suspension Clause of a "Rebellion or Invasion."[15] Second, they debated whether the bill unconstitutionally delegated the final decision whether to suspend to the president. On the latter point, supporters highlighted that the bill had been modeled on the 1863 Act, which had delegated the decision whether and where to suspend to President Lincoln.[16] Notably, during the debates over delegation, several members of Congress invoked Blackstone for the proposition that suspension was a parliamentary power, highlighting the continuing influence both of Blackstone and the English suspension model.[17]

Supporters defended the legislation as absolutely necessary to combat the Klan effectively and to "aid in the restoration of order [and] the protection of the citizen in the exercise of his civil and political rights."[18] They did not deny that suspension is "the last extreme remedy of the Constitution"[19] or that it confers on the executive "a most extraordinary power."[20] But, as Representative Oliver Snyder of Arkansas put it: "severe diseases require severe remedies, and when the disease exists, the sooner the remedy is applied the better."[21]

Fully aware of the potency of the authority vested in the president by the Act, members also conveyed how the Houses would respond in the event that the executive abused his newly-expanded powers. In particular, Representative John Bingham of Ohio declared that "[i]f the President violate[s] the discretionary powers vested in him the people by their Representatives [will] summon him to the bar of the Senate to answer [for his actions]...."[22] In the end, despite substantial opposition in the House, Congress passed the bill and the president signed it into law.

Suspension in South Carolina

President Grant referred to the third and fourth sections of the Act as conferring upon him "extraordinary powers" that he would invoke only "reluctant[ly]" and "in cases of imperative necessity ... for the purpose of securing to all citizens ... enjoyment of the rights guaranteed to them by the Constitution and laws."[23] By the fall of 1871, spurred by reports of "lawlessness and terror" in South Carolina, Grant dispatched Attorney General Akerman to survey existing conditions. Akerman was a curious choice for the job, given that he had served in the Georgia State Guard during the Civil War and was the only southerner to reach cabinet rank during Reconstruction.[24] He was nonetheless deeply committed to his task. He reported back to the president on the total control that the Klan wielded over areas of the state, the extensive violence in the area, and the Klan's success at "depriving the emancipated class of the equal protection of the laws." He also proclaimed that the Klan's actions "amount[ed] to war" and could not "be effectively crushed on any other theory."[25]

As he prepared to invoke his emergency powers, President Grant sent a report to Congress detailing what Akerman and others has told him about the Klan's dominance in South Carolina. As the president described the state of affairs, the Klan sought

> by force and terror, to prevent all political action not in accord with [its] views . . . , to deprive colored citizens of the right to bear arms and of the right to a free ballot, to suppress schools in which colored children were taught, and to reduce the colored people to a condition closely akin to that of slavery; [and the Klan] had rendered the local law ineffectual . . . ; [and] they had perpetrated many murders and hundreds of crimes of minor degree, all of which were unpunished; and . . . witnesses could not safely testify against them unless the more active members were placed under restraint.[26]

Armed with his expanded powers under the 1871 Act but knowing that he did not have sufficient forces to blanket the South, Grant followed the advice of Akerman and military leaders to concentrate efforts on South Carolina and a key Klan stronghold in its upcountry.[27] Complying with the terms of the Act, Grant first ordered Klan members in the area to disperse and turn over all weapons to federal authorities.[28] When unsurprisingly his proclamations went unheeded, Grant next "declare[d] that in [his] judgment the public safety especially requires that the privileges of the writ of *habeas corpus* be suspended, to the end that such rebellion may be overthrown." Specifically, Grant proclaimed the suspension of "the privileges of the writ of *habeas corpus*" in nine upcountry counties for "all persons arrested [by any federal officer] within any one of said counties, charged with any violation of the [1871 Act,] during the continuance of such rebellion."[29]

In the immediate wake of his proclamation, the president ordered military officials in the area, led by Major Lewis Merrill, to conduct widespread arrests of suspected Klan members. As one contemporary newspaper reported, Merrill "gathered up the Ku Klux by the dozen."[30] Akerman later described the arrests as "unavoidably summary and severe."[31] Merrill's aide, Louis Post, wrote that these arrests were "without warrant or specific accusation" of criminal conduct; instead, persons were targeted based solely on their "presume[d] members[hip]" in the Klan. Because Merrill was able to detain suspects without warrant or charges, his aide recounted that "confessions became quite the fashion as arrests multiplied." "For a time the prisoners were silent," Post wrote, "[b]ut as hope of release died out and fears of hanging grew stronger, the weaker ones sought permission to tell Major Merrill what they knew." From this testimony "developed evidence on which to make further arrests."[32] Within just a few months, Merrill's troops had arrested several hundred men suspected of Klan ties, while many others had surrendered.[33] Many of the Klan's leaders and worst offenders, however, had fled the area before the suspension proclamation and therefore escaped Merrill's sweeps.[34]

In time, a sizeable portion of those arrested were indicted on federal charges, typically violations of the criminal provisions in the 1871 Act. Others were released after telling Merrill all they knew. Still others were detained to serve as witnesses for the government in future prosecutions.[35] In the end, the government prosecuted only a handful of those who had been arrested in the sweeps. This followed for primarily two reasons. First, as the chief federal prosecutor in the area recognized, most of the criminal acts for which the government had indicted Klan members had occurred prior to 1871. Violations of the criminal provisions of the 1871 Act, however, could not be applied retroactively without running afoul of the Ex Post Facto Clause.[36] Second, as Attorney General Akerman reported to Congress, the federal courts in the area simply did not have the capacity to try all offenders in a timely fashion.[37]

This extraordinary show of military force by the federal government helped to restore some short-term measure of order in the area by the following year, or so Merrill reported early in 1872. It took only months, however, for Merrill himself to admit that this assessment had been "premature."[38] During this same period, a Senate Report took the position that without an extension of the 1871 Act's suspension authorization, federal efforts were unlikely to achieve any real change in the area. Nonetheless, Congress did not follow the Report's recommendation, allowing an extension bill to stall.[39] Meanwhile, a change in leadership at the Department of Justice brought a new policy of appeasement, culminating in the 1873 decision by President Grant to offer clemency to those Klan members who had not yet been tried and pardons to those who had been convicted in the wake of Merrill's sweeps.[40] It took little time for the Klan to regroup and return to its old ways.

Lessons from the Reconstruction Episode

The Reconstruction example confirms what earlier episodes of suspension had already demonstrated—namely, that suspension serves to expand the scope of executive authority to arrest and detain outside the criminal process. Simply put, Major Merrill had ordered arrests and detentions that would not have been lawful in the absence of the suspension. With the lapsing of the suspension, moreover, all appeared to understand that continuing detention turned entirely upon the criminal process. The Reconstruction period also witnessed the Supreme Court reaffirm that the English Habeas Corpus Act proved the basis of the Suspension Clause. Specifically, in a closely-watched habeas case that challenged Congress's Reconstruction legislation, Ex parte *Yerger*, the Court lauded the Habeas Corpus Act for "firmly guarantee[ing]" the "great writ." Continuing, the Court observed that the Act "was brought to America by the colonists, and claimed as among the immemorial rights descended to them from their ancestors," and that it was given "prominent sanction in the Constitution."[41]

The Reconstruction episode also stands as a second example of Congress delegating to the president the ultimate decision whether to invoke the suspension authority, just as it had during the Civil War. These examples therefore contrast with the proposed suspension that passed in the Senate to address the Burr Conspiracy discussed in Chapter 6, which suspended the privilege outright, as well as the final suspension legislation enacted by the Confederate Congress, explored in the last chapter, in which that Congress suspended the privilege outright throughout the Confederacy after declaring that "the power of suspending the privilege . . . is vested solely in the Congress, which is the exclusive judge of the necessity of such suspension."[42]

As was explored in the last chapter, the issues implicated when Congress leaves the ultimate decision whether to suspend to the president are complex. On the one hand, such legislation may delegate congressional powers improperly to the executive, a branch that does not have the same measure of political accountability to the people and that stands to benefit from expanded authority pursuant to a suspension. Further, such a decision absolves the legislature of engaging in extensive debate on the specific application of an enormously important legislative power, a practice that in the past has led Congress to rebuff presidential requests for a suspension. (Recall the House's rejection of a suspension during the Burr Conspiracy, discussed in Chapter 6.) During the Civil War, moreover, Congress's blanket delegation of the suspension power to Lincoln resulted in a sweeping nationwide suspension—hardly an example of a carefully crafted approach to meet the conditions on the ground to which the executive branch arguably was most keenly attuned. Nor did Congress control the duration of the Civil War suspension, which, as noted, remained in place in many states until 1866. Members of Congress advanced some of these very arguments to defeat a bill in 1872 that would have extended the Reconstruction authorization to empower the executive to suspend as needed.[43]

On the other hand, the Reconstruction suspension suggests that delegation to the executive may result in a narrowly tailored suspension. President Grant exercised the suspension power in only nine counties of the South Carolina upcountry. Permitting such fine-tuning by the executive and his officials on the ground therefore has the potential to result in lesser infringements on liberty interests than forcing Congress to define the scope of the suspension at the outset, when Congress might err on the side of overinclusiveness. Further, the one domestic example of a legislature suspending outright—the final Confederate suspension—declared a suspension across the Confederacy and therefore suggests that there may be advantages to delegating in terms of increasing the potential for narrow tailoring on the ground.

As a threshold matter, whether the ultimate decision to suspend is delegated to the executive or not, in keeping with the terms of Article I, Section 9, Congress must, at a minimum, timely declare that current circumstances constitute a "Rebellion or Invasion" and that the "public Safety . . . require(s)" suspension.[44] In addition, there are strong arguments that Congress must also determine specifically the areas of the country in which such circumstances exist, lest it appear to abdicate the very inquiry the Constitution calls upon the branch to undertake. Similar reasoning supports the argument that Congress must remain engaged with the determination whether circumstances continue to support suspension. This is something that the sunset provision in the Act of 1871 forced Congress to do, whereas the lack of such a provision in the Civil War suspension arguably resulted in that suspension continuing too long.

IN THE AFTERMATH of the Reconstruction suspension, Congress evaluated Grant's actions and concluded that "[t]he results of suspending the writ of *habeas corpus* in South Carolina show that where the membership, mysteries, and power of the organization have been kept concealed this is the most and perhaps only effective remedy for its suppression."[45] Thus, the Reconstruction suspension served as a potent tool for infiltrating a highly secretive organization to uncover its structure and membership. The power to detain without charges also powerfully countered the Klan's pervasive witness intimidation for a time.[46]

The Reconstruction episode is also noteworthy for its purpose. The suspension power is not usually associated with the advancement of civil rights.

Indeed, given its historical office of displacing key protections in the English Habeas Corpus Act, suspension has traditionally been understood as very much in tension with a constitutional framework designed to protect individual liberties. As Representative Stevenson Archer of Maryland said in the debates leading up to the 1871 Act, habeas corpus is "essential to liberty", and "no people can be free without it."[47] Nonetheless, President Grant and his military officers sought the power to engage in preventive detention of Klan members to protect the civil rights of freed slaves and enforce the Reconstruction Amendments in one particularly recalcitrant area of the former Confederacy. Knowing the decades of Klan violence that continued well after this episode, one is left to wonder whether President Grant and Congress went far enough.

After Reconstruction, suspension retreated from American legal discourse and experience. It would take the Japanese bombing of Pearl Harbor on December 7, 1941, and the entry of the United States into World War II for suspension to resurface, this time in the Hawaiian Territory. But as will be seen, the decision by government officials not to suspend habeas corpus on the mainland during the War as it detained tens of thousands of U.S. citizens outside the criminal process was—and remains—not only controversial, but deeply constitutionally problematic.

PART FOUR

The Forgotten Suspension Clause

Notwithstanding the long-settled historical understanding of the Suspension Clause that controlled through Reconstruction, with the Japanese attack on Pearl Harbor on December 7, 1941, everything changed. During World War II and more recently as part of the war on terrorism that followed the terrorist attacks of September 11, 2001, one finds an emerging political and legal acceptance of preventive national security detentions in the absence of suspension legislation—even of U.S. citizens.

In the immediate wake of the bombing of Pearl Harbor and the entry of the United States into World War II, suspension returned to American soil, but it was limited to what was then the Hawaiian Territory. Congress never enacted a suspension applicable to the mainland. Nonetheless, in the western United States, pursuant to President Franklin Delano Roosevelt's Executive Order 9066, the military instituted curfews and designated military areas of exclusion applicable to all persons of Japanese ancestry. Military regulations further ordered evacuated Japanese Americans to report to Assembly Centers, and from there to so-called "Relocation Centers" in turn. The result was unlike anything ever witnessed in American history: over 120,000 Japanese Americans—including over 70,000 U.S. citizens—were forced to leave their homes and report for long-term detention in barren camps, with an average stay of almost three years.

In the lead-up to these events, the attorney general of the United States recognized that any proposed internment of U.S. citizens would violate the Suspension Clause. But the government implemented the policies all the same. When a challenge to the internment eventually came before the Supreme Court, the Court delayed issuing its holding and avoided the important constitutional issues raised in the case, instead deciding it narrowly on non-constitutional grounds. In the meantime, the episode established a precedent that appeared to give constitutional sanction to "a policy of mass incarceration under military auspices."

Over half a century later, debates renewed over the power of the military to detain citizens outside the criminal process in times of war. As part of the war on terrorism that followed the terrorist attacks of September 11, 2001, the government once again defended its authority to detain citizens outside the criminal process and in the absence of a suspension. The Supreme Court in turn held in *Hamdi v. Rumsfeld* that "[t]here is no bar to this Nation's holding one of its own citizens as an enemy combatant." In *Hamdi*'s wake, the Court once again took up the Suspension Clause in an important case raising difficult questions over whether the Clause reaches Guantanamo Bay, Cuba, and if so, what protections it affords those detained there as alleged enemy combatants in the war on terrorism.

10

World War II

SUSPENSION AND MARTIAL LAW IN HAWAII
AND MASS DETENTION OF JAPANESE
AMERICANS ON THE MAINLAND

*[U]nless the writ of habeas corpus is suspended, I do not know
any way in which Japanese born in this country, and therefore
American citizens, could be interned.*

ATTORNEY GENERAL FRANCIS BIDDLE (JANUARY 1942)[1]

*[I]f it a question of safety of the country, the Constitution of
the United States, why the Constitution is just a scrap of
paper to me.*

ASSISTANT SECRETARY OF WAR JOHN J. MCCLOY
(FEBRUARY 1942)[2]

THE BOMBING OF Pearl Harbor on December 7, 1941, finally ushered the
United States into World War II with Congress declaring war on Japan the next
day and Germany three days later. It also set off a dramatic chain of events. In
the hours following the bombing, the governor of the Hawaiian Territory proclaimed a suspension and declared martial law, exercising powers granted him
by the Hawaiian Organic Act of 1900. The mainland, by contrast, never knew
suspension—nor did Congress ever debate the subject. Instead, the military
imposed curfews, designated huge portions of the western United States to be
military areas of exclusion, and ultimately created "relocation centers" across
the west—all aimed at controlling the movements of, and eventually detaining, over 120,000 persons of Japanese ancestry. Those forced into the camps
under military orders during this period included over 70,000 U.S. citizens.

As this chapter explores, in the face of serious constitutional questions
about the propriety of martial law, internment of citizens, and military trials
of civilians, constitutional considerations generally gave way to war hysteria.
But, as many key government actors recognized at the time, the detention of

Habeas Corpus in Wartime. Amanda L. Tyler.
© Oxford University Press 2017. Published 2017 by Oxford University Press.

Japanese American citizens plainly violated the Suspension Clause, standing as it did at odds with the entire history of the suspension framework born out of English legal tradition. As challenges to the relevant military policies spilled over into the courts, the institution arguably best situated to identify and highlight their constitutional infirmities—the Supreme Court—never did so, leaving this episode standing as both a dangerous and deeply problematic precedent in our constitutional history.

Suspension and Martial Law in Hawaii

The government's response to Pearl Harbor was swift and extensive. Within twenty-four hours of the bombing, President Franklin D. Roosevelt issued proclamations designating Japanese, German, and Italian citizens inside the United States to be "alien enemies" and subjecting those "deemed dangerous to the public peace or safety of the United States" to "summary apprehension."[3] In the days that followed, the government arrested hundreds of aliens.[4] By February 1942, almost 3,000 Japanese aliens had been detained on the mainland and in the Hawaiian Territory under this authority.[5] In Hawaii, those detained also included a substantial number of citizens.[6]

That same afternoon of December 7, 1941, Territorial Governor Joseph Poindexter declared martial law and suspended the privilege of the writ of habeas corpus in the Hawaiian Territory "until further notice." Poindexter claimed the authority to do so under the Hawaiian Organic Act of 1900, which delegated to the territorial governor standing authority to suspend the privilege "in case of rebellion or invasion, or imminent danger thereof, when the public safety requires it." The Act also granted the governor the authority to "place the Territory, or any part thereof, under martial law." Under the terms of the Act, any suspension or declaration of martial law remained in effect "until communication can be had with the President and his decision thereon made known."[7] President Roosevelt quickly approved the governor's actions.[8] In the years that followed, the policies that unfolded in Hawaii pushed the boundaries of Suspension Clause jurisprudence and reignited the Civil War debates over the scope of martial law and the propriety of military trial of civilians, culminating in an important Supreme Court opinion embracing and reaffirming *Milligan*'s breadth.

To label as curious the framework that existed for suspending the privilege in Hawaii would be putting it mildly. Indeed, the standing delegation of the authority to suspend found in the Hawaiian Organic Act seems to be inherently problematic under the reasoning of Chief Justice Taney's *Merryman* decision that rebuked President Lincoln's unilateral invocation of the suspension authority. After all, at no point did Congress for itself determine that

circumstances justified declaring a suspension on the Islands or, for that matter, extending the suspension for almost three years. (The only other twentieth-
century U.S. suspension, which took place in the Philippines Territory in
1902, followed under a similar framework.[9]) This being said, there are two
possible reasons that delegation of the suspension authority under these circumstances might have been constitutionally acceptable: first, the Supreme
Court's modern jurisprudence is largely unconcerned with challenges to delegations of congressional authority; and second, the territorial nature of Hawaii
during this period renders the separation-of-powers considerations relating to
delegation less problematic.

On the first point, the Court's jurisprudence respecting congressional
delegations is highly deferential, asking only that Congress give the executive branch "substantial guidance" along with marching orders embodying an
"intelligible principle."[10] One could certainly argue that the Hawaiian Organic
Act passed this test. Nonetheless, the reluctance of many in the Founding
generation to recognize any suspension authority and the decision to vest the
suspension authority in the legislative branch suggest that requiring any decision to suspend to emerge from the arduous process of bicameralism and
presentment—internal checks designed to ensure careful deliberation on
a decision of this magnitude—was an important aspect of the suspension
model adopted by the Founding generation.

As for the second point, the Supreme Court's case law posits that Congress
has broad powers when legislating in the territories.[11] With respect to Hawaii,
however, the Supreme Court has said that "[e]xtraordinary measures [there],
however necessary, are not supportable on the mistaken premise that Hawaiian
inhabitants are less entitled to Constitutional protection than others." This
language stems from the Court's 1946 decision in *Duncan v. Kahanamoku*,
discussed below, in which the Court also said that "[t]he people of Hawaii
are . . . entitled to Constitutional protection to the same extent as the inhabitants of the 48 States."[12] If this is right, then it would seem that the delegation
framework that led to the Hawaiian suspension is highly questionable as a
constitutional matter. In all events, following the governor's proclamation on
December 7, military government quickly took over all governmental affairs in
Hawaii, including the courts. Specifically:

> The Governor's proclamation . . . authorized and requested the
> Commanding General, "during . . . the emergency and until danger
> of invasion is removed, to exercise all the powers normally exercised"
> by the Governor and by "the judicial officers and employees of the
> Territory."

Pursuant to this authorization the Commanding General [Walter Short] immediately proclaimed himself Military Governor and undertook the defense of the Territory and the maintenance of order. On December 8th, both civil and criminal courts were forbidden to summon jurors and witnesses and to try cases. The Commanding General established military tribunals to take the place of the courts.[13]

Thus, "[t]rial by jury and indictment by grand jury were abolished,"[14] and military commissions conducted all criminal trials, even after civilian courts later reopened to hear most other matters.[15] The ramifications swept even further with respect to civil liberties. Under the suspension, "suspected citizens were rounded up and placed in a local inter[n]ment camp," without formal hearings and without charges.[16] As the Supreme Court later observed: "The military undoubtedly assumed that its rule was not subject to any judicial control whatever, for by orders issued on August 25, 1943, it prohibited even accepting of a petition for writ of habeas corpus by a judge or judicial employee or the filing of such a petition by a prisoner or his attorney."[17] Earlier military orders similarly prohibited courts from reviewing habeas petitions.[18]

Nonetheless, the United States District Court for the Territory of Hawaii decided several notable habeas cases during the war. These cases generally involved two categories of petitioners. The first comprised those arrested and detained by military authorities without criminal charges for so-called "subversive" activities. The second encompassed persons who were tried and sentenced by military tribunals during the war. In both contexts, petitioners argued that the military's exercise of emergency powers transgressed the Constitution, the Organic Act, or both.

The first major habeas case in this line was Ex parte *Zimmerman*. The military had arrested and continued to detain Hans Zimmerman, a naturalized citizen of German extraction, for allegedly subversive activities based on an informal hearing before a "Board of Officers and Civilians." His habeas petition, brought by his wife on his behalf in 1942, argued that his hearing's shortcomings, coupled with the unconstitutionality of the territorial suspension that purported to allow it, warranted his release. Despite deeming the petition "well grounded," territorial district judge Delbert E. Metzger denied it in light of General Order No. 57, issued on January 27, 1942, which prohibited the issuance of writs of habeas corpus. In so doing, Judge Metzger reportedly announced that the court was "under duress and is not able to carry out the functions of the court as is its duty."[19] The Ninth Circuit affirmed. As that court saw things in 1942, the ongoing imminent threat of invasion of the Islands by the Japanese more than justified the continuing suspension:

> The emergency inspiring the [Governor's] proclamation [suspending the privilege] did not terminate with the attack on Pearl Harbor. The courts judicially know that the Islands, in common with the whole Pacific area of the United States, have continued in a state of the gravest emergency; and that the imminent threat of a resumption of the invasion persisted. In the months following the 7th of December the mainland of the Pacific coast was subjected to attacks from the sea. Certain of the Aleutian Islands were invaded and occupied. And as late as the early summer of 1942 formidable air and naval forces of Japan were turned back at Midway from an enterprise which appeared to have Hawaii as its ultimate objective.[20]

Against this backdrop, the Ninth Circuit upheld Zimmerman's detention without charges. Nonetheless, the court's opinion is noteworthy for having engaged extensively with the question whether circumstances justified the suspension. Some have argued that such a judicial inquiry is improper because courts are not institutionally designed to assess fairly the existence of a "Rebellion" or "Invasion" sufficient to justify a suspension.[21] At the core of this position is the idea that the decision whether circumstances warrant a suspension should be made in the first and last instance by the political branches. Although it did not address such arguments directly, it is nonetheless noteworthy that the Ninth Circuit in *Zimmerman* never questioned its authority to engage in the relevant inquiry.

The court was right to delve into the matter. Given the dramatic impact on civil liberties that follows under a suspension, the judiciary should ensure that the constitutional prerequisites to suspension exist before sanctioning this emergency state of affairs. To argue, as some have, that the constitutionality of a suspension should be categorically immune from judicial review is equivalent to embracing the proposition that a deprivation of the most fundamental of liberty interests and detention in the absence of any judicial process presents a political question.[22] Such a position is difficult to reconcile with a constitutional tradition that embraces countermajoritarian courts and places the protection of individual liberty among the most important functions of the judicial role. The position is also at odds with a range of historical precedents,[23] including, among many others, the Supreme Court's decision in *Milligan* to opine as to whether Indiana was a part of the active theater of war during the Civil War. It is also in tension with certain Founding-era evidence suggesting an appreciation for an important checking role for the judiciary, lest the suspension power be abused. (Consider, on this score, Massachusetts Chief Justice William Cushing's comments in the Massachusetts ratification debates, detailed in Chapter 5.) Another early example at odds with the idea that evaluating the existence of a rebellion or invasion is not the proper province of the judiciary is the 1792 Calling Forth Act, which set forth detailed standards and procedures governing when and how the president could "call forth" state militias "to repel [an] invasion" or "suppress [an] insurrection."[24] Notably, the second section of the Act required the president to seek certification from a judge in certain circumstances, a procedure that President George Washington followed during the Whiskey Rebellion in 1794, when he put the matter before Associate Justice James Wilson. Washington sent troops to put down the rebellion only after receiving certification from a Supreme Court justice that the situation was dire enough to warrant such a dramatic response.[25]

The Ninth Circuit's opinion in *Zimmerman* is noteworthy for three additional reasons. First, the court explored the purpose and effects of suspension, something that very few American judicial decisions have done. In so doing, it observed that "the purpose of the detention of suspected persons in critical military areas in time of war is to forestall injury and to prevent the commission of acts helpful to the enemy." "Where taken in the genuine interest of the public safety," the court noted, such measures "are not without, but within, the framework of the constitution."[26] Second, the court suggested that it might have disregarded the suspension as legal authorization for Zimmerman's detention if Zimmerman could show that his detention was "unrelated" to the danger threatening the Islands, "arbitrary" in nature, or resulted from "bad faith" on the part of the Board who upheld it.[27] Third, California attorney general Earl Warren, who was at the time running for governor of California and who later served as chief justice of the United States, filed an amicus brief in *Zimmerman* supporting the military's position. Warren, who filed briefs in a number of habeas cases arising out of wartime activities in Hawaii and the western United States (over which the Ninth Circuit presided as the relevant federal appellate court), took the opportunity both to inform the court that "'preventive martial law'" governed in California and to argue that the military should be granted "a wide range of discretion" in exercising the war power.[28] With respect to "[t]he evacuation of persons from military areas or their detention by the military authorities," he wrote, "[s]uch measures are preventive and precautionary only. As no crime is charged, the constitutional rights of an accused are not denied."[29] This latter statement—surely meant to speak to and defend the legality of ongoing developments in California explored below—should raise more than a few eyebrows.

The day before Zimmerman's attorneys filed a petition for certiorari seeking Supreme Court review of his case, the military released him, leading the Supreme Court to deny his petition on mootness grounds.[30] (Release of a prisoner moots a habeas petition because the court's jurisdiction is over the "corpus" or body of the prisoner.) Moving or releasing prisoners to moot judicial proceedings has a long tradition in habeas lore going all the way back to the days leading up to the adoption of the English Habeas Corpus Act of 1679. As discussed in Chapter 1, the Earl of Clarendon regularly dispatched English prisoners in the seventeenth century to "remote islands' garrisons and other places, thereby to prevent them from the benefit of the law." And, as detailed in Chapter 7, during the Civil War, the Johnson administration dispatched several conspirators in Lincoln's assassination to Fort Jefferson in the Florida Keys in an attempt to put them beyond the reach of habeas courts. As will be seen, later in World War II, the government tried to moot the petition in another important habeas case brought by Mitsuye Endo.

In the face of an adverse court ruling in August 1943, the military again chose to release two prisoners detained in Hawaii without criminal charges rather than to keep litigating the matter. The military had arrested the petitioners, two naturalized citizens of German ancestry named Walter Glockner and Edwin Seifert, at different times in the months following Pearl Harbor. It then detained them for allegedly subversive activities. As reports from the period noted, both "had been adjudged dangerous to security after hearings, with the right to retain counsel and to testify, before joint Army and civilian boards."[31] In habeas petitions filed with Judge Metzger, both challenged the legality of the suspension that blanketed the Islands. When the government filed a motion to dismiss for lack of jurisdiction, Metzger denied it, emphasizing that in February 1943, military orders had initiated the restoration of civil government on the Islands and directed the courts to reopen and exercise full authority over all but criminal cases.[32] Judge Metzger also concluded that because the Islands no longer remained in imminent danger of invasion, a suspension could not be defended as necessary.[33] This latter finding possibly followed from General Delos C. Emmons's statement, as early as January 1943, that Hawaii was "safe today under protecting guns of one of the greatest fortresses on earth against any invasion the Japanese currently may be able to organize."[34]

An extraordinary series of events followed. Judge Metzger dispatched a U.S. marshal to serve an order to show cause upon Lieutenant General Robert C. Richardson, Jr., Commanding General of the Army's Hawaiian Department, at his headquarters. Richardson reportedly went to great lengths to evade service.[35] After the marshals finally served process on Richardson, he declined to appear and refused to produce the prisoners. (The many similarities to the events in the *Merryman* case, discussed in Chapter 7, should be apparent.) Not one to be ignored, Judge Metzger held Richardson in contempt and fined him $5,000. This, in turn, triggered General Order No. 31, described above, in which Richardson ordered under threat of fine and imprisonment that the district court could not hear any habeas actions, including the two cases at issue. (To obviate any uncertainty, the orders expressly named the two cases and Judge Metzger.) It took intervention by senior Washington officials, the rescinding of General Order No. 31 following deeply critical press coverage, and the release of the two petitioners to the mainland to defuse the confrontation and moot the habeas petitions.[36]

Hawaiian Martial Law in the Supreme Court

The Supreme Court did hear one pair of habeas cases out of Hawaii during the war, yet once again Suspension Clause issues became moot before the Court could speak to them. *Duncan v. Kahanamoku* involved statutory and constitutional challenges both to the legitimacy of the suspension on the Islands and the criminal trials of civilians by military courts that followed from the declaration of martial law. The two petitioners, Harry E. White and Lloyd C. Duncan, were both U.S. citizens who had been denied a host of procedural rights during their criminal trials by provost courts for charges relating, in White's case, to embezzlement, and in Duncan's, to the assault of two Marine sentries.[37] They had filed their habeas challenges in 1944, a full year after the initiation of the restoration of civilian government and reopening of civilian courts on the Islands. (White had been tried in August of 1942, Duncan in early 1944.)

In Duncan's case, Judge Metzger again held a hearing on the question whether existing conditions justified the suspension in place on the Islands. During the proceedings, the court took testimony from a host of military witnesses on the conditions of the war and the continuing threat posed to the Hawaiian Territory. Among the witnesses to appear during the proceedings was none other than General Richardson, along with Admiral Chester W. Nimitz, the Commander in Chief of the Pacific Ocean Areas.[38] Judge Metzger concluded that "while the Island of Oahu may have" remained in 1944 "subject to possible attack by enemies at war," it is not "in imminent danger of invasion by hostile forces, [nor] in [a state of] rebellion," something that he emphasized the military testimony had underscored. He noted that Territorial Governor Ingram M. Stainback had testified at the hearing that existing conditions demonstrated no necessity for martial law and that "no part of the island of Oahu . . . is a battlefield today nor has it been for over two years. . . ."[39] (Three judges of the territorial courts had also testified that the courts had been able to resume their normal functions for some time.) On this basis, Judge Metzger ordered Duncan's release. His colleague, District Judge J. Frank McLaughlin, likewise ordered discharge in White's case, finding no military necessity supporting the trial of embezzlement charges in the provost courts.[40]

Reversing, the Ninth Circuit relied heavily on its discussion pertaining to the state of the Islands two years earlier in *Zimmerman*. Citing the testimony of Richardson and Nimitz, the court also stressed that in the spring of 1944, "the Islands continued in imminent danger of attack from the air, [and] of submarine forays and commando raids from the sea." Further, the court took judicial notice that "the presence of so many inhabitants of doubtful loyalty posed a continuing threat to the public security," referring to the "tens of thousands of citizens of Japanese ancestry" and Japanese aliens living on the Islands.[41] These conditions, in the court's view, "necessitated" military trials, which were legitimate in any event because "authority for such procedure[s] [was] implicit in the [Hawaiian Organic Act]."[42] Finally, the Ninth Circuit took its lead from the Supreme Court's decision in *Hirabayashi v. United States*, discussed below, in which the Court "observed that the war power . . . extends to every matter and activity so related to war as substantially to affect its conduct and progress" and posited that the judiciary should not "'review . . . the wisdom of the[] action[s]'" of the political branches in times of war "'or substitute its judgment for theirs.'"[43]

Duncan is notable as another example of a wartime court reviewing existing conditions to question the ongoing propriety of a suspension, although the contrasting approaches of the district and circuit courts highlight how influential deference can be in exercising such review. The case also proves something of a cautionary tale. As important as it is for independent, counter-majoritarian courts to ensure that the political branches do not abuse the suspension authority by invoking it in the absence of the required constitutional predicates, it is also important that in so doing courts show sensitivity to military priorities in times of war. Put another way, it is probably fair to say that Admiral Nimitz had better things to do with his time than testify in the *Duncan* proceedings.

In time, *Duncan* advanced to the Supreme Court, with the petitioners continuing to challenge both the lawfulness of the Hawaiian suspension and military rule in the Territory during the war.[44] By the time the case made its way to the Court, the Islands were well along in transitioning back to civil law. Further, President Roosevelt had formally terminated martial law in Hawaii and restored the writ of habeas corpus in an order issued on October 24, 1944.[45] In light of the president's acts, the Supreme Court chose "not [to] pass upon the validity of the order suspending the privilege of habeas corpus," despite having granted review over the matter.[46]

But the Court did reach the merits of the petitioners' challenge to martial law and with it, the propriety of their military trials. The Court began by rejecting outright the notion that such questions should be immune from judicial review. As Chief Justice Harlan Fiske Stone observed in a concurring opinion, "executive action is not proof of its own necessity, and the military's judgment here is not conclusive that every action taken pursuant to the declaration of martial law was justified by the exigency."[47] It followed that asserted military necessity, standing alone, could not sustain the government's actions.

Instead, the Court concluded, any declaration of martial law must be subject to significant judicial scrutiny because it represents the "antithesis" of our system of "[c]ourts and . . . procedural safeguards."[48] Here, the Court found the facts supporting the necessity of martial law wanting:

> [M]ilitary trials of civilians charged with crime, especially when not made subject to judicial review, are so obviously contrary to our political traditions and our institution of jury trials in courts of law, that the tenuous circumstance offered by the Government can hardly suffice to . . . permit[] such a radical departure from our steadfast beliefs.[*]

Justice Hugo Black's majority opinion in *Duncan* listed several historic precedents to support this proposition, including the orders given by Massachusetts governor Bowdoin to General Lincoln during Shays's Rebellion and President Washington's instructions to the military during the Whiskey Rebellion, both of which stressed that the military remained subordinate to civilian authorities and should deliver insurgents to the civilian courts.[49] Black could have also cited James Madison, who as president had taken the same view of martial law in criticizing his wayward military general Andrew Jackson during the War of 1812. As Madison wrote to his acting secretary of war at the time, "[t]he ground

---

[*] Duncan v. Kahanamoku, 327 U.S. 304, 317 (1946). The Court distinguished the "well-established power of the military to exercise jurisdiction over members of the armed forces," as well as "enemy belligerents, prisoners of war, or others charged with violating the laws of war." Id. at 313–314 (citing, among other cases, Ex parte Quirin, 317 U.S. 1 (1942)). It also distinguished the establishment of military tribunals "as part of a temporary military government over occupied enemy territory or territory regained from an enemy where civilian government cannot and does not function." Id. at 314. (Ex parte *Quirin* is detailed in the next chapter.)

on which martial law takes place is that it results from a given military situation; not that it can be introduced or extended in time or place by the authority of a military commander."[50]

The *Duncan* Court continued by relying upon *Milligan*'s "emphatic[] declar[ation] that 'civil liberty and this kind of martial law . . . [are] irreconcilable'" to hold that the Hawaiian Organic Act had not authorized the displacement of civil law any more than absolutely necessary.[51] (It did not matter to the Court that the Act had expressly recognized the declaration of martial law as a wartime possibility.) It followed, the Court held, that the convictions of White and Duncan must be vacated. The Court did not decide the case on constitutional grounds, as it had *Milligan*, but the Constitution loomed large in the backdrop all the same.[52] Years later, Chief Justice William Rehnquist wrote about *Duncan* that the Court's opinion was obviously right. As he put it, "Edwin Stanton at his most autocratic during the Civil War never suggested that military commissions try garden-variety civilian offenses against state law or military orders."[53]

Thus, eight months after the Japanese surrendered to Allied forces, the *Duncan* Court rejected the sweeping imposition of martial law in the Hawaiian Territory that had governed during most of the war. In so doing, the Court embraced a narrow view of martial law grounded in necessity, just as it had in *Milligan*. *Duncan* followed from a concern that any other ruling would have sanctioned the large-scale and years-long displacement of core constitutional protections associated with individual liberty. Further, the strongest argument favoring permitting Congress to establish such a scheme—its broad powers over territories—gave the Court little pause, rejecting as it did the idea that Hawaiian citizens enjoyed lesser claim to those constitutional rights associated with a fair trial.[54]

At its broadest, *Duncan* may be read to promote a narrow view of martial law as critical to ensuring that it is not employed to circumvent the constitutional constraints on suspension and, accordingly, detention outside the criminal process with its full array of procedural protections. Justice Black's view of martial law is, in this regard, consistent with that proffered by Attorney General Caleb Cushing in 1857, which described it as following from the fact that "civil authority has become suspended . . . by the force of circumstances." Thus, Cushing wrote, martial law "must be regarded as the statement of an existing fact, rather than the legal creation of that fact."[55] Unfortunately, the *Duncan* Court never had the opportunity to evaluate the suspension imposed on the Islands during that same period, the duration of which pushed constitutional boundaries.[56] But one military lawyer serving in the Hawaiian Territory during the war did study the problem in depth. The advice that he tendered to his superiors is significant for what it suggested about the events transpiring on the mainland during this same period. In his view, it was *"only in the Territory,"* where martial law and a suspension had been declared, "that internment of citizens is possible."[57]

The Push for Exclusion Orders and Detention of Japanese Americans on the Mainland

In the weeks following the Japanese bombing of Pearl Harbor, internal debates among key government officials quickly began laying the groundwork for President Roosevelt's issuance of Executive Order 9066 on February 19, 1942. That Order, issued ten weeks after the Japanese attack, authorized the secretary of war to designate military zones "from which any or all persons may be excluded" and provided for the regulation of the terms on which persons could enter, remain in, or be forced to leave such areas.[58] By its own terms, 9066 included no language specifically targeting a particular race or ethnicity, nor did it specifically mention detention. But it set in motion what became a massive internment of over 120,000 persons of Japanese ancestry—including over 70,000 citizens—in the western United States.* What followed stands as the most egregious violation of the Suspension Clause in history.

The story, as one historian put it, is nothing short of a "tragedy of democracy." "By arbitrarily confining American citizens of Japanese ancestry, the government violated the essential principle of democracy: that all citizens are entitled to the same rights and legal protections."[59] Many who have written about this period have noted that as early as 1936, Roosevelt had raised the possibility of at least some form of internment in the face of reports that Japanese Americans were making contact with Japanese merchant ships in Hawaii. As he then stated:

> One obvious thought occurs to me—that every Japanese citizen or non-citizen on the island of Oahu who meets these Japanese ships or has any connection with their officers or men should be secretly but definitely identified and his or her name placed on a special list of those who would be the first to be placed in a concentration camp in the event of trouble.[60]

---

* The citizenship numbers may well have been higher had then-existing naturalization laws not discriminated based on race, a practice that ended only with the Immigration and Nationality Act of 1952. See Pub. L. No. 82-414, 66 Stat. 163 (1952).

Fear of additional attacks by the Japanese in the wake of Pearl Harbor surely fueled the developments that preceded and followed issuance of Executive Order 9066. Two days after the bombing of Pearl Harbor, for example, the *Los Angeles Times* reported that "[t]he entire Pacific Coast from British Columbia to San Diego [is] prepared for possible raids."[61] Further, in the days following Pearl Harbor, several Japanese submarines lurking off the West Coast attacked American vessels, sinking at least two tankers.[62] In the weeks that followed, the Japanese captured or forced the surrender of Hong Kong, Manila, and Singapore, and secured other victories, with these early successes magnifying the perceived threat that Japan posed to the Hawaiian Islands and U.S. mainland.

Nonetheless, leading up to and following issuance of 9066, many key participants in the internal government debates expressed great skepticism over whether any evidence existed to support suspicions of widespread disloyalty on the part of persons of Japanese ancestry in the United States. These doubts carried over to the wisdom of evacuation and internment policies directed at such persons. Indeed, just days before issuance of 9066, a key War Department official acknowledged that "no one has justified fully the sheer military necessity for such action."[63] Similarly, at a meeting that took place in the early days of February 1942 between key War Department and Justice Department officials that included Attorney General Francis Biddle, the Justice Department officials remarked that "there is no evidence whatsoever of any reason for disturbing citizens." They therefore proposed a joint departmental statement that "the present military situation does not at this time require the removal of American citizens of the Japanese race."[64] (Biddle was surely influenced by reports he received from Federal Bureau of Investigation (FBI) Director J. Edgar Hoover reporting that the lack of evidence of disloyal activity undermined the arguments favoring relocation proposals.[65]) Then, on February 7, 1942, Biddle informed the president that his Department "believed mass evacuation at this time inadvisable," and that "there were no reasons for mass evacuation." Biddle further "emphasized the danger of the hysteria" so prevalent in the west "moving east."[66] This event marked one of several when the attorney general would counsel pause with respect to wartime policies directed at persons of Japanese ancestry—but, here and elsewhere, Biddle's advice would be ignored.

Early on, General DeWitt, who held the post of Commanding General of the Western Defense Command and would soon promote and subsequently oversee the evacuation and internment policies on the West Coast, apparently had his own doubts about the merits of internment. Initially, he rejected the proposal as out of keeping with "common sense" and likely to "alienate the loyal Japanese."[67] DeWitt also recognized that those persons who were citizens stood legally distinct from Japanese aliens, who were enemy aliens under traditional wartime policies. In fact, during early debates with the Army's provost marshall general over the merits of an internment policy, DeWitt had emphasized: "An American citizen, after all, is an American citizen."[68] Of course, these statements must be compared to later reports documenting that by February, DeWitt was "very anxious about the situation and ha[d] been clamoring for the evacuation of the Japanese of the area surrounding" major ports and areas with airplane factories.[69]

As the push to intern persons of Japanese ancestry—aliens and citizens alike—gained momentum, Attorney General Biddle repeatedly took the position that no detention of citizens could occur without a suspension of the privilege. Biddle, a Harvard-trained lawyer, was the son of a law professor and the direct descendant of Edmund Randolph who, as Chapters 5 and 6 detailed, linked the Suspension Clause to the English Habeas Corpus Act when speaking at the Virginia Ratification debates and later defended Aaron Burr. In this regard, Biddle was perhaps better situated than most to identify the glaring legal problems with any such proposal. Responding to a letter from Representative Leland M. Ford of California advocating that "all Japanese, whether citizens or not, be placed in inland concentration camps,"[70] Biddle wrote: "[U]nless the writ of habeas corpus is suspended, I do not know any way in which Japanese born in this country, and therefore American citizens, could be interned."[71]

This is a remarkable statement given its timing and that it was issued by the chief law enforcement officer of the United States. A report of the meeting held a week later between Justice and War Department officials reveals that Biddle again took the position that his department "will have nothing whatsoever to do with any interference with citizens, whether they are Japanese or not."[72] Biddle also declared that his department would not "recommend the suspension of the writ of habeas corpus."[73] During this same week, Biddle directly informed the president of his view that "American born Japanese, being citizens, cannot be apprehended or treated like alien enemies." This being said, Biddle also informed the president in the same memo that "probably an arrangement can be made, where necessary, to evacuate them from military zones." He also reported that "[s]tudy is being made as to whether, with respect to them, the writ of habeas corpus could be suspended in case of an emergency."[74]

Early on, Secretary of War Henry L. Stimson, also a Harvard-trained lawyer, likewise saw constitutional problems with any detention of citizens, writing in his diary on February 3, 1942: "We cannot discriminate among our citizens on the ground of racial origin." Doing so by ordering second-generation Japanese

American citizens evacuated from the western states, Stimson believed, "will make a tremendous hole in our constitutional system. . . ."[75] There are additional indications, moreover, that Stimson understood the significance of the Suspension Clause as a constraint on the government's ability to detain citizens without criminal charges. For example, in April 1942, Stimson recorded in his diary that upon learning that civil liberties groups were planning to file petitions for writs of habeas corpus on behalf of Japanese American citizens who had been moved from Hawaii to the mainland for detention, he ordered the individuals moved back to Hawaii where a suspension and martial law had been declared and "we can do what we please with them."[76]

These larger concerns, including those particularly grounded in the Suspension Clause, were brought to the attention of the president on more than one occasion. Beyond Biddle raising them, on February 2, lawyer James H. Rowe, Jr., Assistant to the Attorney General, wrote the following to Roosevelt's private secretary Grace Tully:

> Please tell the President to keep his eye on the Japanese situation in California. . . . There is tremendous public pressure to move all of them out of California—citizens and aliens—and no one seems to worry about how or to where. There are about 125,000 of them, and if it happens, it will be one of the great mass exoduses of history. It would probably require suspension of the writ of habeas corpus—and my estimate of the country's present feeling is that we would have another Supreme Court fight on our hands.[77]

Some years later in his memoirs, Attorney General Biddle wrote that in the lead-up to Executive Order 9066, "the President had declared his unwillingness to suspend the writ of habeas corpus [on the mainland]" and ordered the "citizen internees who had been brought over . . . returned to Hawaii,"[78] likely following Secretary Stimson's counsel. Nonetheless, the very actions that Biddle and Rowe had counseled would require a suspension moved forward on the mainland without any such legal imprimatur.[79]

The topic of suspension was not limited to discussions by Justice Department lawyers. Conversations took place inside the War Department about how to reconcile General DeWitt's push for broad exclusion orders with constitutional concerns. Thus, on February 3, in discussing the situation with DeWitt, Assistant Secretary of War John J. McCloy promoted the idea of blanket exclusion orders for military areas as providing "cover . . . with the legal situation." More specifically, McCloy argued that the Constitution posed no problem with respect to excluding both citizens and aliens of all stripes from military areas; such orders, he argued, could issue "without suspending writs of Habeas Corpus and without getting into very important legal complications." (Of course, in the same conversation, McCloy also outlined a plan to "license back into the area" those thought not to pose a danger—in his words, "[e]veryone but the Japs.")[80] But almost immediately, McCloy, another Harvard-trained lawyer in the administration, had changed his tune altogether regarding the "legal complications" to which he had referred in conversation with DeWitt. In a contentious meeting with Attorney General Biddle, McCloy reportedly responded to constitutional objections to the military's proposals by declaring: "[I]f it a question of safety of the country, the Constitution of the United States, *why the Constitution is just a scrap of paper to me.*"[81]

As late as two days before issuance of Executive Order 9066, Attorney General Biddle reportedly was still pushing back against proposals for mass evacuation, writing to the president that his "last advice from the War Department is that there is no evidence of imminent attack and from the F. B. I. that there is no evidence of planned sabotage." Referring to newspaper columnists who were by this point pushing aggressively for evacuation and internment of persons of Japanese ancestry, Biddle told the president that either they "ha[ve] information which the War Department and the F. B. I. apparently do not have, or [they are] acting with dangerous irresponsibility."[82]

In the end, the very serious constitutional concerns that had been raised about proposals for exclusion and internment—including those grounded in questions about citizenship, race, and the Suspension Clause—were all to no effect. The same is true with respect to the well-documented doubts over the existence of any genuine military need for exclusion or internment. Indeed, an important report prepared in January for the Chief of Naval Operations by Lieutenant Commander Kenneth D. Ringle had argued that the so-called " 'Japanese Problem' has been magnified out of its true proportion" and reported that "the most dangerous" were already in custody or "known" to Naval Intelligence and/or the FBI.[83] Reports from the FBI in early February found even less reason to suspect espionage on western shores.[84] Indeed, FBI Director Hoover is reported to have held the view that the push for internment was "based primarily upon public and political pressure rather than on factual data."[85] Executive Order 9066 and the military orders that followed simply glossed over these concerns. The resulting policies are best described as following from a mindset exemplified in the quote above from Assistant Secretary of War McCloy along with a memorandum prepared for the attorney general by three attorneys whose counsel he sought outside his department in the period leading up to 9066. (It is remarkable that the attorney general sought an opinion outside his department on the issue, particularly when all of his immediate subordinates were counseling the unconstitutionality of any internment policy.) As the outsiders advised Biddle and as all key actors seemed to assume in moving forward: "So long as a classification of persons or citizens is reasonably related to a genuine war need and does not under the guise of national defense discriminate . . . for a purpose unrelated to the national defense, no constitutional guaranty is infringed."[86]

By the evening of February 17, Biddle had capitulated and given his "informal approval . . . after a personal conference with the Secretary of War" of what became 9066, which in turn placed the entire matter within the jurisdiction of the War Department.[87] Describing Biddle's change of course, James Rowe later observed: "Frankly, he just folded under, I think."[88] The president issued 9066 two days later, declaring that "the successful prosecution of the war requires every possible protection against espionage and against sabotage to national-defense material, national-defense premises and national-defense utilities. . . ." In addition to authorizing the War Department to designate and regulate military zones, the president further authorized and directed the secretary of war and his military commanders "to take such other steps as he or the appropriate Military Commander may deem advisable to enforce compliance with the restrictions applicable to each Military area. . . ." Finally, President Roosevelt authorized the secretary of war "to provide for residents of any such area who are excluded therefrom, such transportation, food, shelter, *and other accommodations as may be necessary*. . . ."[89] On March 21, 1942, Congress bolstered 9066 with Public Law 503, which made it a criminal offense to violate any restrictions or orders issued by the War Department respecting any designated "military area or military zone."[90]

Following issuance of 9066, General DeWitt swiftly issued a series of military orders designating military zones throughout the western United States and subjecting all alien enemies and "all persons of Japanese ancestry" residing in such zones to exclusion orders, curfew orders, and prohibitions on travel, among many other things. By the end of March, DeWitt prohibited such persons from leaving military areas, a prelude to the orders that followed in May and June, including Civilian Restrictive Order No. 1 and Public Proclamation No. 8, which required "as a matter of military necessity" that "all persons of Japanese ancestry, both alien and non-alien" report to assembly centers. From there, military orders provided that evacuees would be forced into compulsory internment "for their relocation, maintenance and supervision" in ten "War Relocation Centers" spread throughout the western states. At each step, DeWitt provided that violations of the military orders would be subject to criminal penalties under Public Law 503.[91]

And so it was that General DeWitt claimed blanket authority under Executive Order 9066 to regulate in the name of "military necessity," directing his military orders at "person[s] of Japanese ancestry, both alien and nonalien"[92] and spearheading a massive and unprecedented internment policy under threat of criminal sanctions. For good measure, DeWitt promulgated orders prohibiting internees from leaving the camps without prior written authorization. Notably, Congress never passed legislation expressly authorizing the detention of Japanese Americans or providing for penalties in cases of resistance to detention.[93] (To the contrary, the Act of March 21, 1942, criminalized only those actions taken in violation of exclusion orders.)

The camps, situated in barren and desolate areas, were surrounded by barbed wire fences and armed guards at all times. Those forced to live in the camps faced extreme conditions, little in the way of privacy, and substandard food and medical care. In some cases, families were split apart and sent to different camps.[94] Those subject to internment, moreover, had been "permitted to take to the camps only what they could carry." As a result, "they were forced to abandon their homes, farms, furnishings, cars, and other belongings or to sell them off quickly at bargain prices." In other words, "the vast majority of the West Coast Japanese Americans lost all their property."[95] Over time, those persons who answered "no" to key questions on a loyalty test administered by the government were separated out and sent to the camp at Tule Lake, California, where they came to be known as the "no-noes."[96] (Later, thousands who had renounced their citizenship at Tule Lake would win court cases based on judicial findings that such renunciations had not been voluntary.[97]) One could not leave the camps without permission, which only a fraction of those interned received—namely, those who enlisted in the military[98] or successfully managed to line up employment in some of the few communities outside restricted areas that were willing to accept resettling Japanese Americans during the war. The average length of stay in the camps was 900 days.

It was not until 1946 that the government finally resettled the last of the Japanese Americans and closed the last of the Relocation Centers that had detained them, Tule Lake. Over the course of the war, the government had detained upwards of 120,000 persons of Japanese ancestry in the camps, including over 70,000 U.S. citizens. In the wake of the war, Japanese Americans set about rebuilding their lives in the face of hostility and discrimination, having lost extensive property and years of their lives.[99]

Manzanar Relocation Center, 1942
Credit: Dorothea Lange, War Relocation Authority, "Manzanar, California. Dust storm at this War Relocation Authority center where evacuees of Japanese ancestry are spending the duration." July 3, 1942, National Archives and Records Administration.

The Forgotten Suspension Clause

As the military orders grew increasingly restrictive, the controversy spilled over into the courts. Some who were prosecuted and eventually detained filed appeals and habeas petitions seeking relief. As the litigation unfolded, however, Attorney General Biddle's initial reaction to internment proposals—namely, that no detention of Japanese American citizens could occur without a suspension—went unrecognized. (In part this resulted from the fact that most of the legal challenges filed attacked the military regulations providing for curfews, exclusion, and other restrictions that did not directly implicate detention, the core concern of the Suspension Clause.) This point goes a long way to explain why most subsequent assessments of the government's treatment of Japanese Americans during World War II focus upon the racial and ethnic discrimination that drove the government's actions. Race and ethnicity were also highlighted within the debates leading up to the ultimate recommendations made by the War Department to the president and were clearly evident in the military orders themselves, which applied exclusively to "persons of Japanese ancestry." General DeWitt's final recommendations delivered to the president on February 13, 1942, for example, declared: "The Japanese race is an enemy race and while many second and third generation Japanese born on United States soil, possessed of United States citizenship, have become 'Americanized,' the racial strains are undiluted."[100] DeWitt also testified before Congress: "I don't want any of them [persons of Japanese ancestry] here. They are a dangerous element. There is no way to determine their loyalty. . . . It makes no difference whether he is an American citizen, he is still a Japanese. American citizenship does not necessarily determine loyalty."[101] Further, as one historian has argued, President Roosevelt's "view of Japanese Americans as immutably foreign and dangerous was a crucial factor in his approval of the internment."[102] Notably, German Americans and Italian Americans were not subject to similar detention policies during the war. In short, one need not look hard to find indicia of racial and ethnic animus in the lead-up to 9066 and during the events that followed.

But what should be obvious is that there were also very serious—indeed overwhelming—constitutional problems grounded in the Suspension Clause with the government's treatment of Japanese American citizens during the war. Highlighting this fact is not meant in any way to detract from the deeply troubling discriminatory aspects of the exclusion orders. Nonetheless, the simple fact is this: the internment of Japanese American citizens during World War II stands as the most glaring violation of the Suspension Clause in American history. As the preceding chapters have set forth in detail, the animating purpose behind the Suspension Clause as understood at the Founding and well through Reconstruction was to limit the government, even in times of war, from detaining persons who could claim the protection of domestic law outside the criminal process.[103] Yet that is precisely what the government did during World War II without Congress ever enacting a constitutionally required suspension of the privilege. Instead, the internment policy followed exclusively from military orders promulgated by General DeWitt.

The government's asserted justification for the detentions was a generalized and unsubstantiated belief that such persons posed a threat to the war effort and might spy on behalf of the enemy Japanese Empire. No criminal charges supported the mass detentions, nor did the government provide individualized hearings of any kind to those interned before detaining them against their will. Here, it bears noting that even some of those who pushed hardest for compulsory internment—many western state governors— recognized that to do so, "the constitution" might need to "be changed."[104] But of course it never was.

Sign posted by Japanese American grocer in Oakland, California, following the bombing of Pearl Harbor

Credit: Dorothea Lange, War Relocation Authority, "Oakland, Calif., Mar. 1942. A large sign reading 'I am an American' placed in the window of a store, at 13th and Franklin streets, on December 8, the day after Pearl Harbor. The store was closed following orders to persons of Japanese descent to evacuate from certain West Coast areas. The owner, a University of California graduate, will be housed with hundreds of evacuees in War Relocation Authority centers for the duration of the war." Library of Congress.

"[A] Loaded Weapon Ready for the Hand of Any Authority"

As these issues came before the courts, three important cases made their way to the Supreme Court: *Hirabayashi v. United States*, *Korematsu v. United States*, and Ex parte *Endo*. Even when the Court finally confronted the internment policy, however, its decisions all but ignored the Suspension Clause.

Gordon Hirabayashi's case was the first to reach the Court, in 1943. Hirabayashi was a senior at the University of Washington and natural-born citizen whose parents had immigrated from Japan. Hirabayashi refused to register with military authorities as part of the process that would surely result in his relocation to a camp. He also violated the curfew order declared for the area in which he lived so as to force a legal challenge to the regulations. After being prosecuted and convicted in a civilian court for violating both applicable military regulations, Hirabayashi's appeal argued that Congress had delegated too much authority to General DeWitt and that the military orders unconstitutionally discriminated on the basis of race and ethnicity.

A unanimous Supreme Court rejected both arguments, opining with respect to the latter:

> The adoption by Government, in the crisis of war and of threatened invasion, of measures for the public safety, based upon the recognition of facts and circumstances which indicate that a group of one national extraction may menace that safety more than others, is not wholly beyond the limits of the Constitution and is not to be condemned merely because in other and in most circumstances racial distinctions are irrelevant.[105]

Chief Justice Stone wrote the opinion for the Court and expressly limited the Court's holding to the curfew order: "It is unnecessary to consider whether or to what extent such findings would support orders differing from the curfew order." (Even in its limited form, however, the Court's holding included language that swept broadly with respect to Hirabayashi's discrimination claims, positing: "We cannot close our eyes to the fact, demonstrated by experience, that, in time of war, residents having ethnic affiliations with an invading enemy may be a greater source of danger than those of a different ancestry.")[106] The Court was able to avoid wading into questions surrounding the military orders pertaining to registration, evacuation, and internment only because Hirabayashi's sentences for his two convictions had been ordered to run concurrently—in other words, affirming the curfew violation conviction was sufficient to sustain his sentence.

The Supreme Court similarly deferred to military judgment the next year in Fred Korematsu's case. Korematsu, born and raised in Oakland, California, was also the son of Japanese immigrants and also a U.S. citizen. The government had prosecuted him for remaining in a designated military zone when he refused to comply with the military's exclusion orders. On appeal, Korematsu argued that his conviction was unconstitutional. Just as it had one year earlier in *Hirabayashi*, however, the Court declined to "reject as unfounded the judgment of the military authorities and of Congress that there were disloyal members of that population, whose number and strength could not be precisely and quickly ascertained." Continuing, in an opinion written by Justice Black, the Court observed: "We cannot say that the war-making branches of the Government did not have ground for believing that in a critical hour such persons could not readily be isolated and separately dealt with, and constituted a menace to the national defense and safety."[107]

The Court also declined to reach Korematsu's broader attack directed at the assembly centers and internment camps, to which, he correctly noted, he would have been required to report following compliance with the evacuation order he disobeyed. "Our task," the Court observed, "would be simple, our duty clear, were this a case involving the imprisonment of a loyal citizen in a concentration camp because of racial prejudice. . . . [But] we are dealing specifically with nothing but an exclusion order."[108] Concurring, Justice Frankfurter likewise declined to reach the larger issues implicated by the case, while nonetheless going on record to say that the Court's holding should not be read as "approval of that which Congress and the Executive did. *That is their business, not ours.*"[109]

Unlike in *Hirabayashi*, this time the majority's position met with dissent. One dissenter, Justice Owen Roberts, summarized the case as "convicting a citizen as a punishment for not submitting to imprisonment in a concentration camp, based on his ancestry, and solely because of his ancestry, without evidence or inquiry concerning his loyalty and good disposition towards the United States." Justice Roberts argued that the Court had to take into account the larger context in which Korematsu's case fell, lest it "shut [its] eyes to reality."[110] Another dissenter, Justice Frank Murphy, labeled the military framework operating in the west as "fall[ing] into the ugly abyss of racism."[111] The final dissenter, Justice Robert Jackson, after arguing that the Court should not have taken up the case, reduced the principles at issue in *Korematsu* to the following: "[I]f any fundamental assumption underlies our system, it is that guilt is personal and not inheritable."[112]

Korematsu reveals that by 1944, the Court was no longer unified in deferring to the government on wartime matters and that some justices were prepared to reach the elephant in the room: namely, the internment policy. Nonetheless, a majority led by Justice Black (who would sound very different in authoring *Duncan* two years later) upheld Korematsu's conviction. In so doing, the Court established a precedent that, to borrow from Justice Jackson's dissent, "lies about like a loaded weapon ready for the hand of any authority that can bring forward a plausible claim of an urgent need."[113]

The *Korematsu* Court had also been misled as to key underlying facts. Indeed, in both *Hirabayashi* and *Korematsu*, the Court's deference to the government followed expressly from arguments advanced by the government asserting that military necessity justified the military policies. But as noted earlier, the well-documented positions of many key government officials along with a number of intelligence reports from the period immediately preceding

9066 undermine any argument predicated upon military necessity. (Nor, for that matter, had a factual record on the question ever been developed in the courts below in either case, as would normally be required.) This important background led two prominent Justice Department lawyers to concede in briefing both cases that there existed little evidence to support General DeWitt's claims about the threat posed by Japanese Americans in the West. In both cases, superiors removed the concessions. (In *Korematsu*, the government's brief was already at the printer when superiors ordered the changes.)[114] Accordingly, the government incorrectly represented the relevant facts to the justices in these enormously important cases.[115]

On the same day as *Korematsu* in December 1944, the Supreme Court also decided Ex parte *Endo*, a case that finally challenged outright the constitutionality of the detention of citizens of Japanese ancestry. Yet here again the Court declined to reach the constitutionality of the internment policy, despite having formidable arguments grounded in the Suspension Clause presented to it. The case arose out of the wave of suspensions by the State of California of all employees of Japanese ancestry, one of whom was Mitsuye Endo. Endo, a native-born citizen who had worked for the California Department of Motor Vehicles, did not speak Japanese, came from a family that did not subscribe to a Japanese language paper, had not gone to a Japanese language school, was a Methodist, and had a brother serving in the Pacific with the U.S. Army. In this respect, she was, in the words of her attorney James Purcell, "the ideal candidate" for preparing a habeas corpus petition on behalf of all Japanese Americans sent to the Relocation Centers. Purcell, a Stanford-educated attorney practicing in San Francisco, had been originally brought in by the Japanese American Citizens League to challenge the state employment suspensions. But after seeing the deplorable conditions at Tanforan Assembly Center near San Francisco, he chose instead to challenge the internment policy. (Having grown up at Folsom Prison, where his father was a guard, Purcell said of Tanforan: "I was unable to distinguish [it] from the prison except that the walls were barbed wire fences; more frequent gun towers; more difficulty of entering to see a client; and the convicts were better housed than my American citizen clients who were not accused of any crime.") Purcell funded the case entirely out of his own pocket and stayed the course even in the face of threats to his person and his family.[116]

Like so many others, Endo had not only lost her job based on her Japanese ancestry, but had been forced to evacuate the military area encompassing where she lived in Sacramento, California; report to an assembly center; and then report for detention with her family at Tule Lake Camp. Purcell filed Endo's petition for a writ of habeas corpus in July 1942. After a lengthy stay in the district court only to meet defeat, Purcell appealed on Endo's behalf to the United States Court of Appeals for the Ninth Circuit. Meanwhile, the government transferred Endo to the camp at Topaz, Utah. The Ninth Circuit declined to resolve Endo's appeal and instead certified the case to the Supreme Court for resolution. Endo was a determined (indeed, heroic) litigant, for she endured almost two additional years in the camps to keep her habeas petition alive after turning down the government's offer of release, which was conditioned upon not returning to restricted areas on the West Coast.[117] Had she accepted the offer, her case would have become moot like so many other wartime habeas cases before hers. As she later said, "[t]he fact that I wanted to prove that we of Japanese ancestry were not guilty of any crime and that we were loyal American citizens kept me from abandoning the suit."[118]

Purcell's brief to the Court in Endo's case reflected the work of an attorney well versed in the key authorities relating to suspension and martial law. He relied upon *Bollman, Merryman, Milligan,* and Justice Story's *Commentaries on the Constitution,* among other authorities, to argue that the president has no power to hold a citizen outside the criminal process in the absence of a suspension. Quoting extensively from *Milligan,* a case Purcell labeled as "familiar to everyone who has even a smattering of constitutional law," Endo's brief asked:

> Since the military authorities have no jurisdiction by virtue of a Presidential proclamation to *try* a civilian for an alleged offense in a district where the civil Courts are open, how much less right have they to imprison a citizen without any trial at all, when he is neither charged with, nor suspected of, any crime, and when his loyalty (as in this case), is not called into question?

Elaborating, Endo's brief argued that the only means by which the detention of citizens outside the criminal process could be made lawful was through a congressional suspension of the privilege. Finally, Endo's brief contended that no state of martial law existed to justify the internment and more generally that "the existence of a state of war does not suspend constitutional rights."[119] Curiously, the government's brief in response did not even engage with Endo's Suspension Clause arguments and instead primarily recited a descriptive narrative of the history of the military orders issued under the auspices of 9066.

As the litigation unfolded, the government conceded that Endo "was a loyal and law-abiding citizen." Likewise, it "conceded that it is beyond the power of the War Relocation Authority to detain citizens against whom no charges of disloyalty or subversiveness have been made for a period longer

than necessary to separate the loyal from the disloyal and to provide the necessary guidance for relocation."[120] These concessions proved a roadmap for the
narrow Supreme Court opinion that followed under the pen of Justice William
O. Douglas. The Court, he wrote, would "not come to the underlying constitutional issues which have been argued." In a passage proposed by Chief Justice
Stone to Justice Douglas, the Court's opinion nonetheless "noted" that *Endo*
presented different issues than *Milligan*, in part because "Mitsuye Endo is
detained by a civilian agency . . . , not by the military" and because "no questions of military law are involved."[121] As any fair reading of *Milligan* would
reveal, this is an absurdly narrow assessment of the Court's holding in that
case.[122] Recall, as discussed in Chapter 7, that *Milligan* both held that the military trial of Lamdin Milligan had been unconstitutional and that because his
detention was not authorized under the terms of Congress's 1863 suspension
legislation, he was entitled to his freedom.[123]

   Instead, the Court held that the governing regulations required the release
of concededly loyal citizens, such as Endo, from relocation centers because
"[a] citizen who is concededly loyal presents no problem of espionage or sabotage."[124] Justice Douglas "mention[ed]" a list of constitutional provisions—
including the Suspension Clause—"not to stir the constitutional issues which
have been argued at the bar," but instead to explain why the Court would
"give[] a narrower scope," or reading, to the governing legislation and executive orders at issue.[125] (In an interview some years later, Douglas revealed: "I
had the desire to put it on the constitutional grounds but I couldn't get a Court
to do that."[126] His notes from the justices' conference on the case, however, do
not mention any constitutional issues and instead lay out the narrow approach
that his opinion ultimately adopted.[127]) And so, despite the public urging of at
least two justices (and likely a third)—one of whom argued that "[a]n admit-
tedly loyal citizen . . . should be free to come and go as she pleases"—the
Court once again avoided addressing the very serious constitutional issues
implicated by the internment policies and instead delivered an exceedingly
minimalist decision.[128]

   It appears that the Court delayed the announcement of its decision in *Endo*
in order to give the government more time to prepare its response. The Court
also possibly delayed handing down *Endo* until after the 1944 presidential election. Supporting the suggestion of intentional delay generally is an internal
Court memorandum sent by Justice Douglas to the chief justice in November
1944 asking why, if the entire Court was in agreement that the government
was detaining Endo unlawfully, the decision had yet to be announced.[129] Some
weeks later, on December 18, 1944, the decision finally came down, but only
after—by one day—the president essentially rescinded 9066. (Specifically,

Major General Henry C. Pratt issued Public Proclamation No. 21, which declared that as of January 2, 1945, all Japanese American evacuees were free to return to their homes on the West Coast.[130]) In the weeks that followed, the government began the process of closing down the camps. At the time—some three years after the attacks on Pearl Harbor—the camps still detained some 85,000 persons.[131]

"[T]he Constitution Has Never Greatly Bothered Any Wartime President"

In reviewing the Supreme Court decisions arising out of DeWitt's military proclamations, it is fair to label them, as Professor Eugene Rostow did shortly in their wake, a "disaster." It is also remarkable that the Suspension Clause played almost no role in these cases, just as constitutional considerations grounded in the Clause had been pushed aside in the political discussions leading up to 9066 and the resulting military policies. Perhaps this is because until *Endo*, the litigants did not present arguments, other than in passing, grounded in that constitutional provision.[132] Or perhaps it is because the government's attorneys did not engage with such arguments when they were made, implying (incorrectly) that they were easily dismissed. There is also the fact that issues of racial and ethnic discrimination were so obviously central to the military orders that this reality overwhelmed all others. Whatever the reasons, in the end, it was only the dissents of Justices Roberts and Jackson in *Korematsu*, along with Justice Jackson's uncirculated concurrence in *Endo* discussed below, that hint at what Attorney General Francis Biddle had recognized from the very beginning—namely, that any detention of Japanese American citizens could not take place "unless the writ of habeas corpus [wa]s suspended."

Whatever the reason for the Court's approach—whether the targeted and discriminatory aspects of the military orders,[133] excessive deference to the military, the foreign nature of the war, or something else—the contemporary failure to give proper recognition to this glaring constitutional problem with the internment policy is profoundly regrettable. Historical evidence abounds instructing that the core purpose of the Suspension Clause is to prohibit the detention of citizens outside the criminal process in the absence of a valid suspension. Whether discussing the Jacobite sympathizers plotting to regain the throne for the Stuart line, the American colonists fighting for their independence, or those suspected of supporting the Confederacy during the Civil War, the suspension model functioned the same in every episode. Specifically, where those suspected of disloyalty enjoyed the habeas privilege either under the English Habeas Corpus Act or the Suspension Clause, Anglo-American habeas jurisprudence had always required a valid suspension to authorize detention for national security purposes outside the criminal process—*even in wartime*. Indeed, up until World War II, where constitutional, suspension had long been settled as the proper and exclusive means of legalizing detentions outside the criminal process free from judicial interference in times of war.

Thus, contrary to the suggestion of the *Endo* Court, it does not matter whether a person has passed a so-called "loyalty" test—in the absence of a valid suspension, lawful detention in times of war can only be predicated upon timely criminal proceedings. *Endo*, in this regard, missed the forest for the trees. (As Chief Justice Rehnquist wrote of this episode, "[e]ven in wartime, citizens may not be rounded up and required to prove their loyalty.")[134] And although Justice Jackson wrote a concurrence that criticized the Court's emphasis on loyalty and came very close to embracing the proper interpretation of the Suspension Clause, he never cited the Clause itself. He also apparently never circulated his opinion and opened the draft by disclaiming that "[i]f [Endo] were in military custody for security reasons, even if I thought them weak ones, I should doubt our right to interfere for reasons I have stated in Korematsu's case." Nonetheless, Jackson's subsequent language bears highlighting for embracing the Clause's core purpose: " '[P]rotective custody' on an involuntary basis has no place in American law. The whole idea that our American citizens' right to be at large may be conditioned or denied by community prejudice or disapproval should be rejected by this Court the first time it is heard within these walls."[135]

Further, there was no argument that martial law could have somehow justified the mass internment of Japanese Americans in the western United States. After all, to borrow from *Milligan*, the civilian courts in the western United States were fully "open and their process unobstructed." As *Milligan* also held and *Duncan* reaffirmed, martial law is only appropriate within the "theatre of active military operations, where war really prevails . . . [and] no power is left but the military. . . ."[136] Thus, the argument made by then-California attorney general Earl Warren in his *Zimmerman* amicus brief that martial law was in effect in his state and justified the war measures directed at persons of Japanese ancestry is simply wrong. Further, Warren's broader assertion that "the constitutional rights of an accused are not denied" where the "detention by the military authorities" of evacuated persons is "preventive and precautionary only"[137] is at war with everything that the Founding generation thought they were accomplishing in ratifying the Suspension Clause.

Finally, it bears noting that any suspension declared during World War II on the mainland would have been constitutionally problematic, given the lack of any factual support for the internment policy and the months-long delay in implementing such policies following the attacks on Pearl Harbor. Indeed, in evaluating the episode following the war, Justice Department lawyers recognized that because there was no "[r]ebellion" or "[i]nvasion" on the mainland, it "would have been impossible to suspend habeas corpus in the continental United States during World War II."[138] More generally, the notion of widespread disloyalty is impossible to reconcile with the valorous service of Japanese Americans in the U.S. military during this period.

So how did the mass internment of tens of thousands of Japanese Americans happen? Countless commentators have explored this question in an effort to prevent history repeating itself. Decades after the war, a Commission appointed by Congress concluded that the episode was the product of "race prejudice, war hysteria, and a failure of political leadership."[139] There are surely plenty of places to look in assigning responsibility.

To begin, Biddle has been criticized for failing to remain steadfast in his objections. His legacy is certainly not helped by his January 30, 1942, memorandum to the president, which raised suspension on the mainland as a possibility, or the memorandum that he wrote on February 20, 1942 (the day after the president issued 9066), in which he advised the president that 9066 "gives very broad powers to the Secretary of War and the Military Commanders" who could "exercise[]" their authority "with respect to Japanese, irrespective of their citizenship."[140] One of Biddle's lawyers at the Justice Department, Edward Ennis, explained in a 1942 interview that for his boss, "[t]he stakes were too high and the emergency too great. Therefore, the Attorney-General let the Army have its way."[141] This mindset seems to have controlled many of the legal actors as well as military leaders throughout the relevant events, including apparently Solicitor General Charles Fahy in litigating the *Hirabayashi* and *Korematsu* cases in the Supreme Court.

Congress, too, seems to have operated on a similar plane, engaging only one time with any of the decisions that led up to the detention of Japanese Americans when it passed legislation criminalizing disobedience of the military orders that followed under 9066. Congress never debated, much less took a position, with respect to the internment policy. Western politicians, meanwhile, seemed all too comfortable giving in to public hysteria and ignoring the facts on the ground.

Then there is President Roosevelt. Worth asking in all of this is why he issued 9066 granting the broad authority that DeWitt sought in the face of opposition from key advisers. After all, his attorney general and war secretary initially came out against the policies that followed (particularly internment) and FBI Director Hoover and others expressed deep skepticism over the need for such policies.[142] A natural implication to be drawn from these facts is that Roosevelt was a driving force behind the relevant events. Support for this conclusion may be found in historian Greg Robinson's work, which details Roosevelt's extensive involvement in not only the decision to give the military broad authority over Japanese Americans, but also to delay the rescinding of 9066 and closing of the camps until after the November 1944 election. He did so notwithstanding the pendency of *Endo* before the Supreme Court and in the face of key advisers prodding him to move more quickly.[143] Robinson contends that a major factor behind 9066 and the resulting military orders was Roosevelt's predisposition to believe the worst about the potential disloyalty of Japanese Americans.[144] It does seem clear that Roosevelt's actions followed at the least from his strong inclination to defer to the military in wartime. As one biographer has written, for Roosevelt, the military had "primary direct responsibility for the achievement of war victory," which "was prerequisite to all else."[145] Consistent with this conclusion are the details that have emerged of a conversation between Roosevelt and War Department officials in the days leading up to issuance of 9066, in which the president told the War Department to prepare a plan for wholesale evacuation, and specifically noted his approval of the policy encompassing citizens. Following the meeting, Assistant Secretary of War McCloy is reported to have said: " 'We have *carte blanche* to do what we want to as far as the President is concerned.' "[146]

Attorney General Biddle recalls the president's decision this way:

> I do not think [President Roosevelt] was much concerned with the gravity or implications [of signing 9066]. He was never theoretical about things. What must be done to defend the country must be done. The decision was for his Secretary of War, not for the Attorney General, not even for J. Edgar Hoover. . . . Public opinion was on their side, so that there was no question of any substantial opposition. . . . Nor do I think that the constitutional difficulty plagued him—the Constitution has never greatly bothered any wartime President. That was a question of law, which ultimately the Supreme Court must decide.[147]

In the end, then, much of the responsibility for setting in motion and continuing the policies that followed under the auspices of 9066 falls on Roosevelt. His position, moreover, appears to have been heavily influenced by public opinion and political pressure, as is revealed in part by his resistance to rescinding 9066 and closing the camps until after the 1944 presidential election.[148]

There are stark contrasts to be drawn with other wartime episodes during which key political figures made a point of working within the governing legal framework, rather than outside of it. Compare, for example, the actions of the North administration during the American Revolutionary War as detailed in Chapter 3. Recall that the administration sought out legal advice from Lord Mansfield as to the legal status of the American rebels when faced with rising numbers of American prisoners coming to English shores. Once Mansfield advised that Americans could claim the benefit of the Habeas Corpus Act as subjects, Lord North introduced suspension legislation in Parliament to legalize the detention of American rebels "like other prisoners of war." Compare as well President Jefferson, who, as Chapter 6 explored, accepted the House's decision not to pass suspension legislation during the Burr Conspiracy and whose officers then quickly changed their approach from one of military detention to criminal prosecution with respect to the conspirators. As discussed in Chapter 7, moreover, even President Lincoln—the "Great Suspender"—never once suggested during the Civil War that persons suspected of disloyalty could be detained preventively in the absence of a suspension. One is left to wonder why such legal considerations held so little sway in political circles during the World War II period unlike earlier periods. (Consider, in this regard, the prominence of the Suspension Clause to so much of the Civil War legal and political discourse.) Perhaps here is where the issues of ethnicity and suspension intersect, insofar as there were suggestions made by General DeWitt and others in the lead-up to 9066—suggestions given credence by the Supreme Court in *Hirabayashi*[149]—that Japanese Americans were viewed as unassimilable foreigners. Regardless, it is curious that suspension only sporadically entered public discussions during World War II, given the likelihood that had a suspension been proposed, the political climate very likely would have supported its passage.

Nonetheless, some might say—in keeping with Roosevelt's apparent views as recounted above by Biddle—such legal questions were not the proper concern of a wartime president, but instead the proper province of the courts. Putting to the side that the president also takes an oath to uphold the Constitution upon taking office, this proposition only works if the judiciary decides those cases properly presented without "clos[ing] their eyes" to "the Constitution," as Chief Justice John Marshall championed long ago in *Marbury v. Madison*.[150] Measured against this benchmark, the Court's handling of the World War II Japanese American cases was not its finest hour. As legal scholar Eugene Rostow aptly lamented soon after the decisions came down (primarily targeting *Hirabayashi* and *Korematsu*): "This was not the occasion for prudent withdrawal on the part of the Supreme Court, but for affirmative leadership

in causes peculiarly within its sphere of primary responsibility." Indeed, borrowing again from Rostow, "[i]t is hard to imagine what courts are for if not to
protect people against unconstitutional arrest."[151]

The one exception to the critique of the World War II Court is *Duncan*.
But the Court decided *Duncan* after the war, just as it had *Milligan*, a reality
that surely influenced the Court's willingness to rebuke the political branches
in wartime. By contrast, in company with *Hirabayashi* and *Korematsu* is the
German saboteur case of Ex parte *Quirin*,[152] decided early in the war and discussed in the next chapter. On this point, two dissenting justices in *Duncan*
argued that it was "all too easy in this postwar period to assume that the success which our forces attained was inevitable and that military control should
have been relaxed on a schedule based upon such actual developments."[153]

Nonetheless, the inescapable fact is that the mass detention of U.S. citizens during World War II without criminal charges and in the absence of a
valid suspension violated the Suspension Clause, and many key government
officials recognized this fact at the time. By design, the Suspension Clause
recognizes a privilege born out of a judicial writ and made all the stronger by
the English Habeas Corpus Act, the entire purpose of which was to arm the
judiciary to constrain executive excess at the expense of individual rights, *even
in wartime*. The history detailed in these pages, accordingly, raises an enormously important question—at the end of the day, if the courts will not protect
the privilege, then who will?

IT WAS NOT until four years after the camps began closing that a federal court
finally declared that the detention of Japanese Americans had been unconstitutional, and even then it did so only as an aside to litigation brought by
former residents of Tule Lake Camp who challenged their renunciations of
U.S. citizenship made during their time in the camp. The plaintiffs argued, in
most cases successfully, that such renunciations had been made under duress.
In that case, Judge Louis Goodman concluded:

> I have no doubt that there was a complete lack of constitutional author-
> ity for administrative, executive or military officers to detain and
> imprison American citizens at Tule Lake who were not charged crimi-
> nally or subject to martial law.[154]

In the decades since the internment, many Japanese American survivors
have embraced a famous quotation by Chief Justice Charles Evans Hughes
that agrees with Assistant Secretary of War McCloy's assessment of the
Constitution as "just a scrap of paper." Importantly, however, Hughes drew a

different lesson from that premise, highlighting the importance of the people who stand behind the document and make its words real:

> You may think that the Constitution is your security—it is nothing but a scrap of paper. . . . You may think that elaborate mechanism of government is your security—it is nothing at all, unless you have sound and uncorrupted public opinion to give life to your Constitution. . . .[155]

In assessing 9066 and the internment some years later, Justice Tom Clark, having served as Civilian Coordinator for General DeWitt during the war, echoed Hughes's words, observing that "constitutions and laws are not sufficient of themselves," but "must be given life through implementation and strict enforcement." As he further noted, "[d]espite the unequivocal language of the Constitution . . . that the writ of habeas corpus shall not be suspended, and despite the Fifth Amendment's command that no person shall be deprived of life, liberty or property without due process of law, both of these constitutional safeguards were denied by military action under Executive Order 9066."[156]

In 1976, President Ford called "upon the American people to affirm with me this American promise—that we have learned from the tragedy of that long-ago experience forever to treasure liberty and justice for each individual American, and resolve that this kind of action shall never again be repeated."[157] Nonetheless, the inescapable legacy of this episode remains that it established a precedent that gutted the Suspension Clause and gave constitutional sanction to "a policy of mass incarceration under military auspices."[158] As will be seen, this legacy came to influence government policies decades later in the wake of the devastating terrorist attacks of September 11, 2001.

11

Habeas Corpus Today

CONFRONTING THE AGE OF TERRORISM

*There is no bar to this Nation's holding one of its own citizens
as an enemy combatant.*

HAMDI V. RUMSFELD (2004)[1]

THE EXPERIENCE OF World War II and the precedent of the Japanese American
internment dramatically altered the political and legal calculus surrounding habeas corpus and suspension. Indeed, as evidence of the changed
legal dynamic, one need look no further than Congress's enactment of the
Emergency Detention Act of 1950, a product of Cold War and McCarthy-era
anti-communism politics. The Act empowered the president to declare unilaterally an "Internal Security Emergency" and then arrest and detain persons—including citizens—based solely on suspicion of a likelihood of future
engagement in spying or sabotage on behalf of enemies of the United States.
What is perhaps most noteworthy about the Act is that Congress expressly
provided that it was *not* suspending habeas corpus when it passed it. Members
of Congress apparently believed that such a step was unnecessary.[2] (This position was in keeping with advice proffered to Attorney General Tom Clark four
years earlier, when a Justice Department official relied upon the World War
II policies directed at Japanese Americans as a basis for arguing that in the
event of war with Russia, the same approach could be employed "to detain all
Russians and Communists, whether or not American citizens."[3]) Although
the Emergency Detention Act provoked substantial academic criticism, members of Congress overwhelmingly supported its passage along with appropriations for building detention centers.[4] For his part, President Truman vetoed
the bill and called it a "mockery of the Bill of Rights" and a "long step toward
totalitarianism." Notably, Truman also argued:

> [T]he provisions in [the Emergency Detention Act] would very prob-
> ably prove ineffective to achieve the objective sought, since they would

Habeas Corpus in Wartime. Amanda L. Tyler.

not suspend the writ of habeas corpus, and under our legal system to detain a man not charged with a crime would raise serious constitutional questions unless the writ of habeas corpus were suspended.[5]

Both Houses of Congress overrode his veto within a day.

By 1971, things had changed. That year, Congress repealed the Emergency Detention Act, no president having ever invoked its emergency provisions.[6] In its place, Congress adopted the Non-Detention Act, providing that "[n]o citizen shall be imprisoned or otherwise detained by the United States except pursuant to an Act of Congress."[7] A major push for the law's passage came from the Japanese American Citizens League, which three years earlier launched a nationwide effort to repeal the Emergency Detention Act with the hope of preventing anything like the World War II internment of Japanese Americans from ever happening again.[8]

Thirty years later, in the wake of the terrorist attacks of September 11, 2001, questions over the Non-Detention Act and the scope of executive authority to detain prisoners in wartime arose anew. Once again, as it had during World War II, the historical understanding of the suspension framework and the core purpose of the Suspension Clause came under fire. As this chapter explores, nowhere is this point more evident than in the Supreme Court's sanctioning of the concept of the "citizen-enemy combatant" in its 2004 decision in *Hamdi v. Rumsfeld*. As is also explored herein, by blurring the line between the historic office of the Suspension Clause and modern due process jurisprudence, *Hamdi* chipped away at the core of the Suspension Clause's protections in that case. (*Hamdi*'s reliance on the hasty and at least in part misguided World War II decision in Ex parte *Quirin* provided much of the basis for its errors.) As is also explored, *Hamdi* also laid the groundwork for an expansion of the reach of the Clause in other cases—specifically, the habeas cases filed by detainees at Guantanamo Bay, Cuba, that came before the Supreme Court in *Boumediene v. Bush*.

The War on Terrorism in the Supreme Court: The Citizen Cases

On September 11, 2001, terrorists affiliated with al-Qaeda hijacked four commercial airliners. They flew two of them into Manhattan's World Trade Center towers, causing the collapse of the towers, and crashed a third into the Pentagon just across the river from Washington, DC. The fourth plane, likely also headed for Washington, DC, crashed in a Pennsylvania field after its crew and passengers fought back against their hijackers. Together, the attacks claimed almost 3,000 lives and injured thousands more. September 11, 2001, marked one of the darkest days in American history.

Within days of the 9/11 attacks, Congress enacted the Authorization for Use of Military Force (AUMF). The AUMF empowered the executive to "use all necessary and appropriate force against those nations, organizations, or persons he determines planned, authorized, committed, or aided the terrorist attacks that occurred on September 11, 2001 . . . in order to prevent any future acts of international terrorism against the United States by such nations, organizations, or persons."[9] Although there are suggestions that the White House initially proposed that Congress consider enacting a suspension, no one in Congress formally introduced such legislation.[10]

Under the auspices of the AUMF, the United States has waged an ongoing war on terrorism both at home and abroad against an expanding list of terrorist organizations. Initial operations in the wake of 9/11 included military offensives aimed at removing the Taliban government in Afghanistan, capturing or killing members of al-Qaeda linked to the attacks, and preventing future attacks. In the days and months following the attacks, the U.S. government arrested and detained persons without charges in the United States as "persons of interest" and, in some cases, material witnesses to the ongoing investigation of the attacks.[11] Further, as part of its many operations, the U.S. military took hundreds of suspected terrorists and others believed to possess ties to al-Qaeda into custody, including some American citizens. In the case of John Walker Lindh, a U.S. citizen captured fighting with the Taliban in Afghanistan, the government prosecuted him criminally in due course.[12] By contrast, in the cases of José Padilla and Yaser Hamdi, the government labeled the citizens as "enemy combatants" and held them in military detention without criminal charges.

On May 8, 2002, Padilla landed at Chicago's O'Hare International Airport after spending time in the Middle East. Upon his arrival, officers took Padilla into custody pursuant to a material witness warrant tied to the ongoing grand jury investigation of the 9/11 attacks in New York.[13] Approximately one month later, President George W. Bush issued an order declaring that Padilla was an "enemy combatant." In his order, the president wrote that he had "DETERMINE[D]" that Padilla "[was] closely associated with al Qaeda, an international terrorist organization with which the United States is at war"; had carried out "war-like acts, including conduct in preparation for acts of international terrorism" against the United States; "possesse[d] intelligence" that might assist the government in its counterterrorism efforts; and "represent[ed] a continuing, present and grave danger to the national security of the United States." As such, the president declared, Padilla's detention "[was] necessary to prevent him from aiding al Qaeda in its efforts to attack the United States."[14] The president then ordered Padilla's transfer to the custody of the Department of Defense.

In a habeas petition filed in federal court in New York, Padilla attacked the legality of his detention as an enemy combatant. After losing in the district court, Padilla prevailed on appeal before the United States Court of Appeals for the Second Circuit. That court directed that Padilla be released from military custody and concluded that any further detention could only be predicated upon criminal charges or his detention as a material witness. In reaching its decision, the court emphasized the language of the Non-Detention Act, concluding that it "applies to all detentions and that precise and specific language authorizing the detention of American citizens is required to override its protection."[15] On review in the Supreme Court, a five-justice majority concluded that the lower courts never had jurisdiction to reach the merits of Padilla's claims. This followed from the fact that in the days before Padilla filed his petition in New York, the government had moved him to a naval brig in South Carolina, which was located within a different federal judicial district.[16] Writing for four dissenters, Justice John Paul Stevens argued that the Court could and should reach the merits of Padilla's claims:

> At stake in this case is nothing less than the essence of a free society. Even more important than the method of selecting the people's rulers and their successors is the character of the constraints imposed on the Executive by the rule of law. Unconstrained executive detention for the purpose of investigating and preventing subversive activity is the hallmark of the Star Chamber.[17]

Following the Supreme Court's ruling, Padilla filed a new habeas petition in the relevant jurisdiction encompassing South Carolina, winning in the district court. On appeal, the United States Court of Appeals for the Fourth Circuit reversed. In its view, the AUMF gave the president the authority

> to detain militarily a citizen . . . who is closely associated with al Qaeda, an entity with which the United States is at war; who took up arms on behalf of that enemy and against our country in a foreign combat zone of that war; *and* who thereafter traveled to the United States for the avowed purpose of further prosecuting that war on American soil. . . .[18]

When Padilla sought a new round of review of his military detention in the Supreme Court, the government changed course and charged Padilla with various terrorism-related crimes. It then requested court approval to transfer Padilla to civilian authorities for prosecution. The Fourth Circuit rejected the government's request, citing the possibility "that the government may be attempting to avoid consideration of our decision by the Supreme Court" and positing that the case involved questions of such "national importance as to warrant final consideration by that court."[19] (On the first point, there are obvious analogies between the government's conduct in Padilla's case and its handling of both the *Zimmerman* and *Endo* cases, detailed in Chapter 10, in which the government sought to moot habeas cases pending before the Supreme Court by releasing the prisoner, succeeding in *Zimmerman*. Comparisons to the practice of moving prisoners during the Revolutionary and Civil Wars, as detailed in Chapters 3 and 7, are also appropriate.[20]) Nonetheless, the Supreme Court subsequently granted the government's motion to transfer Padilla and denied review of his case, albeit over the recorded dissent of three justices. By that time, the government had detained Padilla in military custody without any pending criminal charges for well over three years.[21]

Yaser Hamdi's case arrived at the Supreme Court at the same time as Padilla's first round of habeas litigation and is the only citizen-enemy combatant case in which the Court reached the merits. Hamdi, born in the United States to Saudi parents, had grown up in Saudi Arabia and made his way to Afghanistan by 2001. Following the American invasion of Afghanistan in the wake of the 9/11 attacks, the Northern Alliance, a U.S. ally in the fight against the Taliban government, captured Hamdi and turned him over to the American military, reporting that Hamdi had been fighting with the Taliban. As the military did with many prisoners captured in the wake of 9/11, it then transported Hamdi to its base at Guantanamo Bay, Cuba, for detention. At this point, the government learned that Hamdi was a U.S. citizen. It therefore transferred him to the United States for detention, with Hamdi winding up at a military installation in South Carolina. Hamdi's father thereafter filed a habeas petition on his son's behalf, challenging the detention as unconstitutional.[22]

Before the Supreme Court, Hamdi's lawyers argued that as a citizen, he could not be detained outside the criminal process in the absence of a suspension. In response, the government argued that Congress had authorized Hamdi's detention in the AUMF and that he was not entitled to independent review of his classification as an "enemy combatant" or his detention on that basis. A fractured Court reached a holding that embraced neither position. Specifically, in a plurality opinion penned by Justice Sandra Day O'Connor, the Court rejected the argument that the Suspension Clause precludes detaining a citizen as the equivalent of a prisoner of war in the absence of a suspension, while also rejecting the government's assertion that the executive could detain a citizen indefinitely without affording him some opportunity to challenge his classification as an enemy combatant.

Writing initially for herself, Chief Justice William Rehnquist, and Justices Anthony Kennedy and Stephen Breyer, Justice O'Connor concluded that the AUMF had authorized the detention of all persons captured as part of the war on terrorism, whether citizens or not. In so holding, she rejected the argument that the Non-Detention Act barred Hamdi's detention as a statutory matter. (Four other justices, by contrast, believed the Non-Detention Act barred Hamdi's detention.)[23] Continuing, and with Justices David Souter and Ruth Bader Ginsburg joining solely to "give practical effect to the conclusions of eight Members of the Court rejecting the Government's position,"[24] Justice O'Connor opined that the Court could not accept the government's arguments across the board. Specifically, her opinion observed that "detention without trial 'is the carefully limited exception'" in our constitutional tradition and cautioned that the Court should "not give short shrift to the values that this country holds dear or to the privilege that is American citizenship."[25]

Turning to Hamdi's arguments predicated upon the Suspension Clause, Justice O'Connor found them wanting, holding that "[t]here is no bar to this Nation's holding one of its own citizens as an enemy combatant"—even in the absence of a suspension.[26] In reaching this conclusion, Justice O'Connor emphasized the "context" of Hamdi's arrest, which involved "a United States citizen captured in a *foreign* combat zone."[27] She also relied heavily on Ex parte *Quirin*, an early World War II case explored at length below, in which the Court upheld the domestic military trial of an individual claiming U.S. citizenship for violations of the laws of war. Quoting *Quirin*, Justice O'Connor took it as accepted that "[c]itizens who associate themselves with the military arm of the enemy government, and with its aid, guidance and direction enter this country bent on hostile acts, are enemy belligerents within the meaning of . . . the law of war."[28] In her view, the power to try and sentence a citizen during wartime under the laws of war led inexorably to the conclusion that citizens also may be held as the equivalent of prisoners of war for the duration of hostilities.

But, Justice O'Connor wrote, this was not the end of the matter. Any citizen detained as an enemy combatant must be given "a meaningful opportunity to contest the factual basis" for his classification "before a neutral decisionmaker." Such a hearing, she wrote, should "balanc[e] [the] serious competing interests" at stake.[29] Relying primarily on the Court's due process jurisprudence developed in cases involving the removal of government benefits, Justice O'Connor posited that the relevant calculus must weigh the individual liberty interests at stake against the government's strong interest in preventing persons captured in battle from returning to the battlefield.[30] Further, in discussing which measures could satisfy due process considerations, she declined to rule out the possibility that the government could rely upon hearsay evidence or that the relevant hearing could proceed before a military tribunal.[31]

Justice Antonin Scalia, joined by Justice Stevens, dissented. Like Justices Souter and Ginsburg, the two argued that the AUMF should not be understood to override the Non-Detention Act. More generally, they rejected the idea that a citizen could be held as an enemy combatant in the absence of a suspension. Instead, they argued, the entire purpose of the Suspension Clause, which was grounded in English legal tradition, was to require that absent suspension, "[c]itizens aiding the enemy [be] treated as traitors subject to the criminal process."[32] As Justice Scalia explained:

> Where the Government accuses a citizen of waging war against it, our constitutional tradition has been to prosecute him in federal court for treason or some other crime. Where the exigencies of war prevent that, the Constitution's Suspension Clause . . . allows Congress to relax the usual protections temporarily. Absent suspension, however, the Executive's assertion of military exigency has not been thought sufficient to permit detention without charge.[33]

Relatedly, the dissent argued that the Founding generation understood the concept of due process to accord with this understanding. Specifically, due process "force[d] the Government to follow those common-law procedures traditionally deemed necessary before depriving a person of life, liberty, or property." "When a citizen was deprived of liberty because of alleged criminal conduct," Justice Scalia asserted, "those procedures typically required committal by a magistrate followed by indictment and trial."[34]

It followed, in the dissent's view, that because the government did not argue that the AUMF was a suspension, Hamdi's detention was unconstitutional. In support of this position, the dissent marshaled extensive historical evidence, beginning with the famous passage of Blackstone's *Commentaries*, invoked by Alexander Hamilton in promoting the Suspension Clause, which counseled that "it is unreasonable to send a prisoner, and not to signify the crimes alleged against him."[35] The dissent also relied upon the development of the law of treason; the 1679 English Habeas Corpus Act and its altering of the law as it stood at the time of the Case of the Five Knights; the role of suspension in the Anglo-American legal tradition, including the Jacobite suspensions, the suspension in response to Shays's Rebellion, the proposed suspension during the Burr Conspiracy, and the Civil War and Reconstruction suspensions; the government's treatment of prisoners during the War of 1812; and the writings of Thomas Jefferson and Justice Story, among others.[36] Putting all of this together, the dissent concluded that a wealth of historical evidence demonstrated that the English Habeas Corpus Act of 1679 along with its mandate "that indefinite imprisonment on reasonable suspicion is not an available option of treatment for those accused of aiding the enemy, absent a suspension of the writ" proved the foundation of the Suspension Clause and dictated that the government could not detain Hamdi as an enemy combatant.[37]

The dissent also relied on *Ex parte Milligan*, discussed in Chapter 7, in which the Supreme Court declared that a citizen could not be tried by a military tribunal for violations of the laws of war " 'where the courts are open and their process unobstructed.' "[38] Although acknowledging that *Quirin*—on which Justice O'Connor had relied heavily—postdated *Milligan*, the dissent labeled the hastily-decided *Quirin* "not this Court's finest hour." (*Quirin* is detailed extensively below.) In the dissent's view, *Milligan*, decided temporally closer to the Founding Era, remained a better "indicator of original meaning" and was in all events more in keeping with "the Founders' general mistrust of military power permanently at the Executive's disposal."* The dissent also distinguished *Quirin* on its facts, noting that there, "it was uncontested that the prisoners were members of enemy forces" or " '*admitted* enemy invaders,' " and emphasizing that the *Quirin* Court characterized its holding as based " 'upon the *conceded* facts.' "[39]

Justice Scalia's dissent concluded by citing a fundamental problem with the plurality's approach:

> If the Suspension Clause does not guarantee the citizen that he will either be tried or released [in the absence of a suspension] . . . ; if it merely guarantees the citizen that he will not be detained unless Congress by ordinary legislation says he can be detained; it guarantees him very little indeed.[40]

It followed that the majority's adoption of a judicial balancing test in this context was especially problematic and fundamentally at odds with the

---

* Note that for Justice Scalia, an avowed originalist, the original meaning of the Suspension Clause carried important weight. Justice Stevens likely joined Scalia's opinion based on his view that "the doctrine of original intent may identify a floor that includes some of a rule's coverage." Where Stevens departs from Scalia is in his view that the same doctrine "is never a sufficient basis for defining the ceiling." Justice John Paul Stevens (Ret.), *Originalism and History*, 48 GA. L. REV. 691, 693 (2014).

constitutional design. (It also reflected, in the dissent's view, a "Mr. Fix-it Mentality.") Instead, Justice Scalia argued, by recognizing a legislative power to suspend the privilege, the Founders "equipped us with a Constitution designed to deal with" the tension between individual liberty and national security that inevitably arises in times of war.[41] Putting all of this together, the dissent argued that the Constitution presented the government with two—and only two—options for detaining Hamdi: either initiate criminal proceedings against him or suspend the privilege of the writ of habeas corpus to legalize his detention outside the criminal process.

Ex parte Quirin*: The Case of the Nazi Saboteurs*

The World War II decision of Ex parte *Quirin* proved a key point of disagreement among the justices in *Hamdi*. For its part, the plurality embraced the decision and read it broadly. By contrast, the dissenting justices read *Quirin* narrowly and more generally attacked its value as precedent. The dissent had good reason to do so. The *Quirin* decision arose out of extraordinary circumstances and the Court's full opinion came down only after the government had already carried out death sentences for six of the German saboteurs whose habeas petitions proved the basis of the case. For this and other reasons explored below, *Quirin* is a deeply problematic precedent.

On June 27, 1942, the FBI announced that it had taken into custody eight German agents who had been trained in military-industrial sabotage and traveled across the Atlantic in German vessels to carry out their orders. Landing in two groups, one in New York and one in Florida, the agents arrived in the dead of night, changed into civilian clothing, and then buried their German uniforms. All of the saboteurs had been born in Germany and lived in the United States at various times before the war, and two, Herbert Hans Haupt and Ernest Peter Burger, arguably held dual German and American citizenship. (The complications generally posed by dual citizenship are discussed further below.) Almost immediately after landing in New York and after encountering a Coast Guard official, two of the saboteurs attempted to turn themselves in to the FBI. An initial attempt to make contact with the Manhattan FBI office appears to have been met with skepticism, and it was not until one of the saboteurs traveled to FBI headquarters in Washington, DC, to turn himself in that the Bureau took the matter seriously.[42]

In the days that followed, the same members of Roosevelt's administration who had months earlier debated the propriety of interning Japanese Americans now debated how to treat the saboteurs. Attorney General Francis

Biddle and Secretary of War Henry Stimson worried that the saboteurs had not taken enough action to warrant lengthy criminal sentences in the civilian courts. Secretary Stimson recorded in his diary that to his "surprise," Biddle was "quite ready to turn them over to a military court."[43] Supreme Court justice Felix Frankfurter had also urged the administration to prosecute the saboteurs in a military tribunal.[44] In all events, on June 30, Biddle recommended that President Roosevelt constitute a military commission for their trial. Biddle argued that a commission could reach judgment more quickly than a civilian court and that trying violations of the laws of war in such a forum would be easier and enable the government to seek the death penalty. (Then-existing federal statutes did not provide for the death penalty as a punishment for the actions of the noncitizen saboteurs.) Biddle also counseled against charging the two citizen-saboteurs with treason, something the president had earlier suggested, because doing so "might give rise to the implication that we should accord [them] the privilege of *habeas corpus* proceedings against the Military Commission." (Proving treason with respect to the citizen-saboteurs would also have been difficult because of the heightened standard of proof that the Constitution requires in treason cases.) Further, Biddle noted that there was evidence that the two dual nationals had forfeited their U.S. citizenship. In sum, by employing a military commission, Biddle argued, all the prisoners could be denied access to civilian courts.[45]

For his part, the president was convinced of the saboteurs' guilt and believed the death penalty an appropriate sentence.[46] Thus, on July 2, Roosevelt created a special military commission to try the saboteurs and prescribed procedures for the commission to follow. Among many differences from standard civilian court procedures, the commission would not empanel juries, as the Constitution requires for criminal trials in the civilian courts, and it would accept a broader range of evidence. Violations of the laws of war were subject to the death penalty and convictions on death-eligible crimes required the approval of only two-thirds of the sitting judges. Finally, the only avenue for appeal for those convicted was to the president himself. In these respects, the rules were similar to those employed by the commission that tried the Lincoln conspirators.

Urged on by Biddle, the president issued a separate proclamation providing that

> all persons who are subjects, citizens or residents of any nation at war
> with the United States or who give obedience to or act under the direc-
> tion of any such nation, and who during time of war enter or attempt
> to enter the United States ... and are charged with committing or

attempting or preparing to commit sabotage, espionage, hostile or war-like acts, or violations of the laws of war, shall be subject to the law of war and to the jurisdiction of military tribunals; and that such persons shall not be privileged to seek any remedy, or maintain any proceeding directly or indirectly or to have any such remedy or proceedings sought on their behalf, in the courts of the United States. . . .[47]

Lest there be any doubt as to the president's intentions, Biddle recounted that Roosevelt said that he would not hand over the saboteurs "to any United States marshal armed with a writ of habeas corpus. Understand?"[48]

Secret proceedings began in earnest against the saboteurs, who were tried together for violations of the Articles of War and more generally, as Milligan had been, with "violation of the law of war."[49] At the conclusion of the presentation of evidence in the saboteurs' trial, military counsel appointed to represent them sought leave to file petitions for writs of habeas corpus in a federal district court, which the court denied within a matter of hours.[50] Counsel next sought to advance their challenges to the commission before the Supreme Court, which announced that it would sit in special session to hear the case and hold arguments in the middle of the saboteurs' ongoing trial.[51] As things quickly unfolded, when the justices met in conference to discuss the case before the first day of oral argument, Justice Roberts reportedly conveyed to his colleagues that Biddle had told him that President Roosevelt was likely to order the execution of the saboteurs regardless of what the Court decided. With the exception of Justice Frank Murphy, moreover, several of the justices with arguable conflicts of interest declined to recuse themselves.[52]

At oral argument before the Supreme Court, defense counsel relied heavily on *Milligan* to attack the commission on multiple grounds, pointing out that the civilian courts remained open and questioning the application of the largely unwritten laws of war to a federal prosecution. (Counsel also attacked as a violation of the Suspension Clause the president's order precluding access to civilian courts.)[53] Biddle himself argued the case for the government, having personally overseen the prosecution below, and at various points urged the Court to overrule *Milligan*. After affording the case two days of oral argument, the Court took it under advisement.

The very next day, the Court issued a brief unsigned opinion that sided with the government, with the promise of a full opinion to be issued some months later. Specifically, after concluding that it had jurisdiction to hear the saboteurs' claims, the Court held that "the military commission was lawfully constituted," the president had the authority to bring the relevant charges against the saboteurs before such a commission, and the petitioners were in lawful custody.[54] Three days later, the commission found the saboteurs guilty of all charges and sentenced them to death.[55] Five days after that, the government carried out the electrocution of six of the saboteurs, including Haupt. (Roosevelt commuted the sentences of the two saboteurs who had betrayed their mission, one of whom was Burger.)

Three months later, the Court issued its explanatory opinion. Written by Chief Justice Harlan Fiske Stone, the opinion followed only after considerable struggle on Stone's part. Indeed, he reportedly described the process of writing the opinion as "a mortification of the flesh" and at times had circulated alternative holdings on certain grounds to his colleagues.[56] In final form, the opinion distinguished *Milligan* as presenting circumstances different from those in the case at bar, largely because Milligan "had never been a resident of any of the states in rebellion" and had "not be[en] a part of or associated with the armed forces of the enemy." Thus, the opinion observed, he could not have been classified as an unlawful combatant or "enemy belligerent" within the law of war. By contrast, the Court held that "upon the conceded facts," the saboteurs were belligerents within the meaning of the law of war because they had come behind enemy lines in disguise to engage in hostile acts. Lawful combatants under the law of war, Stone wrote, are "entitled to be treated as prisoners of war." But unlawful combatants, or "belligerents," are subject to punishment by military commissions.[57] Here, Stone compared the saboteurs to Major John André, the British spy with whom Benedict Arnold had conspired.[58] The Court concluded by reading *Milligan*'s "statement as to the inapplicability of the law of war to Milligan's case as having particular reference to the facts before it."[59]

Then there was the matter of citizenship. Chief Justice Stone had asked his law clerk to research the citizenship of both Burger and Haupt, and his clerk laid out the arguments as to how one or both may have effectively renounced their citizenship by returning to Germany.[60] In the meantime, defense counsel conceded that Burger had renounced his citizenship.[61] It is reported that over the course of writing the opinion, Stone came to question whether Haupt should have been tried for treason in a civilian court, but the final opinion contained no hint of such thinking.[62] (Of course, one must remember that the government had already executed Haupt by the time the Court's opinion came down.) Instead, Stone merely noted that the government challenged Haupt's citizenship and went on to hold any possible citizenship irrelevant. This was, in Stone's words, because "[c]itizenship in the United States of an enemy belligerent does not relieve him of the consequences of belligerency which is unlawful because in violation of the law of war." "[E]ven when committed by a citizen, [an] offense [against the law of war] is distinct from the crime of treason defined in Article III, § 3 of the Constitution, since the absence of uniform essential to one is irrelevant to the other."[63]

And so, on one account, the *Quirin* Court gutted *Milligan* as precedent. Indeed, in a note sent along with the Court's opinion to the president, Biddle asserted that "[p]ractically . . . *Milligan* . . . is out of the way and should not plague us again."[64] Further, shortly after the Court announced *Quirin*, Justice Frankfurter asked a former student and expert on military law what he thought of the opinion. The former student responded that "after *Quirin* it was now possible for military tribunals to try 'persons dangerous to our institutions,' even if they were American citizens and even if they were not members of an invading military force, for offenses against the international law of war. . . ."[65]

But should *Quirin* be read so broadly? Before long, even Justice Frankfurter, who had supported employing a military commission at the outset, came to view the decision as "not a happy precedent."[66] Justice William O. Douglas, too, came to regret the way in which the decision had been rendered, suggesting that the unorthodox delay in issuing the Court's reasoning for its holding revealed that the grounds for it had "crumble[d]."[67] It is hard to dispute that *Quirin* represents, in the words of one critic, a "rush to judgment,"[68] and that it was decided under far from model circumstances. Further, at least one member of the Court at the time, Justice Hugo Black, had urged Stone to "leave the *Milligan* doctrine untouched" and "go no further than to declare that these particular defendants are subject to the jurisdiction of a military tribunal because of the circumstances and purpose of their entry. . . ."[69]

Any modern assessment of *Quirin* must acknowledge, in Justice Scalia's words, that the decision was "not th[e] Court's finest hour." Further, *Quirin* and *Milligan* are exceedingly difficult to reconcile. *Quirin* might be read, as Justice Black suggested, as narrowly decided on conceded facts that do not otherwise call into question the general holding of *Milligan*, at least with respect to citizens. After all, *Quirin* never directly engaged with the fact that Milligan had been charged with violations of the laws of war, just as the saboteurs had, or with *Milligan*'s larger holding that the law of war "can never be applied to citizens in states which have upheld the authority of the government, and where the courts are open and their process unobstructed."[70] This is likely because the foundations of the Court's holding in *Quirin* do not hold up under scrutiny. In lumping citizen and noncitizen saboteurs together as both subject to the laws of war, Stone inescapably suggested that citizen-saboteurs could be subject to the full spectrum of the laws of war, including the recognition that persons may be held upon capture as lawful combatants in a preventive posture as prisoners of war. (Here, however, Stone concluded that circumstances supported a different classification—that of unlawful combatants—for the saboteurs.)

This conclusion is at odds with the historical understanding of the core purpose of the Suspension Clause, which provides a specific tool—suspension—for legalizing the detention of persons who could claim the protection of domestic law in a posture equivalent to that of a prisoner of war. Indeed, the very purpose of suspension has always been to render lawful such otherwise unlawful detentions. Recall the discussion of the early English suspensions, the Revolutionary War suspension, and the Civil War suspensions in Chapters 2, 3, 7 and 8, all of which were adopted to legalize preventive detention of persons who could claim the protection of domestic law. (Recall further that Lord North, in introducing the British suspension targeting the American rebels during the Revolutionary War, called the legislation necessary to treat the rebels "like other prisoners of war.") It follows that if a citizen can never be held in a posture akin to a prisoner of war in the absence of a suspension—that is, as a lawful combatant under the laws of war—that a citizen likewise should not be punishable as an *unlawful* combatant under the laws of war.[71] Of the two decisions, *Milligan* is the only precedent consistent with this long-standing legal framework. In short, if *Quirin* has any legitimacy today with respect to citizens, it must be limited to the Court's emphasis on the "conceded" belligerency of Haupt.

On this score, Stone never fully dealt with the question whether charging Haupt with treason was the proper course. Nor could he have done so persuasively. His position that the government had the choice to prosecute Haupt either for treason in violation of domestic law or under the law of war is at odds with the English legal landscape detailed in Chapter 2, which in turn heavily influenced the long-standing view of treason and allegiance in American law, as detailed in Chapter 4. (Nor was Stone's position helped by the only authority he cited for the proposition—namely, two cases that upheld the government's right to proceed on multiple domestic law charges against criminal defendants—which, of course, included provision for the full panoply of procedural rights that the criminal process offers defendants.[72]) This likely explains why the government prosecuted numerous other naturalized citizens of German origin who had helped the saboteurs in civilian courts, in many cases for treason, as opposed to before military commissions. This group includes Haupt's father, who was convicted of treason for harboring and aiding Haupt's efforts and whose conviction the Supreme Court upheld on review.[73] When another case from this group reached the Supreme Court only three years after *Quirin*, the Court recounted how the Founding generation wrote the Constitution with the "betrayal of Washington by Arnold . . . fresh in mind" and against the backdrop of the Continental Congress's declaration that allegiance was expected of "all persons residing within any colony."[74] In other words, with respect to U.S. citizens, the Court belatedly recognized that the appropriate Revolutionary War comparison in the case of disaffected citizens was Benedict Arnold—*not* British Major John André, as the *Quirin* Court suggested.

Supporting this conclusion is the post-World War II decision in *Kawakita v. United States*, which tackled the question of allegiance and dual citizenship in times of war. Kawakita was born in the United States to Japanese parents, traveled to Japan in 1939, and then took work during the war as an interpreter at a Japanese factory and mine that used American prisoners of war for their labor. When Kawakita returned to the United States after the war, the government prosecuted him for treason based on his treatment of American prisoners at the factory. Before the Supreme Court, Kawakita argued that he had renounced his U.S. citizenship during the war. The Court disagreed and upheld his conviction for treason. Echoing James Wilson and the English understanding of allegiance, the Court emphasized that "American citizenship, until lost, carries obligations of allegiance as well as privileges and benefits." Nothing about dual citizenship, the Court noted, changes this conclusion, for "[o]ne who has dual nationality will be subject to claims from both nations, claims which at times may be competing or conflicting."[75] Continuing, the Court observed that "a person caught in that predicament can resolve the conflict of duty by openly electing one nationality or the other," but "he cannot turn it into a fair-weather citizenship, retaining it for possible contingent benefits but meanwhile playing the part of the traitor."[76] This conclusion is consistent with that reached by Chief Justice Oliver Ellsworth in *Williams' Case*, detailed in Chapter 2, in which Ellsworth observed of a dual citizen: "If he embarrasses himself by contracting contradictory obligations the fault and the folly are his own."[77] As further detailed in Chapters 2 and 3, *Kawakita* is also consistent with pre-ratification English law on these questions, as reflected in the treatment of Jacobites who purported to bear allegiance only to the Stuart line, as well as how the British treated the American rebels during the Revolutionary War. It is also consistent with a host of evidence suggesting that early American legal thinking embraced the same understanding of the difficulties of casually casting off allegiance.[78]

In other words, even dual citizens are bound by their obligations so long as the bond of allegiance is not broken. Importantly, the *Kawakita* Court also reaffirmed that with that bond comes "privileges and benefits"—specifically, the protection of domestic law. *Kawakita*, in this regard, calls into question an earlier decision by a federal appellate court during the war, In re *Territo*,[79] on which Justice O'Connor relied in her *Hamdi* opinion. *Territo* involved a U.S. citizen who was captured fighting for Italy during World War II and then detained as a prisoner of war in the United States without criminal charges during the war. In rejecting Territo's argument that he could not be held as a prisoner of war in light of his citizenship (and in the absence of a suspension on the mainland), the *Territo* court ignored the significance of allegiance within the constitutional suspension framework.[80] Although the Supreme Court never reviewed *Territo*, at a minimum *Kawakita* casts significant doubt upon its soundness today.

Kawakita is also consistent with the post-World War II case of *Duncan v. Kahanamoku*,[81] discussed in the last chapter. Recall that *Duncan* held that the military trials of civilians in the Hawaiian Islands during the war violated the Hawaiian Organic Act. *Duncan* also opined that citizens on the Islands enjoyed the full panoply of procedural rights that the Constitution guarantees to those accused of criminal activity. Notably, *Duncan* relied heavily on *Milligan* in recognizing that the Founding generation was "especially concerned about the potential evils of summary criminal trials and . . . guarded against them by provisions embodied in the constitution itself." To this end, *Duncan* declared: "Courts and their procedural safeguards are indispensable to our system of government."[82] To be sure, *Duncan*'s author, Justice Black, cited *Quirin* and stated that the Court did not mean to call into question the military trial of "enemy belligerents, prisoners of war, or others charged with violating the laws of war."[83] But given Black's earlier reservations about *Quirin*'s treatment of *Milligan*, his extensive reliance on *Milligan* in *Duncan*, and the broader sweep of *Duncan*'s postwar assessment of the subjugation of the military to civilian government in our constitutional system, *Duncan* provides further support for the proposition that *Quirin* should be regarded as a wartime aberration with limited, if any, applicability to legal questions surrounding the detention of citizens today.

Returning to Hamdi *and* Padilla

In the wake of *Hamdi*, some prominent legal scholars applauded the plurality opinion's pragmatic approach, which determined the process required by balancing the individual liberty interests at stake in the case against the government interest in national security.[84] Some have also observed that Hamdi received far more process under Justice O'Connor's opinion than he would have during a suspension. Of course, it is far from obvious that Congress would have pursued a suspension in the wake of a majority opinion ordering

Hamdi's discharge, nor is it clear that the circumstances of Hamdi's capture would have supported a constitutionally permissible suspension covering his case. (Specifically, it is not obvious that the overseas Afghan conflict constituted a "Rebellion or Invasion" that could justify a suspension, although on the domestic front the attacks of September 11 themselves obviously present a much closer question.) In all events, whatever the normative merits of such an approach, there is a basic problem with applying it in cases such as *Hamdi* or *Padilla*—it is entirely at odds with the core understanding of what the Founding generation thought they were accomplishing in ratifying the Suspension Clause.

Consider Padilla's case. There is no principled way to distinguish his situation from that of the Jacobites who plotted to restore James II to the throne or from the English subjects who chose to fight for France during the same period, discussed in Chapters 2 and 3. With respect to the latter group, recall that Lord Mansfield believed that they enjoyed the full protections of English law, a conclusion he offered as instructive on the constraints that limited the Crown's authority to hold rebellious American colonists on English soil without criminal charges during the Revolutionary War. Nor was Padilla's situation distinguishable in principle from those detained outside the criminal process during the Civil War and Reconstruction periods when suspension was deemed necessary, as discussed in Chapters 7, 8, and 9. In Padilla's case, the government ultimately tried him for various federal crimes, but this should not obscure the fact that it did so only after detaining him unconstitutionally as an enemy combatant for several years up to that point.

As for *Hamdi*, some jurists and scholars have distinguished Hamdi from Padilla in part because Hamdi was taken into custody overseas, whereas Padilla was taken into custody on U.S. soil.[85] Indeed, the *Hamdi* plurality emphasized his "capture[] in a *foreign* combat zone" as part of the war in Afghanistan, a more specific conflict than the expansive war on terrorism and one of international character.[86] But here again, historical examples suggest that these distinctions should not matter to the inquiry. To be sure, functional considerations are especially compelling in a battlefield setting. The collection of evidence and securing of witnesses in that setting undoubtedly present tremendous challenges and may impose undesirable distractions from achieving important military objectives. Nonetheless, as detailed in Chapter 2, English law as chronicled by Hale and Coke considered persons owing allegiance "that raise war against the king" to be "not properly enemies but rebels or traitors" and provided that as such "they shall be punished as Traytors." One of the principal forms of treason, of course, was and remains levying war against a government to which one is bound by allegiance, a basic principle reflected in

the U.S. Constitution's Treason Clause and embraced at the Founding, as discussed in Chapter 4.[87] This explains why Parliament's pre-ratification suspensions encompassed those persons who took up arms and actually "levied war"
against the Crown. Consider those who fought with Bonnie Prince Charlie
in Scotland, at whom Parliament directed its 1744 and 1745 suspensions, or
the rebellious American colonists, at whom it directed the 1777 suspension
and its many extensions. The same may be said of President Lincoln's Civil
War suspension proclamations and Congress's 1863 suspension legislation,
both of which encompassed not only disaffected citizens, but also Confederate
soldiers.

Further, once the government transported Hamdi to U.S. soil, any arguments regarding the potential geographic limitations of the Suspension
Clause vanished.[88] By that point, Hamdi's case looked just like that of the
English subjects discussed in Chapter 3 who had gone to fight for the
French flag and whom Lord Mansfield viewed as maintaining their rights
under the Habeas Corpus Act when they were held in custody on English
soil.[89] Parallels may also be drawn to the American rebels captured in battle
on the "sovereignless sea" or other places outside Britain who were then
transported for detention to English soil, where the Habeas Corpus Act
granted its protections to all British subjects. As Lord North declared at
the time, a suspension was necessary to hold the Americans "like other
prisoners of war." And, as Chapter 3 also explored, only after independence
became a foregone conclusion did Parliament view the lines of allegiance
as broken such that it no longer needed a suspension to detain American
soldiers. At this point, Parliament recognized that the law of nations—and
not domestic law—now governed the detention of those Americans remaining in custody.

In sum, the concept of a citizen-enemy combatant recognized in *Hamdi*
cannot be reconciled with the understanding of the suspension model that
governed up to and during the American Revolution, Founding Era, Civil War,
and Reconstruction periods. It is also at odds with Attorney General Biddle's
recognition during World War II that the internment of U.S. citizens violated
the Suspension Clause. As has been shown throughout earlier chapters, the
Founding generation adopted the Suspension Clause to force the government
to choose between criminally prosecuting those suspected of disaffection or
treason who could claim the protection of domestic law, or suspending the
privilege—where permitted—in order to legalize detention outside the criminal process. In short, the detention of citizen-enemy combatants on American
soil stands at odds with the historical understanding of the suspension framework that controlled well through Reconstruction.[90]

The Suspension Clause and Guantanamo Bay

The overwhelming number of those detained as enemy combatants under the auspices of the AUMF were not U.S. citizens, but instead persons captured overseas on Afghan battlefields or in other foreign nations away from the theater of battle who were citizens of other nations, many of which were at peace with the United States. The U.S. military transported those who were captured under such circumstances and designated as enemy combatants to the U.S. military installation at Guantanamo Bay, Cuba, for long-term detention. Possibly taking inspiration from the Earl of Clarendon and Civil War secretary of war Edwin M. Stanton, both of whom dispatched prisoners to far-off islands to avoid the reach of habeas courts, the Bush administration may have chosen Guantanamo Bay in part based on a belief that it would fall outside the habeas jurisdiction of federal courts.[91]

When the Guantanamo detainees sought to challenge their classification as enemy combatants, a protracted interbranch conflict followed over whether the courts should entertain such cases. In the first of three major decisions on the subject, the Supreme Court held in 2004 that the federal habeas statute provided for federal court jurisdiction over such challenges.[92] Congress wasted little time responding, passing two statutes with the objective of stripping federal courts of jurisdiction over all habeas challenges brought by Guantanamo detainees.[93] (The second statute, titled the Military Commissions Act of 2006 (MCA), came in response to the Supreme Court decision in *Hamdan v. Rumsfeld*, which had interpreted the first statute as not applicable to pending cases.[94])

These events set the stage for the Supreme Court's 2008 decision in *Boumediene v. Bush*. In the face of clear statutory language stripping federal court jurisdiction over habeas petitions brought by Guantanamo detainees, the Supreme Court was faced with addressing the question whether the detainees enjoyed a constitutional right to such review.[95] *Boumediene* also raised the subsidiary question whether the procedures established by Congress in the MCA governing the review of enemy combatant classifications provided constitutionally-sufficient process. (Specifically, those procedures provided for review of detainee challenges by military commissions followed by limited review on appeal before Article III federal courts.)

In a 5-4 decision written by Justice Kennedy, the Court held that the Guantanamo detainees could lay claim to "the constitutional privilege of habeas corpus, a privilege not to be withdrawn except in conformance with the Suspension Clause." This conclusion, in the Court's view, meant that the detainees were entitled to challenge their designation as enemy combatants in federal court. As for the procedures set forth in the MCA, the Court held that they were constitutionally deficient on several fronts. It therefore followed that the MCA "operate[d] as an unconstitutional suspension of the writ."[96]

Before analyzing the issues presented in *Boumediene*, the majority had to address a threshold matter never before resolved by the Court—specifically, whether the Suspension Clause provides an affirmative right to judicial review in declaring that "[t]he Privilege of the Writ of Habeas Corpus shall not be suspended, unless when in Cases of Rebellion or Invasion the public Safety may require it." Holding in the affirmative, the Court relied upon a range of sources from the ratification debates, which it concluded revealed that the Founding generation assumed that the availability of the privilege was implicitly guaranteed under the Suspension Clause. In the Court's words, "[t]he Clause . . . ensures that, except during periods of formal suspension, the Judiciary will have a time-tested device, the writ, to maintain the 'delicate balance of governance' that is itself the surest safeguard of liberty."[97] Having resolved this matter, the majority turned to the much harder questions looming in the case.

Most important for present purposes, those questions included whether the petitioners—detained as enemy combatants in the war on terrorism outside the formal territory of the United States—could claim the protections of the U.S. Constitution, including the Suspension Clause, and, if so, what those protections entailed. This required the Court to address the government's argument that "noncitizens designated as enemy combatants and detained in territory located outside [the] Nation's borders have no constitutional rights" and do not enjoy the "privilege of habeas corpus." The Court began by turning to "the history and origins of the writ," observing that "to the extent there were settled precedents or legal commentaries in 1789 regarding the exterritorial scope of the writ or its application to enemy aliens, those authorities can be instructive for the present cases."[98]

On this score, the Court observed that the Founding generation included "specific language in the Constitution to secure the writ" because "[e]xperience [had] taught . . . that the common-law writ all too often had been insufficient to guard against the abuse of monarchial power."[99] It then traced the early origins of the writ as a means of "enforc[ing] the King's prerogative to inquire into the authority of a jailer to hold a prisoner" through its evolution into a judicial instrument for restraining "the King's power." Noting that the "writ remained an imperfect check" during this period, the Court observed that the English Habeas Corpus Act of 1679 had "established procedures for issuing the writ." The Court also recognized that the Act "was the model upon which the habeas statutes of the 13 American colonies were based."

"[S]eeking guidance . . . from founding-era authorities," the Court turned to address the specific question whether "foreign nationals, apprehended and detained in distant countries during a time of serious threats to our Nation's security, may assert the privilege of the writ and seek its protection." In examining this question, the Court sought "to construct a view of the common-law writ as it existed in 1789." Here, the Court first observed that "at common law a petitioner's status as an alien was not a categorical bar to habeas corpus relief." Specifically with respect to enemy aliens, the Court noted that "common-law courts entertained habeas petitions brought by enemy aliens detained in England—'entertained' at least in the sense that the courts held hearings to determine the threshold question of entitlement to the writ."[100] The Court deemed English authorities in this context unclear as to whether courts denied such habeas petitions on the basis of the merits or a lack of jurisdiction, adding in all events that "[t]o the extent these authorities suggest the common-law courts abstained altogether from matters involving prisoners of war, there was greater justification for doing so in the context of declared wars with other nation states."[101]

Turning to the "geographic scope of the writ at common law," the Court found a similarly complicated historical record. After extensive discussion of the availability of the writ in various parts of the British Empire, the Court concluded that "a categorical or formal conception of sovereignty does not provide a comprehensive or altogether satisfactory explanation for the general understanding" that English law took with respect to the reach of the writ during the decades preceding ratification. Thus, in light of "the inherent shortcomings in the historical record," the Court turned to alternative considerations. On this score, the Court highlighted the "unique status of Guantanamo Bay" and observed that "no law other than the laws of the United States applies at the naval station." The Court also referenced "the particular dangers of terrorism in the modern age" and their lack of clear historical analogy.[102]

For its part, the government had argued that because the U.S. does not exercise formal sovereignty over Guantanamo Bay, the naval base is beyond the reach of U.S. courts. The Court acknowledged that Guantanamo Bay is "not formally part of the United States," but it nonetheless took "notice of the obvious and uncontested fact that the United States, by virtue of its complete jurisdiction and control over the base [under its perpetual lease with the Cuban government], maintains *de facto* sovereignty over this territory."[103] Noting as well that prior Court decisions had never maintained a strict geographic tie between application of the Constitution and *de jure* sovereignty, the Court found the government's arguments wanting.

In addressing this aspect of the case, the Court had to confront its earlier World War II decision in *Johnson v. Eisentrager. Eisentrager* declined to award habeas relief to German nationals who had been captured and tried for war crimes in China and later dispatched to serve out their sentences in Germany. In *Eisentrager*, the petitioners claimed that their trial, conviction, and imprisonment violated "Articles I and III of the Constitution, and the Fifth Amendment thereto, and other provisions of the Constitution and laws of the United States and pro- visions of the Geneva Convention governing treatment of prisoners of war."[104] According to Justice Kennedy, it was unclear whether the *Eisentrager* Court rejected the petitioners' claims as a matter of jurisdiction or on the merits—or both. In all events, Justice Kennedy's opinion distinguished *Eisentrager* from the case at bar on three fronts. First, "practical considerations" had played an important role in the case. Second, the United States lacked both *de jure* sover- eignty and plenary control over Landsberg Prison, where the petitioners were being detained. Third, the petitioners in *Eisentrager* "did not contest, it seems, the Court's assertion that they were 'enemy alien[s].' "[105] By contrast, the Court noted, the detainees before the Court disputed their classification as enemy combatants as a threshold matter. Ultimately, the Court concluded, "questions of extraterrito- riality [must] turn on objective factors and practical concerns, not formalism."[106]

More generally, the Court explained that "[t]he Constitution grants Congress and the President the power to acquire, dispose of, and govern ter- ritory, not the power to decide when and where its terms apply." The Court viewed the government's argument against application of the Suspension Clause to Guantanamo Bay as rendering it "possible for the political branches to govern [there] without legal constraint," a proposition that the Court found to be at odds with American constitutional tradition.[107] (As the majority also highlighted, in these cases, "the consequence of error may be detention of persons for the duration of hostilities that may last a generation or more.") Declaring the "writ of habeas corpus . . . an indispensable mechanism for monitoring the separation of powers" and relying upon a host of functional considerations and larger separation-of-powers principles,* the Court held that the Suspension Clause "has full effect at Guantanamo Bay."[108]

---

* Specifically, the Court posited that "at least three factors are relevant in determining the reach of the Suspension Clause":

> (1) the citizenship and status of the detainee and the adequacy of the process by which that status determination was made; (2) the nature of the sites where apprehension and then detention took place; and (3) the practical obstacles inherent in resolving the prisoner's entitlement to the writ.

Boumediene v. Bush, 553 U.S. 723, 766 (2008).

This conclusion, the Court held, meant that the detainees possessed the right to challenge their designations and be afforded an opportunity to secure release in the event of error. It followed that the next question for the Court was whether Congress had afforded the detainees sufficient procedural opportunities in the MCA to do so. Concluding that those procedures did not offer "an adequate substitute for habeas corpus" for a number of reasons,[109] the Court rejected the MCA framework and held that the detainees were entitled to challenge their status as enemy combatants before Article III courts in far more robust proceedings than the MCA provisions permitted. (The Court said little about what such proceedings would entail, leaving much of the details to be worked out by the lower courts.[110])

In the first of two dissenting opinions, Chief Justice John Roberts, joined by Justices Scalia, Clarence Thomas, and Samuel Alito, criticized the Court for "strik[ing] down as inadequate the most generous set of procedural protections ever afforded aliens detained by this country as enemy combatants."[111] Then, after noting that the *Hamdi* plurality had "stated that constitutionally adequate collateral process could be provided 'by an appropriately authorized and properly constituted military tribunal'" for the citizen in that case, Chief Justice Roberts asserted that "surely the Due Process Clause does not afford *non*-citizens in such circumstances greater protection than citizens are due."[112] The chief justice further argued that the majority could have adopted a narrower reading of the MCA to preserve its constitutionality had it wanted to do so.[113] Concluding, the chief justice predicted that the Court's opinion would have little effect in the lower courts and argued that the "majesty [of the Great Writ] is hardly enhanced by its extension to a jurisdictionally quirky outpost, with no tangible benefit to anyone."[114]

Justice Scalia also dissented, joined by the chief justice and Justices Thomas and Alito. For Justice Scalia, "[t]he writ as preserved in the Constitution could not possibly extend farther than the common law provided when the [Suspension] Clause was written."[115] Thus, the relevant inquiry did not need to go further than recognizing that "[t]he writ of habeas corpus does not, and never has, run in favor of aliens abroad." Nor could broader separation-of-powers principles support the Court's holding, Justice Scalia argued, because those principles are not derived "from some judicially imagined matrix, but from the sum total of the individual separation-of-powers principles that the Constitution sets forth."[116] (In other words, he argued that separation-of-powers principles did not establish a freestanding constitutional restraint on government but were instead the product of the design and specific elements of the Constitution.)

In Justice Scalia's view, precedent also foreclosed the majority's holding. Specifically, Justice Scalia quoted from Justice Robert Jackson's opinion for the Court in *Eisentrager*, which stated:

> We are cited to no instance where a court, in this or any other country where the writ is known, has issued it on behalf of an alien enemy who, at no relevant time and in no stage of his captivity, has been within its territorial jurisdiction. Nothing in the text of the Constitution extends such a right. . . .[117]

Justice Scalia also emphasized the *Eisentrager* Court's observation that "in extending constitutional protections beyond the citizenry . . . , it was the alien's presence within its territorial jurisdiction that gave the Judiciary power to act."[118] Further, in his view, "[t]he category of prisoner comparable to these detainees are not the *Eisentrager* criminal defendants, but the more than 400,000 prisoners of war detained in the United States alone during World War II." As he noted, "[n]ot a single one was accorded the right to have his detention validated by a habeas corpus action in federal court—and that despite the fact that they were present on U.S. soil."[119]

As for history, Justice Scalia rejected the notion that the writ followed the king's officers wherever they went, drawing attention in particular to the geographic limitations of the English Habeas Corpus Act and the fact that it did not extend to all parts of the British Empire.[120] Nor, in his view, had things changed with the adoption of the Suspension Clause. That conclusion followed, according to the dissent, directly from the wording of the Clause, which limits suspension "almost entirely to instances of domestic crisis."[121] In concluding, Justice Scalia chided the majority for basing its decision on "an inflated notion of judicial supremacy" and warned that "[t]he Nation will live to regret what the Court has done today."[122]

THERE IS A great deal to unpack from *Boumediene*. To begin, there is the Court's significant holding that the Suspension Clause provides for an affirmative guarantee of judicial review of executive detention. This holding is supported by the extensive evidence detailed in earlier chapters demonstrating that the Founding generation simply took for granted that a constitutional privilege born out of the protections of the Habeas Corpus Act would be available unless suspended. Here, I agree with legal scholars Daniel Meltzer and David Shapiro, both of whom have recognized that the privilege "is essential to the full realization of certain other guarantees" in the Constitution.[123] This is why speakers during the ratification debates declared, among other things, that the habeas "privilege . . . is essential to freedom." To be sure, it is not clear that the Founding generation had fully determined how the privilege would be secured, given that the Constitution does not mandate the creation of inferior federal courts but instead leaves the decision whether to "ordain and establish" such courts to Congress.[124] Given that at the time of the Constitution's ratification, state courts were well established and possessed a wealth of experience with habeas petitions, it is likely that the Founding generation assumed that state courts would fill any void left in the absence of federal courts. (In all events, the First Congress established inferior federal courts and vested them with habeas jurisdiction in the Judiciary Act of 1789.[125])

Beyond this threshold matter, several additional aspects of *Boumediene* warrant discussion. In particular, there is the debate among the justices over the content and significance of history along with the relevant status of both Guantanamo Bay and the detainees. With respect to history, the Court concluded that the historical record was "not dispositive" as to the questions before it, turning instead to larger separation-of-powers principles to reach its holding. Justice Scalia's dissent, by contrast, argued that historically the writ never reached abroad to aliens and as such, the detainees could make no claim to the constitutional privilege.

In many respects, the two sides were talking past one another. To begin, Justice Scalia's dissent correctly highlighted the geographic limitations of the English Habeas Corpus Act and the fact that the habeas privilege associated with the Act did not follow the Crown's officers to all parts of the British empire. As Chapter 3 explored, for example, it was the view of the Crown that the Act did not apply in the American colonies and therefore it was only after colonists set foot on English soil that they could claim the Act's protections. That is why the Revolutionary War suspensions applicable to American "rebels" only covered those transported to England for detention during the war. (Of course, it does not follow automatically that American constitutional law—and specifically the reach of the Suspension Clause—should be interpreted in similarly limited geographic terms. Indeed, modern Supreme Court jurisprudence has held that the Constitution sometimes reaches well beyond the borders of the United States.[126])

The majority opinion, however, disagreed with the dissent's view that Guantanamo Bay should be viewed as "abroad," holding instead that its "unique status" rendered it more like a U.S. territory than an overseas military outpost.[127] (Also, as discussed below, the majority focused less on the Habeas Corpus Act and more on the common law writ, which historians have noted reached further than the Act did as a geographic matter.[128]) Here, an analogy may be drawn to Samuel Mudd's habeas petition filed in federal court in

Florida. As explored in Chapter 7, the government imprisoned Mudd and others convicted in the Lincoln assassination conspiracy at Fort Jefferson in the Dry Tortugas precisely to put them beyond the reach of habeas courts. When Mudd and his fellow petitioners brought a habeas challenge arguing that their military trial was unconstitutional, they lost on the merits. Notably, however, the court never questioned its authority to rule on a habeas petition filed by prisoners detained at the offshore military outpost. Given the perpetual nature of the U.S. foothold at Guantanamo, along with the government's total control over and use of the land for a quintessentially sovereign function (a military installation), there are strong arguments for treating the Guantanamo Bay military base like Fort Jefferson.[129]

Next there is the role, if any, of allegiance. The *Boumediene* majority did not presume that the detainees bore any allegiance to the United States, and did not attach any significance one way or the other to the issue in its analysis. As discussed in earlier chapters, however, historically the concept of allegiance was linked inextricably with the ability to invoke the protections of the Habeas Corpus Act. Recall, for example, the legal treatment of those captured flying French colors in the 1690s, the Seven Men of Moidart who fought with Bonnie Prince Charlie, and the American rebels during the Revolutionary War. As explored in Chapters 2 and 3, in every case the Crown viewed such persons as subjects with a continuing obligation of allegiance. Thus, when brought to England, they could not be held as prisoners of war and instead enjoyed the full protections of the Habeas Corpus Act except during times of its suspension. (Of course, as also detailed in Chapter 2 and later chapters, with allegiance came the "reciprocal" obligation not to commit treason.) Further, once the British government deemed the American rebels to have broken their bond of allegiance, Parliament enacted legislation declaring that in place of any rights under domestic law, they now had to look for protection to the law of nations. And, as Chapters 4 and 5 detailed, this same understanding of the important role of allegiance shaped early American habeas law. In sum, as a historic matter, allegiance was enormously important to habeas jurisprudence and the question whether a person could claim the protection of domestic law.

Without discussing the role of allegiance in the legal calculus, the *Boumediene* majority did note that historically "a petitioner's status as an alien was not a categorical bar to habeas corpus review." This was correct. Indeed, as detailed in Chapter 2 and long recognized in American constitutional law, aliens can owe a "local" or "temporary" allegiance and in so doing claim the protection of domestic law while shouldering its obligations. But historically the treatment of enemy aliens was at best more complicated, and at worst not helpful to the majority's position. As also detailed in Chapter 2, historian Paul Halliday's work reveals that seventeenth- and eighteenth-century habeas proceedings served as a "sorting function" to divide those who could invoke the protections of the Habeas Corpus Act from those who could not, with the existence or lack of allegiance proving one of the critical factors in the legal calculus. Thus, in one of the cases cited by the *Boumediene* majority, *Three Spanish Sailors*, King's Bench concluded that "these men, upon their own shewing, are alien enemies and prisoners of war, and therefore not entitled to any of the privileges of Englishmen; much less to be set at liberty on a habeas corpus."[130] In keeping with this holding, Halliday's survey of hundreds of cases during the seventeenth and eighteenth centuries found that King's Bench "never released a person it concluded had been properly designated as a POW."[131] With discharge being the appropriate remedy under the Habeas Corpus Act, it makes sense that one properly classified as a prisoner of war could not prevail in such proceedings. To be sure, aliens who were subjects of a country with which the Crown was at war were not automatically walled off from domestic law, and as a result could sometimes be both protected and punished by its terms. Recall the case of François Henri de la Motte, the Frenchmen prosecuted for treason for sending information to France during the American Revolutionary War. Because de la Motte lived in England at the time, the attorney general concluded that he fell "under the protection of the laws of this kingdom" and "he owe[d] allegiance to it equal to that of any natural-born subject."[132] It followed that he could also be punished by the laws of the kingdom.

In sum, it is clear that allegiance was enormously important to the relevant legal calculus as a historical matter.[133] The *Boumediene* majority acknowledged that the English courts may have "abstained altogether from matters involving prisoners of war," but ultimately viewed that conclusion, if correct, as more justified "in the context of declared wars with other nation states."[134] This passage proved an important shift in the majority opinion. First, it took the Court away from a historical framing of the questions posed in *Boumediene*. Second, it responded to Justice Scalia's point in dissent that no one had suggested that the thousands of prisoners of war detained in the United States during World War II were entitled to habeas review of their detentions. And finally, perhaps here the majority was also distinguishing *Eisentrager*. There, even while denying habeas relief to the German petitioners, Justice Jackson noted that they possessed rights under international law that they could pursue through diplomatic channels.[135] With respect to the Guantanamo detainees, however, the Court was surely aware that the Bush administration had publicly taken the formal position (whether rightly or wrongly) that a good portion of the Geneva

Conventions did not apply to the Guantanamo detainees[136] and, as a result, many commentators had referred to Guantanamo Bay as a "legal black hole."[137] (There were serious questions on the ground, moreover, about whether a lack of individual review of whether detainees were in fact members of the Taliban or al-Qaeda exacerbated the potential for erroneous detentions.[138]) There are indications in the Court's opinion that this backdrop heavily influenced the outcome in *Boumediene*. Among other things, the Court suggested that "the particular dangers of terrorism in the modern age" did not lend themselves to historical analogies,[139] and it emphasized that if it did not find a constitutional right to habeas review on behalf of the detainees, "the political branches" would be permitted "to govern without legal constraint" at Guantanamo.[140]

In all events, Justice Kennedy's opinion in *Boumediene* suggested that as a methodological matter, history should establish the baseline for the Court's inquiry but not preclude the possibility that the Suspension Clause has expanded in reach and scope over time. In this respect, *Boumediene* reaffirmed what the Court has said in several habeas decisions in recent years, namely, that "'at the absolute minimum,' the Clause protects the writ as it existed when the Constitution was drafted and ratified."[141] But, Justice Kennedy continued, "[t]he Court has been careful not to foreclose the possibility that the protections of the Suspension Clause have expanded along with post-1789 developments that define the present scope of the writ." Because "common-law habeas corpus was, above all, an adaptable remedy" and "[i]ts precise application and scope changed depending upon the circumstances," the *Boumediene* Court concluded that Suspension Clause jurisprudence should do the same.[142] In Justice Kennedy's view, this approach in turn freed the Court to take larger functional and separation-of-powers principles into account in reaching its holding.

As a general proposition, the interpretive approach known as originalism tethers constitutional meaning to the understanding of a particular provision that controlled during the Founding period.[143] By contrast, the interpretive approach embraced by the majority in *Boumediene* by design accepts the proposition that rights can expand under the Constitution as it evolves over time. Such a methodology generally posits that the historical understanding of the Constitution provides a floor below which the government may not go, but not necessarily a ceiling beyond which individual rights may not expand over time. Notably, the only justice to join the *Boumediene* majority and Justice Scalia's dissent in *Hamdi*—Justice Stevens—subscribes to this interpretive methodology.[144] Justice Stevens's position in the two cases suggests a belief that the Suspension Clause can function both as a restraint on certain kinds of executive detention (like that at issue in *Hamdi*) and as a right of access to the courts for a broader category of persons than the Clause may have protected at the time of its ratification (as in *Boumediene*).[145] By contrast, Justice Scalia, an avowed originalist, dissented in both cases, believing history supported Hamdi's claim and at the same time precluded the detainee claims in *Boumediene*. As the different positions taken by Justices Stevens and Scalia in *Boumediene* suggest, one's methodology with respect to constitutional interpretation will strongly influence whether one thinks *Boumediene* was correctly decided.

A related conceptual aspect of *Boumediene* warrants additional discussion. Throughout the Court's opinion, the majority's historical discussion focused almost entirely on the reach and function of the common law writ of habeas corpus. The Court said little about the English Habeas Corpus Act beyond describing it as "establish[ing] procedures for issuing the writ" and recognizing that the Act "was the model upon which the habeas statutes of the 13 American colonies were based."[146] As detailed throughout earlier chapters, the Act wielded enormous influence on early American law and particularly the Suspension Clause. Further, the Act not only codified *procedures* for habeas proceedings, it also established strict—indeed, what one might call *substantive*—limitations on the executive's ability to detain persons who could claim its protections. Specifically, the Act prohibited detention of persons who could claim the protection of domestic law outside the criminal process,* with the purpose of constraining judges and harnessing their common law writ toward this end. This history explains why in Ex parte *Bollman*, Chief Justice John Marshall wrote that the proper remedy for protecting the constitutional privilege is "discharge"—not additional process, as the Court ordered in both *Hamdi* and *Boumediene*.[147]

In this respect, the Court's focus on the common law writ in *Boumediene* led it down a similar path to that taken by the *Hamdi* plurality opinion. In both cases, the Court interpreted the Suspension Clause to promise access to a tribunal to contest the underlying lawfulness of detention, with the legality of the detention to be defined by law external to the Suspension Clause.[148] In this respect, *Boumediene* may have blurred the line between the Court's Suspension Clause jurisprudence and its modern due process case law. As Justice Kennedy wrote, "the privilege of habeas corpus entitles the prisoner to a meaningful opportunity to demonstrate that he is being held pursuant to

---

* As explored throughout earlier chapters and discussed above, as a historical matter, the ability to claim the protection of domestic law has tracked the obligation of allegiance, whether through citizenship or a local or temporary allegiance.

'the erroneous application or interpretation' of relevant law."[149] The chief justice's dissent in *Boumediene* echoed this idea, observing that "[h]abeas is most
fundamentally a procedural right, a mechanism for contesting the legality of
executive detention."[150] Indeed, in *Boumediene*, none of the justices questioned
the government's authority to detain prisoners in the war on terrorism outside
the criminal process as enemy combatants. Instead, the debate between the
two camps centered on whether the detainees had a constitutional right to
greater process to challenge their classification as enemy combatants.

The immediate seeds of this approach are found in *Hamdi*, in which
Justice O'Connor invoked and relied extensively on the Court's due process
balancing framework established in the government benefits case of *Mathews
v. Eldridge*. (This being said, it bears noting that the Court's decisions in the
context of collateral habeas review of criminal convictions have also pointed to
due process as the lodestar of the Suspension Clause inquiry.[151]) Of course, the
link between due process and habeas corpus goes back much further. Indeed,
as explored in Chapter 1, a connection has long been drawn between habeas
and Chapter 39 of Magna Carta, which prohibits detentions in contravention
of "the law of the land." In order to understand this link, it is important to
recall that historically the concept of due process was very different from that
found in the Court's modern due process jurisprudence. As was also explored
in Chapter 1, for example, John Selden argued in the *Case of the Five Knights*
that Chapter 39's admonition that "[n]o freeman shall be imprisoned without
due process of the law" meant that one could be detained solely by "due course
of law, to be either by presentment or by indictment."[152] In other words, the
historical conception of due process long associated with the constitutional
privilege was the process afforded by criminal trial. The modern due process
inquiry on which *Hamdi* and *Boumediene* relied, by contrast, has no fixed content and determines instead what process is due based upon a balancing of
competing interests.

Whatever the merits of such an approach in *Boumediene*, *Hamdi* proves
a cautionary tale of its potential pitfalls. This is because in a case such as
Hamdi, a balancing test will almost always counsel in favor of displacement
of the core protections of the historical habeas privilege. Indeed, it is inevitable that the important and formidable government interest in preserving
national security will weigh heavily in the balance. Further, applying a balancing test in a case such as *Hamdi* ignores the specific trade-offs built into
the very design of the suspension framework. As explored throughout earlier
chapters, that framework prohibits detention outside the criminal process
of persons who can claim the protection of domestic law unless Congress
has taken the extraordinary step of enacting a suspension. Further, the

Constitution carefully limits the circumstances in which a suspension may be declared ("when in Cases of Rebellion or Invasion the public Safety may require it") in order to ensure that this emergency power is rarely employed. In so doing, the framework contemplates that it is only in the most dire of circumstances—those specified in the Suspension Clause—that the government interest in national security may enter the calculus *at all* in order to displace the core privilege long associated with the seventh section of the English Habeas Corpus Act. (Specifically, the Suspension Clause contemplates that interests of national security may enter the legal calculus only as part of legislative debates over whether to take the dramatic step of enacting a suspension.) Put most simply, the suspension framework adopted in the Constitution has already struck the relevant balance between individual liberty and national security, categorically favoring liberty in all but the most extreme circumstances.[153] It follows that applying a balancing test in a case such as *Hamdi* displaces those trade-offs in favor of a more flexible—and less protective—approach that undermines the very core of the Suspension Clause.[154] Connecting the point to the methodological discussion above, *Hamdi* permitted the government to go below the floor established by the Constitution, which prohibits such detentions outright.

Against this backdrop, *Hamdi* and *Boumediene* should be understood as posing distinct questions—*Hamdi* was about identifying the historical substantive prohibitions on detentions embodied in the Suspension Clause, while *Boumediene* was about exploring what procedural rights attach in habeas proceedings. This naturally raises the question whether there is room for both cases under the umbrella of Suspension Clause jurisprudence. Some may argue, as Justice Scalia did in *Boumediene*, that the answer is no. As already noted, Justice Stevens disagreed, joining as he did Justice Scalia's *Hamdi* dissent and the majority opinion in *Boumediene*. Justice Stevens's position would seem to embrace the historical office of the constitutional privilege as prohibiting certain kinds of detention (such as that presented in *Hamdi*), while also interpreting the Suspension Clause to encompass a common law vision of habeas review that promises certain process and can expand to reach new places and persons over time (including the detainees in *Boumediene*).

Alternatively, one could argue that the Suspension Clause and due process elements of the war on terrorism decisions should be rendered conceptually distinct. Doing so would leave the Suspension Clause to function as the Founding generation anticipated it would—namely, as a prohibition of certain kinds of detention in the absence of suspension, with the appropriate remedy being discharge. Further, drawing such a distinction would leave questions about procedural rights, such as those at issue in *Boumediene*, to be addressed by the Court's due process jurisprudence, with the remedy allocating what, if any, further process is due. Doing so arguably would house questions about procedural rights within an area of jurisprudence much better developed to address them.[155] Further, one benefit of this approach would be to guard against the tendency to allow the process-oriented inquiry posed in cases such as *Boumediene* to weaken the substantive limitations historically at the core of the Suspension Clause, as occurred in *Hamdi*.

In the end, whatever one thinks of the merits and basis of the Court's decision in *Boumediene*, the history detailed in these chapters unquestionably supports one important conclusion. Any importing of due process principles into the Suspension Clause analysis should not be permitted to dilute the protections and historical function of the Suspension Clause as understood at the Founding and through much of American history. This is precisely what occurred in *Hamdi*, when the Supreme Court upheld a detention that cannot be reconciled with the core purpose of the Suspension Clause. That purpose, as detailed throughout earlier chapters, was to constrain the executive, in the absence of a valid suspension, from detaining persons entitled to the full protection of domestic law outside the criminal process, *even in wartime*. Put another way, as David Shapiro has written, the Suspension Clause "would be stripped of virtually all meaning if it did not include what might fairly be viewed as the essence of the writ at the time of ratification."[156]

Conclusion

To what purpose are powers limited, and to what purpose is that limitation committed to writing, if these limits may, at any time, be passed by those intended to be restrained?

CHIEF JUSTICE JOHN MARSHALL IN
MARBURY V. MADISON[1]

THE FOUNDING GENERATION ratified the Constitution to establish a structure of government that enabled the United States to function and prosper and also protect the fundamental liberties of the people. As the preceding chapters have detailed, the balance struck in the Suspension Clause between protecting individual liberty and recognizing the need in "extreme emergencies" for expanded government authority to arrest and detain reflects these goals. As the extensive history detailed in these pages has also revealed, the Suspension Clause drew heavily on Anglo-American legal tradition. Indeed, as Chief Justice John Marshall once wrote, the phrase "privilege of the writ of habeas corpus" was "used in the constitution, as one which was well understood."[2] More specifically, those who wrote and ratified the U.S. Constitution knew well Blackstone's glorification of the English Habeas Corpus Act as a "bulwark" of "per[s]onal liberty" and a "second *magna carta*." This explains why the denial of the Act's protections to the colonists in America constituted a major complaint about British rule and contributed to the movement for independence. The colonists wanted to enjoy the benefits of this "second *magna carta*" too.

It is therefore unsurprising to find that in the wake of declaring independence, the Founding generation quickly imported the Act's protections and the concept of suspension into early American law and, in time, the U.S. Constitution. As Alexander Hamilton reported after the delegates met in Philadelphia in 1787 to draft the document, "the *habeas corpus* act [is] provided for in the most ample manner in the plan of the convention." In embracing the Act's core protections, the Founding generation constitutionalized

Habeas Corpus in Wartime. Amanda L. Tyler.

a powerful restraint on executive detention, one that they deemed in no uncertain terms "essential to freedom." Specifically, the core privilege associated with the seventh section of the English Habeas Corpus Act and linked to the concept of suspension had long been understood to prohibit the detention of persons who could claim the protection of domestic law outside the criminal process, *even in wartime.* With the Act, the early seventeenth-century aspiration of John Selden and Sir Edward Coke to prohibit detentions "for matter of state" finally became real.

Having lived through suspensions on both sides of the Atlantic during the American Revolution, the Founding generation also understood the dramatic nature of such a state of affairs and its potential for abuse. Accordingly, although the Suspension Clause recognized an "express provision for exercise of extraordinary authority because of a crisis,"[3] the Founding generation imposed strict constraints on when suspension could be employed by providing that Congress could set aside the privilege only in "Cases of Rebellion or Invasion [when] the public Safety may require it." As Representative James Elliot phrased it in the debates over whether to suspend the privilege during the Burr Conspiracy (quoting Blackstone), suspension of the "writ of liberty . . . ought never to be resorted to but in cases of 'extreme emergency.' " In all other circumstances, the Constitution contemplates that the core habeas privilege will remain inviolate.

As documented in these pages, the understanding of the Suspension Clause that linked the core constitutional privilege with the seventh section of the English Habeas Corpus Act and the parliamentary suspension model remained consistent well through Reconstruction. And although it is true that President Abraham Lincoln erroneously claimed for himself the power to suspend during the Civil War, even Lincoln—the "great suspender"—never once questioned that suspension was a necessary legal predicate to detain Confederate soldiers and those disaffected to the cause of the Union outside the criminal process.

As detailed in Chapter 10, however, the twentieth century witnessed a departure from this long-settled framework with the mass internment of Japanese American citizens during World War II in "Relocation Centers" scattered across the western United States. Notably, at the time, the attorney general and other prominent government lawyers recognized that the internment policy violated the Suspension Clause, at least as it applied to the over 70,000 U.S. citizens forced to report to the camps. Nonetheless, the proposed military policies went into effect and established a dangerous precedent that laid the foundation for policies and judicial decisions that followed in the wake of the terrorist attacks of September 11, 2001. Specifically, by sanctioning the detention of citizens outside the criminal process for national security purposes and in the absence of a suspension, the World War II experience paved the way for the Supreme Court's 2004 decision in *Hamdi v. Rumsfeld* upholding the military detention of a U.S. citizen as an "enemy combatant" in the war on terrorism. But as the pages of this book have shown, the concept of a citizen enemy combatant detained outside the criminal process and in the absence of a suspension cannot be reconciled with the original purpose of the Suspension Clause and the wealth of English and American habeas jurisprudence that informed its ratification and interpretation well through Reconstruction.

The matters explored in these pages remain an active part of the ongoing debate over how to confront terrorism. As noted in the Introduction, several members of Congress proposed that the surviving Boston marathon bomber be treated as an enemy combatant rather than prosecuted criminally. Congress has also recently enacted legislation that revives aspects of the Cold War-era Emergency Detention Act by approving the detention without trial of "unprivileged enemy belligerents," a category from which the statute does not expressly exclude citizens.[4] In signing the bill into law, President Barack Obama stated that his administration would "not authorize the indefinite military detention without trial of American citizens [because] doing so would break with our most important traditions and values as a Nation."[5] Whether President Obama's successors will exercise the same restraint remains to be seen. In all events, both examples highlight how the precedents of World War II and *Hamdi* have led to the erosion of the core constitutional habeas privilege.

This brings us back to where we started: England. There is considerable irony in comparing the unfolding of habeas jurisprudence on both sides of the Atlantic in the years since American independence. In the period following ratification of the U.S. Constitution, Parliament passed several suspensions, putting the robust protections long associated with the privilege under considerable strain.[6] As in the United States, moreover, during the Great War and World War II, there was little political or judicial inclination in the United Kingdom to recognize the protections of the Habeas Corpus Act. Accordingly, during both wars, Parliament vested the Home Secretary with virtually unconstrained authority to detain persons for the public safety and in defense of the realm, a power that the government exercised to detain almost two thousand citizens outside the criminal framework during World War II. (Although not formally styled a suspension, scholars have deemed the relevant World War II regulation as equivalent to a suspension.)[7] During both wars, the Law Lords essentially deferred to the Home Office and in so doing avoided scrutiny of detention decisions made under the governing regulations.[8] But Prime

Minister Winston Churchill, who supported such policies at the outset of World War II, soon turned a critic, writing in the fall of 1943 of the importance of "the great principle of *habeas corpus* and trial by jury, which are the supreme protection invented by the British people for ordinary individuals against the State." More generally, Churchill warned: "[t]he power of the Executive to cast a man into prison without formulating any charge known to the law, and particularly to deny him the judgement of his peers, is in the highest degree odious and is the foundation of all totalitarian government. . . ."[9] In urging that the government end its detention policies in the middle of the war in the face of broad support for their continuance, Churchill also observed that "[p]eople who are not prepared to do unpopular things and to defy clamour are not fit to be Ministers in times of stress."[10] To describe his evolving approach during the war on this score as different from that of his American counterpart would be a dramatic understatement.

Yet it remains the fact that in Great Britain, the Habeas Corpus Act was just that—an Act—and not part of a supreme and binding written constitution. Given that "Parliamentary sovereignty is a fundamental principle of the [unwritten] UK constitution"—a point recently reiterated by the United Kingdom's Supreme Court in its Brexit decision—Parliament possesses "'the right to make or unmake any law whatsoever.'"[11] Thus, it was always the case that Parliament could modify the Habeas Corpus Act through ordinary legislation, which it did in 1971. Specifically, in response to the rise of Irish Republican Army and Loyalist violence, the British government first declared a state of emergency and invoked the emergency powers that had been provided for in the original laws governing the partition of Ireland in 1922.[12] Then, in the Courts Act of 1971, Parliament repealed what was originally the seventh section of the Habeas Corpus Act and in its place adopted legislation authorizing the temporary preventive detention of suspected terrorists, thereby establishing the general foundation of the legal framework that governs the United Kingdom today.[13]

Thus, today in the United Kingdom, the law permits the preventive or investigative detention of suspected terrorists—whether United Kingdom citizens or not—for up to fourteen days. The governing statutory scheme affords persons detained on this basis multiple opportunities for judicial review as well as the opportunity to consult with and be represented by counsel.[14] Parliament has also enacted various other preventive and investigative measures to fight terrorism and exclude terrorists from re-entry to the United Kingdom.[15]

Comparing this regime to that sanctioned in *Hamdi* yields some interesting—and troubling—conclusions. To begin, post-*Hamdi*, American law stands in a similar posture to British law insofar as both permit the detention of citizens for national security purposes outside the criminal process and in the absence of a suspension. Notably, however, U.S. citizens detained as enemy combatants actually enjoy *fewer* legal protections than their British counterparts. Detentions in the United Kingdom are strictly cabined in duration to fourteen days and subject to regular judicial review during that time, whereas *Hamdi* at its broadest holds that citizen enemy combatants may be held for the duration of the war on terrorism—however long that may be— so long as a tribunal determines at the outset of the detention that sufficient evidence exists to support the government's allegations that an individual may be a terrorist.

Chief Justice John Marshall counseled long ago that the provisions in the Constitution are "supreme" and "designed to be permanent."[16] Against this backdrop, the current state of American habeas jurisprudence should trouble anyone who cares about the Constitution. As the early chapters of this book reveal, the *Hamdi* decision and the World War II internment of Japanese Americans stand entirely at odds with everything the Founding generation sought to achieve with the Suspension Clause. To be sure, some have argued that the Suspension Clause is "rudimentary" and dangerously inflexible.[17] Whether or not these criticisms are well founded, they should not be cited as a basis for empowering the government to go below the floor established by the Constitution or, for that matter, relieving the judiciary of exercising its "solemn responsibility" in the constitutional design as Alexander Hamilton described it—namely, "to be an intermediate body between the people and the legislature, in order, among other things, to keep the latter within the limits assigned to their authority."[18] As these pages have demonstrated, the origins and long-standing interpretation of the Suspension Clause understood it to prohibit the government, in the absence of a valid suspension, from detaining persons who can claim the protection of domestic law outside the criminal process, *even in wartime*. Displacing these protections in favor of a balancing test, as the Supreme Court did in *Hamdi*, does a disservice to the Founding generation's long struggle to claim the protections of the "second *magna carta*" as their own and more generally the very idea of a written constitution.

Notes

INTRODUCTION

1. Jeremy Herb & Mike Lillis, *Graham, McCain: Hold Bombing Suspect as "Enemy Combatant,"* THE HILL, Apr. 20, 2013; Ed O'Keefe & Rachel Weiner, *GOP Lawmakers Want Boston Bombing Suspect Treated as "Enemy Combatant,"* WASH. POST, Apr. 20, 2013.

2. Law enforcement officials questioned Tsarnaev without giving him *Miranda* warnings beforehand. See O'Keefe & Weiner, supra note 1.

3. Padilla v. Hanft, 423 F.3d 386, 389 (4th Cir. 2005) (quoting Memorandum from President George W. Bush to Secretary of Defense Donald Rumsfeld (June 9, 2002)).

4. U.S. CONST. art. I, § 9, cl. 2.

5. See Rumsfeld v. Padilla, 542 U.S. 426 (2004); Padilla v. Hanft, 547 U.S. 1062, 1063 (2006) (Kennedy, J., concurring in denial of certiorari).

6. Hamdi v. Rumsfeld, 542 U.S. 507, 519 (2004) (plurality opinion).

7. Habeas Corpus Act of 1679, 31 Car. 2, c. 2, § 1 (Eng.), reprinted in 3 THE FOUNDERS' CONSTITUTION 310, 311 (Philip B. Kurland & Ralph Lerner eds., 1987).

8. 1 WILLIAM BLACKSTONE, COMMENTARIES *126, *131, *133.

9. Address to the People of Great Britain (Oct. 21, 1774), in 1 JOURNALS OF THE CONTINENTAL CONGRESS, 1774–1789, at 81, 88 (Worthington Chauncey Ford ed., 1904).

10. GA. CONST. of 1777, art. LX.

11. See CHARLES FRANCIS JENKINS, BUTTON GWINNETT: SIGNER OF THE DECLARATION OF INDEPENDENCE 109 (1926) ("[T]he House . . . ordered, that 500 copies be immediately struck off, with the Act of Distribution, made in the reign of Charles the Second, and the habeas corpus act annexed. . . .").

Habeas Corpus in Wartime. Amanda L. Tyler.
© Oxford University Press 2017. Published 2017 by Oxford University Press.

12. An Act for the Better Securing the Liberty of the Citizens of this State, and for Prevention of Imprisonments (Feb. 21, 1787), in 1 Laws of the State of New York 369, 369 (New York, Thomas Greenleaf 1792).

13. 3 Joseph Story, Commentaries on the Constitution of the United States § 1335, at 208 (Cambridge, Mass., Brown, Hilliard, Gray & Co. 1833).

14. The Federalist No. 83, at 499 (Alexander Hamilton) (Clinton Rossiter ed., 2003).

15. Debates in the Convention of the Commonwealth of Massachusetts, on the Adoption of the Federal Constitution (Jan. 26, 1788) (statement of Judge Sumner), in 2 The Debates in the Several State Conventions on the Adoption of the Federal Constitution, as Recommended by the General Convention at Philadelphia, In 1787, at 109 (Jonathan Elliot ed., 2d ed., Philadelphia, J.B. Lippincott & Co. 1891).

16. See An Act to Impower his Majesty to Secure and Detain Persons Charged with, or Suspected of, the Crime of High Treason, Committed in any of his Majesty's Colonies or Plantations in *America*, or on the High Seas, or the Crime of Piracy 1777, 17 Geo. 3, c. 9 (Gr. Brit.); 35 H.L. Jour. (1777) 78, 82–83 (Gr. Brit.) (noting royal assent given Mar. 3, 1777); 19 Cobbett's Parliamentary History of England from the Norman Conquest, in 1066 to the Year 180, at 4 (London 1813) (Feb. 6, 1777) (remarks of Lord North).

17. Letter from Abraham Lincoln to Erastus Corning and Others (June 12, 1863), in 6 The Collected Works of Abraham Lincoln 260, 264 (Roy P. Basler et al. eds., 1953).

18. Ex parte Merryman, 17 F. Cas. 144, 151 (C.C.D. Md. 1861) (No. 9487) (quoting 1 Blackstone *136).

19. See Act of Mar. 3, 1863, ch. 81, § 1, 12 Stat. 755, 755; see also, e.g., Proclamation No. 7, 13 Stat. 734, 734 (1863).

20. See, e.g., Abraham Lincoln, First Inaugural Address (Mar. 4, 1861), in Abraham Lincoln: Speeches and Writings, 1859–1865, at 215, 218 (Don E. Fehrenbacher ed., 1989).

21. An Act to enforce the Provisions of the Fourteenth Amendment to the Constitution of the United States, and for other Purposes, ch. 22, § 1, 17 Stat. 13.

22. Ulysses S. Grant, A Proclamation (May 3, 1871), in 9 A Compilation of the Messages and Papers of the Presidents 4088, 4088 (James D. Richardson ed., New York, Bureau of Nat'l Literature, Inc. 1897).

23. 3 C.F.R. 1092 (1942) (repealed 1976).

24. Letter from Attorney Gen. Francis Biddle to Representative Leland Merritt Ford (Jan. 24, 1942), in Documents of the Commission on Wartime Relocation and Internment of Civilians 5739, 5740 (reel 5, 417–418) (Frederick, MD, University Publications of America 1983).

25. Ex parte Endo, 323 U.S. 283 (1944).

26. MORTON GRODZINS, AMERICANS BETRAYED: POLITICS AND THE JAPANESE EVACUATION 374 (1949).

27. Boumediene v. Bush, 553 U.S. 723 (2008).

28. Id. at 746 (2008) (quoting INS v. St. Cyr, 533 U.S. 289, 301 (2001)); see also St. Cyr, 533 U.S. at 301 ("[A]t the absolute minimum, the Suspension Clause protects the writ 'as it existed in 1789.'") (quoting Felker v. Turpin, 518 U.S. 651, 663–664 (1996)).

29. Ex parte Watkins, 28 U.S. 193, 201–202 (1830).

30. Specifically, the Seventh Amendment refers to the traditions of the English common law. See U.S. CONST. amend. VII ("In Suits at common law, where the value in controversy shall exceed twenty dollars, the right of trial by jury shall be preserved."); cf. Wiscart v. Dauchy, 3 U.S. 321, 327 (1796) (Ellsworth, C.J.) (referring to terms of art as "to be understood, when used, according to their ordinary acceptation, unless something appears . . . to controul, modify, or change, the fixed and technical sense which they have previously borne").

31. James Madison, Speech in Congress on the Jay Treaty (Apr. 6, 1796), in JAMES MADISON: WRITINGS 568, 574 (Jack N. Rakove ed., 1999).

32. THE FEDERALIST NO. 37, at 225 (James Madison) ("All new laws, though penned with the greatest technical skill and passed on the fullest and most mature deliberation, are considered as more or less obscure and equivocal, until their meaning be *liquidated* and ascertained by a series of particular discussions and adjudications.").

CHAPTER 1

1. 1 WILLIAM BLACKSTONE, COMMENTARIES, at *135. Blackstone's *Commentaries* grew out of Blackstone's lectures and were published between 1765 and 1769. The timing and circulation of his *Commentaries* meant that they wielded profound influence on the development of early American law.

2. PAUL D. HALLIDAY, HABEAS CORPUS: FROM ENGLAND TO EMPIRE 65 (2010). Historian Paul Halliday's work masterfully tells the story of this development.

3. 1 BLACKSTONE, supra note 1, at *126, *131, *133.

4. GREAT CHARTER OF LIBERTIES, ch. 39 (1215), reprinted in SELECT DOCUMENTS OF ENGLISH CONSTITUTIONAL HISTORY 42, 47 (George Burton Adams & H. Morse Stephens eds., 1904). In the 1225 version of the Great Charter, Chapter 39 became Chapter 29. I refer to the relevant chapter throughout by its original numbering.

5. Within weeks of the events at Runnymede, the pope instructed King John to repudiate the Charter, and John was dead by the end of the next year. Various monarchs issued several revised versions of Magna Carta over the remaining years of the thirteenth century, including two prominent issuances in 1225 by Henry III and 1297 by Edward I.

6. For example, "by the end of the 14th century 'due process of law' and 'law of the land' were interchangeable" in English legal vocabulary. Duncan v. Louisiana,

391 U.S. 145, 169 (1968); see also DANIEL JOHN MEADOR, HABEAS CORPUS AND MAGNA CARTA: DUALISM OF POWER AND LIBERTY 1–38 (1966) (connecting these concepts to modern due process principles and the writ of habeas corpus generally).

7. See SIR EDWARD COKE, THE SECOND PART OF THE INSTITUTES OF THE LAWS OF ENGLAND 54 (London, E & R Brooke 1797) (1628). It would be hard to overstate the influence on the development of English and American law of Coke, who had served as attorney general under Queen Elizabeth and chief justice under James I. For much of the period following its publication, Coke's *Institutes* served as the "lawyer's primer" and heavily influenced developments in English law. HASTINGS LYON & HERMAN BLOCK, EDWARD COKE: ORACLE OF THE LAW 346 (1929); see also Thomas G. Barnes, *Introduction to Coke on Littleton*, in LAW, LIBERTY, AND PARLIAMENT: SELECTED ESSAYS ON THE WRITINGS OF SIR EDWARD COKE 24 (Allen D. Boyer ed., 2004).

8. Codd v. Turback (1615) 3 Bulstrode 109–110, 81 Eng. Rep. 94 (K.B.).

9. Darnel's Case (1627) 3 Cobbett's St. Tr. 1 (Eng.). The knights were Sir Thomas Darnel, Sir John Corbet, Sir Walter Erle, Sir John Heveningham, and Sir Edmund Hampden. See J.A. Guy, *The Origins of the Petition of Right Reconsidered*, 25 HIST. J. 289, 289–291 (1982) (detailing the case). As Halliday notes, Sir Thomas Darnel "had made his submission and been released before arguments" in the case. HALLIDAY, supra note 2, at 392 n. 3.

10. The jurisdiction of the Court of King's Bench reached so-called "pleas of the crown"—that is, most of the cases that involved the Crown in some manner. During this period, its judges were paid by the king and served at his pleasure. See Douglass C. North & Barry R. Weingast, *Constitutions and Commitment: The Evolution of Institutions Governing Public Choice in Seventeenth-Century England*, 49 J. ECON. HIST. 803, 813 (1989).

11. Darnel's Case, 3 Cobbett's St. Tr. at 18 (argument of Selden before King's Bench). Selden represented Sir Edmund Hampden. See Guy, supra note 9, at 293 n.15.

12. Darnel's Case, 3 Cobbett's St. Tr. at 18. Discussing *Darnel's Case*, Professor Daniel Meador notes with insight equally applicable today: "The case is also noteworthy because it shows how the writ of habeas corpus is no greater protector of liberty than the judges' view as to what constitutes lawful custody." MEADOR, supra note 6, at 18.

13. 25 Edw. 3, stat. 5, c. 4 (1351) (Eng.).

14. Darnel's Case, 3 Cobbett's St. Tr. at 38 (argument of Heath before King's Bench).

15. Id. at 37–50. As Paul Halliday's work notes, justices of the peace and other special commissioners still enjoyed summary powers to imprison during this period. See HALLIDAY, supra note 2, at 138.

16. Darnel's Case, 3 Cobbett's St. Tr. at 31.

17. Id. at 50.

18. Id. at 59. As scholars have noted, there was considerable contemporary debate on whether the decisions created precedent or merely constituted a nonprecedential refusal of bail to the knights. See Guy, supra note 9, at 289–294; Mark Kishlansky, *Tyranny Denied: Charles I, Attorney General Heath, and the Five Knights' Case*, 42 Hist. J. 53, 63–64 (1999) (arguing that the case turned on the knights' first return filed and therefore did not resolve questions going to perpetual detention).

19. John Rushworth, Historical Collections of Private Passages of State, Weighty Matters in Law, Remarkable Proceedings in Five Parliaments 420 (1721); Darnel's Case, 3 Cobbett's St. Tr. at 1; see also T. Worthington Barlow, Cheshire: Its Historical and Literary Associations 45–48 (Manchester, John Gray Bell 1855) (discussing Crewe and replicating a letter written by him discussing his dismissal).

20. John Lord Campbell, I The Lives of the Chief Justices of England: from the Norman Conquest till the Death of Lord Mansfield 307 (Philadelphia, Blanchard & Lea 1851); Thomas Birch, I The Court and Times of Charles the First 168–170 (London, Henry Colburn 1849) (replicating correspondence dating to 1626 describing the events); The Journal of Sir Simonds D'Ewes 124 (Wallace Notestein ed., 1923) (replicating MP D'Ewes's journal noting that a motion was made in 1640 to have Crewe testify as to why he had been "putt out of his place" as part of parliamentary investigations into the judges who had supported the king in the Ship-Money case). For more on Ship-Money, see infra note 44 and accompanying text.

21. Halliday, supra note 2, at 138, 222–223; see also id. at 156–160 (elaborating on the king's discretion and prerogative); Kishlansky, supra note 18, at 70, 73, 78–79.

22. 7 A Collection of State-Trials, and Proceedings upon High-Treason, and Other Crimes and Misdemeanors 144 (London 1735)(remarks of Sir Edward Coke in Parliament). Note that Coke had not always held this view. He had once opined that the Privy Council had the power to commit without citing a cause. In discussing his earlier remarks while promoting the Petition of Right, Coke said they were made "by some young student that did mistake" and declared: "I have now better guides." 2 Commons Debates 1628, at 190–193, 213 (Robert C. Johnson & Mary Frear Keeler eds., 1977) [hereinafter Commons Debates] (remarks of Sir Edward Coke given Mar. 29 & 31, 1628). As counsel for the Earl of Shaftsbury later argued in 1677, in Coke's "more mature age he was of another opinion, and accordingly the law is declared in the Petition of Right." See The Case of the Earl of Shaftsbury (1677) 6 Cobbett's St. Tr. 1269, 1285 (Eng.); see also Halliday, supra note 2, at 30 (noting that release rates for prisoners dropped during Coke's tenure on King's Bench).

23. 3 Commons Debates, supra note 22, at 95 (remarks of Sir Edward Coke in Parliament given Apr. 26, 1628). For details on the Petition and why Coke sought

to cloak it in existing law, see ROGER LOCKYER, THE EARLY STUARTS 336–345 (1989).

24. The Petition of Right 1628, 3 Car. 1, c. 1, §§ 5, 8 (Eng.). For more on the origins of the Petition and the parliamentary debates, see Linda S. Popofsky, *Habeas Corpus and "Liberty of the Subject": Legal Arguments for the Petition of Right in the Parliament of 1628*, 41 THE HISTORIAN 257 (1979). For his efforts in promoting the Petition, among other things, John Selden has been called "the chief of learned men reputed in this Land." JOHN MILTON, AREOPAGITICA (1644).

25. The Petition of Right 1628, 3 Car. 1, c. 1, §§ 1, 6, 7.

26. For an overview of the economic context of this struggle, consult North & Weingast, supra note 10, at 808–824.

27. 3 HL JOUR. (1628) 842–844 (Eng.). Among other things, Charles I had pledged support to his uncle, Christian IV of Denmark, in the ongoing wars on the Continent.

28. For details, see Linda S. Popofsky, *The Crisis over Tonnage and Poundage in Parliament in 1629*, 126 PAST & PRESENT 44 (1990); Josh Chafetz, *Executive Branch Contempt of Congress*, 76 U. CHI. L. REV. 1083, 1101–1112 (2009).

29. During this period, Parliament differentiated between bills that became statutes and petitions. The latter, particularly "petitions of right," were viewed as the appropriate means for "addressing the crown on matters of prerogative, as a way of offering counsel, and of presenting grievances." Elizabeth Read Foster, *Petitions and the Petition of Right*, 14 J. BRIT. STUD. 21, 27 (1974). With respect to the Petition of Right presented to King Charles in 1628, there is reason to think that some members of Parliament viewed it as declaring the state of existing law, and thereby hoped to bind judges to the same recognition by securing the king's assent. See E.R. Adair & A.F. Pollard, *Historical Revisions: XIV—The Petition of Right*, 5 HISTORY (n.s.) 99, 101 (1920); Foster, supra, at 43. As noted, the petition followed failed efforts to pass a bill encompassing many of the same terms. See Foster, supra, at 26. Further, although parliamentary adoption of the Petition of Right followed some of the standard procedures for passage of a statute (including witnessing the requisite number of readings in both Houses of Parliament), it did not comply with all such procedures, and the terms of King Charles's assent were distinct from those that he gave to bills having the force of statutes. See Adair & Pollard, supra, at 102. Developments in the wake of the Petition reveal that English historian Henry Hallam's claim that the Petition of Right plainly established that "no freeman could be detained in prison, except upon a criminal charge or conviction, or for a civil debt" gives too much effect to the Petition standing alone. HENRY HALLAM, THE CONSTITUTIONAL HISTORY OF ENGLAND, FROM THE ACCESSION OF HENRY VII TO THE DEATH OF GEORGE II 475 (William Smith ed., New York, Harper & Bros. 1880) (1827).

30. See Chafetz, supra note 28, at 1110–1111 (citing 2 Parl. Hist. Eng. (1628) cols. 490–491) (detailing Finch affair). When Parliament reconvened in 1629, the

House of Commons resolved that Finch had committed "a breach of Privilege of the house" by failing "to obey the commands of the house." Later that year, the Long Parliament ordered that reparations be paid to several of the prisoners. See Stroud's Case (1629) 3 Cobbett's St. Tr. 235, 293–294, 310–315 (Eng.).

31. See generally Parl. Hist. Eng. (1628) cols. 488–490.

32. Stroud's Case, 3 Cobbett's St. Tr. at 281–282.

33. See generally id. at 235–297; John Reeve, *The Arguments in King's Bench in 1629 concerning the Imprisonment of John Selden and Other Members of the House of Commons*, 25 J. BRIT. STUD. 264, 264–287 (1986).

34. Stroud's Case, 3 Cobbett's St. Tr. at 259, 261. Littleton added: "[I]f it be truly treason, then they might have returned treason, and then the party was not to be bailed of right, till there should be a failure of prosecution." Id.

35. Id. at 286.

36. Id. at 288 n.† (citing BULSTRODE WHITELOCK, MEMORIALS OF THE ENGLISH AFFAIRS FROM THE BEGINNING OF THE REIGN OF CHARLES THE FIRST TO THE HAPPY RESTORATION OF KING CHARLES THE SECOND 14 (1682)).

37. WHITELOCK, supra note 36, at 14.

38. Stroud's Case, 3 Cobbett's St. Tr. at 286.

39. Even this outcome was not clear until right before King's Bench was set to announce its opinion. The king originally promised to deliver Selden and Benjamin Valentine to the court, but changed his mind "upon more mature deliberation," deciding that all prisoners should share the same plight and that none would be presented to the court "until we have cause . . . to believe they will make a better demonstration of their modesty and civility." Id. at 287.

40. Id. at 289.

41. See Reeve, supra note 33, at 284–286.

42. Paul Halliday's extensive review of writs filed during this period shows that it remained common practice for subjects to be "imprisoned by means other than presentment or indictment, before 1627 and long after." HALLIDAY, supra note 2, at 139. All the same, Charles I's resistance to the Petition proved part of the story of his downfall.

43. The Habeas Corpus Act of 1641, 16 Car. 1, c. 10 (Eng.).

44. Many have commented on the egregious exercises of arbitrary power by the Star Chamber. See, e.g., F. W. MAITLAND, THE CONSTITUTIONAL HISTORY OF ENGLAND 263 (1908) (calling the Star Chamber "a court of politicians enforcing a policy, not a court of judges administering the law"); see also FRIEDRICH A. HAYEK, THE CONSTITUTION OF LIBERTY 169 (1960) (same). Another example of parliamentary assertions of power from this period may be found in Parliament's decision in 1641 to decry the leveling of Ship-Money and the judicial opinions that had upheld the king's authority to declare an emergency and take the property of subjects for the common defense. For details, see D.L. Keir, *The Case of Ship-Money*, 52 L.Q. REV. 546 (1936).

45. See Halliday, supra note 2, at 226. Halliday tells the story of one noteworthy case in 1643, when the House of Lords arrested Sir Robert Berkeley "while presiding in King's Bench" and tried him only to conclude that he shall remain imprisoned "during the pleasure of this House." Id. at 220 (quoting 6 HL Jour. (1643) 214 (Eng.)); see also id. at 227–229 (detailing additional stories of parliamentary detention insulated from judicial review during the 1640s and 1650s).

46. For details, consult Chafetz, supra note 28, at 1112–1115.

47. See Halliday, supra note 2, at 229–231 (detailing several prominent cases).

48. The Interregnum witnessed some notable progress in habeas law. Starting in 1649, the Commonwealth Parliament enacted several ordinances to make available the writ of *habeas corpus cum causa* to poor prisoners jailed for "debt, breach of promise, contract or convenant." Maxwell Cohen, *Habeas Corpus* Cum Causa—*The Emergence of the Modern Writ—II*, 18 Can. B. Rev. 172, 175–176 (1940) (quoting 2 Henry Scobell, Acts and Ordinances of Parliament 99 (London, H. Hills & J. Field 1658)). The return of the Stuarts led to the abrogation of this legislation. See id. at 178.

49. Earl of Clarendon Case (1667) 6 Cobbett's St. Tr. 317, 330–331 (Eng.) (criticizing Clarendon for doing so "to produce precedents for the imprisoning any other of his majesty's subjects in like manner").

50. 1 Debates of the House of Commons, From the Year 1667 to the Year 1694, at 53 (Anchitell Grey ed., London, D. Henry & R. Cave & J. Emonson 1763) [hereinafter Grey's Debates] (remarks of John Vaughan given Nov. 26, 1667); see also id. at 51 ("The discretion of the Parliament ought to be unconfined.") (remarks of Sir John Littleton given Nov. 25, 1667).

51. 1 Blackstone, supra note 1, at *159 ("Privilege of parliament was principally established, in order to protect it's [sic] members not only from being molested by their fellow-subjects, but also more especially from being oppressed by the power of the crown."). For more on this period, consult Josh Chafetz, Democracy's Privileged Few: Legislative Privilege and Democratic Norms in the British and American Constitutions (2007).

52. 9 HC Jour. (1667) 35–36 (Eng.).

53. 1 Grey's Debates, supra note 50, at 63 (spelling the chief justice's name "Keeling"). After the chief justice testified before the Commons, the House declined to proceed in the matter. See id. at 64.

54. John Milward, Diary Entry (Dec. 13, 1667), in The Diary of John Milward, Esq. 169 (Caroline Robbins ed., 1938) [hereinafter Milward's Diary]; see also Diary Entry (Dec. 11, 1667), in id. at 163; Diary Entry (Dec. 13, 1667), in id. at 166–170 (describing events surrounding the chief justice's testimony before the House). John Milward served in Parliament and kept a diary spanning the years 1666–1668. See id. at ix.

55. See Northey's Notebook 226, in Hill Manuscripts at Lincoln's Inn, London (Pascal term, 19 Charles II, "Feimer's Case"); see also Helen A. Nutting, *The*

Most Wholesome Law—The Habeas Corpus Act of 1679, 65 Am. Hist. Rev. 527, 531 (1960) (discussing case).

56. Diary Entry (Apr. 11, 1668), in Milward's Diary, supra note 54, at 253; id. at 278 (entry dated Apr. 24, 1668); see also id. at 253 (entry dated Apr. 11, 1668), 299 (entry dated May 7, 1668).

57. As Paul Halliday's work explores, the failure of the 1674–1675 bill likely stemmed from the distraction posed by an extraordinary series of contemporary events that witnessed the Commons imprison a group of lawyers in the Tower, the Lords send writs of habeas corpus to the Tower on the lawyers' behalf, and the Commons order the Tower jailer to ignore those writs. See Halliday, supra note 2, at 234.

58. During the debates, one reads many complaints about the practice of sending prisoners to Tangier and other places to escape judicial writs. See, e.g., 2 Grey's Debates, supra note 50, at 364–367.

59. 4 Parl. Hist. Eng. (1673-74) col. 662.

60. 2 Grey's Debates, supra note 50, at 338; see id. (adding "the Ministers say, 'it is his Majesty's Warrant;' a thing very indecent, and unfit to be done!").

61. Id. at 367 (emphasis added); see also 4 Cobbett's St. Tr. at 662 (reporting the same remarks).

62. Id. at 365.

63. Id. at 414.

64. Id. at 424.

65. Hallam, supra note 29, at 475. Hallam was not entirely consistent on this point. See id. at 475–476 (observing that the Act "cut off the abuses by which the government's lust of power . . . had impaired so fundamental a privilege"); see also 2 Thomas Babington Macaulay, The History of England from the Accession of James the Second 3 (New York, Harper & Bros. 1848) (describing the Act as "the most stringent curb that ever legislation imposed on tyranny"); Cohen, supra note 48, at 195 (arguing that the Act improved habeas law). For his part, the English jurist Albert Venn Dicey wrote that the British Habeas Corpus Acts "declare no principle and define no rights, but they are for practical purposes worth a hundred constitutional articles guaranteeing individual liberty." A.V. Dicey, Introduction to the Study of the Law of the Constitution 195 (8th ed., 1915).

66. 3 Blackstone, supra note 1, at *137 (observing that "all other cases of unjust imprisonment" not covered by the Act were "left to the *habeas corpus* at common law").

67. See Nutting, supra note 55, at 539. Earlier in the seventeenth century—specifically, around the time of the Petition of Right—English judges began to employ the writ as a tool for inquiring into both the cause of initial arrest and the cause of continued detention of those who could claim to fall within the protection of domestic law. See Halliday, supra note 2, at 48–53.

68. See 3 Blackstone, supra note 1, at *132–135; Coke, The Second Part of the Institutes, supra note 7, at 54; see also Boumediene v. Bush, 553 U.S. 723, 740 (2008) (citing 9 William Holdsworth, A History of English Law 112 (1926)); 2 James Kent, Commentaries on American Law 30 (New York, O. Halstead 1827) (writing of the Act that "[i]ts excellence consists in the easy, prompt, and efficient remedy afforded for all unlawful imprisonment, and personal liberty is not left to rest for its security upon general and abstract declarations of right").

69. 4 Blackstone, supra note 1, at *432. The writings of Coke and Blackstone represented the most influential sources on English law to which the Founding generation turned in shaping American law. "Coke's *Institutes* were read in the American colonies by virtually every student of the law," Klopfer v. North Carolina, 386 U.S. 213, 225 (1967), and "'seem[ed] to be almost the foundation of [American] law.'" Catherine Drinker Bowen, The Lion and the Throne: The Life and Times of Sir Edward Coke (1552–1634), at 514 (1954) (quoting South Carolina governor, and later Supreme Court justice, John Rutledge). Roscoe Pound once deemed Coke "the oracle of the common law." Roscoe Pound, Criminal Justice in America 94 (1930). Blackstone's *Commentaries* "turned out to be even more influential on American law and lawyers in the formative decades than Coke's *Institutes*." Meador, supra note 6, at 23, 28.

70. Henry Care, English Liberties, or the Free-Born Subject's Inheritance 129 (London, printed by G. Larkin for Benjamin Harris, 1st ed. 1680?).

71. See J. E. Powell, Great Parliamentary Occasions 63–65 (The Queen Anne Press, 1960). Powell relies on the account of the events given by Gilbert Burnet in his *History of His Own Times*, written shortly after passage of the Act.

72. See House of Lords Papers, 20 April 1679 to 4 May 1679, No. 163 (Parliamentary Archives) (recording the evolution of the bill to final form); 4 Parl. Hist. Eng. (1679) cols. 1148–1149 (same); see also Nutting, supra note 55, at 527; Godfrey Davies & Edith L. Klotz, *The Habeas Corpus Act of 1679 in the House of Lords*, 3 Huntington Libr. Q. 469 (1940) (highlighting numerous mistakes in the attendance lists for the House of Lords on the relevant date of the vote). The Lords passed an earlier version of the bill on May 2, prior to the storied vote of May 27. See 13 HL Jour. (1679) 549 (Eng.).

73. See Earl of Shaftsbury Case, 6 Cobbett's St. Tr. at 1298–1302. For extensive details on Shaftsbury's case, see id. at 1269–1310. Shaftsbury was one of three House members sent to the Tower by the Lords.

74. See id. at 1272 n.†.

75. See, e.g., 9 HC Jour. (1647) 584, 616, 618 (Eng.).

76. Nutting, supra note 55, at 527.

77. See Halliday, supra note 2, at 238–239; Nutting, supra note 55, at 540. Relying on the Lords' committee book, Nutting identifies Lord North as having promoted most of the Lords' amendments to the bill.

78. See HALLIDAY, supra note 2, at 239. The Privy Council had imprisoned Holles earlier in his life.

79. 13 HL JOUR. (1679) 595 (Eng.).

80. I MACAULAY, supra note 65, at 232.

81. See, e.g., Nutting, supra note 55, at 542.

82. Habeas Corpus Act of 1679, 31 Car. 2, c. 2, § 1 (Eng.), reprinted in 3 THE FOUNDERS' CONSTITUTION 310, 311 (Philip B. Kurland & Ralph Lerner eds., 1987). Section 8 of the Act specifically disclaimed coverage of civil causes. See id. § 8.

83. Jenkes Case (1676) 6 Cobbett's St. Tr. 1189, 1190, 1196, 1207 (Eng.). The Council had committed Jenkes for contempt but the chief justice of King's Bench and the Lord Chancellor both refused to grant his writ because it came during vacation.

84. 31 Car. 2, c. 2, §§ 2, 3, 5, 6, 9, 10, 11, 12. Section 4 provided that one who failed to petition for habeas corpus for two terms could not obtain habeas corpus during vacation time. See id. § 4.

85. Paul Halliday's work shows that vacation writs were sometimes issued before the Act, see HALLIDAY, supra note 2, at 55–56, but practice was far from uniform and such writs were denied in several high-profile cases in the decade leading up to enactment of the English Act, see id. at 236–237, 239. Halliday's work documents a similar story with respect to the Privy Council's practice of sending prisoners to legal islands, highlighting one case in which the passage of the Act made all the difference. See id. at 240; see also id. at 231 (detailing additional cases).

86. 31 Car. 2, c. 2, § 7 (Eng.) (emphasis added). Over time the relevant language from section 7 moved to section 6 of the Act. Nevertheless, all references here reflect the section's original placement. Judges initially often evaded the Act's protections by setting excessive bail; for that reason, the Declaration of Rights in 1689 outlawed the practice. See Declaration of Rights, 1688, 1 W. & M., sess. 2, c. 2, § 1 (Eng.).

87. Crosby's Case (1694) 88 Eng. Rep. 1167, 1168; see also Ex parte Beeching (1825) 107 Eng. Rep. 1010, 1010 (Abbott, C.J.) ("The object of the Habeas Corpus Act was to provide against delays in bringing persons to trial, who were committed for criminal matters."). Note that "[t]hose charged with misdemeanours were not protected [by this section], probably because they were considered to have a right to be bailed pending trial." JUDITH FARBEY & R.J. SHARPE, THE LAW OF HABEAS CORPUS 160 (3d ed. 2011).

88. The Treason Act of 1351, 25 Edw. 3, stat. 5, c. 2 (Eng.) (establishing the law of high treason that remained largely in effect for five hundred years); see also Clarence C. Crawford, *The Writ of Habeas Corpus*, 42 AM. L. REV. 481, 490 n.30 (1908). "[A]ttempt[s] w[ere] made to fill in the more important gaps" in the original treason statute "by additional legislation and by judicial interpretation," both of which "led to much abuse." Id. In such cases, Parliament often redefined the crime of high treason itself. See id.

89. 4 BLACKSTONE, supra note 1, at *83.

90. Id. Misprision of treason was also a serious crime during this period. It encompassed, among other things, concealing knowledge of treasonous plots. See id. at *120. For more on the crime of high treason during the pre-ratification period, see MICHAEL FOSTER, A REPORT OF SOME PROCEEDINGS ON THE COMMISSION FOR THE TRIAL OF THE REBELS IN THE YEAR 1746 IN THE COUNTY OF SURRY AND OF OTHER CROWN CASES 183–251 (London: W. Clarke & Sons 1809).

91. 4 BLACKSTONE, supra note 1, at *82.

92. ANDREW AMOS, THE ENGLISH CONSTITUTION IN THE REIGN OF KING CHARLES THE SECOND 203 (London, V. & R. Stevens & G.S. Norton 1857) (quoting James II, *For My Son, the Prince of Wales*, in 2 THE LIFE OF JAMES THE SECOND 621 (J.S. Clarke ed., London, Longman, Hurst, Rees, Orme & Brown 1816) (1692)).

93. 4 BLACKSTONE, supra note 1, at *92, *75; see also 3 JOSEPH STORY, COMMENTARIES ON THE CONSTITUTION OF THE UNITED STATES § 1791, at 667–668 (Cambridge, Mass., Brown, Hilliard, Gray & Co. 1833) (discussing the dangers of multiplying types of treason).

94. 1 MATTHEW HALE, HISTORIA PLACITORUM CORONAE [THE HISTORY OF THE PLEAS OF THE CROWN] 86–87 (London, E. & R. Nutt & R. Gosling 1736).

95. See The Treason Act 1695, 7 & 8 Will. 3, c. 3 (Eng.).

96. See U.S. CONST. art. III, § 3, cl. 1.

97. See 7 & 8 Will. 3, c. 3; see also JOHN H. LANGBEIN, THE ORIGINS OF ADVERSARY CRIMINAL TRIAL 67–105 (2003) (detailing background of the Act and observing that it launched a revolution in criminal procedure).

98. See HENRY CARE, ENGLISH LIBERTIES, OR THE FREE-BORN SUBJECT'S INHERITANCE 185 (5th ed., Boston, J. Franklin 1721).

99. As Hayek has written, "[i]ndividual liberty in modern times can hardly be traced back farther than the England of the seventeenth century. It appeared first, as it probably always does, as a by-product of a struggle for power rather than as the result of deliberate aim." HAYEK, supra note 44, at 162.

100. On this development, see generally E.R. Turner, *Parliament and Foreign Affairs, 1603–1760*, 34 ENG. HIST. REV. 172 (1919).

101. See An act for preventing wrongous imprisonment, and against undue delays in trials, Acts of the Parliament of Scotland 1701 (The Criminal Procedure Act of 1701), 12 Will. 3, c. 6 (Scot.) (declaring that "the imprisonment of persons without expressing the reasons thereof, and delaying to put them to trial is contrary to law"); An Act for Better Securing the Liberty of the Subject 1781, 21 & 22 Geo. 3, c. 11, § XVI (Ir.) (importing much of the language of the 1679 Habeas Corpus Act verbatim, with the notable addition of a provision allowing the Irish Council to suspend the act "during such time only as there shall be an actual invasion or rebellion in this kingdom or Great Britain").

102. 1 BLACKSTONE, supra note 1, at *133.

103. 4 id. at *286; see also 1 id. at *133 ("[I]t is unreasonable to send a prisoner [to jail], and not to signify withal the crimes alleged against him."). Here,

Blackstone was paraphrasing Acts 25:27, in which a Roman magistrate explained to St. Paul: "[I]t seemeth to me unreasonable to send a prisoner, and not withal to signify the crimes laid against him." *Acts* 25:27 (King James). Coke also drew on this passage in his speeches. See 2 Parl. Hist. Eng. (1628) cols. 266–271, reprinted in 3 THE SELECTED WRITINGS AND SPEECHES OF SIR EDWARD COKE 1243–1250 (Steve Sheppard ed., 2003) (speech given on Apr. 3, 1628, in Conference with the Lords); see also HALLIDAY, supra note 2, at 1 (noting same).

104. 4 BLACKSTONE, supra note 1, at *288; see also EDWARD COKE, THE FOURTH PART OF THE INSTITUTES OF THE LAWS OF ENGLAND 176 (6th ed. London, W. Rawlins 1681) (1644) (stating that justices of the peace could not issue warrants to arrest on suspicion alone); 2 THOMAS ERSKINE MAY, THE CONSTITUTIONAL HISTORY OF ENGLAND 252 (Boston, Crosby & Nichols 1864) (writing that "[t]he illegality of general warrants" was settled by this time).

105. 3 BLACKSTONE, supra note 1, at *137–*138 (emphasis added).

106. W.B. Gray, *The Scottish Deportees of 1683 and the Habeas Corpus Act*, 35 JURID. REV. 353 (1923).

107. See An Act to Attaint James Duke of Monmouth of High Treason 1685, 1 James II, c. 2 (Eng.) ("Whereas James Duke of Monmouth has in an hostile Manner Invaded this Kingdome and is now in open Rebellion Levying Warr against the King contrary to the Duty of his Allegiance, Bee it enacted. . . . That the said James Duke of Monmouth Stand and be Convicted and Attainted of High-Treason and that he suffer Paines of Death and Incurr all Forfeitures as a Traitor Convicted and Attainted of High Treason.").

108. One year after the passage of the Habeas Corpus Act, a member of Parliament explained this exception this way:

> I have perused the *Habeas Corpus* bill, and do find, that there is not anything in it that doth reach, or can be intended to reach to any commitment made by either house of parliament during session. The preamble of the Act, and all the parts of it, do confine the extent of the Act to cases bailable, and directs such courses for the execution of the act, as cannot be understood should relate to any commitment made by either house. This house is a court of itself, and part of the highest court in the nation, superior to those in Westminster-hall. . . .

II THE HISTORY AND PROCEEDINGS OF THE HOUSE OF COMMONS 1680–1695, at 48–101 (1742) (Chandler) (Dec. 30, 1680) (Remarks of Sir William Jones) (addressing a motion for admitting to bail one committed by order of the House). Indeed, by this time, it was fairly well-settled that the courts could not review orders of the Houses of Parliament. See CHAFETZ, supra note 51, at 28, 32–34. The common defense for parliamentary independence of the royal courts predicated the need for such independence on the Commons being "intrusted with the liberty of the people." Id. at 34 (quoting R. v. Paty (1704), 92 Eng. Rep. 232, 233, 2 Ld. Raym. 1105, 1111–1112).

CHAPTER 2

1. 10 DEBATES OF THE HOUSE OF COMMONS, FROM THE YEAR 1667 TO THE YEAR 1694, at 141 (Anchitell Grey ed., London, D. Henry & R. Cave & J. Emonson 1763) [hereinafter GREY'S DEBATES] (remarks of Sir William Whitlock).

2. PAUL D. HALLIDAY, HABEAS CORPUS: FROM ENGLAND TO EMPIRE 247 (2010). Hampden's argument for expanded executive authority to detain is even more remarkable given the fact that he was the great-nephew of Sir Edmund Hampden, one of the Five Knights imprisoned for failing to pay the king's forced loans some sixty years earlier. See JOHN PHILIPOT, THE VISITATION OF THE COUNTY OF BUCKINGHAM MADE IN 1634, at 70–71 (W. Harry Rylands ed., London 1909) (presenting a genealogical tree of the Hampdens of Buckinghamshire); THE HISTORY OF PARLIAMENT: THE HOUSE OF COMMONS 1604–1629 (Andrew Thrush & John P. Ferris eds., 2010) (entry on John Hampden); THE HISTORY OF PARLIAMENT: THE HOUSE OF COMMONS 1660–1690 (B.D. Henning ed., 1983) (entry on Richard Hampden).

3. A word on terminology is due. As Paul Halliday has noted, heading into the eighteenth century, many of the powers traditionally associated with the king in his person had by then "been transposed into 'the crown.'" Paul D. Halliday, *Blackstone's King*, in RE-INTERPRETING BLACKSTONE'S *COMMENTARIES*: A SEMINAL TEXT IN NATIONAL AND INTERNATIONAL CONTEXTS 169, 179 (Wilfrid Prest ed., 2014) [hereinafter RE-INTERPRETING BLACKSTONE'S *COMMENTARIES*].

4. 9 GREY'S DEBATES, supra note 1, at 129–130. Grey's Debates was derived from the notes of Anchitell Grey, who served in the Commons during this period. Although Grey's notes are not a perfect transcript, they are the best account available of the relevant debates.

5. Id. at 131.

6. Id. (contending that "the Law is sufficient already"). In later debates, Clarges would exclaim: "We have had a struggle for [the Habeas Corpus Act] . . . and now, upon suggested Necessities, to dispense with this Law!" Id. at 268.

7. See Declaration of Rights 1688, 1 W. & M., sess. 2, c. 2, § 2 (Eng.).

8. See 9 GREY'S DEBATES, supra note 1, at 133 (remarks of Heneage Finch). For more on this issue, see Clarence C. Crawford, *The Suspension of the Habeas Corpus Act and the Revolution of 1689*, 30 ENG. HIST. REV. 613, 616–618 (1915).

9. 9 GREY'S DEBATES, supra note 1, at 132.

10. Id. at 136.

11. 14 HL JOUR. (1689) 135 (Eng.).

12. See 9 GREY'S DEBATES, supra note 1, at 136–137 (debates of Mar. 4, 1689). Parliament similarly privileged itself from the suspensions that followed in 1696, 1708, 1715, 1722, and 1744–1745.

13. Although legally distinct from bail, mainprize served a similar function by setting a party at liberty until a stipulated date of appearance.

14. Here the suspension gave the full title and date of the 1679 Act.

15. 1688, 1 W. & M., c. 2 (Eng.); see also 2 THE HISTORY AND PROCEEDINGS OF THE HOUSE OF COMMONS 284–285 (London, n. pub. 1742) [hereinafter HISTORY AND PROCEEDINGS] (noting royal assent granted Mar. 16, 1689). The Statutes at Large do not contain the body of the Act. It may be found in the Statutes of the Realm. See 6 THE STATUTES OF THE REALM 24 (John Raithby ed., London, n. pub. 1819). Historian Clarence Crawford's work highlights that no member of Parliament at the time voiced concerns that the Crown would abuse its new authority. See CLARENCE CORY CRAWFORD, THE SUSPENSION OF THE HABEAS CORPUS ACT IN ENGLAND 28–29 (1906).

16. Here, as in later English suspensions, the Act referenced "persons," not just "subjects," thereby supporting the conclusion that those reached by the suspension, and protected by the Habeas Corpus Act, encompassed at least some aliens.

17. The National Archives (Great Britain) [hereinafter TNA] PC 2/73/47 (replicating March 16, 1689, order in Privy Council Entry Book).

18. TNA PC 2/73/51 (replicating March 16, 1689, order in Privy Council Entry Book).

19. Crawford, supra note 8, at 621–622.

20. See An Act for Impowering His Majestie to Apprehend and Detaine Such Persons as He Shall Finde Just Cause to Suspect Are Conspireing Against the Government, 1688, 1 W. & M., c. 7 (Eng.); 2 HISTORY AND PROCEEDINGS, supra note 15, at 304–305 (noting royal assent granted Apr. 24, 1689). This Act ran to May 25, 1689. See 1 W. & M., c. 7; see also 14 HL JOUR. (1689) 190–191 (Eng.).

21. 1 W. & M., c. 7.

22. TNA PC 2/73/81 (replicating April 25, 1689, order in Privy Council Entry Book). The fact that at least one of the prisoners in the Tower had sought relief at the lapsing of the first suspension seems to have influenced prompt passage of the extension. See Crawford, supra note 8, at 623.

23. Crawford, supra note 8, at 623 (citing the relevant portions of the warrant-book of the home department).

24. Id. at 624.

25. 9 GREY'S DEBATES, supra note 1, at 262–263.

26. See generally id. at 262–276.

27. Id. at 267 ("I think it fit that such a Bill be brought in, in time of danger from abroad, and within the realm; and 'tis only to confine them from doing mischief."). Circumstances must have been dire for Hawles to support the measure, given that during this same period his writings championed an expansive view of the role of the jury in criminal cases. See THOMAS ANDREW GREEN, VERDICT ACCORDING TO CONSCIENCE 252–253, 255–260 (1985).

28. 9 GREY'S DEBATES, supra note 1, at 265.

29. Id. at 267; see also id. at 265 (remarks of Sir Robert Sawyer) (lamenting that the "Bill does not take care for Proof of a Charge against a man" but instead permits commitment "[u]pon a bare Suspicion").

30. Id. at 271.
31. Id. at 274.
32. Id. at 263.
33. An Act for Impowering Their Majestyes to Commit Without Baille Such Persons as They Shall Finde Just Cause to Suspect Are Conspireing Against the Government, 1688, 1 W. & M., c. 19 (Eng.); 2 History and Proceedings, supra note 15, at 321 (noting royal assent granted May 28, 1689). The Act ran until October 23, 1689. See 1 W. & M., c. 19. These debates include the first suggestions that the suspension power could be abused and wielded against political enemies. See 9 Grey's Debates, supra note 1, at 264–267 (remarks of Sir Robert Sawyer, Sir Joseph Tredenham, and Sir Robert Cotton).
34. See Crawford, supra note 15, at 46 (citing 12 A Complete Collection of State Trials and Proceedings for High Treason and Other Crimes and Misdemeanors 598, 613–614 (T.B. Howell ed., London, T.C. Hansard 1816)); see also id. at 44–46 (detailing the bases for numerous arrests made during the suspension); Crawford, supra note 8, at 626–627.
35. See Halliday, supra note 2, at 32.
36. See Paul D. Halliday & G. Edward White, *The Suspension Clause: English Text, Imperial Contexts, and American Implications*, 94 Va. L. Rev. 575, 626–627 & nn. 147, 148 (2008) (detailing some of the cases of prosecution). As Paul Halliday and G. Edward White have observed, "[s]uch high release rates become all the more interesting when we consider who ordered all these prisoners released. The newly appointed King's Bench justices of 1689 were among the chief beneficiaries of the new parliamentary order that these alleged traitors were seen to threaten." Id. at 626–627.
37. Specifically, the House ordered Sir Thomas Jenner, Richard Graham, and Philip Burton taken into custody. See 2 The History and Proceedings of the House of Commons 1680–1695, at 355–373 (1742) (Richard Chandler ed., n. pub. 1742) (Oct. 23, 1689) (detailing events). As the Journal of the House of Commons reports:

> [T]he House being informed, that several of the Prisoners in the Tower were now bailing in the Court of King's Bench, being brought thither by the Governor of the Tower, by virtue of a Habeas Corpus awarded for that Purpose; particularly Sir Thomas Jenner, Mr. Richard Graham, and Mr. Philip Burton. Ordered, That Sir Thomas Jenner, Mr. Richard Graham, and Mr. Philip Burton, be immediately brought to this House, by the Governor of the Tower; to answer such Matters as shall be objected against them.

10 HC Jour. (Oct. 25, 1689) 275 (Eng.). This action followed the prior day's decision by the House to constitute a committee to "inspect . . . Informations given in against the Prisoners in the Tower" as well as "the Informations given against any other Persons in Custody elsewhere than in the Tower"—that is, to review the cases of all persons remaining in custody who had been detained during the suspension. Id. at 273 (Oct. 24, 1689).

38. 10 HC JOUR. (Oct. 26, 1689) 275 (Eng.). The same day, the House of Commons also impeached the Earl of Salisbury and the Earl of Peterborow, "for departing from their Allegiance, and being reconciled to the Church of Rome." The two were imprisoned in the Tower. See id.

39. See 10 GREY'S DEBATES, supra note 1, at 139–145 (detailing debates); id. at 141 (remarks of Sir William Whitlock).

40. See JOCK HASWELL, JAMES II 302–303 (1972).

41. See 4 THOMAS BABINGTON MACAULAY, THE HISTORY OF ENGLAND FROM THE ACCESSION OF JAMES THE SECOND 220–248 (London, Longman, Brown, Green & Longmans 1855).

42. 11 HC JOUR. (Feb. 24, 1696) 465 (Eng.). Details of the plot may be found in RACHEL WEIL, A PLAGUE OF INFORMERS: CONSPIRACY AND POLITICAL TRUST IN WILLIAM III'S ENGLAND 248–275 (2013); 5 COBBETT'S PARLIAMENTARY HISTORY OF ENGLAND 40–41, 987 n.* (London, n. pub. 1809) [hereinafter COBBETT'S PARL. HIST.]. *Cobbett's Parliamentary History* is an account drawn from various sources, including newspapers, pamphlets, memoirs, and diaries. It is relied upon here as one of the best accounts of certain relevant parliamentary debates. Professor Weil notes that two plotters had changed sides and warned the king of the plan. See WEIL, supra, at 249.

43. 15 HL JOUR. (1696) 679 (Eng.); 11 HC JOUR. (1696) 465 (Eng.).

44. 11 HC JOUR. (1696) 465 (Eng.).

45. An Act for Impowering His Majestie to Apprehend and Detain Such Persons as Hee Shall Find Cause to Suspect Are Conspiring Against His Royal Person or Government 1696, 7 & 8 Wlm. 3, c. 11 (Eng.) (running until Sept. 1, 1696); 11 HC JOUR. (1696) 497 (Eng.) (noting royal assent given Mar. 7, 1696).

46. Crawford, supra note 8, at 56. There is no record of any amendments to the bill being introduced in either House.

47. See, e.g., TNA PC 2/76/181v; PC 2/76/182; PC 2/76/190v; PC 2/76/191v; PC 2/76/192v; PC 2/76/198; PC 2/76/204; PC 2/76/205. Professor Weil's study of this episode documents many arrests, noting that the group detained was "much wider" than those ultimately prosecuted. See WEIL, supra note 42, at 260–261.

48. TNA PC 2/76/194v (replicating royal proclamation "requir[ing] all his Loving Subjects to Discover, take & apprehend the Lord Montgomery and Sir John Fenwick wherever they may be found, and to carry them before the next Justice of Peace or Chief Magistrate, who is hereby required to Commit them to the next Gaole, there to remain until they be thence delivered by Due Course of Law"); PC 2/76/205 (ordering a search of Lincoln's Inn for "persons who stand Accused of High Treason [who] are concealed in Lincoln's Inn").

49. See, e.g., (1696) 13 Cobbett's St. Tr. 1 (Eng.) (trial of Sir John Friend for High Treason, convicted and ordered executed); id. at 63 (trial of Sir William Parkyns for High Treason, convicted and ordered executed); id. at 139 (trial of Ambrose Rookwood, convicted and ordered executed); id. at 221 (trial of

Charles Cranburne for High Treason, convicted and ordered executed); id. at 267 (trial of Robert Lowick, for High Treason, convicted and ordered executed); id. at 311 (trial of Peter Cook for High Treason, convicted and ordered executed but later pardoned upon promising never to return to England).

50. See CRAWFORD, supra note 15, at 59.

51. An Act to attaint Sir John Fenwick, Baronet, of high treason, 1697, 8 Wlm. 3, c. 4 (Eng.); see 13 Cobbett's St. Tr. at 537, 758. Parliament also attainted of high treason a number of other alleged conspirators not in custody. See An Act to attaint such of the persons concerned in the late horrid conspiracy, to assassinate his Majesty's royal person, who are fled from justice, unless they render themselves to justice; and for continuing several other of the said conspirators in custody, 1697, 8 Wlm. 3, c. 4 (Eng.).

52. These events generated a Jacobite toast to the mole in question, the so-called "Little Gentleman in Black Velvet."

53. HALLIDAY, supra note 2, at 250 (detailing numerous releases ordered by King's Bench).

54. Bernardi here refers to those tried during the suspension and ordered executed. This group includes those mentioned at note 49.

55. 13 Cobbett's St. Tr. at 759, 768–769; see 1697, 8 Wlm. 3, c. 4 (Eng.) (providing that Bernardi, Counter, Robert Cassells, Robert Meldrum, James Chambers, and Robert Blackburne "shall be detained and kept in Custody without Bail or Mainprise" until January 1, 1698, unless they "shall be sooner bailed or discharged" by an order signed by six members of the Privy Council); see also WEIL, supra note 42, at 271 (noting that witnesses against Bernardi had escaped and been spirited away). Although technically these acts did not attaint of guilt but rather extended detention to await further evidence of the same, they nonetheless applied to specific persons and were passed to circumvent the criminal process and protections of the Habeas Corpus Act, just like bills of attainder.

56. 13 Cobbett's St. Tr. at 770.

57. See JUDITH FARBEY & R.J. SHARPE, THE LAW OF HABEAS CORPUS 158 n.82 (3d ed. 2011); The King against The Earl of Orrery, Lord North and Grey, Bishop of Rochester, Kelly, and Cockran (1722) 88 Eng. Rep. 75 (discussing *Bernardi's Case*). Almost twenty years after the assassination plot, Parliament was not only still ordering the detention of Bernardi, but at least four others who had been implicated in the plot. See An Act for continuing the imprisonment of Robert Blackburn and others, for the horrid conspiracy to assassinate the person of his late sacred Majesty King William the Third 1714, 1 Geo. Stat. 2, c.7 (Gr. Brit.) (ordering continued detention of five prisoners in Newgate based on the events of 1696).

58. Indeed, during the arguments over Fenwick's attainder, one member of Parliament who supported the bill offered: "There is nothing can limit us, but the law of nature, the law of God, and the law of parliaments." 5 COBBETT'S PARL. HIST., supra note 42, at 1034 (remarks of Lord John Cutts). But one historian

surveying this episode views Bernardi's case as raising the question "What does a liberal regime do with persons who are almost certainly guilty and dangerous but cannot be successfully convicted in a court of law?" WEIL, supra note 42, at 279.

59. Lord Aylesbury's Case (1701) 1 Salk. 103 (Eng.); see also The King against The Earl of Ailesbury (1701) 12 Mod. 118 (Eng.).

60. An Act to Impower Her Majesty to Secure and Detain Such Persons as Her Majesty Shall Suspect Are Conspiring Against Her Person or Government 1707, 6 Ann., c. 15 (Gr. Brit.); 18 HL JOUR. (1708) 506 (Gr. Brit.) (noting royal assent given Mar. 11, 1708). This suspension ran to October 23, 1708.

61. An Act to Impower His Majesty to Secure and Detain Such Persons as His Majesty Shall Suspect Are Conspiring Against His Person and Government 1714, 1 Geo., c. 8 (Gr. Brit.); 20 HL JOUR. (1715) 128 (Gr. Brit.) (noting royal assent given July 23, 1715). Parliament renewed this suspension the following year. 1715, 1 Geo., c. 30 (Gr. Brit.); 20 HL JOUR. (1716) 269–270 (Gr. Brit.) (noting royal assent given Jan. 21, 1716). In the same session, Parliament enacted a statute "for the more easy and speedy Trial of such Persons as have levied or shall levy War against his Majesty." 1716, 1 Geo., c. 33 (Gr. Brit.).

62. An Act to Impower His Majesty to Secure and Detain Such Persons, as His Majesty Shall Suspect Are Conspiring Against His Person and Government 1722, 9 Geo., c. 1 (Gr. Brit.) (providing that it shall remain in effect for one year); 22 HL JOUR. (1722) 21–22 (Gr. Brit.) (noting royal assent given Oct. 17, 1722).

63. See 6 Ann., c. 15, 1 Geo., c. 8, 9 Geo., c. 1.

64. In 1708, Louis XIV approved a plan pursuant to which James Edward Stuart would land on the shores of Scotland and seize on resentment over the 1707 Act of Union between Scotland and England to mount Scottish forces. James's ship never landed, and instead sailed back to France.

65. This time, James Edward Stuart did land in Scotland, but with victory unlikely, he abandoned Scotland and again returned to France.

66. Rex versus Wyndham (1723) 1 Strange 3 (KB); see also Old Bailey Proceedings supplementary material, Ebenezer Smith Platt, 19 Feb. 1777, http://www.oldbaileyonline.org/browse.jsp?div=o17770219-1 (discussing Wyndham's case).

67. When the suspension lapsed, a number of prisoners were released rather than prosecuted. Others were not so lucky. Many Jacobites were tried for treason and found guilty, with a number of them being hanged and then taken down still alive to be drawn and quartered publicly in areas that had supported the Jacobite cause. In the wake of Stuart's return to France, most of the remaining prisoners were deported to the American colonies rather than tried. Meanwhile, the Commons impeached a number of the leaders of the rebellion, two of whom were then beheaded at the Tower of London. Parliament deemed other leaders of the rebellion traitors by several acts of attainder. For additional details, see JOHN L. ROBERTS, THE JACOBITE WARS 35–37, 54–55 (2002).

68. As part of the Act of Settlement of 1701 (best known for settling the succession of the English throne), judges now held their commissions during good behavior, subject to removal only by Parliament.

69. 8 Cobbett's Parl. Hist., supra note 42, at 40–41 (Oct. 16, 1722).

70. 1 T. Smollett, The History of England from the Revolution of 1688, to the Death of George II 583–585 (Albany, N.Y., B.D. Packard 1816). As had happened during the 1696 suspension, certain prominent suspects were tried and convicted of treason even during the pendency of the suspension. See id. at 585 (noting that Christopher Layer was tried before King's Bench in November 1722 and found guilty); id. at 586 (noting that Parliament took up and passed two bills of attainder to continue the confinement of certain suspects).

71. The king also detained the Duke of Norfolk on suspicion of treason. In all of these cases, the king requested, and received, the consent of the House of Lords to detain these members, though several Lords protested the commitment of the Duke of Norfolk. See 8 Cobbett's Parl. Hist., supra note 42, at 43–46 (Oct. 17 & 26, 1722).

72. See, e.g., id. at 29 (Oct. 11, 1722) (remarks of the Earls of Anglesea, Cowper, Stafford, and Coningsby, the Lords Trevor, Bathurst, and Bingley); see also id. at 38 (Oct. 16, 1722) (remarks of Spencer Cowper).

73. See id. at 29; see also id. at 35 (reporting formal Protest of these and other members).

74. Id. at 27 (remarks of the Duke of Grafton).

75. Id. at 30 n.* (quoting summary of the arguments published in the *London Journal*). Here, one finds early evidence of an increasing association between the idea of a habeas privilege and the Habeas Corpus Act.

76. The King against The Earl of Orrery, Lord North and Grey, Bishop of Rochester, Kelly, and Cockran, Prisoners in the Tower (1722) 88 Eng. Rep. 75 (KB); 8 Mod. 96 (5th ed. corrected 1795). Note that the king had requested special consent from the House of Lords to detain some of these prisoners as part of his authority conveyed in the 1722 suspension legislation, members of Parliament commonly being privileged from suspensions. See 22 HL Jour. (1722) 21–22 (Gr. Brit.).

77. This case underscores Paul Halliday's observation that "The logic of suspension followed in the wake of statutory extensions of the writ, consuming the judge's autonomy along the way." Halliday, supra note 2, at 217.

78. An Act to Impower His Majesty to Secure and Detain Such Persons as His Majesty Shall Suspect Are Conspiring Against His Person and Government 1744, 17 Geo. 2, c. 6 (Gr. Brit.); 26 HL Jour. (1744) 332, 334–335 (Gr. Brit.) (noting royal assent given Mar. 2, 1744). The Act ran until April 29, 1744.

79. An act for preventing wrongous imprisonment, and against undue delays in trials, 1701, 8 & 9 Wlm. 3, c. 6 (Gr. Brit.) (declaring that "[t]he imprisonment of persons without expressing the reasons thereof, and delaying to put them to trial is contrary to law" and incorporating many of the key provisions of the Habeas

Corpus Act of 1679 including the requirement that one be tried within a specified period of time or discharged).

80. 13 COBBETT'S PARL. HIST., supra note 42, at 683–688 (Mar. 20, 1744) (replicating France's declaration of war); id. at 688–691 (Mar. 31, 1744) (replicating Britain's declaration of war).

81. ROBERTS, supra note 67, at 73, 76.

82. An Act to Impower His Majesty to Secure and Detain Such Persons as His Majesty Shall Suspect Are Conspiring Against His Person and Government 1745, 19 Geo. 2, c. 1 (Gr. Brit.); 26 HL JOUR. (1745) 511 (Gr. Brit.) (noting royal assent given Oct. 21, 1745). This suspension continued the regular practice of exempting members of the Houses of Parliament when in session absent the consent of the relevant House. The Act ran until April 19, 1746. Parliament extended this suspension on the date of its initial expiration. See An Act for Continuing an Act of This Present Session of Parliament, Intituled, *An Act to Impower His Majesty to Secure and Detain Such Persons as His Majesty Shall Suspect Are Conspiring Against His Person and Government* 1746, 19 Geo. 2, c. 17 (Gr. Brit.); 26 HL JOUR. (1746) 565–566 (Gr. Brit.) (noting royal assent given Apr. 19, 1746). Parliament extended the suspension again in November 1746. See An Act for the Further Continuing an Act Made in the Last Session of Parliament, Intituled, *An Act to Impower His Majesty to Secure and Detain Such Persons as His Majesty Shall Suspect Are Conspiring Against His Person and Government* 1746, 20 Geo. 2, c. 1 (Gr. Brit.) (extending the suspension to Feb. 20, 1747); 27 HL JOUR. (1746) 9 (Gr. Brit.) (noting royal assent given Nov. 26, 1746).

83. See ROBERTS, supra note 67, at 175–188.

84. WILLIAM PICKERING, AN OLD STORY RE-TOLD FROM THE "NEWCASTLE COURANT": THE REBELLION OF 1745, at 208 (1881); see also id. at 196–211 (detailing many of the trials); STUART REID, CULLODEN MOOR 1746: THE DEATH OF THE JACOBITE CAUSE 87, 88–90 (2005). The Crown also seized estates of those who had supported the Jacobite cause and Parliament enacted laws disarming Highlanders, demanding oaths of allegiance of them, and banning the wearing of Highland dress. See ROBERTS, supra note 67, at 175–188.

85. Pickering, supra note 84, at 203; see also Rex. v. Townley (1746) 18 Cobbett's St. Tr. 329, 348 (Eng.) (recording rejection of the argument in one trial). The convicted were ordered hanged, but not killed, and then drawn and quartered. "The second half of the year 1746 was a busy time for the hangman in the North of England." PICKERING, supra, at 205.

86. See THE WHOLE PROCEEDINGS IN THE HOUSE OF PEERS UPON THE IMPEACHMENT EXHIBITED BY THE *KNIGHTS, CITIZENS,* AND *BURGESSES,* IN PARLIAMENT ASSEMBLED, IN THE NAMES OF THEMSELVES, AND OF ALL THE COMMONS OF *GREAT BRITAIN;* AGAINST *SIMON* LORD *LOVAT,* FOR HIGH TREASON (London n. pub. 1747); PICKERING, supra note 84, at 218–223 (detailing Lovat's trial and execution); id. at 217. Lord Lovat reportedly made a point of "commend[ing] the abilities" of

his prosecutor in his trial before the House of Lords, Solicitor General William Murray, who would later become the Earl of Mansfield and chief justice of King's Bench. PICKERING, supra, at 222.

87. ROBERTS, supra note 67, at 195–197.

88. This conclusion explains why none of the suspensions during this period or during the Revolutionary War came along with indemnity legislation for officers who committed prisoners in violation of the Habeas Corpus Act—there was simply no need for such legislation. See Amanda L. Tyler, *Suspension as an Emergency Power*, 118 YALE L.J. 600, 613–622 (2009) (expanding upon the point).

89. UNDENIABLE REASONS FOR SUSPENDING THE HABEAS CORPUS ACT, AND SECURING TRAYTORS 2 (Corke, printed by George Bennett Nov. 10, 1722).

90. 1 WILLIAM BLACKSTONE, COMMENTARIES *131–132; see THE FEDERALIST NO. 84, at 511 (Alexander Hamilton) (Clinton Rossiter ed., 2003). In his *American's Blackstone*, St. George Tucker linked this passage with the Suspension Clause in the American Constitution. See 1 ST. GEORGE TUCKER, BLACKSTONE'S COMMENTARIES: WITH NOTES OF REFERENCE, TO THE CONSTITUTION AND LAWS, OF THE FEDERAL GOVERNMENT OF THE UNITED STATES; AND OF THE COMMONWEALTH OF VIRGINIA app. at 292 (Philadelphia, William Young Birch & Abraham Small 1803) (observing in his annotation that the privilege "can be suspended, only, by the authority of congress; but not whenever congress may think proper; for it cannot be suspended, unless in cases of actual rebellion, or invasion"). Tucker's Americanized version of Blackstone's *Commentaries* was "the first major legal treatise on American law" and "one of the most influential legal works of the early nineteenth century." Davison M. Douglas, *Foreword: The Legacy of St. George Tucker*, 47 WM. & MARY L. REV. 1111, 1114 (2006).

91. Indeed, Blackstone's emphasis on Parliament here and elsewhere earned the ire of some critics, who read him to glorify " 'the uncontrolled, absolute, despotic power of Parliament.' " Ruth Paley, *Modern Blackstone: The King's Two Bodies, the Supreme Court and the President*, in RE-INTERPRETING BLACKSTONE'S COMMENTARIES, supra note 3, at 188, 191 (quoting Blackstone critic and Irish Parliament member Charles Francis Sheridan).

92. R.J. SHARPE, THE LAW OF HABEAS CORPUS 13, 91 (1976) (emphasis added).

93. A.V. DICEY, INTRODUCTION TO THE STUDY OF THE LAW OF THE CONSTITUTION 40 (10th ed. 1959) (originally published 1885).

94. See Douglass C. North & Barry R. Weingast, *Constitutions and Commitment: The Evolution of Institutions Governing Public Choice in Seventeenth-Century England*, 49 J. ECON. HIST. 803, 817 (1989).

95. See id. at 824–825. North and Weingast's work suggests that in the wake of the Glorious Revolution, "the emergence of political and civil liberties was inextricably linked with economic freedom." Id. at 829. For more on the link between credible commitments and economic growth during this period, consult JOHN BREWER, THE SINEWS OF POWER: WAR, MONEY, AND THE ENGLISH STATE, 1688–1783 (1989).

96. 1 Blackstone, supra note 90, at *361.

97. 1 Matthew Hale, Historia Placitorum Coronae [The History of the Pleas of the Crown] 159 (E. & R. Nutt & R. Gosling 1736). As evidence of Hale's later influence on American law, note that discussion of his work pervades Chief Justice Marshall's opinion in the treason trial of Aaron Burr. See United States v. Burr, 25 F. Cas. 55 (C.C.D. Va. 1807) (No. 14,693).

98. Edward Coke, The Third Part of the Institutes of the Laws of England 5 (5th ed., London, n. pub. 1671); see also Henry Care, English Liberties, or the Free-Born Subject's Inheritance 65 (5th ed., Boston, J. Franklin 1721).

99. Michael Foster, A Report of Some Proceedings on the Commission of Oyer and Terminer and Goal Delivery for the Trial of the Rebels in the Year 1746 in the County of Surry and of Other Crown Cases 183–190, 193–198, 200–201 (Oxford, Clarendon Press 1762) (observing that "High Treason" is "an Offence committed against the Duty of Allegiance," id. at 183, and that "Protection [of the laws] and Allegiance are reciprocal Obligations," id. at 188); see also Considerations on the Exchange of Seamen, Prisoners of War 9 (printed for J. Noon, London 1758) ("*Allegiance* and *Protection* are reciprocal; where the one may *justly claim'd*, the other is *strictly due*.").

100. 4 Blackstone, supra note 90, at *75 (observing that treason "imports a betraying, treachery, or breach of faith" that happens "only between allies" and is committed by "member[s] of the community"). Blackstone goes on to describe allegiance as "the tie, or *ligament*, which binds the subject to the king in return for that protection which the king affords the subject." 1 Blackstone, supra, at *354.

101. For example, drawing and quartering remained a punishment in use until 1781, with the last to suffer it being David Tyrie, a Scot found guilty of high treason for aiding the French during the American Revolutionary War. See The Trial of David Tyrie for High Treason (1782) 21 Cobbett's St. Tr. 815 (Eng.).

102. TNA, PC 2/76/26-27 (Feb. 1694/1695).

103. Id.

104. See By the King, A Proclamation directing how Prisoners shall bee ordered which are taken at Sea, by men of Warre (London 1628) (directing that prisoners taken at sea during hostilities with France and Spain shall be "kept in Prison and safe custodie . . . until they shall hence bee delivered, and sent backe into their feuetall Countreys, either by way of Exchange for Our Subjects, which shall happen to bee Prisoners there, or otherwise").

105. See, e.g., PC2/76/36 (Feb. 1694/1695) (ordering his Majesty's Commission for Sick & Wounded Seamen, and Exchange of Prisoners at War to "cause so many of the French Kings Subjects now Prisoners in Ireland as they shall judge fit not exceeding Three Hundred, to be exchanged for the like number of his Majesty's Subjects Prisoners in France"); PC 2/76/116v (May 2, 1695) (ordering John Dupuis, "A Frenchman Seized at Exeter by Warrant from

this Board . . . on Suspicion of being a Spy, be delivered into the Commission of Sick and Wounded Seamen and Exchange of Prisoners, who are to cause him to be sent over & Exchanged"). Paul Halliday's work notes additional cases of Frenchmen captured, remanded, and ultimately exchanged. See HALLIDAY, supra note 2, at 171. Part of the impetus for exchanges derived from the obligation of the state to protect its own subjects and negotiate their liberty when taken as prisoner abroad. See generally CONSIDERATIONS ON THE EXCHANGE OF SEAMEN, supra note 99.

106. See Rex v. Barnard Schiever (1759) 97 Eng. Rep. 551–552; HALLIDAY, supra note 2, at 172–173.

107. The Case of the Three Spanish Sailors (1779) 2 Black W. 1324, 96 Eng. Rep. 775–776 (concluding: "we can give them no redress"); HALLIDAY, supra note 2, at 173 (discussing case).

108. HALLIDAY, supra note 2, at 171. The *Schiever* and *Spanish Sailors* cases are discussed in the Supreme Court's decision in *Boumediene v. Bush*, 553 U.S. 723 (2008), explored in Chapter 11.

109. See HALLIDAY, supra note 2, at 170 (discussing Comberford's 1697 petition for habeas relief and citing TNA KB 16/1/6 (23 Jan. 1697); KB 21/25/120); TNA PC 2/76/65v (Privy Council order that Comberford "be discharged and set at Liberty" by the Attorney General after he "hath taken the Oaths" of allegiance before a judge).

110. HALLIDAY, supra note 2, at 170–171.

111. See 108 HALE AND FLEETWOOD ON ADMIRALTY JURISDICTION (M.J. Prichard & D.E.C. Yale eds., London, Selden Society 1993), 332–341 (detailing numerous cases, including that of "John Golden").

112. Id. at 339–340 (detailing case).

113. Williams' Case, 4 Hall L. J. 461, 2 Cranch 82, 29 F. Cas. 1330, 1331 (C.C.D. Conn. 1799) (No. 17,708).

114. For details, see *JOURNAL of the Prince's Imbarkation and Arrival Taken from the Mouth of AeNEAS MACDONALD (a Banker in Paris, and Brother of Kinlochmoidart) when He was in a Messenger's Custody in London, by Dr. BURTON of York*, in I THE LYON IN MOURNING OR A COLLECTION OF SPEECHES LETTERS JOURNALS ETC. RELATIVE TO THE AFFAIRS OF PRINCE CHARLES EDWARD STUART 281–294 (Rev. Robert Forbes ed., 1895).

115. Williams' Case, 4 Hall L.J. 461, 2 Cranch 82, 29 F. Cas. 1330, 1332 (C.C.D. Conn. 1799) (No. 17,708) (Supplemental Note by Cobbett based on the record offered "for the purpose of giving great precision"). The king later pardoned MacDonald. See id.

116. Calvin's Case (1608) 77 Eng. Rep. 377, 383 (Coke, C.J.).

117. COKE, THE THIRD PART OF THE INSTITUTES, supra note 98, at 4–5. That protection could sweep beyond subjecthood likely explains why suspensions commonly referred to the committal of "persons" versus "subjects."

118. TNA PC 2/76/198 (Mar. 26, 1696).
119. (1697) 92 Eng. Rep. 816.
120. The Trial of François Henri de la Motte for High Treason (1781) 21 Cobbett's St. Tr. 687, 709 (KB).
121. Id. at 814–815.
122. Whether de la Motte's and Vienne's cases suggest that the Crown reserved the right to elect whether to treat aliens with prior connections to the Crown as either prisoners of war or domestic criminals is not entirely clear.

CHAPTER 3

1. 19 COBBETT'S PARLIAMENTARY HISTORY OF ENGLAND FROM THE NORMAN CONQUEST, IN 1066 TO THE YEAR 180, at 4 (London, T.C. Hansard 1813) (Feb. 6, 1777) (remarks of Lord North) (emphases added) [hereinafter 19 COBBETT'S PARL. HIST.].
2. 1 JOURNALS OF THE CONTINENTAL CONGRESS, 1774–1789, at 68 (Worthington Chauncey Ford ed., 1904) (replicating 1774 Statement of Violation of Rights).
3. *Observations upon the Charter of the Province of New-York* (1684), in 3 DOCUMENTS RELATIVE TO THE COLONIAL HISTORY OF THE STATE OF NEW-YORK 357, 357 (John Romeyn Brodhead ed., Albany, N.Y., Weed, Parsons & Co. 1853); see David S. Lovejoy, *Equality and Empire: The New York Charter of Libertyes, 1683*, 21 WM. & MARY Q. 493, 510–514 (1964) (detailing story). Following the ascension of William and Mary, the New York Assembly again sought recognition of a range of rights and privileges enjoyed by the English. See An Act Declaring What Are the Rights and Privileges of Their Majesties' Subjects Inhabiting Within the Province of New York (1691) in 3 THE REVISED STATUTES OF THE STATE OF NEW-YORK app. pt. 1, at 2 (Albany, N.Y., Packard & Van Benthuysen 1829) (positing that "no freeman shall be taken and imprisoned . . . but by the lawful judgment of his peers, and by the law of this province"). Nonetheless, as detailed above, the Crown continued to deny the colonists the benefit of the Habeas Corpus Act.
4. An Act for the Better Securing the Liberty of the Subject, and for Prevention of Illegal Imprisonment, ch. 42, 1692–1693 MASS. ACTS 95, 99 (quoting Letter from the Privy Council) (internal quotation marks omitted).
5. PAUL M. HAMLIN & CHARLES E. BAKER, SUPREME COURT OF JUDICATURE OF THE PROVINCE OF NEW YORK 1691–1704, at 389 (1952) (alteration in original) (internal quotation marks omitted).
6. Letter from Lord Bellomont to Lieutenant Governor of New York (June 23, 1699), in 18 CALENDAR OF STATE PAPERS, COLONIAL SERIES, AMERICA AND WEST INDIES, 1700, at 699–700 (Cecil Headlam ed., 1910).
7. EMORY WASHBURN, SKETCHES OF THE JUDICIAL HISTORY OF MASSACHUSETTS FROM 1630 TO THE REVOLUTION IN 1775, at 105–106 (Boston 1840) (recounting statements on the case from six Ipswich residents, including Rev. Mr. John Wise).

8. HAMLIN & BAKER, supra note 5, at 401 (quoting Letter from Cotton Mather to John Cotton (Nov. 1686), in [ser. 4, vol. 8] COLLECTIONS OF THE MASSACHUSETTS HISTORICAL SOCIETY 383, 390 (1868)) (internal quotation marks omitted).

9. [1774] 1 JOURNALS OF THE CONTINENTAL CONGRESS, supra note 2, at 88; see also id. at 107–108 (replicating same complaint). In the 1774 Statement of Violation of Rights, the Continental Congress also set forth their claim that "the inhabitants of the English colonies in North America . . . are entitled to the benefit of such of the English statutes, as existed at the time of their colonization; and which they have, by experience, respectively found to be applicable to their several local and other circumstances." See id. at 68. Given the timing and context of the statement, the Continental Congress surely had the Habeas Corpus Act in mind when registering this claim. (As is described in this and the next chapter, moreover, many of the colonies had undertaken efforts by this time to import its principles into their own legal frameworks, efforts that only increased post-independence.)

10. Id. at 107–108 (replicating Lettre Adressée aux Habitans de la Province de Quebec (Oct. 26, 1774)).

11. Id. at 108; see also id. (listing also "holding lands by the tenure of easy rents" and "freedom of the press"); id. ("These are the rights . . . which we are, with one mind, resolved never to resign but with our lives."). The letter described the role of habeas corpus as follows: "If a subject is seized and imprisoned, tho' by order of Government, he may, by virtue of this right, immediately obtain a writ, termed a Habeas Corpus, from a Judge, whose sworn duty it is to grant it, and thereupon procure any illegal restraint to be quickly enquired into and redressed." Id. at 107.

12. HAMLIN & BAKER, supra note 5, at 400–401.

13. KING GEORGE III, A PROCLAMATION FOR SUPPRESSING REBELLION AND SEDITION (London Aug. 23, 1775).

14. Letter from Edward Thurlow and Alexander Wedderburn to the Earl of Dartmouth (Feb. 11, 1774), The National Archives (Great Britain) [hereinafter TNA] CO 5/160, fo. 40, reprinted in [Transcripts 1774] 8 DOCUMENTS OF THE AMERICAN REVOLUTION 1770–1783, at 47 (K.G. Davies ed., 1975). This advice came in response to a letter from the Earl of Dartmouth seeking counsel on whether the Crown could proceed against the colonists for treason. See Letter from the Earl of Dartmouth to Attorney- and Solicitor-General (Feb. 5, 1774), TNA CO 5/160, fo. 1, reprinted in 8 DOCUMENTS OF THE AMERICAN REVOLUTION, supra, at 37–42 (providing a narrative of the relevant events and asking whether "the acts and proceedings stated in the foregoing case or any of them amount to the crime of high treason" and if so, "who are the persons chargeable with such crime and what will be the proper and legal method of proceeding against them?"). The attorney and solicitor generals advised a host of means by which the Crown could proceed against the suspected traitors. See Letter from Edward Thurlow and

Alexander Wedderburn, supra, in 8 DOCUMENTS OF THE AMERICAN REVOLUTION, supra, at 47–48 (suggesting that the Crown could proceed "either by prosecuting them for their treason in the country in the ordinary course of justice; or arresting them there . . . and transmitting them hither to be tried . . . ; or by sending over a warrant of a Secretary of State, grounded on sufficient information upon oath, to arrest and bring over the offenders to be tried here"). They stressed, however, that "the state of evidence . . . as it stands[,] is scarce sufficient" to sustain charges of high treason "unless [it] can be more distinctly established." Id. at 48. For more details on these events, consult Neil L. York, *Imperial Impotence: Treason in 1774 Massachusetts*, 29 LAW & HIST. REV. 657, 657–676 (2011).

15. ETHAN ALLEN, A NARRATIVE OF COLONEL ETHAN ALLEN'S CAPTIVITY, WRITTEN BY HIMSELF 36 (Burlington H. Johnson & Co. 3d ed. 1838) [hereinafter ALLEN NARRATIVE] (recording Prescott's statement: "I will not execute you now; but you shall grace a halter at Tyburn, God damn you").

16. Extract of Letter from Lieutenant Governor Cramahé to the Earl of Dartmouth (Nov. 9, 1775), TNA SP 44/91/443.

17. ALLEN NARRATIVE, supra note 15, at 38.

18. See Thomas Jefferson, Draft of a Declaration on the British Treatment of Ethan Allen (Jan. 2, 1776), in 1 THE PAPERS OF THOMAS JEFFERSON 276–277 (Julian Boyd ed., Princeton Univ. Press 1950); Letter from George Washington to Lieutenant General Thomas Gage (Aug. 11, 1775), in 3 THE WRITINGS OF GEORGE WASHINGTON 77–79 (Jared Sparks ed., Russell, Ordiorne, & Metcalf, & Hillard, Gray & Co. 1834).

19. Letter from George Washington to General William Howe (Dec. 18, 1775), in 3 THE WRITINGS OF GEORGE WASHINGTON, supra note 18, at 201–202 ("The law of retaliation, is not only justifiable in the eyes of God and man, but absolutely a duty, which in our present circumstances we owe to our relations, friends and fellow citizens."). Washington's threat of retaliation came on the heels of a congressional proclamation that "whatever punishment shall be inflicted upon any persons in the power of our enemies, for favouring, aiding, or abetting the cause of American liberty, shall be retaliated in the same kind and the same degree upon those in our power who have favoured, aided, or abetted, or shall favour, aid, or abet the system of ministerial oppression. The essential difference between our cause and that of our enemies might justify a severer punishment. The law of retaliation will unquestionably warrant one equally severe." [1775] 3 JOURNALS OF THE CONTINENTAL CONGRESS, supra note 2, at 412 (Dec. 6, 1775). "Cartel" was a term commonly used during this period to indicate a formal agreement for the exchange of prisoners.

20. See, e.g., [1775] 3 JOURNALS OF THE CONTINENTAL CONGRESS, supra note 2, at 399–400 (Dec. 2, 1775) ("Resolved, That such as are taken be treated as prisoners of war, but with humanity, and allowed the same rations as the troops in the service of the Continent. . . ."); [1776 January 1–June 4] 4 id. at 119 (Feb.

8, 1776) (adopting the oath prisoners of war must take to be granted parole); id. at 264 (Apr. 9, 1776) (resolving that "a list of the prisoners of war in each colony be made out and transmitted to the house of assembly, convention, council, or committee of safety of such colonies respectively"); [1776 June 5–October 8] 5 id. at 850 (Oct. 7, 1776) (calling for the creation of "a commissary of prisoners of war . . . in each of the United States" that would "make monthly returns of the state and condition of the prisoners" to the Board of War).

21. ALLEN NARRATIVE, supra note 15, at 50; see also id. at 55–56 ("It was a common thing for me to be taken out of close confinement, into a spacious green in the castle, or rather parade, where numbers of gentlemen and ladies were ready to see and hear me.").

22. Id. at 51; see also id. at 56 (recalling that when he asked one spectator for "punch," "he then gave it to me with his own hand, refusing to drink with me in consequence of my being a state criminal").

23. It appears that there may have been a meeting about Allen's case on December 23, 1775—just one day after Allen's arrival at Pendennis. On that day, Lord Germain summoned Thurlow and Wedderburn to meet at Lord Germain's office on the evening of December 23, 1775, to discuss the rebel prisoners. Letter to the Attorney & Solicitor General (Dec. 23, 1775), TNA CO 5/159/75. The *London Evening Post* reports of the prisoners' arrival suggest that even the king knew of Allen's case. See LONDON EVENING POST, Jan. 4, 1776 (noting "[u]pon [Allen's] confinement, a message was sent to Pownall, to know what method should be taken with him. Pownall referred it to Lord G. Germain; he referred it to Lord Dartmouth, and his Lordship laid it before the K---; who ordered them to be continued in confinement until further orders"). The reference to Pownall is to Thomas Pownall, member of Parliament and former colonial governor of Massachusetts.

24. Letter from Alexander C. Wedderburn to William Eden (Dec. 27, 1775), reprinted in [OCT. 18 & NOV. 2, 1898] PROCEEDINGS OF THE VERMONT HISTORICAL SOCIETY app. 147, 147–148 (Burlington, Vt., Free Press Association Printers 1899), also reprinted in 5 B.F. STEVENS'S FACSIMILES OF MANUSCRIPTS IN EUROPEAN ARCHIVES RELATING TO AMERICA NO. 462 (London, Malby & Sons 1890) [hereinafter STEVENS'S FACSIMILES].

25. On the same day as the meeting to determine Allen's fate, Lord Germain wrote the Earl of Sandwich, head of the Lords of Admiralty: "The prisoners from Quebec, now confined in Pendennis Castle, will occasion many difficulties: I wish the general had not sent us such a present." Letter from Lord George Germain to the Earl of Sandwich (Dec. 27, 1775), in 1 THE PRIVATE PAPERS OF JOHN, EARL OF SANDWICH, FIRST LORD OF THE ADMIRALTY 1771–1782, at 85–86 (G.R. Barnes & J.H. Owens eds., 1932).

26. TNA SP 44/91/445 (replicating Dec. 27, 1775 Warrant); Letter from Lord George Germain to the Lords Commanders of the Admiralty (Dec. 27, 1775), TNA CO 5/122/398.

27. *A Letter from Plymouth dated Dec. 31*, LONDON EVENING POST, Jan. 4–6, 1776 (noting that the *Solebay* had already sailed for Ireland); ALLEN NARRATIVE, supra note 15, at 134 (detailing departure on *Solebay* and dating his boarding of the ship on January 8); Letter from Rich. Carne to Brook Watson, Esq. (Jan. 18, 1776), TNA TS 1/526/179 (reporting that the *Solebay* sailed on January 7). Allen would be moved several times upon arrival in America. After several months, the British finally paroled him in New York City and ultimately released him as part of a prisoner exchange in 1778. Notably, even after the administration sent him back to America, Allen was still labeled a "Prisoner of State, not of War" by the British. See Charles A. Huguenin, *Ethan Allen, Parolee on Long Island*, in 25 VERMONT HISTORY 103, 120 (Vermont Historical Society ed., 1957) (quoting British General Riedesel and citing Letter from General Riedesel to General Gates (Oct. 2, 1777) (on file with New York Public Library, Manuscript Room)).

28. 18 COBBETT'S PARLIAMENTARY HISTORY 1196–1197 (London, T.C. Hansard 1813) [hereinafter 18 COBBETT'S PARL. HIST.] (Mar. 5, 1776) (remarks of Lord Richmond).

29. Id. at 1199.

30. Lord Germain's letter to Lord Mansfield from the following summer, discussed below, suggests that Germain was quite concerned over the ability to prosecute Allen successfully. See Letter from Lord George Germain to Lord Mansfield (Aug. 6, 1776), TNA CP 5/43/342, reprinted in [Transcripts 1776] 12 DOCUMENTS OF THE AMERICAN REVOLUTION, supra note 14, at 176–177.

31. 1 THE DIARY AND LETTERS OF HIS EXCELLENCY THOMAS HUTCHINSON, ESQ. 219–220 (Peter Orlando Hutchinson ed., Boston, Houghton, Mifflin 1884) (describing Lord Mansfield's report of the relevant discussions, along with Mansfield's view that "things never would be right until some of them were brought over" to be prosecuted).

32. Letter from the Earl of Dartmouth to Lt. Gen. Thomas Gage (No. 1) (Apr. 9, 1774), TNA CO 5/763 fo. 77, reprinted in 8 DOCUMENTS OF THE AMERICAN REVOLUTION, supra note 14, at 89. This note of caution followed instructions that Gage "employ [his] utmost endeavours to obtain sufficient evidence against the principal actors" and where "upon indictment of them there is a probability of their being brought to punishment, it is His Majesty's pleasure that you do in such case direct the proper steps to be taken for their prosecution." Id. at 88–89. Notably, one historian has observed that "[t]ime and again Attorney General Edward Thurlow and Solicitor General Alexander Wedderburn showed a reluctance to try Americans for treason in English courts, despite their ruling on numerous occasions that treasonous acts had been committed." York, supra note 14, at 700. General Gage had fought with the king's army at Culloden. See JACK RAKOVE, REVOLUTIONARIES: A NEW HISTORY OF THE INVENTION OF AMERICA 67 (2010).

33. Specifically, a friend to the American cause wrote John Hancock in February 1776 with news of "Colonel *Allen*, and the prisoners with him." The author

noted: "Our friends in *London* attended to their case while here, and would have exerted every nerve to effect their release had they not been so unexpectedly removed." Letter from William Palfrey to President of Congress, enclosing letter to John Hancock, Esq., President of Congress dated Feb. 16, 1776 (May 19, 1776), in [ser. 4, vol. 6] American Archives: Consisting of a Collection of Authentick Records, State Papers, Debates, and Letters and Other Notices of Publick Affairs, the Whole Thing Forming a Documentary History of the Origin and Progress of the North American Colonies; of the Causes and Accomplishment of the American Revolution; and of the Constitution of Government for the United States, to the Final Ratification Thereof 508 (Peter Force ed., Washington, D.C. 1846) [hereinafter American Archives]; see also *Extract of a Letter from Dublin, Jan. 8*, London Evening Post, Jan. 23-25, 1776 ("[T]o elude the Habeas Corpus, the Ministry ordered them to be put on board of a man of war, which sailed away with them. . . ."). See also 2 William Gordon, The History of the Rise, Progress, and Establishment, of the Independence of the United States of America 239 (London 1788) ("Ethan Allen and his fellow prisoners, who had been confined in Pendennis Castle, Cornwall: from whence they were removed by direction of government, upon a discovery, that there was an intention of bringing them before the proper magistrate, by the habeas corpus act, in order to ascertain, whether they were legally chargeable with any crime, that could warrant their confinement.") Things happened so quickly in Allen's case that it does not appear that the administration ever drew up a warrant for his commitment. See 10 The Parliamentary Register, or, History of the Proceedings and Debates of the House of Lords 339 (London, J. Almon 1778) (Mar. 31, 1778) (remarks of the Earl of Effingham and Lord Weymouth).

34. Allen Narrative, supra note 15, at 57–58.

35. 18 The Annual Register, or a View of the History, Politics, and Literature for the Year 1775, at 187–188 (London, J. Dodsley 1780). The rifleman was apparently a Virginian captured in Canada. The *London Evening Post* reported that his discharge came as a result of there being "no grounds for his commitment." *Extract of a Letter from Bristol, Jan. 3, 1776*, London Evening Post, Jan. 4-6, 1776.

36. London Evening Post, Jan. 2, 1776 ("Col. Ethan Allen, Mr. George Walker, and 32 other Provincials, sent over in irons from Quebec, and already lodged in Pendenn's Castle, in Cornwall, it is said, have sent up to their friends in town to sue out the writ of Habeas Corpus, to know on what law or authority they are detained in the present state, at a distance from the capital."). This same story ran verbatim contemporaneously in numerous British newspapers.

37. London Evening Post, Jan. 9, 1776. The writer volunteered the sum of five guineas "to so constitutional a purpose."

38. GAZETTEER & NEW DAILY ADVERTISER, Jan. 6, 1776 (London, England) (Issue 14,624); see also CHESTER CHRON. OR COM. INTELLIGENCER, Jan. 8, 1776 (Chester, England) (Issue 37) ("Mr. Dunning and Mr. Alleyne are retained in behalf of Ethan Allen, and the rest of the prisoners lately arrived from America.").

39. Somerset v. Stewart (1772) 98 Eng. Rep. 499 (K.B.) (freeing a slave brought to England from outside the realm on the basis that the positive law of England did not sanction slavery there).

40. Dunning represented Benjamin Franklin in the Hutchinson Letters affair before the Privy Council. See *The Life of Benjamin Franklin*, in 10 THE WRITINGS OF BENJAMIN FRANKLIN 141, 266–268 (Albert Henry Smyth ed., 1907). Alleyne represented the petitioner in *Somersett's Case*. On his role in Sayre and Platt's case, see 20 A COMPLETE COLLECTION OF STATE TRIALS AND PROCEEDINGS FOR HIGH TREASON AND OTHER CRIMES AND MISDEMEANORS FROM THE EARLIEST PERIOD TO THE PRESENT TIME 1296 n.a (T.B. Howell ed., London, T.C. Hansard 1816) [hereinafter STATE TRIALS] (noting that Alleyne was part of Sayre's legal team); WESTMINSTER J. & LONDON POL. MISCELLANY, Issue 1688 (Mar. 1, 1777) (noting that Alleyne represented Platt in his first habeas petition to the Old Bailey).

41. See A HANDBOOK OF DATES FOR STUDENTS OF BRITISH HISTORY 119, 143 (C.R. Cheney ed., Cambridge Univ. Press 2000) (recording the sitting dates for Michaelmas Term 1775 and Hilary Term 1776).

42. The *Old Bailey Proceedings* was a publication that recorded much of what transpired in the Old Bailey. It is now fully digitized and accessible online at http://www.oldbaileyonline.org/. It has no record of any proceedings involving Ethan Allen. Further, a search at the National Archives in London of the King's Bench files comprising entry books and cords of writs of habeas corpus failed to discover any trace of a petition being filed on Allen's behalf before that court. A search of the Treasury Solicitor papers also failed to uncover evidence of a filing.

43. Letter from Lord Hugh Palliser to the Earl of Sandwich (Dec. 29 1775), in 1 THE PRIVATE PAPERS OF JOHN, EARL OF SANDWICH, supra note 25, at 87 (emphasis added).

44. *To the Printer of the Public Advertiser*, PUB. ADVERTISER, Issue 14,474 (Feb. 22, 1776) (referring to Allen's arrival in Corke as resulting from "a Violation of Law" and "criminal too, as it was notoriously done to elude the Habeas Corpus Act").

45. At this time, the book was published in installments in among other places, the *Pennsylvania Packet*. See, e.g., PA. PACKET OR GEN. ADVERTISER (Nov. 11, 1779) (publishing the portion of Allen's *Narrative* discussing his return to America).

46. Letter from Thomas McKean to John Adams (Sept. 19, 1777), in 5 THE PAPERS OF JOHN ADAMS 289 (R.J. Taylor et al. eds., 1983). The case is discussed in Chapter 4.

47. JOHN WILKES, 1 THE SPEECHES OF JOHN WILKES 27 (London 1777); see also JOHN SAINSBURY, DISAFFECTED PATRIOTS: LONDON SUPPORTERS OF REVOLUTIONARY AMERICA 1769–1782, at 13–14 (1987). Indeed, the Wilkites (as Wilkes's radical

camp was known) commonly took on individual causes before the courts to advance various rule-of-law ideals. See John Brewer, *The Wilkites and the Law, 1763–74: A Study of Radical Notions of Governance*, in AN UNGOVERNABLE PEOPLE: THE ENGLISH AND THEIR LAW IN THE SEVENTEENTH AND EIGHTEENTH CENTURIES 128, 136 (John Brewer & John Styles eds., 1980). George III is said to have called Wilkes "that Devil Wilkes." James Lander, *A Tale of Two Hoaxes in Britain and France in 1775*, 49 HIST. J. 995, 998 (2006). Wilkes was also well known in the colonies as a supporter of the American cause. To take one example, his Letter to "The Electors of Great Britain" setting out his position against the war was published in the *Boston Gazette*. BOSTON GAZETTE & COUNTRY J., Dec. 25, 1775, at 1–2; see also BOSTON GAZETTE & COUNTRY J., Jan. 29, 1776, at 2 (replicating Wilkes's October 28, 1775, speech in Parliament opposing the War). He later opposed North's Act in Parliament and contributed to collections made for the benefit of Americans prisoners held in England during the War. See SHELDON S. COHEN, YANKEE SAILORS IN BRITISH GAOLS 154 (1995).

48. Wilkes's imprisonment in the Tower in 1763 lasted only days. See ARTHUR H. CASH, JOHN WILKES: THE SCANDALOUS FATHER OF CIVIL LIBERTY 98–120 (2006) (detailing events).

49. As noted below, Alleyne worked with Wilkes on Stephen Sayre's habeas petition. Dunning earlier represented one of the printers in a civil action arising out of his arrest related to the publication of controversial writing by Wilkes. See id. at 132 (providing details).

50. For details, see JOHN R. ALDEN, STEPHEN SAYRE: AMERICAN REVOLUTIONARY ADVENTURER 33–66, 70–82 (1983). Sayre once served as sheriff for London. See SAINSBURY, supra note 47, at 52.

51. For details, consult the transcript of Sayre's civil action. See The Trial of an Action brought by Stephen Sayre, esq. against the Right Hon. William Henry Earl of Rochford, 20 STATE TRIALS, supra note 40, at 1285–1316 (1776); id. at 1296 n.*. Sayre himself, along with John Reynolds—Wilkes's longtime lawyer and friend—and Coote Purdon, put up bail. Wilkes attended the arguments before Lord Mansfield. See id. Reportedly, Sayre expressed his gratitude to Lord Mansfield for his release on bail, saying that he "hoped his lordship would always act in the like impartial manner according to the constitution." Mansfield, in turn, is said to have responded "I hope so too . . . let us both act according to the constitution, and we shall avoid all difficulties and dangers." ALDEN, supra note 50, at 82–83 (citing contemporary periodical sources). Sayre went before Mansfield alone on a vacation writ, as King's Bench was not in session at this time. See A HANDBOOK OF DATES, supra note 41, at 135, 143 (providing dates for Trinity and Michaelmas Terms, 1775).

52. *The Monthly Chronologer*, in 44 LONDON MAG. OR GENTLEMAN'S MONTHLY INTELLIGENCER 659 (R. Baldwin 1775). For details on Arthur Lee, see SAINSBURY, supra note 47, at 34, 52.

53. See Sayre v. The Earl of Rochford (1776) 96 Eng. Rep. 687, 2 Black. W. 1166. Wilkes, who had been charged with seditious libel only a few years earlier in a widely publicized case arising out of his role in publishing material highly critical of the king, later won a civil trespass suit against those who ransacked his home in the process. Notably, the judge in Wilkes's civil case declared the use of general warrants to search private property illegal, a position later confirmed by King's Bench in 1765. See CASH, supra note 48, at 160–162 (detailing Wilkes's suit); Money v. Leach (1765) 97 Eng. Rep. 1075 (K.B.), 2 Black. W. 1166.

54. Stephen Sayre, esq. against the Right Hon. William Henry Earl of Rochford, 20 STATE TRIALS, supra note 40, at 1285–1316 (1776); id. at 1312 n.*.

55. Letter from Vice Admiral Graves to Mr. Stephens (Dec. 15, 1775), TNA CO 5/123/66. Some coverage of the case of the *Tartar* prisoners lends support to the inference that there was some domestic sympathy for the plight of American prisoners in England. See LONDON EVENING POST, Jan. 11, 1776 ("A letter from Portsmouth says, that people flock from all parts of the country to have a sight of the prisoners . . . ; that a great deal of money has been collected for their support during their residence in England; and that the people pay as much respect to them as if they had saved this nation from destruction."). One has to be careful about extrapolating too much from the *Evening Post*, however, as it was very much a pro-American paper. See SAINSBURY, supra note 47, at 30.

56. Letter from Lord George Germain to The Honorable Major General Howe (Feb. 1, 1776), TNA CO 5/93/16. See also Letter from Lord George Germain to The Lords of Admiralty (Jan. 19, 1776), TNA CO 5/123/168; Letter from Lord George Germain to The Lords of Admiralty (Feb. 2, 1776), TNA CO 5/123/179; Letter from George Germain to Sir Guy Carlton (Aug 22, 1776), TNA CO 43/8/99.

57. Letter from General William Howe to Lord George Germain (July 8, 1777), reprinted in MASSACHUSETTS HISTORICAL SOCIETY, REPORT OF EXCHANGES OF PRISONERS DURING THE AMERICAN REVOLUTIONARY WAR 17 (Boston 1861) [HEREINAFTER MASSACHUSETTS HISTORICAL SOCIETY REPORT].

58. MASSACHUSETTS HISTORICAL SOCIETY REPORT, supra note 57, at 17 (quoting Letter from Lord George Germain to General William Howe (Sept. 3, 1777)); 19 (quoting 5 THE WRITINGS OF GEORGE WASHINGTON; BEING HIS CORRESPONDENCE, ADDRESSES, MESSAGES, AND OTHER PAPERS, OFFICIAL AND PRIVATE 317 n.* (Jared Sparks ed., 1847)).

59. MASSACHUSETTS HISTORICAL SOCIETY REPORT, supra note 57, at 20 (quoting Clinton). One report studying this period describes the British practice as follows: "[W]hile the British Government was unwilling to make that species of convention *durante bello*, which is known to the public law as a cartel between nations at war, they constantly permitted exchanges [in America], under the rules of war, for purposes of military convenience, and in relief of the sufferings of their own officers and privates in captivity." Id. at 23.

60. The pardon relieved the beneficiary of the stigma of criminal wrongdoing. Here, too, one finds evidence of a consistent view that the Americans were traitors and criminals regardless of where they might be found. The creation of commissioners for pardons in America began in early 1776. See Letter from Edward Thurlow and Alexander C. Wedderburn to Lord George Germain (Feb. 22, 1776), TNA CO 5/160/64 (presenting their draft of a commission for accepting pardons). In May of that year, British lieutenant general Henry Clinton issued a proclamation offering amnesty to those who would abandon the American cause (excepting two prominent American soldiers). See Proclamation by Sir Henry Clinton (May 22, 1780), available at NewsBank Archive of Americana, Early American Imprints, ser. 1, no. 43809. In November 1776, General William Howe and Admiral Richard Howe, serving as peace commissions, issued a proclamation offering free and full pardon to Americans who would pledge "peaceable obedience to his Majesty" and "to desist and cease from all such treasonable actings and doings." Proclamation by Lord Howe (Nov. 30, 1776), in [ser. 5, vol. 3] AMERICAN ARCHIVES 928. Efforts to win over Americans with the promise of amnesty continued well into the war.

61. Mansfield, for example, regularly attended Privy Council meetings during the war. See James C. Oldham, *Murray, William, First Earl of Mansfield (1705–1793)*, 39 OXFORD DICTIONARY OF NATIONAL BIOGRAPHY 996–997 (2004).

62. Letter from Lord George Germain to Lord Mansfield (Aug. 6, 1776), TNA CO 5/43/342, reprinted in 12 DOCUMENTS OF THE AMERICAN REVOLUTION, supra note 14, at 176–177.

63. See Account of the Capture of the Yankee, Privateer, Captain Johnson (London, Aug. 10, 1776), in [ser. 5, vol. 1] AMERICAN ARCHIVES, supra note 33, at 756 (describing events); Address to the Lord Mayor of London on the Cruel Treatment of Captain Johnson and his Crew (London, Aug. 5, 1776), in [ser. 5, vol. 1] AMERICAN ARCHIVES, supra, at 754–756 (offering a first person account of the harsh conditions of confinement aboard the *Yankee*); Extract of a Letter from Dover, in England: Capture of the *Yankee*, Privateer, and Ill Treatment of Captain Johnson (July 31, 1776), in [ser. 5, vol. 1] AMERICAN ARCHIVES, supra, at 684 (describing the precautions that the prisoners turned captors took with Captain Johnson and his crew and the complaints of the prisoners); *To the Lord Mayor*, BOSTON GAZETTE & COUNTRY J., Dec. 9, 1776, at 2 (detailing capture).

64. Notably, in his letter, Germain set forth various grounds on which the cases were *politically* distinct, but said nothing as to whether they were *legally* distinct.

65. Letter from Lord George Germain to Lord Mansfield (Aug. 6, 1776), TNA CO 5/43/342, reprinted in 12 DOCUMENTS OF THE AMERICAN REVOLUTION, supra note 14, at 176–177.

66. Letter from Lord Mansfield to Lord George Germain (Aug. 8, 1776), TNA CO 5/43/345, reprinted in 12 DOCUMENTS OF THE AMERICAN REVOLUTION, supra note 14, at 179–180.

67. Id. (noting that despite their convictions, none were executed and all were "sent back").

68. Id. at 180.

69. Letter from Lord Suffolk to Lords of the Admiralty (Aug. 16, 1776), TNA SP 42/ 49/255. Suffolk directed that the crew be put in the king's service on a vessel heading to the East Indies or Mediterranean Station. Id.; see also Letter from Philip Stephens to Vice Admiral Sir James Douglas (Sept. 30, 1776) (ordering the crew put in service on the *Rippon* or otherwise distributed to "other Ships that want Men"), in 6 NAVAL DOCUMENTS OF THE AMERICAN REVOLUTION 619 (William James Morgan ed., 1972).

70. *Downer, Eliphalet*, CONNECTICUT BIOGRAPHICAL DICTIONARY 252 (Caryn Hannan et al. eds., 2008); Deposition of Eliphalet Downer (Mar. 30, 1777) (detailing the surgeon's initial escape), in 8 NAVAL DOCUMENTS OF THE AMERICAN REVOLUTION 723 (William James Morgan ed., 1980); *Independent Chronicle*, Jan. 23, 1777 (reporting Johnson's escape), in 7 NAVAL DOCUMENTS OF THE AMERICAN REVOLUTION 1024 (William James Morgan ed., 1976); 1 GARDNER W. ALLEN, A NAVAL HISTORY OF THE AMERICAN REVOLUTION 267 (1913). Johnson found his way back to America to join the Continental Navy, where he rose to the rank of captain. See ALLEN, supra, at 267.

71. Journal of Timothy Connor, Massachusetts Privateer Brigantine (Forton Prison, July 30, 1777) (reporting of the remaining *Yankee* officers that "four more broke out . . . one got off clear and the other three was re-taken"), in 9 NAVAL DOCUMENTS OF THE AMERICAN REVOLUTION 539–540 (William James Morgan ed., 1986).

72. Letter from Lord Suffolk to the Lords of the Admiralty (Jan. 15, 1777), TNA SP 42/50/33 (giving orders respecting 121 American prisoners arriving on the *Raisonable*); see also, e.g., Letter from Lord Suffolk to the Lords of the Admiralty (Dec. 2, 1776), TNA SP 42/49/292 (giving orders respecting thirteen American prisoners arriving on the *Pallas*); Letter from the Lords of the Admiralty to Lord Suffolk (Dec. 19, 1776), TNA SP 42/49/294 (requesting instructions for nine American prisoners arriving on the *Towey*); Letter from Lord Suffolk to the Lords of the Admiralty (Jan. 8, 1777), TNA SP 42/50/25 (giving orders respecting nine American prisoners arriving on the *Squirrel*); Letter from the Lords of the Admiralty to Lord Suffolk (Jan. 20, 1777), TNA SP 42/50/39 (reporting arrival of captured rebel privateer sloop, *The Charming Sally*, and requesting instructions for treatment of the prisoners taken with the sloop).

73. See Letter from Ebenezer Smith Platt to the Commissioners (Apr. 21, 1778), in 6 THE PAPERS OF JOHN ADAMS 44 (R.J. Taylor et al. eds., 1983); see also Sheldon S. Cohen, *The Odyssey of Ebenezer Smith Platt*, 18 J. AMERICAN STUDIES 255, 258–263 (detailing Platt's involvement in the capture and the circumstances of his arrest).

74. Letter from Ebenezer S. Platt to Captain Hughes of the Centaur (Oct. 4, 1776), TNA TS 11/1057.

75. Letter from Lord Suffolk to the Lords of the Admiralty (Dec. 10, 1776), TNA SP 42/49/298.
76. Letter from Edward Thurlow and Alexander Wedderburn to the Earl of Suffolk (Dec. 10, 1776), TNA TS 11/1057.
77. Letter from Captain Maitland to Wm. Chamberlain (Jan. 10, 1777), TNA TS 11/1057. Notably, the Continental Congress ordered the seized gunpowder to be sent to the aid of General George Washington's troops in Boston, where it played a key role in the Continental forces taking control of the city. See Cohen, supra note 73, at 260–261.
78. The King v. Platt (1777) 168 Eng. Rep. 181, 182, 1 Leach 157, 158 (replicating warrant), TNA TS 11/1057 (copy of original warrant).
79. Letter from W. Cornwallis to Philip Stephens (Dec. 25, 1776), TNA SP 42/49/306 (reporting escape).
80. 35 Hen. VIII, c. 2 ("[A]ll . . . Treasons . . . committed . . . by anye person or persons out of th[e] Realme . . . , shalbe from hensforth . . . determined before the Kings Justices of his Benche. . . ."); 33 Hen. VIII, c. 23.
81. The King v. Platt, 168 Eng. Rep. at 187, 1 Leach at 169–170.
82. 19 COBBETT'S PARL. HIST., supra note 1, at 4 (emphasis added) (Feb. 6, 1777) (remarks of Lord North). North made two additional points. First, he stressed that unlike prior historical episodes of suspension, he "would not be thought to hint at any necessity of trusting ministers at present with such a power in general." Second, North observed that under current law, many of the prisoners "could be legally confined only in the common gaols, which would be entirely impracticable." Id.
83. 20 THE ANNUAL REGISTER, OR A VIEW OF THE HISTORY, POLITICS, AND LITERATURE FOR THE YEAR 1777, at 54 (London, J. Dodsley 1778).
84. 19 COBBETT'S PARL. HIST., supra note 1, at 4–5 (Feb. 7, 1777) (remarks of Lord Germain).
85. Id. at 5–6 (remarks of Governor Johnstone). As with Johnstone's remarks, the Habeas Corpus Act was referred to repeatedly by speakers as a "great palladium of the liberties of the subject" and "the palladium of English liberty." See, e.g., id. at 11 (remarks of Charles James Fox); id. at 40 (remarks of James Luttrell).
86. See id. at 16 (remarks of Paul Feilde).
87. Id. at 7 (remarks of John Dunning); see also id. at 9 (lamenting that under the bill, "[n]o man is exempt from punishment because innocence is no longer a protection"). Charles James Fox raised similar concerns, even invoking the plight of Stephen Sayre. See id. at 12 (remarks of Charles James Fox) ("[T]his Bill cares not a fig whether you are guilty or innocent"); id. ("Suspicions, however ill founded, upon tales, however improbable, are received . . . as facts not to be controverted; witness the information of Richardson against Sayre. . . .").
88. Id. at 9–10 (remarks of Edward Thurlow) ("It was absurd and preposterous to the last degree, to suppose it was framed intentionally to reach or overtake persons presumed to be disaffected to this government, within this realm.").

89. As noted below, the British instituted some screening mechanisms for committing American prisoners in England and yet never prosecuted any American for treason during the war.

90. Id. at 13–14, 16; see id. at 17 (emphasizing that permitting "detaining [persons reached by the bill] till they could be released by a writ of Habeas Corpus" would "controvert[]" the bill's "very principle, the necessity, at this critical season, of strengthening the hands of government").

91. See, e.g., id. at 18 (remarks of James Wallace); id. at 19 (remarks of Serjeant Glynn).

92. Id. at 19 (contending "it was a most extraordinary mode of reasoning to argue against the use of the Bill, from the possible abuse of it").

93. Id. at 30 (remarks of John Wilkes).

94. Id. at 34 (remarks of Richard Rigby); id. at 39 (remarks of Temple Luttrell). The reference to Ireland is curious, given that Ireland's adoption of the Habeas Corpus Act was stymied until 1782 when the Irish Committee of the English Privy Council finally approved such legislation. See KEVIN COSTELLO, THE LAW OF HABEAS CORPUS IN IRELAND 6, 16 (2006).

95. See, e.g., 19 COBBETT'S PARL. HIST., supra note 1, at 9 (remarks of John Dunning) ("[W]hatever the title of the Bill may be, it is not an American, so much as it is a British suspension of the Habeas Corpus Act."); id. at 11 (remarks of Charles James Fox) ("[E]xpressing his astonishment . . . at the insolence and temerity of ministers, who could thus dare to snatch [the Habeas Corpus Act] from the people, by mandate manufactured by themselves. . . ."); id. at 17 (remarks of George Dempster) (referring to "the propriety of suspending the Habeas Corpus Act"); id. at 17–18 (remarks of Abel Moysey) (same); id. at 30 (remarks of John Wilkes) (observing that "[the] Bill . . . is to suspend the Habeas Corpus Act"); id. at 37–38 (remarks of the Attorney General) (connecting the proposed legislation to prior acts of suspension). In debating an extension of the original bill, many members of Parliament continued to refer to it as a suspension. See id. at 465–466 (remarks of Edmund Burke) (referring to "suspending the Habeas Corpus" and warning that "this suspension may become a standing suspension, and consequently, the eternal suspension and destruction of the Habeas Corpus"); see also id. at 464 (remarks of William Baker) (referring to "the late bill for the suspension of the Habeas Corpus Act").

96. Id. at 38 (remarks of the Attorney General).

97. The summary of the debates in the *Annual Register* directly supports this explanation for why the bill did not expressly suspend the Habeas Corpus Act. See 20 ANNUAL REGISTER, supra note 83, at 59. It is curious all the same that the legislation does not mention the Habeas Corpus Act by name. Nonetheless, it was routinely deemed a suspension by virtually everyone who referred to it during this period, including countless members of Parliament both in the original debates and the renewal debates over the course of the war.

98. See, e.g., 19 Cobbett's Parl. Hist., supra note 1, at 18–19 (remarks of John Morton) (raising such concerns); id. at 22 (remarks of Thomas Powys) (same). It did not matter that Lord North had claimed the "the inhabitants of Great Britain . . . were not within the Act." Id. at 17.

99. John Dunning proposed the clarifying amendment, which was amended in turn by Charles Wolfran Cornwall and then adopted. See id. at 49. The ultimate language included in the Act is quoted. See 17 Geo. 3, c. 9, pt. IV, pmbl. (1777) (Gr. Brit.).

100. See 19 Cobbett's Parl. Hist., supra note 1, at 51.

101. See id. at 51–53.

102. An Act to Impower his Majesty to Secure and Detain Persons Charged with, or Suspected of, the Crime of High Treason, Committed in any of his Majesty's Colonies or Plantations in *America*, or on the High Seas, or the Crime of Piracy 1777, 17 Geo. 3, c. 9 (Gr. Brit.); see 35 H.L. Jour. (1777) 78, 82–83 (Gr. Brit.) (noting royal assent given Mar. 3, 1777).

103. 17 Geo. 3, c. 9, pmbl. & pt. II (1777) (Gr. Brit.).

104. Letter from Lord Suffolk to the Lords of the Admiralty (Mar. 4, 1777), TNA SP 42/50/61 (stating that he was writing on the day of assent).

105. Letter from the Lords of the Admiralty to Lord Suffolk (Mar. 6, 1777), TNA SP 42/50/63. The prisons were run by the Board for Sick and Hurt Seamen, which operated under the auspices of the Admiralty Lords. See Catherine M. Prelinger, *Benjamin Franklin and the American Prisoners of War in England during the American Revolution*, 32 Wm. & Mary Q. 261, 264 (1975).

106. Letter from Lord Suffolk to the Lords of Admiralty (Apr. 16, 1777), TNA SP 42/50/98; Letter from Lord Suffolk to the Lords of Admiralty (Apr. 23, 1777), TNA SP 42/50. American prisoners were also held in smaller numbers in other locations, including Kinsale in Ireland. See Cohen, supra note 47, at 30; see also Francis D. Cogliano, American Maritime Prisoners in the Revolutionary War 131 (2001). The British detained approximately 15 Americans during the War in Edinburgh Castle, where prisoner graffiti, in the form of a carving of the Stars and Stripes, remains to this day.

107. George Washington, *Manifesto of General Washington, Commander in Chief of the Forces of the United States of America, in Answer to General Burgoyne's Proclamation* (July 19, 1777), in 47 The Gentleman's Magazine, And Historical Chronicle for the Year 1777, at 456–457 (Sylvanus Urban ed., London, D. Henry Sept. 1777), reprinted in Continental J. & Wkly. Advertiser (Boston), Mar. 5, 1778, at 3.

108. See TNA TS 11/1057 (Order of the Court of King's Bench receiving and filing Platt's petition); TNA KB 21/41 (King's Bench Entry Book).

109. An Argument in the Case of Ebenezer Smith Platt, Now Under Confinement for High Treason 2 (London G. Kearsly 1777). These quotations are derived from the notes taken and published by a "Gentleman of the

Law" who observed the arguments and purported to transcribe Lord Mansfield's speech in delivering the court's decision in Platt's case, which constitutes the best source available recording what transpired.

110. Id. at 6.

111. Id. at 11–13. Here Mansfield's opinion echoes the brief filed on behalf of the Crown, which made this argument and relied on earlier suspension acts that had used the same language. See Brief For the Crown, The King against Platt, TNA TS 11/1057.

112. Here, too, Mansfield relied upon arguments levied in the Crown's brief arguing against bail. See Brief For the Crown, The King against Platt, TNA TS 11/1057. Notably, Mansfield stated in announcing his opinion that he was "taking it now all along that the Case is clearly within the 7th Section of the Habeas Corpus Act, just as a Case of High-Treason in *England* would have been," while also noting that "there is a Provision with Regard to foreign Crimes in the 16th Section of the Act." In other words, Mansfield did not question—though he suggested a basis on which one could—whether the full benefits of Section 7 of the Act would have governed Platt's case in the absence of a suspension. An Argument in the Case of Ebenezer Smith Platt, supra note 109, at 14. The very existence of the suspension, however, demonstrates that it was predicated upon a parliamentary belief that the benefits of Section 7 would apply to royal subjects brought to England for detention. (After all, the suspension only applied to cases arising out of treasonous practices in America and on the high seas.)

113. Mansfield reasoned that as "no single Judge can try" a party for treason, the prohibition against any "judge" awarding bail or other relief, if construed as Platt would have it, would be pointless insofar as it would constrain a party from doing something that it could not have done in the first instance.

114. See id. at 11–17. Correspondence from one supporter of the American cause in London to Benjamin Franklin suggests that Lord Mansfield gave extrajudicial advice to Platt. The March 1777 letter reports that Mansfield recommended Platt petition the king directly and take an oath of allegiance to win his freedom. Letter from Elizabeth Wright to Benjamin Franklin (Mar. 10, 1777), in 23 The Papers of Benjamin Franklin 457, 458 (William B Wilcox et al. eds., 1983) [hereinafter Franklin Papers].

115. TNA KB 21/41 (King's Bench Entry Book, 1777).

116. Letter from Ebenezer Smith Platt to Benjamin Franklin (Newgate, Mar. 10, 1777), in 23 Franklin Papers, supra note 114, at 457.

117. See 22 Geo. 3, c. 1 (1782) (Gr. Brit.); 21 Geo. 3, c. 2 (1781) (Gr. Brit.); 20 Geo. 3, c. 5 (1780) (Gr. Brit.); 19 Geo. 3, c. 1 (1779) (Gr. Brit.); 18 Geo. 3, c. 1 (1778) (Gr. Brit.).

118. Letter from Matthew Ridley to the American Commissioners (Apr. 3, 1778), in 26 Franklin Papers 227 (William B Wilcox et al. eds., 1987). In January 1778,

Platt directly petitioned Lord Suffolk requesting that he be brought to trial or admitted to bail. See Letter from Ebenezer Smith Platt to the Earl of Suffolk (Jan. 8, 1778), TNA TS 11/1057. For more on how Platt came to Franklin's attention, consult Prelinger, supra note 105, at 265–266.

119. 19 COBBETT's PARL. HIST., supra note 1, at 462-463 (remarks of Edmund Burke, quoting Lord Stormont); see also 21 THE ANNUAL REGISTER, OR A VIEW OF THE HISTORY, POLITICS, AND LITERATURE FOR THE YEAR 1778, at 58 (London, J. Dodsley 1800) (noting same). Stormont recorded his response as worded slightly differently, but to the same effect: "The King's Ambassador receives no applications from rebels, unless they come to implore his Majesty's mercy." Prelinger, supra note 105, at 263 (citing Report from Lord Stormont to Lord Weymouth (Apr. 3, 1777), TNA SP 78/302).

120. 19 COBBETT's PARL. HIST., supra note 1, at 463 (remarks of Edmund Burke).

121. Id. at 561 (remarks of the Duke of Richmond).

122. Id. at 561 (remarks of the Lord Chancellor).

123. For example, several American newspapers reported on the motion by Sir Grey Cooper in November 1780 for a bill to extend North's Act for a fourth time on the basis that "should [the Act] expire in January next (which was the present limitation of its existence) no prisoner charged with such offences could be detained after that period, and three or four hundred persons now in confinement must of course be set at liberty." See, e.g., *House of Commons, Nov. 10*, INDEP. LEDGER & AM. ADVERTISER, Apr. 9, 1781, at 1. Of course, Grey's statements are not entirely true, as the option of trying the Americans as traitors remained available, at least in theory. Grey's motion spurred some in the opposition to complain about the detention of Americans in Britain "without benefit of our equal laws and free constitution." See id. (reporting remarks of Sir George Younge). William Baker in turn remarked on the inconsistency of committing the American prisoners on charges of high treason "and then exchang[ing them] in cartels." Id.

124. Russell's account is detailed in COGLIANO, supra note 106. See id. at 42 (quoting Russell's journal). Many first-person accounts of life in Mill and Forton Prisons exist, including *A Yankee Privateersman in Prison in England, 1777–1779*, in 30 NEW ENG. HIST. & GENEALOGICAL REG. 343–352 (John Ward Dean ed., 1876). Several others are discussed in COHEN, supra note 47; Olive Anderson, *The Treatment of Prisoners of War in Britain during the American War of Independence*, 28 INST. HIST. RES., BULL 63, 76 n.1 (1955); and Jesse Lemisch, *Listening to the Inarticulate: William Widger's Dream and the Loyalties of American Revolutionary Seamen in British Prisons*, 3 J. SOC. HIST. 1, 5–29 (1969).

125. COGLIANO, supra note 106, at 46 (quoting CHARLES HERBERT, RELIC OF THE REVOLUTION 44 (Boston, C.H. Peirce 1847)). A similar journal account described how "three justices" examined a group of nine Americans both separately and together for four hours before their committal to Mill Prison for

High Treason. See *Samuel Cutler's Diary*, NEW ENG. HIST. & GENEALOGICAL REG. 184, 186 (Rev. Samuel Cutler ed., Boston, David Clapp & Son 1878). Yet another talked about being "examined[,] tryed & committed . . . as Rebels & Pirates" by warrants issued by "commissioners." John K. Alexander, *Forton Prison during the American Revolution: A Case Study of British Prisoner of War Policy and the American Prisoner Response to That Policy*, in 103 ESSEX INSTITUTE HISTORICAL COLLECTIONS 365, 369 (1967). One British historian described the general framework as permitting detention on charge of treason or piracy "provided adequate evidence could be submitted to the committing magistrate of their capture on an armed vessel." See Anderson, supra note 124, at 66.

126. COGLIANO, supra note 106, at 47 (quoting Russell's journal).
127. Alexander, supra note 125, at 369 (citing sources).
128. See COGLIANO, supra note 106, at 69, 142–165 (comparing the British prisons in England and America and detailing Russell's stay on the *Jersey* upon his second capture at the hands of the British); Lemisch, supra note 124, at 9–13, 14–15, 17–20. How well the American prisoners were treated in Britain is the subject of some dispute among historians. John Alexander explains some of the "strikingly divergent views" as resulting in large part from whether scholars have relied upon primarily British or American sources. Alexander, supra note 125, at 365.
129. Compare Anderson, supra note 124, at 72, 83 (noting that the Americans received two-thirds of the bread rations of regular prisoners of war); and COHEN, supra note 47, at 174 (detailing a 1782 letter sent by Mill prisoners to the Lords of the Admiralty complaining about lesser bread rations, and the Admiralty's defensive response that the bread quality was comparably better than that given to prisoners of other nations); with COGLIANO, supra note 106, at 54–55 (noting that the Americans divided the standard rations for four men by six prisoners).
130. See Anderson, supra note 124, at 67. France and Great Britain entered a formal cartel for the exchange of prisoners in March 1780. See id. at 71. In time, the British also detained Spanish and Dutch prisoners at the prisons originally designated for detaining Americans. See COGLIANO, supra note 106, at 49 n.52 (citing archival documents and correspondence).
131. COGLIANO, supra note 106, at 131, 133. The British Navy tried to lure defectors "before they were committed to prison," for "[o]nce charged with treason and piracy, would-be enlistees required pardons from the king before they could enter the navy." Id. at 116.
132. See Prelinger, supra note 105, at 262. On the securing of pardons in such cases, see COHEN, supra note 47, at 143. Later in the war, this requirement appears to have been dispensed with in such cases. See id. at 177. On the prisoner exchanges negotiated by Benjamin Franklin, see, e.g., id. at 150–160; Sheldon S. Cohen, *William Hodgson: An English Merchant and Unsung Friend to American Revolutionary Captives*, 123 PA. MAG. HIST. & BIOGRAPHY 57, 68–72 (1999).

133. MASSACHUSETTS HISTORICAL SOCIETY REPORT, supra note 57, at 25. The absence of compulsion to try rebels for treason in America followed from the absence of the protections of the Habeas Corpus Act there.

134. Letter from Lord George Germain to Governor Haldimand (Mar. 17, 1780), TNA CO 43/8/191. Notably, Germain contrasted the situation in Canada, observing that in Nova Scotia, "the same objections to their detention will probably not occur." "[O]n that account," Germain counseled, "I should recommend your sending to Halifax such disaffected Persons of whose Guilt you have no doubt, but against whom you cannot support the Charge by sufficient Evidence to secure their Commitment in England & yet judge it proper to send out of the Province." Id.

135. Letter from Lord George Germain to Governor Haldimand (Mar. 17, 1780), TNA CO 43/8/192.

136. Letter from Governor Haldimand to Lord George Germain (Oct. 25, 1780), TNA CO 42/40/168 ("The many Inconveniences, we are daily exposed to, from the Number of Rebel Prisoners now in the Province, Where some of them have been confined these four Years, has induced me to send them by the present Fleet to England."). Haldimand noted that some government buildings, including a prison, had been destroyed in battle and that there were so many prisoners, many were escaping with the help of "Ill disposed Inhabitants." The governor also requested that Germain send a vessel to pick up yet more prisoners. See id. at 168–169.

137. See RAKOVE, supra note 32, at 236–238 (detailing events); Henry Laurens, *Journal and Narrative of Capture Confinement in and the Tower of London* [hereinafter LAURENS NARRATIVE], in 15 THE PAPERS OF HENRY LAURENS: DECEMBER 11, 1778–AUGUST 31, 1782, at 332–334 (David R. Chestnut et al. eds., 2000) [hereinafter LAURENS PAPERS]. Incredibly, Laurens had practically predicted his fate in 1775, when he wrote his young son of the possible effects of the war that was then inevitable. Laurens speculated: "I may be a prisoner; in Chains & under Sentence of Death," on account of his role in "Striving to transmit that Liberty to my Children, which was mine by birthright & compact." RAKOVE, supra, at 213–214 (quoting 10 LAURENS PAPERS, supra, at 139–141) (internal quotations omitted).

138. Curiously, when ordered sent to England by Rear Admiral Edwards in Newfoundland, Laurens was called a "Prisoner of War." Letter from Rear Admiral Rich. Edwards to Captain Berkeley of His Majesty's Ship *Vestal* (Sept. 26, 1780), TNA CO 5/131/300. As is discussed above, once he arrived in England, the administration consistently treated him as a criminal.

139. 15 LAURENS PAPERS, supra note 137, at 436 (replicating *Examination of Henry Laurens*, printed in LONDON EVENING POST, Oct. 5–7, 1780 ("When he was told that he was to be committed to the Tower, he told them it was violating the law of nations to detain an Ambassador. . . ."); see also DAVID DUNCAN WALLACE, THE LIFE OF HENRY LAURENS 358–363 (1915).

140. Warrant for the Commitment of Henry Laurens to the Tower of London, TNA WO 94/10/518; SP 44/96/91; CO 5/43/485 (copy with Mansfield's approval and signature). For additional details of these events, consult LAURENS NARRATIVE, supra note 137, at 340–343.

141. Letter from Moses Young to Benjamin Franklin (Feb. 5, 1782), in 36 Papers of Benjamin Franklin, available at http://www.franklinpapers.org/franklin/framedVolumes.jsp.

142. LAURENS NARRATIVE, supra note 137, at 391 (replicating Burke's letter recounting these events); see also id. at 421, 423, 424–425. Laurens detailed his time in the Tower in a journal that he kept during his stay.

143. 22 COBBETT'S PARL. HIST. 853 (London, T.C. Hansard 1814) (Dec. 17, 1781) (remarks of Edmund Burke).

144. "In the early part of the war," Burke observed, "the conduct of [the] administration was not so rigid towards the Americans who were brought prisoners into England, as to confine them, without ever admitting them to be exchanged or released." Burke specifically invoked the detention of Ethan Allen, who he noted "had been brought to England in irons; but he was sent back without irons, and exchanged in America." Laurens, by contrast, had fallen victim to "a new project . . . for narrowing the scale, upon which the King's pardon was to have been granted to those who had opposed his government." Id.

145. Id. at 857; see also 25 THE ANNUAL REGISTER, OR A VIEW OF THE HISTORY, POLITICS, AND LITERATURE FOR THE YEAR 1782, at 147 (London, J. Dodsley 1783) (reporting on the same debates).

146. 22 COBBETT'S PARL. HIST., supra note 143, at 877 (remarks of Mr. Mansfield) (emphasis added). See also id. at 876–877 (remarks of Lord North) (making similar remarks).

147. WALLACE, supra note 139, at 357–358; MASSACHUSETTS HISTORICAL SOCIETY REPORT, supra note 57, at 22. For extensive discussion of the life of John Laurens, consult RAKOVE, supra note 32, at 212–241, 276.

148. 22 COBBETT'S PARL. HIST. , supra note 143, at 874–875 (Dec. 20, 1781) (remarks of Lord North); id. at 877–878 (replicating petition to House of Commons from Henry Laurens). This petition followed an earlier one directed to Hillsborough, Stormont, and Germain. See WALLACE, supra note 139, at 374–380 (replicating petition). Earlier attempts to sway Laurens to throw off his support of the American cause failed, as did efforts by his supporters to convince him to seek a pardon. See id. at 369–372, 383–384. In conjunction with his petition to the House of Commons, Laurens also directed a renewed appeal for his exchange to Congress. See 15 LAURENS PAPERS, supra note 137, at 458–459.

149. Letter from James Wallace to Earl of Hillsborough (Dec. 24, 1781), TNA SP 37/15, and quoted in LAURENS NARRATIVE, supra note 137, at 395 n.138.

150. LAURENS NARRATIVE, supra note 137, at 397.

151. See WALLACE, supra note 139, at 388; DANIEL J. McDONOUGH, CHRISTOPHER GADSDEN AND HENRY LAURENS: THE PARALLEL LIVES OF TWO AMERICAN PATRIOTS 259 (2000). A copy of the Record of Bail taken may be found at 10 STEVENS'S FACSIMILES, supra note 24, at 295 (No. 988). Laurens's British friend Richard Oswald reportedly posted his bond. Oswald soon represented Lord Shelburne in early negotiations with the American commissioners in Paris over a possible peace. For details, see RAKOVE, supra note 32, at 273.

152. WALLACE, supra note 139, at 393–395. A copy of the entry of the Order of Discharge of Laurens's recognizance may be found at 10 STEVENS'S FACSIMILES, supra note 24, at 303 (No. 990). While bailed, Laurens traveled to Bath to recover his health and later visited Mill Prison. He also worked with Franklin promoting the exchange of American prisoners.

153. LAURENS NARRATIVE, supra note 137, at 400 (reporting Shelburne's remarks).

154. 10 STEVENS'S FACSIMILES, supra note 24, at 5 (No. 920); see also TNA SP 44/96/90.

155. Letter from Thomas Digges to John Adams (Nov. 22, 1780), in 10 THE PAPERS OF JOHN ADAMS 365 (Gregg L. Lint et al. eds., 1996). Digges wrote of the events at the time: "Since the news of Adjut. Genl. Andre's Execution in the Rebel Washingtons Camp nothing has been talkd of here but 'making Examples,' acts of retaliation, &ca. &ca. A person of the name of Trumbull was taken up for high Treason on Sunday night and committed Irond to Prison. A search has been made after a Companion of His a Mr. Tyler who I am told got away some days ago." Id. The original warrant for Trumbull ordered only that his papers and person be secured, but with Tyler's escape, he was charged with treason. Trumbull details his ordeal at length in his autobiography. THE AUTOBIOGRAPHY OF COLONEL JOHN TRUMBULL 58–72 (Theodore Sizer ed., 1953).

156. Id. at 67 n.32 (noting that the writ of commitment was dated Nov. 20, 1780). Trumbull was given a choice of prisons, although as he notes in his autobiography, many had recently been destroyed in the Gordon Riots. He decided against the Tower of London "as I should have to pay dearly for the honor, in the exorbitance of fees" and instead chose to remain at Tothill-fields Bridewell. Id. at 68.

157. Id. at 70–71.

158. Id. at 71–72; Letter from William Hodgson to Benjamin Franklin (Sept. 4, 1781), in 35 THE PAPERS OF BENJAMIN FRANKLIN 439 (Barbara B. Oberg ed., 1999).

159. As testament to the island's importance in the war, Lord Stormont reportedly declared before Parliament in 1778 that "if Sint Eustatius had sunk into the sea three years before, the United Kingdom would already have dealt with George Washington."

160. Rodney also ordered sent with them another prisoner, Dr. John Witherspoon, Jr., an American whose father was the President of the College of New Jersey, member of the Continental Congress, and signatory to the Declaration of

Independence. Witherspoon's treatment was reportedly harsh but his deten-
tion in England brief, his release having been quickly negotiated by Benjamin
Franklin. See Letter from James Lovell for the Committee of Foreign Affairs to
Benjamin Franklin (May 9, 1781), in 35 Franklin Papers, supra note 158, at
48 (requesting Franklin to give "particular Attention to the Exchange of these
Persons"); Letter from Samuel Curson and Isaac Gouverneur to John Adams
(Sept. 1, 1781), in 11 The Papers of John Adams 475 (Gregg L. Lint et al. eds.,
2003); David Walker Woods, Jr., John Witherspoon 253–254 (1906).

161. Letter from Lord George Germain to the Attorney & Solicitor General (July 5,
1781), TNA CO 5/160/149.

162. Report of the Attorney & Solicitor General (July 21, 1781), TNA CO 5/160/153.

163. See Sheldon S. Cohen, British Supporters of the American
Revolution: 1775–1783, at 22–50 (2004).

164. Letter from William Hodgson to Benjamin Franklin (Dec. 21, 1781), in 36
Franklin Papers 277 (Ellen R. Cohn et al. eds., Yale Univ. Press 2001).

165. See James J. Kirschke, Gouverneur Morris: Author, Statesman, and Man
of the World 38, 249–250 (2005).

166. Lord Rockingham had earlier contributed to financial collections on behalf of
American prisoners held in England. See Cogliano, supra note 106, at 63.

167. An Act for the Better Detaining, and More Easy Exchange, of *American
Prisoners Brought into Great Britain* 1782, 22 Geo. 3, c. 10 (Gr. Brit.) (emphases added); see also 36 H.L. Jour. (1782) 425–426 (Gr. Brit.) (noting royal assent
given Mar. 25, 1782).

168. Letter from Benjamin Franklin to John Adams (Apr. 21, 1782), in 8 The
Writings of Benjamin Franklin 430, 431 (Albert Henry Smyth ed., 1907);
see also Prelinger, supra note 105, at 290 ("[I]n 1782, the official British posture respecting prisoners, as well as its attitude toward the war in general,
changed fundamentally. Parliament enacted legislation that recognized captured Americans as prisoners of war rather than rebels.").

169. Letter from William Hodgson to Benjamin Franklin (Apr. 9, 1782), in 37
Franklin Papers 124, 125 (Ellen R. Cohn et al. eds., Yale Univ. Press 2003).

170. See Harry T. Dickinson, *The Impact of the War on British Politics*, in The Oxford
Handbook of the American Revolution 355 (Edward G. Gray & Jane
Kamensky eds., 2013). By September 1782, Shelburne had directed his emis-
saries to acknowledge their counterparts as representatives "of the Thirteen
United States of America." Rakove, supra note 32, at 278.

171. 25 Annual Register, supra note 145, at 321–324 (replicating preliminary articles of peace, which provided in Article VII that "all prisoners on both sides
shall be set at liberty").

172. See, e.g., Cohen, supra note 47, at 206; Alexander, supra note 125, at 387.
By September 1783, Great Britain had formally recognized American independence in the Treaty of Paris, which also provided for the release of any

remaining prisoners of war. See Definitive Treaty of Peace, U.S.-Gr. Brit., art. 8, Sept. 3, 1783, 8 Stat. 80.

173. COGLIANO, supra note 106, at 55 (citing Russell Journal, 28 Apr. 1782, 4:45). The Cowdry to whom Russell refers ran Mill Prison during this period. See id. at 50.

174. COHEN, supra note 47, at 181.

175. COGLIANO, supra note 106, at 133 (noting that Lord Shelburne wrote to the Lords of Admiralty asking for a list of all remaining American prisoners, which Shelburne then forwarded to the king).

CHAPTER 4

1. 3 JOHN STETSON BARRY, THE HISTORY OF MASSACHUSETTS: THE COMMONWEALTH PERIOD 178 (Boston, Henry Barry 1857) (discussing the comments of the Boston delegates with respect to the draft habeas clause in the Massachusetts Constitution of 1780). Barry paraphrases Alden Bradford's earlier account of the relevant events. See 2 ALDEN BRADFORD, HISTORY OF MASSACHUSETTS 186 (Boston, Wells & Lilly 1825) ("They wished the provision respecting the privilege of habeas corpus to be more accurately defined, and more liberally granted, so that the citizens should not be subject to confinement on suspicion.").

2. Letter from General Thomas Gage to the Earl of Hillsborough (Oct. 31, 1768), in 1 THE CORRESPONDENCE OF GENERAL THOMAS GAGE WITH THE SECRETARIES OF STATE 1763–1775, at 204 (Clarence Edwin Carter ed., Yale University Press, 1931). Around this same time, the British attorney general said of the Americans: "Look into the papers and see how well these Americans are versed in Crown Law." I DEBATES OF THE HOUSE OF COMMONS DURING THE THIRTEENTH PARLIAMENT OF GREAT BRITAIN 196 (Jan. 26, 1769) (Henry Cavendish ed., London 1841).

3. 1 THE WORKS OF EDMUND BURKE, WITH A MEMOIR 230 (New York 1860); see also JACK RAKOVE, REVOLUTIONARIES 68 (2010) (collecting additional quotes on point by Gage and Burke).

4. See William B. Stoebuck, *Reception of English Common Law in the American Colonies*, 10 WM. & MARY L. REV. 393, 413 (1968).

5. The fifth edition of Henry Care's *English Liberties, or the Free-Born Subject's Inheritance*, was published in 1721 in Boston and widely circulated. As noted in Chapter 1, Care's treatise included copies of the Magna Carta, Petition of Right, English Habeas Corpus Act, and Declaration of Rights. On the place of Care, Blackstone and others in the Founding generation's studies, consult Forrest McDonald, *A Founding Father's Library*, 1 LITERATURE OF LIBERTY 4, 7 (1978). To give an idea of Blackstone's profound influence, 2,500 copies of his *Commentaries* had been sold in the colonies by the time of the Declaration of Independence, and two American editions were published in the 1770s. See ROSCOE POUND, CRIMINAL JUSTICE IN AMERICA 82 (1972). As Roscoe Pound observed, "From the

beginning, Blackstone was the foundation of American legal education, and was treated by bench and bar as an authoritative statement of the English law which we had inherited or received. Even Blackstone's occasional errors passed into our law." Similarly, Pound noted that the *Commentaries* "with their readable exposition of the immemorial rights of Englishmen, furnished convenient weapons in the political controversies leading to independence." Id. at 82, 106–107.

6. Nonetheless, the book invokes the phrase "Founding generation" as shorthand for those who participated in the Convention as well as those who subsequently debated the merits of the Constitution of 1787 during ratification proceedings, although scholars have sometimes argued that the phrase obscures the nuances of that political moment. See, e.g., RAKOVE, supra note 3, at 16.

7. THOMAS HUTCHINSON, THE HISTORY OF THE PROVINCE OF MASSACHUSETTS BAY, FROM 1749 TO 1774, at 479–487 (London 1828) (replicating resolves and petitions arising out of the 1765 Convention). The Congress in 1774 resolved: "[o]ur ancestors, who first settled these colonies, were, at the time of their emigration from the mother country, entitled to all the rights, liberties and immunities of free and natural-born subjects within the realm of England," and "by such emigration they by no means forfeited, surrendered or lost any of their rights. . . ." Declaration and Resolves of the First Continental Congress (Oct. 14, 1774), in [ser. 4, vol. 1] AMERICAN ARCHIVES: CONSISTING OF A COLLECTION OF AUTHENTICK RECORDS, STATE PAPERS, DEBATES, AND LETTERS AND OTHER NOTICES OF PUBLICK AFFAIRS, THE WHOLE THING FORMING A DOCUMENTARY HISTORY OF THE ORIGIN AND PROGRESS OF THE NORTH AMERICAN COLONIES; OF THE CAUSES AND ACCOMPLISHMENT OF THE AMERICAN REVOLUTION; AND OF THE CONSTITUTION OF GOVERNMENT FOR THE UNITED STATES, TO THE FINAL RATIFICATION THEREOF 910–911 (Peter Force ed., Washington, D.C. 1837) [hereinafter AMERICAN ARCHIVES].

8. For an extensive explication of the basis for drawing geographic distinctions in the application of English law, consult St. George Leakin Sioussat, *The Theory of the Extension of English Statutes in the Plantations*, in 1 SELECT ESSAYS ON ANGLO-AMERICAN LEGAL HISTORY 416 (1907). Blackstone took the position that the colonies were equivalent to conquered lands, which meant that English law, including the common law, was not automatically received in the colonies. See 1 WILLIAM BLACKSTONE, COMMENTARIES, at *106–108.

9. 1 BLACKSTONE, supra note 8, at *133.

10. Massachusetts's failed attempt to adopt the Act was well known to leading early American legal voices. See, e.g., James Wilson, Lectures on Law, in 2 COLLECTED WORKS OF JAMES WILSON 901–902 (Kermit L. Hall & Mark David Hall eds., 2007) (discussing episode); 1 JOSEPH STORY, COMMENTARIES ON THE CONSTITUTION OF THE UNITED STATES § 76, at 62 (1833) (same). The Massachusetts effort paralleled a similar one in the Barbardos colony, where its Assembly passed a habeas corpus bill that was rejected in 1702 by the Privy Council and Board of Trade. For details,

see PAUL D. HALLIDAY, HABEAS CORPUS: FROM ENGLAND TO EMPIRE 273 (2010). Mary Sarah Bilder details the processes by which supervision of royal charter obligations occurred in MARY SARAH BILDER, THE TRANSATLANTIC CONSTITUTION: COLONIAL LEGAL CULTURE AND THE EMPIRE 35–36, 54–69 (2004).

11. GEORGE CHALMERS, 1 POLITICAL ANNALS OF THE PRESENT UNITED COLONIES FROM THEIR SETTLEMENT TO THE PEACE OF 1763, at 677 (1780).

12. See KEVIN COSTELLO, THE LAW OF HABEAS CORPUS IN IRELAND 6, 16 (2006).

13. A.H. Carpenter, *Habeas Corpus in the Colonies*, 8 AM. HIST. REV. 18, 24–26 (1902) (replicating proclamation). The legality of the proclamation has been questioned, given that it did not embody a parliamentary act. See id.; see also 1 WILLIAM GORDON, THE HISTORY OF THE RISE, PROGRESS, AND ESTABLISHMENT, OF THE INDEPENDENCE OF THE UNITED STATES OF AMERICA 100–101 (London 1788). Nonetheless, both houses of the Virginia Assembly proclaimed their thankfulness for her "majesty's late favor, in allowing us the benefit of the Habeas Corpus act, and in appointing courts of oyer and terminer, for the more speedy execution of justice, and relief from long imprisonments." GORDON, supra, at 100.

14. An Act to impower the Right Honourable the Governour of this Province, the Lords Deputies, the Chief Justice or the Justices of the Peace, and other Officers or Ministers within this Province, to execute and put in force in the same, an Act made in the Kingdom of England in the thirty-first year of the Reign of the late King Charles the Second, entitled *An Act for the better securing the Liberty of the Subject, and for the prevention of Imprisonments beyond the Seas, commonly called the Habeas Corpus Act* (Dec. 12, 1712), in 2 THE STATUTES AT LARGE OF SOUTH CAROLINA 399, 400 (Thomas Cooper ed. 1837) [hereinafter STAT. SO. CAR.]; see also An Act to impower the several Magistrates, Justices, Ministers, and Officers within this part of this Province to execute and put in force an Act made in the Kingdom of England, Anno 31, Caroli 2, Regis, commonly called the Habeas Corpus Act, in 2 STAT. SO. CAR., supra, at 74 (Oct. 15, 1692). Section 5 of the 1712 Act repealed the 1692 Act. It appears that the earlier Act was in any event disallowed by the Lords Proprietors (the British nobility designated to oversee the colony) as unnecessary because the people of the Province were "of the King's allegiance, which makes them subject to the laws of England," a proposition that in its broadest sweep seems at odds with the Crown's position with respect to contemporary events to the north. See 1 EDWARD McCRADY, HISTORY OF SOUTH CAROLINA UNDER THE PROPRIETARY GOVERNMENT 1670–1719, at 247–248 (1897). The 1712 Act came alongside a general codification of much of the English statutory law in South Carolina. See McCRADY, supra, at 517.

15. See Carpenter, supra note 13, at 23 (noting that there is no record of formal sanction of the South Carolina statute by the Crown). Research has failed to locate any record of formal sanction.

16. See BILDER, supra note 10, at 58–63 (detailing practices).

17. 1 Royal Instructions to British Colonial Governors 1670–1776 §§ 464, 466, at 334–338 (Leonard Woods Larabee ed., 1935) [hereinafter Royal Instructions] (replicating instructions).

18. For example, judges who improperly delayed or denied the writ were to "incur the forfeiture of [their] place" as opposed to substantial monetary penalties. See id. This means that by not providing for automatic penalties, removal was left to the executive who had appointed the judges—a check that history had shown to be ineffective.

19. An Act for the Prevention of Suits and Disturbances to His Majesty's Judges and Magistrates in this Province, on Account of the Habeas Corpus Act (May 4, 1733), 3 Stat. So. Car., supra note 14, at 347.

20. For details on these events, consult Edward McCrady, The History of South Carolina under the Royal Government: 1719–1776, at 151–163 (New York 1899); see also Journal of the Commissioners for Trade and Plantations (Jan. 1728–1729 to Dec. 1734), 375–376 (London 1928) (reporting the Commissioners' vote that the South Carolina law be repealed).

21. See 3 Stat. So. Car., supra note 14, at 348 (replicating Privy Council's disallowance of the law dated Apr. 11, 1734).

22. This being said, the South Carolina Attorney General and Chief Justice in 1756 reportedly advised the colonial governor that the Habeas Corpus Act limited his options for detaining or expelling Acadians from the state, a story that underscores the Act's evolving influence on the legal framework governing executive detention in the colony. See James Oldham & Michael J. Wishnie, *The Historical Scope of Habeas Corpus and INS v. St. Cyr*, 16 Geo. Imm. L.J. 485, 497–499 (2002) (detailing story).

23. Journal of the General Assembly of South Carolina, March 26, 1776–April 11, 1776, at 21, 24, 26 (1906).

24. 1 An Alphabetical Digest of the Public Statute Law of South-Carolina 394 (Joseph Brevard ed., 1814) (reprinting 31 Car. 2, c.2 (Eng.)).

25. L. 1715, ch. 31, §§ 5–7, in 1 Revised Statutes of the State of North Carolina xi (1837).

26. See Royal Instructions, supra note 17, §§ 464, 466, at 334–338 (replicating instructions); Instructions to George Burrington concerning the government of North Carolina §§ 51–60 (Dec. 14, 1730), in 3 Colonial Records of North Carolina 104–106 (William L. Saunders ed., Raleigh 1886).

27. 23 Acts of the North Carolina General Assembly, 1749, at 317 (1905) (providing that the enumerated English laws, starting with the Magna Carta and including the English Habeas Corpus Act, "are hereby to be in as full Force, Power, and Virtue, as if the same had been specially Enacted and made for this Province, or as if the same had been made and Enacted there in, by any General Assembly thereof").

28. Order of the Privy Council of Great Britain concerning acts of the North Carolina General Assembly, 5 COLONIAL AND STATE RECORDS OF NORTH CAROLINA 116 (William Laurence Saunders ed., 1887) (order dated Apr. 8, 1754).

29. JOHN V. ORTH, THE NORTH CAROLINA STATE CONSTITUTION 62 (1993) (observing that "[t]he absence of a specific reference [to habeas in the original North Carolina Constitution] was of no practical import since England's Habeas Corpus Act (1679) was accepted as part of the state's common law").

30. Carpenter, supra note 13, at 20; see also PAUL M. HAMLIN & CHARLES E. BAKER, SUPREME COURT OF JUDICATURE OF THE PROVINCE OF NEW YORK 1691–1704, at 403 (1952). All the same, many colonies enacted statutes generally granting jurisdiction to the courts to issue writs of habeas corpus.

31. This incorporation "in practice," which was sometimes realized through wide departures from settled theories of English law, resulted in a "common law [that] was not the same in any two of the Colonies." James Madison, *Report on the Resolutions*, in 6 THE WRITINGS OF JAMES MADISON 341, 373 (Gaillard Hunt ed., 1906); see also Paul Samuel Reinsch, *The English Common Law in Early American Colonies*, in 1 SELECT ESSAYS ON ANGLO-AMERICAN LEGAL HISTORY, supra note 8, at 367, 369; Bernadette Meyler, *Towards a Common Law Originalism*, 59 STAN. L. REV. 551 (2006).

32. William Kilty, *A report of all such English statutes as existed at the time of the first emigration of the people of Maryland, and which by experience have been found applicable to their local and other circumstances; . . .* , 143 ARCHIVES OF MARYLAND 176 (Annapolis 1811) ("Kilty's Report"). Kilty's Report was the product of Chancellor Kilty's exhaustive survey of the status of English statutory law in Maryland in 1776.

33. See MD. CONST. of 1776, Declaration of Rights ¶ 3; 63 ARCHIVES OF MARYLAND, PROCEEDINGS AND ACTS OF THE GENERAL ASSEMBLY OF MARYLAND, 1771, at 81 (1946) (resolving that the province enjoyed the common law and such statutes of England "as are securitative of the Rights and Liberties of the Subject. . . ."). A list of earlier enactments by the Maryland General Assembly to the same effect may be found in ELIZABETH GASPAR BROWN & WILLIAM WIRT BLUME, BRITISH STATUTES IN AMERICAN LAW 1776–1836, at 95 n.63 (1964). Both Hurd's and Church's popular treatises on habeas corpus observe that Maryland did not pass a provincial habeas act, but "the act was recognized and practically adopted." WILLIAM S. CHURCH, A TREATISE OF THE WRIT OF HABEAS CORPUS § 42, at 34 (1884) (citing ROLLIN C. HURD, A TREATISE ON THE RIGHT OF PERSONAL LIBERTY, AND ON THE WRIT OF HABEAS CORPUS 100 (Frank H. Hurd ed., 2d ed., Albany, N.Y., W.C. Little & Co. 1876) (1858)).

34. See Kilty's Report, supra note 32, at 178.

35. THE PROCEEDINGS RELATIVE TO CALLING THE CONVENTIONS OF 1776 AND 1790 THAT FORMED THE PRESENT CONSTITUTION OF PENNSYLVANIA 54 (Harrisburg 1825) (entry dated Sept. 27, 1776).

36. An Act for the Better Securing Personal Liberty, and Preventing Wrongful Imprisonments (Feb. 18, 1785), GENERAL LAWS OF PENNSYLVANIA 142 (James Dunlop, 2d ed. 1849).

37. The applicability of the English Act in the state at this point may have followed most immediately under the Act of January 28, 1777, which declared that the common law and those English statutory laws that had heretofore been in force in the province would continue to be in force. See An Act to Revive and Put in Force Such and So Much of the Late Laws of the Province of Pennsylvania as is Judged Necessary to be in Force in this Commonwealth and [to] Revive and Establish the Courts of Justice and for Other Purposes Therein Mentioned (1777), 9 STATUTES AT LARGE OF PENNSYLVANIA 29 (1903). Other original states enacted similar statutes. For examples, consult BROWN & BLUME, supra note 33, at 54, 63, 95 (discussing Rhode Island, Vermont, and Maryland). Other states included such provisions in their initial constitutions. See, e.g., BROWN & BLUME, supra, at 95, 103 (discussing Maryland and Delaware).

38. Letter from Thomas McKean to John Adams, Sept. 19, 1777, in 5 THE PAPERS OF JOHN ADAMS No. PJA05d178 (Massachusetts Historical Society Digital Edition) (2017).

39. JOURNAL AND PROCEEDINGS OF THE GENERAL ASSEMBLY OF THE COMMON-WEALTH OF PENNSYLVANIA 88 (John Dunlap, Philadelphia 1777).

40. See ROYAL INSTRUCTIONS, supra note 17, §§ 464, 466, at 334–338.

41. GA. CONST. of 1777, art. LX; see also CHARLES FRANCIS JENKINS, BUTTON GWINNETT: SIGNER OF THE DECLARATION OF INDEPENDENCE 109 (1926) ("[T]he House . . . ordered, that 500 copies be immediately struck off, with the Act of Distribution, made in the reign of Charles the Second, and the habeas corpus act annexed. . . .").

42. A CODIFICATION OF THE STATUTE LAW OF GEORGIA INCLUDING THE ENGLISH STATUTES OF FORCE 300 (2d ed. William A. Hotchkiss ed., 1848). In the meantime, the verbatim adoption of the Act had presented the need for clarifying legislation to ensure that properly named Georgia judicial officers (as opposed to their British counterparts) had the authority to issue writs. See An Act to amend an act entitled "An Act to revise and amend the Judiciary System of this State § 7 (Feb. 16, 1799), in DIGEST OF THE LAWS OF THE STATE OF GEORGIA 419–420 (Oliver H. Prince ed., 2d ed. 1837).

43. See HAMLIN & BAKER, supra note 30, at 390–400 (listing example of New York lawyers and judges in the eighteenth century invoking the English Act); LEONARD W. LEVY, ORIGINS OF THE BILL OF RIGHTS 57–58, 61, 63 (1999) (detailing New York cases from the period). There are many other stories of the English Act being cited in colonial courts. See, e.g., Carpenter, supra note 13, at 22 (citing a New Hampshire case from 1684 in which the petitioner appears to have successfully relied upon the Act).

44. The Declaration of Independence para. 22 (U.S. 1776) (decrying the king "[f]or abolishing the free System of English Laws in a neighbouring Province, establishing therin an Arbitrary government, and enlarging its Boundaries so as to render it at once an example and fit instrument for introducing the same absolute rule into these Colonies").

45. 1 Journals of the Continental Congress, 1774–1789, at 88 (Worthington Chauncey Ford ed., 1904) [hereinafter J. Cont. Cong.].

46. Id. at 107–108 (replicating Lettre Adressée aux Habitans de la Province de Quebec (Oct. 26, 1774)).

47. [ser. 4, vol. 4] American Archives 1631 (Peter Force ed., Washington, D.C. 1843) (replicating Resolution of Jan. 3, 1776).

48. 4 J. Cont. Cong., supra note 45, at 358 (Resolution of May 15, 1776).

49. 5 id. at 475 (replicating Resolution of June 24, 1776). It bears noting here that "Anglo-American law has never held that allegiance is simply a question of citizenship." Carlton F.W. Larson, *The Forgotten Constitutional Law of Treason and the Enemy Combatant Problem*, 154 U. Pa. L. Rev. 863, 867 (2006). The 1776 Continental Congress defined allegiance and protection to encompass "all persons passing through, visiting, or making a temporary stay in any of the said colonies." 4 J. Cont. Cong., supra note 45, at 475 (June 24, 1776); see also Philip Hamburger, *Beyond Protection*, 109 Colum. L. Rev. 1823, 1851 (2009) (observing that during the Founding period, "not only citizens, but also lawfully visiting aliens who joined an enemy would have had the protection of the law, and they would therefore have gone free, unless tried . . . and convicted of treason or another offense").

50. The Declaration of Independence para. 32 (U.S. 1776).

51. 5 J. Cont. Cong., supra note 45, at 475.

52. Hamburger, supra note 49, at 1855; see also Brian F. Carso, Jr., "Whom Can We Trust Now?" 62–63 (2006).

53. 6 J. Cont. Cong., supra note 45, at 1045–1046 (replicating Resolution of Dec. 27, 1776).

54. 9 id. at 1069 (replicating Resolution of Dec. 30, 1777).

55. 5 id. at 693 (replicating Resolution of Aug. 21, 1776).

56. Thomas Paine, *Common Sense*, in 1 The Complete Writings of Thomas Paine 43–44 (Philip S. Foner, ed., 1945).

57. Commonly, states adopted most, if not all, of the procedural guarantees for treason cases granted under English law. See Carso, supra note 52, at 62; Trial of Treasons Act 1696, 7 & 8 Will. 3, c. 3 (Eng.).

58. An Act Declaring What Shall Be Treason, and What Other Crimes and Practices Against the State Shall Be Misprision of Treason §§ 2–3, in The Acts of the General Assembly of the Commonwealth of Pennsylvania 18, 18 (Thomas M'Kean ed., Philadelphia, Francis Bailey 1782).

59. An Act Declaring What Crimes and Practices Against the State Shall Be Treason, and What Shall be Misprision of Treason, and Providing Punishments Adequate

to Crimes of Both Classes, and for Preventing the Dangers Which May Arise from the Persons Disaffected to the State § 1, in 24 THE STATE RECORDS OF NORTH CAROLINA 9, 9 (Walter Clark ed., 1905) (1777) (defining treasonous activities).

60. 8 J. CONT. CONG., supra note 45, at 695 (replicating Resolution of Aug. 28, 1777).

61. See RAKOVE, supra note 3, at 133 (detailing the British Navy movements); Hamburger, supra note 49, at 1911–1917 (detailing events surrounding the detention of Quakers).

62. JOURNAL AND PROCEEDINGS OF THE GENERAL ASSEMBLY OF THE COMMON-WEALTH OF PENNSYLVANIA 88 (John Dunlap ed., 1777).

63. An Act to Empower the Supreme Executive Council of this Commonwealth to Provide for the Security Thereof in Special Cases Where No Provision Is Already Made by Law, ch. 762, pmbl. (1777), in 9 THE STATUTES AT LARGE OF PENNSYLVANIA FROM 1682 TO 1801, at 138, 138–140 (James T. Mitchell & Henry Flanders eds., 1903); id. §§ 1, 2; see id. § 3 (providing that the Act "shall be in force to the end of the first sitting of the next general assembly of the commonwealth and no longer"). To make sure that the council would be protected for past conduct, the legislature appended an indemnity bill to insulate the council for actions taken before the suspension. See id. § 2.

64. 8 J. CONT. CONG., supra note 45, at 694 (replicating Resolution of Aug. 28, 1777).

65. EXILES IN VIRGINIA 112 (Thomas Gilpin ed., Philadelphia, C. Sherman 1848) (replicating Resolution of Sept. 9, 1777).

66. Letter from Thomas McKean to John Adams, Sept. 19, 1777, in 5 THE PAPERS OF JOHN ADAMS No. PJA05d178 (Massachusetts Historical Society Digital Edition) (2017).

67. An Act to Punish Certain Crimes and Misdemeanors, and to Prevent the Growth of Toryism, ch. 20, § 12 (Feb. 5, 1777), in 1 THE LAWS OF MARYLAND 338, 340–341 (Virgil Maxcy ed., Philip H. Nicklin & Co. 1811).

68. 7 J. CONT. CONG., supra note 45, at 285–286 (replicating Resolution of Apr. 19, 1777).

69. An Ordinance to Empower the President or Commander-in-Chief for the Time Being, with the Advice of the Privy Council, to Take Up and Confine All Persons Whose Going at Large May Endanger the Safety of this State (Oct. 17, 1778), in 4 STAT. SO. CAR., supra note 14, at 458; id. § 1; id. § 2. State legislators exempted themselves in large measure from the suspension. See id. at 459.

70. See JOURNAL OF THE GENERAL ASSEMBLY OF SOUTH CAROLINA, MARCH 26, 1776–APRIL 11, 1776, at 21, 24, 26 (1906).

71. An Act Appointing Commissioners for Detecting and Defeating Conspiracies and Declaring Their Powers, ch. 3 (1778), in 1 LAWS OF THE STATE OF NEW YORK 8, 9 (Albany, Weed, Parsons & Co. 1886); see also THOMAS B. ALLEN, TORIES: FIGHTING FOR THE KING IN AMERICA'S FIRST CIVIL WAR 196 (2010) (discussing the New York State Committee and Commission for Detecting and Defeating Conspiracies); see also James Westfall Thompson, *Anti-Loyalist Legislation during the American*

Revolution, 3 ILL. L. REV. 81, 152–153 (1908). Other states also constituted committees of safety during the war. See Thompson, supra, at 87 (discussing Connecticut's committee).

72. An Act More Effectually to Prevent the Inhabitants of this State from Trading with the Enemy, or Going Within Their Lines, and for Other Purposes Therein Mentioned §§ 1, 9 (1780), in ACTS OF THE FIFTH GENERAL ASSEMBLY OF THE STATE OF NEW-JERSEY 11, 15 (Trenton, N.J., Isaac Collins 1781). The Act ran for one year and from then to the end of the next sitting of the General Assembly.

73. See HENRY P. JOHNSTON, THE YORKTOWN CAMPAIGN AND THE SURRENDER OF CORNWALLIS, 1781, at 29 (New York, Harper & Brothers 1881).

74. An Act for Giving Certain Powers to the Governour and Council, and for Punishing Those Who Shall Oppose the Execution of the Laws, ch. 7 (1781), in 10 THE STATUTES AT LARGE; BEING A COLLECTION OF ALL THE LAWS OF VIRGINIA, FROM THE FIRST SESSION OF THE LEGISLATURE, IN THE YEAR 1619, at 413, 413–414 (William Waller Hening ed., Richmond, Va., George Cochran 1822). The Act remained in effect through the end of the next session of the assembly. See id. at 416.

75. See R.B. BERNSTEIN, THOMAS JEFFERSON 45 (2003); RAKOVE, supra note 3, at 308–309 (relaying Jefferson's account of the British pursuing him at Monticello and his narrow escape).

76. An Act for Taking Up and Restraining Persons Dangerous to this State, ch. 45, § 1 (1777), in 5 THE ACTS AND RESOLVES, PUBLIC AND PRIVATE, OF THE PROVINCE OF THE MASSACHUSETTS BAY 401, 401 (Boston, Wright & Potter Printing Co. 1886); id. § 3 (alterations in original). This Act had a one-year sunset provision. Id. § 4.

77. RAKOVE, supra note 3, at 195; see id. at 193–195 (describing the drafting process). Much of the history of the drafting of the Massachusetts Constitution is described in detail in THE POPULAR SOURCES OF POLITICAL AUTHORITY: DOCUMENTS ON THE MASSACHUSETTS CONSTITUTION OF 1780, at 52 (Oscar Handlin & Mary Handlin eds., 1966) [hereinafter POPULAR SOURCES], which collects and presents all of the town returns.

78. MASS. CONST. of 1780, pt. 2, ch. VI, art. VII.

79. POPULAR SOURCES, supra note 77, at 763 (emphasis added); see also 3 BARRY, supra note 1, at 177–178 (describing Boston's Return as seeking a stronger habeas clause to ensure "that citizens should not be subject to confinement on mere suspicion").

80. POPULAR SOURCES, supra note 77, at 790.

81. Id. at 680.

82. See id. at 661 (observing that a twelve-month suspension would be "longer than is necessary; and that a suspension of the Benefit of the act referred to in the

Article, for so long a Term, might be of dangerous Consequence to the Liberties of the Subject").

83. Id. at 649.

84. Richard D. Brown, *Shays's Rebellion and the Ratification of the Federal Constitution in Massachusetts, in* BEYOND CONFEDERATION: ORIGINS OF THE CONSTITUTION AND AMERICAN NATIONAL IDENTITY 113, 113 (Richard Beeman, Stephen Botein & Edward C. Carter II eds., 1987).

85. See, e.g., DAVID P. SZATMARY, SHAYS' REBELLION 43 (1980); CHARLES MARTYN, THE LIFE OF ARTEMAS WARD 263 (1921); ROBERT J. TAYLOR, WESTERN MASSACHUSETTS IN THE REVOLUTION 103–122 (1954).

86. See MARTYN, supra note 85, at 263–264, 267 n.30. Many members of the General Court feared that the insurgents were infected with Toryism. See, e.g., TAYLOR, supra note 85, at 118, 119.

87. An Act to Suspend the Privilege of the Writ of Habeas Corpus for Six Months, ch. 2, 1782–1783 MASS. ACTS 6, 7 (1782) (including a non obstante clause referencing "any Law, Usage or Custom to the contrary notwithstanding").

88. An Act to Suspend the Privilege of the Writ of Habeas Corpus for Four Months, ch. 34, 1782–1783 MASS. ACTS 105 (1783) (emphasis added).

89. An Act directing the Process in *Habeas Corpus* § 13 (Mar. 16, 1785), 1 MASS. GEN. LAWS ch. 72, § 13 (1784).

90. See 3 BARRY, supra note 1, at 232–246.

91. TAYLOR, supra note 85, at 148.

92. EDWARD EVERETT HALE, THE STORY OF MASSACHUSETTS 306 (Boston, D. Lothrop Co. 1891) ("'Burning barns and blazing haystacks' were the tokens of the punishment by which lawless men showed their resentment against friends of the Government.").

93. See, e.g., TAYLOR, supra note 85, at 149–150 (detailing communications to Governor Bowdoin conveying these fears while noting that the insurgents denied British involvement).

94. See 3 BARRY, supra note 1, at 232, 176, 238.

95. GEORGE RICHARDS MINOT, THE HISTORY OF THE INSURRECTIONS, IN MASSACHUSETTS, IN THE YEAR MDCCLXXXVI, AND THE REBELLION CONSEQUENT THEREON 62 (Worcester, Mass., Isaiah Thomas 1788).

96. See 2 BRADFORD, supra note 1, app. at 366 (replicating the February 3, 1787, speech given by Governor Bowdoin to the General Court expressing fear of civil war); see also MINOT, supra note 95, at 80, 96–97.

97. See MINOT, supra note 95, at 52–66 (detailing legislative delays).

98. An Act for Suspending the Privilege of the Writ of Habeas Corpus, ch. 41, 1786–1787 MASS. ACTS 102–103 (1786) (providing that the suspension would be in effect for eight months).

99. Accounts of the events include 2 BRADFORD, supra note 1, app. at 363, 365
    (replicating Governor Bowdoin's February 3, 1787, speech to the General Court
    discussing arrests ordered pursuant to state warrants); MINOT, supra note 95,
    at 77–79 (mentioning one round of arrests by state warrants); TAYLOR, supra
    note 85, at 162 (reporting on another round of arrests on state warrants); see
    also LEONARD L. RICHARDS, SHAYS'S REBELLION: THE AMERICAN REVOLUTION'S
    FINAL BATTLE 19–21 (2002) (providing another account). Bowdoin wrote the
    leader of the state militia, General Benjamin Lincoln, who had served as
    George Washington's second-in-command at Yorktown, with instructions:

    > to protect the Judicial Courts . . . , to assist the civil magistrates in executing
    > the laws; and in repelling or apprehending all and every such person [who
    > shall] . . . attempt or enterprise the destruction, detriment or annoyance of
    > this Commonwealth; and also to aid . . . in apprehending . . . all such per-
    > sons, as may have been named in the state warrants. . . .

    MINOT, supra note 95, at 99–100.
100. See id. at 79.
101. 3 BARRY, supra note 1, at 243.
102. See MINOT, supra note 95, at 161, 162–163 (noting the adoption of a severe
    disqualification law stripping participants in the insurgency of various rights);
    3 BARRY, supra note 1, at 254 ("As disturbances had now in a great measure
    subsided, the legislature turned its attention to the trial of those who had been
    seized and imprisoned."); id. at 255 (discussing trials); 2 BRADFORD, supra note
    1, at 307–308 (same).
103. Thomas B. Wait, Editorial, CUMBERLAND GAZETTE, Dec. 15, 1786.
104. Minot, supra note 95, at 65.
105. 3 BARRY, supra note 1, at 258.
106. See THE FEDERALIST NOS. 6, 21, 25, 28, 74 (Alexander Hamilton), No. 43
    (James Madison) (Clinton Rossiter ed., 2003); see id. at THE FEDERALIST No. 28
    (Alexander Hamilton), at 174 (referring to Shays's Rebellion when observing
    "[a]n insurrection . . . eventually endangers all government"); THE FEDERALIST
    No. 21 (Alexander Hamilton), at 135–136 (including the rebellion within a
    broader discussion of the defects of the existing Articles and observing that "[a]
    successful faction may erect a tyranny on the ruins of order and law, while no
    succor could constitutionally be afforded by the Union to the friends and sup-
    ports of the government").
107. Letter from George Washington to James Madison (Nov. 5, 1786), in 4 THE
    PAPERS OF GEORGE WASHINGTON 331, 332 (W.W. Abbot & Dorothy Twohig eds.,
    1995). The rebellion also figured prominently in the ratification debates, as
    many supporters of the new Constitution labeled their opponents "Shaysites."
    See RICHARDS, supra note 99, at 139.
108. Maryland's 1776 Constitution purported to entitle its inhabitants to "the benefit
    of such of the English statutes, as existed at the time of their first emigration,

and which, by experience, have been found applicable to their local and other circumstances, and of such others as have been since made in England, or Great Britain, and have been introduced, used and practiced by the courts of law or equity"—a provision that likely provided at least part of the basis for operation of the English Habeas Corpus Act in that state during the war, necessitating in turn a suspension of the "habeas corpus act" when the British threatened to invade. MD. CONST., art. III (1776). Similar provisions found their way into the early constitutions of several other states. See, e.g., N.J. CONST., art. XXII (1776); DEL. CONST., art. XXV (1776); N.Y. CONST., art. XXXV (1777).

109. See, e.g., MASS. CONST. of 1780, pt. 2, ch. VI, art. VII; N.H. CONST. pt. 2, art. XCI (1784) ("The privilege and benefit of the habeas corpus, shall be enjoyed in this state, in the most free, easy, cheap, expeditious, and ample manner, and shall not be suspended by the legislature, except upon the most urgent and pressing occasions, and for a time not exceeding three months."); VT. CONST., art. XII (1836) (providing that "[t]he Writ of Habeas Corpus shall in no case be suspended" and declaring that "[i]t shall be a writ, issuable of right").

110. An Act directing the mode of suing out and prosecuting writs of habeas corpus (1784), 11 VA. STATUTES AT LARGE ch. 35, 408–410 (William Waller Hening ed., 1823).

111. An Act for the Better Securing Personal Liberty, and Preventing Wrongful Imprisonments (Feb. 18, 1785), GENERAL LAWS OF PENNSYLVANIA 142 (James Dunlop, 2d ed. 1849).

112. An Act directing the Process in *Habeas Corpus* (Mar. 16, 1785), 1 MASS. GEN. LAWS ch. 72, § 13 (1784).

113. An Act for better securing personal liberty, and easily and speedily redressing all wrongful restraints thereof § 3 (Feb. 2, 1793), 2 DEL. LAWS 1056 (New-Castle, Del. 1797).

114. Act for preventing the injury of illegal confinement, and better securing the liberty of the people § 7 (Mar. 11, 1795), N.J. LAWS 193 (Trenton, N.J., 1821) (adopting Section 7 and other relevant provisions of the English Habeas Corpus Act almost verbatim).

115. An Act for the Better Security of Personal Liberty § 9, 1 N.C. REV. STAT. 314, ch. 55 (1837).

116. See In re Bryan, 60 N.C. 1, 43 (1863) (Pearson, C.J.).

117. See DIGEST OF THE LAWS OF THE STATE OF GEORGIA vii, 313, 571–576 (Oliver H. Prince ed. 1822).

118. An Act declaratory of certain rights of the people of this State, R.I. PUBLIC LAWS 66, 67 (1798) (Miller & Hutchens 1822).

119. See also An Act in Addition to an Act, Entitled an Act Constituting the Supreme Court of Judicature, and Country Courts, Defining their Powers, and Regulating Judicial Proceedings §§ 2–3, 7 (Nov. 11, 1814), 3 VT. LAWS 21, 21–22, 24 (Fay, Davison & Burt 1817) (declaring that "the writ of Habeas Corpus is a writ of

right," while promising discharge under threat of penalty to the judge where a "prisoner is imprisoned or restrained of personal liberty without due process of law"); An Act to prevent unjust imprisonment, and to secure the privilege and benefit of the Writ of Habeas Corpus § 1 (June 26, 1815), 2 N.H. LAWS 11, ch. 45 (1815); An Act relative to Bail and the writ of Habeas Corpus, ch. II (May 1808), 1 PUBLIC STAT. LAW OF CONN. 69 (Hudson & Goodwin 1808); An Act to provide for issuing the writ of Habeas Corpus § 2, PUBLIC STATUTE LAWS OF CONN. 265 (1821).

120. An Act for the Better Securing the Liberty of the Citizens of this State, and for Prevention of Imprisonments (Feb. 21, 1787), in 1 LAWS OF THE STATE OF NEW YORK 369, 369 (New York, Thomas Greenleaf 1792). As Chancellor Kent noted in his *Commentaries*, "[t]he substance of [New York's] statute provisions on the subject . . . closely followed" the terms of the English Act. 2 JAMES KENT, COMMENTARIES ON AMERICAN LAW 24, 29 (New York, O. Halsted 1827).

121. 2 KENT, supra note 120, at 24; see also id. at 23 ("[T]he statute of 31 Charles II. c. 2. . . . has been re-enacted or adopted, if not in terms, yet in substance and effect, in all these United States.").

122. 3 STORY, supra note 10, § 1335, at 208.

123. See, e.g., id. § 1333, at 206; See 2 KENT, supra note 120, at 22 (calling the writ of habeas corpus as a "writ of right").

CHAPTER 5

1. Debates in the Convention of the Commonwealth of Massachusetts, on the Adoption of the Federal Constitution (Jan. 26, 1788) (statement of Judge Sumner), in 2 THE DEBATES IN THE SEVERAL STATE CONVENTIONS ON THE ADOPTION OF THE FEDERAL CONSTITUTION, AS RECOMMENDED BY THE GENERAL CONVENTION AT PHILADELPHIA, IN 1787, at 109 (Jonathan Elliot ed., 2d ed., Philadelphia, J.B. Lippincott 1891) [hereinafter ELLIOT'S DEBATES].

2. ARTICLES OF CONFEDERATION, art. IV. For additional details on the Articles as well as a survey of the literature on them, consult Jack Rakove, *The Legacy of the Articles of Confederation*, 12(4) PUBLIUS 45 (1982).

3. U.S. CONST. art. I, § 9, cl. 2.

4. See Rakove, supra note 2, at 55.

5. Washington described the Articles of Confederation as having created "a half-starved, limping government, that appears to be always moving upon crutches, and tottering at every step." Letter from George Washington to Benjamin Harrison (Jan. 18, 1874), reprinted in 27 THE WRITINGS OF GEORGE WASHINGTON FROM THE ORIGINAL MANUSCRIPT SOURCES 305–306 (John C. Fitzpatrick ed., 1939). See also generally JOSEPH J. ELLIS, THE QUARTET: ORCHESTRATING THE SECOND AMERICAN REVOLUTION, 1783–1789 (2015).

6. U.S. CONST. art. III, § 1 (providing that "[t]he judicial Power of the United States, shall be vested in one supreme Court, and in such inferior Courts as the Congress

may from time to time ordain and establish" and that judges "shall hold their Offices during good Behaviour").

7. THE FEDERALIST No. 78 (Alexander Hamilton), at 465 (Clinton Rossiter ed., 2003) (quoting Montesquieu's SPIRIT OF LAWS) (positing that "complete independence of the courts of justice is peculiarly essential" and that limits on legislative authority "can be preserved in practice no other way than through the medium of courts of justice. . . ." Id.

8. Id. at 466. Madison espoused a similar view of the judicial role, declaring two years later that "independent tribunals of justice will consider themselves in a peculiar manner the guardians of [the Bill of Rights]; they will be an impenetrable bulwark against every assumption of power in the legislative or executive. . . ." James Madison, *Amendments to the Constitution*, in 12 JAMES MADISON, THE PAPERS OF JAMES MADISON 196, 207 (Robert A. Rutland, William M.E. Rachal, Barbara D. Ripel & Fredrika J. Teute eds., 1973) (speech to the House of Representatives, June 8, 1789).

9. *Letter IV*, from *Four Letters on Interesting Subjects* (Philadelphia, Styner & Cist 1776), reprinted in JACK N. RAKOVE, DECLARING RIGHTS: A BRIEF HISTORY WITH DOCUMENTS 73 (1998). Professor Rakove writes that the anonymous author may have been Thomas Paine. See id. at 70. Notably, the author expressly references the Habeas Corpus Act.

10. See Amendments to the Articles of Confederation Proposed by a Grand Committee of Congress (Aug. 7, 1786), reprinted in 1 THE DOCUMENTARY HISTORY OF THE RATIFICATION OF THE CONSTITUTION 165, 167 (John P. Kaminski & Gaspare J. Saladino eds., 1984) [hereinafter DOCUMENTARY HISTORY] (replicating Article XIX, which, like the other proposed amendments was never formally considered by the Congress). Charles Pinckney had proposed the idea of constituting a committee to propose amendments to the Articles. See id. at 165.

11. See Ordonnance Pour la Sûreté de la Liberté du Sujet dans la Province de Québec, et pour Empêcher les Emprisonnemens hors de Cette Province, 1784, 24 Geo. 3, c. 1 (Que.), reprinted in both English and French in Ordinances Made and Passed by the Governor and Legislative Council of the Province of Quebec 57 (William Vondenvelden 1795); see id. § 8, at 63 (incorporating Section 7 of the English Act).

12. 1 ELLIOT'S DEBATES, supra note 1, at 148 (replicating Charles Pinckney's draft plan, Article VI). Here, a note on sources is in order. Elliot's Debates, originally published in 1830 and an outgrowth of the official records of the Convention, see Mary Sarah Bilder, *How Bad Were the Official Records of the Federal Convention?*, 80 GEO. WASH. L. REV. 1620, 1626 (2012), reprints the draft plan with the notation that the "[p]aper [was] furnished by Mr. Pinckney." 1 ELLIOT'S DEBATES, supra, at 145. The other source commonly relied upon for collecting various records of the Convention, Max Farrand's *Records of the Federal Convention of 1787*, concludes that Pinckney's original draft plan was lost and the reprinted one was

a copy of a draft sent by him to John Adams well after the Convention. See 3 THE RECORDS OF THE FEDERAL CONVENTION OF 1787, at 602 (Max Farrand ed., 1911) [hereinafter FARRAND'S RECORDS]. Farrand questions in his own replication of the draft plan the ordering and particulars of Pinckney's proposal, see FARRAND'S RECORDS, supra, at 609, but given Pinckney's attendant notes in his "Observations," discussed below, it seems fairly clear that the draft included a habeas provision of some kind.

13. An Act for Better Securing the Liberty of the Subject, 1781, 21 & 22 Geo. 3, c. 11, § XVI (Ir.). For details on the Irish Act, see KEVIN COSTELLO, THE LAW OF HABEAS CORPUS IN IRELAND 6, 16 (2006).

14. Charles Pinckney, *Observations on the Plan of Government Submitted to the Federal Convention, in Philadelphia, on the 28th of May, 1787*, in 3 FARRAND'S RECORDS, supra note 12, at 106, 122 (replicating Observations, which were published in New York by Francis Childs in 1787 and reprinted in the *State Gazette of South Carolina* later that year).

15. Delaware delegate John Dickinson's draft plan dated June 18 did call for "[p]rovision to be made for securing the Benefits of the writ of Habeas Corpus and Trial by Juries in proper Cases." John Dickinson, Plan of Government (I) (June 18, 1787), reprinted in James H. Hutson, *John Dickinson at the Federal Constitutional Convention*, 40 WM. & MARY Q. 256, 266 (1983). Although there is no evidence that Dickinson introduced his plan, perhaps because the timing coincided with Alexander Hamilton presenting his own, see id. at 262, it stands as another example from this period that linked the benefits of habeas corpus with the jury trial right. Also during this period, the Congress approved the Northwest Ordinance, which provided that "[t]he inhabitants of the said territory shall always be entitled to the benefits of the writ of *habeas corpus*, and of the trial by jury." Art. II, An Act to provide for the Government of the Territory Northwest of the river Ohio, ch. 8, 1 Stat. 50, 52 n. a (July 13, 1787, re-enacted Aug. 7, 1789).

16. James Madison, Notes on the Constitutional Convention (Aug. 20, 1787) [hereinafter Madison's Notes], in 2 FARRAND'S RECORDS, supra note 12, at 340 n.4 (quoting Madison's notes); id. at 334, 341 (quoting proposal) (omission in original) (internal quotation marks omitted); see also 1 ELLIOT'S DEBATES, supra note 1, at 249 (replicating same wording, except "benefit" is "benefits," along with slight variations in punctuation and capitalization, and noting that the proposal was referred to the committee of five). Here, again, a word is in order on sources. An important new study by historian Mary Sarah Bilder reveals that Madison revised his Notes on the Convention over the course of many years following the Convention and to a far greater extent than scholars have previously recognized. See MARY SARAH BILDER, MADISON'S HAND: REVISING THE CONSTITUTIONAL CONVENTION (2015). Absent reason to question the description in Madison's Notes of the Convention debates over the privilege, I rely on them here.

17. MASS. CONST. of 1780, pt. 2, ch. VI, art. VII ("The privilege and benefit of the writ of habeas corpus shall be enjoyed in this commonwealth, in the most free, easy, cheap, expeditious, and ample manner; and shall not be suspended by the legislature, except upon the most urgent and pressing occasions, and for a limited time, not exceeding twelve months."); N.H. CONST. of 1784, pt. 2, art. XCI ("The privilege and benefit of the habeas corpus, shall be enjoyed in this state, in the most free, easy, cheap, expeditious, and ample manner, and shall not be suspended by the legislature, except upon the most urgent and pressing occasions, and for a time not exceeding three months.").

18. The Treason Clause provides: "Treason against the United States, shall consist only in levying War against them, or in adhering to their Enemies, giving them Aid and Comfort. No Person shall be convicted of Treason unless on the Testimony of two Witnesses to the same overt Act, or on Confession in open Court." U.S. CONST. art. III, § 3, cl. 1. Shortly after ratification, Wilson observed that the clause was "transcribed from a part of the statute of Edward the third." 2 JAMES WILSON, *Of Crimes, Immediately Against the Community*, in THE WORKS OF JAMES WILSON 663, 665 (Robert Green McCloskey ed., 1967); see also 3 JOSEPH STORY, COMMENTARIES ON THE CONSTITUTION OF THE UNITED STATES § 1793, at 669 (1833) (noting the same).

19. Madison's Notes (Aug. 28, 1787), in 2 FARRAND'S RECORDS, supra note 12, at 438.

20. Id. at 438 (internal quotation marks omitted).

21. 5 ELLIOT'S DEBATES, supra note 1, at 346 (replicating Morris's remarks on July 21, 1787). For details on Morris, see JAMES J. KIRSCHKE, GOUVERNEUR MORRIS: AUTHOR, STATESMAN, AND MAN OF THE WORLD 174–180 (2005).

22. Madison's Notes, in 2 FARRAND'S RECORDS, supra note 12, at 438 (alteration in original).

23. BRIAN F. CARSO, JR., "WHOM CAN WE TRUST NOW?" 61, 66 (2006); 2 WILSON, supra note 18, at 663–669 (echoing Blackstone and others in arguing that "the law of treason should . . . be determinate [and] . . . stable"). Wilson had also served as defense counsel in several prominent treason prosecutions during the Revolutionary War.

24. Madison's Notes, in 2 FARRAND'S RECORDS, supra note 12, at 438; see also 1 ELLIOT'S DEBATES, supra note 1, at 270 (reporting the approval of Morris's proposed wording).

25. Luther Martin Before the Maryland House of Representatives (Nov. 29, 1787), reprinted in 3 FARRAND'S RECORDS, supra note 12, at 151, 157 (replicating statement that represents an earlier stage of Martin's *Genuine Information*, discussed below).

26. Madison's Notes, in 2 FARRAND'S RECORDS, supra note 12, at 438.

27. The two provisions together comprised Article XI, Section 4. See 2 FARRAND'S RECORDS, supra note 12, at 576.

28. Report of Committee of Style (Sept. 12, 1787), in 2 FARRAND'S RECORDS, supra note 12, at 590, 596, 601; U.S. CONST. art. III, § 2, cl. 3 (Jury Clause).

29. Report of Committee of Style (Sept. 12, 1787), in 2 FARRAND'S RECORDS, supra note 12, at 596.

30. 3 STORY, supra note 18, § 1774, at 653 ("So long, indeed, as this palladium remains sacred and inviolable, the liberties of a free government cannot wholly fall.").

31. Id. § 1773, at 652 (discussing jury right); 1 WILLIAM BLACKSTONE, COMMENTARIES, at *133 (calling habeas privilege a "bulwark" of liberty). The jury trial right was practically sacred to the former colonists. For example, the New Jersey Constitution of 1776 provided "that the inestimable right of trial by jury shall remain confirmed as part of the law of this Colony, without repeal, forever," and further required all state legislators to take an oath promising to oppose any attempt to "annul or repeal" the provision "respecting the trial by jury." N.J. CONSTITUTION OF 1776, arts. XXII, XXIII. The importance of the jury trial right to the Founding generation helps explain why one of the most controversial aspects of the draft Constitution was its failure to provide for a jury right in civil cases. As one Anti-Federalist argued, without the right, federal courts sitting without juries might be "ready to protect the officers of government against the weak and helpless citizen." *Essay of a Democratic Federalist* (1787), reprinted in 3 THE COMPLETE ANTI-FEDERALIST 58, ¶ 3.5.9, at 61 (Herbert J. Storing ed., 1981).

32. See U.S. CONST. art. I, § 9, cl. 3 ("No Bill of Attainder or ex post facto Law shall be passed."). For more on the Attainder Clause, see 3 STORY, supra note 18, § 1338, at 209–211; 1 ST. GEORGE TUCKER, BLACKSTONE'S COMMENTARIES: WITH NOTES OF REFERENCE, TO THE CONSTITUTION AND LAWS, OF THE FEDERAL GOVERNMENT OF THE UNITED STATES; AND OF THE COMMONWEALTH OF VIRGINIA app. at 292–293 (Philadelphia, William Young Birch & Abraham Small 1803) (describing bills of attainder as "legislative declaration of the guilt of the party, without trial" and observing that the practice had largely died out in Britain by the time of Ratification).

33. 3 STORY, supra note 18, § 1334, at 207. The Constitution's prohibition on bills of attainder followed on the heels of the adoption of similar provisions at the state level. See, e.g., VT. CONST., ch. 2, § 17 (1786) ("No person ought, in any case, or in any time, to be declared guilty of treason or felony by the Legislature.") The Constitution also constrained another historical means of circumventing the Habeas Corpus Act, namely parliamentary impeachment, or "legislative criminal justice" as Roscoe Pound once called it. See ROSCOE POUND, CRIMINAL JUSTICE IN AMERICA 96 (1972).

34. James Madison highlighted the importance of the state ratification debates in a speech before Congress in 1796, observing that "the sense of [those who attended the Philadelphia Convention] could never be regarded as the oracular guide in expounding the Constitution. As the instrument came from them it was nothing more than the draft of a plan. . . . If we were to look, therefore, for the meaning of the instrument beyond the face of the instrument, we must look for it . . . in the State Conventions." 5 ANNALS OF CONG. 776 (1796) (remarks of James Madison).

35. Brutus, *To the Citizens of New York, Second Essay Opposing the Constitution*, in 41(44) THE NEW YORK JOURNAL AND WEEKLY REGISTER (Nov. 1, 1787) (New York, Thomas Greenleaf). Many believe that New York's Robert Yates, who had attended the Philadelphia Convention, authored the Brutus essays.

36. 3 ELLIOT'S DEBATES, supra note 1, at 461. Many participants made similar arguments during the state debates. See, e.g., Robert Whitehill, Remarks at the Pennsylvania Ratifying Convention (Nov. 28, 1787), reprinted in 2 DOCUMENTARY HISTORY, supra note 10, at 398–399. Cf. Jack P. Greene, *Ideas and the American Revolution*, 17 AM. Q. 592, 594 (1965) (noting that during this period a "dominant" theory of politics viewed power as "by its very nature a corrupting and aggressive force, and . . . liberty []as its natural victim"). For greater discussion of the ratification debates, consult Eric M. Freedman, *The Suspension Clause in the Ratification Debates*, 44 BUFF. L. REV. 451, 463–465 (1996).

37. See, e.g., William Grayson, Remarks at the Virginia Ratifying Convention (June 16, 1788), reprinted in 10 DOCUMENTARY HISTORY, supra note 10, at 1332; John Smilie, Remarks at the Pennsylvania Ratifying Convention (Nov. 28, 1787), reprinted in 2 DOCUMENTARY HISTORY, supra, at 392; Letter from Thomas B. Wait to George Thatcher, (Jan. 8, 1788), reprinted in 5 DOCUMENTARY HISTORY, supra, at 646.

38. Edmund Randolph, Remarks at the Virginia Ratifying Convention (June 17, 1788), reprinted in 10 DOCUMENTARY HISTORY, supra note 10, at 1348.

39. Thomas Tredwell, Remarks at the New York Ratifying Convention (July 2, 1788), in 2 ELLIOT'S DEBATES, supra note 1, at 399.

40. THE FEDERALIST No. 84 (Alexander Hamilton), at 513.

41. Id. at 511.

42. THE FEDERALIST No. 83 (Alexander Hamilton), 498–499.

43. THE FEDERALIST No. 84 (Alexander Hamilton), at 511 (quoting 1 BLACKSTONE *136).

44. Id. at 509–515.

45. Letter IV from the Federal Farmer to the Republican (Oct. 12, 1787), reprinted in 14 DOCUMENTARY HISTORY, supra note 10, at 42, 45 (positing that "the 9th and 10th Sections in Art. I. in the proposed constitution, are no more nor less, than a partial bill of rights; they establish certain principles as part of the compact upon which the federal legislators and officers can never infringe" and arguing that "this bill of rights ought to be carried farther").

46. Barron v. Baltimore, 32 U.S. (7 Pet.) 243, 250 (1833). Ten years earlier, Justice Bushrod Washington opined that the "right . . . to claim the benefit of the writ of habeas corpus" was among "the particular privileges and immunities of citizens, which are clearly embraced by the general description of privileges deemed to be fundamental" in the Constitution. Corfield v. Coryell, 6 F.Cas. 546 (C.C.E.D. Pa. 1823) (No. 3,230).

47. Letter XVI from the Federal Farmer to the Republican (Jan. 20, 1788) (emphasis added), reprinted in 17 DOCUMENTARY HISTORY, supra note 10, at 348; see also id. at 347–348.

48. Jasper Yeates, Remarks at the Pennsylvania Ratifying Convention (Nov. 30, 1787), reprinted in 2 DOCUMENTARY HISTORY, supra note 10, at 435; see also id. at 437.

49. John Smilie, Remarks at the Pennsylvania Ratifying Convention (Nov. 28, 1787), reprinted in 2 DOCUMENTARY HISTORY, supra note 10, at 392.

50. Luther Martin, *The Genuine Information VIII*, Baltimore Maryland Gazette (Jan. 22, 1788), reprinted in 15 DOCUMENTARY HISTORY, supra note 10, at 434.

51. Justus Dwight Journal (Jan. 26, 1788), reprinted in 7 DOCUMENTARY HISTORY, supra note 10, at 1813.

52. A Native of Virginia, Observations upon the Proposed Plan of Federal Government (Apr. 2, 1788), reprinted in 9 DOCUMENTARY HISTORY, supra note 10, at 691; see also Independent Chronicle (Nov. 1, 1787), reprinted in 4 DOCUMENTARY HISTORY, supra note 10, at 90–91 (discussing "[t]he new ship *Federal Constitution* . . . containing the habeas corpus act").

53. See, e.g., Thomas Hartley, Remarks at the Pennsylvania Ratifying Convention (Nov. 30, 1787), reprinted in 2 DOCUMENTARY HISTORY, supra note 10, at 430 (observing that "it has occasionally been found necessary to make laws for the security of the subject, a necessity that has produced the writ of *habeas corpus*, which affords an easy and immediate redress for the unjust imprisonment of the person, and the trial by jury" and celebrating that "the writ of *habeas corpus* . . . [is] here expressly provided for").

54. See, e.g., James Iredell, Remarks at the North Carolina Ratifying Convention (July 28, 1788), in 4 ELLIOT'S DEBATES, supra note 1, at 145 ("The greatest danger from ambition is in criminal cases. But here they have no option. The trial must be by jury, in the state wherein the offence is committed; and the writ of *habeas corpus* will in the mean time secure the citizen against arbitrary imprisonment. . . ."); Cassius VI, Massachusetts Gazette (Dec. 18, 1787), reprinted in 5 DOCUMENTARY HISTORY, supra note 10, at 481–482 (referencing the Suspension Clause as "expressly providing for securing the right of the subject . . . to . . . be[] tried in his own state"); American Herald (Jan. 14, 1788), reprinted in 5 DOCUMENTARY HISTORY, supra note 10, at 712 (equating suspension with a "poor man perhaps never hav[ing] an opportunity for a trial"); Judge Increase Sumner, Remarks at the Massachusetts Ratifying Convention (Jan. 26, 1788), reprinted in 6 DOCUMENTARY HISTORY, supra note 10, at 1359–1360 (explaining the writ as a vehicle for a judge to review a person's imprisonment along "with the crime on which he was committed" and defending the provision for suspension as necessary to address an enemy who "may lay plans to destroy us, and so artfully as to prevent any evidence against him").

55. John Adams, Defence of the Constitutions of Government of the United States, Letter XXIII: "Recapitulation," reprinted in THE POLITICAL WRITINGS OF JOHN ADAMS 132 (George W. Carey ed., 2000).

56. James Iredell, Remarks at the North Carolina Ratifying Convention (July 29, 1788), in 4 ELLIOT'S DEBATES, supra note 1, at 171.

57. Edmund Randolph, Remarks at the Virginia Ratifying Convention (June 10, 1788), reprinted in 9 DOCUMENTARY HISTORY, supra note 10, at 1099; see also Centinel II, *Philadelphia Freeman's Journal* (Oct. 24, 1787), reprinted in 13 DOCUMENTARY HISTORY, supra, at 466 ("The new plan, it is true, does propose to secure the people the benefit of personal liberty by the *habeas corpus*. . . ."); Brutus, *Second Essay,* supra note 35 ("Does this constitution any where grant the power of suspending the habeas corpus . . . ?"); Remarks of James McHenry Before the Maryland House of Delegates (Nov. 29, 1787), in 3 FARRAND'S RECORDS, supra note 12, app. A at 144, 149 ("Public Safety may require a suspension of the Ha: Corpus in cases of necessity.").

58. George Nicholas, Remarks at the Virginia Ratifying Convention (June 3, 1788), in 3 ELLIOT'S DEBATES, supra note 1, at 19. William Grayson also used the phrase in reference to the English Habeas Corpus Act in the Virginia debates. See William Grayson, Remarks at the Virginia Ratifying Convention (June 21, 1788), in 3 ELLIOT'S DEBATES, supra note 1, at 569 ("The British government does it when the *habeas corpus* is to be suspended—when the *salus populi* is affected.").

59. See, e.g., Dr. John Taylor, Remarks at the Massachusetts Ratifying Convention (Jan. 26, 1788), reprinted in 6 DOCUMENTARY HISTORY, supra note 10, at 1359.

60. Virginia Debates, reprinted in 10 DOCUMENTARY HISTORY, supra note 10, at 1552; see also North Carolina Debates, 4 ELLIOT'S DEBATES, supra note 1, at 243 (suggesting similar language); Rhode Island Debates, 1 ELLIOT'S DEBATES, supra note 1, at 334 (same); New York Declaration of Rights and Form of Ratification, Poughkeepsie Country Journal (July 29, 1788), reprinted in 18 DOCUMENTARY HISTORY, supra note 10, at 298 (suggesting similar wording with additional recognition of the power to suspend). The House of Representatives passed the Virginia language as an amendment and sent it on to the Senate, where it failed. See JOURNAL OF THE SENATE OF THE UNITED STATES OF AMERICA, 1789–1793 (Sept. 8, 1789), at 74.

61. James Wilson, Remarks at the Pennsylvania Ratifying Convention (Dec. 4, 1787), in 2 ELLIOT'S DEBATES, supra note 1, at 455.

62. See, e.g., Dr. John Taylor, Remarks at the Massachusetts Ratifying Convention (Jan. 26, 1788), reprinted in 6 DOCUMENTARY HISTORY, supra note 10, at 1359; Samuel Nasson, Remarks at the Massachusetts Ratifying Convention (Feb. 1, 1788), reprinted in 6 DOCUMENTARY HISTORY, supra note 10, at 1400.

63. See Recommendatory Amendments of the Convention of This State to the New Constitution, Poughkeepsie Country Journal (Aug. 12, 1788), reprinted in 18 DOCUMENTARY HISTORY, supra note 10, at 301–302.

64. See, e.g., Judge Francis Dana, Remarks at the Massachusetts Ratifying Convention (Jan. 26, 1788), reprinted in 6 DOCUMENTARY HISTORY, supra note 10, at 1359.

65. Luther Martin, *The Genuine Information VIII,* Baltimore Maryland Gazette (Jan. 22, 1788), reprinted in 15 DOCUMENTARY HISTORY, supra note 10, at 434.

66. See, e.g., Judge Francis Dana, Remarks at the Massachusetts Ratifying Convention (Jan. 26, 1788), reprinted in 6 DOCUMENTARY HISTORY, supra note 10, at 1359 (opining also that the Massachusetts provision was inferior in this respect because it permitted suspension "as often as the[] legislature judge[s] the most urgent and pressing occasions' call for it"); see also George Nicholas, Remarks at the Virginia Ratifying Convention (June 6, 1788), reprinted in 9 DOCUMENTARY HISTORY, supra, at 1002 ("The suspension of the writ of *habeas corpus* is only to take place in cases of rebellion or invasion. . . . In no other case can [Congress] suspend our laws—and this is a most estimable security.").

67. Remarks of James McHenry Before the Maryland House of Delegates (Nov. 29, 1787), in 3 FARRAND'S RECORDS, supra note 12, app. A at 144, 149.

68. It bears highlighting here that Cushing's remarks were not delivered; they nonetheless reflect the views of a prominent legal figure during this time. William Cushing, Undelivered Speech (c. Feb. 4, 1788), reprinted in 6 DOCUMENTARY HISTORY, supra note 10, at 1436. Cushing also held the view that "where the Jurisdiction of the State Judges is not clearly taken away, that Jurisdiction must remain untouched." Id.; cf. Tarble's Case, 80 U.S. (13 Wall.) 397 (1871) (holding that state judges could not issue writs running against federal officers).

69. Specifically, Tucker wrote that Congress could only suspend "in cases of actual rebellion, or invasion. A suspension under any other circumstances, whatever might be the pretext, would be unconstitutional, and consequently must be disregarded by those whose duty it is to grant the writ." 1 ST. GEORGE TUCKER, BLACKSTONE'S COMMENTARIES: WITH NOTES OF REFERENCE, TO THE CONSTITUTION AND LAWS, OF THE FEDERAL GOVERNMENT OF THE UNITED STATES; AND OF THE COMMONWEALTH OF VIRGINIA app. at 292 (1803).

70. Letter from Thomas Jefferson to James Madison (Dec. 20, 1787), reprinted in 8 DOCUMENTARY HISTORY, supra note 10, at 250; see also Letter from Thomas Jefferson to Alexander Donald (Feb. 7, 1788), reprinted in 8 DOCUMENTARY HISTORY, supra, 353, 354 (expressing a hope that the Constitution would be amended with "a declaration of rights . . . which shall stipulate . . . no suspensions of the habeas corpus"); see also Letter from Thomas Jefferson to William Stephens Smith (Feb. 2, 1788), in 14 DOCUMENTARY HISTORY, supra, at 500.

71. Letter from Thomas Jefferson to James Madison (July 31, 1788), reprinted in 13 THE PAPERS OF THOMAS JEFFERSON 440, 442 (Julian P. Boyd ed., 1956) [hereinafter JEFFERSON PAPERS].

72. Cf. I JAMES KENT, COMMENTARIES ON AMERICAN LAW 638 (7th ed. 1851) ("In addition to the benefit of the writ of habeas corpus, which operates merely to *remove* all unlawful imprisonment, the party aggrieved is entitled to his private action of trespass to recover damages for the false imprisonment. . . .").

73. Letter from Thomas Jefferson to James Madison (July 31, 1788), reprinted in 13 JEFFERSON PAPERS, supra note 71, at 440, 442.

74. Letter from James Madison to Thomas Jefferson (Oct. 17, 1788), in 5 THE WRITINGS OF JAMES MADISON 272–274 (Gaillard Hunt ed., 1904).

75. On this point, after Madison forwarded a copy of his original draft bill of rights (including twelve amendments) to Jefferson, the latter responded: "I like it as far as it goes; but I should have been for going further." Specifically, Jefferson suggested the following additional amendment:

> No person shall be held in confinement more than ___ days after he shall have demanded and been refused a writ of habeas corpus by the judge appointed by law, nor more than ___days after such a writ shall have been served on the person holding him in confinement, and no order given on due examination for his remandment or discharge, nor more than ___ hours in any place of greater distance than ___ miles from the usual residence of some judge authorized to issue the writ of habeas corpus; nor shall the writ be suspended for any term exceeding one year, nor in any place more than ___ miles distant from the station or encampment of enemies or insurgents.

Letter from Thomas Jefferson to James Madison (Aug. 28, 1789), in 5 WORKS OF THOMAS JEFFERSON 487, 493 (Paul Ford ed. 1904).

76. Gerald L. Neuman, *The Habeas Corpus Suspension Clause after* INS v. St. Cyr, 33 COLUM. HUM. RTS. L. REV. 555, 600 (2002).

77. Saikrishna Bangalore Prakash, *The Sweeping Domestic War Powers of Congress*, 113 MICH. L. REV. 1337, 1341 (2015).

78. Examples of scholarship advancing this reading include WILLIAM F. DUKER, A CONSTITUTIONAL HISTORY OF HABEAS CORPUS 126–156 (1980); and Akhil Reed Amar, *Of Sovereignty and Federalism*, 96 YALE L.J. 1425, 1509 & n.329 (1987).

79. Richard H. Fallon, Jr. & Daniel J. Meltzer, *New Law, Non-retroactivity, and Constitutional Remedies*, 104 HARV. L. REV. 1731, 1779 (1991).

80. James Wilson, Remarks at the Pennsylvania Ratifying Convention (Dec. 4, 1787), in 2 ELLIOT'S DEBATES, supra note 1, at 455.

81. THE FEDERALIST No. 83 (Alexander Hamilton), at 499.

82. Ex parte Bollman, 8 U.S. (4 Cranch) 75, 94 (1807).

83. Id. at 95 (emphasis added).

84. See Boumediene v. Bush, 553 U.S. 723 (2008).

85. George Nicholas, Remarks at the Virginia Ratifying Convention (June 3, 1788), in 3 ELLIOT'S DEBATES, supra note 1, at 19.

86. James Wilson, Lectures on Law, in 2 COLLECTED WORKS OF JAMES WILSON 901–902 (Kermit L. Hall & Mark David Hall eds., 2007).

87. 3 STORY, supra note 18, § 1335, at 207, 208.

88. 1 STORY, supra note 18, § 453, at 438. In this passage, Justice Story highlights the relevance of the English backdrop to interpreting what many would call constitutional "terms of art," or what James Madison called "the technical phrases." See JAMES MADISON, REPORT ON THE RESOLUTIONS, in 6 THE WRITINGS OF JAMES MADISON 341, 375–376 (Gaillard Hunt ed., 1906)

(observing that "particular parts of the common law may have a sanction from the Constitution, so far as they are necessarily comprehended in the technical phrases" of the document).

89. Marbury v. Madison, 5 U.S. (1 Cranch) 137, 176 (1803).

CHAPTER 6

1. Ex parte Watkins, 28 U.S. (3 Pet.) 193, 202 (1830) (Marshall, C.J.).

2. THE FEDERALIST NO. 37 (James Madison), at 225 (Clinton Rossiter ed., 2003) ("All new laws, though penned with the greatest technical skill, and passed on the fullest and most mature deliberation, are considered as more or less obscure and equivocal, until their meaning be liquidated and ascertained by a series of particular discussions and adjudications.").

3. Act of April 30, 1790, ch. 9, §§ 1–2, 1 Stat. 112.

4. See 2 JAMES WILSON, *Of Crimes, Immediately against the Community*, in THE WORKS OF JAMES WILSON 663, 665–666 (Robert Green McCloskey ed., 1967) ("In the monarchy of Great Britain, protection and allegiance are universally acknowledged to be rights and duties reciprocal."); id. at 666–668; see also WILLIAM RAWLE, A VIEW OF THE CONSTITUTION OF THE UNITED STATES OF AMERICA 93 (2d ed., Philadelphia, Philip H. Nicklin 1829) (noting "the reciprocal compact of protection and allegiance").

5. Pennsylvania did not suspend the privilege either. Instead, the legislature authorized the governor "to engage . . . the militia" to "restor[e] peace and order." An Act to Provide for Suppressing an Insurrection in the Western Counties of this Commonwealth, ch. 1779, § 1 (1794), in 15 THE STATUTES AT LARGE OF PENNSYLVANIA FROM 1682 TO 1801, at 195, 195–196 (James T. Mitchell & Henry Flanders eds., 1911).

6. Proclamation of President George Washington, Cessation of Violence and Obstruction of Justice in Protest of Liquor Laws in Pennsylvania (Aug. 7, 1794), published in *Claypoole's Daily Advertiser* (Aug. 11, 1794). Washington called forth the militia only after seeking certification from a member of the Supreme Court that such conditions existed, as was required by the original calling-forth statute. Only after Justice James Wilson agreed with Washington's assessment of the situation did Washington proceed. See id.

7. ROBERT W. COAKLEY, THE ROLE OF FEDERAL MILITARY FORCES IN DOMESTIC DISORDERS, 1789–1878, at 55 (1988); see also WILLIAM HOGELAND, THE WHISKEY REBELLION 215 (2006).

8. COAKLEY, supra note 7 at 52 (recounting how Washington rejected the idea that the army would "bring offenders to a military Tribunal" but instead promised that they would "merely aid the civil magistrates" (quoting 4 THE DIARIES OF GEORGE WASHINGTON, 1748–1799, at 216 (John C. Fitzpatrick ed., 1925)) (internal quotation mark omitted).

9. These orders were set forth in Letter from Alexander Hamilton to Henry Lee (Oct. 20, 1794), in 1 AMERICAN STATE PAPERS: DOCUMENTS, LEGISLATIVE AND EXECUTIVE, OF THE CONGRESS OF THE UNITED STATES 112, 112 (Walter Lowrie & Walter S. Franklin eds., Washington, D.C., Gales & Seaton 1834).

10. COAKLEY, supra note 7, at 50. Ultimately, the military arrested only a handful of insurgents, thirty-five of whom were charged with "levying war against the United States." BRIAN F. CARSO, JR., "WHOM CAN WE TRUST NOW?" 92 (2006) (internal quotation marks omitted). Eventually, only two were convicted of treason. See CARSO, supra, at 92. President Washington later pardoned them. See COAKLEY, supra, at 63.

11. WILLIAM FINDLEY, HISTORY OF THE INSURRECTION, IN THE FOUR WESTERN COUNTIES OF PENNSYLVANIA: IN THE YEAR M.DCC.XCIV 179 (Philadelphia, Samuel Harrison Smith 1796). Once the civil justice system took over, however, there were enormous pressures levied on judges not to release suspected insurgents even in cases of limited evidence. See HOGELAND, supra note 7, at 223. The Supreme Court reviewed one such commitment on a petition for a writ of habeas corpus in *United States v. Hamilton*, 3 U.S. (3 Dall.) 17 (1795), and admitted to bail one of the insurgents charged with High Treason. As for John Fries and his lieutenants, the government successfully prosecuted them for treason. CARSO, supra note 10, at 94.

12. See Letter from Secretary of the Navy Jones to Commodore Isaac Chauncey (July 14, 1813), reprinted in 2 THE NAVAL WAR OF 1812: A DOCUMENTARY HISTORY 500, 501 (William S. Dudley ed., 1992) (observing that "[t]he moment is critical" in the war).

13. In re Stacy, 10 Johns. 328, 333–334 (N.Y. Sup. Ct. 1813) ("A military commander is here assuming criminal jurisdiction over a private citizen, is holding him in the closest confinement, and contemning the civil authority of the state."). For more on this period, see Ingrid Brunk Wuerth, *The President's Power to Detain "Enemy Combatants": Modern Lessons from Mr. Madison's Forgotten War*, 98 NW. U. L. REV. 1567 (2004).

14. See Smith v. Shaw, 12 Johns. 257, 265 (N.Y. Sup. Ct. 1815) (concluding that an American citizen "might be amenable to the civil authority for treason; but could not be punished, under martial law, as a spy"). The court upheld a generous award of damages on the basis that "[if] the defendant was justifiable in doing what he did, every citizen of the *United States* would, in time of war, be equally exposed to a like exercise of military power and authority." Id. at 266. Another case from this period, in which the military held a citizen as a prisoner of war and then moved the prisoner to Vermont to avoid habeas proceedings in New Hampshire, resulted in criminal contempt proceedings being brought against a military official. For details, see Eric M. Freedman, *Habeas Corpus in Three Dimensions: Dimension II: Habeas Corpus as a Legal Remedy*, 8 NE. U. L.J. 1, 7–23 (2016).

15. Opinion of the President (Oct. 20, 1812), in Case of Clark the Spy (1812), reprinted in Mil. Monitor & Am. Reg. (N.Y.), Feb. 1, 1813, at 121.

16. Articles of War of 1806, ch. 20, § 2, 2 Stat. 359, 371. Congress modified this provision during the Civil War to permit greater flexibility in the trial of Rebel spies. See Act of Feb. 13, 1862, 12 Stat. 339–340 (1862); Act of Mar. 3, 1863, 12 Stat. 731, 737 (1863).

17. Letter from Alexander James Dallas to Andrew Jackson (July 1, 1815), published in the National Intelligencer (Nov. 3, 1828); Matthew Warshauer, Andrew Jackson and the Politics of Martial Law 35–39 (2006) (detailing these events).

18. 16 Annals of Cong. 39 (1807) (message from President Thomas Jefferson to the Senate and House of Representatives of the United States dated January 22, 1807); see also Carso, supra note 10, at 96–100 (describing background of Burr's Conspiracy). For more on the life of Aaron Burr, see generally Herbert S. Parmet & Marie B. Hecht, Aaron Burr (1967).

19. Letter from Thomas Jefferson to John Langdon (Dec. 22, 1806), in 19 The Writings of Thomas Jefferson 157, 157 (Andrew A. Lipscomb & Albert Ellery Bergh eds., 1903). To Congress, Jefferson had posited that Burr's objects included "the severance of the Union of these States by the Alleghany mountains" and "an attack on Mexico." 16 Annals of Cong. 41 (1807).

20. See R. Kent Newmyer, The Treason Trial of Aaron Burr 36 (2012) (describing how "[t]he man who had been Burr's partner now became his chief accuser and the government's chief witness"); Peter Charles Hoffer, The Treason Trials of Aaron Burr 38 (2008) (describing Wilkinson's role as a secret agent for Spain and his receipt of "regular payments from Spain for reporting on American aims and movements").

21. See 3 Albert J. Beveridge, The Life of John Marshall 332–333 (1919); Carso, supra note 10, at 103.

22. See United States v. Bollman, 24 F. Cas. 1189, 1190 (C.C.D.C. 1807) (No. 14,622) (reporting that the petition for habeas corpus filed in the D.C. Circuit alleged that Bollman and Swartwout were "confined in the city of Washington, at the marine barracks, under a military guard"); William Plumer's Memorandum of Proceedings in the United States Senate, 1803–1807, at 596 (Everett Somerville Brown ed., 1923) [hereinafter Plumer's Memorandum of Proceedings] (reporting that the prisoners were "guarded, night & day, by an officer & 15 soldiers of the Marine Corps").

23. Plumer's Memorandum of Proceedings, supra note 22, at 616 (internal quotation marks omitted) (entry of February 20, 1807). The chief justice of Maryland referenced his decision to discharge both in habeas corpus proceedings in a subsequent published opinion. See *In re* Roberts, 2 Am. L. J. 192, 195–196 (John E. Hall ed., 1809) (Nicholson, C.J.) (noting that he wrote the president over the matter explaining that they could not be held in military custody without charges).

24. Letter from President Thomas Jefferson to Governor W.C.C. Claiborne (Feb. 3, 1807), in 11 THE WRITINGS OF THOMAS JEFFERSON, supra note 19, at 150, 151 (Andrew A. Lipscomb & Albert Ellery Bergh eds., 1905). Jefferson continued:

> The Feds, and the little band of Quids, in opposition, will try to make something of the infringement of liberty by the military arrest and deportation of citizens, but if it does not go beyond such offenders as Swartwout, Bollman, Burr, [and two others], they will be supported by the public approbation.

Id. In his retirement, Jefferson reflected on these actions (and the Louisiana Purchase) with the same emphasis on "public preservation":

> A strict observance of the written laws is doubtless *one* of the high duties of a good citizen, but it is not *the highest*. The laws of necessity, of self-preservation, of saving our country when in danger, are of higher obligation. To lose our country by a scrupulous adherence to written law, would be to lose the law itself, with life, liberty, property and all those who are enjoying them with us; thus absurdly sacrificing the end to the means.

Letter from Thomas Jefferson to John B. Colvin (Sept. 20, 1810), in 11 THE WORKS OF THOMAS JEFFERSON 146 (Paul Leicester Ford ed., 1905).

25. Letter from President Thomas Jefferson to General James Wilkinson (Feb. 3, 1807), in 11 THE WRITINGS OF THOMAS JEFFERSON, supra note 19, at 147, 149. Wilkinson also apparently recognized the dubious legality of his actions, telling the president that he would "look to our country for protection" if he was later sued by Bollman and Swartwout for damages for false imprisonment. 3 BEVERIDGE, supra note 21, at 334 (quoting Letter from General James Wilkinson to President Thomas Jefferson (Dec. 14, 1806), in NAT'L INTELLIGENCER (D.C.), Jan. 23, 1807) (internal quotation marks omitted). Presumably, Wilkinson meant that he would seek indemnification from the government for any damages levied against him, a common practice during this period. See James E. Pfander & Jonathan L. Hunt, *Public Wrongs and Private Bills: Indemnification and Government Accountability in the Early Republic*, 85 N.Y.U. L. REV. 1862, 1866 (2010).

26. Letter from President Thomas Jefferson to General James Wilkinson (Feb. 3, 1807), supra note 25, at 149. As for Burr, a month earlier, Senator William Plumer wrote that "[t]he president of the United States, a day or two since, informed me that he knew of no evidence sufficient to convict [Burr] of either high crimes or misdemeanors." 3 BEVERIDGE, supra note 21, at 338 n.2 (quoting Letter from William Plumer to Jeremiah Mason (Jan. 4, 1807)) (internal quotation mark omitted) (citing additional Plumer letters). On January 22, however, Jefferson told Congress that Burr's "guilt is placed beyond question." 16 ANNALS OF CONG. 40 (1807).

27. 16 ANNALS OF CONG. 43 (1807); id. at 39–41; but see id. at 43 (stating that the conspirators will be turned over for the "course of trial").

28. See S. JOURNAL, 9th Cong., 2d Sess. 130–131 (1807); PLUMER'S MEMORANDUM OF PROCEEDINGS, supra note 22, at 585.

29. See, e.g., 3 BEVERIDGE, supra note 21, at 346–347; WILLIAM F. DUKER, A CONSTITUTIONAL HISTORY OF HABEAS CORPUS 135 (1980); 1 CHARLES WARREN, THE SUPREME COURT IN UNITED STATES HISTORY 302 (1922); but see LEONARD W. LEVY, JEFFERSON & CIVIL LIBERTIES: THE DARKER SIDE 205 n.45 (1963) (deeming it "most unlikely . . . that the bill originated in the White House"). One account suggests that the first request for a suspension during this episode came from Navy Secretary Smith two months earlier, who asked for it "in a panic." IRVING BRANT, JAMES MADISON: SECRETARY OF STATE, 1800–1809, at 349 (1953).

30. See LEVY, supra note 29, at 74.

31. Thomas Jefferson, First Inaugural Address (Mar. 4, 1801), in 33 THE PAPERS OF THOMAS JEFFERSON 148–152 (Barbara B. Oberg ed., 2006); see also Letter from Thomas Jefferson to Albert Gallatin (Nov. 9, 1803), in 10 THE WORKS OF THOMAS JEFFERSON 46 (Paul Leicester Ford ed., 1905) (calling "trial by jury . . . , the habeas corpus, the freedom of the press, [and] freedom of religion" the "first principles of liberty").

32. These debates, although not those of the very First Congress, constituted the first major debates regarding suspension at a federal level and came only twenty years after the Convention. It is therefore fair to say that they "afford us precious insight into how the constitution was understood by those charged with making it a reality." David P. Currie, *The Constitution in Congress: The First Congress and the Structure of Government, 1789–91*, 2 U. CHI. L. ROUNDTABLE 161, 161 (1995).

33. See S. JOURNAL, 9th Cong., 2d Sess. 130–131 (1807); 1 MEMOIRS OF JOHN QUINCY ADAMS 445–446 (Charles Francis Adams ed., Philadelphia, J.B. Lippincott 1874); PLUMER'S MEMORANDUM OF PROCEEDINGS, supra note 22, at 585; LEVY, supra note 29, at 85–86. The main sources describing the debates are John Quincy Adams's diaries and Plumer's summaries of the proceedings. For more on the context of the debates, see DAVID P. CURRIE, THE CONSTITUTION IN CONGRESS: THE JEFFERSONIANS, 1801–1829, at 131–133 (2001).

34. PLUMER'S MEMORANDUM OF PROCEEDINGS, supra note 22, at 585, 586, 588.

35. Id. at 587, 589. The quoted text retains the original spelling.

36. Specifically, Plumer lamented that the House's subsequent failure to pass the bill meant that General Wilkinson would "probably fall a victim" and be "harrassed [*sic*] by suits" brought "by those whom he has arrested." Id. at 592. Soon thereafter, Plumer regretted his support for the bill. See id. at 617–619 (Feb 21, 1807) ("I rejoice the bill to suspend the writ of *habeas corpus* did not pass into a law. I hope that I shall never again consent to . . . passing an important law in haste.").

37. 16 ANNALS OF CONG. 402 (1807) (replicating bill). John Quincy Adams wrote that only Senator James Bayard voted against the bill. 1 MEMOIRS OF JOHN QUINCY ADAMS, supra note 33, at 445–446. Plumer reported that "3 or 4" senators voted against it. PLUMER'S MEMORANDUM OF PROCEEDINGS, supra note 22, at 590.

38. See 16 ANNALS OF CONG. 402–425 (1807) (reporting on the debates). The *Annals* were not a verbatim transcript but were derived from newspaper reports. This

book quotes and relies upon them here as the best account available of this important debate.

39. Id. at 419 (statement of Rep. John Randolph).

40. Id. at 404, 405 (1807) (statement of Rep. William Burwell) (emphasis added). Burwell read Jefferson's statement to suggest that "there was sufficient evidence to authorize their commitment" in part because "[s]everal months would elapse before their final trial, which would give time to collect evidence." Id.

41. Id. at 405.

42. 1 WILLIAM BLACKSTONE, COMMENTARIES, at *132 ("In like manner this experiment ought only to be tried in cases of extreme emergency; and in these the nation parts with its liberty for a while, in order to preserve it for ever.").

43. 16 ANNALS OF CONG. 406–408 (1807) (statements of Rep. James Elliot).

44. Id. at 411 (statement of Rep. John Eppes).

45. 16 ANNALS OF CONG. 409, 411 (statement of Rep. John Eppes).

46. Id. at 411–413 (statement of Rep. Joseph Varnum).

47. Id. at 416 (statement of Rep. Barnabas Bidwell) ("Want of legal evidence to show, by oath or affirmation, probably cause for detention, would be a ground of discharge . . . by virtue of a habeas corpus."). For his part, Bidwell was satisfied as to the existence of a rebellion. See id. at 415 ("To constitute a rebellion, in the sense of the Constitution, . . . it [is not] necessary that a battle should have been fought, or even a single gun fired. If troopers were enlisted, assembled, organized, and armed, for the purpose of effecting a treasonable object, it amounted to actual rebellion."). He questioned whether public safety nonetheless supported the measure, arguing as well that such a determination involved "a matter of opinion, rather than of fact." Id.

48. Id. at 412–413 (statement of Rep. Joseph Varnum).

49. Id. at 413–414 (statement of Rep. Roger Nelson).

50. Id. at 422 (statements of Rep. John Smilie).

51. Id. at 422–423. Similarly, William Burwell feared that "under the sanction" of such a law the executive could "harass and destroy the best men of the country." Id. at 406 (statement of Rep. William Burwell).

52. Id. at 422 (statements of Rep. John Smilie).

53. Id. at 419 (statement of Rep. John Randolph); see also id. at 406–409 (remarks of James Elliot).

54. Id. at 424 (statement of Rep. Samuel W. Dana).

55. Id. at 424.

56. See United States v. Bollman, 24 F. Cas. 1189, 1190 (C.C.D.C. 1807) (No. 14,622) (noting that the original petition was filed on January 24); see also Ex parte Bollman, 8 U.S. (4 Cranch) 75, 75 (1807) (noting that separate counsel later renewed the motion on behalf of Bollman).

57. Bollman, 24 F. Cas. at 1190; see id. at 1189.

58. Id. at 1190. The order for Bollman and Swartwout's commitment is replicated in the Supreme Court's opinion. See Bollman, 8 U.S. (4 Cranch) at 75–76.

59. Bollman, 24 F. Cas. at 1192 (Cranch, C.J., dissenting); see id. ("No political motives, no reasons of state, can justify a disregard of [the court's] solemn [duty]."). In a letter to his father, Chief Judge Cranch wrote of his dissent:

> I had no doubt whatever that the Constitution did not justify a commitment upon such evidence; and although I felt that the public interest might be benefitted by committing those gentlemen for trial, yet I could not consent to sacrifice the most important constitutional provision in favor of individual liberty, to reasons of State.

1 WARREN, supra note 29, at 304 (quoting letter).

60. Bollman, 24 F. Cas. at 1193 (Cranch, C.J., dissenting).

61. Ex parte Burford, 7 U.S. (3 Cranch) 448, 452 (1806).

62. Bollman, 8 U.S. (4 Cranch) at 95, 101.

63. See id. at 135, 137. The Court's review of the evidence in *Bollman* and order of discharge followed on the example set in the Whiskey Rebellion case of *United States v. Hamilton*, 3 U.S. (3 Dall.) 17 (1795), in which the Court bailed a prisoner detained on charges of high treason.

64. Martin later argued the famous case of *McCulloch v. Maryland*, 17 U.S. (4 Wheat.) 316 (1819), as attorney general of Maryland and eventually died at the home of Aaron Burr.

65. Former senator Wilson Cary Nicholas also withdrew from grand jury service in the matter. John Randolph reported the bill of indictment out of the grand jury against Burr and other alleged conspirators. See 1 THE TRIAL OF COL. AARON BURR, ON AN INDICTMENT FOR TREASON 12 (T. Carpenter ed., 1807); SAMUEL L. KNAPP, 4 THE LIFE OF AARON BURR 146–148 (1835). The grand jury came very close to indicting one of the government's key witnesses against Burr, General Wilkinson, for misprision of treason, and John Randolph was among those who voted in favor of doing so. See R. KENT NEWMYER, THE TREASON TRIAL OF AARON BURR: LAW, POLITICS, AND THE CHARACTER WARS OF THE NEW NATION 104–106 & n.84 (2012).

66. See United States v. Burr, 25 F. Cas. 55, 201 (C.C.D. Va. 1807) (No. 14,693). For general details of the Burr trial, see 1 WARREN, supra note 29, at 308–315.

67. For a highly critical assessment, see LEVY, supra note 29, at 70–92; see also Letter from John Adams to Benjamin Rush (Feb. 2, 1807), in THE SPUR OF FAME: DIALOGUES OF JOHN ADAMS AND BENJAMIN RUSH, 1805–1813, at 75–77 (The Huntington Library, John A. Schutz & Douglass Adair eds., 1966) ("[I]f [Burr's] guilt is as clear as the noonday sun, the first magistrate ought not to have pronounced it so before a jury had tried him.").

68. See, e.g., 16 ANNALS OF CONG. 410 (1807) (statement of Rep. John Eppes) ("The Constitution . . . vested this power in Congress.").

69. Similar views may be gleaned from a review of the House debate that followed some weeks later on a bill that would have provided for penalties where the writ was not honored. The comments consistently suggest that everyone in the

House took for granted that the military arrests during this period were illegal. See, e.g., 16 ANNALS OF CONG. 506, 520 (1807) (statement of Rep. James Broom); id. at 510 (statement of Rep. William Burwell); id. at 513 (statement of Rep. John Eppes). Eppes, for example, stated that President Jefferson "ought most certainly to have delivered over these persons to the civil authority." Id. at 515 (statement of Rep. John Eppes); see also id. at 579 ("In this country, no man can be legally committed, or detained in custody, but by the civil authority.").

70. 1 WARREN, supra note 29, at 304. As this passage indicates, there was also strong opposition to the fact that the prisoners had been moved from where the alleged conspiracy took place, a fact that the Supreme Court also deemed problematic in *Bollman*. See 8 U.S. (4 Cranch) at 111.

71. Ex parte Watkins, 28 U.S. (3 Pet.) 193, 201 (1830).

72. Watkins, 28 U.S. (3 Pet.) at 201–202 (emphasis added); see also Judiciary Act of 1789, ch. 20, § 14, I Stat. 73, 81–82 (granting federal judges power to grant writs of habeas corpus). Justice Story described the origins of the Suspension Clause similarly while riding circuit in 1813: "What is the writ of habeas corpus? What is the privilege which it grants? The common law, and that alone, furnishes the true answer. The existence . . . of the common law is not only supposed by the constitution, but is appealed to for the construction and interpretation of its powers." United States v. Coolidge, 25 F. Cas. 619, 619 (C.C.D. Mass. 1813) (No. 14,857), rev'd on other grounds, 14 U.S. (1 Wheat.) 415, 416–417 (1816).

73. Watkins, 28 U.S. (3 Pet.) at 201–202. For discussion of Marshall's earlier interpretation of Section 14 in Ex parte Bollman, 8 U.S. (4 Cranch) 75 (1807), see Chapter 5.

74. Ex parte Yerger, 75 U.S. (8 Wall.) 85, 95 (1868).

75. Letter from Abraham Lincoln to Erastus Corning and Others (June 12, 1863), in 6 THE COLLECTED WORKS OF ABRAHAM LINCOLN 260, 264 (Roy P. Basler et al. eds., 1953).

CHAPTER 7

1. Ex parte Merryman, 17 F. Cas. 144, 151 (C.C.D. Md. 1861) (No. 9487). I borrow the phrase "the Great Suspender" from Saikrishna Bangalore Prakash, *The Great Suspender's Unconstitutional Suspension of the Great Writ*, 3 ALB. GOV'T L. REV. 575 (2010).

2. Abraham Lincoln, First Inaugural Address (Mar. 4, 1861), in ABRAHAM LINCOLN: SPEECHES AND WRITINGS, 1859–1865, at 215, 218 (Don E. Fehrenbacher ed., 1989) (arguing that secession was illegal and that "the Union [was] unbroken").

3. See, e.g., Letter from Abraham Lincoln to Winfield Scott (Apr. 25, 1861), in 4 THE COLLECTED WORKS OF ABRAHAM LINCOLN 344, 344 (Roy P. Basler et al. eds., 1953) [hereinafter COLLECTED WORKS] (authorizing suspension of the privilege in Maryland in situations of the "extremest necessity"); Letter from Abraham

Lincoln to Winfield Scott (Apr. 27, 1861), in 4 COLLECTED WORKS, supra, at 347, 347 (authorizing suspension of the privilege in the face of "resistance" encountered between Philadelphia and Washington). This order was not issued publicly and so many were entirely unaware of it until the arrest of John Merryman that followed. See MARK E. NEELY, JR., THE FATE OF LIBERTY: ABRAHAM LINCOLN AND CIVIL LIBERTIES 9 (1991). In the months following this order, the military arrested the Baltimore police chief and four commissioners, members of the Maryland legislature, and the mayor of Baltimore, among others. See id. at 14–18; JAMES M. MCPHERSON, BATTLE CRY OF FREEDOM: THE CIVIL WAR ERA 289 (1998).

4. Ex parte Merryman, 17 F. Cas. 144 (C.C.D. Md. 1861) (No. 9487).
5. Taney's unwillingness to grant Cadwalader the postponement has earned him many critics, including the late chief justice William Rehnquist. See WILLIAM H. REHNQUIST, ALL THE LAWS BUT ONE: CIVIL LIBERTIES IN WARTIME 25, 40–41 (1998). For a suggestion that Cadwalader may have exceeded his authority and additional criticism of Taney's choice not to avoid a constitutional showdown with the President, see David Farnham, *"A High and Delicate Trust": How Ignorance and Indignation Combined to Expand President Lincoln's Claimed Power to Suspend* Habeas Corpus *in the Case of John Merryman*, 24 J. S. LEGAL HIST. 109 (2016).
6. Some estimates put the crowd in and outside the courtroom at two thousand people. See BRIAN MCGINTY, THE BODY OF JOHN MERRYMAN: ABRAHAM LINCOLN AND THE SUSPENSION OF HABEAS CORPUS 28 (2011). Chief Justice Taney reportedly announced the following summary of his decision:
   First—The President, under the Constitution and laws of the United States cannot suspend the privilege of the writ of habeas corpus, nor authorize any military officer to do so. Second—A military officer has no right to arrest and detain a person, nor subject him to the rules and articles of war for an offence against the laws of the United States, except in aid of the judicial authority, and subject to its control, and if the party is arrested by the military, it is the duty of the officer to deliver him over immediately to the civil authority, to be dealt with according to law.

   Affairs in Baltimore.; Habeas Corpus Cask—Return of the Sheriff—Action of Chief Justice Taney—President's Instructions to Gen. Cadwallader, Suspending the Writ, etc., NEW YORK TIMES, May 29, 1861.
7. Merryman, 17 F. Cas. at 148.
8. Id. at 148, 150–151.
9. Id. at 150, 151 (quoting 1 WILLIAM BLACKSTONE, COMMENTARIES, at *136).
10. Id. at 150.
11. For more details on *Merryman*, see MCGINTY, supra note 6; JONATHAN W. WHITE, ABRAHAM LINCOLN AND TREASON IN THE CIVIL WAR: THE TRIALS OF JOHN MERRYMAN 46–52, 59–60 (2011) (detailing the stalled treason prosecution).

Other decisions from the war were consistent with *Merryman*. See, e.g., In re Kemp, 16 Wis. 384 (1863).

12. See, e.g., Proclamation No. 7, 12 Stat. 1260 (May 10, 1861) (suspending the privilege in Florida); Letter from Abraham Lincoln to Winfield Scott, U.S. Commanding General (June 20, 1861), in 4 COLLECTED WORKS, supra note 3, at 414 (authorizing suspension of the privilege with respect to Major-General William Henry Chase Whiting of the Engineer Corps of the Army, whom Lincoln "alleged to be guilty of treasonable practices"); Letter from Abraham Lincoln to Winfield Scott, U.S. Commanding General (July 2, 1861), in 4 COLLECTED WORKS, supra, at 419 (authorizing suspension of the privilege between Washington and New York where resistance was encountered); Letter from Abraham Lincoln to Winfield Scott, U.S. Lieutenant General (Oct. 14, 1861), in 4 COLLECTED WORKS, supra, at 554 (suspending the privilege as far north as Maine); Letter from Abraham Lincoln to Henry W. Halleck, U.S. Major General (Dec. 2, 1861), in 5 COLLECTED WORKS, supra, at 35 (authorizing suspension of the privilege in Missouri); Executive Order (Aug. 8, 1862), in 7 A COMPILATION OF THE MESSAGES AND PAPERS OF THE PRESIDENTS 3322 (James D. Richardson ed., New York, Bureau of National Literature, Inc. 1897) [hereinafter MESSAGES AND PAPERS] (suspending the privilege with respect to all draft evaders and "all persons arrested for disloyal practices"); Proclamation No. 1, 13 Stat. 730 (Sept. 24, 1862) (providing that "the writ of habeas corpus is suspended in respect to all persons arrested, or who are now or hereafter during the rebellion shall be, imprisoned in any fort, camp, arsenal, military prison, or other place of confinement by any military authority or by the sentence of any court-martial or military commission").

13. See Abraham Lincoln, Message to Congress in Special Session (July 4, 1861), in 4 COLLECTED WORKS, supra note 3, at 421, 430. The original version of Lincoln's statement here read: "I violated no law." Id. at 430 n.53.

14. Bates's defense of Lincoln's position argued primarily that the president must enjoy the power to suspend as part of his obligation to "preserve, protect, and defend the Constitution" as commander in chief. See Letter from the Attorney General to the Speaker of the House of Representatives (July 5, 1861), in H.R. EXEC. DOC. NO. 37-5, at 6 (1st Sess. 1861). Bates also defended the president's right to ignore a writ once issued when the president has proclaimed a suspension, arguing "the whole subject-matter is political and not judicial" in nature. Id. at 8. Finally, Bates pointed to impeachment as the means by which executive abuses of the power may be checked. See id. at 7–8, 12.

15. *The Secession Rebellion: Special Dispatch from Washington*, N.Y. TIMES, May 28, 1861 ("The intention of Judge TANEY, in issuing a writ of habeas corpus for the prisoner retained by Gen. CADWALLADER at Baltimore, is to bring on a collision between the Judicial and the Military Departments of the Government, and if possible to throw the weight of the judiciary against the United States and in favor of the rebels."); *Martial Law—Habeas Corpus*, N.Y. DAILY TRIBUNE,

May 30, 1861; *Gen. Cadwallader and Judge Taney*, CHI. TRIBUNE, June 1, 1861 (opinion that Taney had "take[n] sides with traitors who are exerting every energy to subvert [the Constitution]"); *Taney vs. Taney*, N.Y. WORLD, June 7, 1861 (calling the opinion "a gratuitous manifestation of hostility to the government and sympathy with the rebels"); *Civil and Martial Law at Baltimore*, N.Y. TIMES, May 30, 1861 (opining that Taney will "go down through history as the Judge who draggled his official robes in the pollutions of treason").

16. *The Habeas Corpus Case*, BALT. AM. & COMMERCIAL ADVERTISER, June 4, 1861; see also *Opinion of Chief Justice Taney*, BALT. SUN, June 4, 1861 ("Long after this terrible conflict shall have been brought to an end . . . , the grand, true, cogent, restless influence of this document . . . will live, at once a vindication of the principles of the republic, and of the fundamental rights of the people. . . ."); *Habeas Corpus*, N.Y. WEEKLY J. COMM., June 6, 1861 ("The writ was originally and always intended as a defence of the subject against the tyranny of the government; and nowhere is such defence more needed than under a government like our own. . . .").

17. See HORACE BINNEY, THE PRIVILEGE OF THE WRIT OF HABEAS CORPUS UNDER THE CONSTITUTION (Philadelphia, C. Sherman & Son, 2d ed. 1862) [hereinafter BINNEY, FIRST PART]; HORACE BINNEY, SECOND PART: THE PRIVILEGE OF THE WRIT OF HABEAS CORPUS UNDER THE CONSTITUTION (Philadelphia, John Campbell 1862). Binney's argument may be described as relying on an expansive notion of executive power coupled with the assertion that analogies to English law were flawed. See BINNEY, FIRST PART, supra, at 32 (positing that "the clause is entirely un-English . . . it is truly American"). A leading opposition pamphlet was THE SUSPENDING POWER AND THE WRIT OF HABEAS CORPUS (Philadelphia, John Campbell 1862) (originally published anonymously and now considered the work of James F. Johnston). For a list of pamphlets published during this period, consult Sydney G. Fisher, *The Suspension of Habeas Corpus During the War of the Rebellion*, 3 POL. SCI. Q. 454, 485–488 (1888).

18. See Ex parte Bollman, 8 U.S. (4 Cranch) 75, 101 (1807) (Marshall, C.J.) ("If at any time the public safety should require the suspension of the powers vested by [the Judiciary Act] in the courts of the United States, it is for the legislature to say so."); 3 JOSEPH STORY, COMMENTARIES ON THE CONSTITUTION OF THE UNITED STATES § 1336, at 208–209 (1833) ("[T]he power is given to congress to suspend the writ of habeas corpus in cases of rebellion or invasion.").

19. As discussed in Chapter 5, moreover, Charles Pinckney's proposed language for the Suspension Clause that triggered substantive debate made specific reference to the legislature, providing that "[t]he privileges and benefit of the Writ of Habeas corpus . . . shall not be suspended by the Legislature except upon the most urgent and pressing occasions. . . ." James Madison, Notes on the Constitutional Convention (Aug. 20, 1787), in 2 THE RECORDS OF THE FEDERAL CONVENTION OF 1787, at 340 n.4 (Max Farrand ed., 1911) (quoting Madison's

original notes); id. at 334, 341 (quoting proposal) (omission in original) (internal quotation marks omitted).

20. See 1 BLACKSTONE, supra note 9, at *132, *136.

21. Declaration of Rights, 1688, 1 W. & M., sess. 2, c. 2, § 1 (Eng.).

22. To borrow from Justice Jackson's famous explication of executive wartime authority, "emergency powers are consistent with free government only when their control is lodged elsewhere than in the Executive who exercises them." Youngstown Sheet & Tube Co. v. Sawyer, 343 U.S. 579, 652 (1952) (Jackson, J., concurring); see also Brown v. United States, 12 U.S. (8 Cranch) 110, 129 (1814) (observing with respect to the war power: "Like all other questions of policy, it is proper for the consideration of a department which can modify it at will [the legislature]; not for the consideration of a department which can pursue only the law as it is written").

23. See, e.g., MD. CONST. of 1776, Decl. of Rights, § VII ("That no power of suspending laws, or the execution of laws, unless by or derived from the Legislature, ought to be exercised or allowed."); see also VT. CONST. of 1786, Decl. of Rights, § XVII; N.H. CONST. of 1784, art. 1, Bill of Rights, § XXIX; MASS. CONST. of 1780, pt. 1, art. VII, XX; DEL. CONST. OF 1776, Decl. of Rights, § VII; N.C. CONST. of 1776, Decl. of Rights, § V; VA. CONST. of 1776, Bill of Rights, § VII.

24. See, e.g., MASS. CONST. of 1780, pt. 2, ch. VI, art. VII (providing that "[t]he privilege and benefit of the writ of habeas corpus . . . shall not be suspended by the legislature, except upon the most urgent and pressing occasions, and for a limited time, not exceeding twelve months. . . ."); N.H. CONST. of 1784, pt. 2, art. XCI (providing that the privilege "shall not be suspended by the legislature, except upon the most urgent and pressing occasions, and for a time not exceeding three months."); CONN CONST. of 1818, art. I, § 14 ("The privileges of the writ of habeas corpus shall not be suspended, unless, when in case of rebellion or invasion, the public safety may require it; nor in any case, but by the legislature."); R.I. Const. of 1842, art. I, § 9 ("The privilege of the writ of habeas corpus shall not be suspended, unless when in cases of rebellion or invasion the public safety shall require it; nor ever without the authority of the general assembly.").

25. Not only does the Suspension Clause require the existence of a "Rebellion or Invasion," but any decision to suspend must also emerge from the arduous process of bicameralism and presentment, internal checks on the political branches that ensure careful deliberation on a decision of such magnitude. The meaningfulness of this check is demonstrated by the fact that the proposed suspension during the Jefferson administration stalled in the House, as discussed in the last chapter. It is also reflected in the fact that Congress deliberated for two years before finally authorizing suspension during the Civil War. For an outstanding explication of the position that suspension is a congressional power, see Prakash, supra note 1, at 591–613.

26. See Abraham Lincoln, Message to Congress in Special Session, in 4 COLLECTED WORKS, supra note 3, at 421, 430–431 ("[A]s the provision was plainly made for a dangerous emergency it cannot be believed the framers of the instrument intended, that in every case, the danger should run its course until Congress could be called together; the very assembling of which might be prevented, as was intended in this case, by the rebellion."). Here, it bears noting that the Irish Habeas Corpus Act secured approval by the Irish Committee of the English Privy Council in 1782 only after the addition of a provision permitting suspension by executive proclamation, which contemporaries recounted was added to address the long intervals between parliamentary sittings in Ireland. See KEVIN COSTELLO, THE LAW OF HABEAS CORPUS IN IRELAND 16 & n.54 (2006).

27. See, e.g., John Yoo, Merryman *and* Milligan *(and* McCardle*)*, 34 J. SUP. CT. HIST. 243, 258 (2009).

28. See CONG. GLOBE, 37th Cong., 3d Sess. 22 (1863) (statement of Rep. Stevens) ("I do doubt the authority of the President of the United States to suspend the privilege of the writ of *habeas corpus* except when there is an absolute necessity for him to have that power, or an emergency when Congress is not in session."); see also CONG. GLOBE, 37th Cong., 1st Sess. 341 (1861) (statement of Sen. Cowan) (making a similar point). For scholarly commentary, see Prakash, supra note 1, at 589–590 (exploring this proposition); Henry P. Monaghan, *The Protective Power of the Presidency*, 93 COLUM. L. REV. 1 (1993) (exploring protective presidential power generally). More recently, Justice Souter suggested such a power might be appropriate, observing that "in a moment of genuine emergency, when the Government must act with no time for deliberation, the Executive may be able to detain a citizen if there is reason to fear he is an imminent threat to the safety of the Nation and its people." Hamdi v. Rumsfeld, 542 U.S. 507, 552 (2004) (Souter, J., joined by Ginsburg, J., concurring in part, dissenting in part, and concurring in the judgment).

29. U.S. CONST. art. II, § 3.

30. The Appollon, 22 U.S. 362, 366–367 (1824) (Story, J.).

31. As Lincoln famously phrased it: "[A]re all the laws, but one, to go unexecuted, and the government itself go to pieces, lest that one be violated?" Abraham Lincoln, Message to Congress in Special Session (July 4, 1861), in 4 COLLECTED WORKS, supra note 3, at 421, 430. Notably, this statement was made as part of Lincoln's defense of acting at the outset of the Civil War before Congress had assembled; nonetheless, many point to it as a more general defense of Lincoln's actions even after Congress assembled. See also Letter from Abraham Lincoln to A.G. Hodges (Apr. 4, 1864), in 7 COLLECTED WORKS, supra, at 281–282 ("[M]easures otherwise unconstitutional might become lawful by becoming indispensable to the preservation of the nation.").

32. For a forceful elaboration of this position, consult Richard H. Fallon, Jr., *Executive Power and the Political Constitution*, 2007 UTAH L. REV. 1, 21.

33. Congress did enact loosely-worded legislation in August 1861 declaring that "All the acts, proclamations, and orders of the President . . . respecting the army and navy of the United States, and calling out or relating to the militia or volunteers from the States, are hereby approved and in all respects legalized and made valid" and stating that all such acts should be viewed as having been "done under the previous express authority and direction of the Congress." Act of Aug. 6, 1861, 12 Stat. 326. Although some have argued otherwise, given the protracted debates that Congress undertook over whether to enact suspension legislation— debates that spanned from 1861 to 1863—it is a stretch to read this legislation as intended to approve formally of Lincoln's suspension proclamations, and the statute does not say anything specifically about suspension.

34. Letter from Abraham Lincoln to Erastus Corning and Others (June 12, 1863), in 6 COLLECTED WORKS, supra note 3, at 260, 264 (internal citation omitted). Similarly, Lincoln wrote that the Suspension Clause distinguishes between "arrests by process of courts, and arrests in cases of rebellion." Id. at 264–265. As to the latter category, Lincoln observed that it is "directed at sudden and extensive uprisings against the government, which, at most, will succeed or fail, in no great length of time." Id. at 264. The *New York Tribune* published Lincoln's letter and the Loyal Publication Society distributed some 500,000 copies of the letter as a pamphlet. Lincoln wrote the public letter to New York Democrats in large part to defend the military's arrest of Clement Vallandigham, a Copperhead from Ohio and former member of the House of Representatives who had decided to test General Ambrose Burnside's Order No. 38, which prohibited expressing sympathy for the enemy, by giving a speech doing just that. Vallandigham's arrest and trial are discussed infra at note 65; see also Geoffrey R. Stone, *Abraham Lincoln's First Amendment*, 78 N.Y.U. L. REV. 1 (2003) (discussing the case).

35. Letter from Abraham Lincoln to Erastus Corning and Others (June 12, 1863), in 6 COLLECTED WORKS, supra note 3, at 260, 264. It followed, in Lincoln's view, that suspension allows even for "instances of arresting innocent persons," something "always likely to occur in such cases." Id. at 263.

36. Id. at 265. In the wake of *Merryman*, Lincoln had written to Congress that suspension was necessary to "arrest, and detain, without resort to the ordinary processes and forms of law, such individuals as he might deem dangerous to the public safety." Abraham Lincoln, Message to Congress (July 4, 1861), in 4 COLLECTED WORKS, supra note 3, at 421, 429.

37. Civil War historian Mark Neely found numerous record-keeping failures, yet concluded from his extensive research on the question that "far more than" the often-cited number of "13,535 civilians were arrested." NEELY, supra note 3, at 130; see also id. at 44, 136, 233–234 (detailing the waves of arrests during key periods and the kinds of arrests undertaken). Obviously, Union troops captured thousands of Confederate soldiers during the war. See id. at 136 (noting that "329,363 Confederate prisoners of war" were "paroled or exchanged during the war").

38. See id. at 26, 52–53, 60–64, 69–71, 131–132, 186; see also McPHERSON, supra
    note 3, at 436 (discussing many of the early arrests and noting that many
    were political in nature and that such prisoners were released in the spring
    of 1862). In the first year of the war, Secretary of State William Seward super-
    vised military arrests and reportedly bragged to a British ambassador that he
    could "touch a bell on my right hand" and order the arrest of any "citizen." The
    story continues with Seward asking: "Can the Queen of England do so much?"
    See Prakash, supra note 1, at 613 (quoting JOHN M. TAYLOR, WILLIAM HENRY
    SEWARD: LINCOLN'S RIGHT HAND 169 (1991)) (internal quotation marks omit-
    ted). The War Department took over managing arrests and detentions in 1862.
39. JAMES G. RANDALL, CONSTITUTIONAL PROBLEMS UNDER LINCOLN 150 (1926)
    (observing that the object of these detentions was "precautionary"); id. at 149
    (noting that during the early months of the war, "hundreds of prisoners were
    apprehended"). Randall further observed: "That all this procedure was arbitrary,
    that it involved the withholding of constitutional guarantees normally available,
    is of course evident." Id. at 152. Secretary of State William Seward reportedly
    defended arrests made in Kentucky by stating: "I don't care a d—n whether they
    are guilty or innocent. I saved Maryland by similar arrests, and so I mean to hold
    Kentucky." NEELY, supra note 3, at 30 (internal quotation marks and citation
    omitted).
40. Letter from Edward Bates to R. J. Lackey (Jan. 19, 1863), in [ser. 2] 5 WAR OF
    THE REBELLION: A COMPILATION OF THE OFFICIAL RECORDS OF THE UNION
    AND CONFEDERATE ARMIES 190, 191 (Washington, D.C., Government Printing
    Office 1899).
41. See McPHERSON, supra note 3, at 791 (discussing the negotiation of pris-
    oner exchanges during the Civil War); see also JOHN FABIAN WITT, LINCOLN'S
    CODE: THE LAWS OF WAR IN AMERICAN HISTORY 142 (2012) (noting that Lincoln
    initially treated secessionists as criminals versus enemies).
42. Proclamation No. 1, 13 Stat. 730 (1862).
43. *A Policy at Last*, N.Y. TIMES, Sept. 26, 1862.
44. Executive Order (Aug. 8, 1862), in 7 MESSAGES AND PAPERS, supra note 12,
    at 3322.
45. NEELY, supra note 3, at 53; see also McPHERSON, supra note 3, at 493–494.
46. Merryman sued Cadwalader in February 1863. See WHITE, supra note 11,
    at 92–95.
47. The matter was the subject of discussion at a cabinet meeting on April 18, 1862,
    at which President Lincoln referred to one of the lawsuits as "'a matter which
    deeply concerns the public welfare as well as the safety of the individual offi-
    cers of the government.'" James G. Randall, *The Indemnity Act of 1863: A Study
    in the Wartime Immunity of Governmental Officers*, 20 MICH. L. REV. 589, 592
    (1922) (quoting Lincoln). In the wake of the meeting, Attorney General Bates
    drew up a draft bill and delivered it to the Senate. See EDWARD BATES, THE DIARY

OF EDWARD BATES, 1859–1866, at 252 (Howard K. Beale ed., 1933) (diary entry for April 21, 1862).

48. Act of Mar. 3, 1863, ch. 81, § 1, 12 Stat. 755, 755.

49. See CONG. GLOBE, 37th Cong., 3d Sess. 1186 (1863) (statement of Sen. Trumbull) (observing that both those who believed the power to suspend resides in Congress and those who thought it resides with the president could vote for a bill worded in this fashion); CONG. GLOBE, 37th Cong., 3d Sess. 1094 (1863) (statement of Sen. Bayard) (referring to the measure as "intentionally ambiguous . . . [and] intended to be so framed that it may be read two ways").

50. For example, Senator Jacob Collamer of Vermont, the principal author of the 1863 Act, declared that the purpose of a suspension is to "enable [the Executive] to take and to hold persons independent of their committing crimes, for State reasons, for public safety, for the public security." CONG. GLOBE, 37th Cong., 3d Sess. 1206 (1863) (statement of Sen. Jacob Collamer). Similarly, Senator James Doolittle of Vermont posited that under the Act, the president "will be authorized to seize upon [not only] those who are guilty of the crime of treason . . . [but also] those whom he knows, or has every reason to believe, are about to join the enemy, or give them aid or comfort; for it is to reach that class of men that it is necessary that the Executive should be clothed with this power." Id. at 1194 (statement of Sen. James Doolittle); see also id. at 1472 (statement of Sen. Edgar Cowan) (observing that, as the English understood it, the purpose of a suspension was to arrest persons "out of excessive caution"); id. at 1200 (statement of Sen. Morton Wilkinson) (opining that a suspension was necessary because "there are a great many ways in a rebellion of this magnitude in which a party can oppose the Government without committing those overt acts which render him liable to an indictment for treason"); id. at 1092 (statement of Sen. Lyman Trumbull) (equating suspension with "allow[ing] . . . a temporary arrest of parties," including those "preparing plots not yet matured so that you can arrest them for treason"). For more on the details of this legislation and the congressional debates, consult Amanda L. Tyler, *Suspension as an Emergency Power*, 118 YALE L.J. 600, 637–655 (2009).

51. Act of Mar. 3, 1863, ch. 81, § 2, 12 Stat. at 755.

52. Id. § 4, at 756. Later sections provided for removal of suits against federal officers from state courts and imposed a two-year statute of limitations on any suit or prosecution attacking "any arrest or imprisonment made, or other trespasses or wrongs done or committed" during the rebellion. See id. §§ 5, 7, at 756–757. These provisions originated in the House bill introduced by Representative Thaddeus Stevens that was directed at protecting the president and his officers from suits attacking their actions in the period leading up to the 1863 Act. See Tyler, supra note 50, at 641–642.

53. Proclamation No. 7, 13 Stat. 734, 734 (1863). Lincoln's proclamation also encompassed those in the U.S. military, military deserters, and draft dodgers. See id.

Lincoln issued another arguably redundant suspension proclamation on July 5, 1864, applicable to Kentucky. See Proclamation No. 16, 13 Stat. 742, 743 (1864).

54. As explored in Chapter 2, historically, prisoner of war status tracked being in the service of a foreign sovereign. The use of the term "prisoners of war" in both the Act and the presidential proclamation that followed should not obscure the fact that the Union did not view the Confederacy in such terms.

55. For details, consult generally NEELY, supra note 3. Union detention facilities stretched the entire nation. Indeed, under military orders, "leading secessionists" were ordered confined on Alcatraz Island in the San Francisco Bay. See Letter from Asst. Adj.-Gen. R.C. Drum to Lieut. Col. Harvey Lee (Sept. 12, 1862), in [ser. 1] 50 WAR OF THE REBELLION: A COMPILATION OF THE OFFICIAL RECORDS OF THE UNION AND CONFEDERATE ARMIES 116 (Washington, DC, Government Printing Office 1897).

56. See NEELY, supra note 3, at 160–184. "The jurisdiction of [military] tribunals extended to 'all Rebels and Insurgents, their aiders and abettors within the United States, and all persons discouraging volunteer enlistments, resisting militia drafts, or guilty of any disloyal practice, affording aid and comfort to Rebels against the authority of the United States.'" DANIEL FARBER, LINCOLN'S CONSTITUTION 20 (2003).

57. Randall, supra note 39, at 166; see also George Clarke Sellery, *Lincoln's Suspension of Habeas Corpus as Viewed by Congress*, 1 BULL. UNIV. WIS. HIST. SERIES 217, 267–268 n.14 (1908). Another Lincoln expert documents the turning over of one list—"late and reluctantly"—by the War Department. Mark E. Neely, Jr., *The Lincoln Administration and Arbitrary Arrests: A Reconsideration*, 5 J. ABRAHAM LINCOLN ASSOC. 6, 21 (1983).

58. See ROBERT B. WARDEN, AN ACCOUNT OF THE PRIVATE LIFE AND PUBLIC SERVICES OF SALMON PORTLAND CHASE 546 (Cincinatti, Ohio, Wilstach, Baldwin & Co. 1874).

59. The Lincoln administration interpreted Sections 2 and 3 not to apply to "'aiders or abettors of the enemy' and all other prisoners who had previously been deemed 'amenable to military law.'" David J. Barron & Martin S. Lederman, *The Commander in Chief at the Lowest Ebb—A Constitutional History*, 121 HARV. L. REV. 941, 1005 (2008) (quoting Abraham Lincoln, Proclamation, 13 Stat. 734 (Sept. 15, 1863)). For more details, consult WHITE, supra note 11, at 84.

60. The president on occasion actively intervened to direct his inferior officers *not* to comply with court orders issued pursuant to Section 2 of the Act. See In re Dugan, 6 D.C. 131 (1865) (upholding refusals to comply with Section 2 because the president has the inherent power to suspend). The Supreme Court granted review in *Dugan*, 69 U.S. (2 Wall.) 134 (1865), only to hold the case over and see it mooted upon Dugan's release. See CHARLES FAIRMAN, 6 THE OLIVER WENDELL HOLMES DEVISE HISTORY OF THE SUPREME COURT OF THE UNITED STATES: RECONSTRUCTION AND REUNION 1864–88, pt. 1, at 57–58 (1971).

61. Specifically, Johnson lifted the suspension's application to a number of states in December 1865, to several more in April 1866, and finally to the last remaining state in August 1866. See Andrew Johnson, A Proclamation (Dec. 1, 1865), in 8 MESSAGES AND PAPERS, supra note 12, at 3531 (lifting suspension in all states except "the States of Virginia, Kentucky, Tennessee, North Carolina, South Carolina, Georgia, Florida, Alabama, Mississippi, Louisiana, Arkansas, and Texas, the District of Columbia, and the Territories of New Mexico and Arizona"); Andrew Johnson, A Proclamation (Apr. 2, 1866), in 8 MESSAGES AND PAPERS, supra, at 3627, 3630 (lifting the suspension in Virginia, Tennessee, North Carolina, South Carolina, Georgia, Florida, Alabama, Mississippi, Louisiana, and Arkansas); Andrew Johnson, A Proclamation (Aug. 20, 1866), in 8 MESSAGES AND PAPERS, supra, at 3631, 3636 (ending suspension in Texas and declaring that the "insurrection is at an end and that peace, order, tranquility, and civil authority now exact in and throughout the whole of the United States of America"); see also id. at 3635 (deeming suspension "in time of peace dangerous to public liberty, incompatible with the individual rights of the citizen, [and] contrary to the genius and spirit of our free institutions").

62. Ex parte Milligan, 71 U.S. (4 Wall.) 2, 6 (1866); see REHNQUIST, supra note 5, at 85–87.

63. See REHNQUIST, supra note 5, at 86–88. President Johnson later commuted Milligan's sentence to a life sentence. See id. at 104. This followed after Justice Davis, who was circuit justice for the circuit including Indiana, and another judge who reviewed Milligan's habeas petition, wrote the president urging commutation of the sentence. See id. at 116–117.

64. Milligan, 71 U.S. (4 Wall.), at 127. For greater discussion of the implications of this observation, see Chapter 10. See also Amanda L. Tyler, *Is Suspension a Political Question?*, 59 STAN. L. REV. 333 (2006).

65. Milligan, 71 U.S. (4 Wall.) at 121. The decision in *Milligan* stands in stark contrast to the Supreme Court's actions in Clement Vallandigham's case, which challenged his conviction by military commission for violating a military order prohibiting expressing "sympathy for those in arms against the government of the United States." There, the Court ruled that it did not have jurisdiction to review the decision of a military tribunal. See Ex parte Vallandigham, 68 U.S. 243, 251–254 (1863).

66. Milligan, 71 U.S. (4 Wall.), at 124–125 (quoting THE DECLARATION OF INDEPENDENCE).

67. Id. at 20, 120–121.

68. Id. at 126; see also id. at 125–126 (observing that "in a great crisis," it is "essential" that "there should be a power somewhere of suspending the writ of *habeas corpus*" because "[i]n the emergency of the times, an immediate public investigation according to law may not possible; and yet, the peril to the country may be too imminent to suffer such persons to go at large").

69. Specifically, the Court noted that Milligan had not been indicted by the next sitting grand jury in the Circuit Court for the District of Indiana after his arrest.

70. Milligan, 71 U.S. (4 Wall.) at 132.

71. The Court presided over two challenges to the military tribunals used in such states during Reconstruction. Before it could reach the merits in Ex parte *McCardle*, Congress repealed the basis of the Supreme Court's appellate jurisdiction in that case. See Ex parte McCardle, 74 U.S. (7 Wall.) 506 (1868). When another case came before it on an alternative jurisdictional basis, the Court upheld its jurisdiction, setting the stage for it to reach the merits in a subsequent round of arguments. See Ex parte Yerger, 75 U.S. (8 Wall.) 85 (1868). But before the Court had a chance to do so, the military turned the petitioner over to civilian authorities for prosecution, mooting his challenge.

72. *Reconstruction* (Remarks of Thaddeus Stevens in Congress dated Jan. 3, 1867), in 2 THE SELECTED PAPERS OF THADDEUS STEVENS: APRIL 1865–AUGUST 1868, at 212 (Beverly Wilson Palmer & Holly Byers Ochoa eds., 1998). For examples of press accounts, see REHNQUIST, supra note 5, at 133–134.

73. See Act of Mar. 2, 1867, ch. 155, 14 Stat. 432, 432–433. The concurring justices had argued that congressional approval of military tribunals to try civilians would render their use constitutional. For more on this and related legislation, see Tyler, supra note 50, at 652–655; see also Act of May 11, 1866, ch. 80, 14 Stat. 46.

74. For details, see NEELY, supra note 3, at 176–179; Yoo, supra note 27, at 256 (stating that "[f]rom the end of the war until January 1, 1869, the Union army conducted 1,435 military trials, although the number of such trials steadily declined throughout this period," while noting that some of these trials "were of Union soldiers").

75. Order of the War Department (May 27, 1865), in 8 MESSAGES AND PAPERS, supra note 12, at 3537 (ordering that "in all cases of sentences by military tribunals of imprisonment during the war the sentence be remitted and that the prisoners be discharged").

76. The eight—seven men and one woman—were Samuel Arnold, George A. Atzerodt, David E. Herold, Samuel A. Mudd, Michael O'Laughlin (sometimes spelled O'Laughlen), Lewis Payne (who sometimes went by Lewis Powell), Edward Spangler (sometimes called Edman Spangler), and Mary E. Surratt. I have chosen to follow the spelling of their names in the War Department Special Orders applicable to their trial. See Special Orders, No. 211 (May 6, 1865), in 8 MESSAGES AND PAPERS, supra note 12, at 3533. The plot that concluded with Lincoln's assassination had begun as one to kidnap him and send him to Richmond. See MICHAEL W. KAUFFMAN, AMERICAN BRUTUS: JOHN WILKES BOOTH AND THE LINCOLN CONSPIRACIES 133–134 (New York, Random House, 2004). Mary Surratt's son, John Surratt, remained a fugitive until 1867, when he was captured in Egypt and returned to stand trial before a civilian court, with

a hung jury resulting. See EDWARD STEERS, JR., THE TRIAL: THE ASSASSINATION OF PRESIDENT LINCOLN AND THE TRIAL OF THE CONSPIRATORS XII (Lexington, University Press of Kentucky 2003); see also GERARD N. MAGLIOCCA, AMERICA'S FOUNDING SON: JOHN BINGHAM AND THE INVENTION OF THE FOURTEENTH AMENDMENT 107 (2013).

77. See Executive Chamber (May 1, 1865), in 8 MESSAGES AND PAPERS, supra note 12, at 3532–3533.

78. See BATES, supra note 47, at 483 (diary entry for May 25, 1865). Bates was equally critical of the proposal to try Jefferson Davis before a military tribunal. See id. at 483–484.

79. See 2 GIDEON WELLES, DIARY OF GIDEON WELLES, SECRETARY OF THE NAVY UNDER LINCOLN AND JOHNSON 303 (Boston and New York, Houghton Mifflin Co. 1911) (entry dated May 9, 1865).

80. Military Commissions, 11 Op. Att'y Gen. 305 (1865). Speed defended the choice of military tribunal in an opinion submitted to Congress, arguing that "if the persons who are charged with the assassination of the President committed the deed as public enemies . . . they not only can, but ought to be tried before a military tribunal" under the laws of war. Id. at 316.

81. According to Welles's diary, he again argued for a civilian court for Davis's trial, but others, including Secretary of State William Seward pushed for a military commission, "for he had no confidence in proceeding before a civil court." 2 WELLES, supra note 79, at 335–336 (entry dated July 18, 1865); see also id. at 337–339 (entry dated July 21, 1865). Davis ultimately spent two years in military custody before being bailed and charged with treason, but he was never tried. Interestingly, a group of northerners, including Horace Greeley and prominent abolitionist Gerrit Smith, posted bond for Davis. Smith reportedly said he signed the bond because Davis "was entitled either to his trial or to his liberty." Gerrit Smith, *On the Bailing of Jefferson Davis* (Peterboro, June 6, 1867). For more on the Davis case, see David K. Watson, *The Trial of Jefferson Davis: An Interesting Constitutional Question*, 24 YALE L.J. 669 (1915); Cynthia Nicoletti, *Did Secession Really Die at Appomattox?: The Strange Case of* U.S. v. Jefferson Davis, 41 UNIV. OF TOLEDO L. REV. 587 (2010).

82. See STEERS, supra note 76, at XVIII.

83. See Executive Chamber (May 1, 1865), in 8 MESSAGES AND PAPERS, supra note 12, at 3533; EDWARD STEERS, JR., BLOOD ON THE MOON: THE ASSASSINATION OF ABRAHAM LINCOLN 222–223 (2001).

84. MAGLIOCCA, supra note 76, at 89 (quoting Bingham's argument); see also id. at 89–107 (detailing Bingham's role in the prosecution of the Lincoln conspirators).

85. Id. at 94.

86. Id. (quoting Senator Johnson's argument). Senator Johnson is infamous for having argued and won the *Dred Scott* case. Johnson had also earlier published his views on *Merryman*, concluding that Lincoln's unilateral exercise of the suspension

authority was "perfectly constitutional." McGinty, supra note 6, at 107–109 (detailing Johnson's opinion and quoting Reverdy Johnson, *The Power of the President to Suspend the Habeas Corpus Writ*, in The Rebellion Record: A Diary of American Events 193 (Frank Moore ed., New York, G.P. Putnam 1862)).

87. Magliocca, supra note 76, at 96 (quoting Representative Bingham's argument).

88. See General Court-Martial Orders, No. 356 (Report of Judge Advocate General Joseph Holt to President Andrew Johnson), in 8 Messages and Papers, supra note 12, at 3540–3543; Executive Order (July 5, 1865), in id. at 3545–3546 (approving of the sentences and setting the execution date for four conspirators). The government did not charge the conspirators with treason.

89. In the meantime, an attempt of the officers to convince the president to grant Mary Surratt clemency failed. President Johnson did not stop the execution and later claimed that he never saw the letter sent to him by the officers, although that fact remains disputed. See Magliocca, supra note 76, at 102–103 (providing details).

90. For example, Representative Henry Winter Davis wrote to President Johnson that he had "found *not one* person who does not deplore this form of trial." Letter from Henry Winter Davis to President Andrew Johnson (May 13, 1865), in 8 The Papers of Andrew Johnson 65, 66 (Paul H. Bergeron ed., 1989). Similarly, David Dudley Field, the brother of Supreme Court Justice Stephen J. Field who later presented one of the arguments in *Milligan*, wrote to the president asserting that the military trial of the Lincoln conspirators was "a matter of great embarrassment to all of us who have been educated to dread encroachments upon the Constitution." Letter from David Dudley Field to President Andrew Johnson (June 8, 1865), in The Papers of Andrew Johnson, supra, at 201.

91. Surratt's petition is replicated in The Assassination of President Lincoln and the Trial of the Conspirators 250 (Benn Pitman ed., Moore, Wilstach & Baldwin, 1865) [hereinafter Pitman's Transcript], reprinted in Steers, supra note 76. It argued:

> at the time of the commission of the said offense she was a private citizen of the United States, and in no manner connected with the military authority of the same, and that said offense was committed within the District of Columbia, said District being at the time within the lines of the armies of the United States. . . . [And] the said crime was an offense simply against the peace of the United States, properly and solely cognizable under the Constitution and laws of the United States, by the Criminal Court of this District, and which said court was and is now open for the trial of such crimes and offenses.

Id.

92. Here, Johnson is presumably referencing the 1863 suspension legislation and Lincoln's subsequent declaration of a nationwide suspension.

93. The court order along with Hancock's return and the president's "Indorsement" are all replicated in Pitman's Transcript, supra note 91, at 250.

94. 2 WELLES, supra note 79, at 334 (diary entry dated July 17, 1865, describing events of July 11). My appreciation goes to John Gordon III for bringing this entry in Welles's diary to my attention. President Johnson originally ordered that the prisoners be confined at the penitentiary at Albany, New York. See Executive Order (July 5, 1865), in 8 MESSAGES AND PAPERS, supra note 12, at 3545–3546. After the *Pawnee* discussion, Johnson modified the order to send them to the Tortugas. See Executive Order (July 15, 1865), in 8 MESSAGES AND PAPERS, supra, at 3546; see also ROBERT K. SUMMERS, DR. SAMUEL A. MUDD AT FORT JEFFERSON 42–43 (2008) (replicating a letter to Dr. Mudd's attorney from a colleague speculating that the prisoners were transferred to "preclude" the use of habeas corpus).

95. See 6 COBBETT'S COMPLETE COLLECTION OF STATE TRIALS AND PROCEEDINGS FOR HIGH TREASON AND OTHER CRIMES AND MISDEMEANORS 317, 330–331 (London, T.C. Hansard 1810) (reporting on the 1667 impeachment proceedings against Clarendon). For greater discussion of Clarendon, see Chapter 1.

96. See Letter from Sarah Mudd to President Andrew Johnson (June 28, 1866), in 10 THE PAPERS OF ANDREW JOHNSON 632, 632 (Paul H. Bergeron ed., 1992).

97. Ex parte Mudd, 17 F. Cas. 954 (S.D. Fl. 1868). Note that the opinion in *Mudd* was nowhere reported and the original records from the Southern District of Florida for this period have been lost. The version of the opinion quoted here was recovered by the Surratt Society and authenticated from a contemporary newspaper publication. As things unfolded, by the next year, President Johnson had pardoned all three, with Mudd being singled out for having treated victims of yellow fever during an outbreak at Fort Jefferson in 1867.

98. See Chapter 2 (detailing trials that occurred during the suspensions of 1696, 1722, and 1745–1746).

99. See Ex parte Quirin, 317 U.S. 1 (1942); Hamdi v. Rumsfeld, 542 U.S. 507 (2004).

100. Ex parte Milligan, 71 U.S. (4 Wall.) 2, 126 (1866).

101. See, e.g., CONG. GLOBE, 37th Cong., 1st Sess. 341 (1861) (statement of Sen. Edgar Cowan) (opining that the Union may take as a prisoner of war "a citizen of our own who has cut himself away from the Government and severed his allegiance"); *The Law of Conquest the True Basis of Reconstruction*, 24 NEW ENGLANDER 111, 120 (1865) (opining that the rebels "have no longer any right of protection from our government or any right of citizenship under it, and become *de facto* foreigners" and that "[a]gainst them the government possesses full belligerent rights under the laws of war"); GROSVENOR P. LOWREY, THE COMMANDER-IN-CHIEF 16 (New York, G.P. Putnam 1862) ("[T]he armed rebel, ha[s] voluntarily withdrawn from the protection of the Constitution and submitted himself to the arbitrament of war.").

102. See, e.g., Proclamation No. 5, 12 Stat. 1258, 1259 (1861) (asserting in a presidential proclamation the legal authority to institute a blockade under "the laws of the United States and of the law of nations").

103. 67 U.S. (2 Black) 635, 672–674 (1862). Notably, the Court also suggested that these questions might be political in nature—that is, the president's decisions on this score were immune from judicial review:

> Whether the President in fulfilling his duties, as Commander-in-chief, in suppressing an insurrection, has met with such armed hostile resistance, and a civil war of such alarming proportions as will compel him to accord to them the character of belligerents, is a question to be decided *by him*, and this Court must be governed by the decisions and acts of the political department of the Government to which this power was entrusted.

    Id. at 673.

104. Id. at 666, 667. See 1 EMMERICH DE VATTEL, THE LAW OF NATIONS §§ 292–293, at 424–425 (London, n. pub. 1787) (1758).

105. Id. at 674. Even as it made this point, the Court highlighted the inherent legal tensions raised by the Civil War by referring to the Rebels as "traitors." See id. ("All persons residing within this territory whose property may be used to increase the revenues of the hostile power are, in this contest, liable to be treated as enemies, though not foreigners. They have cast off their allegiance and made war on their Government, and are none the less enemies because they are traitors.").

106. For example, during the war, Lincoln offered those who had supported the Confederacy the opportunity to affirm their allegiance to the Union and, in many cases, earn a presidential pardon. See Amanda L. Tyler, *The Story of Klein: The Scope of Congress's Authority to Shape the Jurisdiction of the Federal Courts*, in FEDERAL COURTS STORIES 87, 88–91 (Vicki C. Jackson & Judith Resnik eds., 2010) (detailing the terms of Lincoln's Amnesty Proclamation).

107. For details, see WITT, supra note 41, at 145–146 (noting also that Navy Secretary Welles referred to Lincoln's policy as embodying a "strange inconsistency"); see also id. at 160–161 (further discussing the administration's position when dealing with the British that the conflict was an insurrection as opposed to a war).

108. Proclamation dated July 4, 1868, in 14 THE PAPERS OF ANDREW JOHNSON 332 (Paul H. Bergeron ed., 1997); see also Proclamation dated May 25, 1865, in 8 PAPERS OF ANDREW JOHNSON, supra note 90, at 317–318 (providing for a similar pardon, albeit with exceptions for those "under presentment or indictment in any court of the United States . . . upon a charge of treason or other felony").

109. See, e.g., War Department General Orders, No. 109 (June 6, 1865), in 8 MESSAGES AND PAPERS, supra note 12, at 3538–3539.

110. Traditionally, English law viewed martial law as a law of necessity. Thus, Hale described it as "in Truth and Reality . . . not a Law, but something indulged rather than allowed as a Law." SIR MATTHEW HALE, THE HISTORY OF THE COMMON LAW OF ENGLAND 40 (n.p., J. Nutt 1713). And Coke contrasted a state of martial law in which "the courts of justice be *as it were* shut up" with

times "[w]hen the courts of justice be open, and *the judges and ministers of the same may by law protect men from wrong and violence*, and *distribute justice to all.*" W.F. Finlason, A Review of the Authorities as to the Repression of Riot or Rebellion, with Special Reference to Criminal or Civil Liability 50 (London, Stevens & Sons 1868) (quoting 1 Sir Edward Coke, The First Part of the Institutes of the Laws of England § 412 (Francis Hargrave & Charles Butler eds., Philadelphia, Robert H. Small 1853)) (internal quotation marks omitted); see also Finlason, supra, at 98 ("Martial law is quite different from ordinary military law, that it is justified by paramount necessity, and proclaimed by a military chief." (quoting 1 James Kent, Commentaries on American Law 370 n.a (7th ed., New York, William Kent 1851)) (internal quotation marks omitted).

111. Martial Law, 8 Op. Att'y Gen. 374 (1857); see also Milligan, 71 U.S. (4 Wall.) at 127 (describing martial law as limited to "the theatre of active military operations, where war really prevails").

112. See Neely, supra note 3, at 36–38.

113. G.M. Wharton, Remarks on Mr. Binney's Treatise on the Writ of Habeas Corpus 12 (2d ed., Philadelphia, John Campbell 1862).

CHAPTER 8

1. Letter from President Jefferson Davis to the Senate and House of Representatives of the Confederate States of America, Feb. 3, 1864, in 3 Journal of the Congress of the Confederate States of America 669, 671 (1904) [hereinafter 3 J. Cong. C.S.A.]

2. See Constitution of the Confederate States, in 1 Journal of the Congress of the Confederate States of America 909–924 (1904); see id. Art. II § 1(1) (presidential term); id. Art. I § 9(4) (prohibiting laws "denying or impairing" rights of slaveholders); id. Art. I § 9(3) (Suspension Clause); id. Art. III § 3 (Treason Clause). For more on the Confederate Constitution, see G. Edward White, *Recovering the Legal History of the Confederacy*, 68 Wash. & Lee L. Rev. 467, 496–509 (2011).

3. David P. Currie, *Through the Looking-Glass: The Confederate Constitution in Congress, 1861–1865*, 90 Va. L. Rev. 1257, 1260 (2004).

4. 5 Jefferson Davis, Constitutionalist: His Letters, Papers, and Speeches 198, 199 (Dunbar Rowland ed., 1923) [hereinafter Jefferson Davis, Constitutionalist]. This critique married with Davis's earlier reproach of the idea that the "Executive possesses the power of suspending the writ of habeas corpus, and of delegating that power to military commanders, at his discretion." *Message of President Davis*, Daily Dispatch (Richmond, Va.), July 22, 1861.

5. *Suspension of Habeas Corpus*, The Standard, Apr. 15, 1863 (Raleigh, North Carolina paper's reprinting of an article from *The Charleston Mercury*, lauding in turn an editorial from *The Richmond Enquirer*) ("By the suspension of the writ,

President Lincoln can arrest and cast into prison any citizen he pleases, and there is no power by which the citizens can be released, but his arbitrary will.").

6. 5 JEFFERSON DAVIS, CONSTITUTIONALIST, supra note 4, at 199. As these examples reveal, Davis's statements were "meticulously written with an eye to their propaganda value." James W. Silver, *Propaganda in the Confederacy*, 11 J. SOUTH. HIST. 487, 489 (1945).

7. See WILLIAM M. ROBINSON, JR., JUSTICE IN GREY: A HISTORY OF THE JUDICIAL SYSTEM OF THE CONFEDERATE STATES OF AMERICA 385 (Harvard Univ. Press 1941). The War Department established review procedures for those taken into military custody, a process that sometimes resulted in release upon taking an oath of loyalty to the Confederacy. See id. at 386–389.

8. An act to authorize the suspension of the writ of habeas corpus in certain cases, Act of Feb. 27, 1862, ch. 2, Pub. Laws, 1st Cong., 1st sess., in THE STATUTES AT LARGE OF THE CONFEDERATE STATES OF AMERICA 1, 1 (James M. Matthews ed., Richmond 1862) [hereinafter CSA STATUTES AT LARGE, FIRST SESSION]. The bill "was passed in secret session without debate in the upper house and with only slight maneuvering in the lower house." ROBINSON, supra note 7, at 390.

9. Proclamation by the President of the Confederate States (Feb. 27, 1862) (proclaiming martial law and suspension of the privilege in Norfolk and Portsmouth, Virginia); in 1 A COMPILATION OF THE MESSAGES AND PAPERS OF THE CONFEDERACY, INCLUDING THE DIPLOMATIC CORRESPONDENCE 1861–1865, at 219, 219 (James D. Richardson ed., 1904) [hereinafter MESSAGES AND PAPERS]; General Orders No. 8 (Mar. 1, 1862) (proclaiming both in Richmond), in 1 id. at 220, 220–221; General Orders No. 11 (Mar. 8, 1862) (proclaiming both in Petersburg, Virginia), in 1 id. at 221, 221–222; General Orders No. 15 (Mar. 14, 1862) (proclaiming both in additional Virginia counties), in 1 id. at 222, 222–223; General Orders No. 18 (Mar. 29, 1862) (proclaiming both in additional counties), in 1 id. at 223, 223–224; General Orders No. 21 (Apr. 8, 1862) (proclaiming both in East Tennessee), in 1 id. at 224, 224–225; General Orders No. 33 (May 1, 1872) (proclaiming both in portions of South Carolina), in 1 id. at 225, 225–226; General Orders No. 19 (May 3, 1862) (proclaiming both in additional Virginia counties), in 1 id. at 226, 226–227.

10. Robinson, supra note 7, at 390 (citing war records).

11. See id. at 390, 393; John B. Robbins, *The Confederacy and the Writ of Habeas Corpus*, 55 GA. HIST. QUARTERLY 83, 85 (1971) (citing primary sources); see also JAMES M. MCPHERSON, BATTLE CRY OF FREEDOM: THE CIVIL WAR ERA 433 (1998). Prior to this time, late in 1861, a military official had declared martial law in Tennessee. See ROBINSON, supra note 7, at 389.

12. See, e.g., Special Orders No. 129 (June 5, 1862) (suspending the privilege in Salisbury, North Carolina), in 3 THE WAR OF THE REBELLION: A COMPILATION OF THE OFFICIAL RECORDS OF THE UNION AND CONFEDERATE ARMIES SER. II, at 890 (Washington, D.C., Gov't Printing Office 1898); Special Orders No. 206 (Sept. 3,

1862) (suspending the privilege in Atlanta, Georgia), in 1 HISTORY OF ATLANTA, GEORGIA 175 (Wallace P. Reed ed., 1889).

13. See ROBINSON, supra note 7, at 394, 396; White, supra note 2, at 533 (noting that the military imposed martial law in western Virginia; eastern Tennessee; areas of South Carolina; Mobile, Alabama; and parishes around New Orleans); White, supra, at 535 (expanding the list of states into the summer of 1862); MARK E. NEELY, JR., SOUTHERN RIGHTS: POLITICAL PRISONERS AND THE MYTH OF CONFEDERATE CONSTITUTIONALISM 32–38 (1999) (noting that martial law was sometimes related to the suppression of alcohol sales); FRANK LAWRENCE OWSLEY, STATE RIGHTS IN THE CONFEDERACY 156–163 (1925) (noting that May witnessed all of Texas fall under martial law); Robbins, supra note 11, at 86 (adding Mississippi).

14. For discussion of extensive critical reaction in the Confederate Congress, see Currie, supra note 3, at 1335–1336; see also McPHERSON, supra note 11, at 434 (detailing press criticizing and supporting the early measures taken in Richmond).

15. ROBINSON, supra note 7, at 395 (quoting Representative Robert Baldwin of Virginia); see also Robbins, supra note 11, at 86–87 (citing Senator Williamson S. Oldham of Texas, among others, as a critic).

16. Act of Apr. 19, 1862, ch. 44, Pub. Laws, 1st Cong., 1st Sess., in CSA STATUTES AT LARGE, FIRST SESSION, supra note 8, at 40, 40.

17. See ROBINSON, supra note 7, at 392 (discussing North Carolina suspension); Paul D. Lack, *Law and Disorder in Confederate Atlanta*, 66 GA. HIST. Q. 171, 183 (1982) (noting that the Atlanta suspension followed on the heels of the declaration of martial law in the area, which was reversed within a month).

18. 5 JOURNAL OF THE CONGRESS OF THE CONFEDERATE STATES OF AMERICA 376–377 (1905) (arguing that if martial law "is properly styled law" then "it can only be established or authorized by Congress"). The report also declared that "it has long been well settled that Congress alone can authorize a suspension of the writ of habeas corpus. . . ." Id. at 376.

19. As legal historian G. Edward White has written, martial law "replaces the civilian legal authorities in [an] area with military authorities," resulting in "all detained persons" in a covered area being "eligible for trial and possible punishment by military tribunals under the laws of war." This contrasts with suspension, the chief impact of which is "on cases in which the detaining authority wants to confine, on a preventive basis, persons ordinarily eligible for trials in civilian courts." White, supra note 2, at 533–535. Professor White notes, however, that one could well view suspension as "having a broader potential effect on the civil liberties of civilians in wartime than martial law declarations because of their potential duration and the fact that they relieve the authorities of providing any kind of a trial to those detained." Id. at 535.

20. Robbins, supra note 11, at 88.

21. An Act authorizing the suspension of the writ of habeas corpus, Act of Oct. 13, 1862, ch. 51, § 1, Pub. Laws, 1st Cong., 2d Sess., in THE STATUTES AT LARGE OF

THE CONFEDERATE STATES OF AMERICA 84, 84 (James M. Matthews ed., Richmond 1862) [hereinafter CSA STATUTES AT LARGE, SECOND SESSION]. An amendment that would have required the president to report every arrest made upon his warrant to the Confederate Congress failed. See ROBINSON, supra note 7, at 402 (providing details).

22. Currie, supra note 3, at 1329.

23. ROBINSON, supra note 7, at 405. For example, the president waited several months following the October enactment before re-proclaiming suspension in one area of North Carolina. See id. Mark Neely's work questions the idea that Davis invoked the power to declare martial law and suspend sparingly, observing that "[i]n fact, Davis employed the power for social ends beyond the constitutionally described ends of repelling invasion and providing for public safety"— including to promote prohibition of alcohol. NEELY, supra note 13, at 42.

24. See OWSLEY, supra note 13, at 173 (detailing Governor Zebulon Vance's protests relating to the arrest and detention of forty persons for suspected disloyalty).

25. Letter from Adjutant and Inspector General S. Cooper to General John H. Forney (Nov. 10, 1862), in [ser. 1, vol. 15] THE WAR OF REBELLION: A COMPILATION OF THE OFFICIAL RECORDS OF THE UNION AND CONFEDERATE ARMIES 859, 859 (Washington, D.C., Government Printing Office 1886).

26. Ex parte *Milligan* is discussed at length in Chapter 7.

27. Act of Oct. 13, 1862, ch. 51, § 2, in CSA STATUTES AT LARGE, SECOND SESSION, supra note 21, at 84.

28. See Currie, supra note 3, at 1330. The War Department named several prominent lawyers as commissioners for reviewing arrests during this and the subsequent suspension. See ROBINSON, supra note 7, at 387–389, 409–411. Nonetheless, inaction was sometimes the order of the day, resulting in ongoing military custody for some arrested during these periods. See NEELY, supra note 13, at 81–85.

29. See 6 JOURNAL OF THE CONGRESS OF THE CONFEDERATE STATES OF AMERICA 7 (1905) [hereinafter 6 J. CONG. C.S.A.]; see also White, supra note 2, at 536 & n.440.

30. See ROBINSON, supra note 7, at 405–406 (detailing some legislative actions); White, supra note 2, at 536–537 (same).

31. Letter from President Jefferson Davis, Feb. 3, 1864, in 3 J. CONG. C.S.A., supra note 1, at 670. One case from March 1864 highlights the import of suspension in such circumstances. In Virginia, a man was arrested for aiding Union troops as a guide, but prosecutors located only one witness to testify to the treasonous acts. The Confederate prosecutor and military officials therefore decided to detain the accused under the terms of the February 15, 1864, suspension. See ROBINSON, supra note 7, at 382.

32. See Robbins, supra note 11, at 91 (detailing North Carolina events).

33. See id. at 670–671.

34. See id. at 671 ("England, whose reverence for this great writ of right is at least as strong as our own . . . has repeatedly, with the last hundred years, resorted to this remedy when only threatened with invasion.").

35. An Act to suspend the privilege of the writ of habeas corpus in certain cases, Act of Feb. 15, 1874, ch. 37, pmbl., Pub. Laws., 1st Cong., 4th Sess., in THE STATUTES AT LARGE OF THE CONFEDERATE STATES OF AMERICA 187, 187 (James M. Matthews ed., Richmond 1864) [hereinafter CSA STATUTES AT LARGE, FOURTH SESSION].

36. Act of Feb. 15, 1874, ch. 37, § 1, in CSA STATUTES AT LARGE, FOURTH SESSION, supra note 35, at 188.

37. See McPHERSON, supra note 11, at 435.

38. Message from President Jefferson Davis to the House of Representatives of the Confederate States of America (May 20, 1864), in 1 MESSAGES AND PAPERS, supra note 9, at 452, 453.

39. Act of Feb. 15, 1874, ch. 37, § 2, in CSA STATUTES AT LARGE, FOURTH SESSION, supra note 35, at 188.

40. See Act of Feb. 15, 1874, ch. 37, § 4, in CSA STATUTES AT LARGE, FOURTH SESSION, supra note 35, at 189. The statute also relieved military officials from having to appear before judicial officials or produce prisoners in court; instead, an officer need only supply a certificate given under oath stating that a prisoner was held within the terms of the suspension after which habeas proceedings were to cease. See id. § 3, in CSA STATUTES AT LARGE, FOURTH SESSION, supra note 35, at 188–189.

41. See House Bill No. 113—Secret (introduced Feb. 4, 1864), in 6 J. CONG. C.S.A., supra note 29, at 762.

42. For additional details on the War Department's implementation of procedures, see ROBINSON, supra note 7, at 409–410 (noting that War Department regulations established the standard for detention as turning on the existence of "reasonable and probable cause").

43. Message from President Jefferson Davis to the House of Representatives of the Confederate States of America (May 20, 1864), in 1 MESSAGES AND PAPERS, supra note 9, at 452, 452–453.

44. H. COMM. ON THE JUDICIARY, 2ND CONFEDERATE CONG., REPORT OF THE COMMITTEE ON THE JUDICIARY UPON THE SUSPENSION OF THE HABEAS CORPUS 1–2 (1864) [hereinafter HOUSE REPORT ON SUSPENSION], in 7 JOURNAL OF THE CONGRESS OF THE CONFEDERATE STATES OF AMERICA 101 (1905) [hereinafter 7 J. CONG. C.S.A.].

45. Id. at 7. The Report specifically rejected that this function of suspension is superseded by the constitutional guarantee of due process, id. at 5, a point on which the committee Minority Report disagreed, see H. COMM. ON THE JUDICIARY, 2ND CONFEDERATE CONG., MINORITY REPORT OF THE COMMITTEE ON THE JUDICIARY 8–9 (1864) (arguing that suspension cannot displace the right to due process,

defined as "judicial process" and speedy trial), in 7 J. Cong. C.S.A., supra note 44, at 111. In this respect, the Minority Report built on similar arguments made two months earlier by Vice President Alexander Stephens. See *Speech on the State of the Confederacy, Delivered Before the Georgia Legislature, At Milledgeville, Georgia* (Mar. 16, 1864), in Alexander H. Stephens in Public and Private with Letters and Speeches, before, during, and since the War 761, 767–770 (Henry Cleveland ed., 1866) [hereinafter Stephens Papers]. Such arguments had been made in the North by three members of Congress seeking to filibuster the Union suspension bill. See Amanda L. Tyler, *Suspension as an Emergency Power*, 118 Yale L.J. 600, 643–644 (2009). The argument presumes that the Bill of Rights amendments superseded and nullified the recognition of a power to suspend in the Suspension Clause. See Martin H. Redish & Colleen McNamara, *Habeas Corpus, Due Process and the Suspension Clause: A Study in the Foundations of American Constitutionalism*, 96 Va. L. Rev. 1361 (2010) (elaborating the argument). This position is exceedingly difficult to reconcile with the Founding-era and early Republic debates, all of which assumed the opposite, as well as the dominant understanding of suspension that controlled in both the Union and Confederacy during the Civil War.

46. House Report on Suspension, supra note 44, at 7.

47. See White, supra note 2, at 537 (citing sources); Robinson, supra note 7, at 414–415. In November, Davis called for suspension to combat "a dangerous conspiracy" in several states (Virginia, North Carolina, and Tennessee), highlighting again his administration's inability, in the absence of suspension, to detain spies and others "holding treasonable communication with the enemy" due to the lack of "legal proof" to sustain criminal charges. Message from President Jefferson Davis to the Senate and House of Representatives of the Confederate States of America (Nov. 9, 1864), in 1 Messages and Papers, supra note 9, at 498, 498.

48. See *Jeff. Davis Special Message*, Chi. Tribune (Mar. 24, 1865) (quoting from a "confidential message to the two Houses of the Rebel Congress" sent by Davis).

49. Owsley, supra note 13, at 177.

50. See Robbins, supra note 11, at 92.

51. Resolutions on the Suspension of Habeas Corpus (Mar. 19, 1864), in Acts of the General Assembly of the State of Georgia Passed in Milledgeville at the Called Session in March 1864, 1864 Ga. Laws 152–154. Curiously, on the same day, the Georgia Assembly passed a resolution registering support for President Davis. See A resolution expressive of the confidence of this General Assembly in the integrity and patriotism of President Davis (Mar. 19, 1864), in Acts of the General Assembly of the State of Georgia, supra, at 154.

52. *Speech on the State of the Confederacy*, supra note 45, in Stephens Papers, supra note 45, at 767, 782–783. Days earlier, Georgia's Governor also urged a resolution condemning suspension. See *Speech of Governor Joseph E. Brown to the*

Senate and House of Representatives, in II THE CONFEDERATE RECORDS OF THE STATE OF GEORGIA 587, 619 (Allen D. Candler ed., 1909) ("[W]hat will we have gained when we have achieved our independence of the Northern States, if in our efforts to do so, we have . . . lost *Constitutional liberty* at home?"). For more on the complex debates in Georgia, see Robbins, supra note 11, at 93–95; Donald W. Wilkes, Jr., *From Oglethorpe to the Overthrow of the Confederacy: Habeas Corpus in Georgia, 1733-1865*, 45 GA. L. REV. 1015, 1048–1054 (2011).

53. See, e.g., RESOLUTIONS OF THE LEGISLATURE OF THE STATE OF MISSISSIPPI IN RELATION TO THE RECENT ACT OF THE CONGRESS OF THE CONFEDERATE STATES SUSPENDING THE PRIVILEGE OF THE WRIT OF HABEAS CORPUS (Apr. 5, 1864), in LAWS OF THE STATE OF MISSISSIPPI PASSED AT A CALLED SESSION OF THE MISSISSIPPI LEGISLATURE HELD IN MACON, MARCH AND APRIL 1864, 1864 MISS. LAWS 91-93; see also 4 JOURNAL OF THE CONGRESS OF THE CONFEDERATE STATES OF AMERICA 34 (1904); OWSLEY, supra note 13, at 177–191 (surveying state resistance and discussing North Carolina resolutions condemning the third suspension); ROBINSON, supra note 7, at 413; Robbins, supra note 11, at 95–96 & n.60 (detailing Mississippi events); Amos E. Simpson & Vincent Cassidy, *The Wartime Administration of Governor Henry W. Allen*, 5 LA. HIST. 257, 266–267 (1964) (discussing Louisiana Governor Henry Allen's complaints to President Davis). For a general discussion of North Carolina's disagreement with many war measures, see Marc W. Kruman, *Dissent in the Confederacy: The North Carolina Experience*, 27 CIVIL WAR HIST. 293 (1981).

54. The role of suspension and related policies in the downfall of the Confederacy has provoked considerable debate among scholars. Compare, e.g., OWSLEY, supra note 13, at 202 (labeling this period as the "turning of the tide against the Confederacy"), with White, supra note 2, at 538 n.452 ("It is hard to imagine how preventive detention of residents of the Confederacy in the years after 1863 would have effectively distinguished turncoats from the general mass of the war weary, or improved Confederate military resistance to invading Union armies."). One chronicler of the period argues that regardless which position is correct, "there can be no doubt that the efficiency of the executive branch . . . was much lowered by the failure of the Congress to grant it a continuous right to suspend constitutional guarantees." ROBINSON, supra note 7, at 415.

55. See JAMES M. MCPHERSON, EMBATTLED REBEL: JEFFERSON DAVIS AS COMMANDER IN CHIEF 74 (2014).

56. NEELY, supra note 13, at 1 (estimating the number to be at least 4,000 prisoners); see also id. at 87 (noting that "a phrase commonly appearing next to the name of a civilian prisoner in Confederate records was 'Union man'"). Neely's work highlights that Confederacy prisoner records, like those of the Union, are incomplete. One estimate reveals that the Confederate Army captured 211,411 Union soldiers during the war, holding approximately 194,743 as prisoners of war and paroling the rest. Approximately 30,000 Union soldiers died in captivity.

See Dora L. Costa & Matthew E. Kahn, *Surviving Andersonville: The Benefits of Social Networks in POW Camps*, 97 AM. ECON. REV. 1467, 1468 (2007).

57. NEELY, supra note 13, at 10.

58. During one hiatus between suspensions, Davis wrote to one of his generals lamenting that he no longer had the power to authorize suspension. See Letter from Jefferson Davis to Theophilus H. Holmes (Feb. 26, 1863), in 9 THE PAPERS OF JEFFERSON DAVIS 74 (Lynda Lasswell Crist ed., 1997).

59. See NEELY, supra note 13, at 154–157.

60. See *The Essay on* Habeas Corpus *in the Judge Sharkey Papers*, 23 MISS. VALLEY HIST. REV. 243, 244–246 (F. Garvin Davenport ed., 1936).

61. *Speech on the State of the Confederacy*, supra note 45, in STEPHENS PAPERS, supra note 45, at 774.

62. H. COMM. ON THE JUDICIARY, MINORITY REPORT OF THE COMMITTEE ON THE JUDICIARY (1864), supra note 45, at 4–5.

63. Currie, supra note 3, at 1332.

64. Ableman v. Booth, 62 U.S. (21 How.) 506 (1859) (overturning two orders of discharge of a federal prisoner by the Wisconsin state courts, one directed to Booth's federal custodian and one directed to a federal court); Tarble's Case, 80 U.S. (13 Wall.) 397, 409 (1871); see also id. at 411 ("If a party thus held be illegally imprisoned, it is for the courts or judicial officers of the United States, and those courts or officers alone, to grant him release.").

65. See Charles Warren, *Federal and State Court Interference*, 43 HARV. L. REV. 345, 353–358 (1930).

66. See In re Stacy, 10 Johns. 328 (N.Y. Sup. Ct. 1813); In re Roberts, 2 AM. L.J. 192, 195–196 (John E. Hall ed., 1809) (Nicholson, C.J.) (discussing and contrasting the discharge he ordered in the cases of John Adair and Peter Ogden during the Burr episode).

67. For discussion, see RICHARD H. FALLON, JR., JOHN F. MANNING, DANIEL J. MELTZER & DAVID L. SHAPIRO, HART & WECHSLER'S THE FEDERAL COURTS AND THE FEDERAL SYSTEM 430–436 (7th ed. 2015). To the extent that the Constitution promises a core habeas privilege, which Chapter 5 argues it does, some court must be open to hear the argument that the privilege has been suspended unconstitutionally. In keeping with this position is an opinion issued by Attorney General H. S. Legare in 1841, in which Legare posited that although federal courts should be the preferred venue for habeas actions brought against federal officials, "it would in my opinion be a very strong proposition to advance, that a man imprisoned against law, under a color of authority from the government of the United States, should be deprived of the protection of the State courts, by means of the great and speedy remedy of the *habeas corpus* act, where there is no means of resorting to the federal tribunals." Enlistment of Aliens, 3 Op. Att'y Gen. 670, 673 (1841). (Note Legare's reference to "the *habeas corpus* act," which underscores the

continuing influence of the English Habeas Corpus Act on American constitutional habeas jurisprudence.)

68. See White, supra note 2, at 509–529. For a general overview of the courts of the
Confederacy, see ROBINSON, supra note 7.

69. Robbins, supra note 11, at 90; see id. (discussing and citing cases reflecting various approaches).

70. Mims v. Wimberly, 33 Ga. 587, 596 (1863) (noting, however, that state courts
could not question imprisonment following under order of a Confederate court).
See also Ex parte Hill, 38 Ala. 458, 461 (1863) (concluding, over the dissent of
the chief justice, that state courts have at least the power to second-guess actions
of Confederate officials acting outside their "official cognizance"). In one case,
the North Carolina Supreme Court defended its jurisdiction to review War
Department conscription laws and discharged a soldier it believed to be exempt
from service. See In re Bryan, 60 N.C. 1, 19 (1863) (Pearson, C.J.); id. at 22 (distinguishing detentions following under court order). Decisions in keeping with
these may also be found in Texas, see infra note 74.

71. Mims, 33 Ga. at 591, 598; see id. at 592 (contrasting the U.S. Constitution and
observing that the Confederate Constitution "works no transfer of sovereignty").

72. See id. at 598; In re Stacy, 10 Johns. 328, 333–334 (N.Y. Sup. Ct. 1813). The *Stacy*
case is discussed in Chapter 6. A later New York decision notes that jurisdiction
was not contested in *Stacy*. See In re Hopson, 40 Barb. 34, 49–50 (N.Y. Sup. Ct.
1863), which is notable because Kent had earlier questioned state court jurisdiction in a decision preceding Stacy. See In re Ferguson, 9 Johns. 239, 240–241
(N.Y. Sup. Ct. 1812).

73. See OWSLEY, supra note 13, at 193–198 (noting that judges in Virginia and Texas
were well known to grant discharge in such cases); Robbins, supra note 11, at
90 (citing Confederate District Judge James Halyburton as often granting such
petitions).

74. See, e.g., State v. Sparks, 27 Tex. 705 (1864); State v. Sparks, 27 Tex. 627 (1864)
(holding that even under a suspension, the writ should issue to a Confederate
official holding one on suspicion of treasonous activities); compare Ex parte
Peebles, 1864 WL 4870 (Tex. 1864) (recognizing that "it would be the duty of the
Court to respect" a military official's order "to arrest and detain parties charged
with the offences enumerated in the [suspension] statute").

75. William L. Shaw, *The Confederate Conscription and Exemption Acts*, 6 AM. J. LEGAL
HIST. 368, 398 (1962); OWSLEY, supra note 13, at 181. Mark Neely writes that "[i]t
is not clear that Pearson ever recognized a dual sovereignty." NEELY, supra note
13, at 74.

76. In re Cain, 60 N.C. 525 (1864).

77. In re Roseman, 60 N.C. 368 (1863) ("[T]here is no precedent in this country or in
England where the privilege of the writ has ever been suspended in *civil cases*, all
the precedents are in cases of *political offenses*, treason, sedition and the like.").

78. See also ROBINSON, supra note 7, at 209.

79. In re Rafter, 60 N.C. 537 (N.C. 1864) (Manly, J.). As Justice Manly wrote in one case, "[t]he officer's return, in the case before me, pursued the form prescribed [in the statute]; and that, by the terms of the act, puts an end to all further inquiry." Id. at 538. For more details on the North Carolina conscription cases, see Jennifer Van Zant, *Confederate Conscription and the North Carolina Supreme Court*, 72 No. CAR. HIST. REV. 54 (1995).

80. For examples of state courts declining jurisdiction over conscription challenges during the War, see, e.g., In re Spangler, 11 Mich. 298 (1863) (concluding that jurisdiction over such challenges is exclusive to federal courts); In re Hopson, 40 Barb. 34, 49–50 (N.Y. Sup. Ct. 1863) (same). Other decisions are more equivocal, but also decline jurisdiction. See, e.g., Ex parte Anderson, 16 Iowa 595 (1864) (declining to give effect to the operative nationwide suspension and defending its jurisdiction over federal officers by citing pre-Civil War state court practices, while ultimately eschewing review of a case involving a deserter currently under court martial); Shirk's Case, 3 Grant 460 (Pa. 1863) (defending state court jurisdiction generally but declining to exercise it in desertion cases, relying on *Booth*). An example of an early state court wartime decision discharging a minor who enlisted without his parent's consent may be found in Dabb's Case, 21 How. Pr. 68 (Sup. Ct. N.Y. 1861).

81. Act of Mar. 3, 1863, ch. 81, § 5, 12 Stat. at 756.

82. See Act of Feb. 16, 1866, ch. 690, 1866 Ky. Acts 54; Act of Feb. 5, 1866, ch. 372, 1866 Ky. Acts 25. For additional details on the resistance to removal, see JAMES G. RANDALL, CONSTITUTIONAL PROBLEMS UNDER LINCOLN 196–197 (1926).

83. The court in In re *Fagan* dismissed habeas petitions brought by draftees in light of the president's suspension while observing that a suspension "preclude[s the court] from granting the privilege, benefit, or relief" sought by them. See 8 F. Cas. 947, 948 (D. Mass. 1863) (No. 4604). Often cited as in tension with *Fagan* is an Indiana case that contains language supporting a different understanding. See Griffin v. Wilcox, 21 Ind. 370 (1863). Nonetheless, *Griffin*, which involved a false imprisonment action, held that the suspension could not be read to sanction military trial of civilians in that state.

84. In re Rafter, 60 N.C. 537 (N.C. 1864) (Manly, J.) (interpreting Confederate suspension to require dismissal of conscription challenge); see also id. ("I see no sufficient reason for holding the law invalid for defect of power.").

85. See *The Pennsylvania Decision against the Conscription Act*, N.Y. TIMES (Nov. 13, 1863) (noting that the court "granted injunctions to restrain the Provost-Marshals from proceeding with the draft").

86. See Act of Mar. 2, 1867, ch. 155, 14 Stat. 432, 432–433.

87. See, e.g., Act of Oct. 13, 1862, ch. 49, in CSA STATUTES AT LARGE, SECOND SESSION, supra note 21, at 80–81 (1864) (providing for military trial of charges of passing or importing counterfeit notes for the Union); Currie, supra note 3,

at 1338–1339 (noting that some viewed passing or importing counterfeit Union notes as a war crime).

88. See Neely, supra note 13, at 124 & n.25 (citing Letter from Wake Keys to James A. Seddon (Nov. 18, 1863) (on file with National Archives, Washington, D.C., Letters Received by the Confederate Secretary of War, 1861–1865, RG 109, microcopy 437, K(WD)127, reel 99)); see also Robinson, supra note 7, at 380–381 (detailing Confederacy debates on this question).

89. For extensive details, consult Currie, supra note 3, at 1338–1343; see also Robinson, supra note 7, at 381 (discussing military trial of bridge-burners in East Tennessee); Neely, supra note 13, at 123–124 (describing one military court in Virginia).

90. See Robinson, supra note 7, at 385.

CHAPTER 9

1. Ulysses S. Grant, Second Inaugural Address (Mar. 4, 1873), in 9 A Compilation of the Messages and Papers of the Presidents 4175–4177 (James D. Richardson ed., New York, Bureau of Nat'l Literature, Inc. 1897) [hereinafter Messages and Papers].
2. U.S. Const. am. XIII.
3. U.S. Const. am. XIV.
4. U.S. Const. am. XV.
5. See Lou Falkner Williams, The Great South Carolina Ku Klux Klan Trials: 1871–1872, at 19–39 (1996) (describing Klan atrocities); Lou Falkner Williams, *The Constitution and the Ku Klux Klan on Trial: Federal Enforcement and Local Resistance in South Carolina, 1871–72*, 2 Ga. J. S. Legal Hist. 41, 50 (1993) ("Klan brutality reached fearsome proportions in . . . the [South Carolina] upcountry. . . . [M]asked riders rode almost nightly . . . terrorizing black families until they were forced to sleep in the woods and swamps in the dead of winter for fear of their lives.").
6. Robert J. Kaczorowski, The Politics of Judicial Interpretation: The Federal Courts, Department of Justice and Civil Rights, 1866–1876, at 81 (1985); see also District of Columbia v. Carter, 409 U.S. 418, 425–426 (1973) (observing the same); Kermit L. Hall, *Political Power and Constitutional Legitimacy: The South Carolina Ku Klux Klan Trials, 1871–1872*, 33 Emory L.J. 921, 925 (1984) (noting that local law enforcement undermined federal efforts to restore order to the region).
7. See Letter from Ulysses S. Grant to the House of Representatives (Apr. 19, 1872), in H.R. Exec. Doc. No. 42-268, 2d Sess., at 1 (1872) (recounting report of Attorney General Akerman that the Klan "control[s] juries in the State courts and sometimes in the court of the United States"); Stephen Budiansky, The Bloody Shirt: Terror after Appomattox 125, 133 (2008) (noting that Major Merrill described proceedings in South Carolina federal courts as a "farce"); J. Michael Martinez, Carpetbaggers, Cavalry, and the Ku Klux Klan 138–139 (2007).

8. Department of Justice, Annual Report of the Attorney General of the United States, H.R. Exec. Doc. No. 42-55, 2d Sess., at 4 (1871) [hereinafter 1871 Annual Report].

9. Letter from Ulysses S. Grant to the Senate and House of Representatives (Mar. 23, 1871), in 9 Messages and Papers, supra note 1, at 4081, 4081.

10. An Act to enforce the Provisions of the Fourteenth Amendment to the Constitution of the United States, and for other Purposes, ch. 22, § 1, 17 Stat. 13. Sections 2 and 6 also provided for civil causes of action on specific terms.

11. See id. §§ 2, 5, 17 Stat. at 13–15.

12. See id. §§ 3, 4, 17 Stat. at 14–15.

13. See § 4, 17 Stat. at 15.

14. See, e.g., Cong. Globe, 42d Cong., 1st. Sess. app. at 82 (1871) (statement of Rep. Bingham) ("The people grant discretionary power to the President, they trust and confide in him, and have reason to believe that he will faithfully do his duty."); id. app. at 154 (statement of Rep. Garfield) ("[T]his section provides no safeguard for citizens who may be arrested during the suspension of the writ."); id. app. at 260 (statement of Rep. Holman) ("[U]pon his discretion alone rest the guarantees of liberty. . . ."); id. at 367 (statement of Rep. Arthur) (referencing the executive's "boundless power"); id. at 362 (statement of Rep. Swann) (observing that the bill "confers . . . unlimited military power upon the President of the United States"); id. at 479–480 (statement of Rep. Leach) (calling suspension a "tremendous power" and lamenting that it "can be used for subjugating a free people").

15. See, e.g., id. at 368 (statement of Rep. Arthur) ("I do not believe a case to justify [the bill] exists. . . ."); id. app. at 210 (statement of Rep. Blair) ("No war really and in fact exists, but we will create one by legal enactment"); id. app. at 219 (statement Rep. Johnston) ("[T]his fourth section authorizes a suspension of the *habeas corpus* in a great many more cases than that of rebellion."); id. at 373 (statement of Rep. Archer) ("The meaning of the term rebellion is totally perverted"). Among those opposed on this ground were Senator Trumbull. See id. at 581 (statement of Sen. Trumbull) (denying that the present state of affairs constituted a rebellion); id. at 705 (moving to strike entirely the fourth section conferring suspension authority upon the president).

16. See, e.g., id. at 352 (statement of Rep. Beck) ("The power cannot be delegated to the President or anyone else. The people have a right to have the action of their Representatives, under all their responsibilities, acting on the existing facts. . . ."); id. at 373 (statement of Rep. Archer) ("I am aware that in 1863 this power was delegated to the President, but a bad precedent or an innovation can never shake a great and fundamental principle."); id. at 483 (statement of Rep. Wilson) (invoking the Civil War model as precedent for the Act's terms); id. app. at 160 (statement of Rep. Golladay) ("It is well decided that Congress alone has the power, and Congress alone having the power, has the exclusive right to

judge whether the exigency has arisen."); id. app. 245 (statement of Sen. Bayard) ("There is no proposition more undeniable, no one more accepted by all authority, than that a delegated power cannot be delegated by the person in whom it is vested.").

17. See, e.g., id. at 411 (statement of Rep. Van Trump).

18. Id. app. at 316 (statement of Rep. Burchard); see also id. at 477 (statement of Rep. Dawes); id. app. at 273 (statement of Rep. Porter ("Ku Klux troops are marching from one point to another, and from one State to another, to engage in the slaughter of loyal men, and gentlemen here are doubting the power of Congress to protect citizens . . . from systematic outrage in the States!"); id. at 820 (statement of Sen. Sherman) ("This bill will enable the President to again meet force with force, and I do not hide from myself the terrors of this kind of warfare, or the dangerous precedent we set for this kind of legislation.").

19. Id. at 477 (statement of Rep. Dawes); see also id. app. at 182 (statement of Rep. Mercur) (making a similar observation); id. app. at 315 (statement of Rep. Burchard) (same).

20. Id. at 761 (statement of Sen. Stevenson).

21. Id. app. at 202 (statement of Rep. Snyder). Some even complained that the suspension did not vest enough discretion in the executive to combat the Klan. See id. at 567–568 (statement of Sen. Edmunds) (opposing incorporation of Section 2 of the 1863 Act).

22. Id. app. at 82 (statement of Rep. Bingham).

23. Ulysses S. Grant, A Proclamation (May 3, 1871), in 9 MESSAGES AND PAPERS, supra note 1, at 4088, 4088.

24. Akerman was northern-born. See William S. McFeely, *Amos T. Akerman: The Lawyer and Racial Justice*, in REGION, RACE, AND RECONSTRUCTION: ESSAYS IN HONOR OF C. VANN WOODWARD 395–415 (J. Morgan Kousser & James M. McPherson eds., 1982); WILLIAMS, supra note 5, at 44.

25. Akerman also reportedly remarked at the time that "no community 'normally civilized, has been so fully under the domination of systematic and organized depravity.'" WILLIAMS, supra note 5, at 44 (citing original sources).

26. Letter from Ulysses S. Grant to the House of Representatives (Apr. 19, 1872), in H.R. EXEC. DOC. NO. 42-268, 2d Sess., at 1–2 (1872) (recounting Akerman's report).

27. See CHARLES W. CALHOUN, CONCEIVING A NEW REPUBLIC: THE REPUBLICAN PARTY AND THE SOUTHERN QUESTION, 1869–1900, at 31 (2006); see also ROBERT W. COAKLEY, THE ROLE OF FEDERAL MILITARY FORCES IN DOMESTIC DISORDERS 1789–1878, at 310–311 (1988) (noting that a military report in June 1871 "painted a grim picture of Klan domination in the area" and reported that up to three-fourths of the white men in the region were Klan members).

28. Ulysses S. Grant, A Proclamation, (Oct. 12, 1871), in 9 MESSAGES AND PAPERS, supra note 1, at 4089–4090; Ulysses S. Grant, A Proclamation, (Nov. 3, 1871), in

9 MESSAGES AND PAPERS, supra, at 4092–4093; see also COAKLEY, supra note 27, at 312 (detailing failure of dispersal orders).

29. Ulysses S. Grant, A Proclamation (Oct. 17, 1871), in 9 MESSAGES AND PAPERS, supra note 1, at 4090–4092 (naming the counties of Spartanburg, York, Marion, Chester, Laurens, Newberry, Fairfield, Lancaster, and Chesterfield); Ulysses S. Grant, A Proclamation, (Nov. 10, 1871), in 9 MESSAGES AND PAPERS, supra, at 4093–4095 (replacing Marion County with Union County).

30. FARMER'S CABINET, Nov. 22, 1871, at 2. In just a few months, Merrill arrested hundreds of men suspected of Klan ties. After the raids, the empty streets of Yorkville "took on a haunted look." MARTINEZ, supra note 7, at 150. For more details, consult Hall, supra note 6, at 925; BUDIANSKY, supra note 7, at 135; COAKLEY, supra note 27, at 312. Merrill had been investigating the Klan in the area since March, but his efforts were frustrated by the secrecy and compartmentalization of the organization. See David Everitt, *1871 War on Terror*, 38 AM. HIST. 26, 30 (2003).

31. 1871 ANNUAL REPORT, supra note 8, at 5.

32. Louis F. Post, A "Carpetbagger" in South Carolina, 10 J. NEGRO HIST. 10, 41, 43–44 (1925) ("By this means [Merrill] gathered an accumulating mass of testimony, each day bringing forth further clues for further arrests."); see also WILLIAMS, supra note 5, at 47 (noting several murders that came to light under these circumstances).

33. See Letter from Attorney General George H. Williams to President Ulysses S. Grant (Apr. 19, 1872) (reporting 501 arrests), in H.R. EXEC. DOC. No. 42-268 at 3 (1872); 1871 ANNUAL REPORT, supra note 8, at 5 (1871) (reporting 472 arrests); Williams, supra note 5, at 53, 55 (noting that many Klan members surrendered to federal authorities).

34. See WILLIAMS, supra note 5, at 46–47.

35. See Letter from Attorney General George H. Williams, supra note 33, exhibit A, at 8 (listing many witnesses held without charges, including one "very important witness for Government"); see also JAMES E. SEFTON, THE UNITED STATES ARMY AND RECONSTRUCTION 1865–1877, at 226 (1967); WILLIAMS, supra note 5, at 47, 49, 56, 61.

36. See Letter from District Attorney D.T. Corbin to Attorney General Amos T. Akerman, Nov. 13, 1871, microformed on RG 60, Microcopy 947, Reel 1, National Archives, Washington, D.C. The Constitution's ban on "ex post facto Law[s]" prohibits retroactive application of criminal statutes to prior conduct. See U.S. CONST. art. I, § 9, cl. 3.

37. See 1871 ANNUAL REPORT, supra note 8, at 5; Letter from District Attorney D.T. Corbin to Attorney General George H. Williams, Feb. 20, 1872 ("It must be apparent that the present facilities for bringing the Ku-Klux causes to trial are utterly inadequate, and Congress ought to afford some more speedy and effective means. It must do so or permit most of the prosecutions to fail."), in H.R.

EXEC. DOC. NO. 42-268, 2d Sess., at 19 (1872); see also WILLIAMS, supra note 5, at 111 (noting that 1188 Enforcement Act cases remained pending in South Carolina alone at the end of 1872).

38. Richard Zuczek, *The Federal Government's Attack on the Ku Klux Klan: A Reassessment*, 97 S.C. HIST. MAG. 47, 62–64 (1996) (quoting Merrill); see also Francis B. Simkins, *The Ku Klux Klan in South Carolina, 1868–1871*, 12 J. NEGRO HIST. 606, 646 (1927) (noting that Merrill's 1872 report stated that order had been restored to the area).

39. S. REP. NO. 42-41, pt. 1, at 99 (1872) (recommending that the Act's "protective measures" be "continued until there remains no further doubt of the actual suppression and disarming of this wide-spread and dangerous conspiracy"). Senate Bill 656 would have extended the Act's emergency provisions, but failed.

40. See WILLIAMS, supra note 5, at 122–125.

41. Ex parte Yerger, 75 U.S. (8 Wall.) 85, 95 (1869). *Yerger* came after Ex parte *McCardle*, 74 U.S. 506 (1868). Both cases challenged the constitutionality of the Military Reconstruction Act. The *Yerger* decision followed from the first round of argument in the case over the Court's jurisdiction to decide the merits of Yerger's petition. In the end, the Court never reached the merits of Yerger's claims because the government transferred him to state authorities rather than try him before a military commission. See CHARLES FAIRMAN, 6 HISTORY OF THE SUPREME COURT OF THE UNITED STATES: RECONSTRUCTION AND REUNION, 1864–1888, PART ONE A 589 (1971).

42. An Act to suspend the privilege of the writ of habeas corpus in certain cases, Act of Feb. 15, 1874, ch. 37, pmbl., Pub. Laws., 1st Cong., 4th Sess., in THE STATUTES AT LARGE OF THE CONFEDERATE STATES OF AMERICA 187, 187 (James M. Matthews ed., Richmond 1864).

43. See, e.g., CONG. GLOBE, 42d Cong., 2nd. Sess. app. at 665 (1872) (statement of Sen. Thurman) (quoting Blackstone and discussing the history of parliamentary suspension of the Habeas Corpus Act); see also id. app. at 507–510 (statement of Sen. Stevenson); id. at 3714 (statement of Sen. Vickers); id. at 3719 (statement of Sen. Hamilton); id. at 4373 (statement of Sen. Saulsbury).

44. As is explored in the next chapter, the suspension invoked in the Hawaiian Territory during World War II fails this test, insofar as it followed under a standing delegation to the territorial governor of the power to suspend that dated back to the Hawaiian Organic Act of 1900.

45. S. REP. NO. 42-41, pt. 1, at 99 (1872).

46. See COAKLEY, supra note 27, at 312 (highlighting the suspension's use to detain suspected Klansmen to obtain information on Klan hierarchy); id. at 308–309 (discussing witness intimidation); see also 1871 ANNUAL REPORT, supra note 8, at 4 (noting that witness protection was one purpose behind the suspension).

47. CONG. GLOBE, 42d Cong., 1st. Sess. at 373 (1871) (statement of Rep. Archer).

CHAPTER 10

1. Letter from Attorney Gen. Francis Biddle to Representative Leland Merritt Ford (Jan. 24, 1942), in DOCUMENTS OF THE COMMISSION ON WARTIME RELOCATION AND INTERNMENT OF CIVILIANS 5739, 5740, reel 5, 417–418 (Frederick, Md., University Publications of America 1983).

2. Transcript of Telephone Conversation, Major Karl R. Bendetsen, assistant to the Judge Advocate Gen., Major Gen. Allen W. Gullion, Provost Marshal Gen. of the U.S. Army, and Gen. Mark W. Clark, Deputy Chief of Staff of the Army Ground Forces 2 (Feb. 4, 1942), in DOCUMENTS OF THE COMMISSION ON WARTIME RELOCATION, supra note 1, at 5936, 5937, reel 5, 579 ("That is what McCloy said.") (statement of General Gullion).

3. Proclamation No. 2525, 6 Fed. Reg. 6321 (Oct. 10, 1941); Proclamation No. 2526, 6 Fed. Reg. 6323 (Dec. 8, 1941); Proclamation No. 2527, 6 Fed. Reg. 6324 (Dec. 8, 1941). War Department instructions expanded those subject to the proclamations to dual citizens in Hawaii. See Harry N. Scheiber, Jane L. Scheiber & Benjamin Jones, *Hawai'i's Kibei under Martial Law: A Hidden Chapter in the History of World War II Internments*, 22 W. LEGAL HIST. 1, 19 n.56 (2009) (citing Adams (War Department) to Commanding Gen., Fort Shafter, radiogram, Dec. 11, 1941, U.S. District Court case no. 730, exhibit C, RG 21, National Archives, San Bruno, CA).

4. Letter from Federal Bureau of Investigation Director J. Edgar Hoover to Presidential Secretary Major Gen. Edwin M. Watson (Dec. 10, 1941) (on file with Franklin D. Roosevelt Presidential Library, Hyde Park, NY [hereinafter FDR Library], Franklin D. Roosevelt Papers, President's Official File 10-B: Justice Department; FBI Reports, 1941; Box 15 (including maps detailing FBI arrests of 1,212 Japanese, 620 German, and 98 Italian aliens); see also ANNUAL REPORT OF THE ATTORNEY GENERAL FOR FISCAL YEAR ENDED JUNE 30, 1942, at 14 (1943) [hereinafter ANNUAL REPORT] (reporting that 2,971 enemy aliens were taken into custody in the early weeks of the war).

5. See PETER IRONS, JUSTICE AT WAR: THE STORY OF THE JAPANESE AMERICAN INTERNMENT CASES 19 (1983); ANNUAL REPORT, supra note 4, at 14 (discussing arrests during this period).

6. See Scheiber, Scheiber & Jones, supra note 3, at 24–38, 67–68 (noting that many were evacuated to the mainland).

7. Ch. 339, 31 Stat. 141, id. § 67, 31 Stat. at 153. For more details, consult Duncan v. Kahanamoku, 327 U.S. 304, 307–308 (1946); Garner Anthony, *Martial Law, Military Government and the Writ of Habeas Corpus in Hawaii*, 31 CALIF. L. REV. 477, app. 1 (1943) (reprinting the full text of the Governor's Proclamation).

8. See Duncan, 327 U.S. at 308 & n.2; id. at 348 (Burton, J., dissenting); Anthony, supra note 7, at 478 (detailing communications between Territorial Governor Poindexter and President Roosevelt).

9. In legislation governing the Philippine Territory, Congress provided that the privilege "shall not be suspended, unless when in cases of rebellion, insurrection, or invasion the public safety may require it," and that "the same may be suspended by the President, or by the Governor-General with the approval of the Philippine Commission, wherever during such period the necessity for such suspension shall exist." Act of July 1, 1902, ch. 1369, § 5, 32 Stat. 691, 692. Shortly thereafter, the governor suspended the writ in two provinces for a period of approximately nine months. See Fisher v. Baker, 203 U.S. 174, 179–181 (1906). The suspension came in response to an "open insurrection" led by organized bands of ladrones against authorities in the provinces, which were experiencing a breakdown of the judicial process due to "a state of insecurity and terrorism among the people." Id. at 179–180 (noting that the governor had concluded that "there exists a state of insecurity and terrorism among the people which makes it impossible in the ordinary way to conduct preliminary investigations before justices of the peace and other judicial officers"). During this period, persons were detained without charges. See Barcelon v. Baker, 5 PHIL. REP. 87, 89–91 (S.C., Sept. 30, 1905). "To legally detain them, certain legal requirements had to be satisfied. But conditions then existing did not permit compliance with such requirements. Hence, the suspension." Estelito P. Mendoza, *The Suspension of the Writ of Habeas Corpus: Suggested Amendments*, 33 PHIL. L.J. 630, 632 (1958).

10. Whitman v. American Trucking Ass'ns, Inc., 531 U.S. 457, 472, 475 (2001) (internal quotation marks omitted); cf. United States v. Curtiss-Wright Export Corp., 299 U.S. 304 (1936) (deferring to delegations in the foreign affairs arena). For additional discussion of delegation questions in the suspension context, see Amy Coney Barrett, *Suspension and Delegation*, 99 CORNELL L. REV. 251 (2014).

11. See American Ins. Co. v. Cantor, 1 Pet. (26 U.S.) 511, 546 (1828) (Marshall, C.J.) ("In legislating for [the territories], Congress exercises the combined powers of the general, and of a state government.").

12. 327 U.S. 304, 318–319 (1946). Well before this time, the Court's jurisprudence treated "incorporated" territories such as Alaska and Hawaii differently from other territories, such as those taken as spoils in war. With respect to the latter context, the Court held in a series of early twentieth century decisions that every provision of the Constitution does not automatically apply. One case distinguishing "incorporated" versus "unincorporated" territories and recognizing Hawaii's status as being distinct from those territories acquired after the Spanish-American War is *Downes v. Bidwell*, 182 U.S. 244 (1901), commonly known as one of the *Insular Cases*. See id. at 304–306; id. at 345 (Gray, J., concurring); cf. *Reid v. Covert*, 354 U.S. 1, 14 (1957) (Black, J.) (plurality opinion) (distinguishing the *Insular Cases* as involving "the power of Congress to provide rules and regulations to govern temporarily territories with wholly dissimilar traditions and institutions."). Depending on the reach and continuing force of

the *Insular Cases*, similar standing delegations to suspend found today in several territorial organic acts could also be constitutionally suspect. See, e.g., An Act to Provide a Civil Government for Porto Rico, and for Other Purposes, Bill of Rights § 2, 39 Stat. 951, 951 (1917); An Act to Provide a Civil Government for the Virgin Islands of the United States § 34, 49 Stat. 1807, 1815 (1936); An Act to Provide a Civil Government for Guam, and for Other Purposes § 6(b), 64 Stat. 384, 386 (1950).

13. Duncan, 327 U.S. at 308. General Short's orders were as follows: "Under the direction of the Commanding General, Hawaiian Department, all courts of the Territory of Hawaii will be closed until further notice." Letter from Commanding General Walter Short to Chief Justice Samuel Kemp (Dec. 8, 1941), quoted in J. Garner Anthony, Hawaii under Army Rule 10 (1955). General Short was relieved of his command within days of the attack on Pearl Harbor and succeeded by General Delos C. Emmons.

14. Anthony, supra note 7, at 481.

15. As the Ninth Circuit noted during this period, "because of the prohibition against the assembling or empaneling of juries[, the courts] were wholly disabled from trying criminal cases in the constitutional sense." Ex parte Duncan, 146 F.2d 576, 579 (9th Cir. 1944).

16. See Anthony, supra note 7, at 503 (noting that the hearings "apparently consist of reports of investigations and cross examination of the suspected individuals," and "[t]he proceedings are secret"). For an extensive discussion of conditions in Hawaii during the war, see Harry N. Scheiber & Jane L. Scheiber, Bayonets in Paradise: Martial Law in Hawai'i during World War II (2016).

17. Duncan, 327 U.S. at 309.

18. See, e.g., General Orders No. 29 (Dec. 16, 1941) (banning circuit courts from issuing writs of habeas corpus), quoted in Robert S. Rankin, *Hawaii under Martial Law*, 5 J. Politics 270, 274–275(1943).

19. Ex parte Zimmerman, 132 F.2d 442, 443–444 & n.1 (9th Cir. 1942) (describing the district court decision); *Habeas Corpus Denied: Honolulu Judge Says Court Is under Military Duress*, N.Y. Times, Feb. 22, 1942, at 9. The order's text is reprinted at Garner Anthony, *Martial Law in Hawaii*, 30 Cal. L. Rev. 371, 396 (1942).

20. 132 F.2d 442, 445 (9th Cir. 1942). The court added that "[i]t is common knowledge that the Hawaiian Islands, owing to their position and the inclusion in their population of so large an element presumptively alien in sympathy, are peculiarly exposed to fifth-column activities." Id. at 446. For criticism, see Anthony, supra note 7, at 485 n.37.

21. Most recently, Justice Scalia advocated this position in *Hamdi v. Rumsfeld*. See 542 U.S. 507, 564, 577–578 (2004) (Scalia, J., dissenting); see also id. at 594 n.4 (Thomas, J., dissenting) (same).

22. For detailed discussion of arguments on both sides of the debate and a defense of the justiciability of suspension, see Amanda L. Tyler, *Is Suspension a Political*

Question?, 59 STAN. L. REV. 333, 354–362 (2006). Although one could certainly argue in favor of deferring to the political branches when they deem a suspension necessary, deference should not equate with disclaiming judicial review altogether. See United States v. Nixon, 506 U.S. 224, 239–252 (1993) (White, J., concurring in the judgment) (exploring this important distinction); see also Tyler, supra, at 408–412 (same).

23. In a speech given in the wake of World War II, Justice Robert Jackson endorsed the proposition that "courts might inquire whether the conditions existed which permit [a] suspension." Robert H. Jackson, Wartime Security and Liberty Under Law (address delivered at Buffalo Law School, May 9, 1951), available at http:// www.roberthjackson.org/the-man/bibliography/wartime-security-and-liberty-under-law. Along similar lines, in the context of reviewing declarations of martial law, the Court has posited that "[w]hat are the allowable limits of military discretion, and whether or not they have been overstepped in a particular case, are judicial questions." Sterling v. Constantin, 287 U.S. 378, 401 (1932); see also JOHN HART ELY, WAR AND RESPONSIBILITY 55 (1993) ("[T]he Supreme Court has routinely decided 'foreign affairs' and 'national security' cases throughout the nation's history. . . ."); id. at 176 n.46 (citing numerous cases).

24. 1792 Calling Forth Act, ch. 28, §§ 1, 3, 1 Stat. 264 (repealed 1795).

25. Proclamation of President George Washington, (Aug. 7, 1794), in *Dunlap and Claypoole's American Daily Advertiser*, Aug. 11, 1794 (internal quotation marks omitted).

26. Ex parte Zimmerman, 132 F.2d 442, 446 (9th Cir. 1942) (citing Ex parte Milligan, 71 U.S. (4 Wall.) 2, 125 (1866); Moyer v. Peabody, 212 U.S. 78, 84, 85 (1909)); see id. ("[A] prime purpose of the suspension of the writ is to enable the executive, as a precautionary measure, to detain without interference persons suspected of harbouring designs harmful to the public safety."); see also McCall v. McDowell, 15 F. Cas. 1235, 1245 (C.C.D. Cal. 1867) (No. 8673) (holding that "[t]he suspension being the virtual authorization of arrest without the ordinary legal cause or warrant, it follows that such arrests, pending the suspension . . . are practically legal").

27. Although he dissented in *Zimmerman*, Judge Haney agreed that so long as "the action of the military [was] reasonably necessary for it 'to execute the Laws of the Union, suppress Insurrections and repel Invasions' and to protect each of the states 'against invasion,'" it was proper. 132 F.2d at 451, 453 (Haney, J., dissenting) (quoting U.S. CONST. art. I, § 8, cl. 15; id. art. IV).

28. Brief for the State of California as Amicus Curiae at 34, Ex parte Zimmerman, 132 F.2d 442 (9th Cir. 1942) (on file with author) (quoting FREDERICK BERNAYS WIENER, A PRACTICAL MANUAL OF MARTIAL LAW (1940)); id. at 11. Warren also gave a speech promoting an expansive view of martial law the same year. See Earl Warren, Address to the Stanford Law Society: Martial Rule in Time of War (June 4, 1942), California State Archives, Earl Warren Papers.

29. Id. at 10; see also id. at 5 (observing that "[t]he exigencies of the war on the Pacific Coast may require the imposition of additional controls by the military authorities"). California's brief argued that Justice Holmes's decision for the Supreme Court in *Moyer v. Peabody*, 212 U.S. 78 (1909), recognized broad authority for the state to displace individual rights in times of crisis. See id. at 26 (quoting Moyer, 212 U.S. at 85 ("When it comes to a decision by the head of the State upon a matter involving its life, the ordinary rights of individuals must yield to what he deems the necessities of the moment.")). The Supreme Court's later decision in *Sterling v. Constantin*, 287 U.S. 378 (1932), calls into question *Moyer's* breadth. See id. at 399 ("What are the allowable limits of military discretion and whether or not they have been overstepped in a particular case, are judicial questions.").

30. See Zimmerman v. Walker, 319 U.S. 744 (1943) ("Petition . . . denied on the ground that the cause is moot, it appearing that Hans Zimmerman, on whose behalf the petition is filed, has been released from the respondent's custody."). For additional details, see Anthony, supra note 7, at 486 (noting that the government had earlier moved him to Wisconsin and then back to Hawaii because of the suspension in effect there). Zimmerman later filed a civil suit for damages against government officials, see Zimmerman v. Poindexter, 78 F. Supp. 421 (D. Hawaii 1947) (denying several motions to dismiss), losing at trial, see Zimmerman v. Emmons, 225 F.2d 97, 98 (9th Cir. 1955).

31. *Call Martial Law Vital to Hawaii: War Chiefs Say Continuance Is Essential for Security There and Continental Defense*, N.Y. TIMES, Sept. 16, 1943. The cases were Ex parte *Seifert*, U.S.D.C. (Haw.) No. 296, and Ex parte *Glockner*, U.S.D.C. (Haw.) No. 295. In yet another case, the government also released a prisoner to avoid Supreme Court review. See Steer v. Spurlock, 146 F.2d 652 (9th Cir. 1944) (upholding provost court sentence and denying petition for a writ of habeas corpus); J. Garner Anthony, *Hawaiian Martial Law in the Supreme Court*, 57 YALE L.J. 27, 36–37 (1947) (noting that once Spurlock sought review in the Supreme Court, he was pardoned and released, after which the government argued that the case was moot).

32. See Robert S. Rankin, *Martial Law and the Writ of Habeas Corpus in Hawaii*, 6 J. POLITICS 213, 221 (1944). The Ninth Circuit later rejected this reasoning in the *Duncan* case. See Ex parte Duncan, 146 F.2d. 576, 578 (9th Cir. 1944) ("[T]he later proclamation was not intended to terminate the suspension and did not have that effect.").

33. See Anthony, supra note 7, at 486–487; H. Brett Melendy, *Delbert E. Metzger, Hawai'i's Liberal Judge*, 35 HAWAIIAN J. HIST. 43, 54 (2001) (citing archival documents); Rankin, supra note 32, at 221 (quoting the court) ("'True, a state of war exists, but that is not sufficient to authorize the suspension, and the governor's proclamation clearly manifests that in his executive judgment civilian government functions and laws should be resumed. . . .'").

34. Bob Dye, Hawaiʻi Chronicles III: World War Two in Hawaiʻi, From the Pages of Paradise of the Pacific 160 (2000) (quoting Emmons) (internal quotation marks omitted).

35. For details, see Rankin, supra note 32, at 222; Anthony, supra note 7, at 487–488. One newspaper article reports that the marshals were "manhandled" and "forcibly removed" from the premises. *Justice, War Depts. Confer on Court Move*, Honolulu Advertiser, Aug. 18, 1943.

36. See Anthony, supra note 7, at 486–492 (detailing events); Rankin, supra note 32, at 219–226; Melendy, supra note 33, at 54–55; Scheiber & Scheiber, supra note 16, at 263–270. Reportedly, the resolution followed "[a] series of conferences among the War, Interior and Justice Departments. . . ." *Army, Court Controversy in Hawaii at White Heat*, Wash. Post, Aug. 27, 1943. Judge Metzger eventually reduced General Richardson's fine to $100, which was never paid because President Roosevelt granted a full pardon to Richardson. See Rankin, supra, at 226. For press criticism, see, e.g., *Habeas Corpus*, Wash. Post, Sept. 2, 1943 ("It is by no means clear whence General Richardson derives the right, which he claims to have, of suspending the writ. . . . That section of the Constitution which forbids Congress to suspend the writ except in cases of invasion or rebellion by clear implication vests the right of suspension in such cases solely with Congress.").

37. Duncan v. Kahanamoku, 327 U.S. 304, 307, 311 (1946).

38. Admiral Nimitz's testimony is detailed in Ex parte *Duncan*, 146 F.2d 576, 587–588 (9th Cir. 1944) (en banc) (Wilbur, J., concurring).

39. Ex parte Duncan, 66 F. Supp. 976, 979, 980–981 (D. Haw. 1944); see id. at 979 (highlighting that the territorial governor had begun reintroducing civilian rule in February 1943).

40. See Duncan, 66 F. Supp. at 982; Ex parte White, 66 F. Supp. 982, 989 (D. Haw. 1944). In *White*, Judge McLaughlin emphasized three points: (1) after the Battle of Midway concluded successfully in June 1942, the Islands no longer remained in any danger of a land invasion by the Japanese; (2) the Army had conceded that no acts of sabotage had been committed "by the Japanese population of the Territory"; and (3) the Hawaiian courts were open and ready to hear criminal cases. Id. at 984–985. These cases are discussed at length in Scheiber & Scheiber, supra note 16, at 274–284.

41. Duncan, 146 F.2d at 580 ("Thus was afforded ideal cover for the activities of the saboteur and the spy.").

42. Id. at 581.

43. Id. at 583 (quoting Hirabayashi v. United States, 320 U.S. 81, 93 (1943)). Only after the war, a member of the Ninth Circuit panel published the dissent that he had circulated to the panel at the time but withheld until the conclusion of the war. See Ex parte Duncan, 153 F.2d 943 (9th Cir. 1946) (Stephens, J., dissenting).

44. Duncan v. Kahanamoku, 327 U.S. 304 (1946). One of the two questions on which the Court granted certiorari read: "Was the privilege of the writ of habeas corpus suspended as to this case on April 20, 1944?" Petition for Writ of Certiorari at 7, Duncan, 327 U.S. 304 (No. 791).

45. See Proclamation No. 2627, 3 C.F.R. 41 (1943–1948) (Oct. 24, 1944). Details on the transition to civil law may be found in Anthony, supra note 7, at 482–483. Some news accounts pointed to Judge Metzger's role in spearheading the demise of martial law in the Islands. See, e.g., *Two Years Too Late*, CHI. TRIBUNE, Oct. 28, 1944 ("[Roosevelt] would not have yielded to the obvious even now if it had not been for the resolute courage of Judge Delbert E. Metzger. . . ."); see also *Two Years Too Late*, supra ("Mr. Roosevelt has ended martial law in Hawaii, two years too late and less than two weeks before the election.").

46. Duncan, 327 U.S. at 312 n.5.

47. Id. at 336 (Stone, C.J., concurring).

48. Duncan, 327 U.S. at 322. Before the Ninth Circuit, Duncan's lawyers "described a typical provost court judge as a soldier sitting on the bench with a gun on one side, a gas mask on the other, and 'a big cigar in his mouth.'" *Charge Abuse of Civilians in Army Courts: Tell of Judges in Hawaii with Guns at Side*, CHI. DAILY TRIBUNE, July 2, 1944.

49. Duncan, 327 U.S. at 320–321 (noting also that the Petition of Right came in response to the king "speedily punishing all types of crimes committed by civilians"). For Discussion of Shays's Rebellion and the Whiskey Rebellion, see Chapters 4 & 6. The Court also called into question a number of decisions upholding military trials of civilians following major labor strikes, see Duncan, 327 U.S. at 322, a passage that further calls into question the continuing precedential value of *Moyer v. Peabody*, 212 U.S. 78 (1909), discussed supra note 29.

50. Letter from James Madison to A.J. Dallas (May 17, 1815), quoted in 6 IRVING BRANT, JAMES MADISON 384 (1961).

51. Id. at 324 (quoting Ex parte Milligan, 71 U.S. (4 Wall.) 2, 124, 125 (1866)); see also id. at 325 (Murphy, J., concurring) ("Th[e] supremacy of the civil over the military is one of our great heritages. . . ."). Chief Justice Stone went further in his concurring opinion, writing that a review of the record showed clearly that even in February 1942, "the civil courts were capable of functioning, and that trials of petitioners in the civil courts no more endangered the public safety than the gathering of the populace in saloons and places of amusement, which was authorized by military order." Id. at 337 (Stone, C.J., concurring).

52. In the Chief Justice's view, the Court had a long history of case law defining martial law as "a law of necessity." He argued, in turn, that the relevant precedents must inform the Court's interpretation of the Hawaiian Organic Act. Id. at 620 (Stone, C.J., concurring).

53. WILLIAM H. REHNQUIST, ALL THE LAWS BUT ONE: CIVIL LIBERTIES IN WARTIME 217 (1998).

54. Duncan, 327 U.S. at 318 ("[C]ivilians in Hawaii are entitled to the Constitutional guarantee of fair trial to the same extent as those who live in any other part of our country.").

55. Martial Law, 8 Op. Att'y Gen. 374 (1857). For a similar view, see Judge Haney's dissent in *Zimmerman* at the Ninth Circuit, which argued that "military government is not established by merely proclaiming it. It comes into being and exists solely by reason of the fact that strife prevents operation of the civil government." Ex parte Zimmerman, 132 F.2d 442, 450 (9th Cir. 1942) (Haney, J., dissenting) (citing Milligan, 71 U.S. at 127).

56. Justice Department lawyer Edward Ennis, who argued *Duncan* for the government, referred to suspension in Hawaii as of January 1944 as " 'probably unconstitutional.' " SCHEIBER & SCHEIBER, supra note 16, at 310 (quoting Memorandum from Edward Ennis to the Solicitor Gen., Jan. 21, 1944); see also *Editorial: Study Army Gag on Hawaii: The Military Tyrant*, CHI. DAILY TRIBUNE, Aug. 27, 1943 ("There is no rebellion in Hawaii and Hawaii is not invaded and is in no danger of invasion.").

57. Scheiber, Scheiber & Jones, supra note 3, at 65 (quoting Memorandum from Maj. Louis F. Springer to Col. William Morrison (Dec. 31, 1943)) (emphasis added) (internal quotation marks omitted).

58. 3 C.F.R. 1092 (1942) (repealed 1976). This section relies heavily on the interviews and archival sources identified in the work of Morton Grodzins, Peter Irons, and Greg Robinson.

59. GREG ROBINSON, BY ORDER OF THE PRESIDENT: FDR AND THE INTERNMENT OF JAPANESE AMERICANS 5–6 (2001).

60. Memorandum of President Franklin Delano Roosevelt to the Chief of (Naval) Operations (Aug. 10, 1936) (on file with National Archives, Washington, D.C. [hereinafter National Archives, DC], RG 80: Dept. of the Navy, 1798–1947, entry UD 8 Office of the Secretary of the Navy (General Records), Formerly Confidential Correspondence, 1927–1939, Box 216, File A 8-5). As late as 1944, President Roosevelt was still using the term. See ROBINSON, supra note 59, at 2 (quoting presidential statement in November 21, 1944, press conference). Once instituted, the government labeled the camps "relocation centers." In 1946, however, former Roosevelt administration interior secretary Harold L. Ickes said that "they were concentration camps nonetheless." *Man to Man: Wartime Abuse of American Japanese Should Now Be Corrected by U.S.*, WASH. EVENING STAR, Sept. 23, 1946.

61. *Enemy Planes Sighted over California Coast*, L.A. TIMES, Dec. 9, 1941.

62. U.S. DEP'T OF WAR, FINAL REPORT: JAPANESE EVACUATION FROM THE WEST COAST, 1942, at 8 (1943), cited in IRONS, supra note 5, at 27.

63. Memorandum from Major Karl R. Bendetsen, assistant to the Judge Advocate Gen., "Alien Enemies on the West Coast (and Other Subversive Persons)," to Major Gen. Allen W. Gullion, Provost Marshal Gen. 4 (Feb. 4, 1942), in

DOCUMENTS OF THE COMMISSION ON WARTIME RELOCATION, supra note 1, at 5945, 5948, reel 5, 588. As Professor Irons notes, just days later the same official drafted a final recommendation to Commanding General of the Western Defense Command John L. DeWitt asserting that mass evacuation was required "by military necessity," which DeWitt adopted in turn. Id. at 50; see Lieutenant Gen. John L. DeWitt, Final Report, Japanese Evacuation from the West Coast, 1942 (submitted February 13, 1942). In the months leading up to the Pearl Harbor attack, intelligence officers had uncovered a West Coast espionage ring aiding Japanese efforts. But by the time of the attack, the Office of Naval Intelligence, the FBI, and Army investigators all believed that they had broken up the ring. As one FBI memo reported a month before the bombing of Pearl Harbor, "no evidence ha[d] been obtained" to suggest that any persons not previously investigated had committed any criminal offenses tied to espionage. IRONS, supra note 5, at 23 (citing, inter alia, G-2 Periodic Report (Feb. 7, 1942) (on file with Federal Records Center, Suitland, Md., Western Defense Command records, Box 28)).

64. Transcripts of Telephone Conversations, Bendetsen, Gullion, and Clark, supra note 2, at 1 (statement of General Gullion) (describing meeting).

65. See FRANCIS BIDDLE, IN BRIEF AUTHORITY 221–224 (1962) (discussing reports that he had received from Hoover); see also ROBINSON, supra note 59, at 100.

66. Memorandum from Attorney Gen. Francis Biddle, "Luncheon Conversation with the President" 2 (Feb. 7, 1942) (on file with the FDR Library, supra note 4, Francis Biddle Papers, Box 3, Roosevelt, Franklin D. Correspondence Folder).

67. IRONS, supra note 5, at 29 (quoting Transcript of Telephone Conversation, Commanding Gen. of the Western Defense Command John L. DeWitt and Provost Marshal Gen. of the U.S. Army Major Gen. Allen W. Gullion (Dec. 26, 1941) (internal quotation marks omitted) (reporting DeWitt to have said: "if we go ahead and arrest the 93,000 Japanese [in California], native born and foreign born, we are going to have an awful job on our hands and are very liable to alienate the loyal Japanese," and that he was "very doubtful that it would be common sense procedure" to intern the Japanese American population)).

68. IRONS, supra note 5, at 30 (quoting Transcript of Telephone Conversation, DeWitt and Gullion, supra note 67) (internal quotation marks omitted). Additional examples of DeWitt's earlier reluctance over internment proposals are detailed in BIDDLE, supra note 65, at 215.

69. Henry L. Stimson, Diary 85 (Feb. 3, 1942) (on file with Henry L. Stimson Papers, Yale University Library, reel 7).

70. Letter from Representative Leland Ford to Attorney Gen. Francis Biddle (Jan. 23, 1942) (on file with Bancroft Library, University of California, Berkeley, Japanese Evacuation and Relocation Study Papers, reel 1). Ford urged the same policy in letters to Secretary of the Navy William Franklin Knox and FBI Director J. Edgar Hoover on January 16, 1942. See MORTON GRODZINS, AMERICANS BETRAYED: POLITICS AND THE JAPANESE EVACUATION 65 (1949) (quoting letter). On

the House floor, Ford argued that "a patriotic native-born Japanese, if he wants to make his contribution, will submit himself to a concentration camp." IRONS, supra note 5, at 38 (quoting floor statement) (internal quotation marks omitted).

71. Letter from Attorney Gen. Francis Biddle to Representative Leland Merritt Ford (Jan. 24, 1942), in DOCUMENTS OF THE COMMISSION ON WARTIME RELOCATION, supra note 1, at 5739, 5740, reel 5, at 417–418; see also BIDDLE, supra note 65, at 215 (repeating what he had written). Biddle also wrote to Ford three days later: "This Department has not deemed it advisable at this time to attempt to remove all persons of the Japanese race into the interior of the country." In support, Biddle cited policies already in place along with "the legal difficulties presently involved in attempting to intern or evacuate the thousands of American born persons of Japanese race, who are, of course, American citizens." Letter from Attorney Gen. Francis Biddle to Representative Leland Merritt Ford (Jan. 27, 1942) (on file with Bancroft Library, University of California, Berkeley, Japanese Evacuation and Relocation Study Papers, reel 1. The archived copy of the letter includes a signature by Edward Ennis after the notation "No intention & no plans yet to evacuating citizens." Jan. 27 Letter from Attorney Gen. Francis Biddle, supra. A Justice Department directive issued to the FBI only days after the Pearl Harbor attacks took the same position regarding citizens of German extraction, advising that "[c]itizens may only be apprehended if some probable cause exists for criminal proceedings against them." Memorandum from Assistant Attorney Gen. Francis Shea to FBI Director J. Edgar Hoover (Dec. 10, 1941), in DOCUMENTS OF THE COMMISSION ON WARTIME RELOCATION, supra note 1, at 5780, reel 6, at 458.

72. Transcript of Telephone Conversation, Bendetsen, Gullion, and Clark, supra note 2, at 1 (statement of General Gullion). Biddle also reportedly stated in the meeting: "the Department of Justice would be through if [the War Department] interfered with citizens and [the] write [*sic*] of habeas corpus. . . ." Id. Biddle later wrote of the significance of citizenship, observing that Japanese American citizens' "constitutional rights were the same as those of the men who were responsible for the program." BIDDLE, supra note 65, at 213.

73. Id. at 217. Biddle dates the meeting on February 1, 1942. See id. at 216.

74. Memorandum from Attorney Gen. Francis Biddle to President Franklin Delano Roosevelt (Jan. 30, 1942) (on file with Bancroft Library, University of California, Berkeley, Japanese Evacuation and Relocation Study Papers, reel 1). (Professor Grodzins notes in his work that two different drafts exist of a memorandum dated this day written by Biddle to the president. The shorter version conveys essentially the same message. See GRODZINS, supra note 70, at 255 & n.58.) Biddle reportedly made a similar statement at a cabinet meeting on January 30, 1942. According to Secretary of the Interior Harold Ickes's diary, Biddle suggested that "the time might come that there would be certain areas where the President might suspend the writ of Habeas Corpus." Harold Ickes, Diary 6303

(Feb. 1, 1942) (on file with Harold Ickes Papers, Library of Congress, reel 5). The Department was clearly evaluating the possibility of a suspension. See GRODZINS, supra, at 256 (quoting Letter from Edward J. Ennis to Director J. Edgar Hoover (Feb. 13, 1942) (noting he was "studying the uses to which a statute suspending the writ of habeas corpus might be put")).

75. Henry L. Stimson, Diary, supra note 69, at 85 (Feb. 3, 1942); id. at 102 (Feb. 10, 1942).

76. See id. at 116–117 (Apr. 15, 1942); see also ROBINSON, supra note 59, at 151 (detailing these events and reporting that Stimson suggested that the president consider suspension on the mainland).

77. Memorandum from Assistant to the Attorney Gen. James H. Rowe, Jr. to Grace Tully, Private Secretary to President Franklin Delano Roosevelt (Feb. 2, 1942) (on file with FDR Library, supra note 4, James H. Rowe, Jr. Papers, Assistant to the Attorney Gen. Files, Alien Enemy Control Unit, Box 33).

78. BIDDLE, supra note 65, at 223. During this time, President Roosevelt also heard from John Franklin Carter, who served in a special intelligence role for the president and reported directly to him. Carter sent the president a memo in January 1942 noting that Congress had before it a proposal to strip citizenship of suspected foreign spies and that the Department of Justice was working on a draft Executive Order and a Joint Resolution to allow the arrest and 90-day detention of citizens based on " 'Certificates of Probable Cause' for consorting with Axis agents etc." Carter acknowledged such a measure would "be a modification of Habeas Corpus," and informed the president that "Biddle . . . was not ready to sponsor any such drastic move as yet." Memorandum from John Franklin Carter to President Franklin Delano Roosevelt (Jan. 19, 1942) (on file with FDR Library, supra note 4, John Franklin Carter File, Jan.–Feb. 1942, President's Secretary's File, Box 122, p. 108).

79. Some commentators have suggested that by reporting that his department was studying the possibility of calling for a suspension, Biddle may have encouraged the events that followed. See, e.g., ROBINSON, supra note 59, at 100 ("Biddle's reassurance that the legal obstacles to removing citizens from restricted areas could be evaded in an emergency was an invitation to the President to ignore constitutional issues entirely.").

80. IRONS, supra note 5, at 47 (quoting Transcript of Telephone Conversation, Commanding Gen. of the Western Defense Command John L. DeWitt and Assistant Secretary of War John J. McCloy (Feb. 2, 1942) (on file with National Archives, DC, supra note 60, at RG 389)) (internal quotation marks omitted).

81. Transcript of Telephone Conversation, Bendetsen, Gullion, and Clark, supra note 2, at 2 ("That is what McCloy said. But they are just a little afraid DeWitt hasn't enough grounds to justify any [mass] movements. . . .") (statement of General Gullion) (emphasis added); see also id. (reporting that as of the February 4 call, Secretary Stimson was "against any mass movement").

82. Memorandum from Attorney Gen. Francis Biddle to President Franklin Delano Roosevelt (Feb. 17, 1942) (on file with FDR Library, supra note 4, President's Office File 18: Navy Department, March–April 1942, Box 7). Biddle referred specifically to columnists Walter Lippman and Westbrook Pegler, the latter of whom had written that "[t]he Japanese in California should be under armed guard to the last man and woman right now, and to hell with habeas corpus until the danger is over." Westbrook Pegler, WASH. POST, Feb. 15, 1942, at B7. Additional examples of Justice Department resistance to proposals are detailed in GRODZINS, supra note 70, at 257–262.

83. See Lt. Commander Kenneth D. Ringle to Chief of Naval Operations, "Report on Japanese Question" (Jan. 26, 1942) (on file with National Archives, DC, supra note 60, File ASW 014.311, RG 107); see IRONS, supra note 5, at 202–206 (discussing Ringle Report). Ringle was the Assistant District Intelligence Officer for the Eleventh Naval District in Los Angeles.

84. See BIDDLE, supra note 65, at 221–222 (detailing a report that Director Hoover sent to Attorney General Biddle on February 9 as well as similar doubts raised by the Federal Communications Commission).

85. BIDDLE, supra note 65, at 224 (quoting from a memo sent by Hoover to Biddle). Commentators have also noted that only 10 percent of the western Japanese American population lived near strategic areas. See GRODZINS, supra note 70, at 158; see id. at 159 (noting higher numbers for Italian Americans).

86. GRODZINS, supra note 70, at 257 (quoting Memorandum of Benjamin Cohen to Attorney Gen. Francis Biddle, undated; probably near Feb. 10, 1942) (internal quotation marks omitted); see also IRONS, supra note 5, at 53–55 (discussing same memorandum and quoting Memorandum, The Japanese Situation on the West Coast, File 146-13-7-2-0, Records of the Alien Enemy Control Unit, Department of Justice files); see also ROBINSON, supra note 59, at 103–104. Some of the sources of West Coast pressure are detailed in GRODZINS, supra note 70, at 19–88. Among those pushing for evacuation was California attorney general Earl Warren. See GRODZINS, supra note 70, at 93–94, 96–98 (discussing Warren's role). For details on "the starkest contradiction in [Warren's] public career"—namely his support for the evacuation policy, see G. EDWARD WHITE, EARL WARREN: A PUBLIC LIFE 57, 67–77 (1982).

87. Memorandum of Harold D. Smith, Director, Bureau of the Budget, for President Franklin Delano Roosevelt (Feb. 19, 1942) (on file with FDR Library, supra note 4, President's Official File 4805: Military Areas, 1941–1942) (presenting the president with a draft of Executive Order 9066 reportedly prepared by James Rowe from the Justice Department and Karl Bendetsen from the War Department). For details of James Rowe's recollection of this meeting, see GRODZINS, supra note 70, at 266.

88. James H. Rowe, interview in *The Earl Warren Oral History Project: Japanese-American Relocation Reviewed: Volume 1, Decision and Exodus* (Regional Oral

History Office, University of California Berkeley, 1976), at 9, available at: http://
content.cdlib.org/view?docId=ft667nb2x8&brand=calisphere&doc.view=entire_
text.

89. 3 C.F.R. 1092 (1942) (repealed 1976) (emphasis added). Later, the president established the War Relocation Authority by executive order, which in turn managed the camps. See Executive Order 9102, 3 C.F.R. 1123 (1942).

90. Act of Mar. 21, 1942, Pub. L. No. 77-503, 56 Stat. 173 (repealed 1976).

91. See, e.g., Public Proclamation No. 3, 7 Fed. Reg. 2543 (Mar. 24, 1942) (establishing an 8:00 pm to 6:00 am curfew for "all enemy aliens and all persons of
Japanese ancestry" within designated military areas, limiting travel, and prohibiting possession of firearms, shortwave radios, cameras, and other items);
Public Proclamation No. 4, 7 Fed. Reg. 2601 (Mar. 27, 1942) (prohibiting "all
alien Japanese and persons of Japanese ancestry" from leaving Military Area
No. 1); Public Proclamation No. 8, 7 Fed. Reg. 8346 (June 27, 1942) (compelling "persons of Japanese ancestry who have been evacuated from Military Areas
Nos. 1 and 2" to report to "Relocation Centers for their relocation, maintenance
and supervision" and that "[a]ll persons of Japanese ancestry, both alien and
nonalien, . . . are required to remain within the bounds of . . . War Relocation
Project Area[s]"); see also Civilian Restrictive Order 1, 8 Fed. Reg. 982 (May 19,
1942) (prohibiting "all persons of Japanese ancestry, both alien and non-alien,"
within "Assembly Centers, Reception Centers or Relocation Centers pursuant to
exclusion orders" from leaving such areas without prior written authorization).
For additional discussion, see Ex parte Endo, 323 U.S. 283, 289 (1944).

92. See, e.g., Public Proclamation No. 8, 7 Fed. Reg. 8346 (June 27, 1942).

93. See Ex parte Endo, 323 U.S. 208, 300 (1944) ("Neither the Act nor the [executive]
orders use the language of detention.").

94. Irons, supra note 5, at 73 (describing terrible conditions).

95. Robinson, supra note 59, at 4–5.

96. This stigma made reassimilation all the more difficult following the war. See
Norimitsu Onishi, *At Internment Camp, Exploring Choices of the Past*, N.Y. Times,
July 8, 2012.

97. See John Christgau, *Collins versus the World: The Fight to Restore Citizenship
to Japanese American Renunciants of World War II*, 54 Pac. Hist. Rev. 1 (1985)
(detailing the litigation, which spanned decades).

98. Japanese American units, including the 100th Infantry Battalion and the 442nd
Regimental Combat Team, fought for the United States with great distinction
during the war.

99. On the discrimination and losses such persons faced, see, e.g., *Army Ban on
Return of Nisei to Coast Is Lifted; Protests Seen*, Seattle Star, Dec. 18, 1944, at A1
(covering return of Japanese Americans to previously restricted areas); Paul A.
Shackel, Myth, Memory, and the Making of the American Landscape 93
(2001) (documenting extensive discrimination suffered by Japanese Americans

following the war); COMMISSION ON WARTIME RELOCATION AND INTERNMENT OF CIVILIANS, PERSONAL JUSTICE DENIED, PART 2: RECOMMENDATIONS 5 (1983).

100. Lieutenant Gen. John L. DeWitt, Final Report, Japanese Evacuation from the West Coast (1942).

101. Testimony of John L. DeWitt, Apr. 13, 1943, before the House Naval Affairs Subcommittee to Investigate Congested Areas, Part 3, 739–740 (78th Cong., 1st Sess.), cited in Korematsu v. United States, 323 U.S. 214, 218 (1944) (Murphy, J., dissenting); see also GRODZINS, supra note 70, at 88–89, 281–283 (detailing additional examples); IRONS, supra note 5, at 39–41, 58–59 (same).

102. ROBINSON, supra note 59, at 7.

103. American constitutional law has always included citizens (and some aliens) in the category of persons who could claim the Constitution's protection. This discussion is limited to citizens because historically American law has treated enemy aliens differently. Since 1798, some version of an Alien Law has provided for apprehension or other limitations on the freedom of aliens living in the United States who are citizens or subjects of a nation with which the United States is in a declared state of war. See Act of July 6, 1798, 1 Stat. 577; see also Johnson v. Eisentrager, 339 U.S. 763 (1950) ("Executive power over enemy aliens, undelayed and unhampered by litigation, has been deemed, throughout our history, essential to war-time security."). As noted, the numbers of Japanese American citizens would certainly have been higher had then-existing naturalization laws not discriminated based on race and precluded naturalization by Japanese Americans not born in the U.S.

104. This statement was made by Utah governor Herbert Maw at a Governor's Meeting in early April, after he complained that "the Army and the WRA were much too concerned about the constitutional rights of Japanese-American citizens." Report on meeting with Governors and other officials regarding relocation of Japanese, Salt Lake City, Utah (Apr. 7, 1942) (on file with National Archives, DC, supra note 60, at 19, RG 220, pp. 4188–4216).

105. Hirabayashi v. United States, 320 U.S. 81, 101 (1943). The Court vacated a companion case to *Hirabayashi* and remanded it for resentencing on a conviction of violating a curfew order, the validity of which the Court never questioned. See Yasui v. United States, 320 U.S. 115 (1943).

106. Id. at 101, 105. Three justices wrote separate concurring opinions.

107. Korematsu v. United States, 323 U.S. 214, 218 (1944); see id. at 219–220 ("Compulsory exclusion of large groups of citizens from their homes, except under circumstances of direst emergency and peril, is inconsistent with our basic governmental institutions. But when . . . our shores are threatened by hostile forces, the power to protect [must prevail]."). Korematsu had violated Civilian Exclusion Order No. 34. See 7 Fed. Reg. 3967 (May 3, 1942).

108. Korematsu, 323 U.S. at 223. The majority deemed it "unjustifiable to call" the camps "concentration camps with all the ugly connotations that the term

implies." Id. (Other government officials were not so reluctant. See GRODZINS, supra note 70, at 66.)

109. Korematsu, 323 U.S. at 225 (Frankfurter, J., concurring) (emphasis added).

110. Id. at 226, 232 (Roberts, J., dissenting); id. at 230 (calling the camps "concentration camps" and "prison[s]"). Justice Roberts compared *Hirabayashi* as "a case of keeping people off the streets at night." Id. at 225. Earlier, Justice Roberts oversaw the Roberts Commission, which studied the Japanese attack on Pearl Harbor. For details, see ROBINSON, supra note 59, at 94–96.

111. Korematsu, 323 U.S. at 234 (Murphy, J., dissenting); see also id. ("[U]nder our system of law individual guilt is the sole basis for deprivation of rights.").

112. Id. at 243 (Jackson, J., dissenting).

113. Id. at 246.

114. As Peter Irons documents, Justice Department lawyer Edward J. Ennis, who had been involved from the outset as in discussions leading up to 9066 and who also litigated the *Duncan* case, and his colleague John L. Burling believed that the Department had a "duty" to inform the Supreme Court of the Ringle Report. See IRONS, supra note 5, at 204, 278–292 (detailing events). Professor Irons places ultimate responsibility for the brief submission on Solicitor General Charles Fahy. See id.; see also Peter Irons, *How Solicitor General Charles Fahy Misled the Supreme Court in the Japanese American Cases: A Reply to Charles Sheehan,* 55 AM. J. LEGAL HIST. 208 (2015).

115. IRONS, supra note 5, at 287–292; see also supra, text accompanying note 83 (discussing Ringle Report). Both Justice Murphy's and Justice Jackson's dissents drew attention to the potential importance of this development. Jackson, for example, asked "How does the Court know that these orders have a reasonable basis in necessity? No evidence whatsoever on that subject has been taken by this or any other court." Korematsu, 323 U.S. at 245 (Jackson, J., dissenting); see also Korematsu, supra, at 241 (Murphy, J., dissenting) ("[T]here [is] no adequate proof that the [FBI] and the military and naval intelligence services did not have the espionage and sabotage situation well in hand. . . .").

116. Letter from James C. Purcell to Peter Linzer (June 11, 1975) (on file with author) (detailing his representation of Endo); see also Public Hearings of the Commission on Wartime Relocation and Internment, San Francisco, CA 689–695 (Aug. 13, 1981) (on file with National Archives at College Park, College Park, Md., ARC identifier 734681, RG 220) (testimony of James C. Purcell); Letter from Elizabeth Purcell to Amanda L. Tyler (Aug. 29, 2016) (on file with author); BILL HOSOKAWA, NISEI: THE QUIET AMERICANS: THE STORY OF A PEOPLE 426 (1969) (quoting interview with Purcell). Purcell selected Endo as the ideal petitioner based upon a questionnaire that he had distributed to the suspended California employees.

117. The government's brief to the Supreme Court alludes to this fact. See Brief for the United States at 3, Endo, 323 U.S. 283 (No. 70) (noting that Endo had been

granted "leave clearance" but "refuses to apply" for the necessary conditional permit to leave the camps). For additional details, see IRONS, supra note 5, at 102–103.

118. Letter from Mitsuye [Endo] Tsutsumi to Anne Saito Howden (June 5, 1989) (on file with author).

119. See Opening Brief for Appellant, at 16–31, 31, Endo, 323 U.S. 283 (No. 70). (Joining Purcell on the brief were his law partner, William Ferriter, and Wayne Collins, the latter of whom handled *Korematsu* and thousands of renunciation cases after the war.) Two amicus briefs from the local and national chapters of the American Civil Liberties Union also made Suspension Clause arguments and went further to argue that even if Congress had enacted a suspension, it would not have been valid insofar as there was no rebellion or invasion on the mainland. See, e.g., Brief for the American Civil Liberties Union, Amicus Curiae, at 5–7, Endo, 323 U.S. 283 (No. 70) ("[T]here is no basis under our constitutional system for the indefinite detention of American citizens even during wartime unless charges are preferred against them under the safeguards contained in the Fifth and Sixth Amendments to the Constitution.").

120. 323 U.S. 283, 294 (1944).

121. Id. at 298. For details on Stone's proposal, see Patrick O. Gudridge, *Remember Endo?*, 116 HARV. L. REV. 1933, 1962 n.141 (2003) (citing William O. Douglas, Galley dated Nov. 2, 1944 and marked "not circulated/ C.J. copy showing suggestions/ 11/8/44," at ii (on file with the Library of Congress, Manuscript Division, Papers of William O. Douglas, Box 116, Folder No. 70/ Endo v. Eisenhower/ Galley draft/ O.T. 1944)).

122. On this point, see Eugene V. Rostow, *The Japanese American Cases—A Disaster*, 54 YALE L.J. 489, 527 (1945) (asking about Endo in 1945: "Why doesn't the *Milligan* case apply *a fortiori*? If it is illegal to arrest and confine people after an unwarranted military trial, it is surely even more illegal to arrest and confine them without any trial at all").

123. Ex parte Milligan, 71 U.S. (4 Wall.) 2, 131 (1866).

124. Id. at 297, 302 ("Loyalty is a matter of the heart and mind, not of race, creed, or color. . . . When the power to detain is derived from the power to protect the war effort against espionage and sabotage, detention which has no relationship to that objective is unauthorized."). This aspect of the Court's opinion has been the subject of extensive criticism by scholars for denying any accountability for the internment policies to the relevant political actors. See, e.g., Jerry Kang, *Watching the Watchers: Enemy Combatants in the Internment's Shadow*, 68 L. & Contemp. PROB. 260, 268–271 (2005).

125. See id. at 299–300 (applying a clear statement rule).

126. Transcript of Interviews by Walter F. Murphy with William O. Douglas (May 23, 1962) (on file with Seeley G. Mudd Manuscript Library, Princeton University, Princeton, N.J.), quoted in Gudridge, supra note 121, at 1953. See id. ("Black,

Frankfurter, Stone, were very clear that that was not unconstitutional but that . . . Endo would have to turn upon the construction of the regulations."). Douglas's law clerk wrote memoranda suggesting that the case be decided either by avoiding the constitutional issues or else on equal protection grounds, the latter of which suggested new precedential territory. It does not appear that she briefed Suspension Clause issues to the justice. See Jennie Berry Chandra, *Lucile Lomen: The First Female United States Supreme Court Law Clerk*, in CHAMBERS: STORIES OF SUPREME COURT LAW CLERKS AND THEIR JUSTICES 206, 207 (Todd C. Peppers & Artemus Ward eds., 2012).

127. Douglas's notes read: "U.S. concedes clearance implied determination that she was not disloyal. . . . once loyalty is shown basis for military decision disappears—this woman is entitled to summary release." Justice William O. Douglas Conference Notes (Oct. 16, 1944), Ex parte Endo, 323 U.S. 283 (1944) (on file with Stanford University Libraries, Stanford, Cal., Dept. of Special Collections and University Archives, Lucile Lomen Collection (SC0776), Box 1, Folder 11).

128. Justice Roberts questioned the Court's interpretation of the military regulations and made the above constitutional argument. Id. at 208–310 (Roberts, J.). Justice Murphy would have held the internment to be a product of "the unconstitutional resort to racism." Id. at 307 (Murphy, J., concurring). Justice Jackson's files reveal that he made notes on a draft of Justice Douglas's *Endo* opinion suggesting he too would have reached the constitutional issues and found for Endo: "Finds no constitutional vice/Seems to sanction mass detention without individual charges of disloyalty." Robert H. Jackson, Handwritten Note (marginal note on first page of Douglas opinion in Ex parte Endo, circulated Nov. 8, 1944) (on file with the Library of Congress, Manuscript Division, Papers of Robert H. Jackson, Container No. 133), quoted in Gudridge, supra note 121, at 1959. Justice Jackson also penned a concurrence that he never circulated suggesting as much. See Gudridge, supra, at 1959, 1969–1970. That draft is discussed further below.

129. See Memorandum from William O. Douglas to Harlan Stone (Nov. 28, 1944) (on file with Library of Congress, Manuscript Division, Papers of William O. Douglas, Box 116, Folder No. 70 O.T. 1944, Endo v. Eisenhower, Certiorari, Conference & Misc. Memos) (arguing that a government request for delay should be ignored and that "Endo . . . is a citizen, insisting on her right to be released—a right which we all agree she has. I feel strongly that we should act promptly and not lend our aid in compounding the wrong through our inaction any longer than necessary to reach a decision."); see also Gudridge, supra note 121, at 1953–1964 (detailing the justices' deliberations in *Endo*); IRONS, supra note 5, at 344–345; ROBINSON, supra note 59, at 230 (noting the widely reported rumor that Justice Frankfurter tipped off the War Department as to the forthcoming holding).

130. Public Proclamation No. 21, 10 Fed. Reg. 53 (Dec. 17, 1944) (effective Jan. 2, 1945).

131. PERSONAL JUSTICE DENIED, PART 2, supra note 99, at 3.

132. Note, however, that Hirabayashi's brief contended:

> In time of invasion or rebellion the Constitution authorizes the suspension of the writ of habeas corpus. The power of the Executive to order the detention of persons on suspicion without possibility of judicial review thus exists. But it must be confined to the circumstances described in the Constitution and be exercised in the manner there provided.

Brief for Appellant at 19–20, Hirabayashi, 320 U.S. 81 (No. 870). Korematsu's brief argued generally that the executive has no power to effect "an outright suspension of the Constitution." Brief for Appellant at 29, 39–40, Korematsu, 323 U.S. 214 (No. 22). Note that the Suspension Clause arguments presented in *Endo* are especially significant for transcending issues of race given that the Supreme Court had not yet decided *Bolling v. Sharpe*, 347 U.S. 497 (1954), which held that the federal government is constrained by equal protection principles.

133. Unlike earlier historical episodes of suspension, 9066 targeted a group of persons viewed by many Americans as unassimilable foreigners, despite their citizenship status, see, e.g., generally LISA LOWE, IMMIGRANT ACTS: ON ASIAN AMERICAN CULTURAL POLITICS (1996), a point that received express recognition in the Supreme Court's *Hirabayashi* decision and is found throughout public statements and government documents. See, e.g., Memorandum, "Alien Enemies on the West Coast (and Other Subversive Persons)," supra note 63, at 2 (observing that "a substantial number of the Nisei [citizens of Japanese ancestry born to immigrant parents] bear allegiance to Japan [and] are well controlled and disciplined by the enemy").

134. REHNQUIST, supra note 53, at 206. The majority opinion emphasized loyalty in reaching its holding, noting: "He who is loyal is by definition not a spy or saboteur. When the power to detain is derived from the power to protect the war effort against espionage and sabotage, detention which has no relationship to that objective is unauthorized." Ex parte Endo, 323 U.S. 283 (1944).

135. Robert H. Jackson, Undated Typescript entitled "Endo" (n.d.) (on file with the Library of Congress, Manuscript Division, Papers of Robert H. Jackson, Container No. 133), reproduced in Gudridge, supra note 121, at 1969–1970; see id. at 1969 ("There is no way by which trial techniques can establish what is in a man's heart. . . ."). Justice Jackson also wrote:

> [U]nder our form of government it has never been thought that a citizen must prove or be admitted to be harmless in order to be free. On the contrary, it has been supposed that it must be charged that he has committed or conspired or attempted or threatened to commit some crime before he could be temporarily detained, and the charge must be speedily proved if he is to be held.

Id.

136. Ex parte Milligan, 71 U.S. (4 Wall.) 2, 127 (1866).

137. Brief for the State of California, supra note 28, at 10.

138. The ACLU Brief made these arguments in *Endo*. See also Memorandum from Assistant Attorney Gen. for the Criminal Division, Theron L. Caudle, "Detention of Communists in the event of sudden difficulty with Russia," to Attorney Gen. Tom C. Clark 6 (July 11, 1946), in Documents of the Commission on Wartime Relocation, supra note 1, at 3067–3075, reel 3, 283–291.

139. Personal Justice Denied, Part 2, supra note 99, at 5. The Commission also concluded that "no documented acts of espionage, sabotage or fifth column activity were shown to have been committed by any identifiable American citizen of Japanese ancestry or resident Japanese alien on the West Coast" in the period leading up to the orders. Id. at 3.

140. Memorandum from Attorney Gen. Francis Biddle to President Franklin Delano Roosevelt (Feb. 20, 1942) (on file with Bancroft Library, University of California, Berkeley, Japanese Evacuation and Relocation Study Papers, reel 1). This being said, Biddle's memorandum never references internment but instead evacuation orders and restrictions on the movement "of certain racial classes, whether American citizens or aliens, in specified defense areas," which he opined clearly fell under the president's "general war powers" free of any need for legislation. Id.; see also Memorandum from Attorney Gen. Francis Biddle to President Franklin Delano Roosevelt (Jan. 30, 1942), supra note 74.

141. Grodzins, supra note 70, at 271 (quoting interview with Edward Ennis, Sept. 17, 1942). Professor Grodzins criticized the Justice Department for "abdicating their own authority over matters of internal security [and] allow[ing] the War Department to proceed with a large-scale program of evacuation of alien enemies and American citizens." See id. at 267; see also id. at 268–273.

142. First Lady Eleanor Roosevelt also voiced opposition and/or took steps to support those detained in the camps during the war. See Robinson, supra note 59 at 122, 171–172, 189, 215.

143. Robinson, supra note 59, at 214, 216–221 (noting that War Secretary Stimson and Interior Secretary Ickes raised points favoring lifting exclusion orders with the president in May 1944, while noting also that Biddle counseled against it until after the election), 222–223 (detailing the influence of political advisers), 235 (providing additional details); Commission on Wartime Relocation and Internment of Civilians, Personal Justice Denied, Part 1, at 215 (1982).

144. Robinson, supra note 59, at 118–121 (surveying a range of evidence from Roosevelt's lifetime).

145. Kenneth S. Davis, FDR: The War President, 1940–43, at 424 (2000).

146. Biddle, supra note 65, at 218 (quoting McCloy); see also Robinson, supra note 59, at 106 (quoting Stimson's diary about the meeting in which Stimson described Roosevelt as "very vigorous"); see also Robinson, supra, at 109

(noting that Roosevelt defended 9066 in cabinet meetings on the basis that he should defer to military claims of necessity). Consistent with the notion that Roosevelt placed a high value on deferring to the military, he deferred to the War Department when it decided against a broad evacuation policy in Hawaii despite his strong support for the idea. See ROBINSON, supra, at 158.

147. BIDDLE, supra note 65, at 219. In all of this, Biddle believed that opposition from Stimson would have swayed the president to chart a different course. See ROBINSON, supra note 59, at 116 (quoting Biddle).

148. See PERSONAL JUSTICE DENIED, PART I, supra note 143, at 215 (highlighting the importance of the election); ROBINSON, supra note 59, at 234 (noting that Roosevelt only came around after months of prodding by advisers, three days after the election).

149. See Hirabayashi v. United States, 320 U.S. 81, 96–99 (1943) (discussing the high number of dual Japanese and American citizens and remarking that "[t]here is support for the view that [circumstances] have in large measure prevented the[] assimilation" of Japanese Americans).

150. 5 U.S. (1 Cranch) 137, 178 (1803); see also Korematsu v. United States, 323 U.S. 214, 226, 232 (1944) (Roberts, J., dissenting) (arguing that the Court should not "shut [its] eyes to reality").

151. See Rostow, supra note 122, at 504, 511. Another early scholarly evaluation was equally harsh. See GRODZINS, supra note 70, at 358 (criticizing the Court for ignoring the "extreme gravity of the civil liberties deprivation; its racial character; the fact that people were condemned en masse rather than according to the principles of individual liability; and the belief held by many that evacuation was the result of public pressures and racial animosity rather than the result of carefully conceived military policy"). This being said, with the benefit of hindsight, the fact that the Court never actually ruled on the merits of the Suspension Clause challenge in *Endo* could be a good thing. Considering *Hirabayashi* and *Korematsu*, it is possible that the Court may have announced a misguided precedent upholding the internment policy against constitutional challenge at least in part.

152. 317 U.S. 1 (1942).

153. Duncan, 327 U.S. at 351 (Burton, J., dissenting, joined by Frankfurter, J.).

154. Abo v. Clark, 77 F. Supp. 806, 811 (N.D. Ca. 1948), affirmed in part and reversed and remanded in part, McGrath v. Abo, 186 F.2d 766 (9th Cir. 1951); see also Acheson v. Murakami, 176 F.2d 953 (9th Cir. 1949) (affirming district court findings that renunciations of citizenship at Tule Lake were not voluntary and therefore void).

155. MERLO J. PUSEY, CHARLES EVANS HUGHES 175–176 (1951). Hughes made the statement while running for governor of New York in 1906.

156. Tom C. Clark, *Epilogue* to EXECUTIVE ORDER 9066: THE INTERNMENT OF 110,000 JAPANESE AMERICANS 110–111 (Maisie & Richard Conrat eds., 1992).

157. Proclamation No. 4417, 41 Fed. Reg. 35,7741 (Feb. 19, 1976). Subsequently, federal courts vacated the convictions of Fred Korematsu and Gordon Hirabayashi. Presidents Clinton and Obama awarded Korematsu, Hirabayashi, and Yasui the Presidential Medal of Freedom. Endo, who died in 2006, should receive the same recognition.

158. Grodzins, supra note 70, at 374.

CHAPTER 11

1. 542 U.S. 507, 519 (2004) (plurality opinion).

2. Pub. L. No. 81-831, tit. II, § 102, 64 Stat. 1019, 1021 (repealed 1971) (authorizing the president to arrest and detain "each person as to whom there is a reasonable ground to believe that such person probably will engage in, or probably will conspire with others to engage in, acts of espionage or sabotage"); see id. § 116, 64 Stat. at 1030. Congress passed the Emergency Detention Act as part of the Internal Security Act of 1950, known as the "McCarran Act," Pub. L. No. 81-831, 64 Stat. 987 (repealed 1971).

3. Memorandum from Assistant Attorney Gen. for the Criminal Division, Theron L. Caudle, "Detention of Communists in the event of sudden difficulty with Russia," to Attorney Gen. Tom C. Clark 2 (July 11, 1946), in Documents of the Commission on Wartime Relocation and Internment of Civilians 3067–3075 (reel 3, 283–291) (Frederick, Md., University Publications of America 1983).

4. See 96 Cong. Rec. 15,726 (1950) (reporting Senate vote); 96 Cong. Rec. 15,632–15,633 (1950) (reporting House vote). On the appropriations and aftermath related to the Act, see David Cole, *The Priority of Morality: The Emergency Constitution's Blind Spot*, 113 Yale L.J. 1753, 1770 (2004) (discussing the Act). For timely criticism of the Act, see Zechariah Chafee, Jr., *The Most Important Human Right in the Constitution*, 32 B.U. L. Rev. 143, 160 (1952).

5. Veto of the Internal Security Bill, 150 Pub. Papers 645 (Sept. 22, 1950).

6. See Louis Fisher, Cong. Research Serv., RS22130, Detention of U.S. Citizens 1 (Apr. 28, 2005) (noting that "[s]ix detention camps were established but never used").

7. Pub. L. No. 92-128, 85 Stat. 347 (1971) (codified in scattered sections of the U.S. Code); 18 U.S.C. § 4001(a) (2017).

8. See Fisher, supra note 6, at 2, 4.

9. Pub. L. No. 107-40, 115 Stat. 224 (2001) (codified at 50 U.S.C. § 1541 note (2006)).

10. See, e.g., Jonathan Alter, *Keeping Order in the Courts*, Newsweek, Dec. 10, 2001, at 48 ("When Attorney General John Ashcroft sent the secret first draft of the antiterrorism bill to Capitol Hill in October, it contained a section explicitly titled: 'Suspension of the Writ of Habeas Corpus.'"); Steven Brill, After: How America Confronted the September 12 Era 73–74 (2003) (reporting that the

initial draft of the USA PATRIOT Act of 2001, Pub. L. No. 107-56, 115 Stat. 272, included a proposal to suspend the writ for an undefined period); Petitioners' Brief on the Merits at 14 n.12, Rasul v. Bush, 542 U.S. 466 (2004) (No. 03-334), 2004 WL 162758 (collecting cites and reporting reaction of Representative James Sensenbrenner to proposal).

11. "Within 2 months of the attacks, law enforcement authorities had detained, at least for questioning, more than 1,200 citizens and aliens nationwide. Many of these individuals were questioned and subsequently released without being charged with a criminal or immigration offense. Many others, however, were arrested and detained for violating federal immigration law." U.S. Dep't of Justice, Office of the Inspector Gen., The September 11 Detainees: A Review of the Treatment of Aliens Held on Immigration Charges in Connection with the Investigation of the September 11 Attacks (2003), available at https://oig.justice.gov/special/0306/full.pdf.

12. The government charged Lindh with various crimes, but not treason; eventually, he pleaded guilty to two charges. See Katharine Q. Seelye, *Regretful Lindh Gets 20 Years in Taliban Case*, N.Y. Times, Oct. 5, 2002, at A1.

13. For discussion of how the use of material witness warrants can run afoul of the Suspension Clause, see Amanda L. Tyler, *The Forgotten Core Meaning of the Suspension Clause*, 125 Harv. L. Rev. 901, 1015 (2012).

14. See Rumsfeld v. Padilla, 542 U.S. 426, 430–432, 432 n.3 (2004); Padilla v. Hanft, 423 F.3d 386, 389 (4th Cir. 2005) (quoting Memorandum from President George W. Bush to Secretary of Defense Donald Rumsfeld (June 9, 2002)).

15. Padilla v. Rumsfeld, 352 F.3d 695, 718–722, 724 (2d Cir. 2003). In support, the Second Circuit detailed the background to the Non-Detention Act:

> Both the sponsor of the Act and its primary opponent repeatedly confirmed that the Act applies to detentions by the President during war and other times of national crisis. The legislative history is replete with references to the detentions of American citizens of Japanese descent during World War II, [as] authorized both by congressional acts and by orders issued pursuant to the President's war power. This context convinces us that military detentions were intended to be covered.

Id. at 718–719.

16. See Padilla, 542 U.S. at 430, 451.

17. Id. at 465 (Stevens, J., dissenting); see id. ("[I]f this Nation is to remain true to the ideals symbolized by its flag, it must not wield the tools of tyrants even to resist an assault by the forces of tyranny."). Justice Stevens also took issue with the government holding Padilla incommunicado and denying him access to counsel. See id.

18. Padilla v. Hanft, 423 F.3d 386, 389 (4th Cir. 2005); see also Padilla v. Hanft, 389 F. Supp. 2d 678, 692 (D.S.C. 2005).

19. Padilla, 432 F.3d at 583.

20. An additional example from the Reconstruction period is particularly close to the mark. When the Supreme Court held in Ex parte *Yerger*, 75 U.S. (8 Wall.) 85 (1868), that it possessed jurisdiction to review Yerger's challenge to his forthcoming military trial, and with it the Reconstruction policies that authorized it, the military turned him over for prosecution to civilian authorities.

21. See Padilla v. Hanft, 546 U.S. 1084 (2006) (granting government's motion); Padilla v. Hanft, 547 U.S. 1062 (2006) (denying petition for certiorari). A jury eventually convicted Padilla of various terrorism-related crimes. With respect to the delay leading up to the filing of charges against Padilla, the government later contended, successfully, that speedy trial rights do not apply "to those not yet accused" of a crime. See Government's Opposition to Defendant Padilla's Motions to Dismiss for Lack of Speedy Trial and for Pre-indictment Delay at 6, United States v. Padilla, No. 04-60001-CR (S.D. Fla. Apr. 9, 2007). For more details on Padilla's case, see generally Jenny S. Martinez, *Process and Substance in the "War on Terror,"* 108 COLUM. L. REV. 1013, 1032–1041 (2008).

22. Hamdi v. Rumsfeld, 542 U.S. 507, 510–511 (2004) (plurality opinion).

23. See id. at 517 (O'Connor, J.). The dissenters on this point were Justices Stevens, Scalia, Souter, and Ginsburg. See id. at 543, 553 (Souter, J., joined by Ginsburg, J., concurring in part, dissenting in part, and concurring in the judgment) ("Congress . . . adopted § 4001(a) for the purpose of avoiding another *Korematsu*."); id. at 554 (Scalia, J., joined by Stevens, J., dissenting). Justice Thomas wrote that the president likely possesses inherent authority to detain enemy combatants, but concluded that, regardless, Congress had approved Hamdi's detention in the AUMF. See id. at 587 (Thomas, J., dissenting).

24. Justices Souter and Ginsburg specifically noted that they "do not adopt the plurality's resolution of constitutional issues that [they] would not reach"; they joined the plurality for purposes of "ordering remand on terms closest to those [they] would impose." Id. at 553 (Souter, J., joined by Ginsburg, J., concurring in part, dissenting in part, and concurring in the judgment).

25. Id. at 529, 532 (plurality opinion) (quoting United States v. Salerno, 481 U.S. 739, 755 (1987)).

26. Id. at 519.

27. Id. at 523. Justice O'Connor criticized Justice Scalia for ignoring these circumstances. See id. at 523–524 (plurality opinion).

28. See id. at 519 (plurality opinion) (alteration in original) (quoting Ex parte Quirin, 317 U.S. 1, 37–38 (1942)) (internal quotation marks omitted).

29. Id. at 509, 529 (plurality opinion); see also id. at 553 (Souter, J., joined by Ginsburg, J., concurring in part, dissenting in part, and concurring in the judgment). Justice Thomas would have required no such review under the circumstances. See id. at 579 (Thomas, J., dissenting).

30. See id. at 528–531 (citing Mathews v. Eldridge, 424 U.S. 319 (1976)). Justice O'Connor also relied upon decisions establishing procedures for civil commitment

of the mentally ill and pretrial detention. See id. (citing Heller v. Doe, 509 U.S. 312, 330–331 (1993); Zinermon v. Burch, 494 U.S. 113, 127–128 (1990); United States v. Salerno, 481 U.S. 739, 746 (1987); Schall v. Martin, 467 U.S. 253, 274–275 (1984); Addington v. Texas, 441 U.S. 418, 425 (1979)).

31. See id. at 528–538; id. at 533–534 ("Hearsay, for example, may need to be accepted as the most reliable available evidence from the Government in such a proceeding."); id. at 538 ("There remains the possibility that the standards we have articulated could be met by an appropriately authorized and properly constituted military tribunal.").

32. Id. at 559 (Scalia, J., dissenting). Justice Scalia posited that long-standing acceptance of civil commitment in certain circumstances presented an entirely inapposite set of considerations. See id. at 556 (discussing commitment of the mentally ill and quarantines of infectious persons).

33. Id. at 554.

34. Id. at 555–556.

35. Id. at 555 (citing 1 WILLIAM BLACKSTONE, COMMENTARIES *131–*133); see id. at 561–562 (relying upon Blackstone's description of the role of suspension).

36. See id. at 556–567.

37. Id. at 564.

38. Id. at 567 (quoting Ex parte Milligan, 71 U.S. (4 Wall.) 2, 121 (1866)).

39. Id. at 567 n.1, 568, 569, 571 (quoting Quirin, 317 U.S. at 46–47) (emphasis added). In the dissent's view, "where those jurisdictional facts are *not* conceded [and] where the petitioner insists that he is *not* a belligerent—*Quirin* left the pre-existing law in place." Id. at 571–572.

40. Id. at 575. The dissent spoke exclusively to citizens held on U.S. soil, noting that the detention of noncitizens might present a different case, as would a situation in which a citizen is captured and held outside the United States. See id. at 574 n.5, 577.

41. Id. at 579.

42. See G. Edward White, *Felix Frankfurter's "Soliloquy" in* Ex parte Quirin: *Nazi Sabotage & Constitutional Conundrums*, 5 GREEN BAG 2d 423 (2002). Many of the key details of the saboteurs' case were set forth in the Supreme Court's written opinion issued in the fall. See Ex parte Quirin, 317 U.S. 1 (1942); see also David Danelski, *The Saboteurs' Case*, 1 J. SUP. CT. HIST. 61 (1996).

43. Henry L. Stimson, Diary 130–132 (June 29, 1942) (on file with Henry L. Stimson Papers, Yale University Library, reel 7); see also Danelski, supra note 42, at 66. As one government lawyer at the time later recalled, the likely maximum sentence available under federal law for the alleged offenses was two years' imprisonment. See Boris I. Bittker, *The World War II German Saboteurs' Case and Writs of Certiorari before Judgment by the Court of Appeals*, 14 CONST. COMMENTARY 431, 434 (1997).

44. See White, supra note 42, at 433.

Notes to pages 254–256

45. Francis Biddle, Memorandum for the President (June 30, 1942) (on file with Franklin D. Roosevelt Papers, Franklin D. Roosevelt Presidential Library, Hyde Park, N.Y. [hereinafter FDR Papers]), quoted in Danelski, supra note 42, at 65.

46. Franklin D. Roosevelt, Memorandum for the Attorney General (June 30, 1942) (on file with FDR Papers, supra note 45), quoted in Danelski, supra note 42, at 65 (quoting Roosevelt as saying: "'Surely they are just as guilty as it is possible to be . . . and it seems to me that the death penalty is almost obligatory.'").

47. Proclamation No. 2561, 7 Fed. Reg. 5101 (July 2, 1942), reprinted in 56 Stat. 1964 (1942). Danelski details Biddle's advice behind these orders. See Danelski, supra note 42, at 66–67.

48. FRANCIS BIDDLE, IN BRIEF AUTHORITY 331 (1962).

49. Ex parte Quirin, 317 U.S. 1, 23 (1942) (replicating charges).

50. See Ex parte Quirin, 47 F. Supp. 431 (D.D.C. 1942) (deeming the president's orders preclusive of any federal court jurisdiction).

51. See Lewis Wood, *Supreme Court Is Called in Unprecedented Session to Hear Plea of Nazi Spies*, N.Y. TIMES, July 28, 1942, at 1, 10. The fact that the saboteurs skipped first seeking relief in the federal appellate court before the Supreme Court led Justice Frankfurter to question the Court's jurisdiction over the case, which led to the lodging of a notice of appeal with the Court of Appeals and filing of a petition for a writ of certiorari with the Supreme Court in the *middle* of the Supreme Court's two days of oral argument. See generally Bittker, supra note 43.

52. Chief Justice Stone's son worked on the defense team, Justice Frankfurter had earlier counseled the administration in favor of instituting a military commission to try the saboteurs, and Justice James Byrnes had been advising the administration for several months—so much that Biddle apparently thought he had taken leave from the Supreme Court. (As it was, Byrnes, a former senator, served only fifteen months on the Court before joining the administration.) Murphy enlisted as an infantry officer during the war and appeared at conference in uniform before recusing himself at Frankfurter's suggestion. See Danelski, supra note 42, at 69.

53. See Danelski, supra note 42, at 68–69.

54. Ex parte Quirin, 317 U.S. 1 (1942) (per curiam).

55. The commission offered few written explanations for its procedures and holdings; this included offering "no written explanation . . . of the elements of the violations of the laws of war." See JOHN YOO, CRISIS AND COMMAND: THE HISTORY OF EXECUTIVE POWER FROM GEORGE WASHINGTON TO GEORGE W. BUSH 274–276 (2009).

56. See Danelski, supra note 42, at 72–79 (quoting ALPHEUS T. MASON, HARLAN FISKE STONE: PILLAR OF THE LAW 659 (1956)); White, supra note 42, at 430–435. During this period, Justice Robert Jackson circulated a memorandum concluding that the Court never should have taken the case. See Danelski, supra, at 76 (quoting Memorandum of Justice Robert Jackson (Oct. 23, 1942) (on file with

Robert H. Jackson Papers, Library of Congress, Box 124)). The Court had to wrestle with a number of additional issues beyond those discussed here, including the application of the procedures set forth in the Articles of War adopted by Congress.

57. Quirin, 317 U.S. at 35.

58. Id. at 31 n.9.

59. Id. at 45.

60. His law clerk reported that Burger's case presented a likelier argument for renunciation. See Ross E. Davies, *Some Clerical Contributions to Ex Parte Quirin*, 19 GREEN BAG 2D 283, 286 & App. A (2016) (replicating clerk's memorandum).

61. See Danelski, supra note 42, at 81 n.32.

62. Danelski, supra note 42, at 73 (quoting memorandum from Stone to his law clerk). For this, Stone has been much criticized. See, e.g., Michal R. Belknap, *The Supreme Court Goes to War: The Meaning and Implications of the Nazi Saboteur Case*, 89 MIL. L. REV. 59, 87 (1980) ("Stone's purpose was not to elucidate the law, but rather to justify as best he could a dubious decision. Stone realized Haupt should have been tried for treason in a civil court.").

63. Danelski, supra note 42, at 20, 37, 38.

64. Francis Biddle, Memorandum for the President (Oct. 29, 1942), OF 3603 (on file with FDR Papers, supra note 45), quoted in Danelski, supra note 42, at 79.

65. White, supra note 42, at 436 (quoting letters from Frederick Bernays Weiner to Felix Frankfurter from 1942–1943, Felix Frankfurter Papers).

66. Felix Frankfurter, Memorandum, *Rosenberg v. United States* (June 4, 1953) (on file with Felix Frankfurter Papers, Harvard Law School Library, Cambridge, Mass. [hereinafter Felix Frankfurter Papers], Box 65), quoted in Danelski, supra note 42, at 80. Interestingly, during the exchange of drafts preceding release of the opinion, Frankfurter wrote to Stone that he believed "the President has the power to suspend the writ, and so believing I conclude also that his determination whether an emergency calls for such suspension is not subject to judicial review." Nonetheless, Frankfurter suggested that the Court need not speak to the issue in writing about Roosevelt's attempt to close civilian courts to the saboteurs. Letter from Felix Frankfurter to Harlan Fiske Stone (Oct. 15, 1942) (on file with Felix Frankfurter Papers, supra, at Box 172), quoted in Danelski, supra note 42, at 76. For additional discussion on the question whether suspension is a political question, see Chapter 10.

67. Transcript of Interviews by Walter F. Murphy with William O. Douglas 204–205 (1961–1963) (on file with Seeley G. Mudd Manuscript Library, Princeton University, Princeton, N.J.), quoted in Danelski, supra note 42, at 80.

68. Danelski, supra note 42, at 69.

69. Letter from Justice Hugo Black to Chief Justice Harlan Fiske Stone (Oct. 2, 1942) (on file with Hugo L. Black Papers, Library of Congress, Box 269). As Justice Black wrote, "I seriously question whether Congress could constitutionally

confer jurisdiction to try all . . . violations [of the Laws of War] before military tribunals." He further noted that such inquiry must ask whether "the offense charged" and "the person charged with committing the offense . . . come within that group of offenses and person which the Constitution contemplates may fall within the jurisdiction of military tribunals rather than the courts." Id.

70. Ex parte Milligan, 71 U.S. (4 Wall.) 2, 6, 121 (1866).

71. In *Hamdi*, Justice Scalia correctly criticized Justice O'Connor for misunderstanding *Milligan* in another important respect. As he noted, the *Milligan* Court initially decided the legitimacy of Milligan's military trial before separately deciding whether Milligan's detention could be upheld under the suspension then in place. As Justice Scalia observed, the Court discussed whether Milligan could be considered a "prisoner of war" only in addressing the second, and not the first question. See Hamdi, 542 U.S. at 570–571 (Scalia, J., dissenting). As explored in Chapter 7, the 1863 suspension legislation excepted persons labeled as "prisoners of war" (surely a reference to Confederate soldiers) from the reporting requirements in Section 2 of that statute. Because Milligan could not, on any fair reading of the facts, be so classified, the Court held that his detention was not authorized under the terms of the suspension. (Specifically, the Court noted that Milligan had not been indicted by the next sitting grand jury in the Circuit Court for the District of Indiana after his arrest, as Section 2 required.)

72. See Quirin, 317 U.S. at 38 (citing Morgan v. Devine, 237 U.S. 632 (1915); Albrecht v. United States, 273 U.S. 1 (1927)).

73. See Haupt v. United States, 330 U.S. 631 (1947).

74. Cramer v. United States, 325 U.S. 1, 8–12 (1945). For more details on the civilian court prosecutions of those who helped the saboteurs, see LOUIS FISHER, NAZI SABOTEURS ON TRIAL 68–71 (2d ed. 2005).

75. The lower court in *Kawakita* also observed that American law follows English tradition in recognizing the concept of "temporary allegiance," by which is meant "the obligation of fidelity and obedience which the individual owes to the government under which he lives, or to his sovereign in return for the protection he receives. . . ." United States v. Kawakita, 96 F. Supp. 824, 826–827 (S.D. Cal. 1950). On this point, see also Carlisle v. United States, 83 U.S. 147 (1872); Charles Warren, *What Is Giving Aid and Comfort to the Enemy?*, 27 YALE L. J. 331, 346–347 (1918); Carlton Larson, *The Forgotten Constitutional Law of Treason and the Enemy Combatant Problem*, 154 U. PA. L. REV. 863, 893 (2006) ("[A]ny person present in the United States, other than in the company of an invading military force, owes at least a temporary or local allegiance to the United States and can be tried for treason against the United States.").

76. 343 U.S. 717, 733–736 (1952). In rejecting the renunciation argument, the Court cited the fact that Kawakita had asserted his U.S. citizenship in a passport application in December 1945 and returned to the United States in 1946.

77. Williams' Case, 4 Hall L. J. 461, 2 Cranch 82, 29 F. Cas. 1330, 1331 (C.C.D. Conn. 1799) (No. 17,708).

78. See, e.g., Shanks v. Dupont, 28 U.S. (3 Pet.) 242, 246 (1830) (Story, J.) ("The general doctrine is, that no persons can by any act of their own, without the consent of the government, put off their allegiance, and become aliens."); see also WILLIAM RAWLE, A VIEW OF THE CONSTITUTION OF THE UNITED STATES OF AMERICA 93 (2d ed., Philadelphia, Philip H. Nicklin 1829) (noting "the reciprocal compact of protection and allegiance" and positing that "[t]he citizen who unites himself with a hostile nation, waging war against his country, is guilty of a crime of which the foreign army is innocent; with him it is treason, with his associates it is, in the code of nations, legitimate warfare."). As Thomas Jefferson once wrote:

    > [T]he laws do not admit that the bare commission of a crime amounts of itself to a divestment of the character of citizen, and withdraws the criminal from their coercion. They would never prescribe an illegal act among the legal modes by which a citizen might disinfranchise himself; nor render treason, for instance, innocent by giving it the force of a dissolution of the obligation of the criminal to his country.

    Letter from Thomas Jefferson to the United States Minister of France Gouverneur Morris (Aug. 16, 1793), in 6 THE WRITINGS OF THOMAS JEFFERSON 371, 381 (Paul Leicester Ford ed., New York, G.P. Putnam's Sons 1895).

79. 156 F.2d 142 (9th Cir. 1946).

80. In *Territo*, the Ninth Circuit relied on *Quirin* to reject the argument that "citizenship . . . necessarily affects the status of one captured on the field of battle." Id. at 145.

81. 327 U.S. 304, 322 (1946).

82. Id. (citing Ex parte Milligan, 71 U.S. (4 Wall.) 2 (1866)). Ironically, the Court cited *Quirin* for the latter proposition.

83. Id. at 313–314.

84. See, e.g., DANIEL A. FARBER & SUZANNA SHERRY, JUDGMENT CALLS: PRINCIPLE AND POLITICS IN CONSTITUTIONAL LAW 137 (2009); Richard H. Fallon, Jr. & Daniel J. Meltzer, *Habeas Corpus Jurisdiction, Substantive Rights, and the War on Terror,* 120 HARV. L. REV. 2029, 2091 (2007); Trevor W. Morrison, Hamdi's *Habeas Puzzle: Suspension as Authorization?*, 91 CORNELL L. REV. 411, 416 (2006).

85. See, e.g., Hamdi v. Rumsfeld, 337 F.3d 335, 344 (4th Cir. 2003) (Wilkinson, J., concurring in the denial of rehearing *en banc*) ("To compare this battlefield capture to the domestic arrest in *Padilla v. Bush* is to compare apples and oranges."); Fallon & Meltzer, supra note 84, at 2072 (contrasting *Hamdi* and *Padilla* by pointing to "[t]he crucial fact [of] Hamdi's seizure on a foreign battlefield"). Only Justice Breyer voted with the plurality in *Hamdi* and with the dissent in *Padilla*, suggesting possibly that he drew the same distinction between the cases.

86. Hamdi v. Rumsfeld, 542 U.S. 507, 521, 523 (2004) (plurality opinion).

87. See U.S. CONST. art. III, § 3 (defining "[t]reason against the United States" as encompassing "levying War against them, or . . . adhering to their Enemies, giving them Aid and Comfort"). Note that English law defined treason as encompassing, among other things, aiding nonstate actors who were waging war against the Crown.

88. It bears noting that modern Supreme Court jurisprudence has also interpreted certain provisions of the Constitution to protect citizens well beyond U.S. borders. See, e.g., Reid v. Covert, 354 U.S. 1 (1957) (holding that spouse of serviceperson stationed overseas was entitled to jury trial in capital murder proceedings).

89. As detailed in Chapter 3, when advising Lord North's administration on the proper treatment of American colonists captured during the Revolutionary War, Lord Mansfield highlighted the cases of "many French officers" who "were in gaol as rebels, being either born in the King's dominions or if born abroad the sons of British subjects." As he noted, "they were tried and condemned," rather than held as prisoners of war. It was on this basis that he advised that so long as the American privateers "claim to be considered as subjects and apply for a *habeas corpus*, it is their own doing; *they force a regular commitment for their crime.*" Letter from Lord Mansfield to Lord George Germain (Aug. 8, 1776), in 12 DOCUMENTS OF THE AMERICAN REVOLUTION, 1770–1783, at 179, 179–180 (K.G. Davies ed., 1976) (emphasis added). Additional analogous cases are detailed in Chapter 2.

90. As noted above, the government eventually prosecuted Padilla in civilian court. Following the Supreme Court's decision in Hamdi's case, the government offered him release to Saudi Arabia predicated on several conditions, including his forfeiture of any claims to citizenship. See Press Release, U.S. Dept. of Justice, Regarding Yaser Hamdi (Sept. 22, 2004), http://www.usdoj.gov/opa/pr/2004/September/04_opa_640.htm.

91. In the lead-up to these events, government lawyers asked to evaluate the jurisdictional question opined that precedent supported the conclusion that Guantanamo Bay was beyond the jurisdiction of the courts. See Memorandum from Patrick F. Philbin, Deputy Assistant Attorney Gen., and John C. Yoo, Deputy Assistant Attorney Gen. on Possible Habeas Jurisdiction over Aliens Held in Guantanamo Bay, Cuba, to William J. Haynes II, Gen. Counsel, Dep't of Defense (Dec. 28, 2001). Participants in the relevant discussions have stated that there were additional arguments favoring the choice of Guantanamo Bay for detention facilities. See John Bellinger, *Guantanamo Redux: Why It Was Opened and Why It Should Be Closed (and Not Enlarged)* (Mar. 12, 2017), available at https://www.lawfareblog.com/guantanamo-redux-why-it-was-opened-and-why-it-should-be-closed-and-not-enlarged.

92. Rasul v. Bush, 542 U.S. 466 (2004).

93. Detainee Treatment Act of 2005, Pub. L. No. 109-148, 119 Stat. 2739; Military Commissions Act of 2006, Pub. L. No. 109-366, 120 State. 2600 (codified in relevant part at 28 U.S.C. § 2241(e) (2017)).

94. 548 U.S. 557 (2006).
95. The Court heard the case only after reversing an earlier ruling denying review. For details of this extraordinary change of course, see Daniel J. Meltzer, *Habeas Corpus, Suspension, and Guantanamo: The* Boumediene *Decision*, 2008 SUP. CT. REV. 1, 7–9.
96. Boumediene v. Bush, 553 U.S. 723, 732–733 (2008). Justices Stevens, Souter, Ginsburg, and Breyer joined the majority opinion.
97. Id. at 745.
98. Id. at 739.
99. Id. at 739–740.
100. Id. at 746–748 (citing the Case of the Three Spanish Sailors (1779) 2 Black. W. 1324, 96 Engl. Rep. 775 (C.P.), King v. Schiever (1759) 2 Burr. 765, 97 Eng. Rep. 551 (K.B.), Du Castro's Case (1697) Fort. 195, 92 Eng. Rep. 816 (K.B.)).
101. Boumediene, 553 U.S. at 747.
102. Id. at 751, 752.
103. Id. at 753, 755.
104. Johnson v. Eisentrager, 339 U.S. 763, 767 (1950).
105. Boumediene, 553 U.S. at 763, 766.
106. Id. at 764.
107. Id. at 765.
108. Id. at 742, 743; see also id. at 746–755 ("[T]he Framers deemed the writ to be an essential mechanism in the separation-of-powers scheme.").
109. The Court primarily found fault with the relevant provisions because it interpreted them not to permit detainees to present exculpatory evidence during Article III proceedings. See id. at 771–792.
110. Id. at 766, 785. For an overview of how the D.C. Circuit and district courts have handled these cases in the wake of *Boumediene*, see RICHARD H. FALLON, JR., JOHN F. MANNING, DANIEL J. MELTZER & DAVID L. SHAPIRO, HART & WECHSLER'S THE FEDERAL COURTS AND THE FEDERAL SYSTEM 1238–1240 (7th ed. 2015).
111. 553 U.S. at 801 (Roberts, C.J., dissenting).
112. Id. at 804; see id. at 811 ("[T]he *Hamdi* plurality concluded that this type of review would be enough to satisfy due process, even for citizens.").
113. See id. at 808–824.
114. Id. at 826.
115. Id. at 832 (Scalia, J., dissenting).
116. Id. at 827, 833.
117. Id. at 834–835 (quoting Eisentrager 339 U.S. at 768) (internal quotation marks omitted); see also Eisentrager, 339 U.S. at 781 (adding that "no right to the writ of *habeas corpus* appears").
118. Boumediene, 553 U.S. at 835 (Scalia, J., dissenting) (quoting 339 U.S. at 770–771).

119. Id. at 841.

120. Id. at 845–846 ("The Habeas corpus Act . . . confirms the consensus view of scholars and jurists that the writ did not run outside the sovereign territory of the Crown.").

121. Id. at 848.

122. Id. at 842, 850.

123. David L. Shapiro, *Habeas Corpus, Suspension, and Detention: Another View*, 82 NOTRE DAME L. REV. 59, 64–65 (2006), quoted in Meltzer, supra note 95, at 14; see also Meltzer, supra, at 11–12 ("It seems more than plausible to suggest that it would have astonished the Framers to think that they had protected the writ against suspension . . . but that Congress could achieve the same result . . . simply by precluding the federal courts from making it available in the first place.").

124. U.S. CONST. art. III, § 1.

125. For additional discussion of Chief Justice John Marshall's opinion in Ex parte *Bollman*, 8 U.S. (4 Cranch) 75 (1807), and the "obligation" that the First Congress must have felt to provide for such jurisdiction, see Chapter 5. On the importance of state courts, see Henry M. Hart, Jr., *The Power of Congress to Limit the Jurisdiction of Federal Courts: An Exercise in Dialectic*, 66 HARV. L. REV. 1362, 1372 (1953) (arguing that it is "a necessary postulate of constitutional government—that a court must always be available to pass on claims of constitutional right to judicial process, and to provide such process if the claim is sustained"); id. at 1401 ("[State courts] are the primary guarantors of constitutional rights, and in many cases they may be the ultimate ones.").

126. See, e.g., United States v. Verdugo-Urquidez, 494 U.S. 259 (1990); Reid v. Covert, 354 U.S. 1 (1957). The Court in *Eisentrager*, moreover, was divided, with Justice Black arguing for three justices in dissent: "I would hold that our courts can exercise [habeas corpus review] whenever any United States official illegally imprisons any person in any land we govern. Courts should not for any reason abdicate this, the loftiest power with which the Constitution has endowed them." 339 U.S. at 798 (Black, J., dissenting).

127. See, e.g., Boumediene, 553 U.S. at 751 ("[N]o law other than the laws of the United States applies at the naval station.").

128. See generally PAUL D. HALLIDAY, HABEAS CORPUS: FROM ENGLAND TO EMPIRE (2010).

129. Whether the holding in *Boumediene* should be extended beyond Guantanamo Bay has been the subject of considerable debate and litigation. See, e.g., Al Maqaleh v. Gates, 605 F.3d 84, 92–99 (D.C. Cir. 2010) (reversing a lower court and holding that *Boumediene* does not extend to the American military base in Bagram, Afghanistan).

130. The Case of the Three Spanish Sailors (1779) 2 Black W. 1324, 96 Eng. Rep. 775–776 ("[W]e can give them no redress."); HALLIDAY, supra note 128, at 173 (discussing case).

131. HALLIDAY, supra note 128, at 171.

132. The Trial of François Henri de la Motte for High Treason, 21 Cobbett's St. Tr. 687, 709 (Jan. 1781) (KB).

133. For additional discussion, see Philip Hamburger, *Beyond Protection*, 109 COLUM. L. REV. 1823 (2009).

134. Boumediene, 553 U.S. at 747.

135. With respect to the petitioners' claims predicated upon the Geneva Convention, Justice Jackson wrote that it was "the obvious scheme" of the Convention "that responsibility for observance and enforcement of these rights is upon political and military authorities. Rights of alien enemies are vindicated under it only through protests and intervention of protecting powers." *Eisentrager*, 339 U.S. at 789 n.14.

136. For discussion of the complex international law issues posed by the War on Terrorism and the Guantanamo detainees, see JACK GOLDSMITH, THE TERROR PRESIDENCY 110–120, 136–140 (2007). For a different view on certain points, see JONATHAN HAFETZ, HABEAS CORPUS AFTER 9/11: CONFRONTING AMERICA'S NEW GLOBAL DETENTION SYSTEM 15–16, 185–187 (2011).

137. See Charles Babington & Michael Abramowitz, *U.S. Shifts Policy on Geneva Conventions*, WASH. POST, July 12, 2006.

138. See GOLDSMITH, supra note 136, at 118–119. Legal scholar Jack Goldsmith, who served in the Bush administration, has argued that the administration's approach on this issue, along with its general reluctance to work with Congress, partly explains the Supreme Court's rejection of the administration's position in several War on Terrorism cases. See generally id.

139. On this score, as the Court noted, because of the nature of the War on Terrorism, detainees could be subject to indefinite detention. There is also the problem of clearly defining what is an "enemy combatant"—something the Court has yet to do—along with determining in a war where combatants do not wear uniforms whether a party captured is properly identified as the enemy. See, e.g., Meltzer, supra note 95, at 15.

140. Boumediene, 553 U.S. at 764–765. As one commentator noted, "[t]he divisions in American society, and criticism from Europe, unsurprisingly might have [had] an effect on human judges" deciding the case. Ruth Wedgwood, *The Supreme Court and the Guantanamo Controversy*, in TERRORISM, THE LAWS OF WAR, AND THE CONSTITUTION: DEBATING THE ENEMY COMBATANT CASES 182 (Peter Berkowitz ed., 2005); see also Meltzer, supra note 95, at 5 ("[C]oncerns about military practice, when set against the Executive's broad assertions of executive power and its limited respect for international law, very

likely motivated the Court's invalidation of the judicial review regime established by Congress."). Among other matters garnering press coverage in the lead-up to *Boumediene* that may have influenced the Court were the events at Abu Ghraib prison in Iraq, details of which became public in 2004 and revealed horrific mistreatment of prisoners by U.S. officials.

141. Boumediene, 553 U.S. at 746 (quoting INS v. St. Cyr, 533 U.S. 289, 301 (2001)).

142. Id. at 746 (citing St. Cyr, 533 U.S. at 300–301); id. at 780. For a defense of a common law model of habeas lauding the normative value of its adaptability, see Fallon & Meltzer, supra note 84; see also Willard Hurst, *The Role of History*, in Supreme Court and Supreme Law 55, 61 (Edmond Cahn ed., 1954) (quoting legal scholar Paul Freund's remarks at a 1953 symposium) ("[W]hether or not a specific wrong could be redressed by habeas corpus . . . as of 1787 is not controlling, because the whole history of habeas corpus shows that the courts in England were capable of developing the writ, and we did not adopt an institution frozen as of that date."); see also id. ("My point is that there is involved in such institutions or practices a dynamic element which itself was adopted by the framers.").

143. The literature surveying constitutional interpretive methodology is vast. A general introduction to originalism along with some of the classic responses to its tenets may be found in the essays collected in Antonin Scalia, A Matter of Interpretation: Federal Courts and the Law (1997).

144. Justice Stevens's methodological approach, which looks to history as a guide to the constitutional floor but not a ceiling, is discussed above.

145. One might also put Justice Black's dissent in *Eisentrager*, discussed above, in this camp. As is also discussed above, these considerations included the incentives created by the governing legal framework for government actors, the practical realities of war, and perhaps the background role of international law.

146. Boumediene, 553 U.S. at 742; see also id. at 746–755.

147. 4 Cranch 75 (1807); id. at 136 (observing that where one is imprisoned unlawfully, the court "can only direct [the prisoner] to be discharged").

148. See Stephen I. Vladeck, Boumediene's *Quiet Theory: Access to Courts and the Separation of Powers*, 84 Notre Dame L. Rev. 2107, 2110 (2009) ("Reading *Boumediene*, one is left with the distinct impression that for Justice Kennedy, at least, the writ of habeas corpus is in part a means to an end—a structural mechanism protecting individual liberty *by* preserving the ability of the courts to check the political branches."). As Professor Zechariah Chafee once observed, the import of the writ "depends on the location of the line between lawful and unlawful imprisonments." Chafee, supra note 4, at 159.

149. Boumediene, 553 U.S. at 779.

150. Id. at 802 (Roberts, C.J., dissenting).

151. See Swain v. Pressley, 430 U.S. 372, 381 (1977) (inquiring in habeas petition whether procedures followed in petitioner's criminal trial were "adequate or

effective"); United States v. Hayman, 342 U.S. 205, 223 (1952) (applying same standard to collateral review of federal court criminal proceedings). To be sure, Justice Kennedy did not fully embrace this blending of the two inquiries. See Boumediene, 553 U.S. at 785 ("Even if we were to assume that the [military commissions at issue] satisfy due process standards, it would not end our inquiry.").

152. Darnel's Case (1627) 3 Cobbett's St. Tr. 1, 18 (Eng.).

153. Hamdi v. Rumsfeld, 542 U.S. 507, 576 (2004) (Scalia, J., dissenting) ("The role of habeas corpus is to determine the legality of executive detention, not to supply the omitted process necessary to make it legal."). See also Hart, supra note 125, at 1382 (cautioning that one must be careful not to "turn[] an ultimate safeguard of law into an excuse for its violation").

154. Cf. Konigsberg v. State Bar, 366 U.S. 36, 61 (1961) (Black, J., dissenting) (arguing that "the men who drafted our Bill of Rights did all the 'balancing' that was to be done in that field" and that "the very object of adopting" the Bill of Rights "was to put the freedoms protected there completely out of the area of any congressional control that may be attempted . . . to 'balance' the Bill of Rights out of existence").

155. See U.S. Const. amend. V ("[N]or shall any person . . . be deprived of life, liberty, or property, without due process of law. . . ."). For additional discussion of the intersection between the Suspension Clause and due process, see, e.g., Joshua Alexander Geltzer, *Of Suspension, Due Process, and Guantanamo: The Reach of the Fifth Amendment after* Boumediene *and the Relationship between Habeas Corpus and Due Process*, 14 J. Const. L. 719 (2012); Gerald L. Neuman, *The Extraterritorial Constitution after* Boumediene v. Bush, 82 S. Cal. L. Rev. 259 (2009); Vladeck, supra note 148.

156. Shapiro, supra note 123, at 74.

CONCLUSION

1. Marbury v. Madison, 5 U.S. (1 Cranch) 137, 176 (1803).

2. Ex parte Watkins, 28 U.S. 193, 201 (1830).

3. Youngstown Sheet & Tube Co. v. Sawyer, 343 U.S. 579, 650 (1952) (Jackson, J., concurring).

4. National Defense Authorization Act of 2012 (NDAA), Pub. L. No. 112-81, 125 Stat. 1298 § 1021.

5. Statement by the President on H.R. 1540, Office of the Press Sec'y, White House (Dec. 31, 2011), https://www.whitehouse.gov/the-press-office/2011/12/31/statement-president-hr-1540.

6. See 2 Thomas Erskine May, The Constitutional History of England since the Accession of George the Third 1760–1860, at 255 (1864).

7. The best source on the implementation of Regulation 18B during World War II is A.W. BRIAN SIMPSON, IN THE HIGHEST DEGREE ODIOUS (2005). As Simpson notes, "it is hard to see what difference it would have made" if habeas had been suspended during the war. See id. at 380.

8. See Liversidge v. Anderson [1942] A.C. 206 (H.L.) (appeal taken from Eng.) (concluding that detention of British subject under Regulation 18B (which was declared pursuant to the Emergency Powers (Defence) Act of 1939), based upon the Home Secretary's determination that subject was "of hostile origin or associations" was not subject to judicial review); King v. Halliday [1917] A.C. 260 (H.L.) (appeal taken from Eng.) (leaving undisturbed detention of naturalized British subject without charges pursuant to Regulation 14B of the Defence of the Realm Regulations, 1914).

9. Churchill nonetheless recognized that "when extreme danger to the State can be pleaded," and "only" when such danger exists, "this power may be temporarily assumed by the Executive, and even so its working must be interpreted with the utmost vigilance by a Free Parliament." Cable from Prime Minister Winston Churchill to Home Secretary Herbert Morrison (Nov. 21, 1943), reprinted in 5 WINSTON S. CHURCHILL, THE SECOND WORLD WAR: CLOSING THE RING 679 (1951). Days later, Churchill argued for the repeal of the specific regulation in question, 18B, counseling "strongly" that "such powers . . . are contrary to the whole spirit of British public life and British history." Cable from Prime Minister Winston Churchill to Deputy Prime Minister Clement Attlee and Home Secretary Herbert Morrison (Nov. 25, 1943), reprinted in 5 id. at 680. Churchill's uneasiness with Regulation 18B's infringement of the classic role of habeas corpus arose early, although initially he directly his criticism at the specifics of the implementation of Regulation 18B. See SIMPSON, supra note 7, at 148-250.

10. Cable from Prime Minister Winston Churchill to Home Secretary Herbert Morrison (Nov. 29, 1943), reprinted in 5 CHURCHILL, supra note 9, at 681. In another stark contrast to his American counterparts, Churchill advised the Home Secretary that "[a]ny unpopularity you have incurred through correct and humane exercise of your functions will be repaid in a few months by public respect." Cable from Prime Minister Winston Churchill to Home Secretary Herbert Morrison (Nov. 25, 1943), reprinted in 5 id. at 680.

11. R (Miller) v. Secretary of State for Exiting the European Union [2017] UKSC 5, (appeal taken from Eng. and Wales) (quoting A.V. DICEY, INTRODUCTION TO THE STUDY OF THE LAW OF THE CONSTITUTION 38 (8th ed. 1915)).

12. Pursuant to those powers, the government claimed the right to hold persons for a range of purposes and, in extreme cases, for an indefinite period upon an executive determination that "internment was expedient in the interests of the preservation of peace." See Ireland v. United Kingdom, 2 Eur. Ct. H.R. (ser. B) 25, ¶¶ 81–84 (1978).

13. See Act of 1971, c. 23, § 56(4) (Eng.).
14. See Terrorism Act 2000, c. 11 (Eng.), as amended, Protection of Freedoms Act 2012, c. 9 Pt. 4 § 57(1) (Eng.) ("In paragraph 36(3)(b)(ii) of Schedule 8 to the Terrorism Act 2000 (maximum period of pre-charge detention for terrorist suspects) for '28 days' substitute '14 days.' ").
15. Terrorism Prevention and Investigation Measures Act 2011, c. 23, § 1 (Eng.); see also Counter-Terrorism and Security Act (CTSA) 2015, c. 6, § 20(1) (Eng.) (permitting the Home Secretary to implement Terrorism Exclusion Orders). The Terrorism Prevention and Investigation Measures Act of 2011 repealed the earlier legislative scheme that permitted the Home Secretary to impose control orders on people who were suspected of involvement with terrorism. See Prevention of Terrorism Act 2005, c. 2 (Eng.) (repealed).
16. Marbury, 5 U.S. (1 Cranch) at 176.
17. See, e.g., Bruce Ackerman, *The Emergency Constitution*, 113 YALE L. J. 1029, 1041 (2004) (calling the Suspension Clause a "rudimentary emergency provision"); DANIEL A. FARBER & SUZANNA SHERRY, JUDGMENT CALLS: PRINCIPLE AND POLITICS IN CONSTITUTIONAL LAW 137 (2009) (arguing that Justice Scalia's position in *Hamdi* would put the government in a "straightjacket" unable to account for "changing conditions" and observing that "if invoked [a suspension] might be far more destructive of civil liberties than a judicially defined solution"); Trevor W. Morrison, *Suspension and the Extrajudicial Constitution*, 107 COLUM. L. REV. 1533, 1539 (2007) (lauding Justice O'Connor's position in *Hamdi* and arguing that Congress should enjoy "some leeway to authorize extraordinary executive detention without suspending the writ").
18. THE FEDERALIST No. 78 (Alexander Hamilton), at 466; see also Chambers v. Florida, 309 U.S. 227, 241 (1940) (Black, J.) (referring to the "solemn responsibility" of the judiciary to "translat[e] into living law and maintain[] this constitutional shield deliberately planned and inscribed for the benefit of every human being subject to our Constitution—of whatever race, creed, or persuasion").

Index

Figures are indicated by "f" following page numbers.